COLLECTOR'S EDITION

Fruits Basket

NATSUKI TAKAYA

8

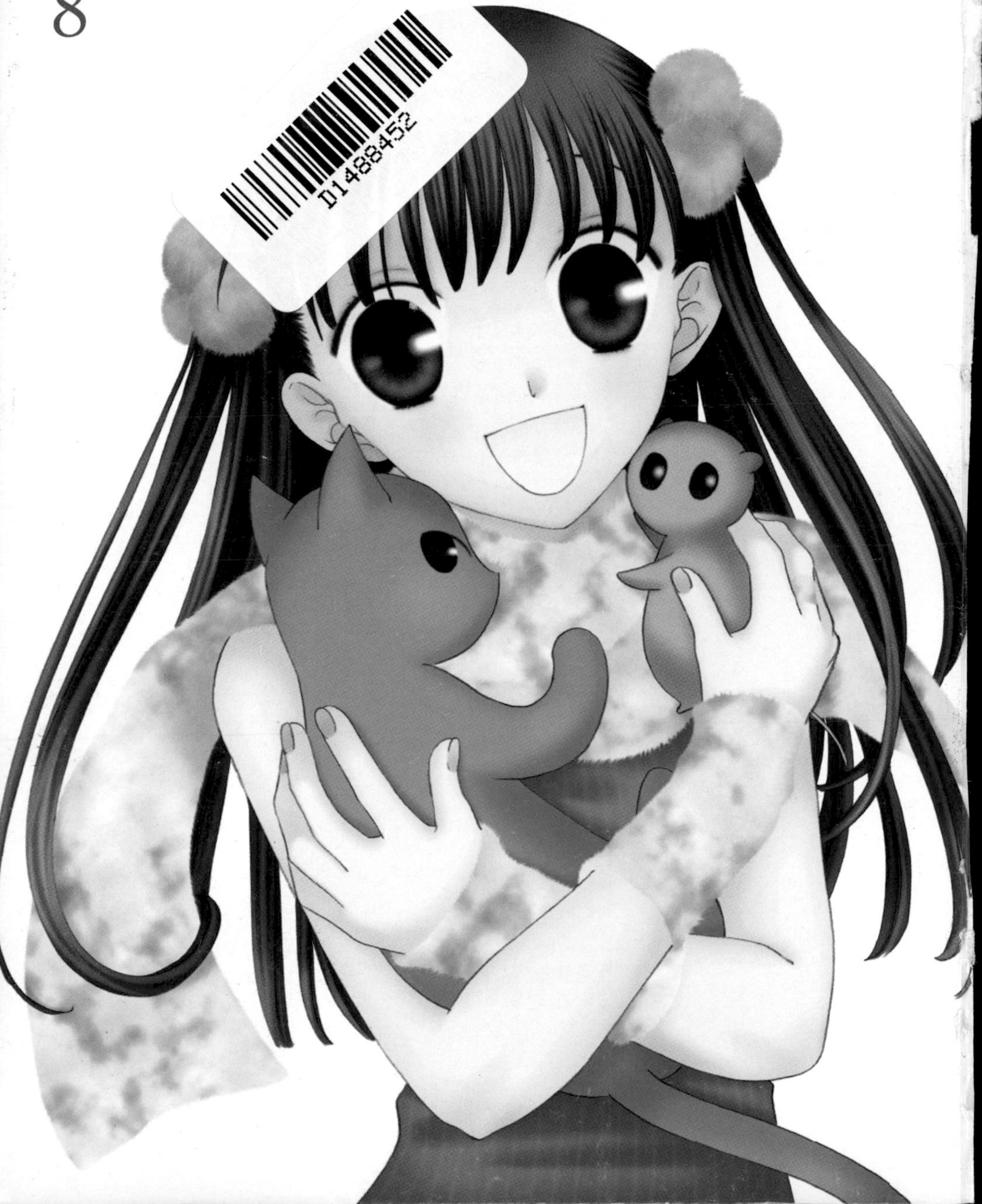

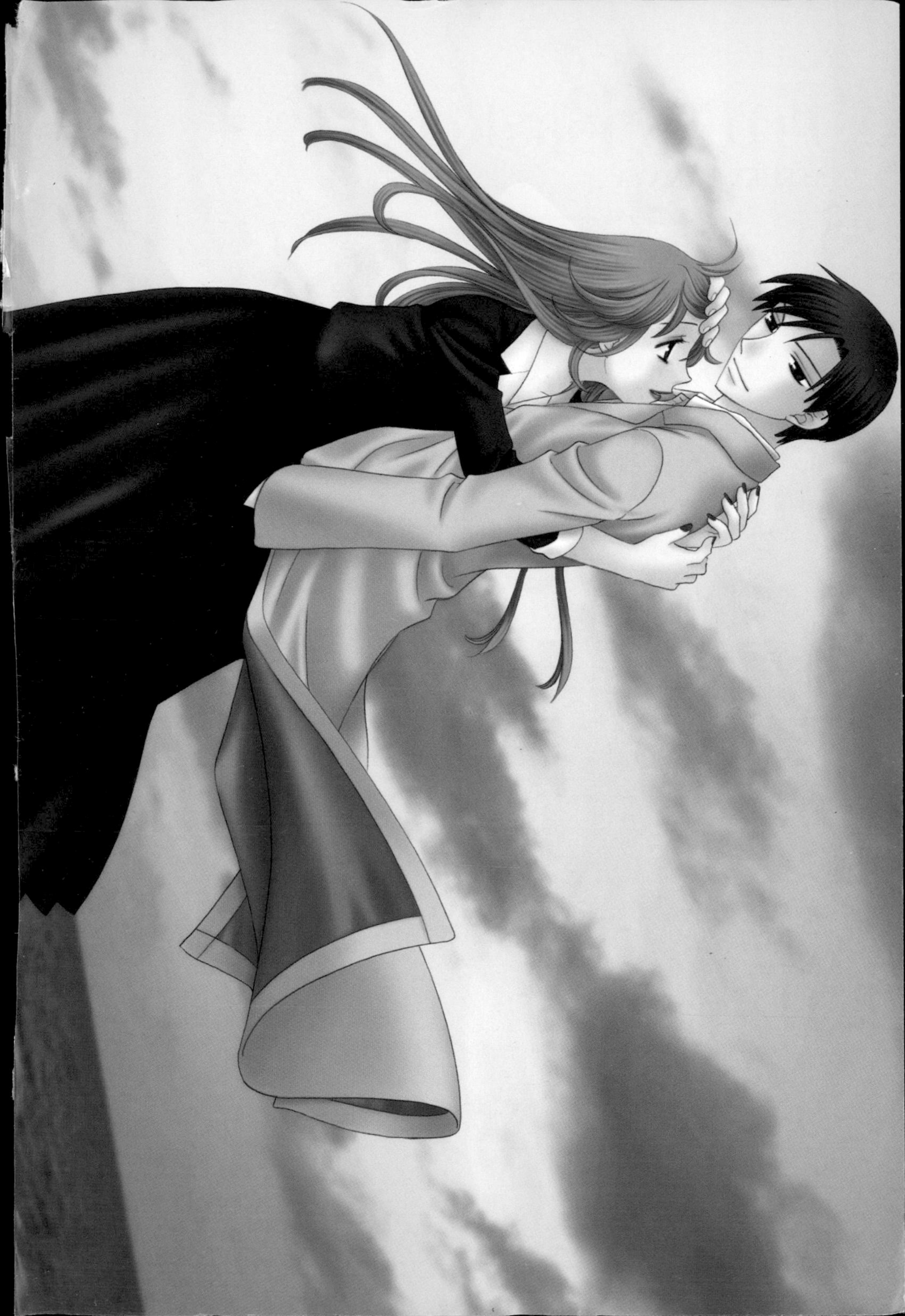

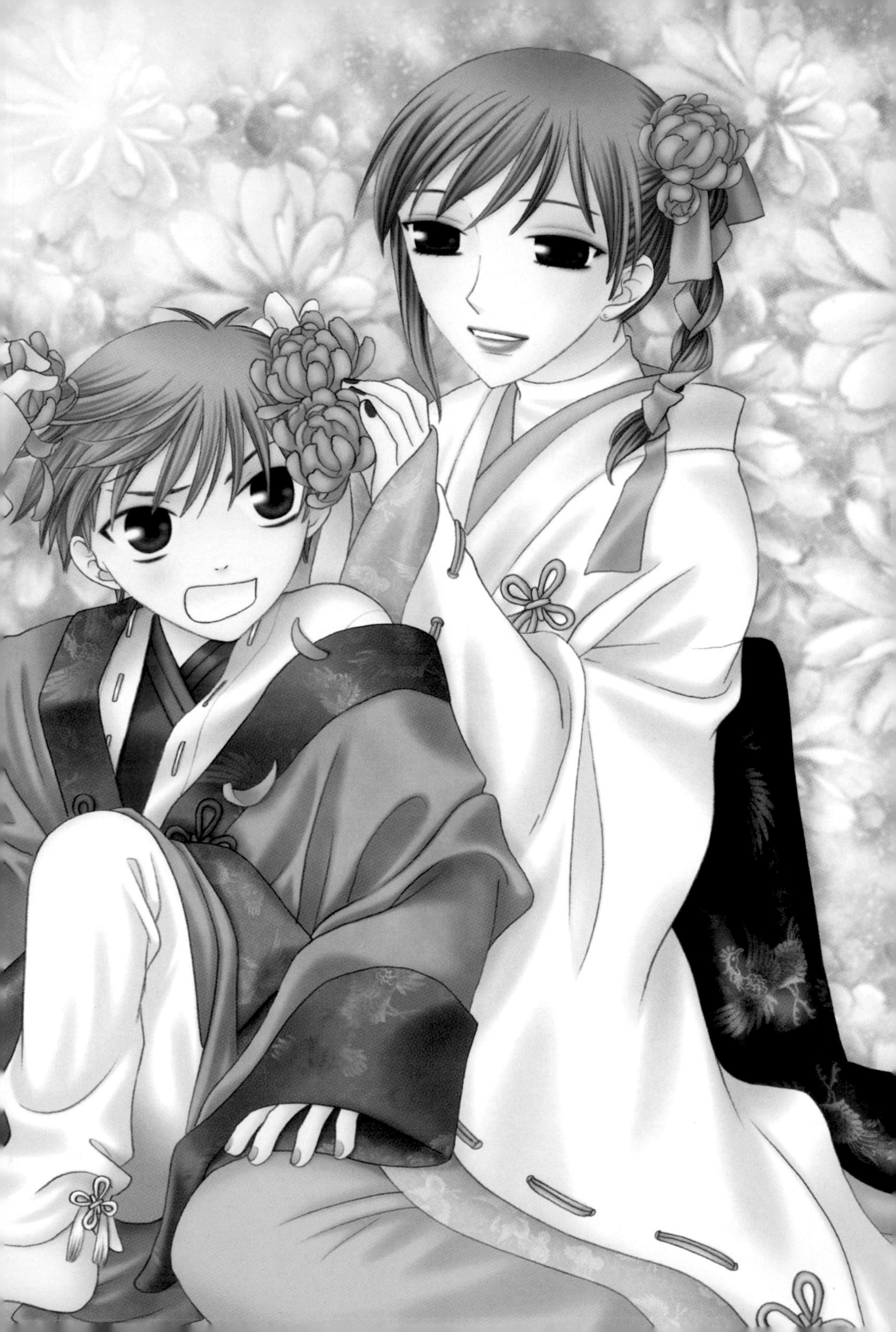

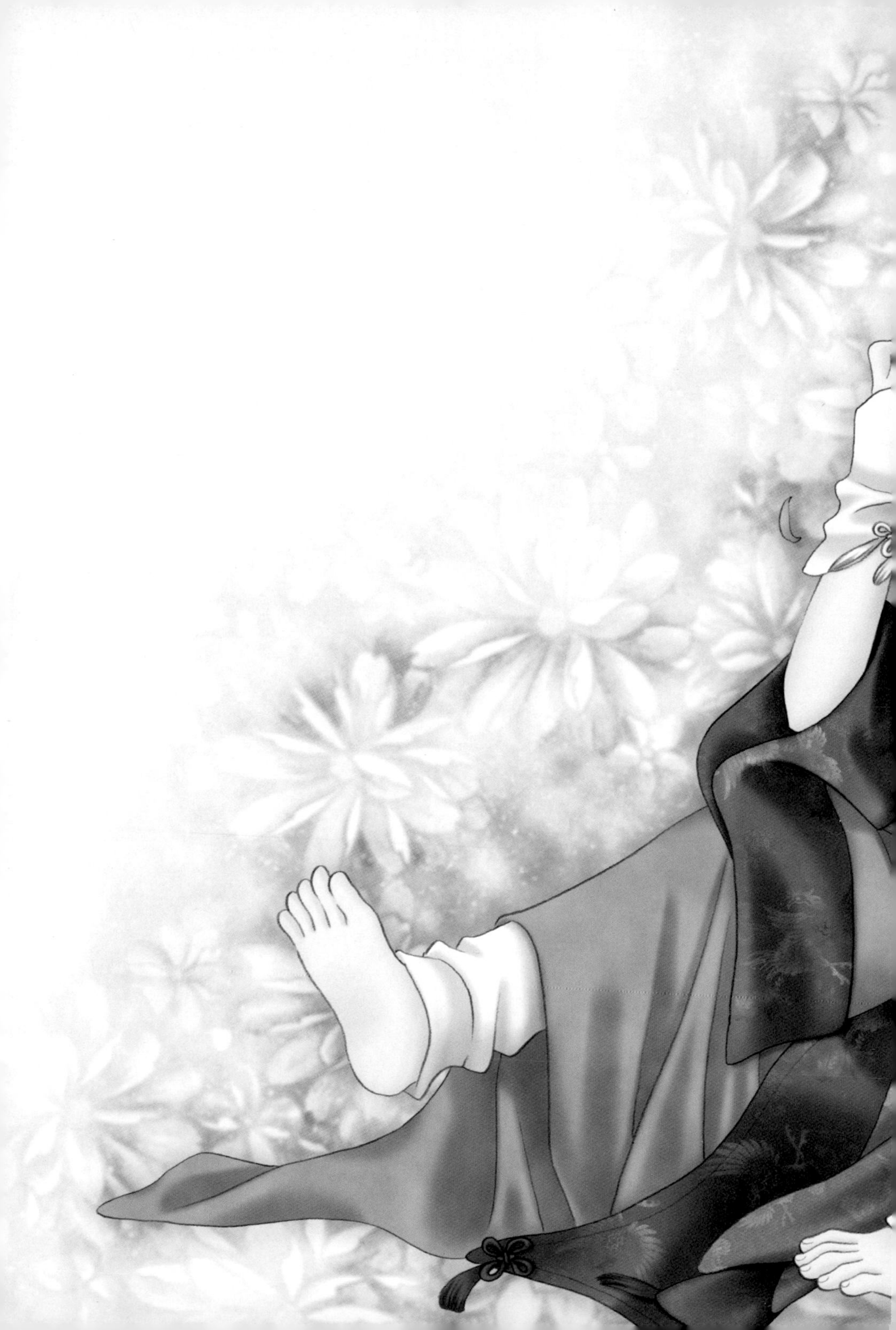

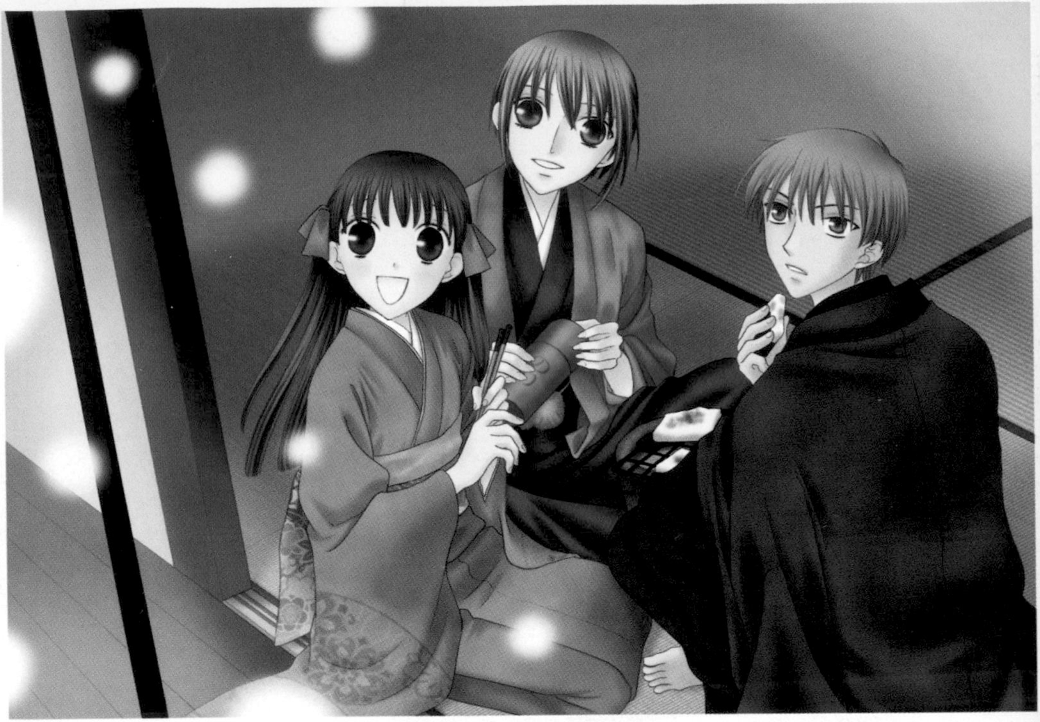
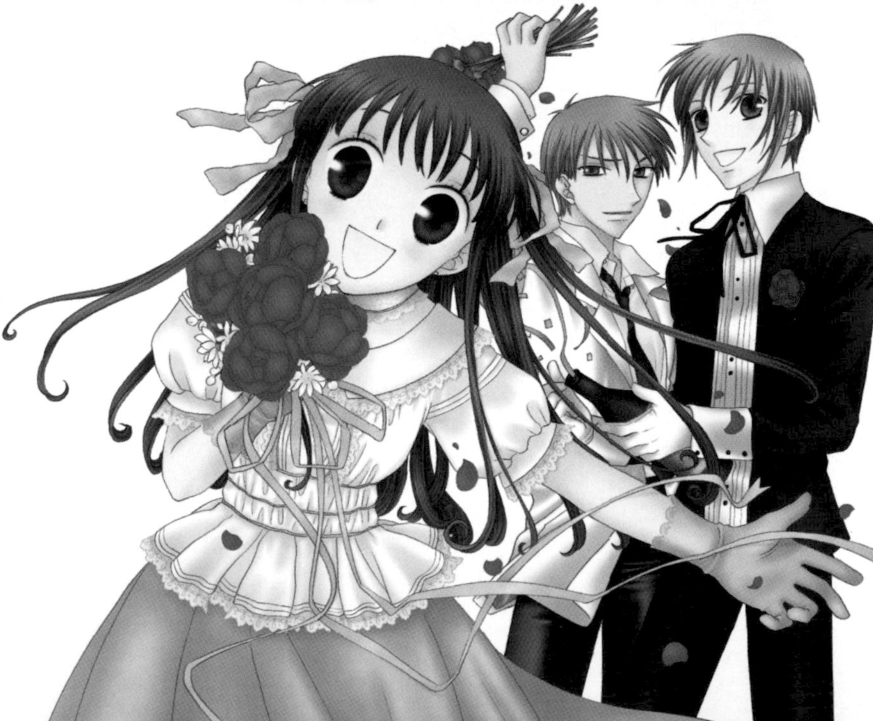

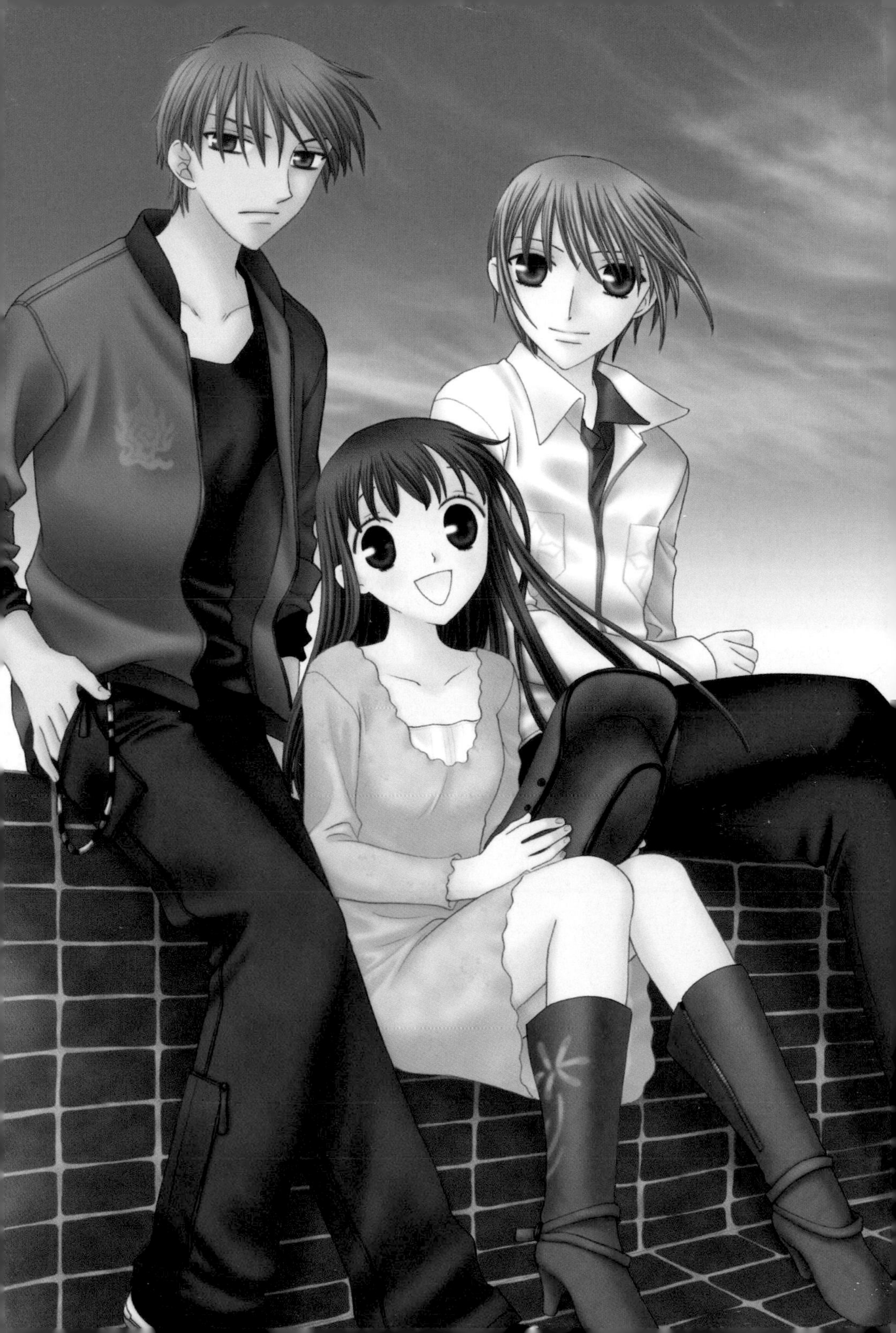

TABLE OF CONTENTS
COLLECTOR'S EDITION

Chapter 84···········9

Chapter 85··········39

Chapter 86··········69

Chapter 87·········100

Chapter 88·········133

Chapter 89·········163

Chapter 90·········194

Chapter 91········227

Chapter 92········257

Chapter 93········287

Chapter 94········317

Chapter 95········347

Special Thanks

··························· 377

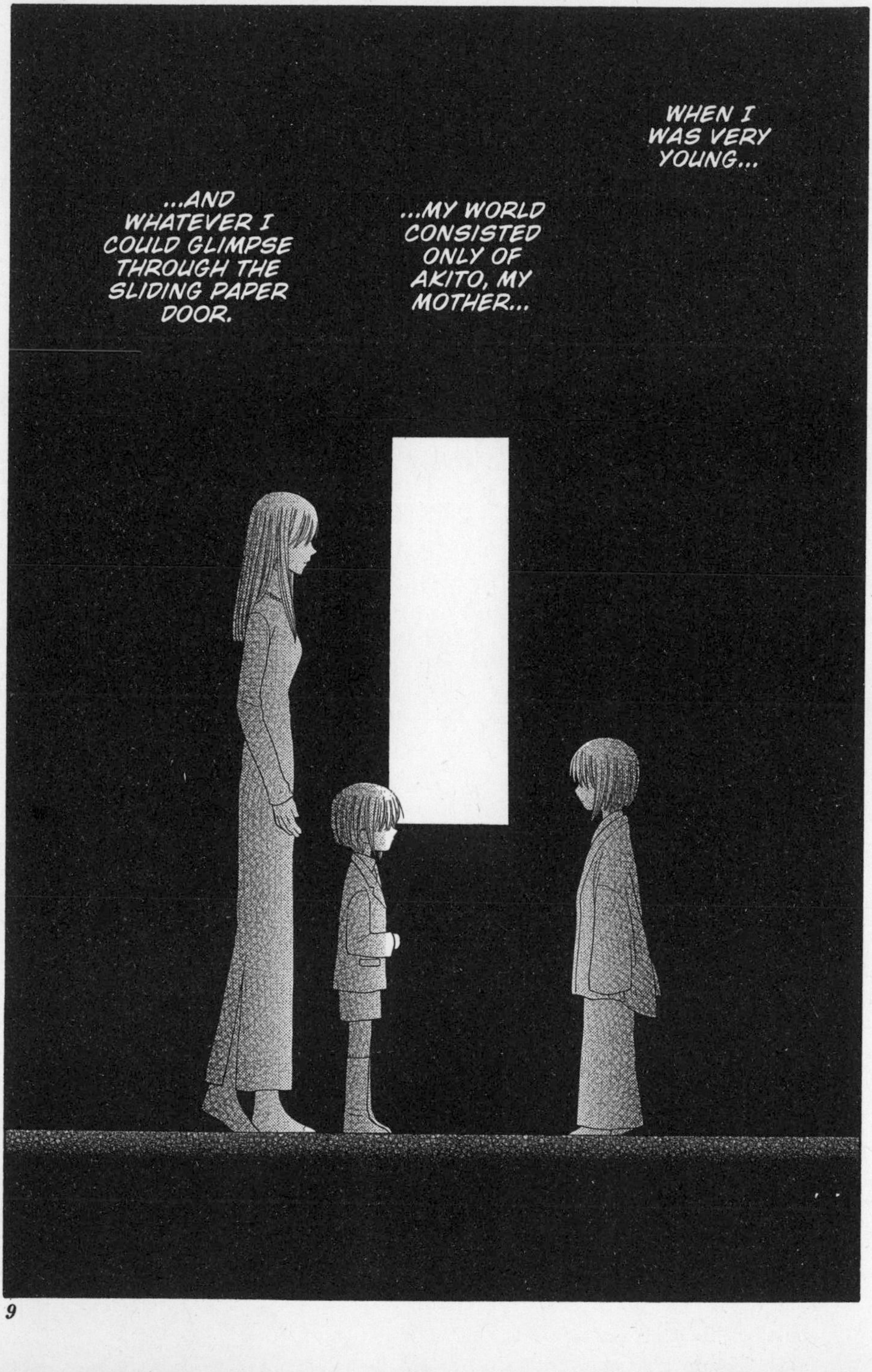
WHEN I WAS VERY YOUNG...
...MY WORLD CONSISTED ONLY OF AKITO, MY MOTHER...
...AND WHATEVER I COULD GLIMPSE THROUGH THE SLIDING PAPER DOOR.

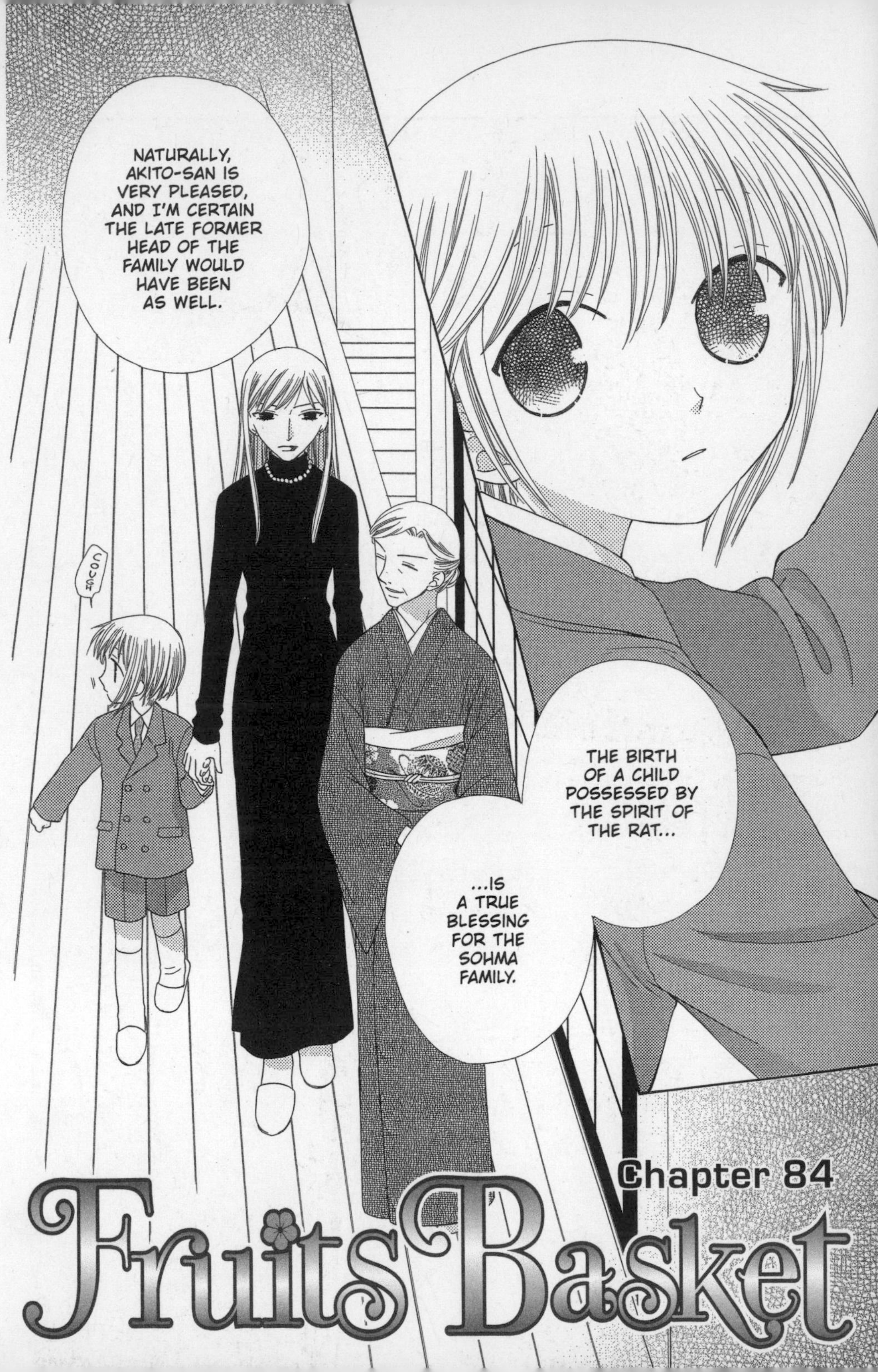
THE BIRTH OF A CHILD POSSESSED BY THE SPIRIT OF THE RAT...
...IS A TRUE BLESSING FOR THE SOHMA FAMILY.
NATURALLY, AKITO-SAN IS VERY PLEASED, AND I'M CERTAIN THE LATE FORMER HEAD OF THE FAMILY WOULD HAVE BEEN AS WELL.
COUGH
Chapter 84
Fruits Basket

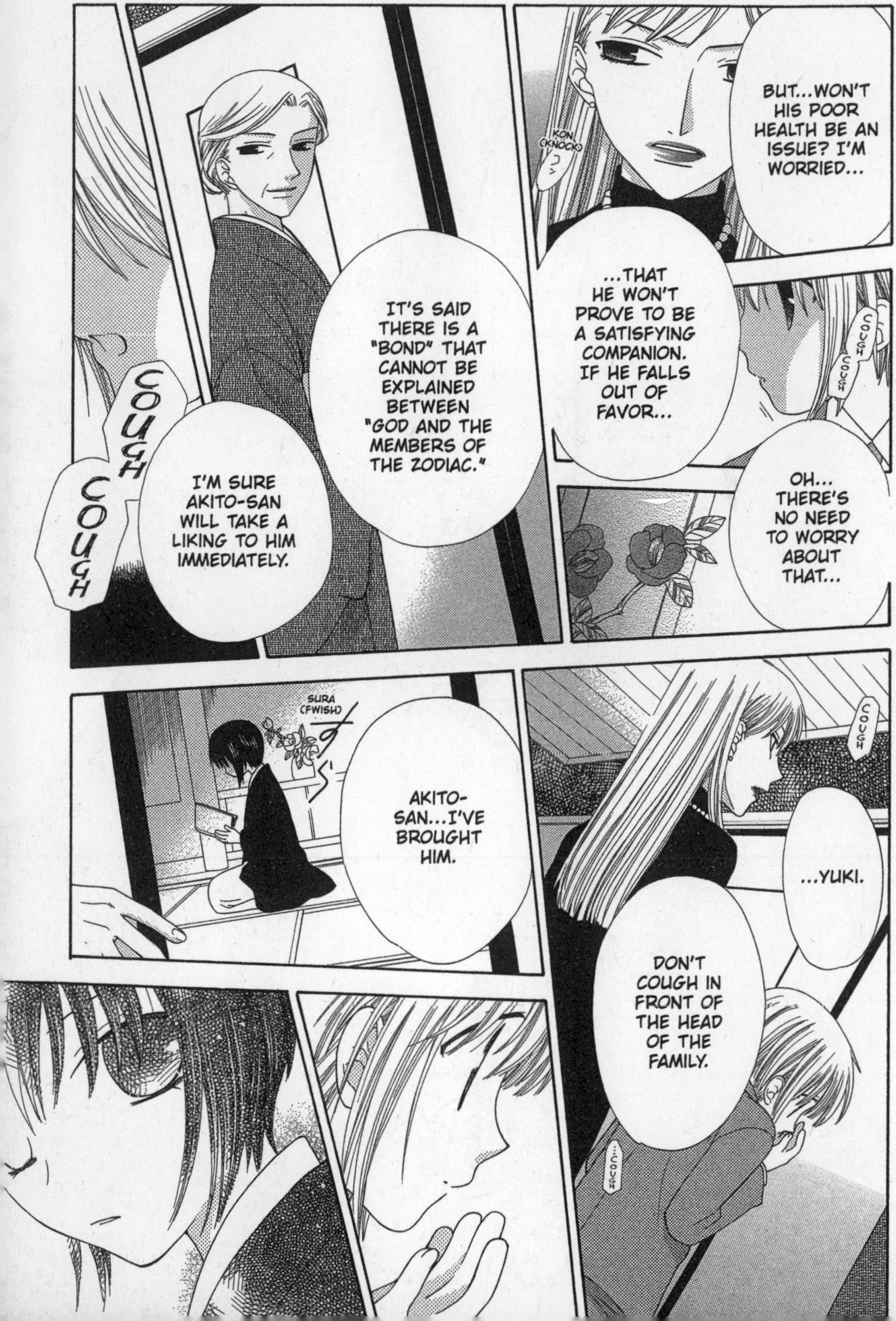
KON (KNOCK)
BUT...WON'T HIS POOR HEALTH BE AN ISSUE? I'M WORRIED...
COUGH COUGH
...THAT HE WON'T PROVE TO BE A SATISFYING COMPANION. IF HE FALLS OUT OF FAVOR...
OH... THERE'S NO NEED TO WORRY ABOUT THAT...
IT'S SAID THERE IS A "BOND" THAT CANNOT BE EXPLAINED BETWEEN "GOD AND THE MEMBERS OF THE ZODIAC."
I'M SURE AKITO-SAN WILL TAKE A LIKING TO HIM IMMEDIATELY.
COUGH COUGH
COUGH
...YUKI.
DON'T COUGH IN FRONT OF THE HEAD OF THE FAMILY.
...COUGH
SURA (FWISH)
AKITO-SAN...I'VE BROUGHT HIM.

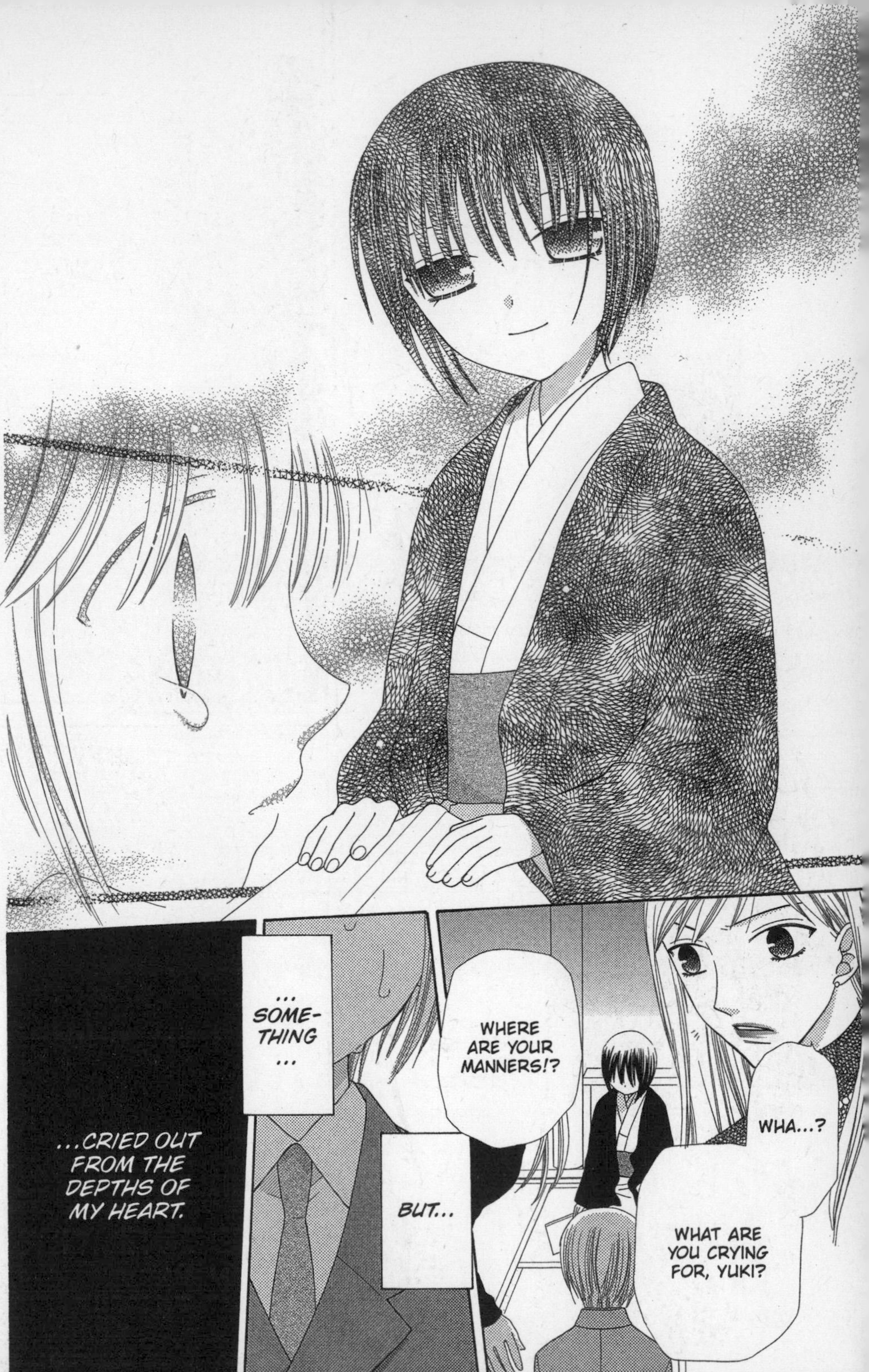
WHA...?
WHAT ARE YOU CRYING FOR, YUKI?
WHERE ARE YOUR MANNERS!?
BUT...
...SOMETHING...
...CRIED OUT FROM THE DEPTHS OF MY HEART.

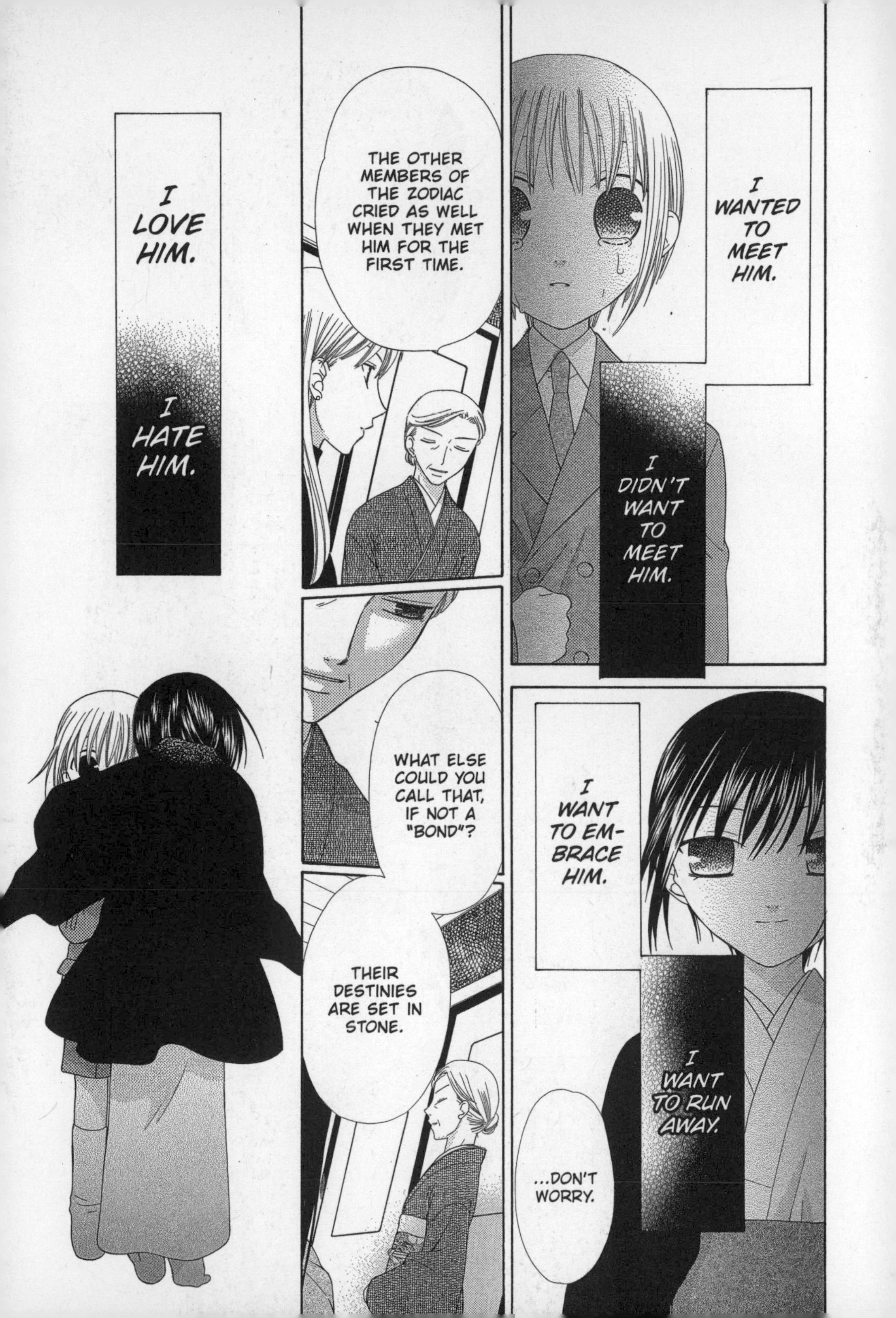
I WANTED TO MEET HIM.
I DIDN'T WANT TO MEET HIM.
THE OTHER MEMBERS OF THE ZODIAC CRIED AS WELL WHEN THEY MET HIM FOR THE FIRST TIME.
WHAT ELSE COULD YOU CALL THAT, IF NOT A "BOND"?
I WANT TO EM-BRACE HIM.
I WANT TO RUN AWAY.
...DON'T WORRY.
THEIR DESTINIES ARE SET IN STONE.
I LOVE HIM.
I HATE HIM.

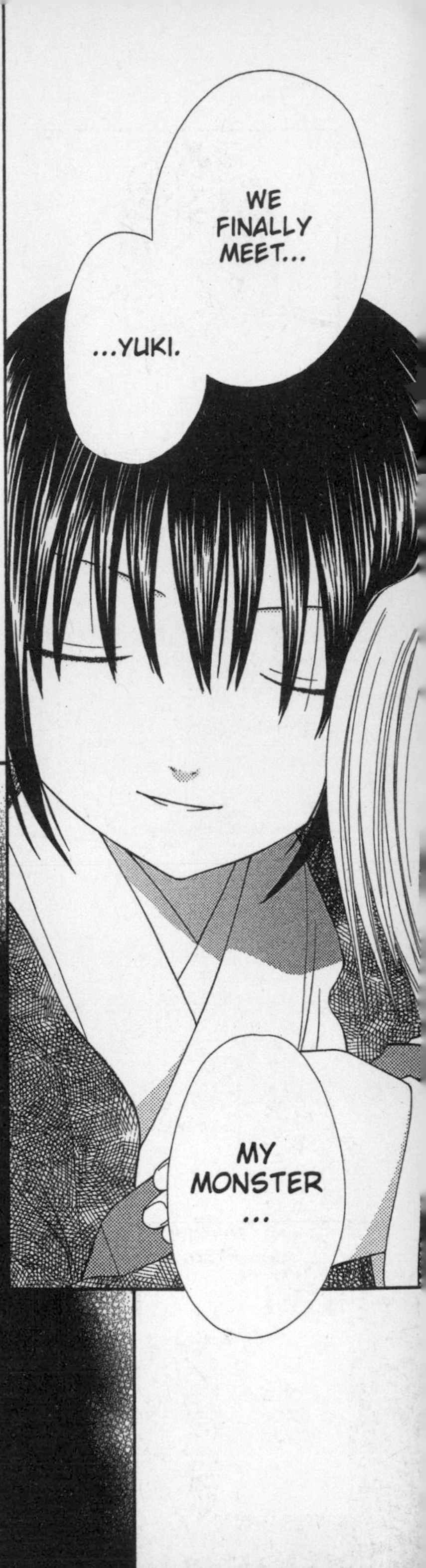
WE FINALLY MEET...
...YUKI.
MY MONSTER...

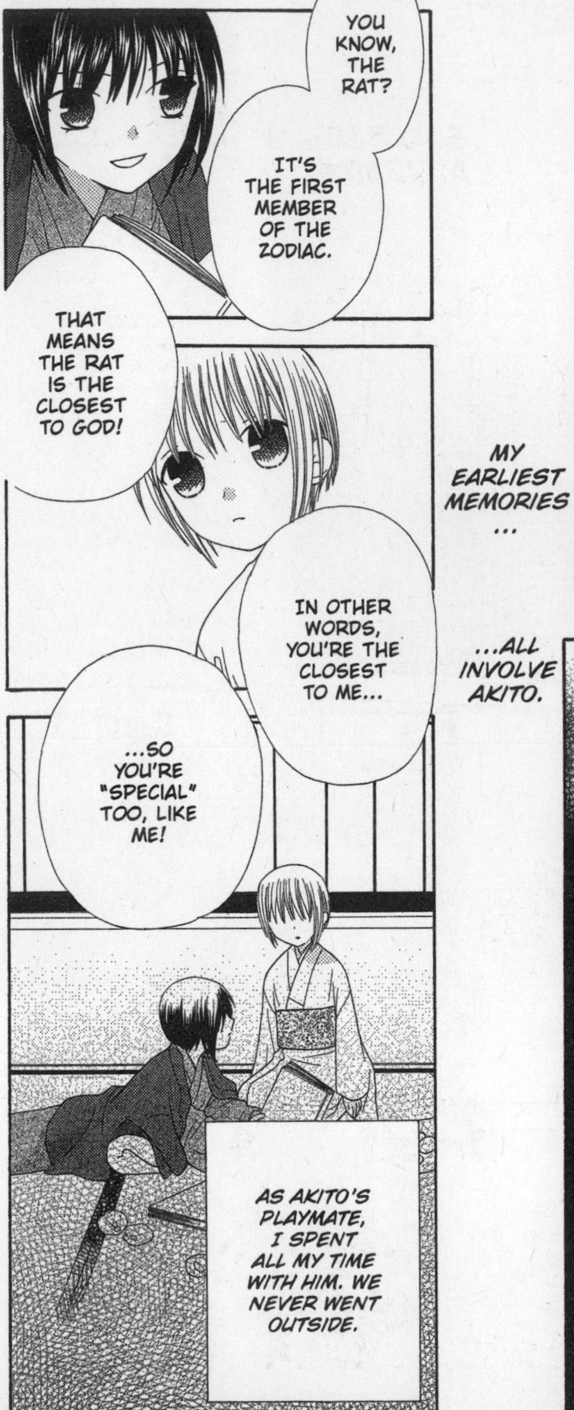
YOU KNOW, THE RAT?
IT'S THE FIRST MEMBER OF THE ZODIAC.
THAT MEANS THE RAT IS THE CLOSEST TO GOD!
MY EARLIEST MEMORIES...
IN OTHER WORDS, YOU'RE THE CLOSEST TO ME...
...ALL INVOLVE AKITO.
...SO YOU'RE "SPECIAL" TOO, LIKE ME!
AS AKITO'S PLAYMATE, I SPENT ALL MY TIME WITH HIM. WE NEVER WENT OUTSIDE.

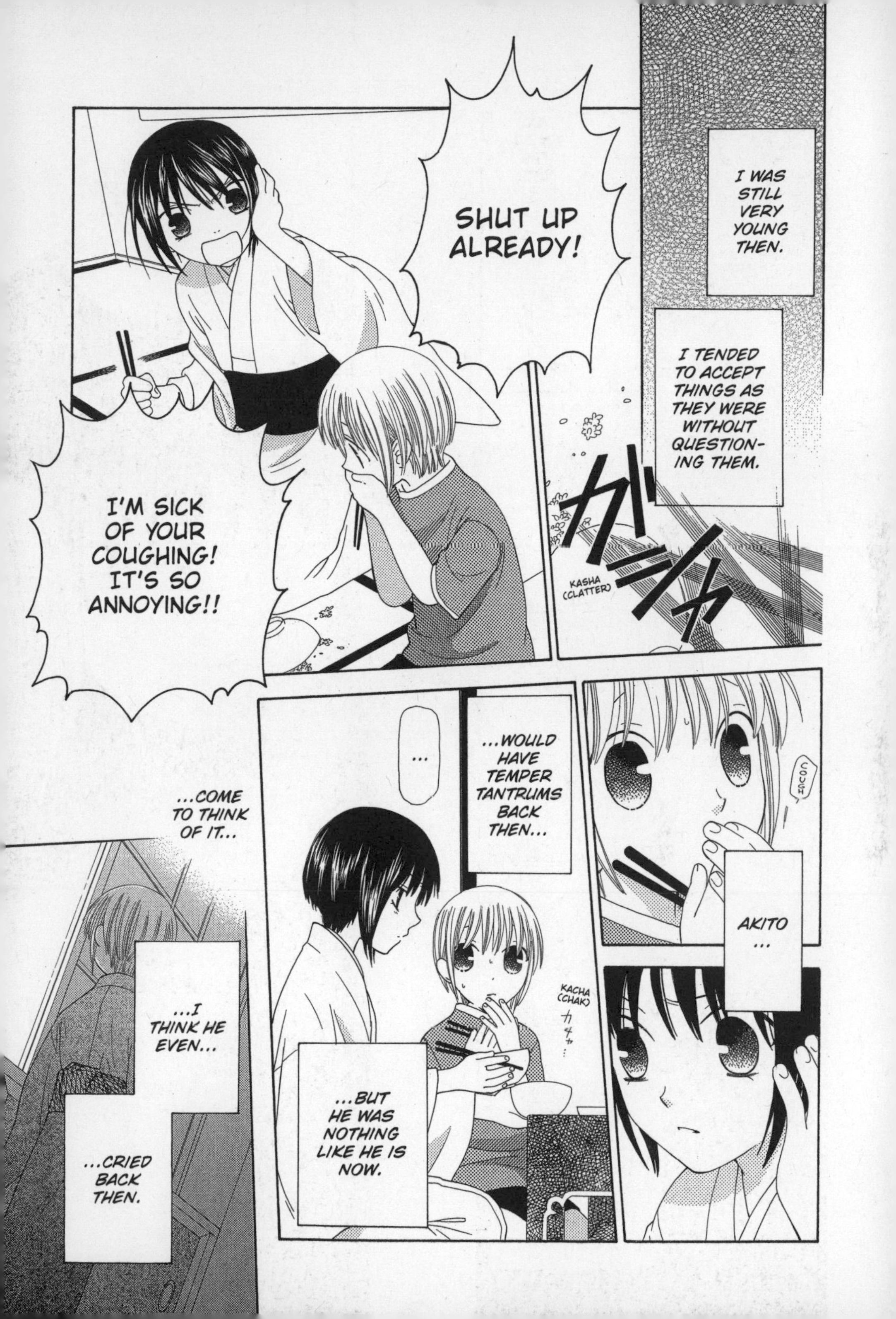
I WAS STILL VERY YOUNG THEN.
I TENDED TO ACCEPT THINGS AS THEY WERE WITHOUT QUESTIONING THEM.
KASHA (CLATTER)
SHUT UP ALREADY!
I'M SICK OF YOUR COUGHING! IT'S SO ANNOYING!!
COUGH
AKITO ...
...
...WOULD HAVE TEMPER TANTRUMS BACK THEN...
KACHA (CHAK)
...BUT HE WAS NOTHING LIKE HE IS NOW.
...COME TO THINK OF IT...
...I THINK HE EVEN...
...CRIED BACK THEN.

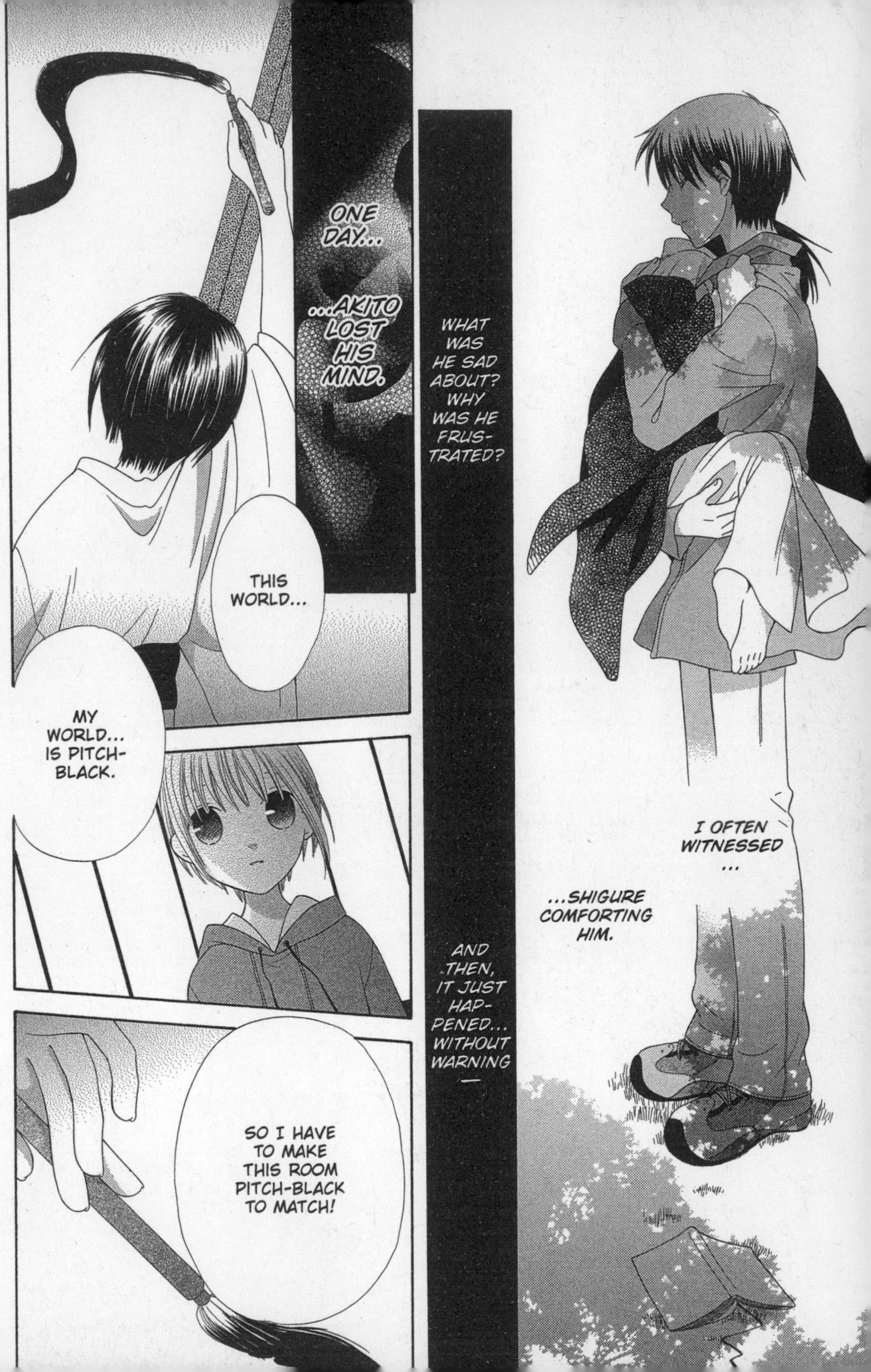
I OFTEN WITNESSED ...
...SHIGURE COMFORTING HIM.
WHAT WAS HE SAD ABOUT? WHY WAS HE FRUS-TRATED?
AND THEN, IT JUST HAP-PENED... WITHOUT WARNING —
ONE DAY...
...AKITO LOST HIS MIND.
THIS WORLD...
MY WORLD... IS PITCH-BLACK.
SO I HAVE TO MAKE THIS ROOM PITCH-BLACK TO MATCH!

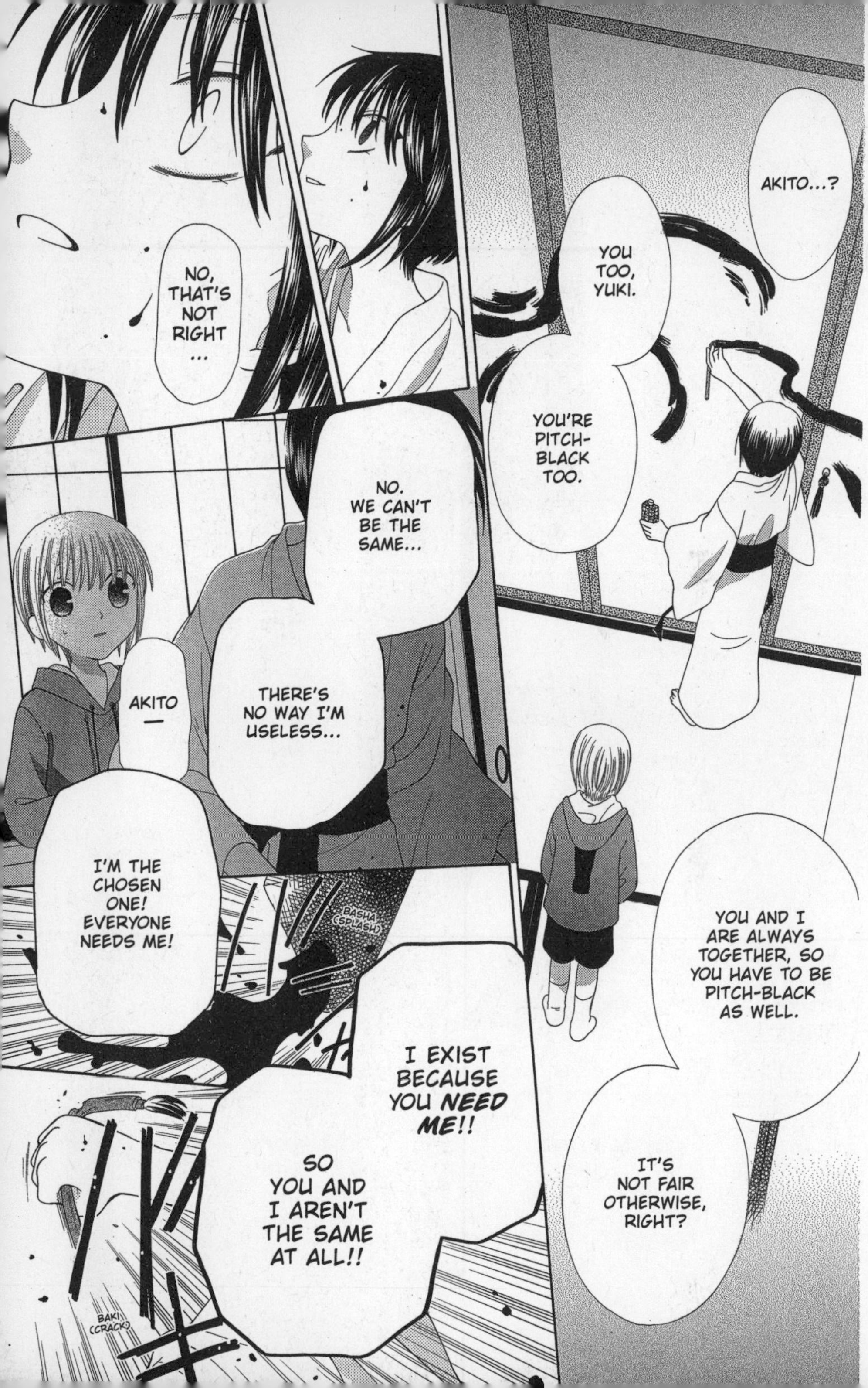

AKITO...?
YOU TOO, YUKI.
YOU'RE PITCH-BLACK TOO.
YOU AND I ARE ALWAYS TOGETHER, SO YOU HAVE TO BE PITCH-BLACK AS WELL.
IT'S NOT FAIR OTHERWISE, RIGHT?
NO, THAT'S NOT RIGHT...
NO. WE CAN'T BE THE SAME...
THERE'S NO WAY I'M USELESS...
AKITO—
I'M THE CHOSEN ONE! EVERYONE NEEDS ME!
BASHA (SPLASH)
I EXIST BECAUSE YOU **NEED ME**!!
SO YOU AND I AREN'T THE SAME AT ALL!!
BAKI (CRACK)

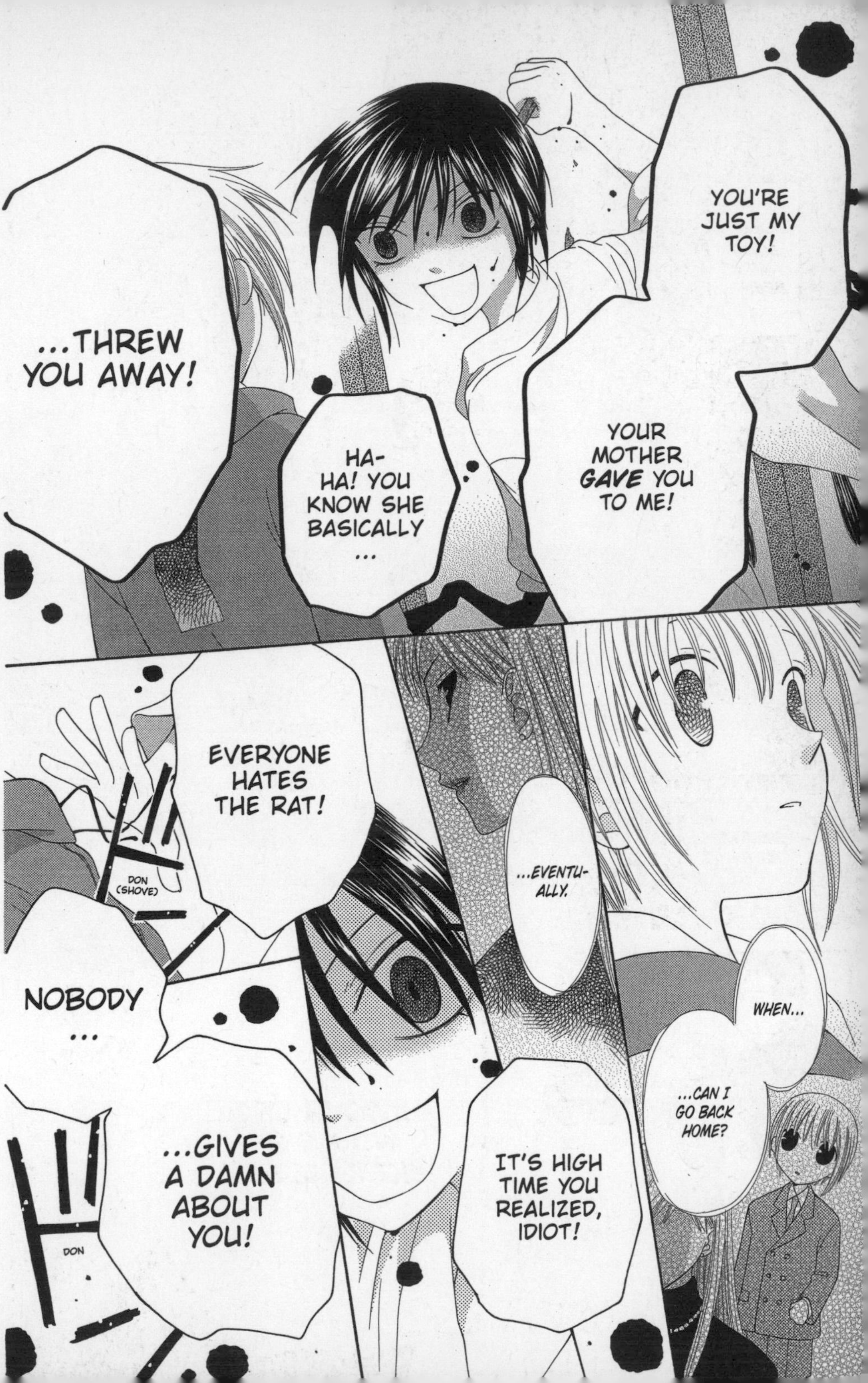
YOU'RE JUST MY TOY!
YOUR MOTHER GAVE YOU TO ME!
HA-HA! YOU KNOW SHE BASICALLY ...
...THREW YOU AWAY!
WHEN...
...EVENTU-ALLY.
...CAN I GO BACK HOME?
EVERYONE HATES THE RAT!
DON (SHOVE)
NOBODY ...
...GIVES A DAMN ABOUT YOU!
IT'S HIGH TIME YOU REALIZED, IDIOT!
DON

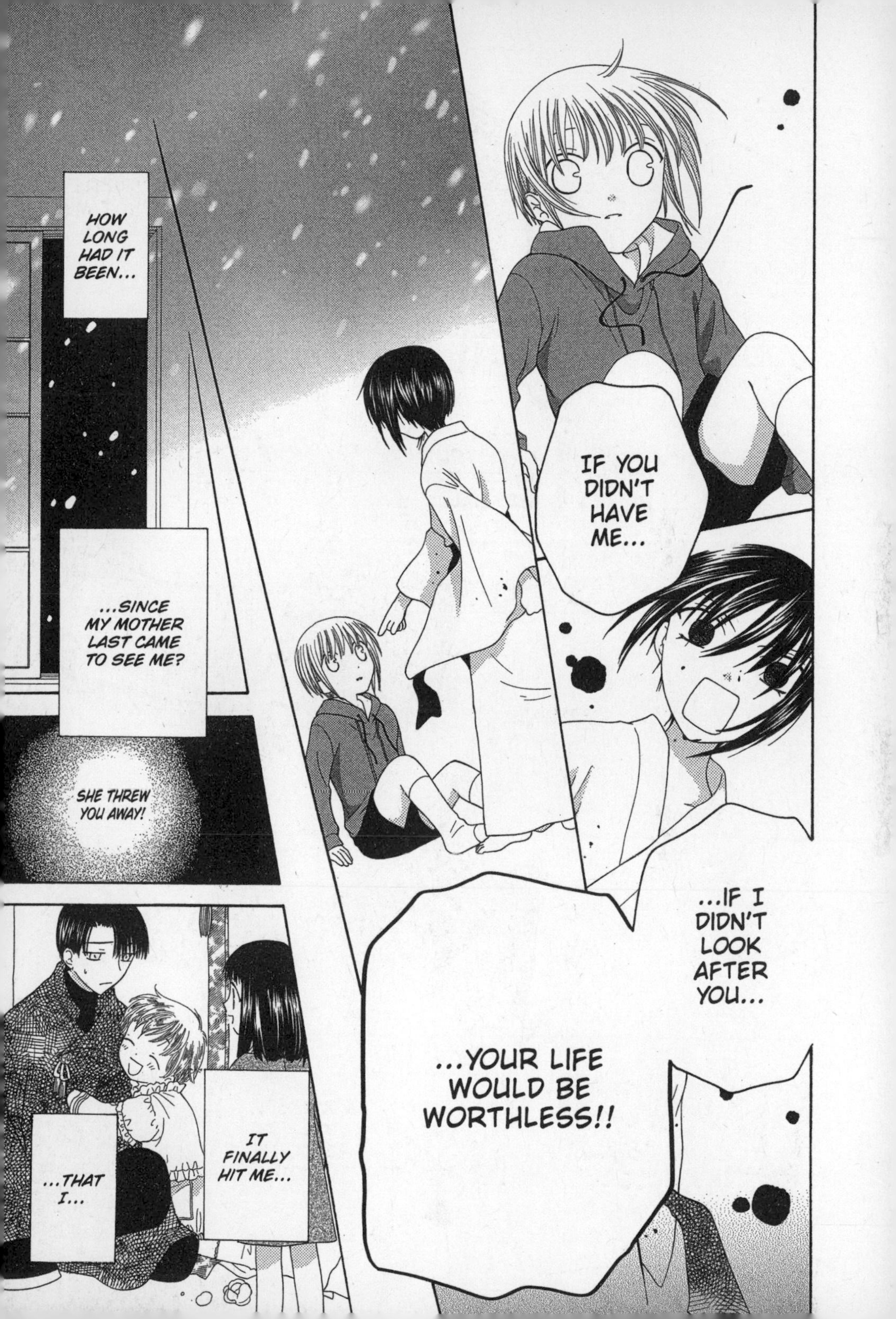
IF YOU DIDN'T HAVE ME...
...IF I DIDN'T LOOK AFTER YOU...
...YOUR LIFE WOULD BE WORTHLESS!!
HOW LONG HAD IT BEEN...
...SINCE MY MOTHER LAST CAME TO SEE ME?
SHE THREW YOU AWAY!
IT FINALLY HIT ME...
...THAT I...

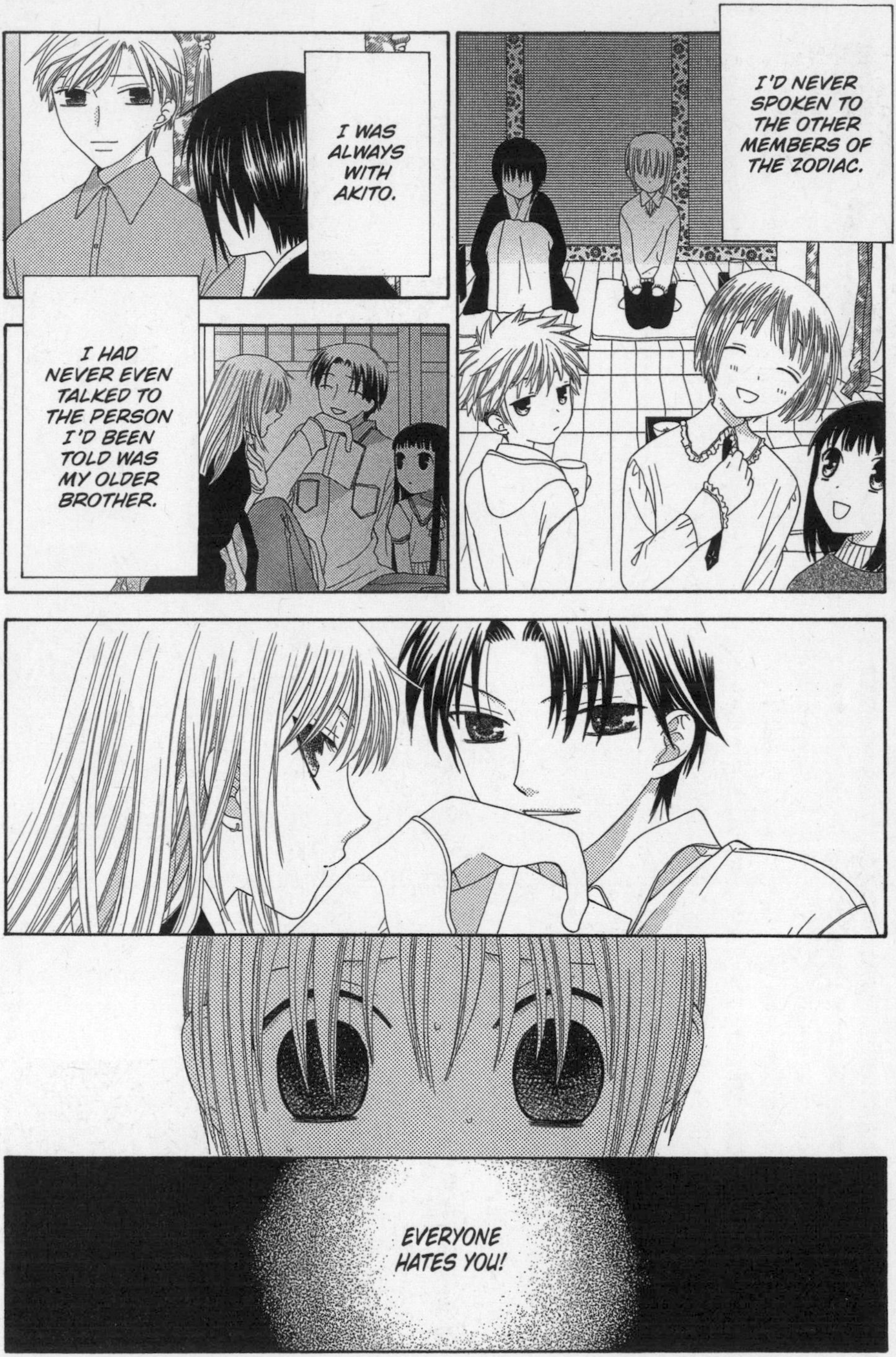
I'D NEVER SPOKEN TO THE OTHER MEMBERS OF THE ZODIAC.
I WAS ALWAYS WITH AKITO.
I HAD NEVER EVEN TALKED TO THE PERSON I'D BEEN TOLD WAS MY OLDER BROTHER.
EVERYONE HATES YOU!

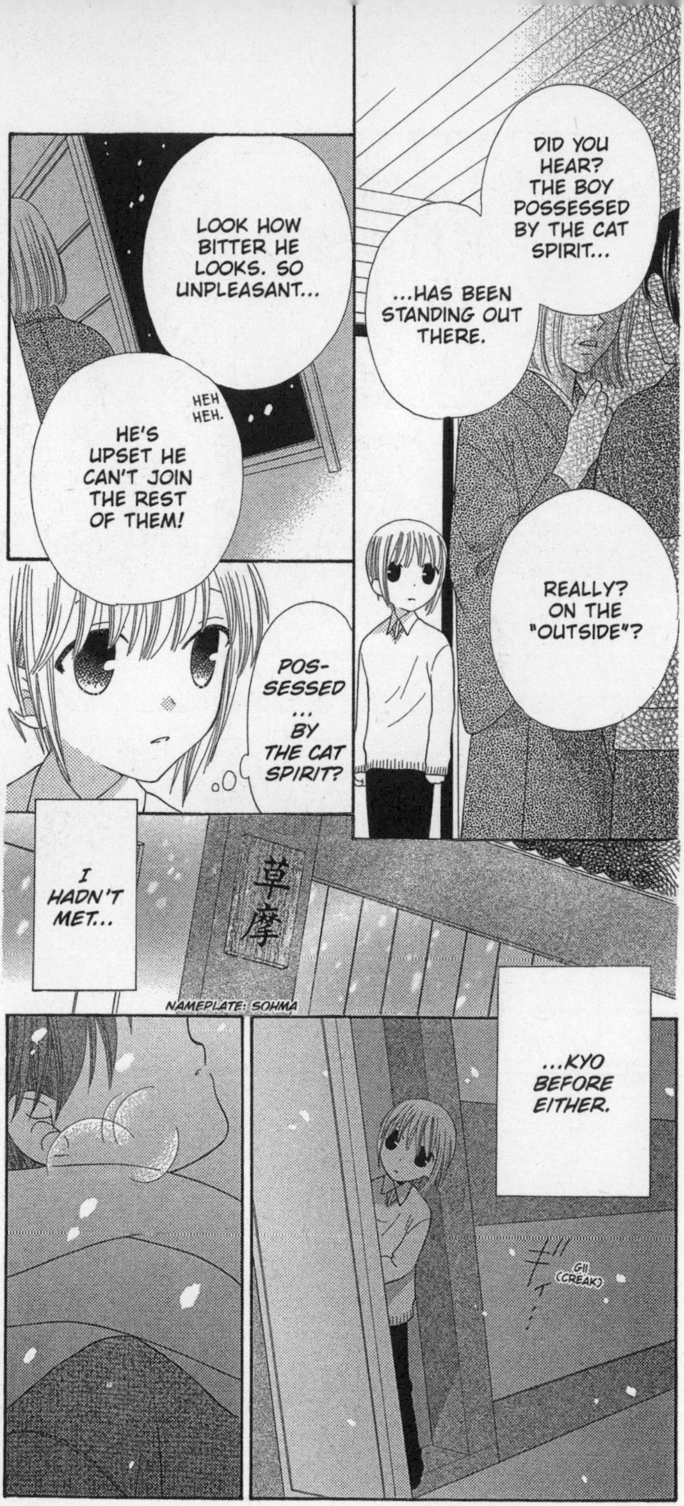
DID YOU HEAR? THE BOY POSSESSED BY THE CAT SPIRIT...
...HAS BEEN STANDING OUT THERE.
REALLY? ON THE "OUTSIDE"?
LOOK HOW BITTER HE LOOKS. SO UNPLEASANT...
HEH HEH.
HE'S UPSET HE CAN'T JOIN THE REST OF THEM!
POS-SESSED ... BY THE CAT SPIRIT?
I HADN'T MET...
草摩
NAMEPLATE: SOHMA
...KYO BEFORE EITHER.
GII (CREAK)

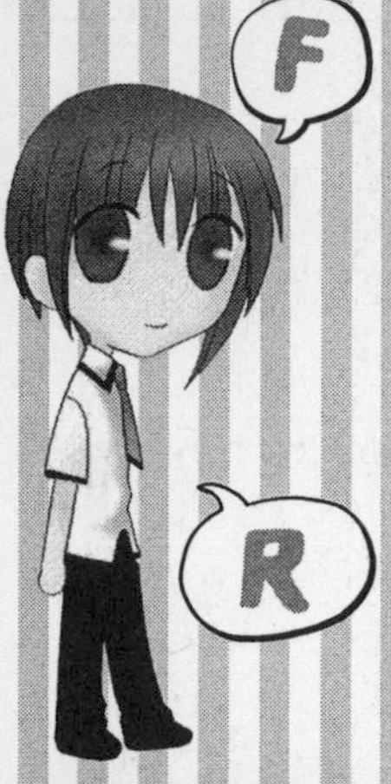
F
R

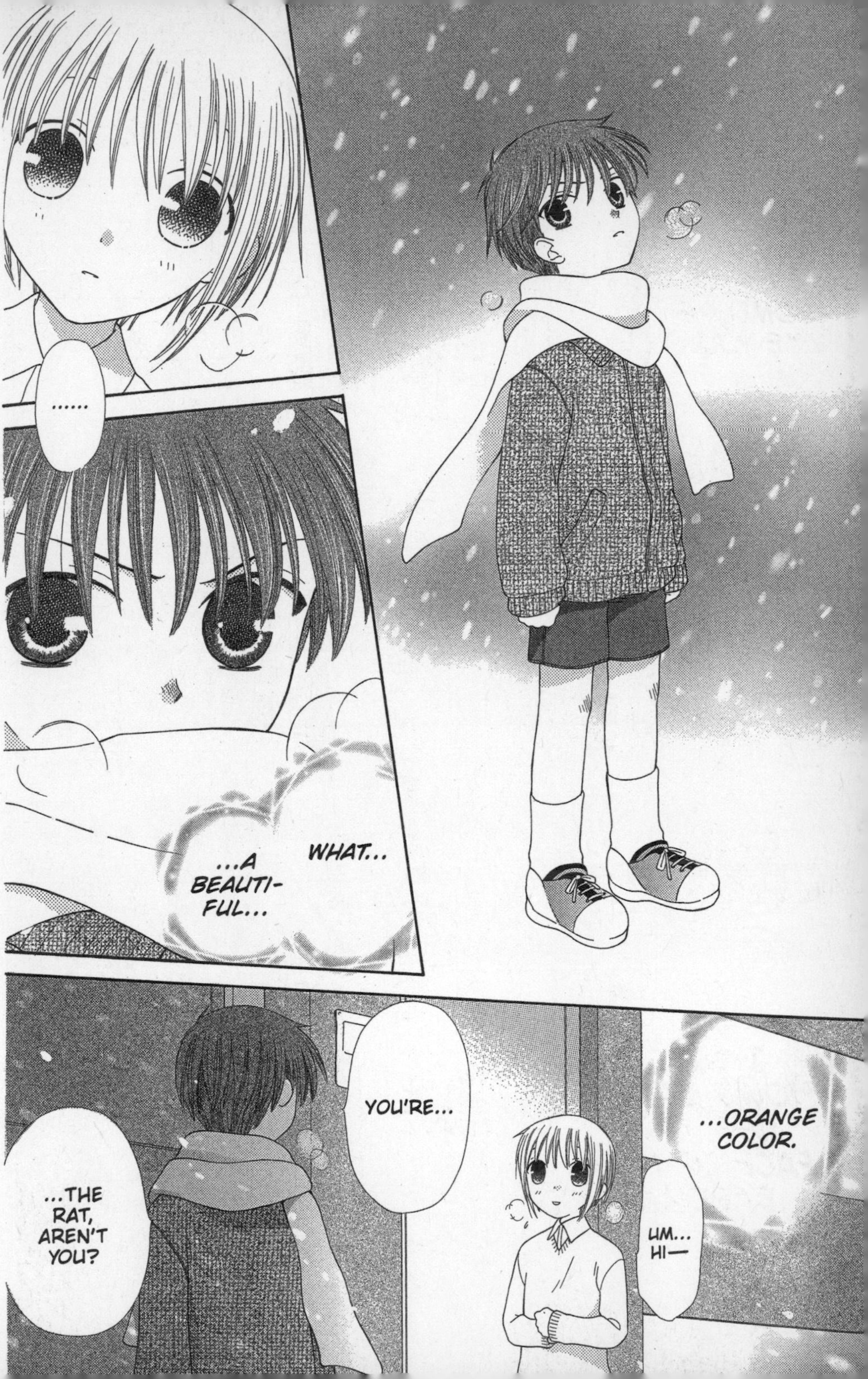
......
WHAT...
...A BEAUTIFUL...
...ORANGE COLOR.
UM... HI—
YOU'RE...
...THE RAT, AREN'T YOU?

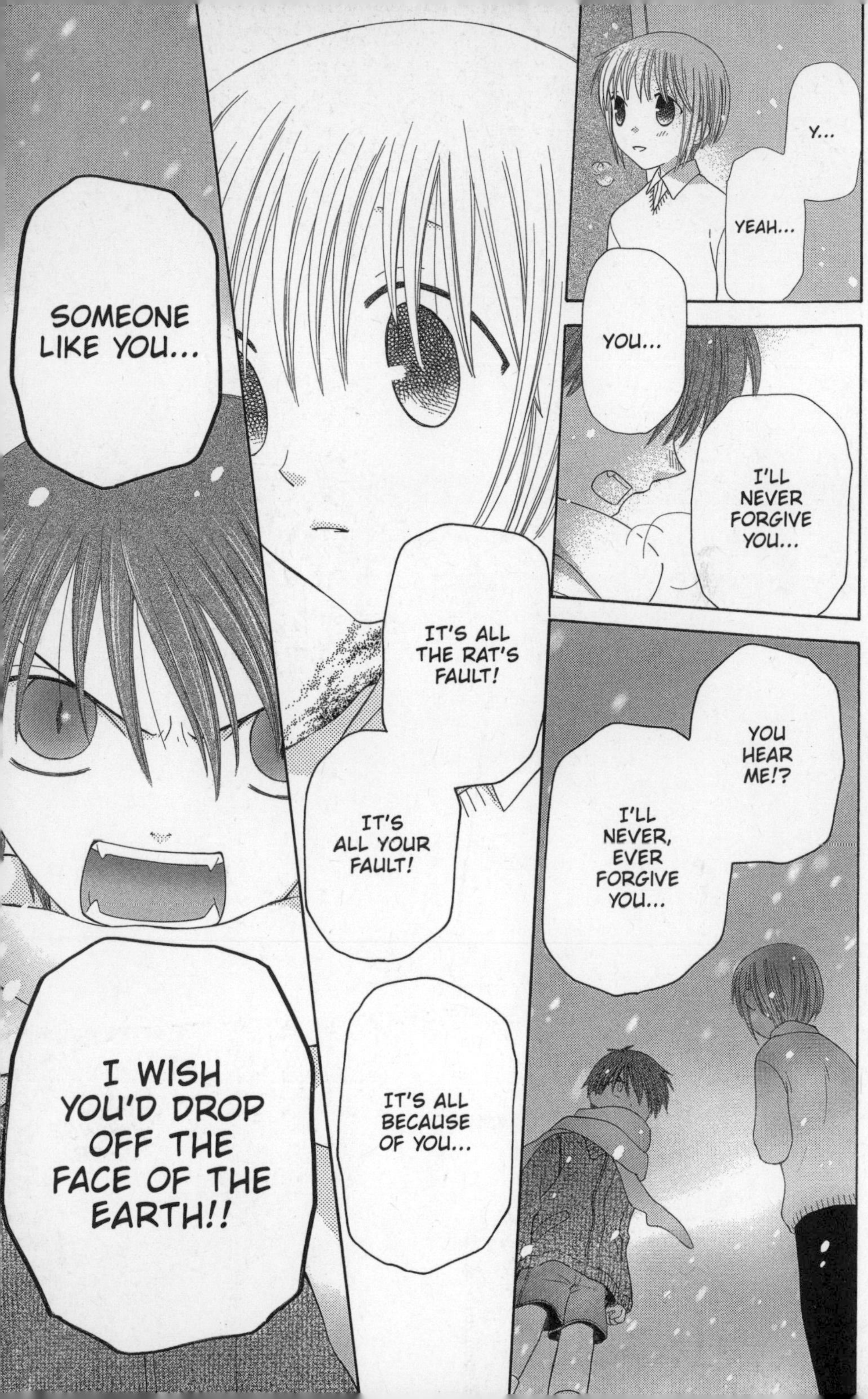
Y...
YEAH...
YOU...
I'LL NEVER FORGIVE YOU...
YOU HEAR ME!?
I'LL NEVER, EVER FORGIVE YOU...
IT'S ALL THE RAT'S FAULT!
IT'S ALL YOUR FAULT!
IT'S ALL BECAUSE OF YOU...
SOMEONE LIKE YOU...
I WISH YOU'D DROP OFF THE FACE OF THE EARTH!!

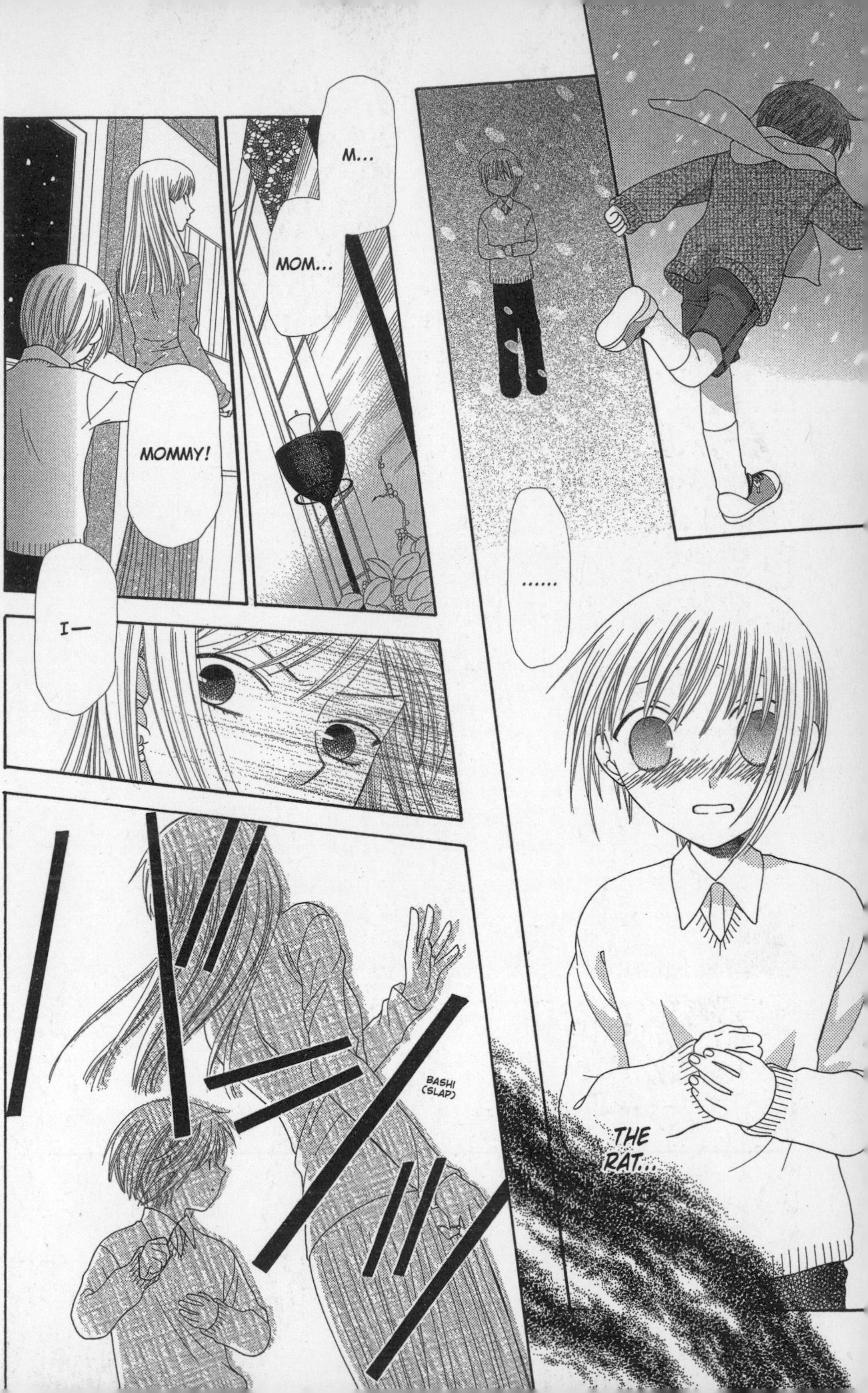
......
THE RAT...
M...
MOM...
MOMMY!
I—
BASHI (SLAP)

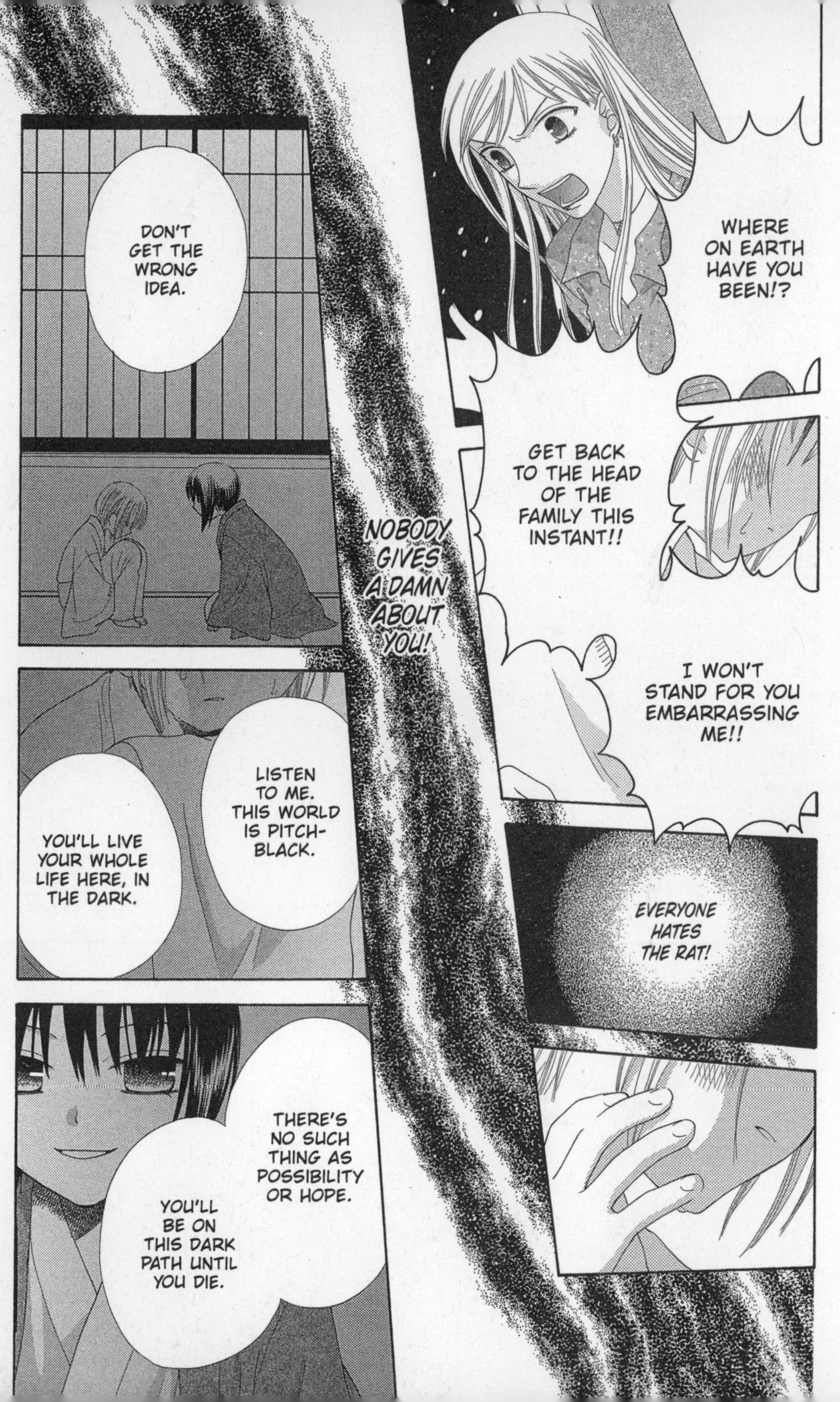
WHERE ON EARTH HAVE YOU BEEN!?
GET BACK TO THE HEAD OF THE FAMILY THIS INSTANT!!
I WON'T STAND FOR YOU EMBARRASSING ME!!
EVERYONE HATES THE RAT!
NOBODY GIVES A DAMN ABOUT YOU!
DON'T GET THE WRONG IDEA.
LISTEN TO ME. THIS WORLD IS PITCH-BLACK.
YOU'LL LIVE YOUR WHOLE LIFE HERE, IN THE DARK.
THERE'S NO SUCH THING AS POSSIBILITY OR HOPE.
YOU'LL BE ON THIS DARK PATH UNTIL YOU DIE.

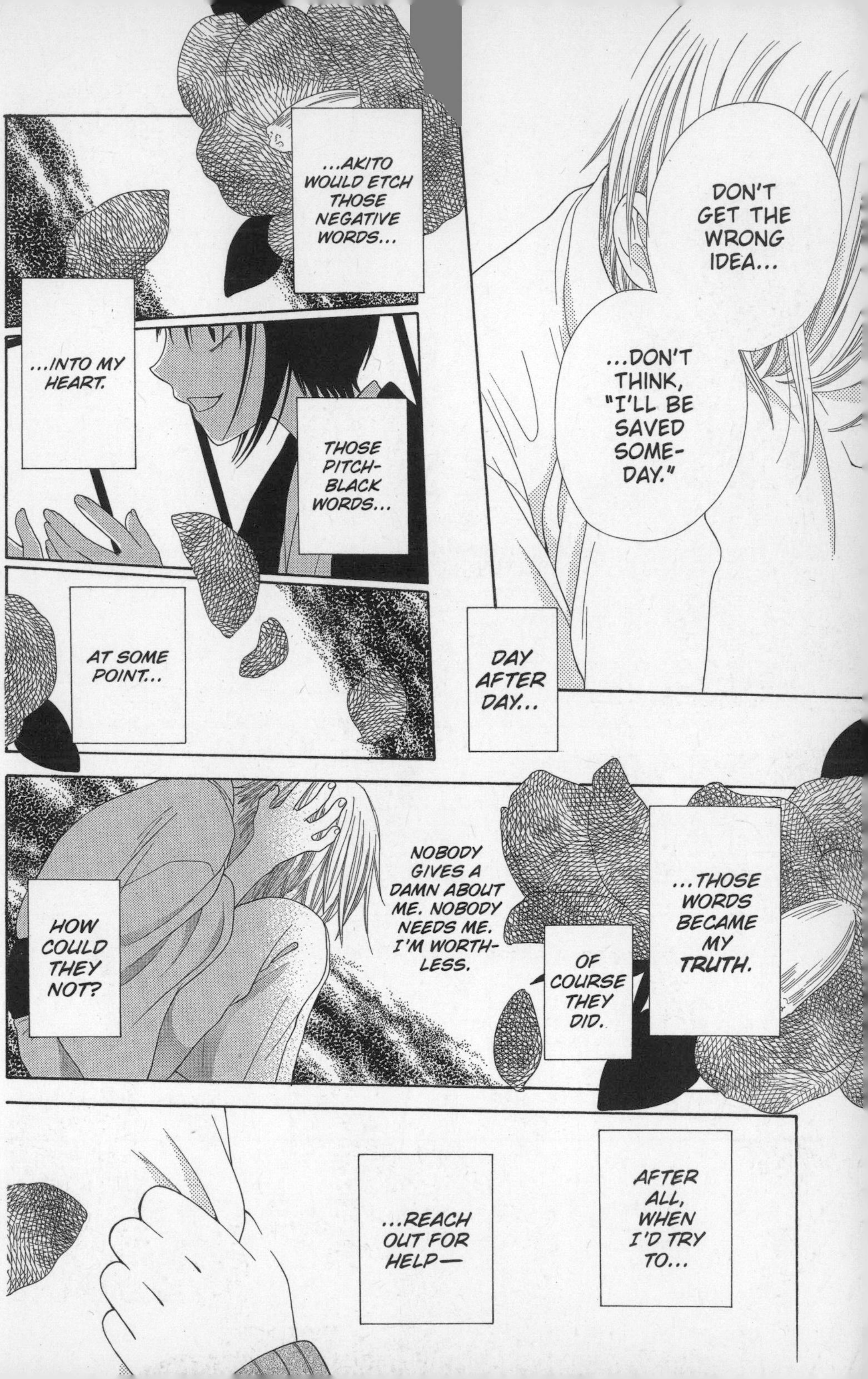
DON'T GET THE WRONG IDEA...
...DON'T THINK, "I'LL BE SAVED SOME-DAY."
DAY AFTER DAY...
...AKITO WOULD ETCH THOSE NEGATIVE WORDS...
...INTO MY HEART.
THOSE PITCH-BLACK WORDS...
AT SOME POINT...
...THOSE WORDS BECAME MY TRUTH.
OF COURSE THEY DID.
NOBODY GIVES A DAMN ABOUT ME. NOBODY NEEDS ME. I'M WORTH-LESS.
HOW COULD THEY NOT?
AFTER ALL, WHEN I'D TRY TO...
...REACH OUT FOR HELP—

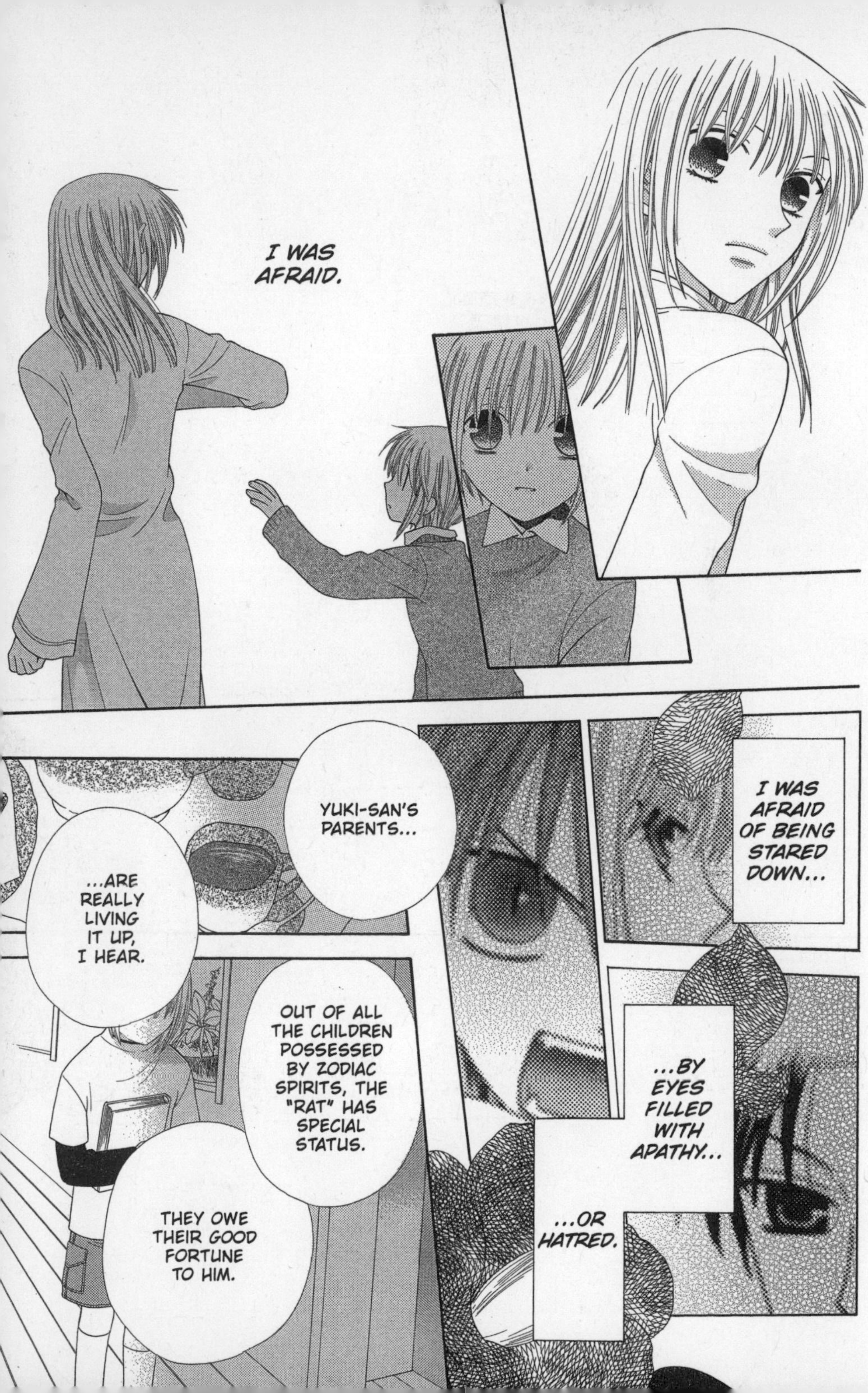
I WAS AFRAID.
I WAS AFRAID OF BEING STARED DOWN...
...BY EYES FILLED WITH APATHY...
...OR HATRED.
YUKI-SAN'S PARENTS...
...ARE REALLY LIVING IT UP, I HEAR.
OUT OF ALL THE CHILDREN POSSESSED BY ZODIAC SPIRITS, THE "RAT" HAS SPECIAL STATUS.
THEY OWE THEIR GOOD FORTUNE TO HIM.

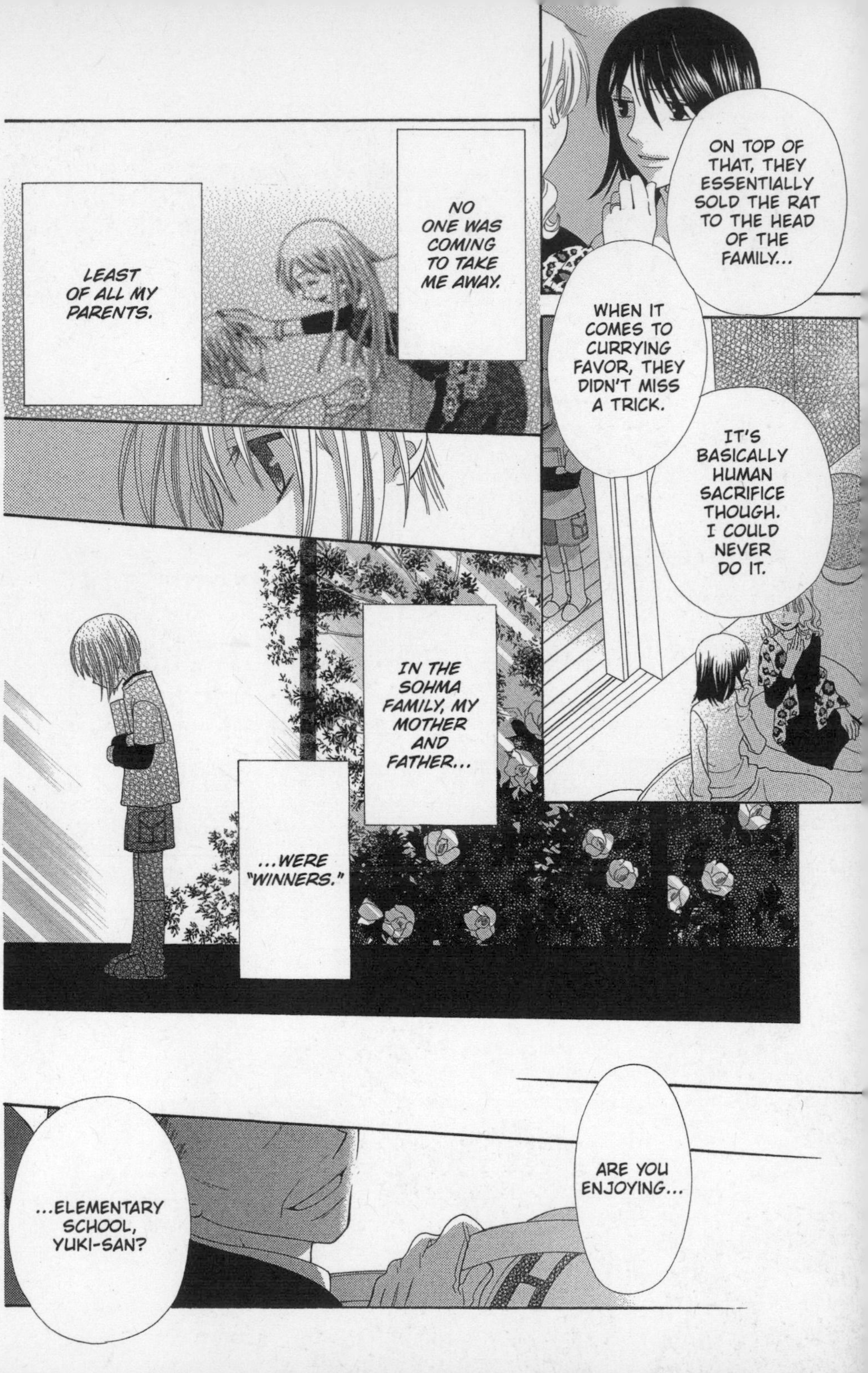
ON TOP OF THAT, THEY ESSENTIALLY SOLD THE RAT TO THE HEAD OF THE FAMILY...
WHEN IT COMES TO CURRYING FAVOR, THEY DIDN'T MISS A TRICK.
IT'S BASICALLY HUMAN SACRIFICE THOUGH. I COULD NEVER DO IT.
NO ONE WAS COMING TO TAKE ME AWAY.
LEAST OF ALL MY PARENTS.
IN THE SOHMA FAMILY, MY MOTHER AND FATHER...
...WERE "WINNERS."
ARE YOU ENJOYING...
...ELEMENTARY SCHOOL, YUKI-SAN?

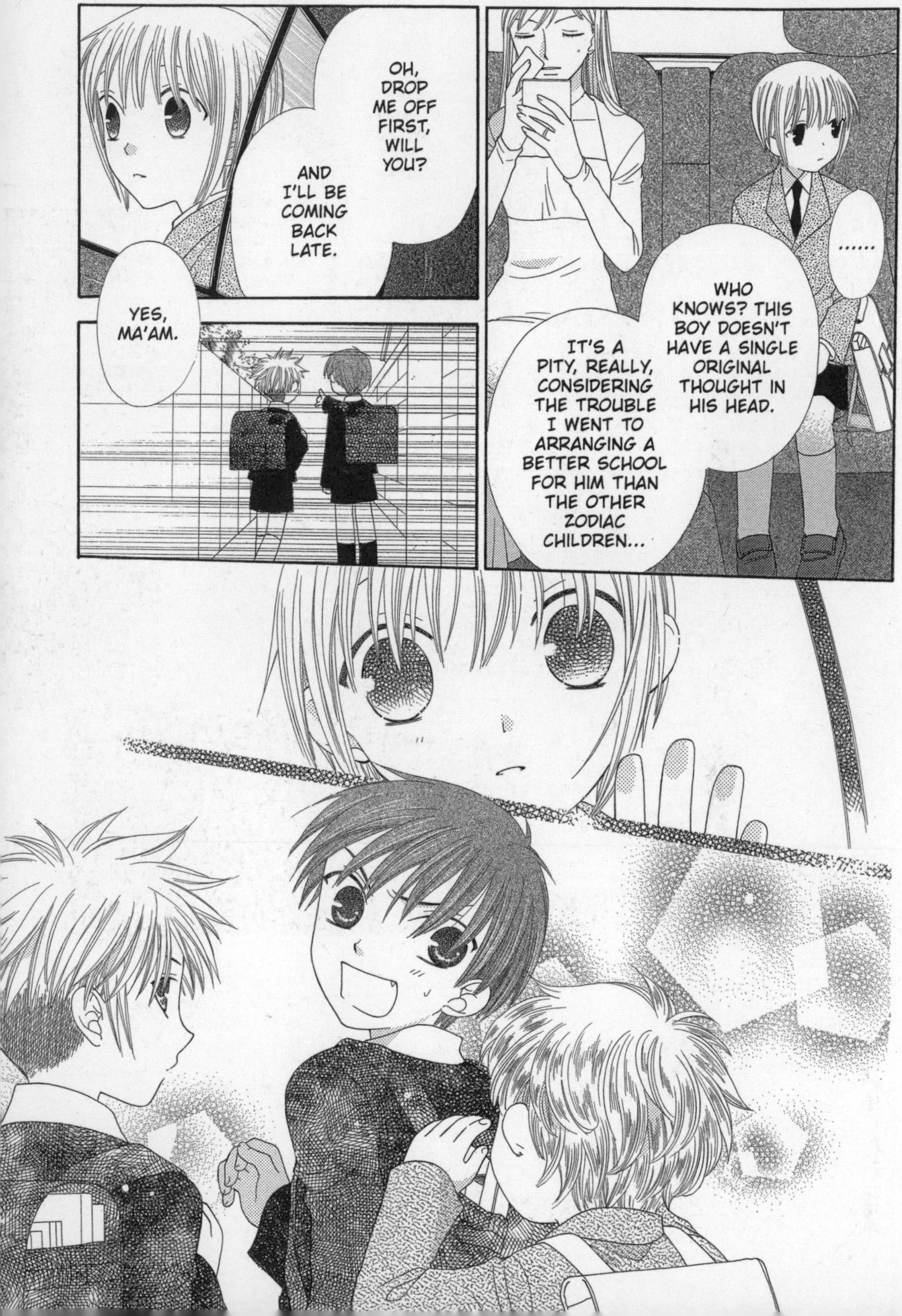
......
WHO KNOWS? THIS BOY DOESN'T HAVE A SINGLE ORIGINAL THOUGHT IN HIS HEAD.
IT'S A PITY, REALLY, CONSIDERING THE TROUBLE I WENT TO ARRANGING A BETTER SCHOOL FOR HIM THAN THE OTHER ZODIAC CHILDREN...
OH, DROP ME OFF FIRST, WILL YOU?
AND I'LL BE COMING BACK LATE.
YES, MA'AM.

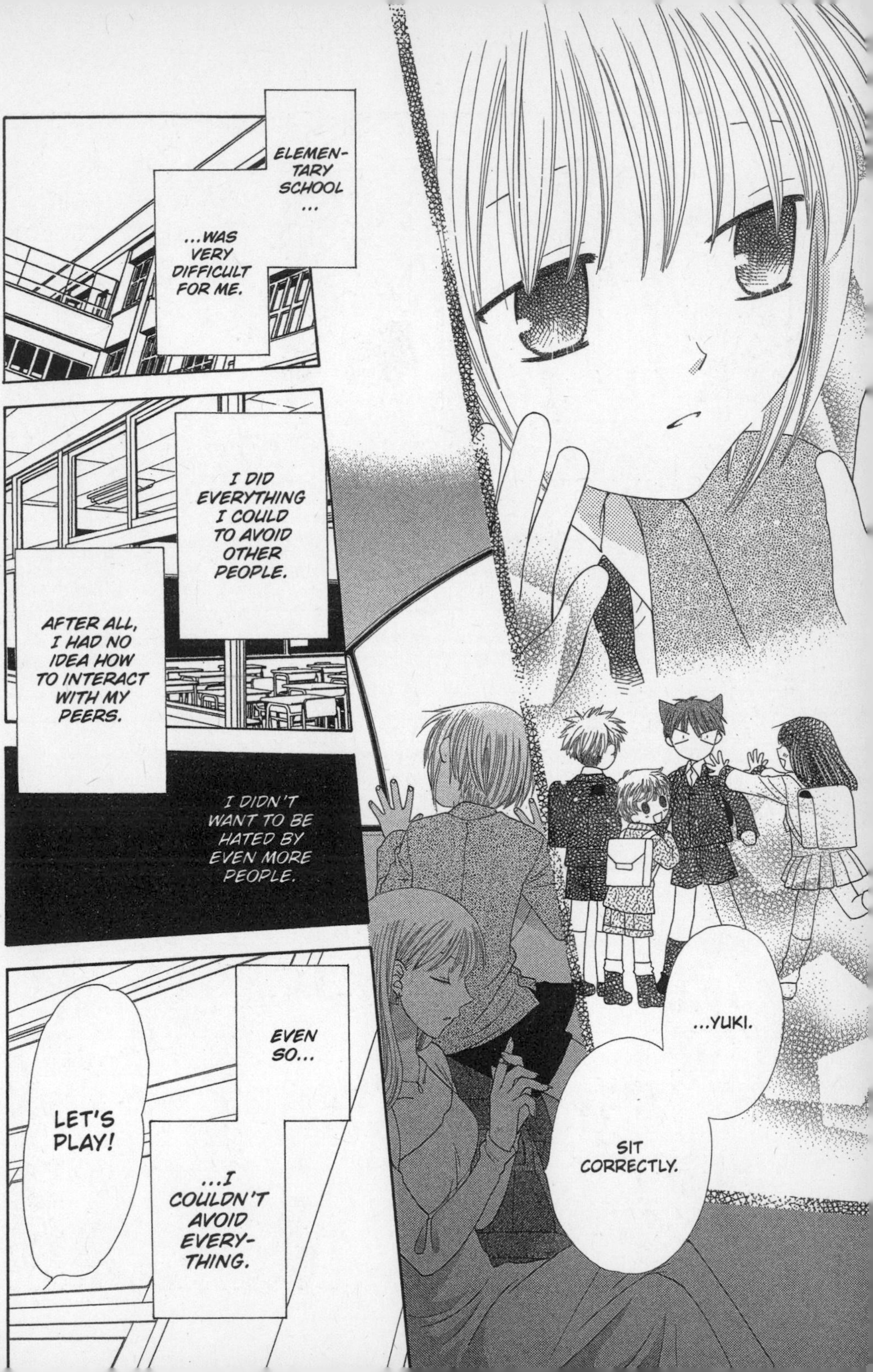

...YUKI.
SIT CORRECTLY.
ELEMEN-TARY SCHOOL ...
...WAS VERY DIFFICULT FOR ME.
I DID EVERYTHING I COULD TO AVOID OTHER PEOPLE.
AFTER ALL, I HAD NO IDEA HOW TO INTERACT WITH MY PEERS.
I DIDN'T WANT TO BE HATED BY EVEN MORE PEOPLE.
EVEN SO...
LET'S PLAY!
...I COULDN'T AVOID EVERY-THING.

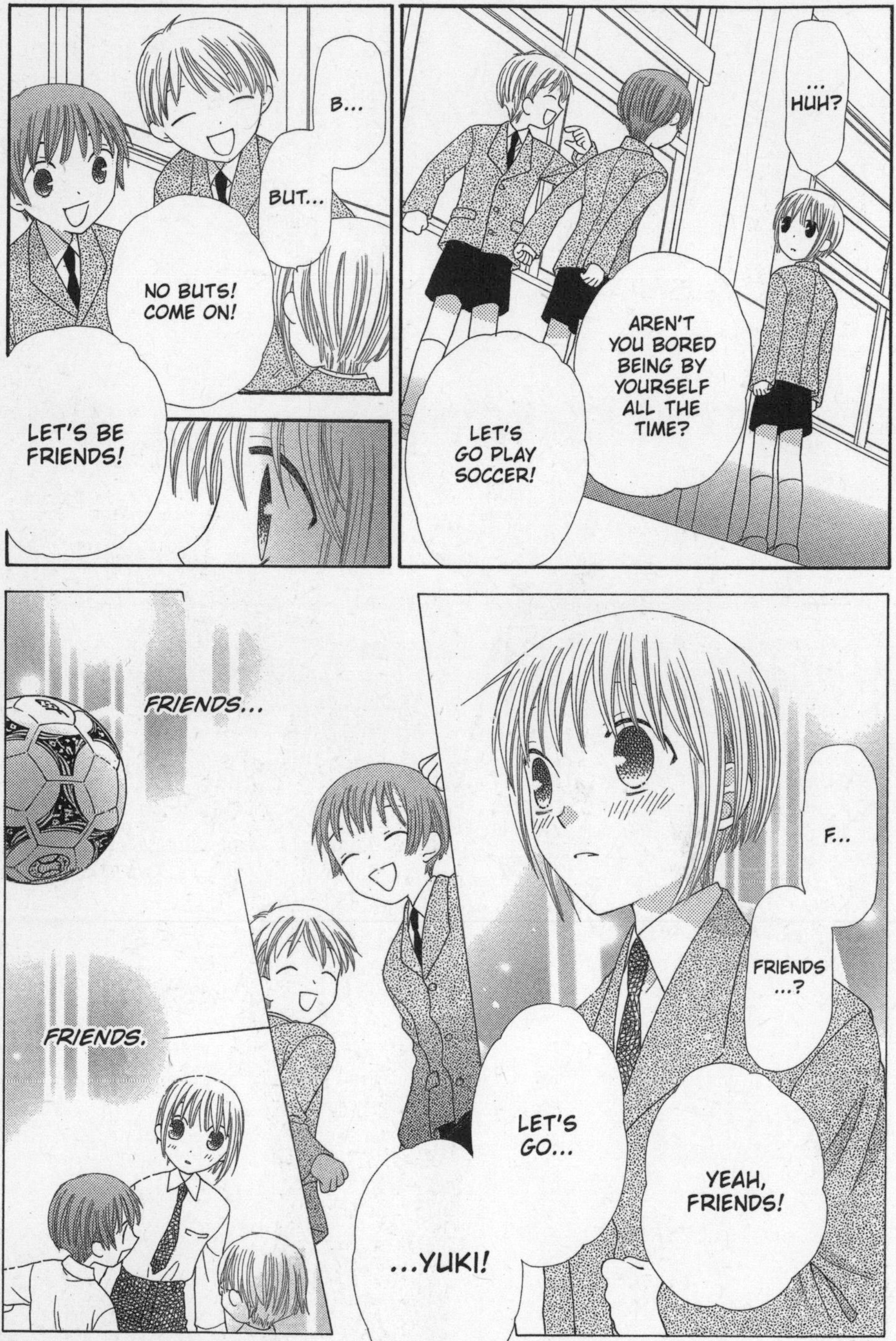
...HUH?
AREN'T YOU BORED BEING BY YOURSELF ALL THE TIME?
LET'S GO PLAY SOCCER!
B...
BUT...
NO BUTS! COME ON!
LET'S BE FRIENDS!
F...
FRIENDS ...?
YEAH, FRIENDS!
LET'S GO...
...YUKI!
FRIENDS...
FRIENDS.

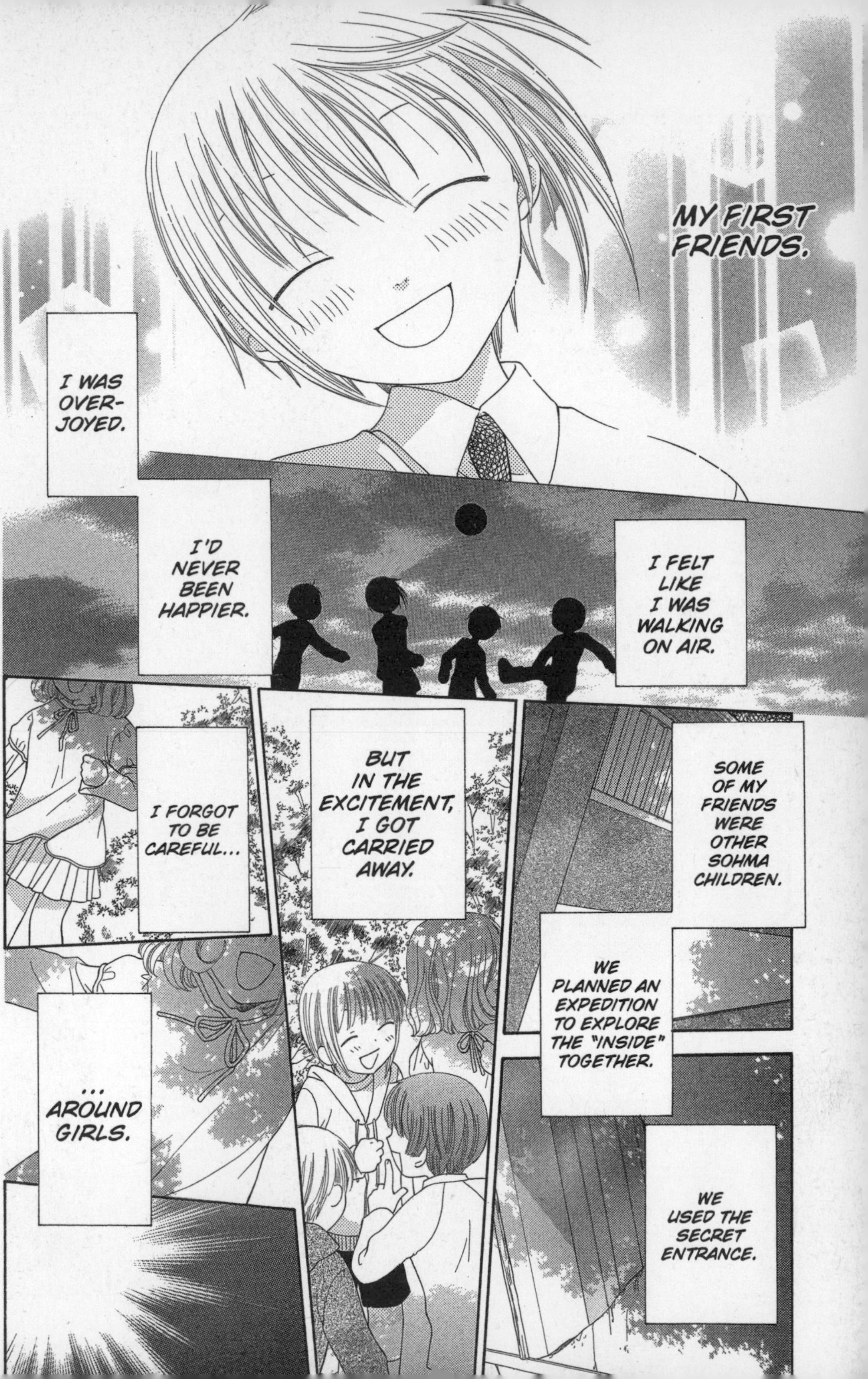
MY FIRST FRIENDS.
I WAS OVER-JOYED.
I FELT LIKE I WAS WALKING ON AIR.
I'D NEVER BEEN HAPPIER.
SOME OF MY FRIENDS WERE OTHER SOHMA CHILDREN.
WE PLANNED AN EXPEDITION TO EXPLORE THE "INSIDE" TOGETHER.
WE USED THE SECRET ENTRANCE.
BUT IN THE EXCITEMENT, I GOT CARRIED AWAY.
I FORGOT TO BE CAREFUL...
...AROUND GIRLS.

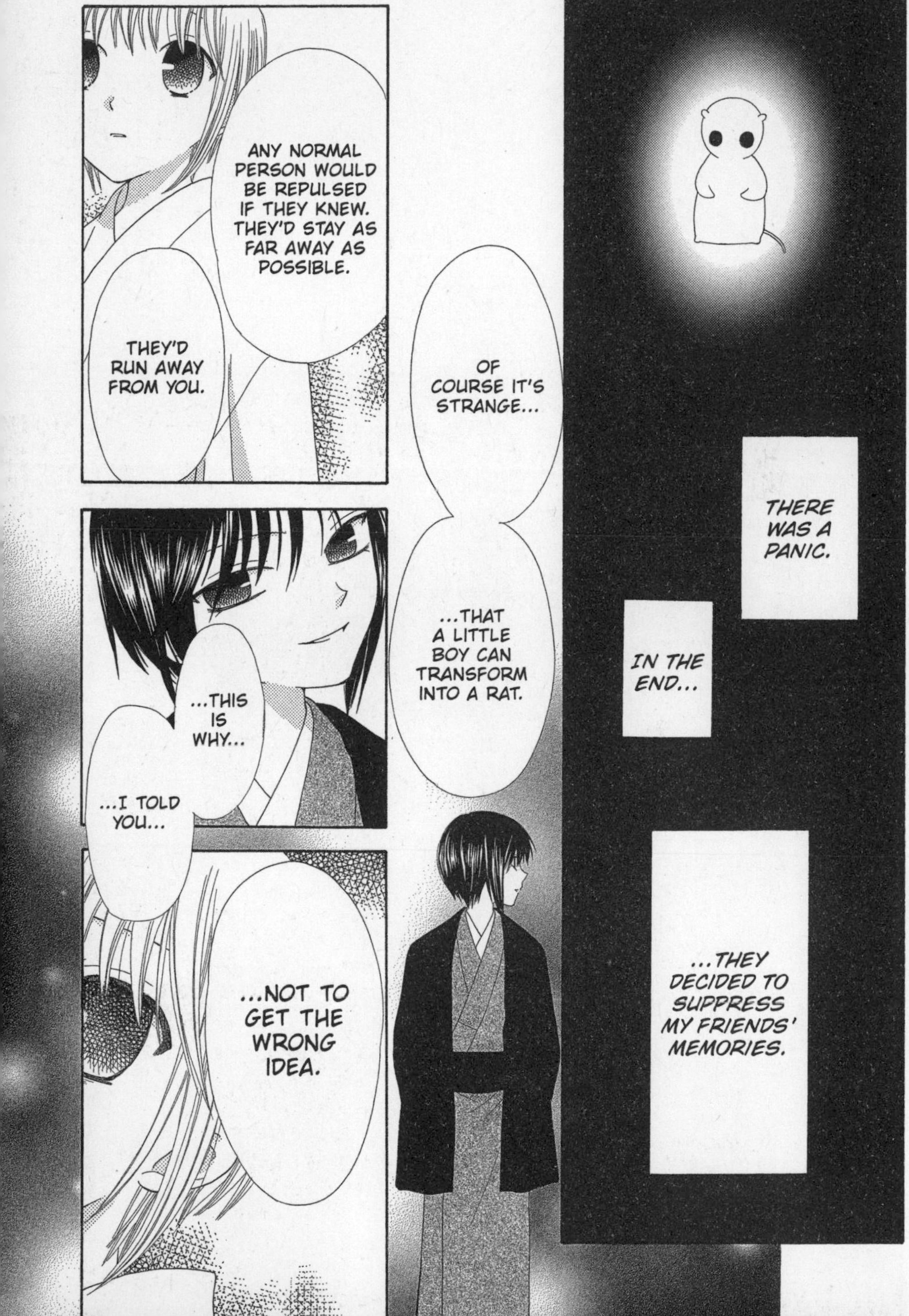
THERE WAS A PANIC.
IN THE END...
...THEY DECIDED TO SUPPRESS MY FRIENDS' MEMORIES.
ANY NORMAL PERSON WOULD BE REPULSED IF THEY KNEW. THEY'D STAY AS FAR AWAY AS POSSIBLE.
THEY'D RUN AWAY FROM YOU.
OF COURSE IT'S STRANGE...
...THAT A LITTLE BOY CAN TRANSFORM INTO A RAT.
...THIS IS WHY...
...I TOLD YOU...
...NOT TO GET THE WRONG IDEA.

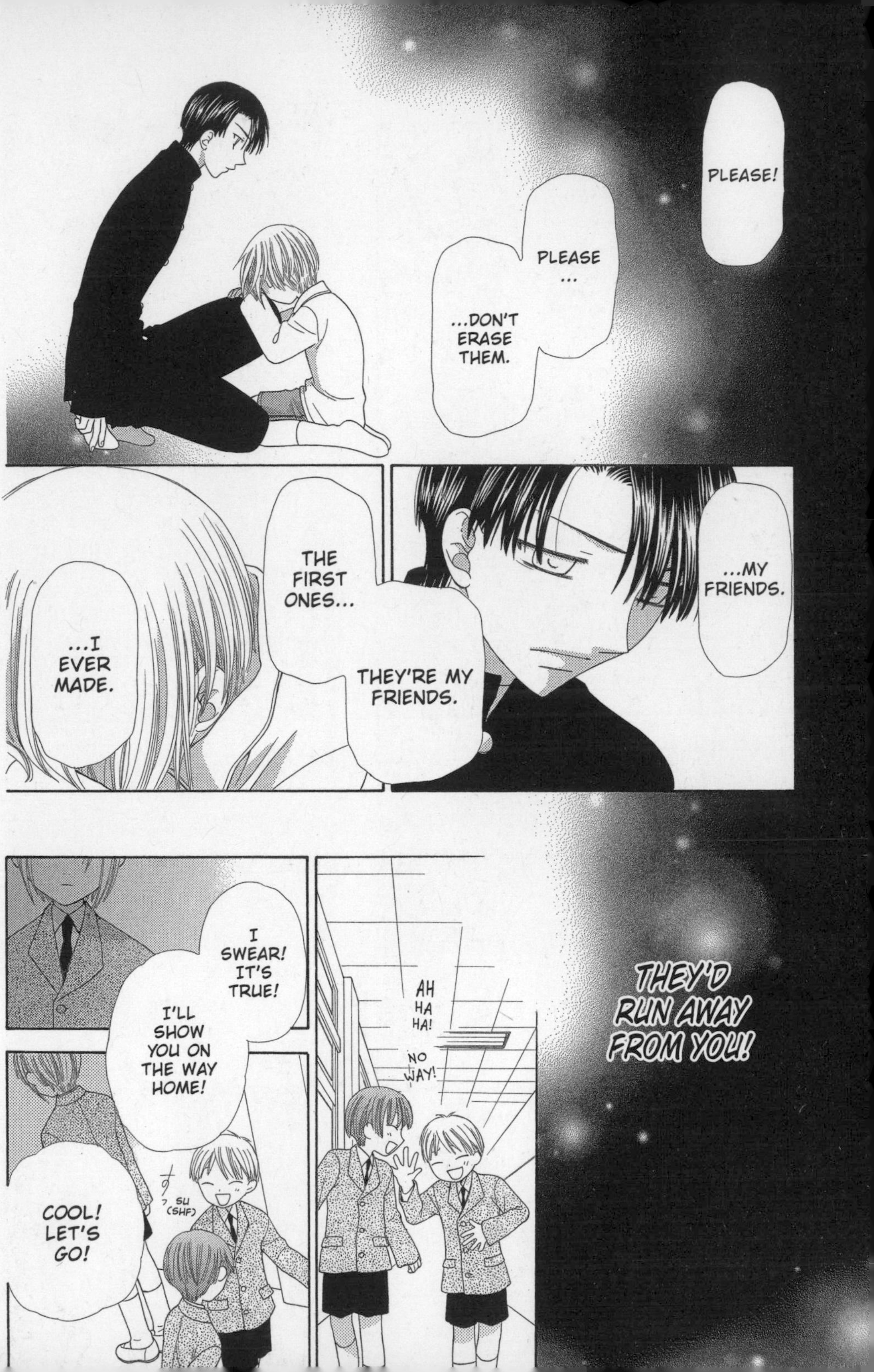
PLEASE!
PLEASE ...
...DON'T ERASE THEM.
...MY FRIENDS.
THEY'RE MY FRIENDS.
THE FIRST ONES...
...I EVER MADE.
THEY'D RUN AWAY FROM YOU!
AH HA HA!
NO WAY!
I SWEAR! IT'S TRUE!
I'LL SHOW YOU ON THE WAY HOME!
す SU (SHF)
COOL! LET'S GO!

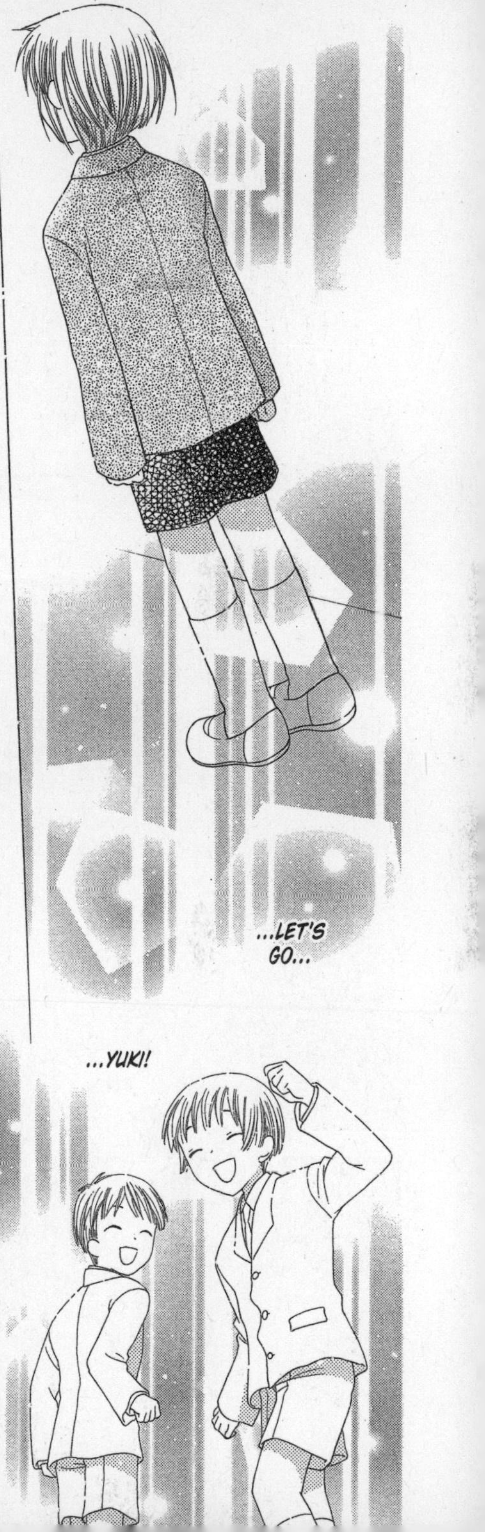
...LET'S GO...
...YUKI!

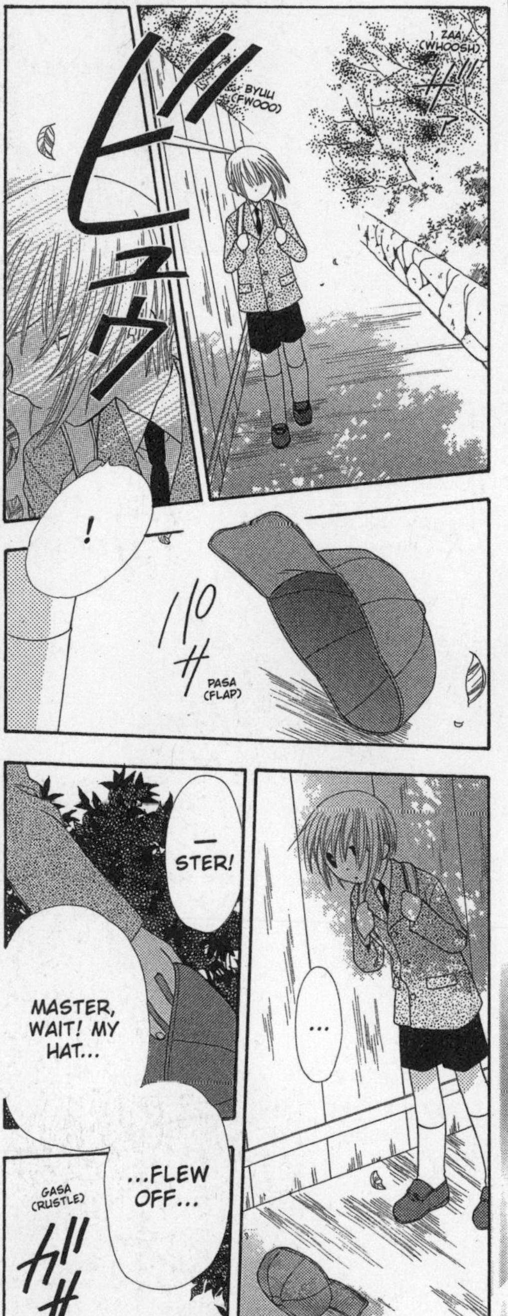
ZAA (WHOOSH)
ザァ
BYUU (FWOOO)
ビュウ
!
パサ
PASA (FLAP)
—STER!
...
MASTER, WAIT! MY HAT...
...FLEW OFF...
GASA (RUSTLE)
ガサ

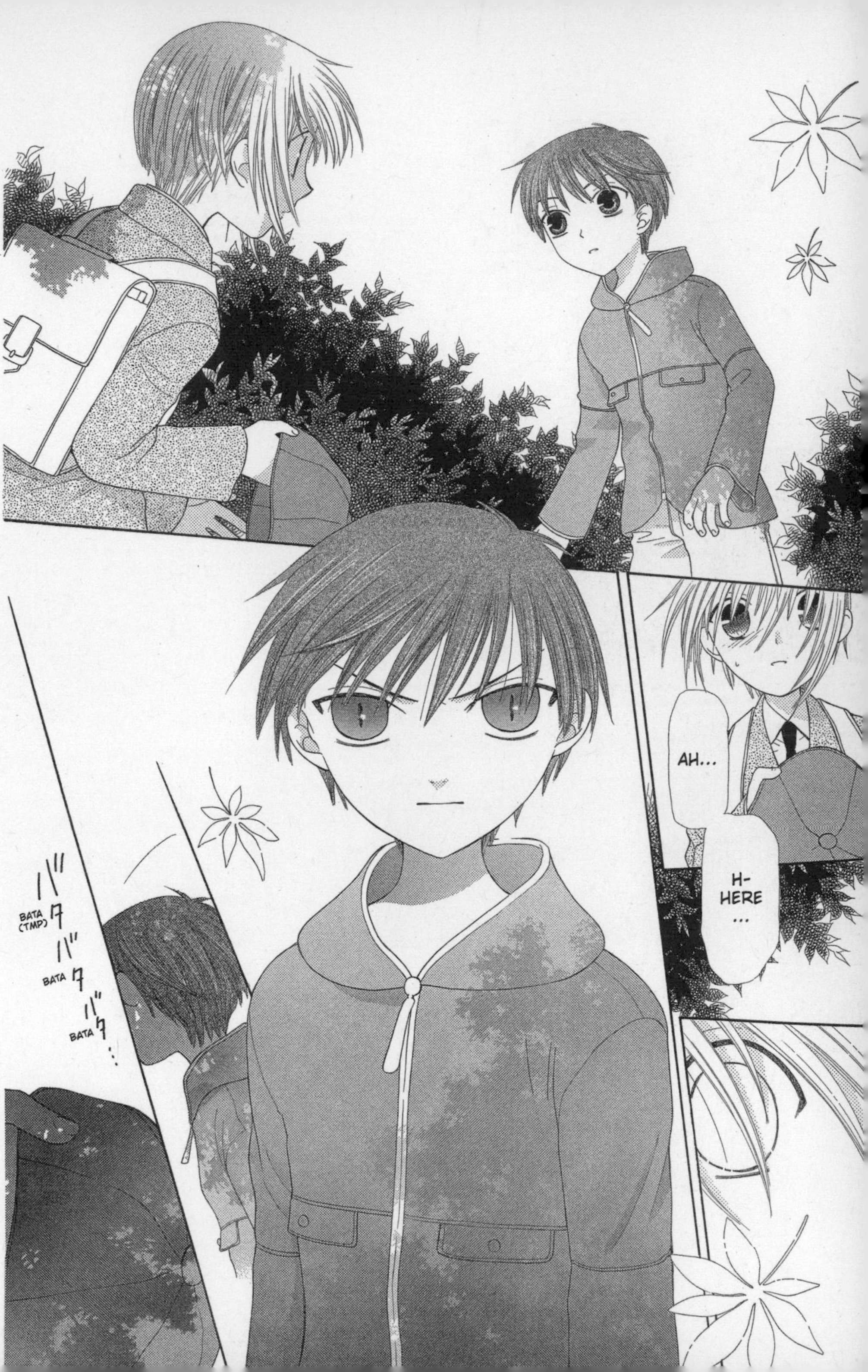
AH...
H-HERE...
バタ
BATA (TMP)
バタ
BATA
バタ
BATA

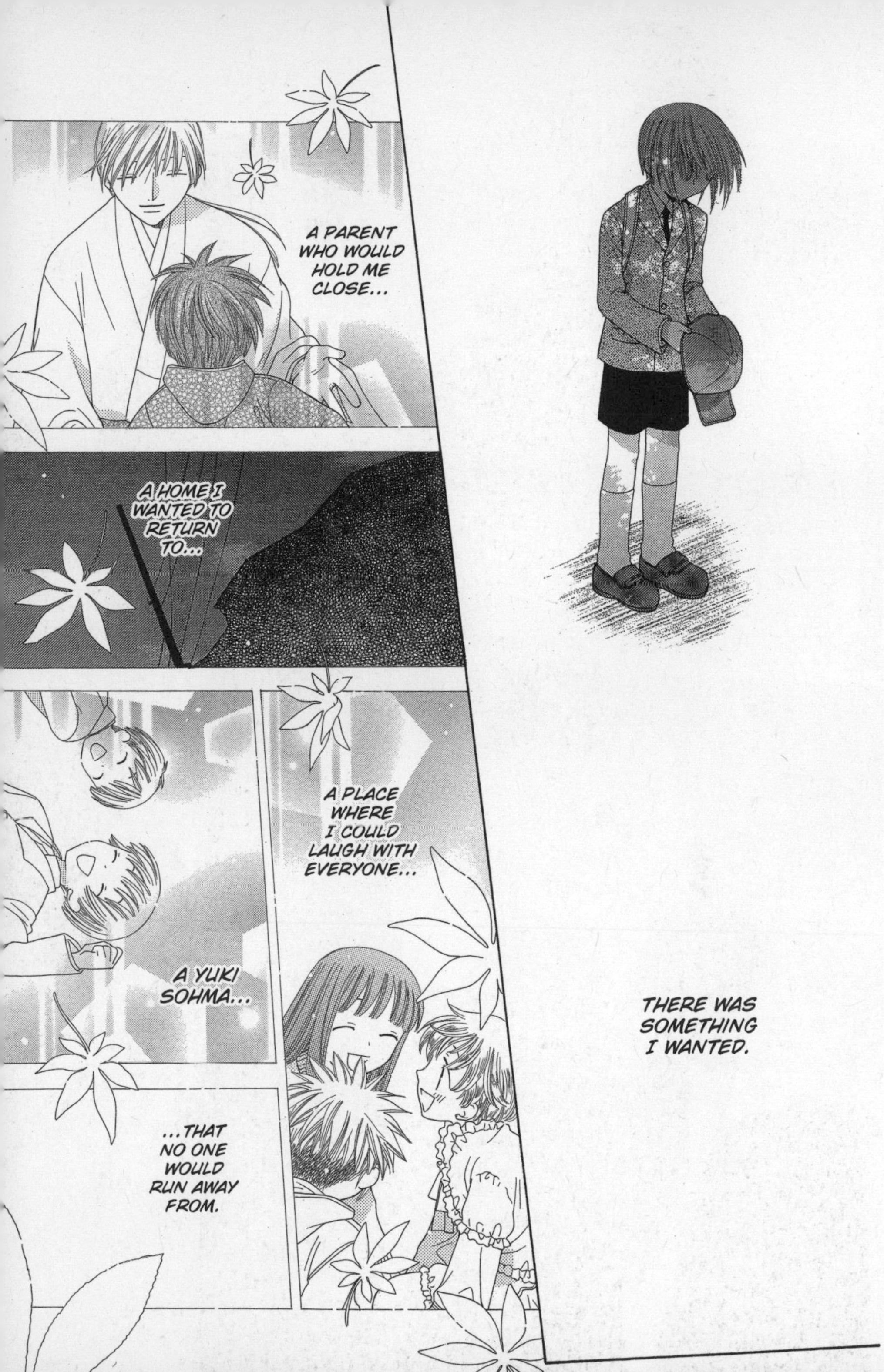
THERE WAS SOMETHING I WANTED.
A PARENT WHO WOULD HOLD ME CLOSE...
A HOME I WANTED TO RETURN TO...
A PLACE WHERE I COULD LAUGH WITH EVERYONE...
A YUKI SOHMA...
...THAT NO ONE WOULD RUN AWAY FROM.

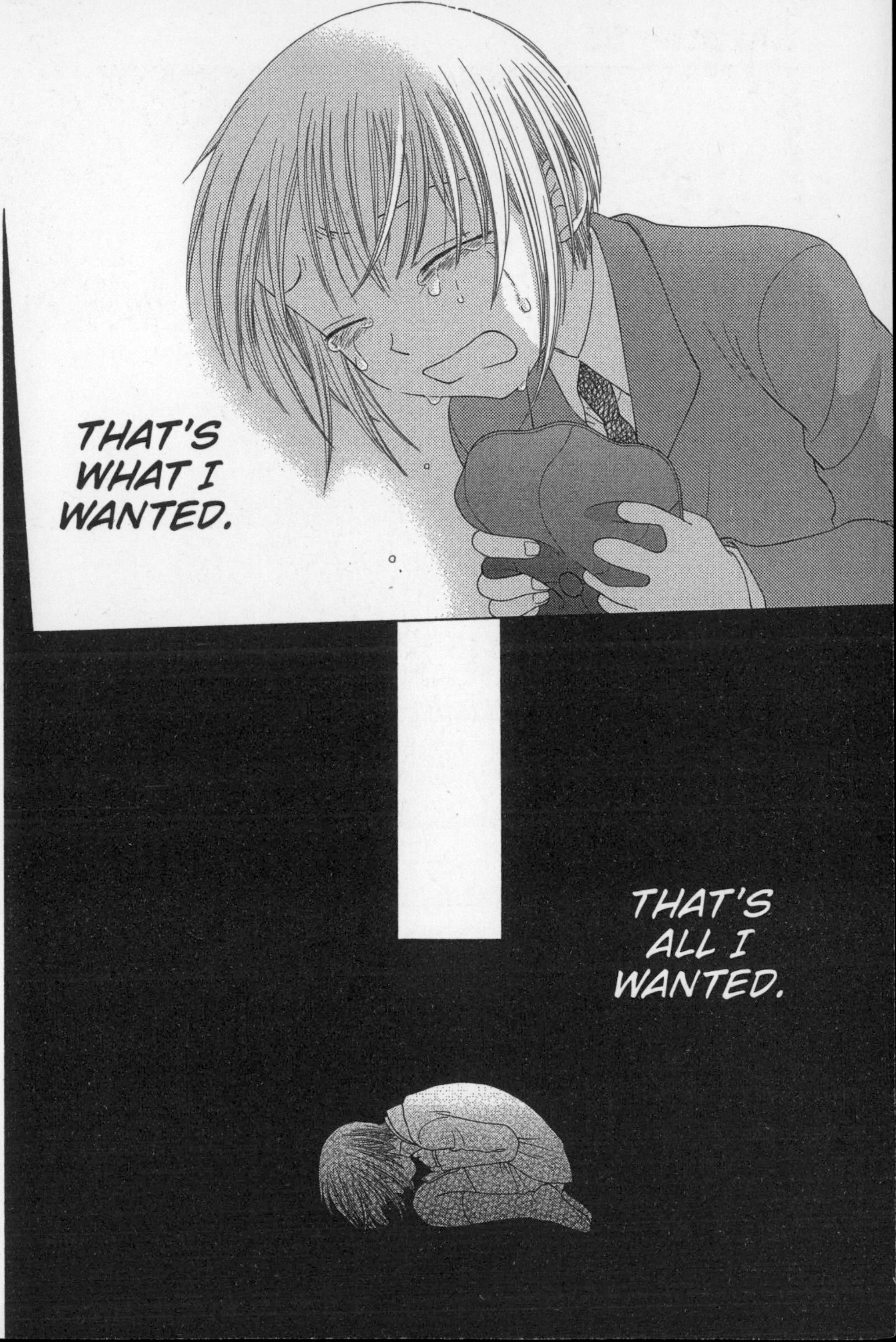
THAT'S WHAT I WANTED.
THAT'S ALL I WANTED.

Chapter 85

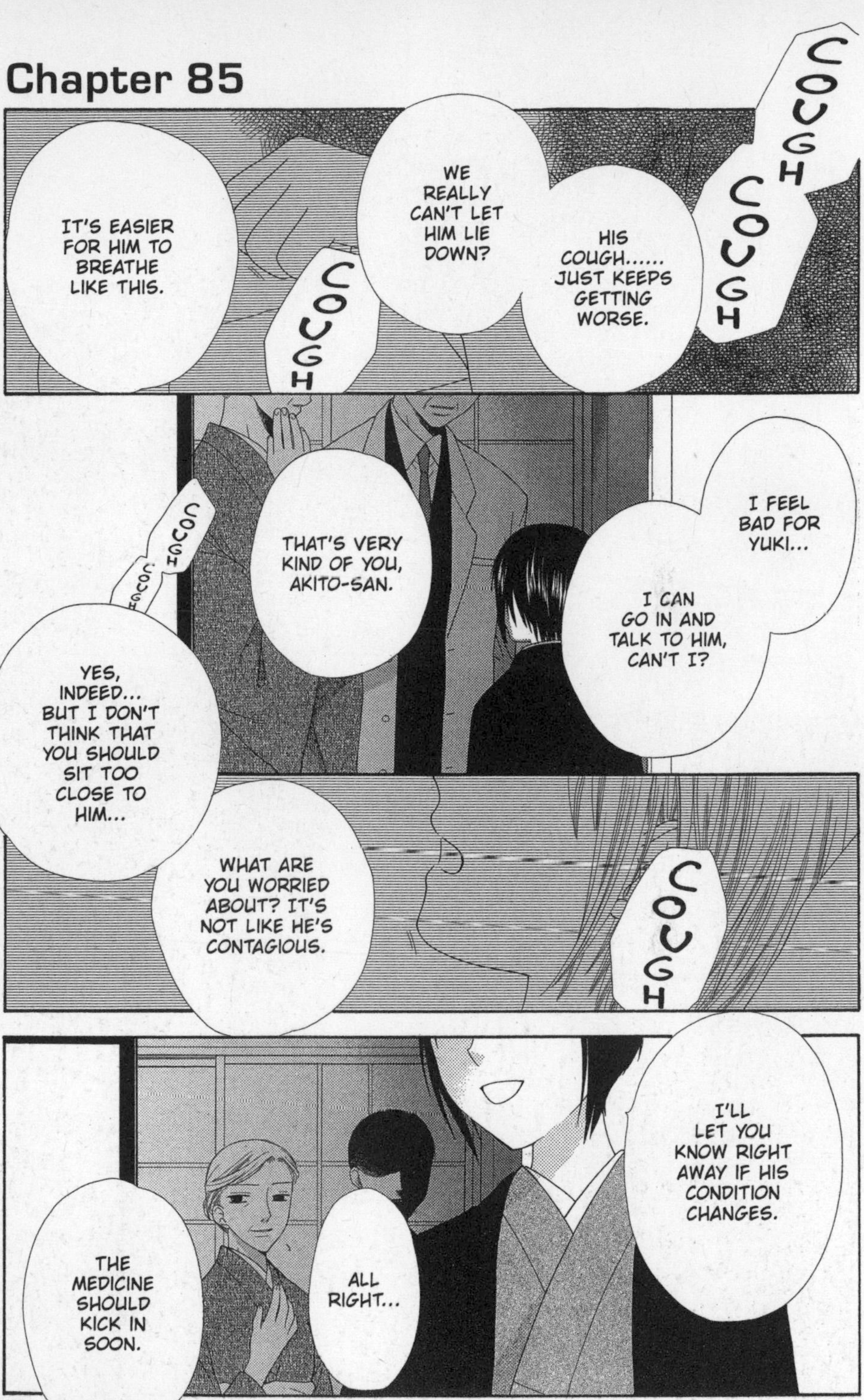
COUGH
COUGH
HIS COUGH...... JUST KEEPS GETTING WORSE.
WE REALLY CAN'T LET HIM LIE DOWN?
COUGH
IT'S EASIER FOR HIM TO BREATHE LIKE THIS.
I FEEL BAD FOR YUKI...
I CAN GO IN AND TALK TO HIM, CAN'T I?
THAT'S VERY KIND OF YOU, AKITO-SAN.
COUGH
COUGH
YES, INDEED... BUT I DON'T THINK THAT YOU SHOULD SIT TOO CLOSE TO HIM...
COUGH
WHAT ARE YOU WORRIED ABOUT? IT'S NOT LIKE HE'S CONTAGIOUS.
I'LL LET YOU KNOW RIGHT AWAY IF HIS CONDITION CHANGES.
ALL RIGHT...
THE MEDICINE SHOULD KICK IN SOON.

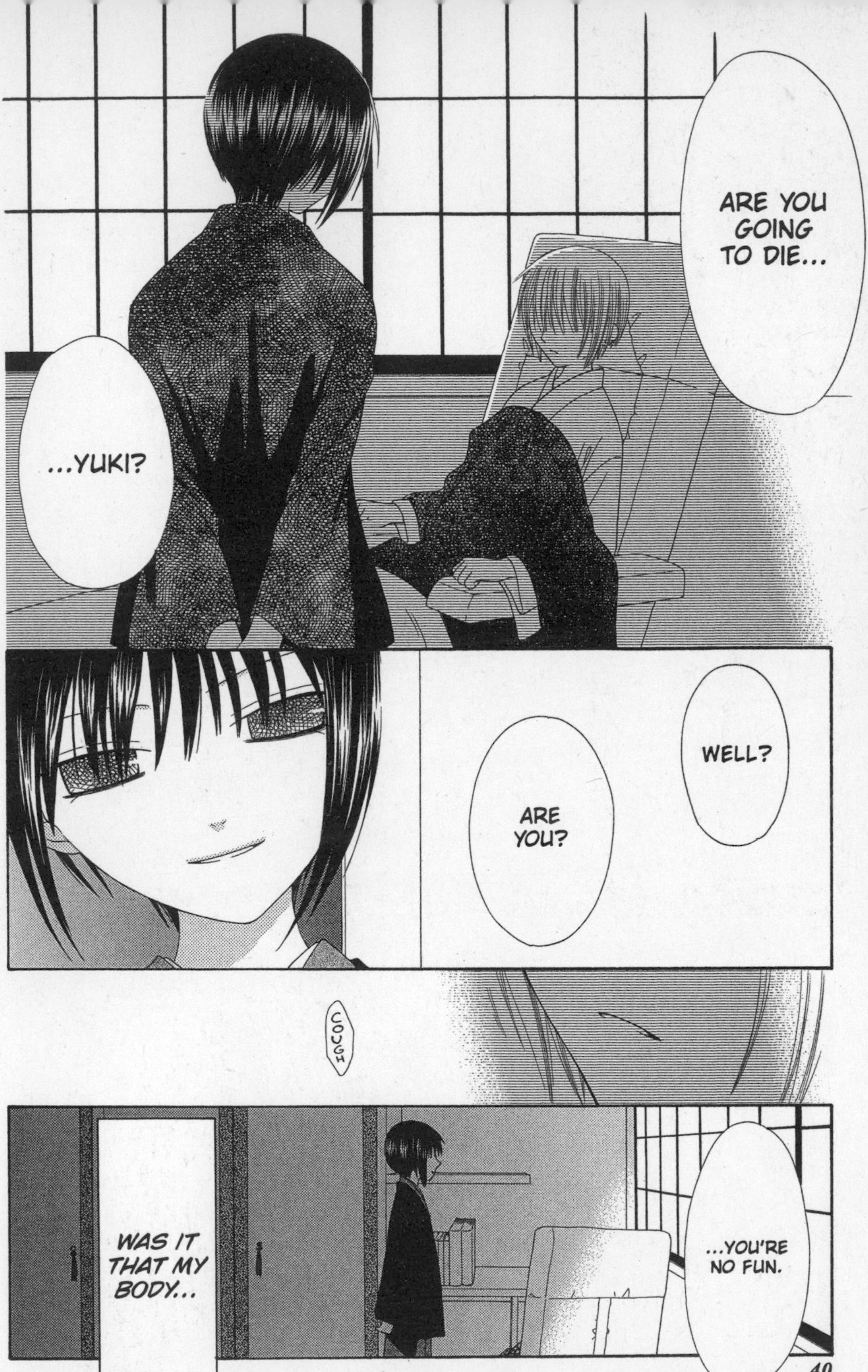
ARE YOU GOING TO DIE...
...YUKI?
WELL?
ARE YOU?
COUGH
...YOU'RE NO FUN.
WAS IT THAT MY BODY...

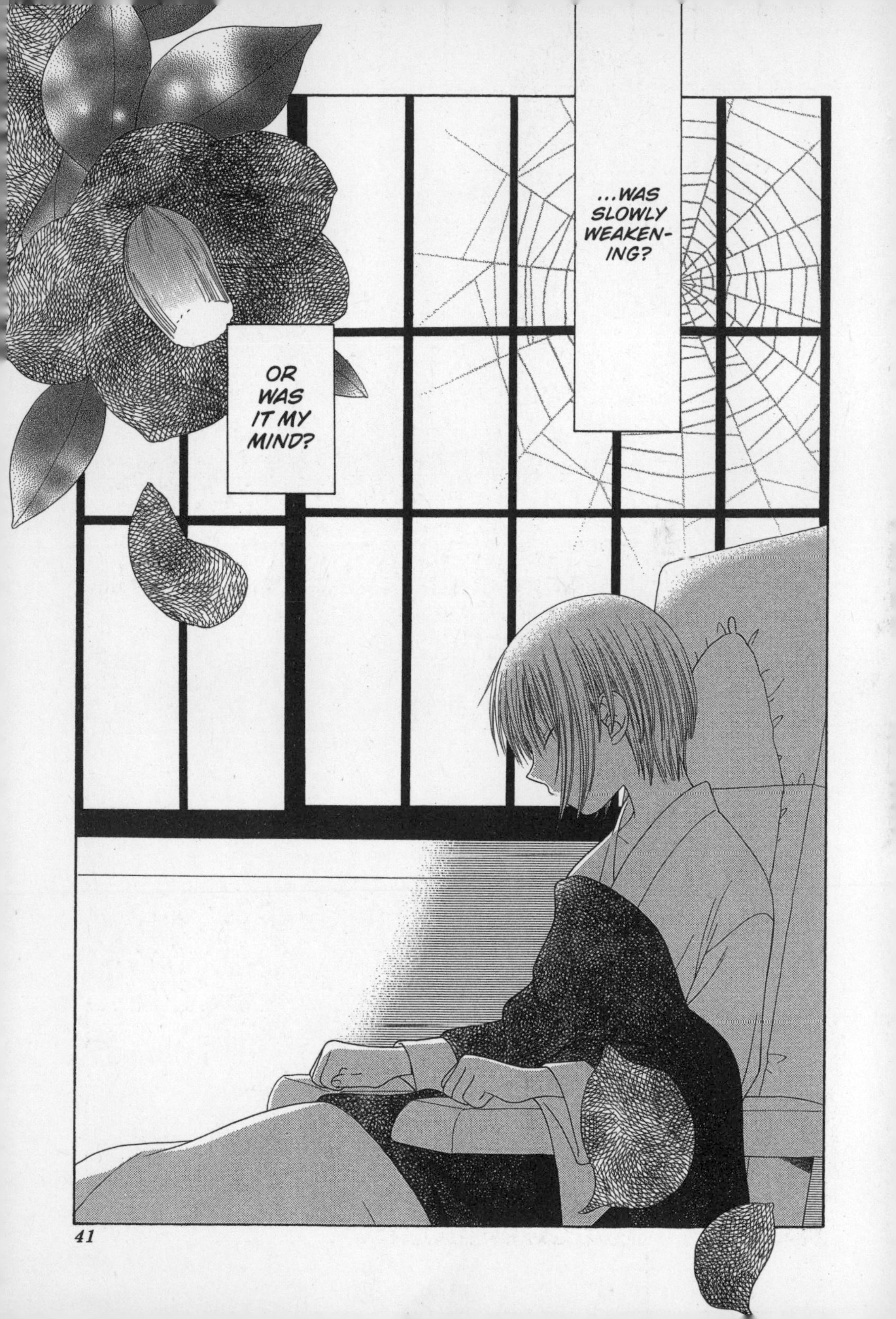
...WAS SLOWLY WEAKEN-ING?
OR WAS IT MY MIND?

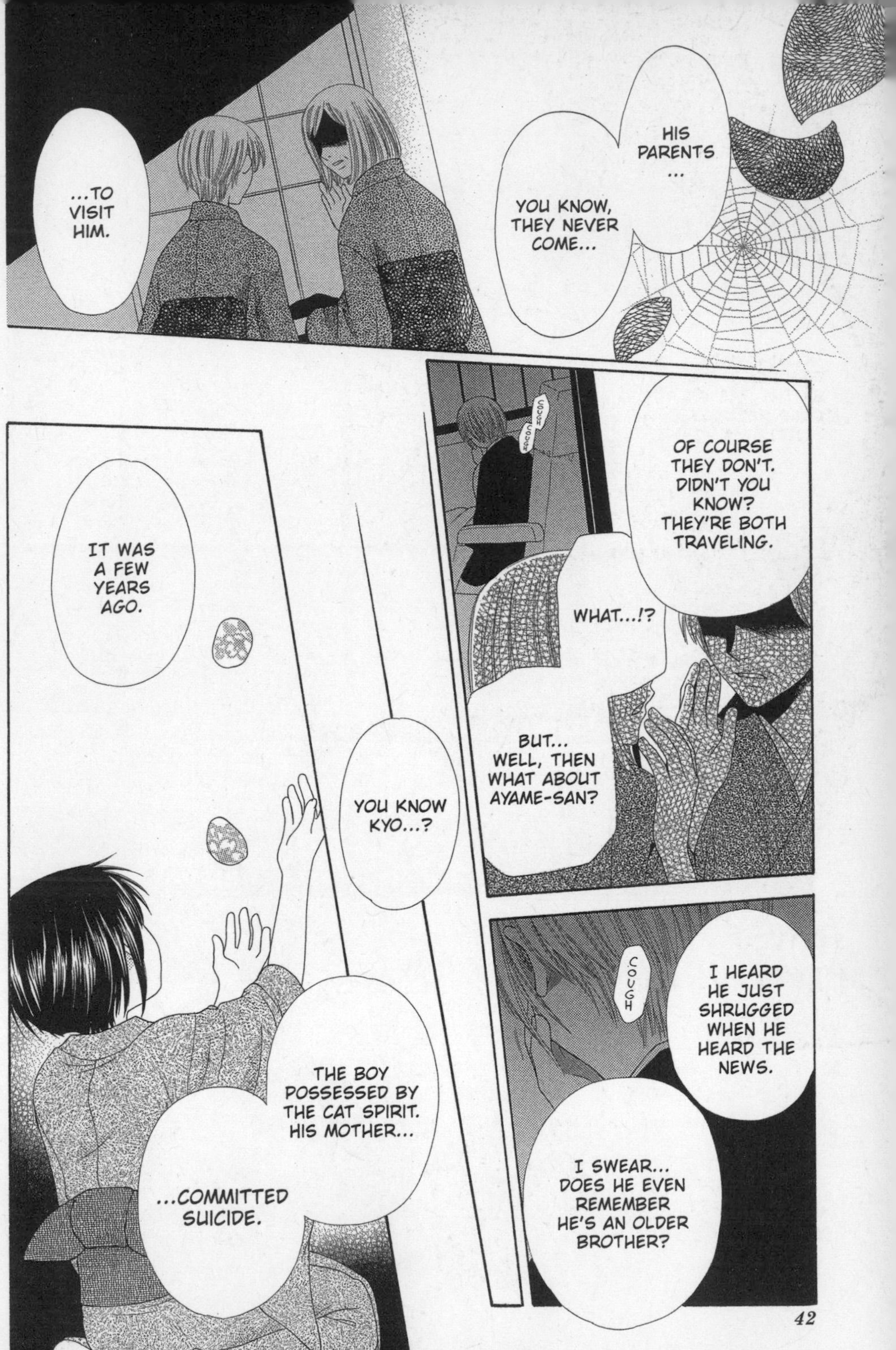
HIS PARENTS ...
YOU KNOW, THEY NEVER COME...
...TO VISIT HIM.
COUGH COUGH
OF COURSE THEY DON'T. DIDN'T YOU KNOW? THEY'RE BOTH TRAVELING.
WHAT...!?
BUT... WELL, THEN WHAT ABOUT AYAME-SAN?
COUGH
I HEARD HE JUST SHRUGGED WHEN HE HEARD THE NEWS.
I SWEAR... DOES HE EVEN REMEMBER HE'S AN OLDER BROTHER?
YOU KNOW KYO...?
IT WAS A FEW YEARS AGO.
THE BOY POSSESSED BY THE CAT SPIRIT. HIS MOTHER...
...COMMITTED SUICIDE.

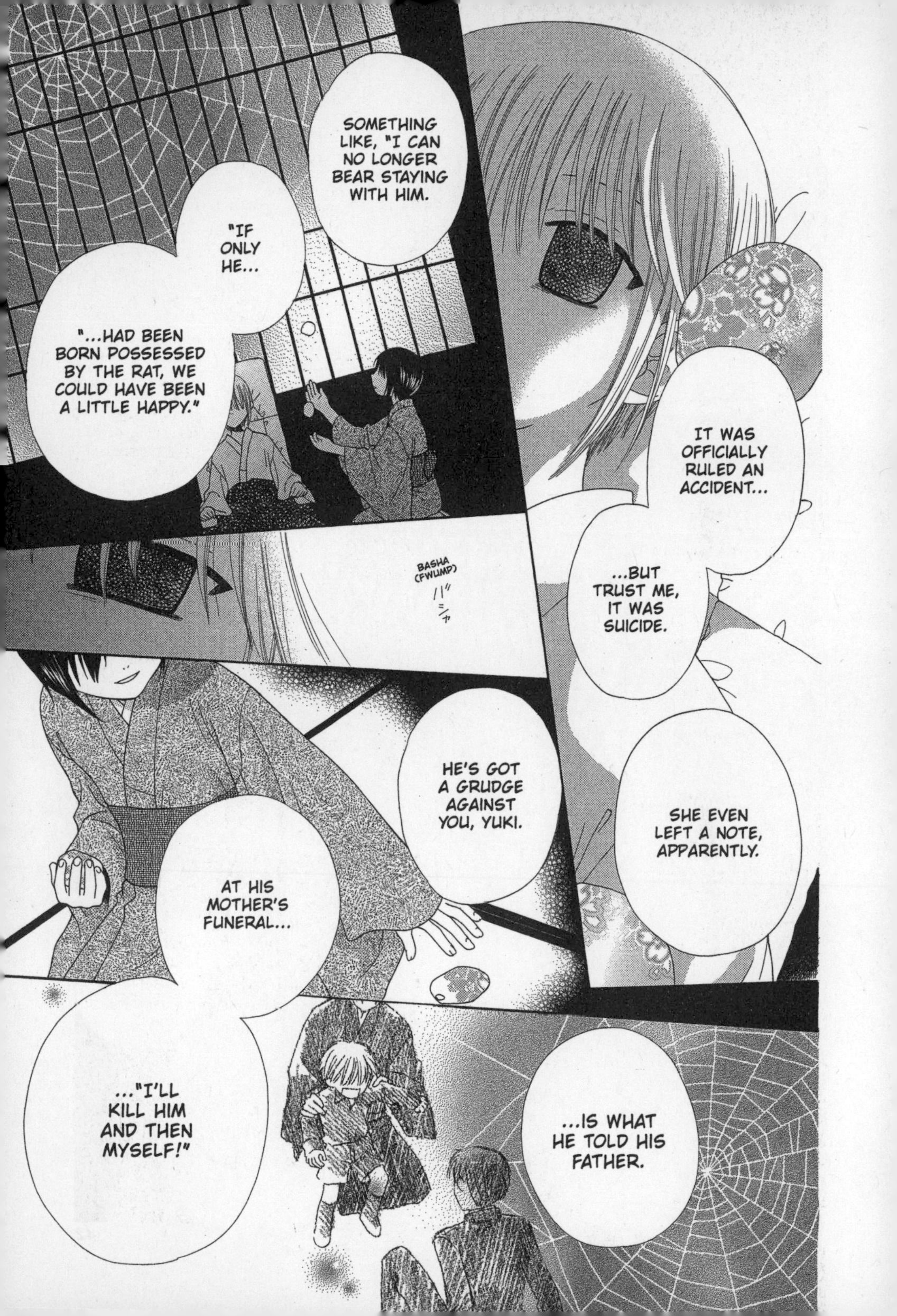
IT WAS OFFICIALLY RULED AN ACCIDENT...
...BUT TRUST ME, IT WAS SUICIDE.
SHE EVEN LEFT A NOTE, APPARENTLY.
SOMETHING LIKE, "I CAN NO LONGER BEAR STAYING WITH HIM.
"IF ONLY HE...
"...HAD BEEN BORN POSSESSED BY THE RAT, WE COULD HAVE BEEN A LITTLE HAPPY."
BASHA (FWUMP)
バシャ
HE'S GOT A GRUDGE AGAINST YOU, YUKI.
AT HIS MOTHER'S FUNERAL...
..."I'LL KILL HIM AND THEN MYSELF!"
...IS WHAT HE TOLD HIS FATHER.

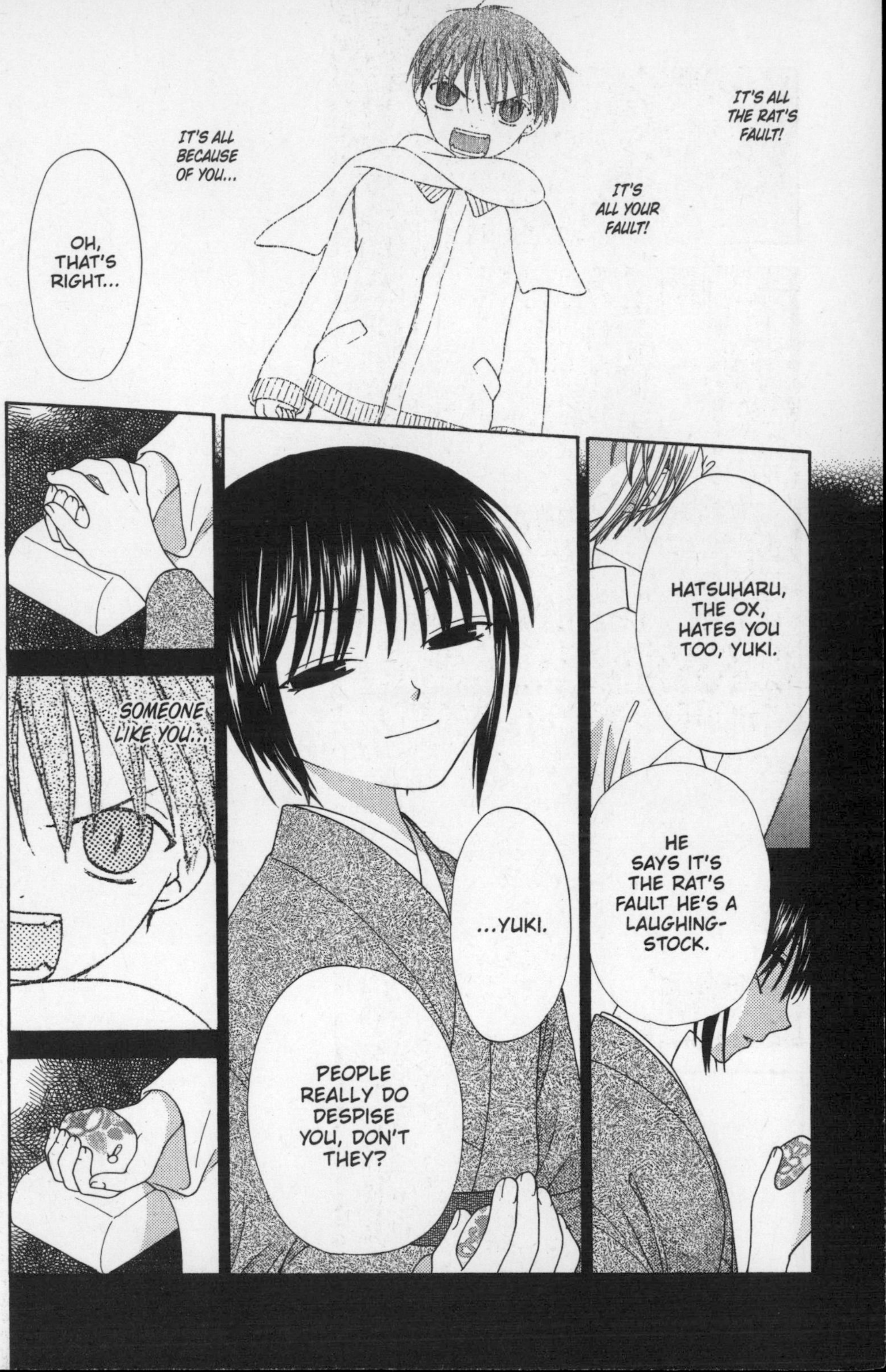
IT'S ALL THE RAT'S FAULT!
IT'S ALL YOUR FAULT!
IT'S ALL BECAUSE OF YOU...
OH, THAT'S RIGHT...
HATSUHARU, THE OX, HATES YOU TOO, YUKI.
HE SAYS IT'S THE RAT'S FAULT HE'S A LAUGHING-STOCK.
...YUKI.
PEOPLE REALLY DO DESPISE YOU, DON'T THEY?
SOMEONE LIKE YOU...

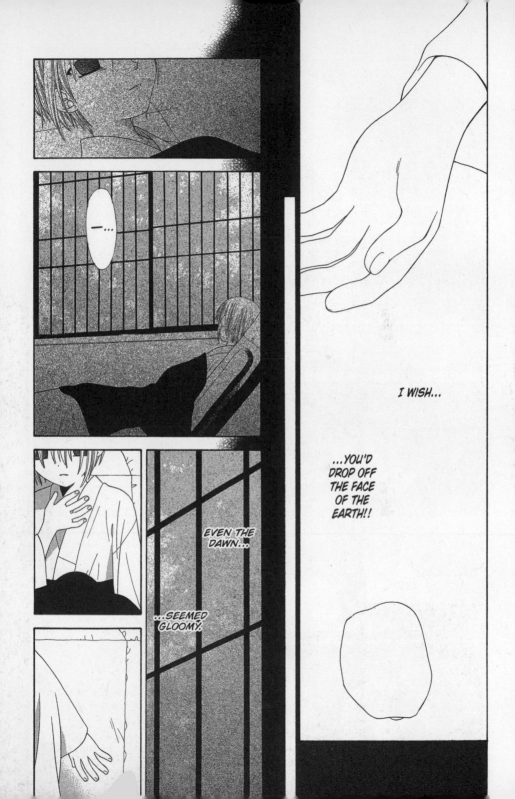

I WISH...

...YOU'D DROP OFF THE FACE OF THE EARTH!!

EVEN THE DAWN...

...SEEMED GLOOMY.

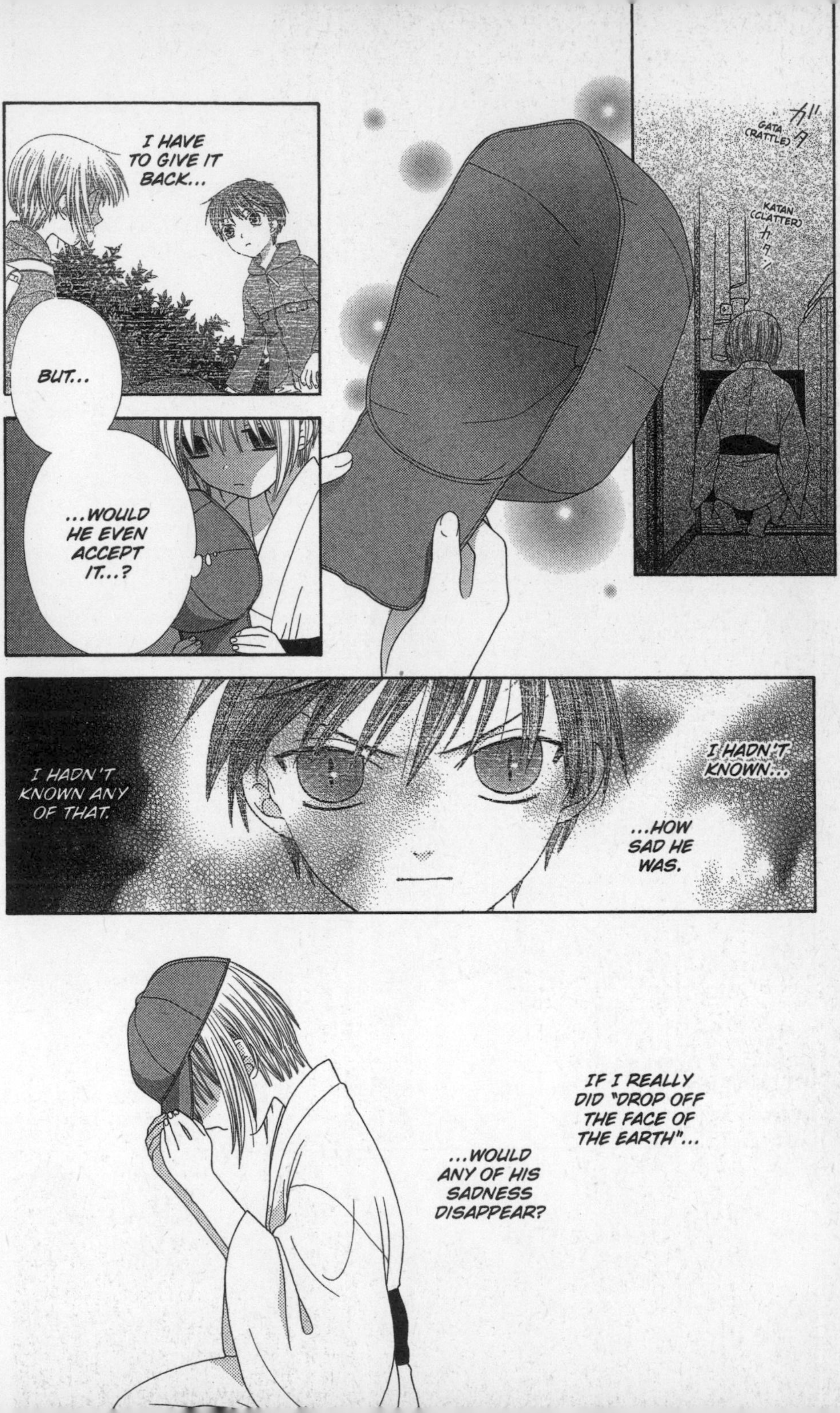
GATA (RATTLE)
KATAN (CLATTER)
I HAVE TO GIVE IT BACK...
BUT...
...WOULD HE EVEN ACCEPT IT...?
I HADN'T KNOWN...
...HOW SAD HE WAS.
I HADN'T KNOWN ANY OF THAT.
IF I REALLY DID "DROP OFF THE FACE OF THE EARTH"...
...WOULD ANY OF HIS SADNESS DISAPPEAR?

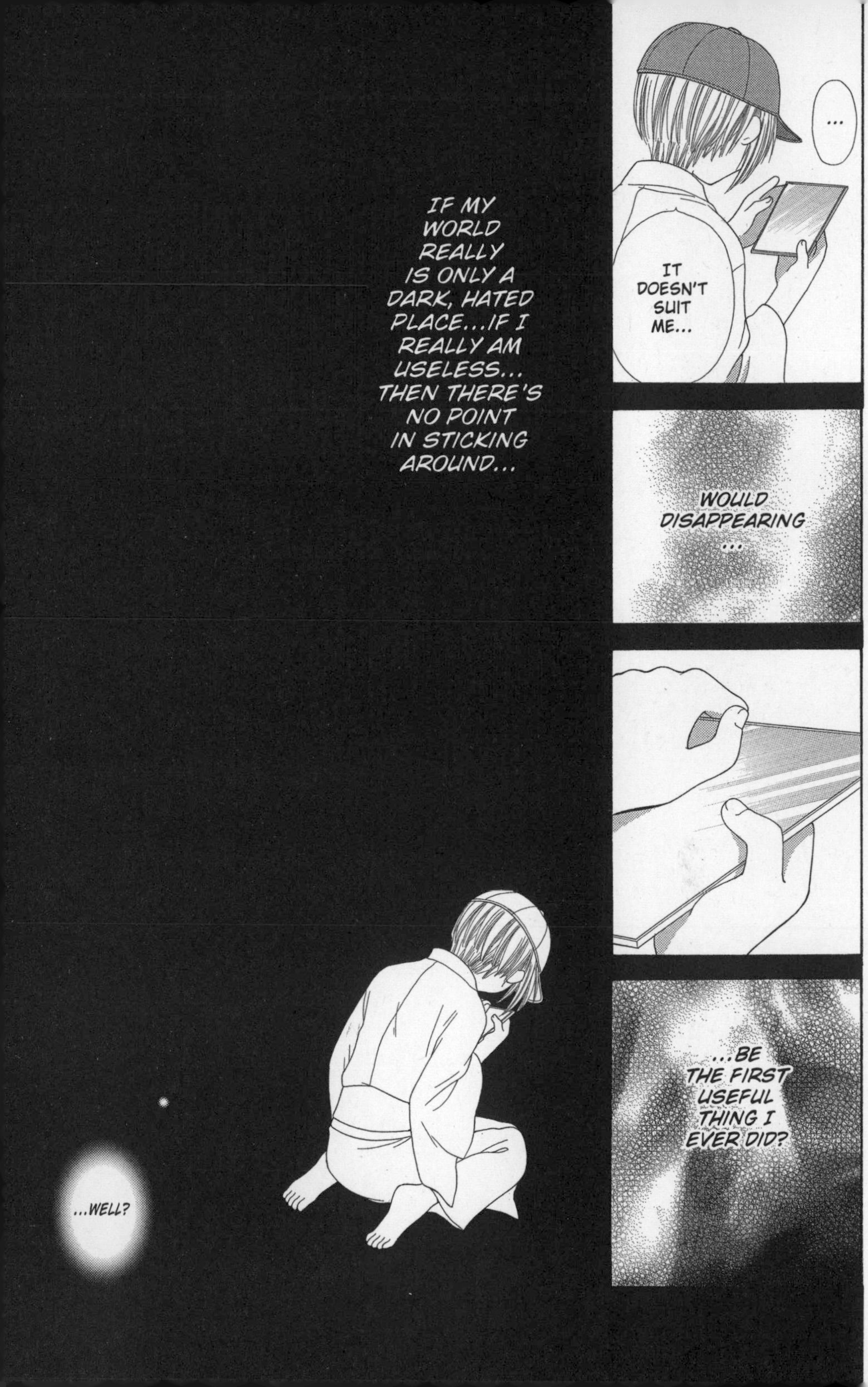
...
IT DOESN'T SUIT ME...
WOULD DISAPPEARING...
...BE THE FIRST USEFUL THING I EVER DID?
IF MY WORLD REALLY IS ONLY A DARK, HATED PLACE...IF I REALLY AM USELESS... THEN THERE'S NO POINT IN STICKING AROUND...
...WELL?

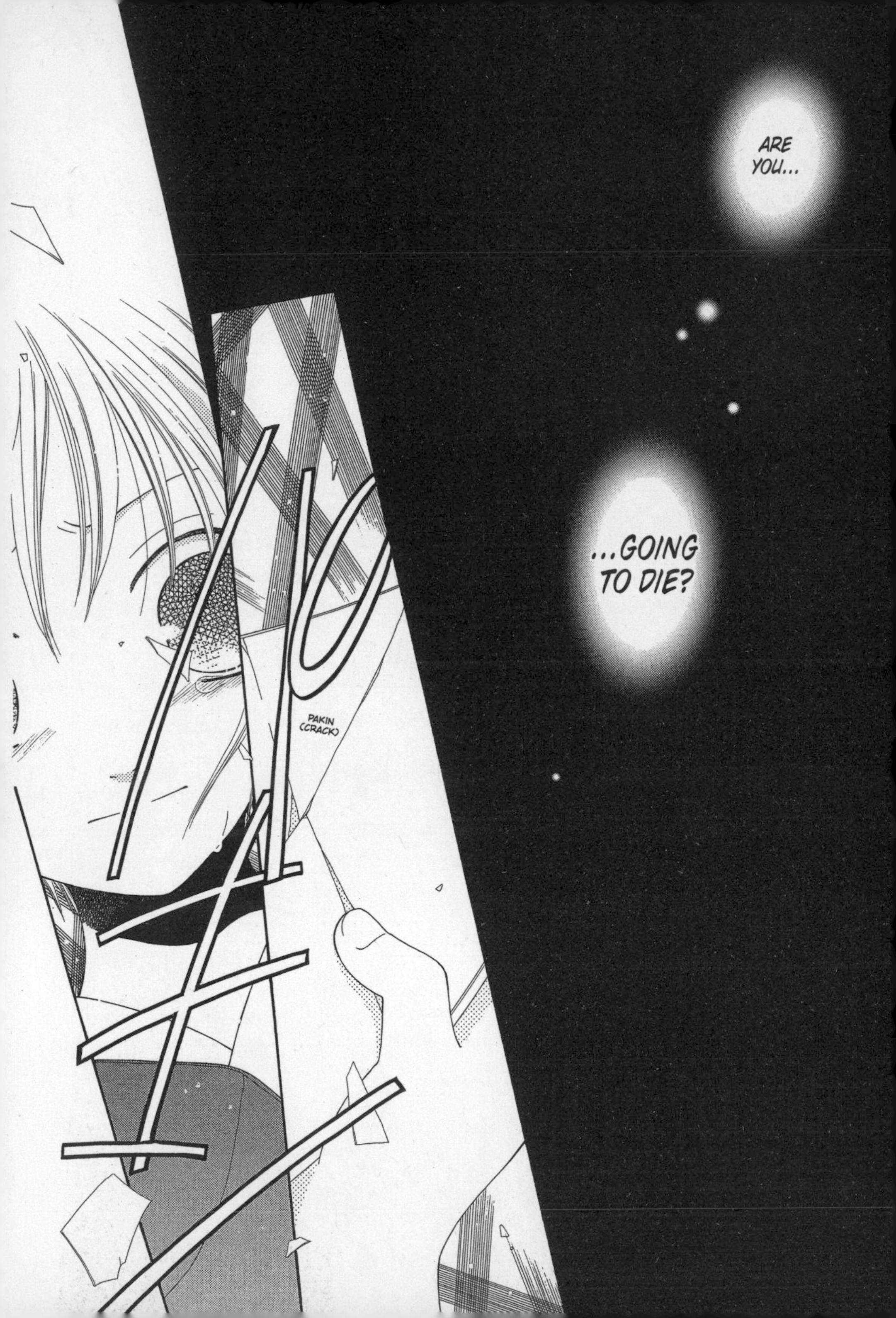
ARE YOU...
...GOING TO DIE?
PAKIN (CRACK)

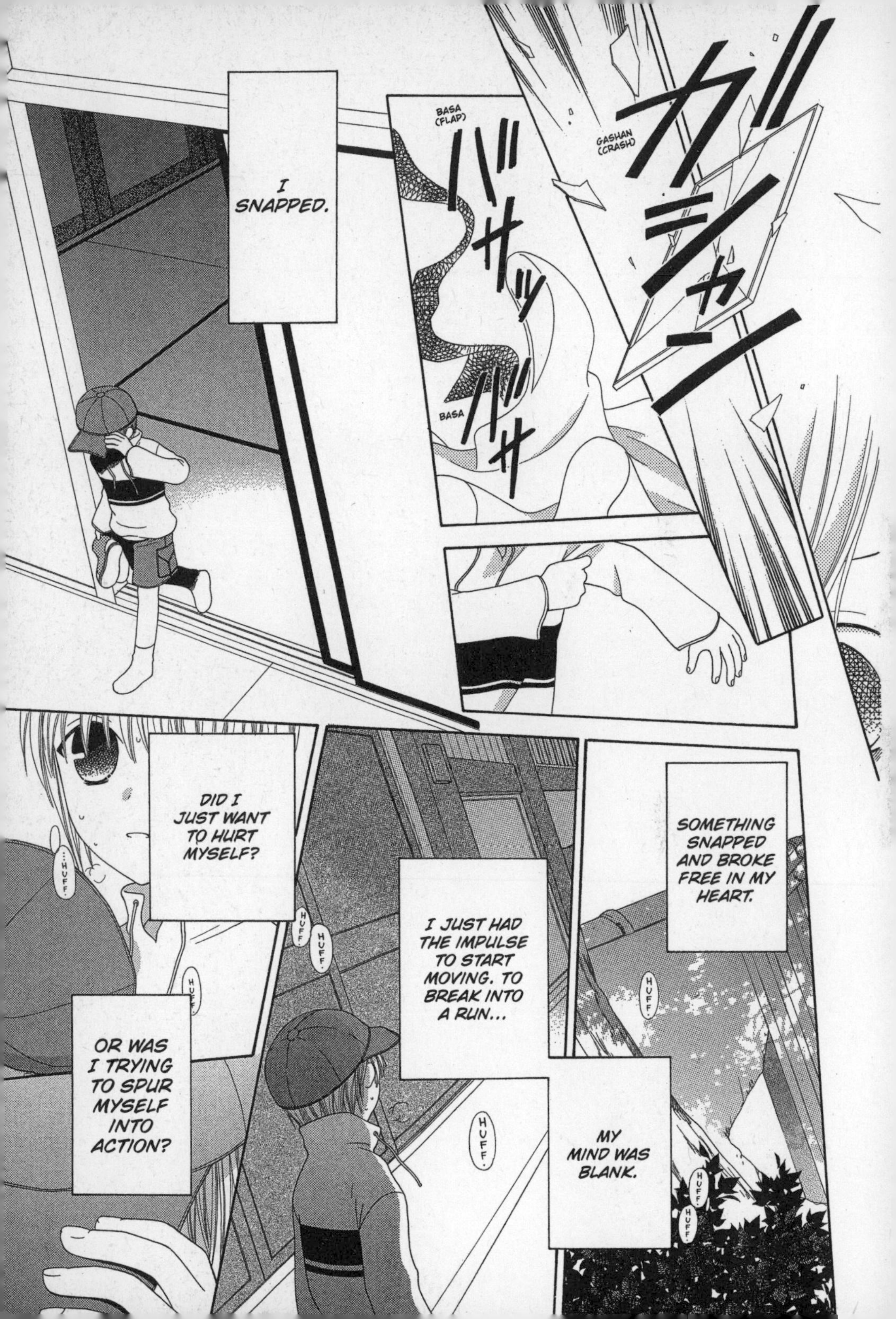
ガシャーン
GASHAN (CRASH)
バサッ
BASA (FLAP)
バサ
BASA
I SNAPPED.
SOMETHING SNAPPED AND BROKE FREE IN MY HEART.
HUFF.
MY MIND WAS BLANK.
HUFF.
HUFF.
I JUST HAD THE IMPULSE TO START MOVING. TO BREAK INTO A RUN...
HUFF.
DID I JUST WANT TO HURT MYSELF?
...HUFF.
HUFF.
HUFF.
HUFF.
OR WAS I TRYING TO SPUR MYSELF INTO ACTION?

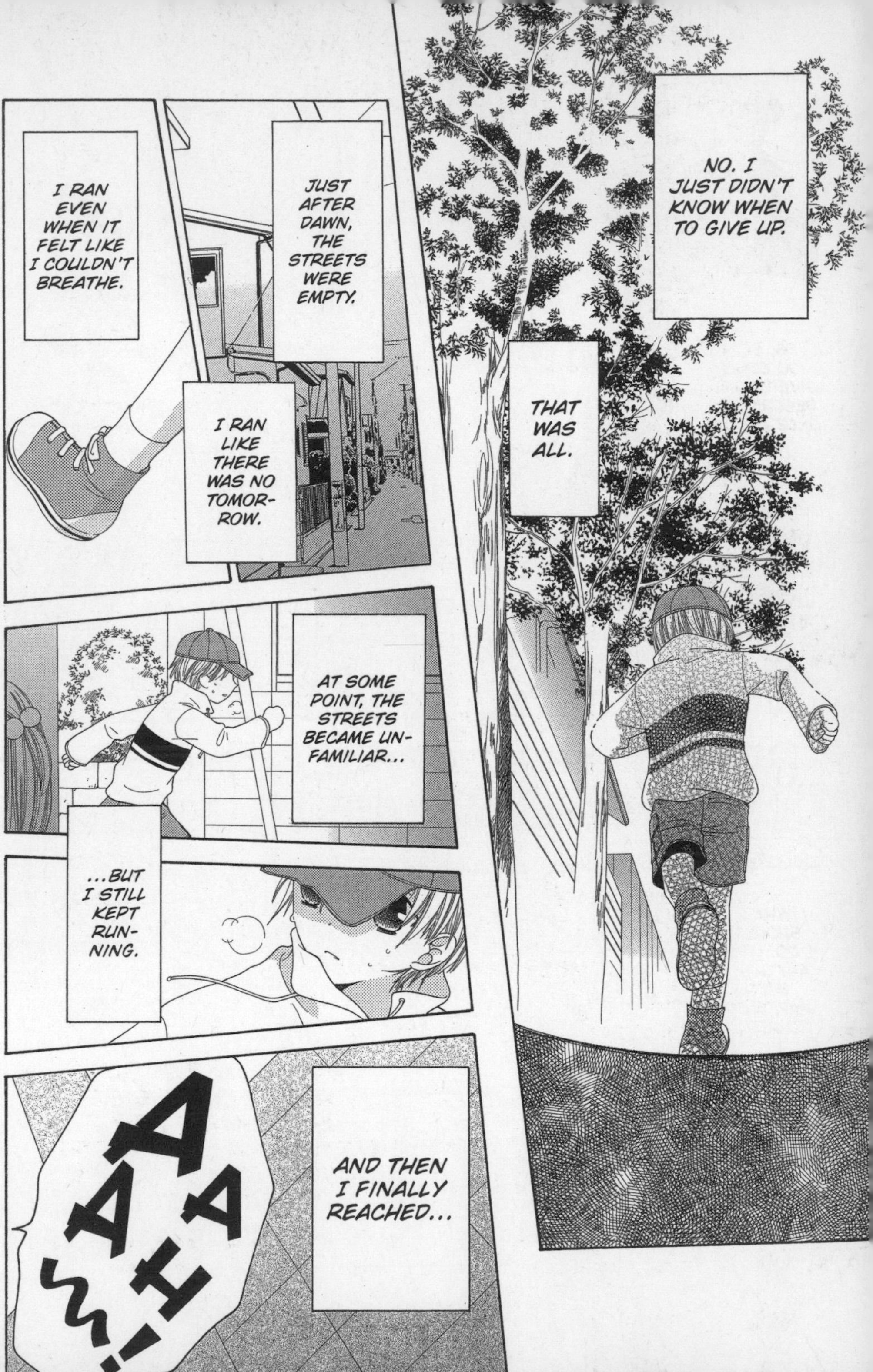
NO. I JUST DIDN'T KNOW WHEN TO GIVE UP.
THAT WAS ALL.
JUST AFTER DAWN, THE STREETS WERE EMPTY.
I RAN LIKE THERE WAS NO TOMORROW.
I RAN EVEN WHEN IT FELT LIKE I COULDN'T BREATHE.
AT SOME POINT, THE STREETS BECAME UNFAMILIAR...
...BUT I STILL KEPT RUNNING.
AND THEN I FINALLY REACHED...
AAAH~!

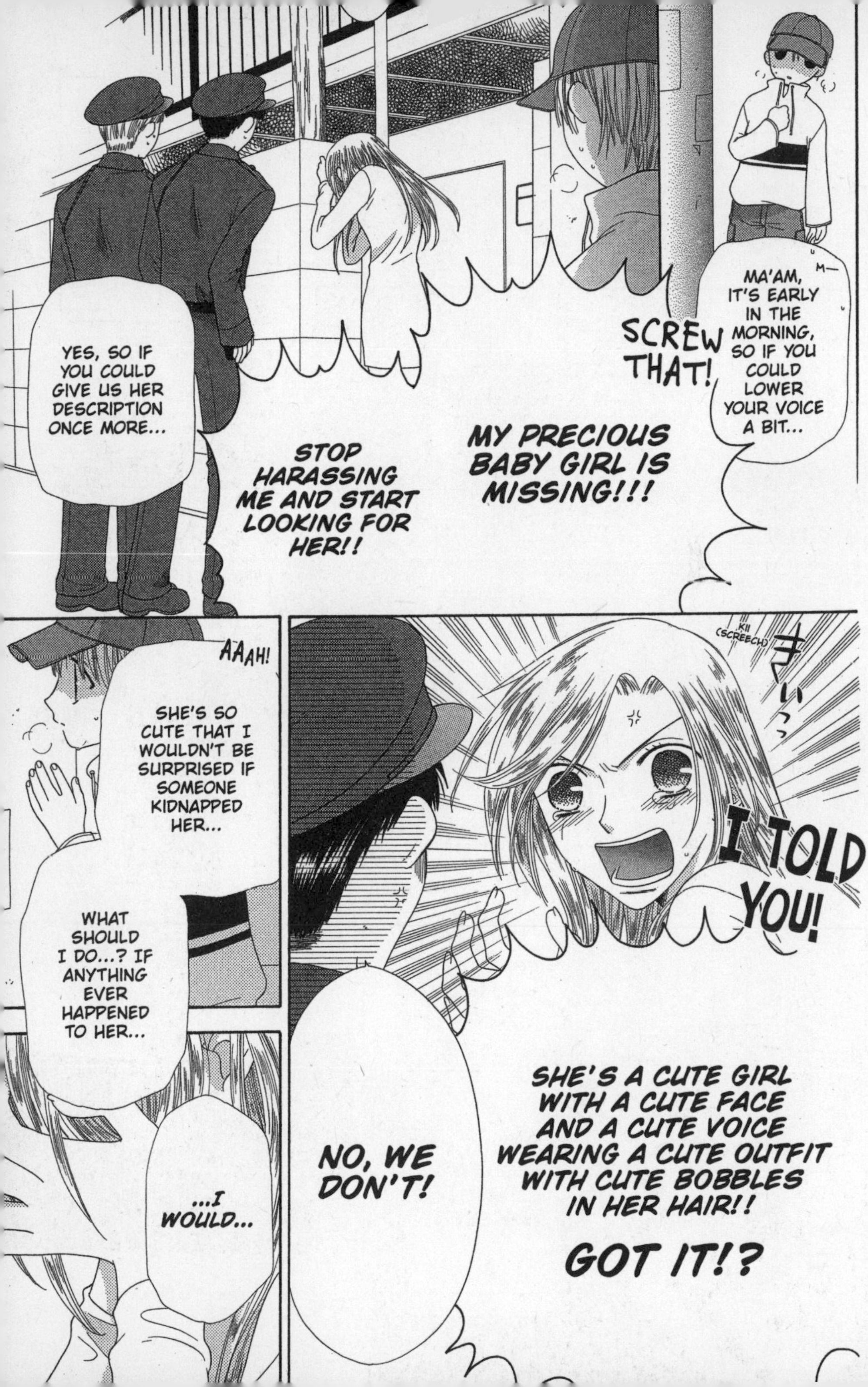
M—
MA'AM, IT'S EARLY IN THE MORNING, SO IF YOU COULD LOWER YOUR VOICE A BIT...
SCREW THAT!
MY PRECIOUS BABY GIRL IS MISSING!!!
STOP HARASSING ME AND START LOOKING FOR HER!!
YES, SO IF YOU COULD GIVE US HER DESCRIPTION ONCE MORE...
KII (SCREECH)
I TOLD YOU!
SHE'S A CUTE GIRL WITH A CUTE FACE AND A CUTE VOICE WEARING A CUTE OUTFIT WITH CUTE BOBBLES IN HER HAIR!!
GOT IT!?
NO, WE DON'T!
AAAH!
SHE'S SO CUTE THAT I WOULDN'T BE SURPRISED IF SOMEONE KIDNAPPED HER...
WHAT SHOULD I DO...? IF ANYTHING EVER HAPPENED TO HER...
...I WOULD...

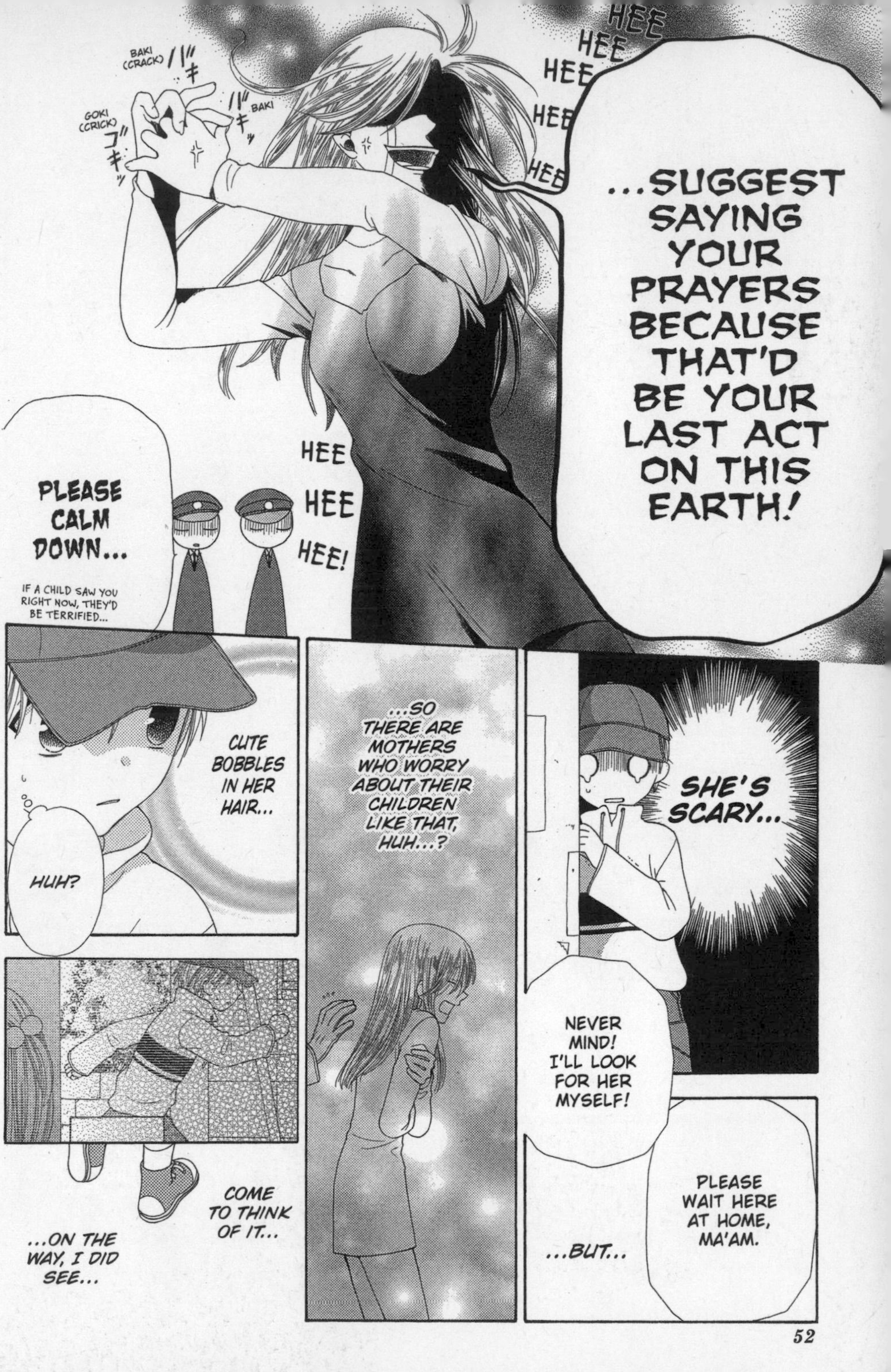
HEE
HEE
HEE
HEE
HEE
...SUGGEST SAYING YOUR PRAYERS BECAUSE THAT'D BE YOUR LAST ACT ON THIS EARTH!
BAKI (CRACK) バキ
バキッ BAKI
GOKI (CRICK) ゴキッ
HEE
HEE
HEE!
PLEASE CALM DOWN...
IF A CHILD SAW YOU RIGHT NOW, THEY'D BE TERRIFIED...
SHE'S SCARY...
NEVER MIND! I'LL LOOK FOR HER MYSELF!
PLEASE WAIT HERE AT HOME, MA'AM.
...BUT...
...SO THERE ARE MOTHERS WHO WORRY ABOUT THEIR CHILDREN LIKE THAT, HUH...?
COME TO THINK OF IT...
CUTE BOBBLES IN HER HAIR...
HUH?
...ON THE WAY, I DID SEE...

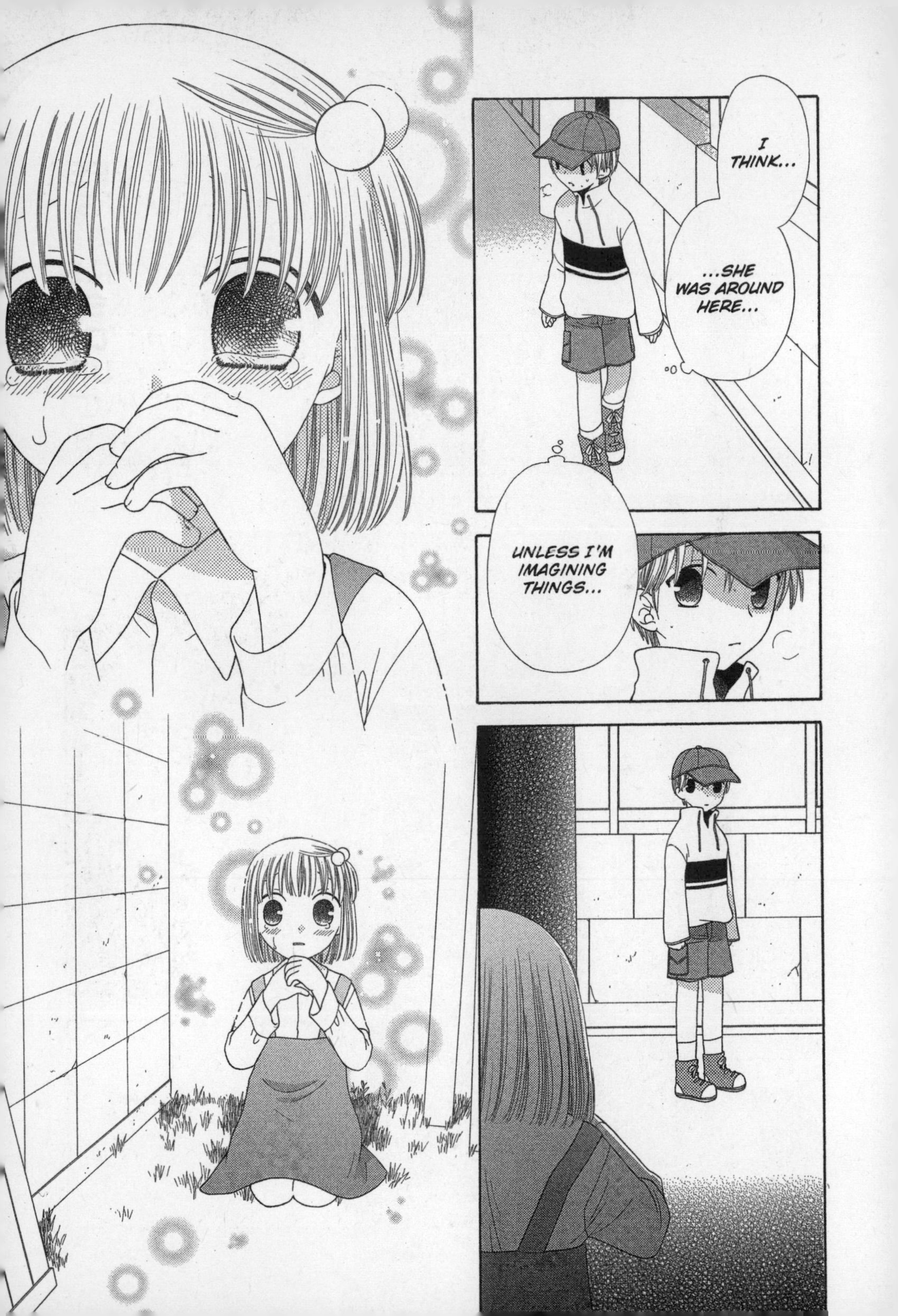
I THINK...
...SHE WAS AROUND HERE...
UNLESS I'M IMAGINING THINGS...

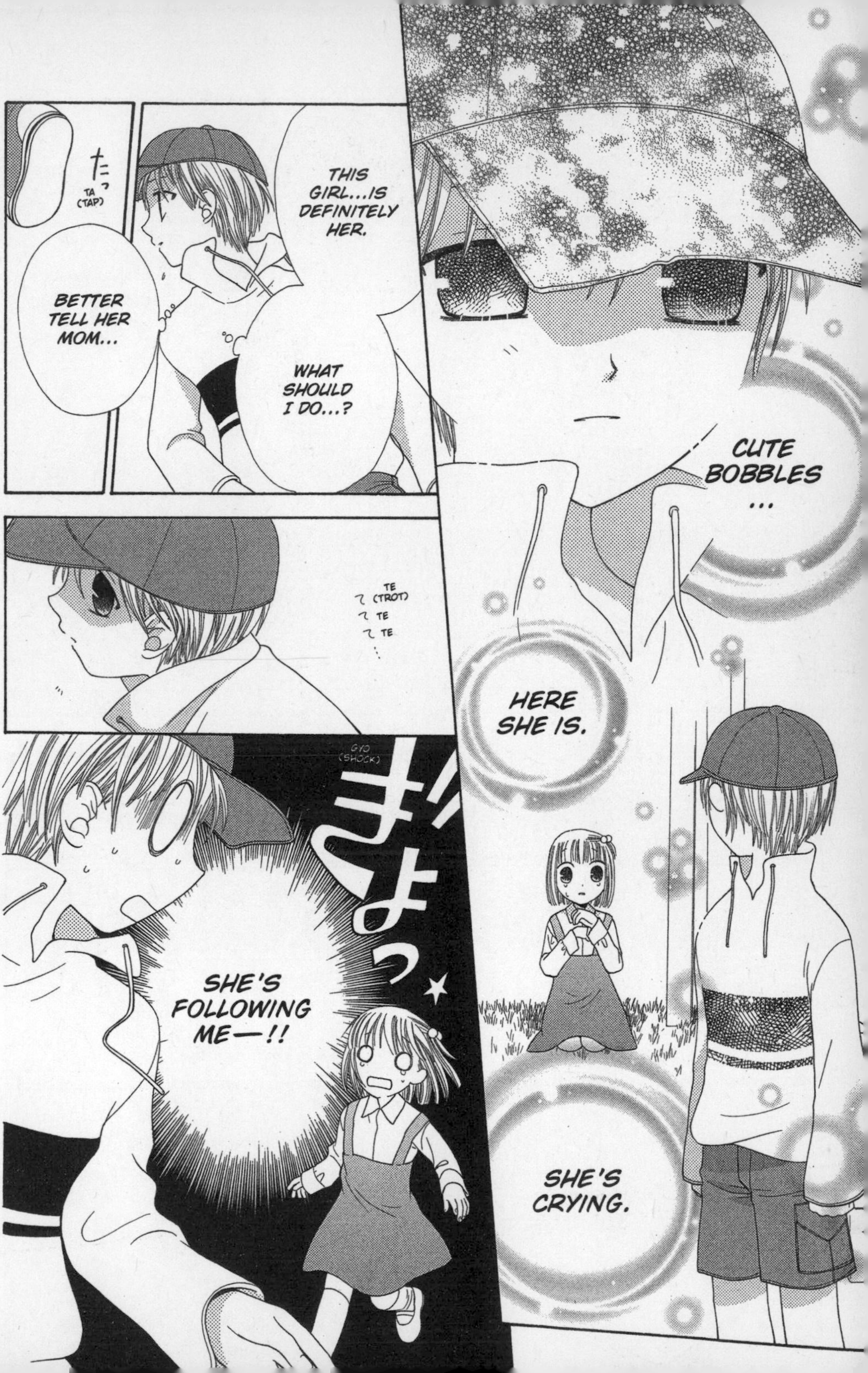
CUTE BOBBLES ...
HERE SHE IS.
SHE'S CRYING.
THIS GIRL...IS DEFINITELY HER.
WHAT SHOULD I DO...?
BETTER TELL HER MOM...
たっ
TA (TAP)
てててて...
TE (TROT) TE TE
ぎょっ
GYO (SHOCK)
SHE'S FOLLOWING ME—!!

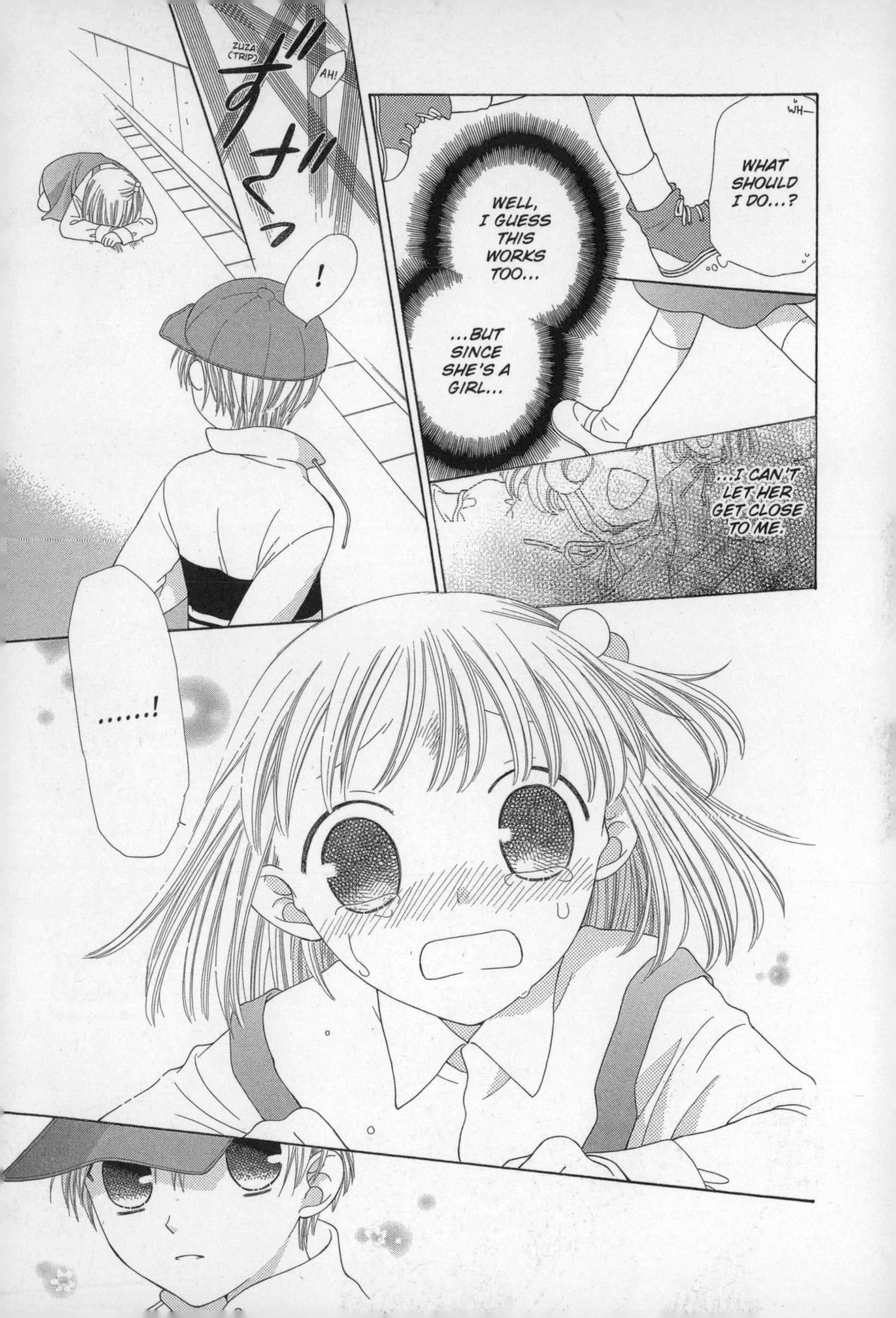
WH—
WHAT SHOULD I DO...?
WELL, I GUESS THIS WORKS TOO...
...BUT SINCE SHE'S A GIRL...
...I CAN'T LET HER GET CLOSE TO ME.
ずざっ
ZUZA (TRIP)
AH!
!
......!

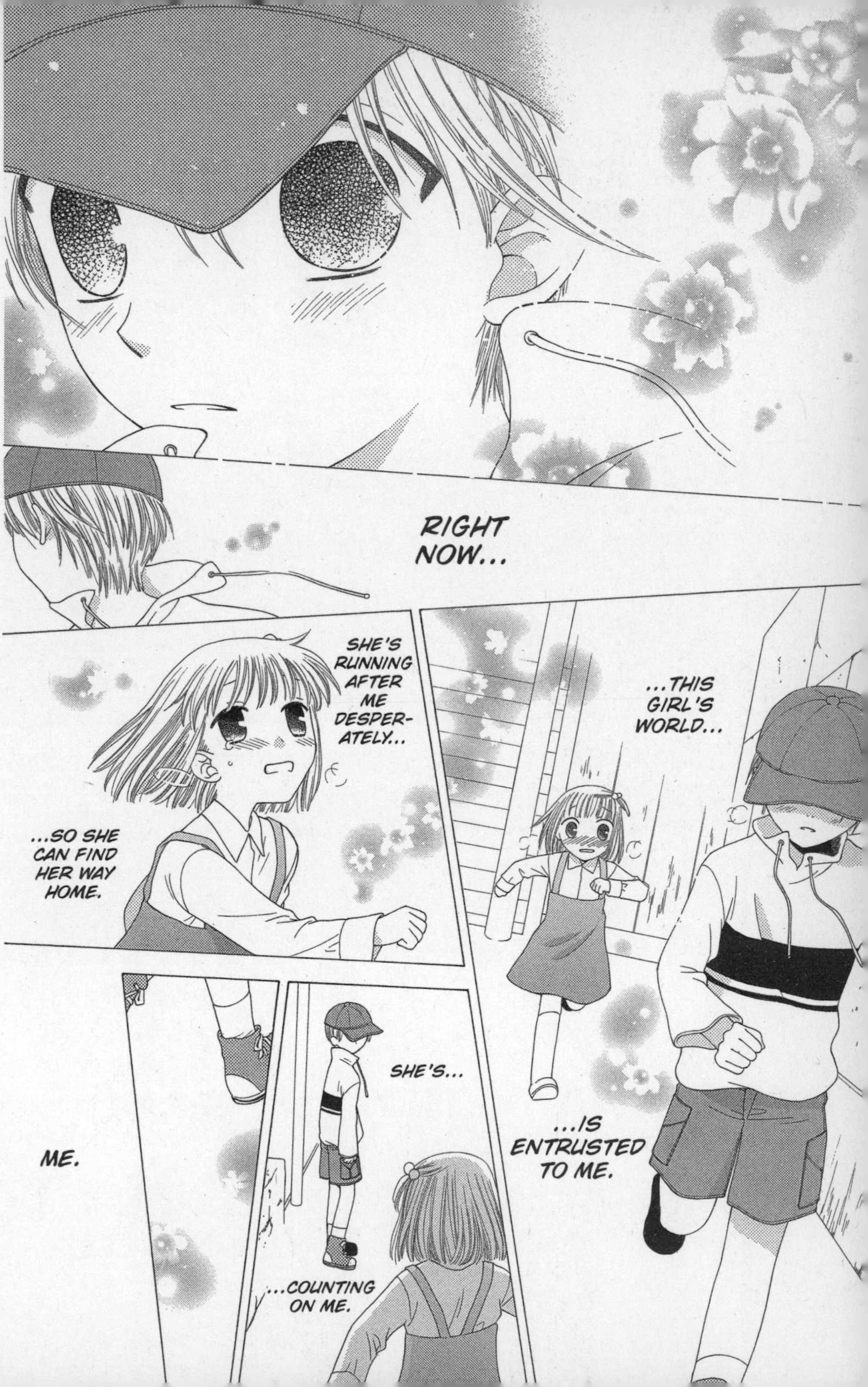
RIGHT NOW...
...THIS GIRL'S WORLD...
...IS ENTRUSTED TO ME.
SHE'S RUNNING AFTER ME DESPERATELY...
...SO SHE CAN FIND HER WAY HOME.
SHE'S...
...COUNTING ON ME.
ME.

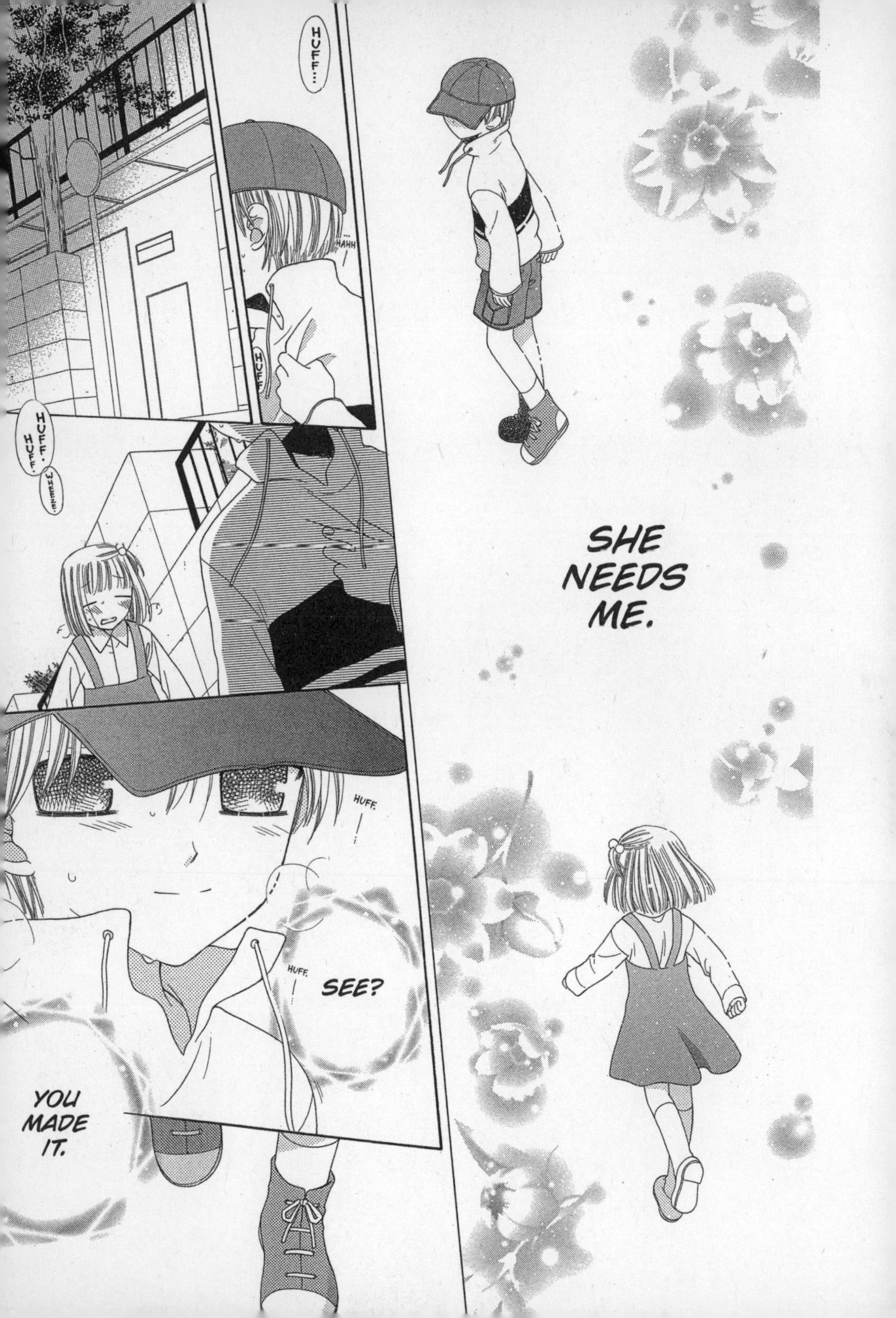
SHE NEEDS ME.
...HAHH
HUFF
HUFF...
HUFF. HUFF.
WHEEZE.
HUFF.
HUFF.
SEE?
YOU MADE IT.

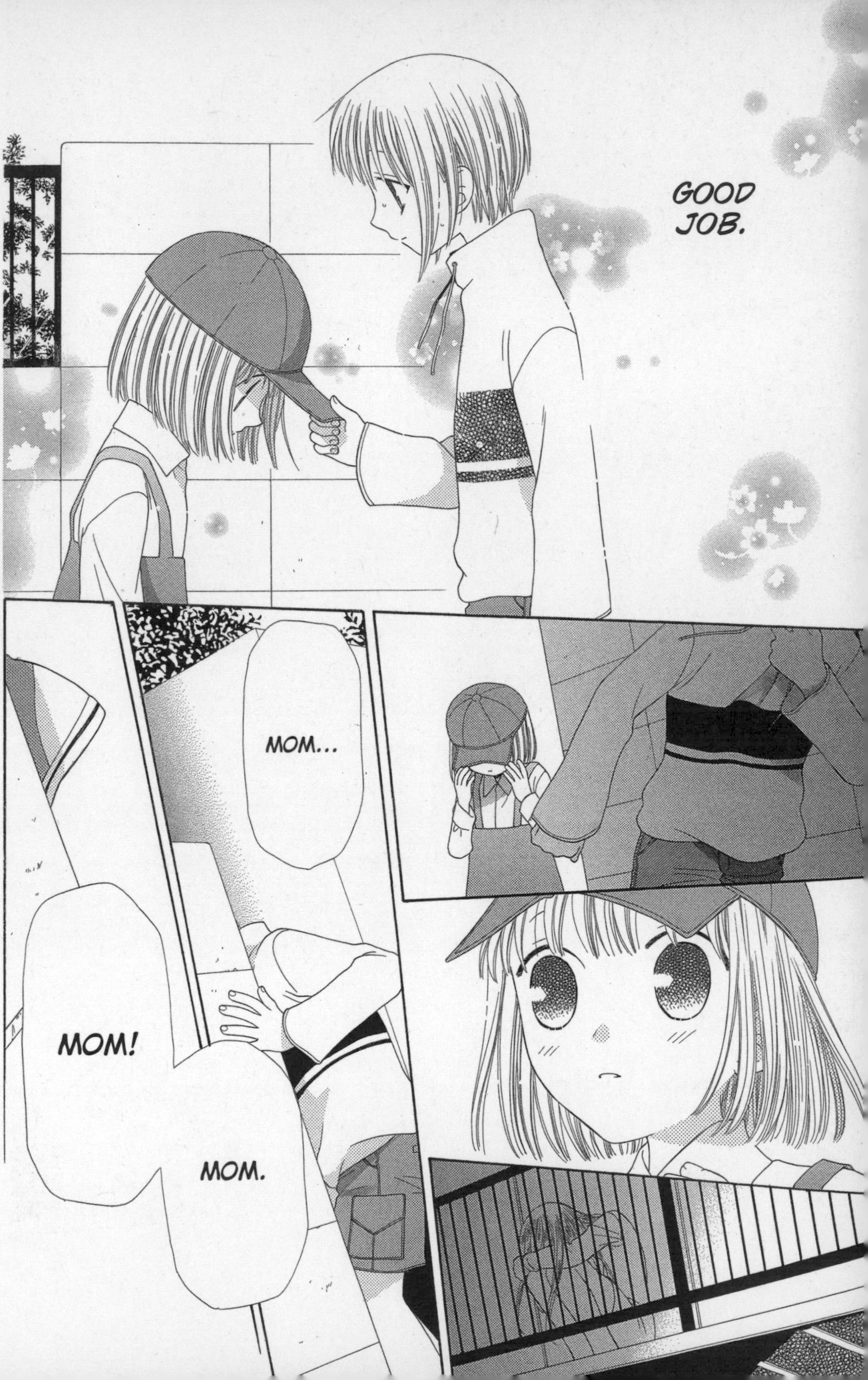
GOOD JOB.
MOM...
MOM!
MOM.

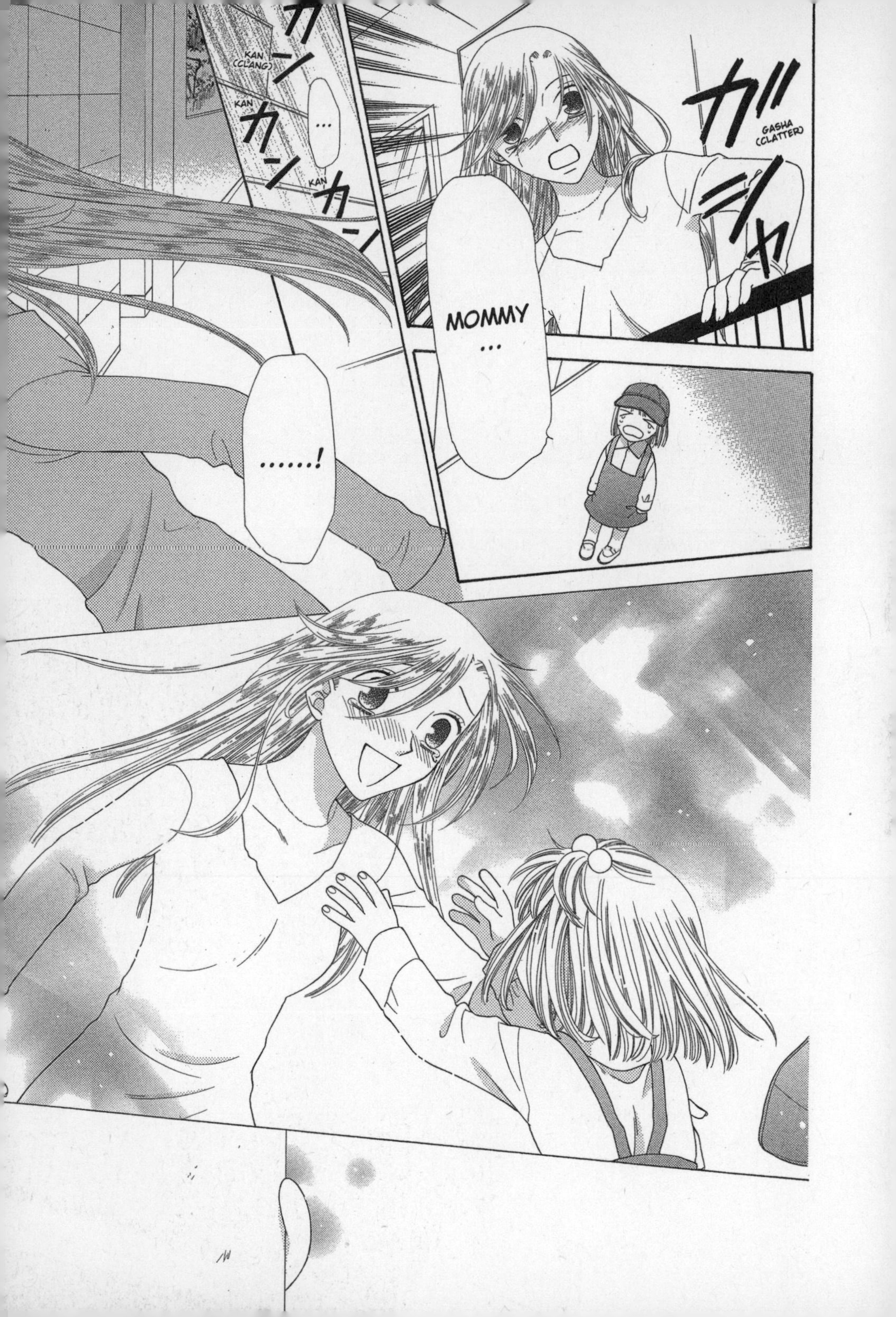
ガシャ
GASHA (CLATTER)
MOMMY ...
カンカンカン
KAN (CLANG)
KAN
KAN
...
......!

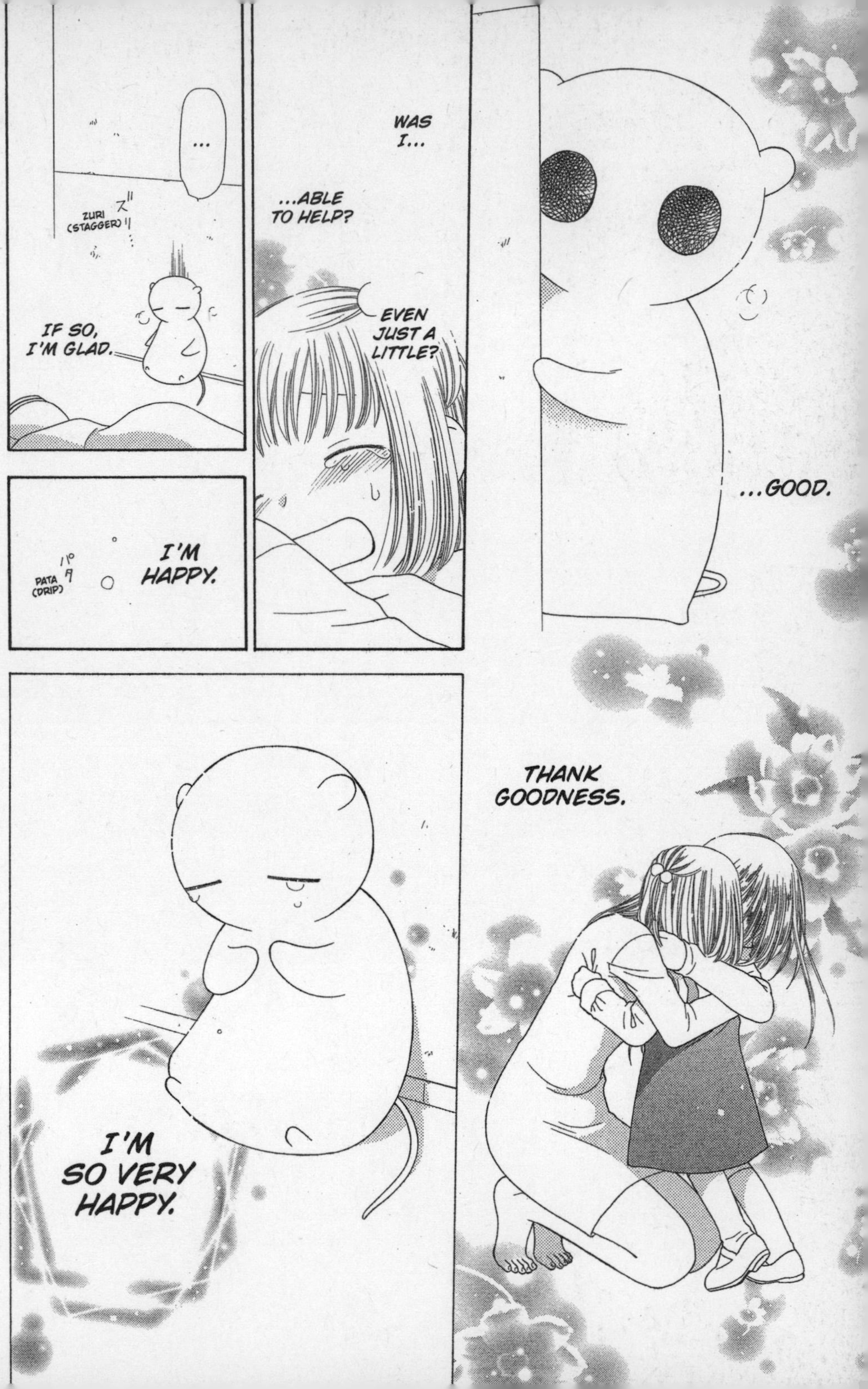
...GOOD.
WAS I...
...ABLE TO HELP?
EVEN JUST A LITTLE?
...
ズリ
ZURI (STAGGER)
IF SO, I'M GLAD.
I'M HAPPY.
パタ
PATA (DRIP)
THANK GOODNESS.
I'M SO VERY HAPPY.

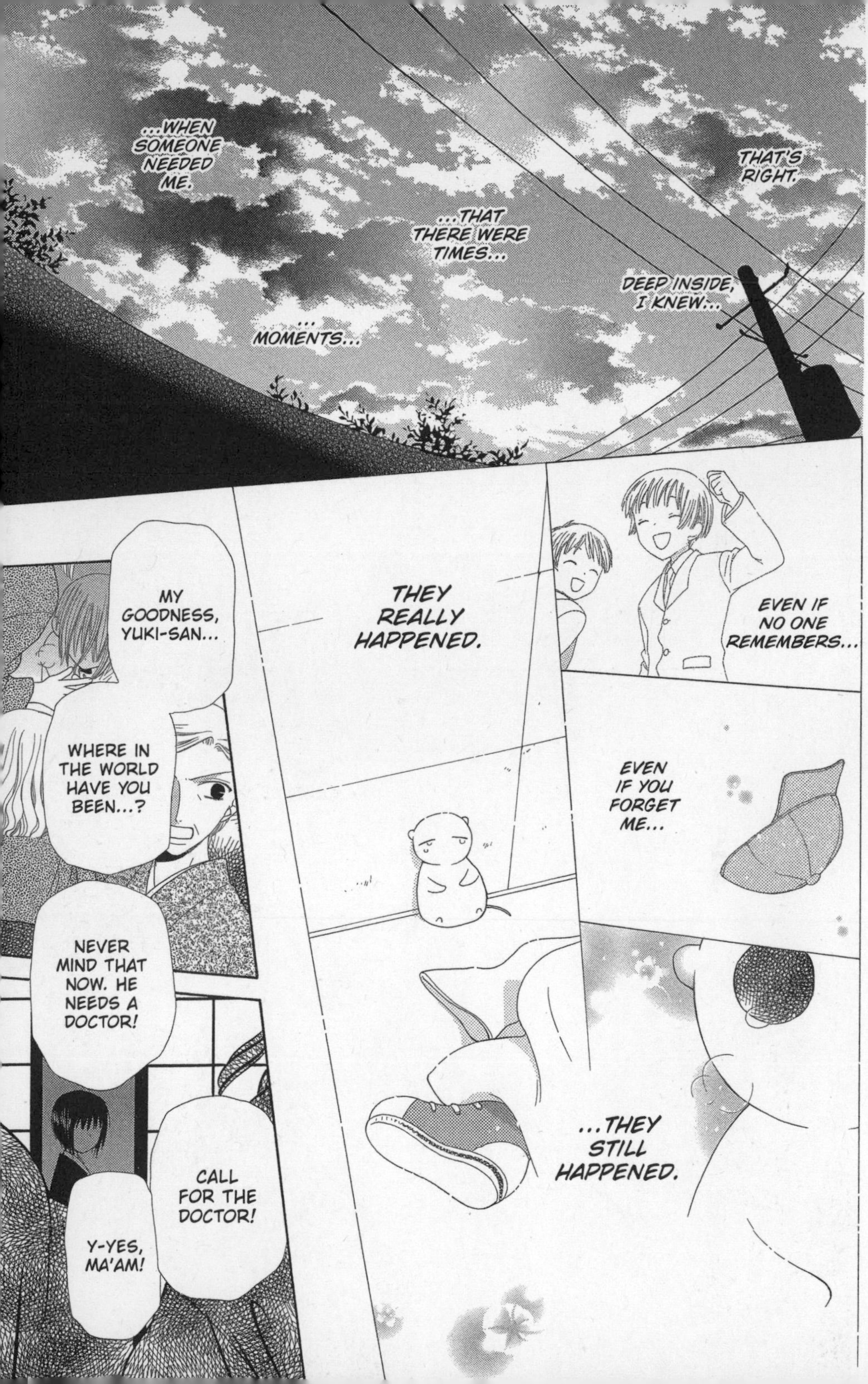
THAT'S RIGHT.
DEEP INSIDE, I KNEW...
...THAT THERE WERE TIMES...
...WHEN SOMEONE NEEDED ME.
...MOMENTS...
EVEN IF NO ONE REMEMBERS...
EVEN IF YOU FORGET ME...
...THEY STILL HAPPENED.
THEY REALLY HAPPENED.
MY GOODNESS, YUKI-SAN...
WHERE IN THE WORLD HAVE YOU BEEN...?
NEVER MIND THAT NOW. HE NEEDS A DOCTOR!
CALL FOR THE DOCTOR!
Y-YES, MA'AM!

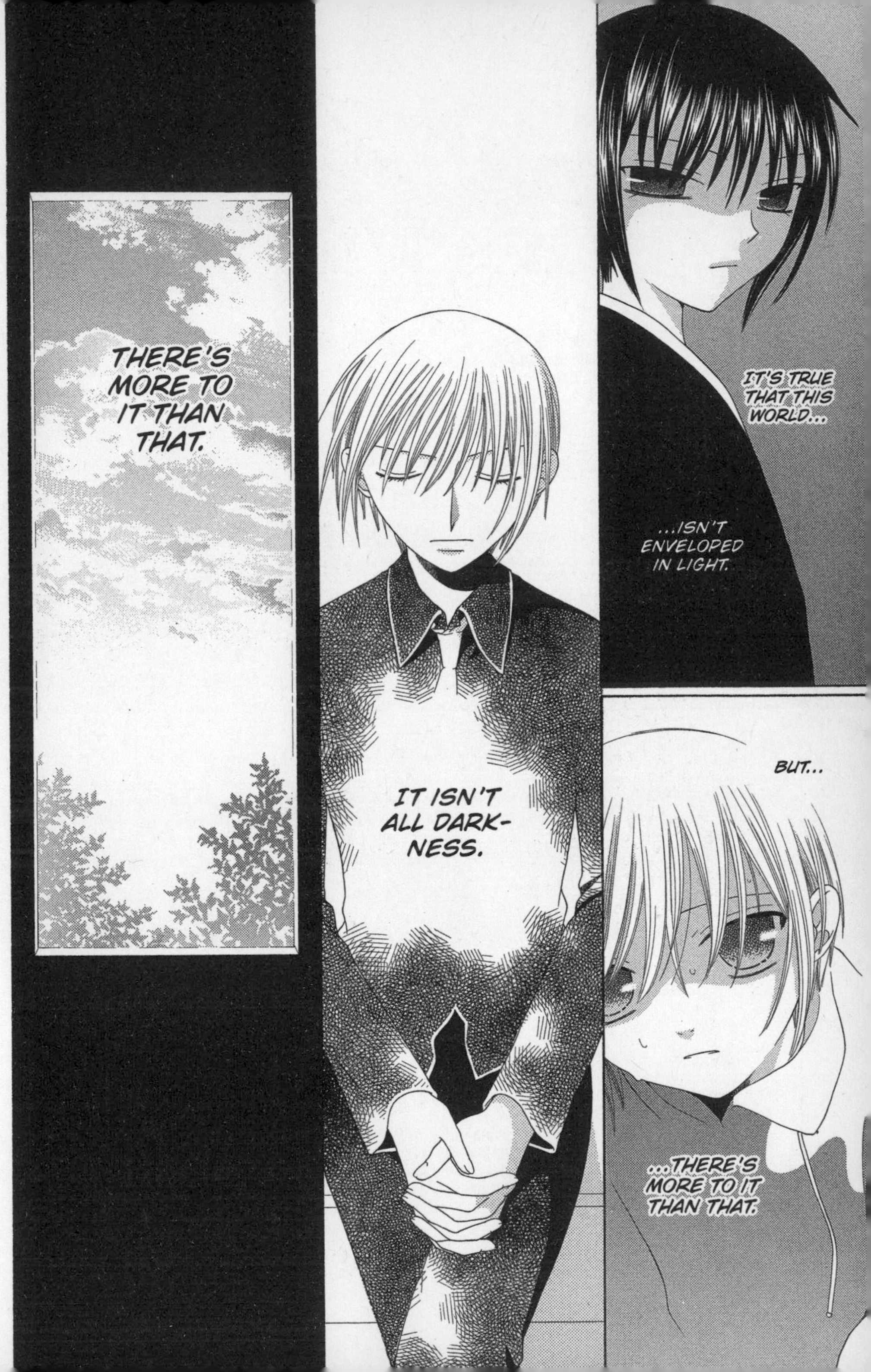
IT'S TRUE THAT THIS WORLD...
...ISN'T ENVELOPED IN LIGHT.
BUT...
...THERE'S MORE TO IT THAN THAT.
IT ISN'T ALL DARK-NESS.
THERE'S MORE TO IT THAN THAT.

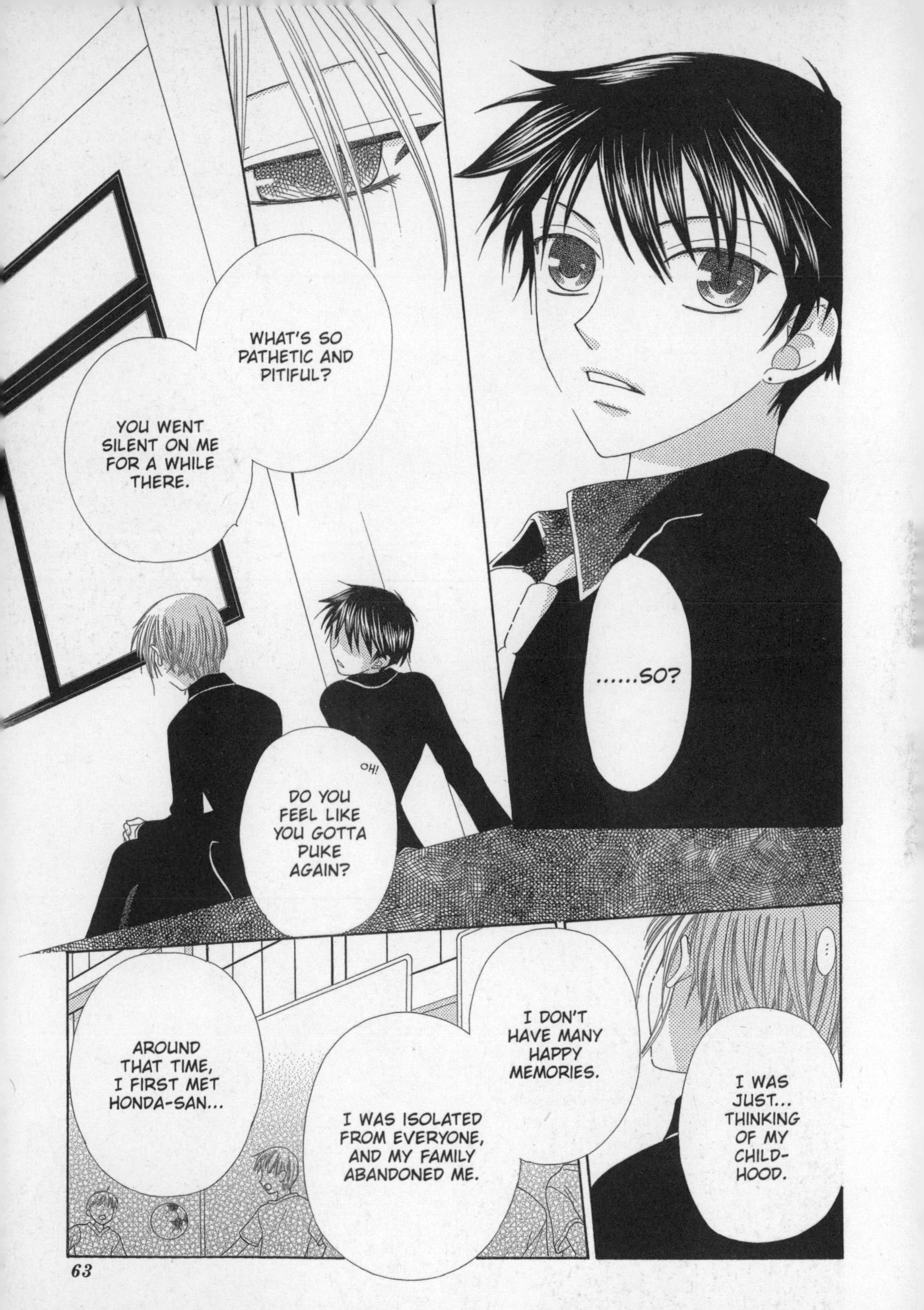
......SO?
WHAT'S SO PATHETIC AND PITIFUL?
YOU WENT SILENT ON ME FOR A WHILE THERE.
OH!
DO YOU FEEL LIKE YOU GOTTA PUKE AGAIN?
I WAS JUST... THINKING OF MY CHILD-HOOD.
I DON'T HAVE MANY HAPPY MEMORIES.
I WAS ISOLATED FROM EVERYONE, AND MY FAMILY ABANDONED ME.
AROUND THAT TIME, I FIRST MET HONDA-SAN...

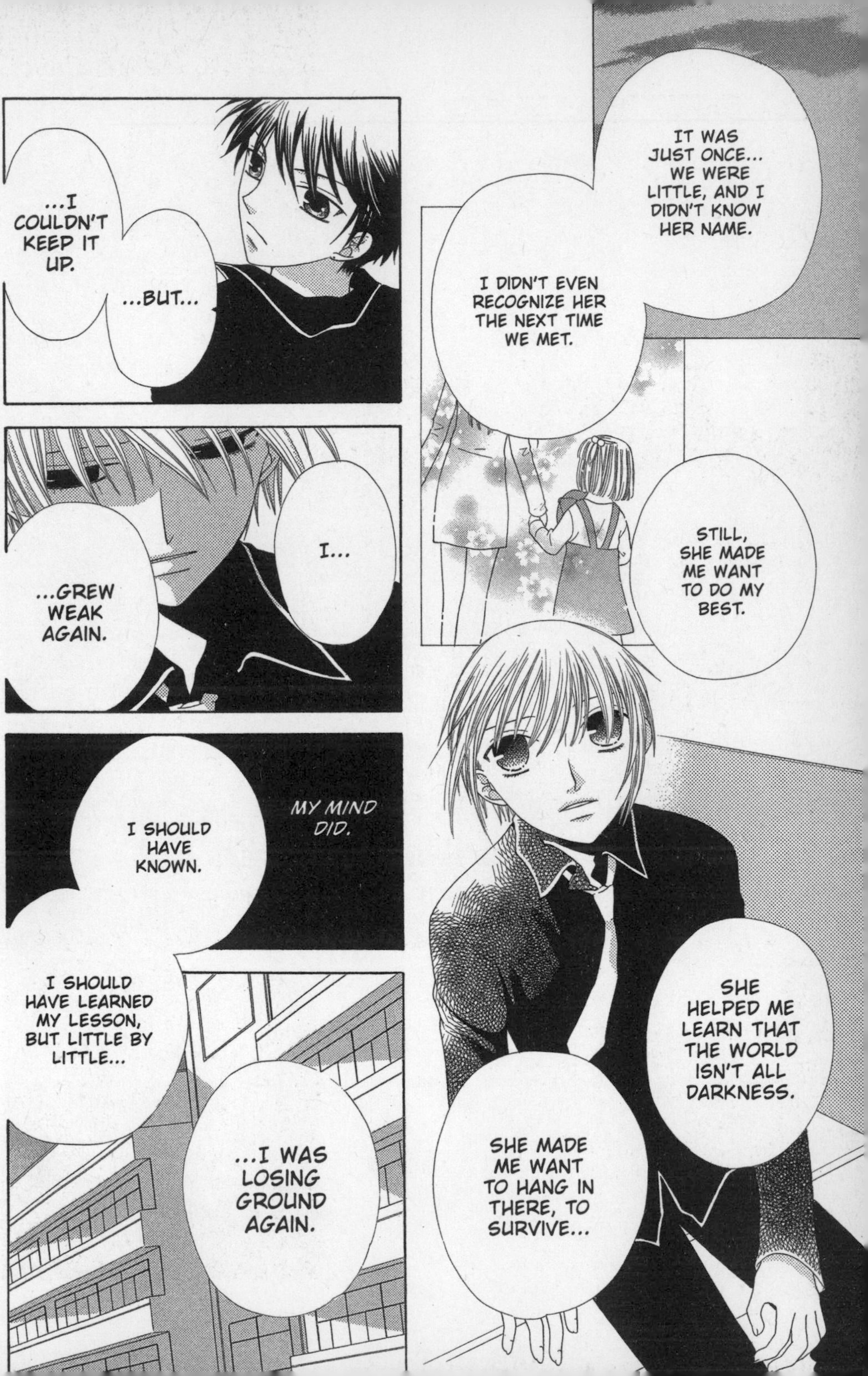
IT WAS JUST ONCE... WE WERE LITTLE, AND I DIDN'T KNOW HER NAME.
I DIDN'T EVEN RECOGNIZE HER THE NEXT TIME WE MET.
STILL, SHE MADE ME WANT TO DO MY BEST.
SHE HELPED ME LEARN THAT THE WORLD ISN'T ALL DARKNESS.
SHE MADE ME WANT TO HANG IN THERE, TO SURVIVE...
...BUT...
...I COULDN'T KEEP IT UP.
I...
...GREW WEAK AGAIN.
MY MIND DID.
I SHOULD HAVE KNOWN.
I SHOULD HAVE LEARNED MY LESSON, BUT LITTLE BY LITTLE...
...I WAS LOSING GROUND AGAIN.

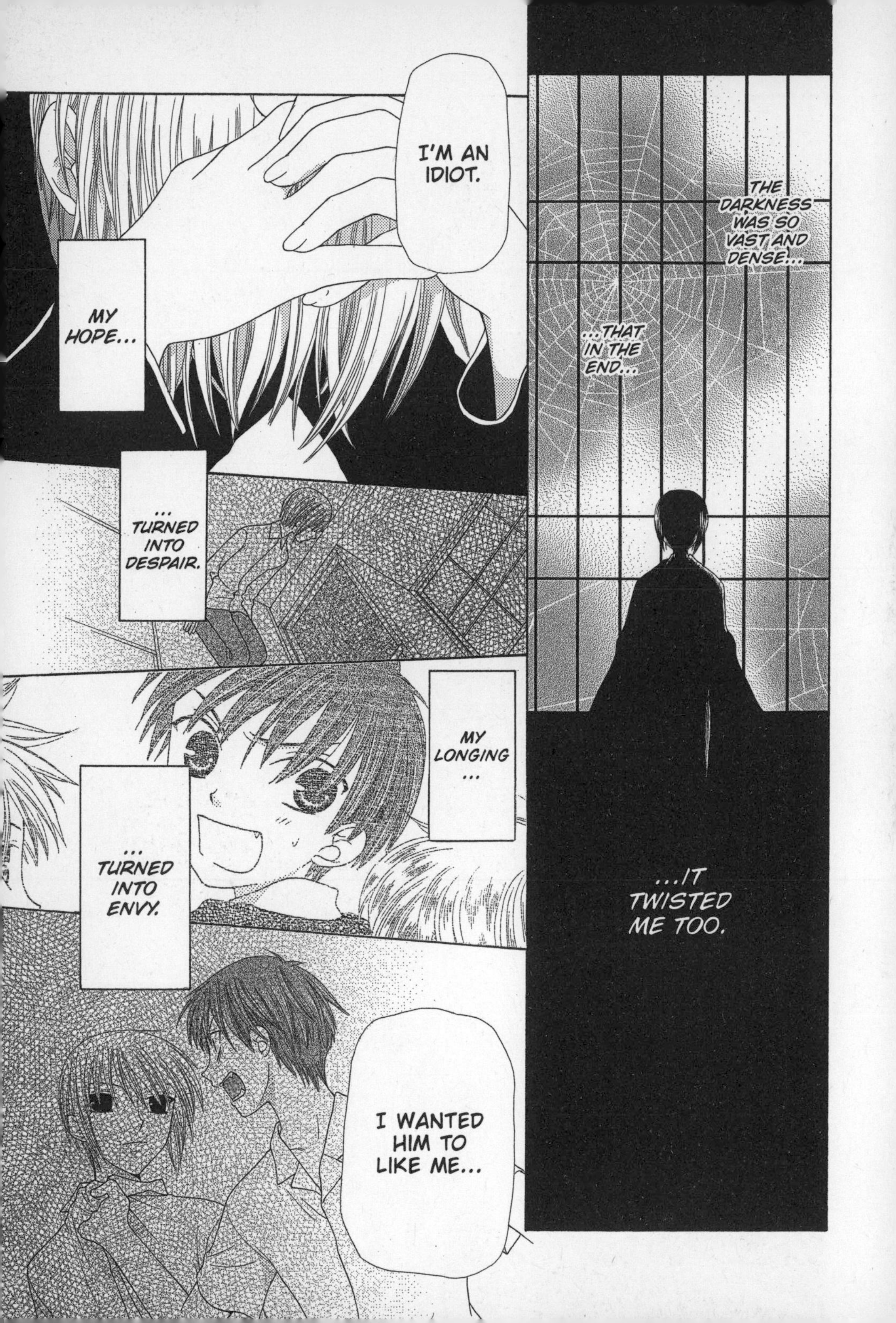
THE DARKNESS WAS SO VAST AND DENSE...
...THAT IN THE END...
...IT TWISTED ME TOO.
I'M AN IDIOT.
MY HOPE...
...TURNED INTO DESPAIR.
MY LONGING...
...TURNED INTO ENVY.
I WANTED HIM TO LIKE ME...

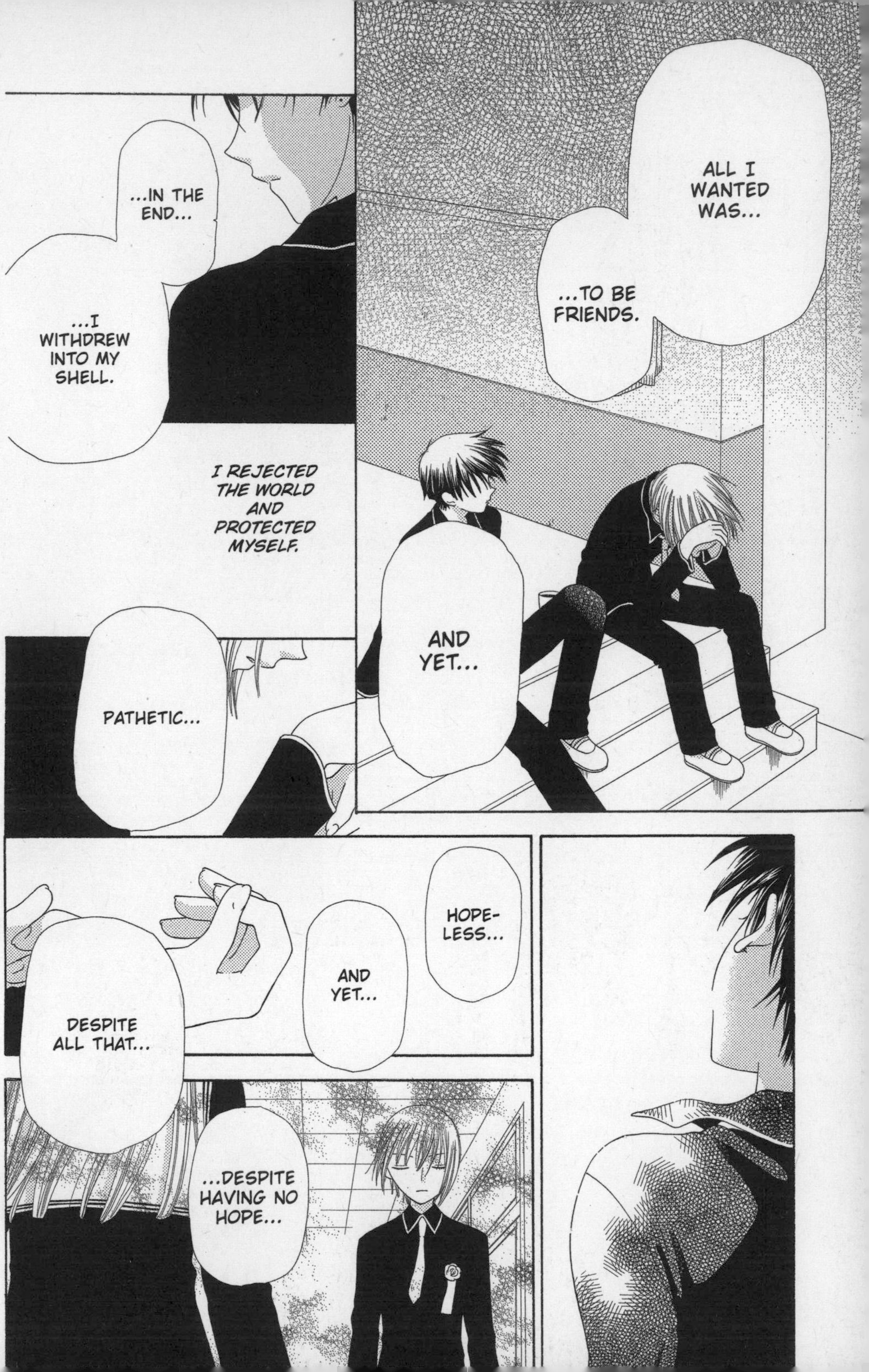
ALL I WANTED WAS...
...TO BE FRIENDS.
AND YET...
...IN THE END...
...I WITHDREW INTO MY SHELL.
I REJECTED THE WORLD AND PROTECTED MYSELF.
PATHETIC...
HOPE-LESS...
AND YET...
DESPITE ALL THAT...
...DESPITE HAVING NO HOPE...

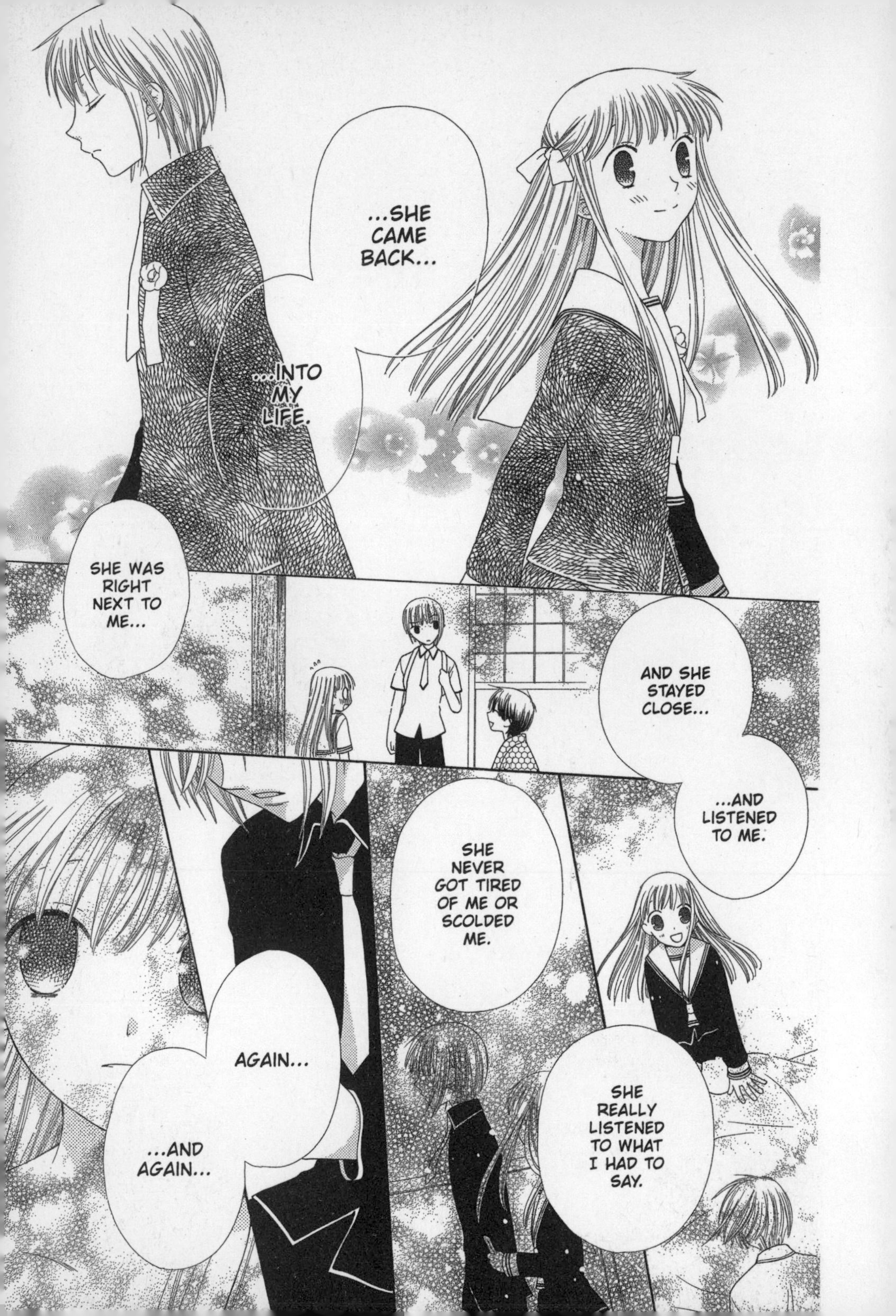
...SHE CAME BACK...
...INTO MY LIFE.
SHE WAS RIGHT NEXT TO ME...
AND SHE STAYED CLOSE...
...AND LISTENED TO ME.
SHE NEVER GOT TIRED OF ME OR SCOLDED ME.
SHE REALLY LISTENED TO WHAT I HAD TO SAY.
AGAIN...
...AND AGAIN...

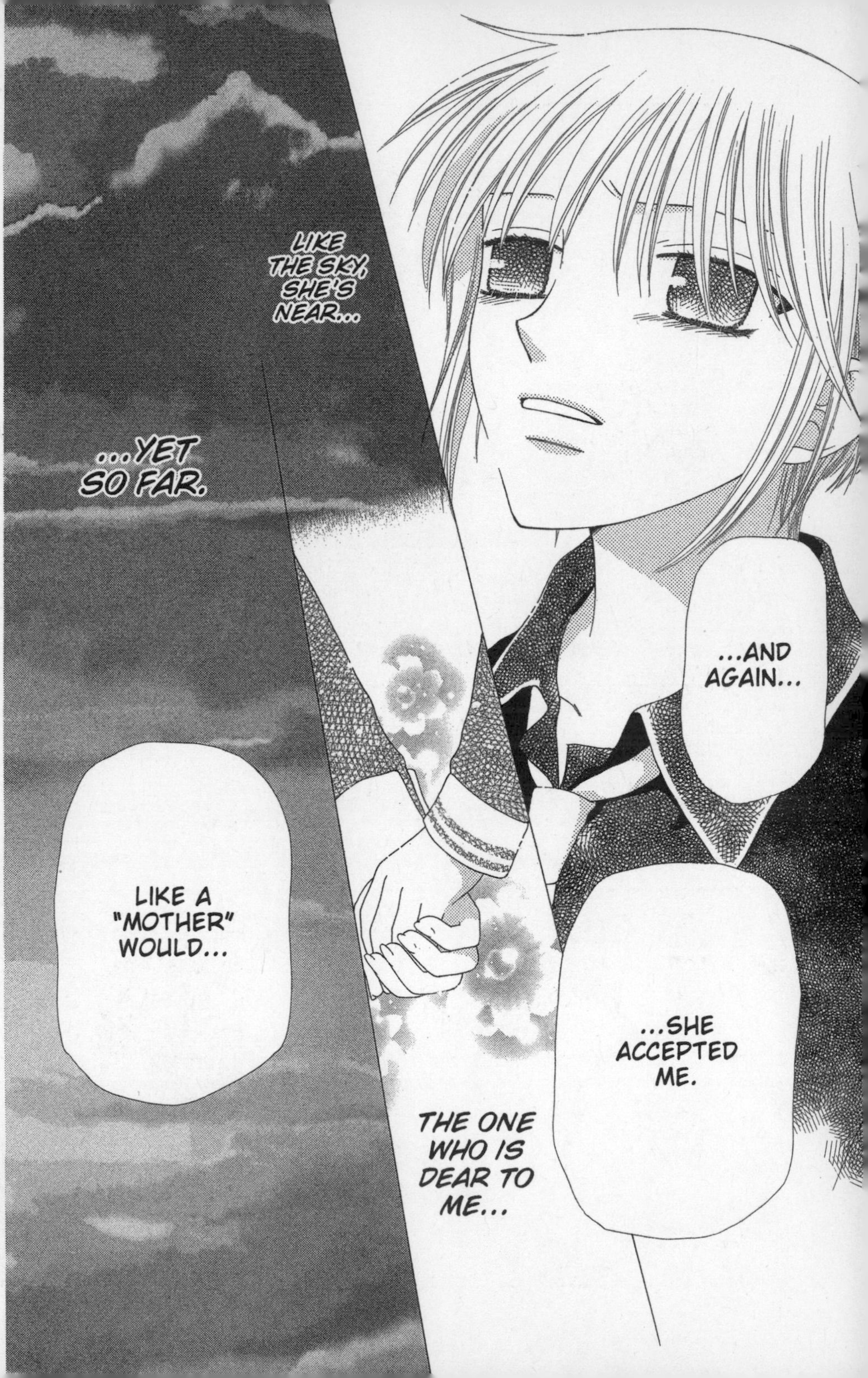
LIKE THE SKY, SHE'S NEAR...
...YET SO FAR.
...AND AGAIN...
...SHE ACCEPTED ME.
THE ONE WHO IS DEAR TO ME...
LIKE A "MOTHER" WOULD...

Chapter 86

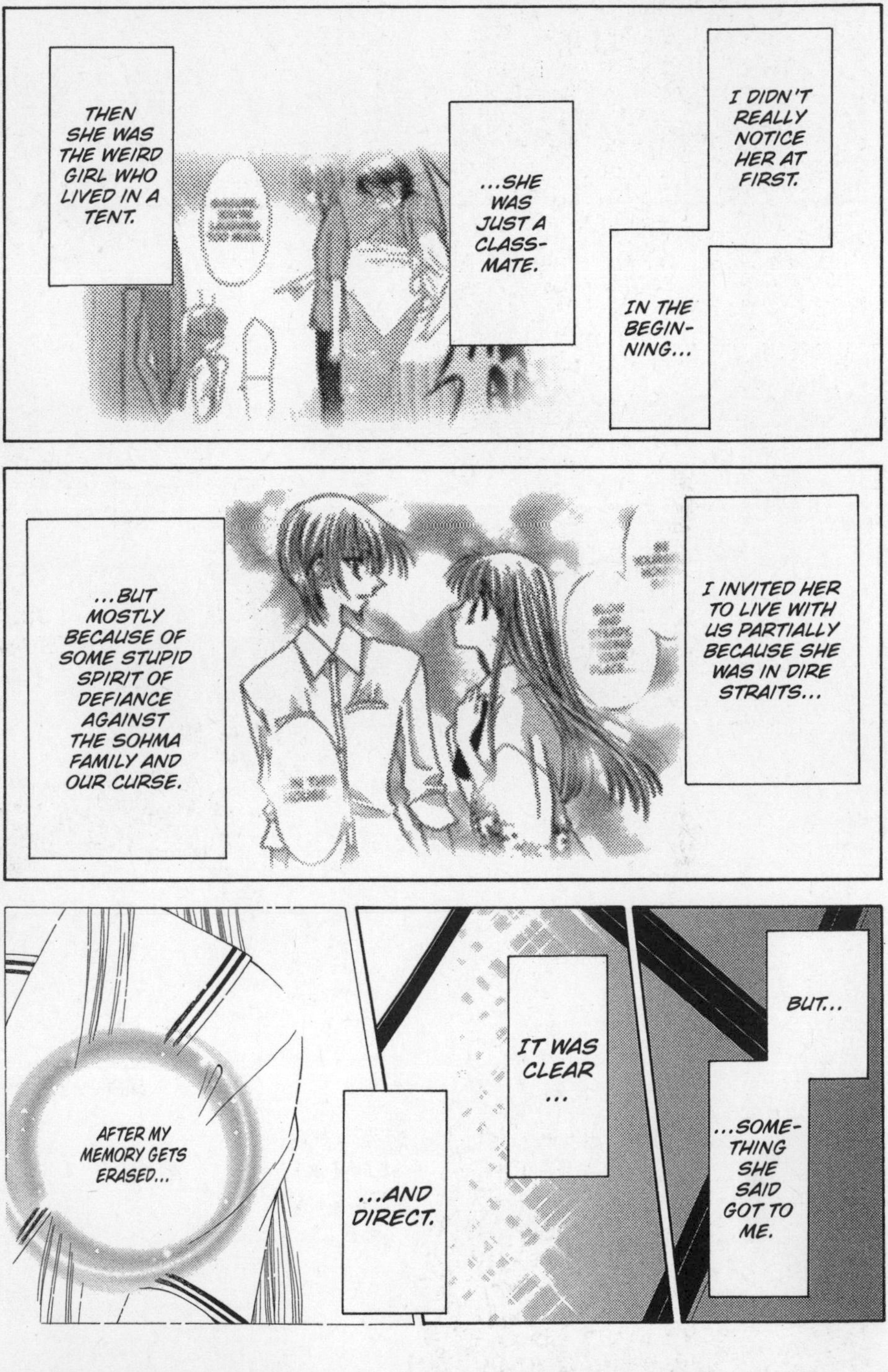

I DIDN'T REALLY NOTICE HER AT FIRST.
IN THE BEGINNING...
...SHE WAS JUST A CLASSMATE.
THEN SHE WAS THE WEIRD GIRL WHO LIVED IN A TENT.
I INVITED HER TO LIVE WITH US PARTIALLY BECAUSE SHE WAS IN DIRE STRAITS...
...BUT MOSTLY BECAUSE OF SOME STUPID SPIRIT OF DEFIANCE AGAINST THE SOHMA FAMILY AND OUR CURSE.
BUT...
...SOMETHING SHE SAID GOT TO ME.
IT WAS CLEAR...
...AND DIRECT.
AFTER MY MEMORY GETS ERASED...

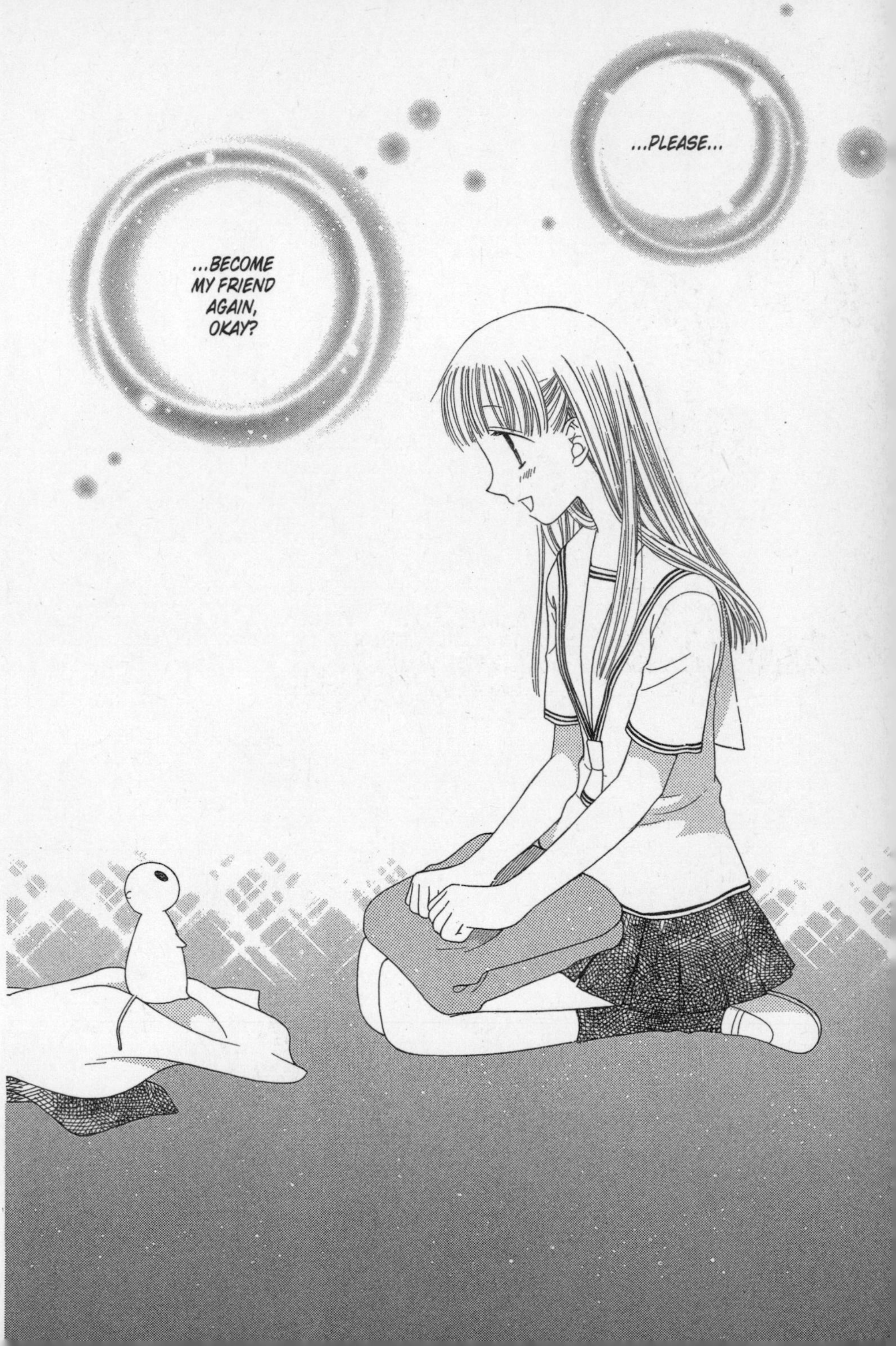
...PLEASE...
...BECOME MY FRIEND AGAIN, OKAY?

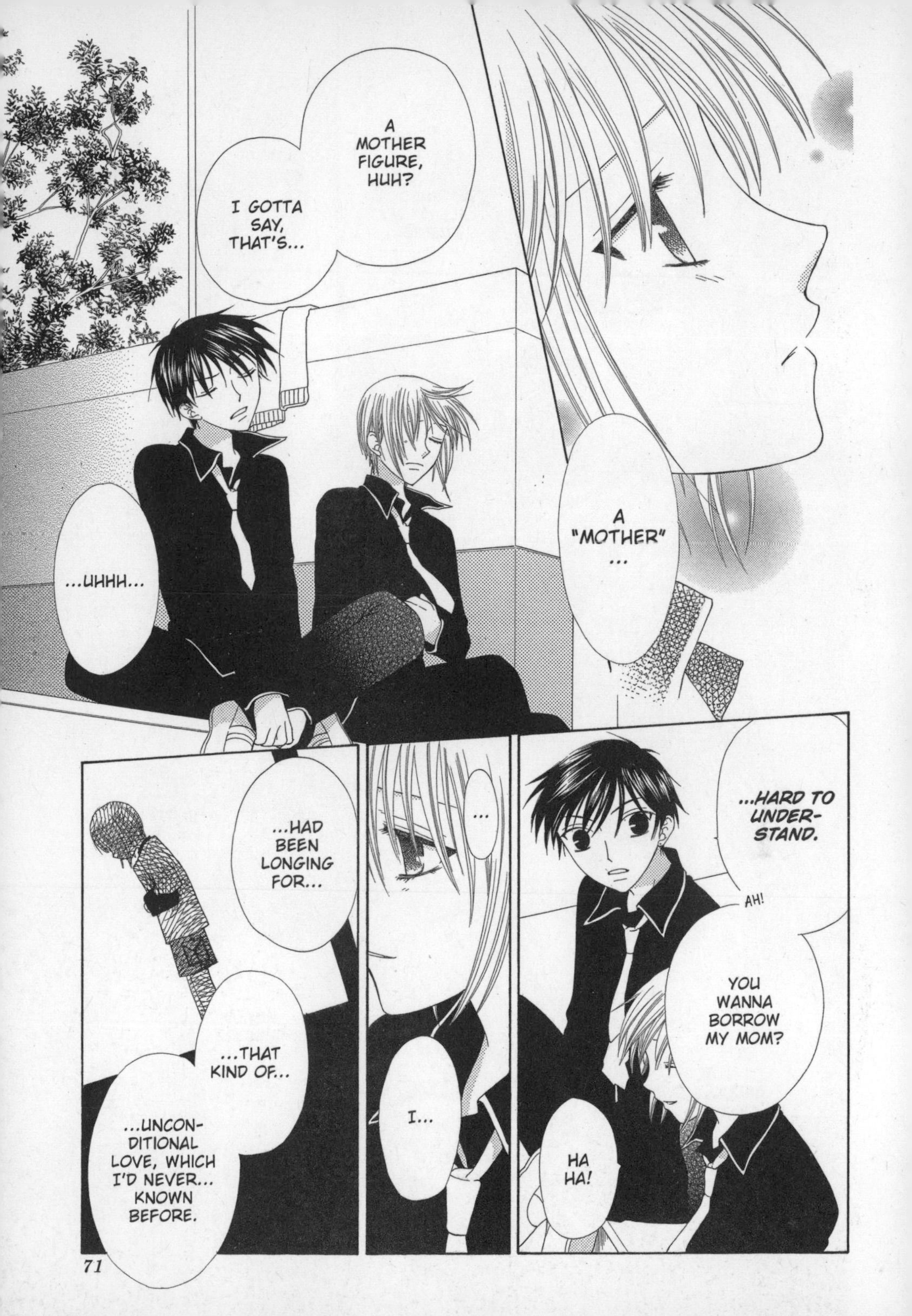
A "MOTHER" ...
A MOTHER FIGURE, HUH?
I GOTTA SAY, THAT'S...
...UHHH...
...HARD TO UNDER-STAND.
AH!
YOU WANNA BORROW MY MOM?
HA HA!
...
I...
...HAD BEEN LONGING FOR...
...THAT KIND OF...
...UNCON-DITIONAL LOVE, WHICH I'D NEVER... KNOWN BEFORE.

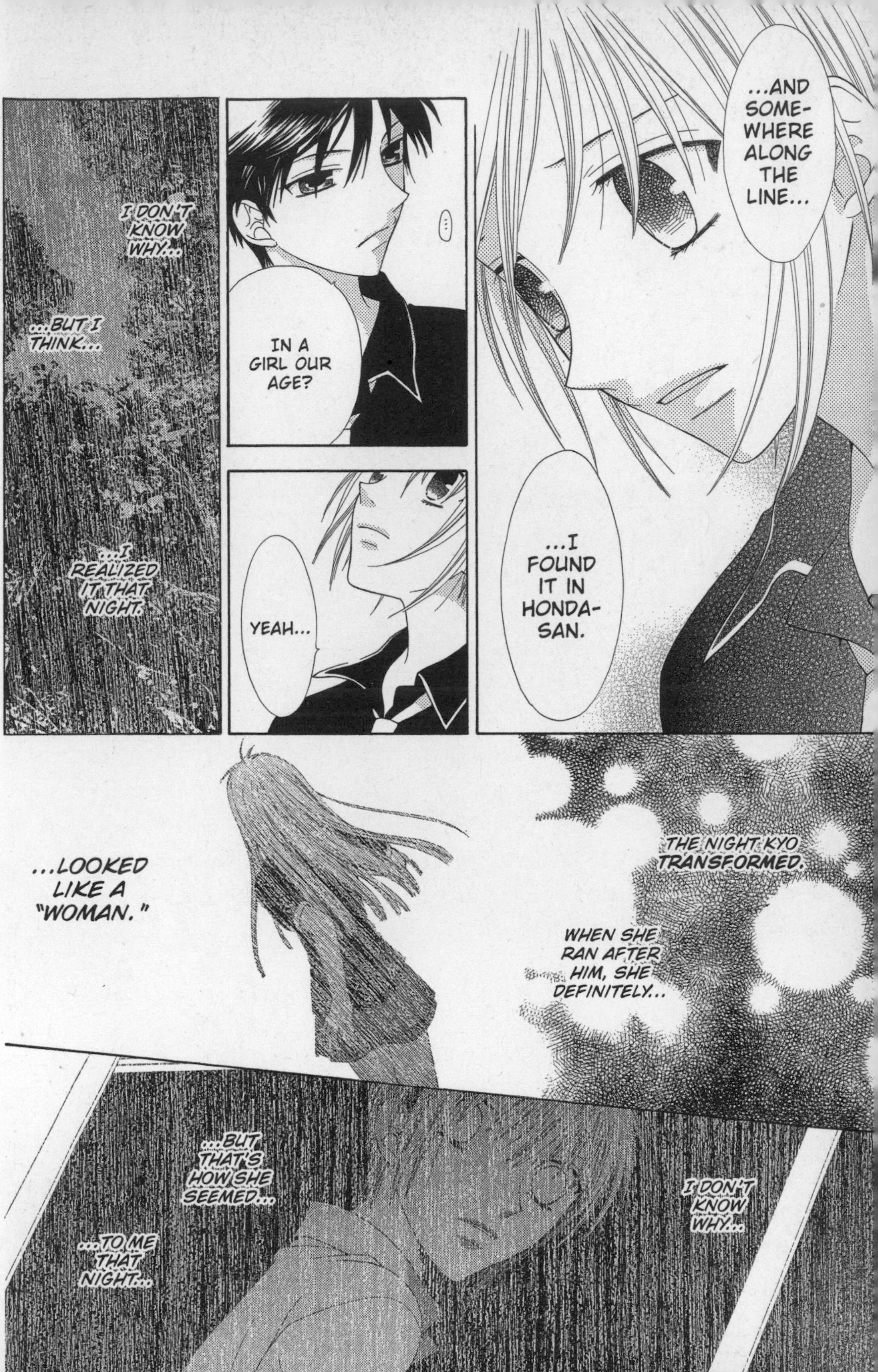
...AND SOME-WHERE ALONG THE LINE...
...I FOUND IT IN HONDA-SAN.
...
IN A GIRL OUR AGE?
YEAH...
I DON'T KNOW WHY...
...BUT I THINK...
...I REALIZED IT THAT NIGHT.
THE NIGHT KYO TRANSFORMED.
WHEN SHE RAN AFTER HIM, SHE DEFINITELY...
...LOOKED LIKE A "WOMAN."
I DON'T KNOW WHY...
...BUT THAT'S HOW SHE SEEMED...
...TO ME THAT NIGHT...

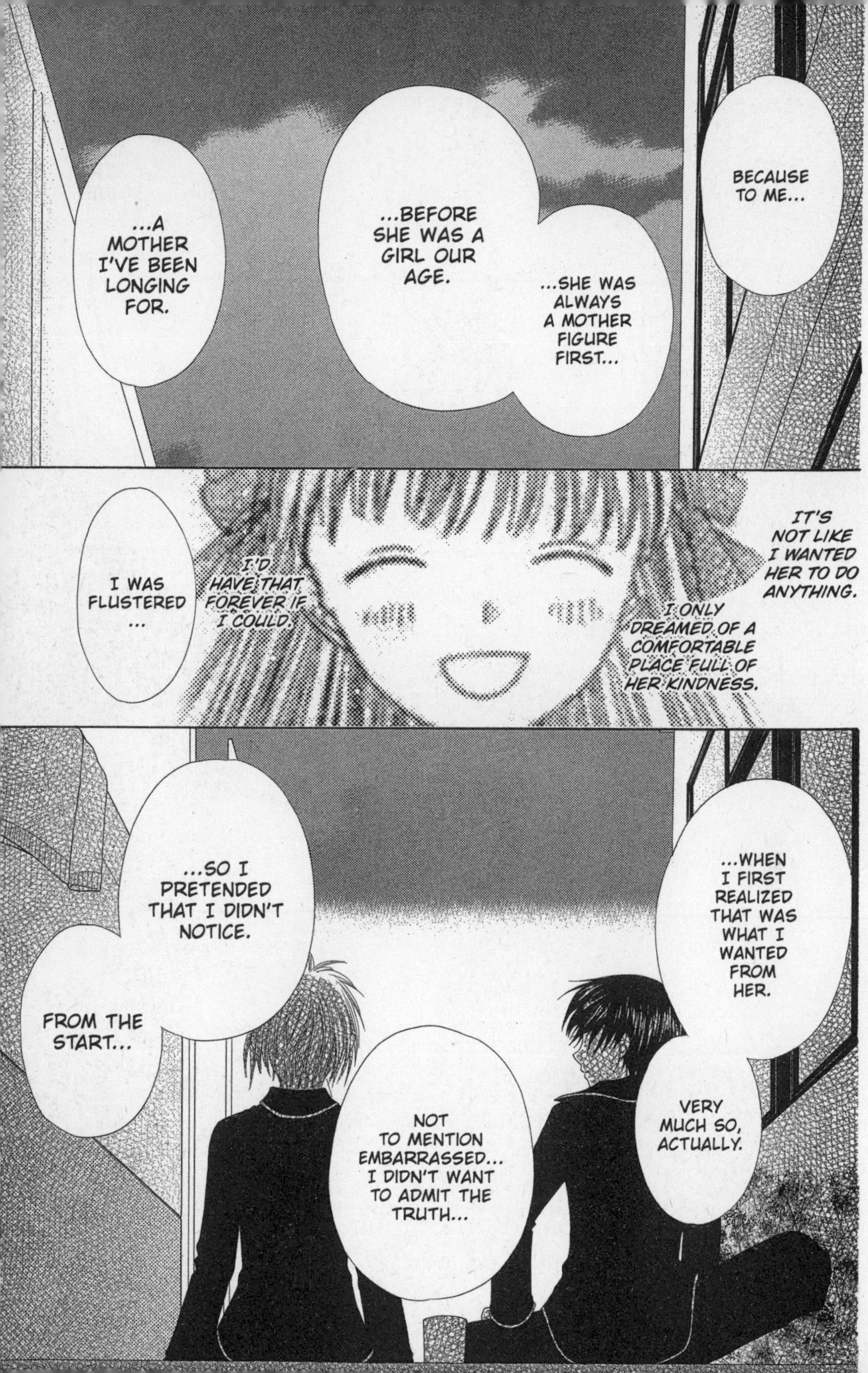
BECAUSE TO ME...
...SHE WAS ALWAYS A MOTHER FIGURE FIRST...
...BEFORE SHE WAS A GIRL OUR AGE.
...A MOTHER I'VE BEEN LONGING FOR.
IT'S NOT LIKE I WANTED HER TO DO ANYTHING.
I ONLY DREAMED OF A COMFORTABLE PLACE FULL OF HER KINDNESS.
I'D HAVE THAT FOREVER IF I COULD.
I WAS FLUSTERED ...
...WHEN I FIRST REALIZED THAT WAS WHAT I WANTED FROM HER.
VERY MUCH SO, ACTUALLY.
NOT TO MENTION EMBARRASSED... I DIDN'T WANT TO ADMIT THE TRUTH...
...SO I PRETENDED THAT I DIDN'T NOTICE.
FROM THE START...

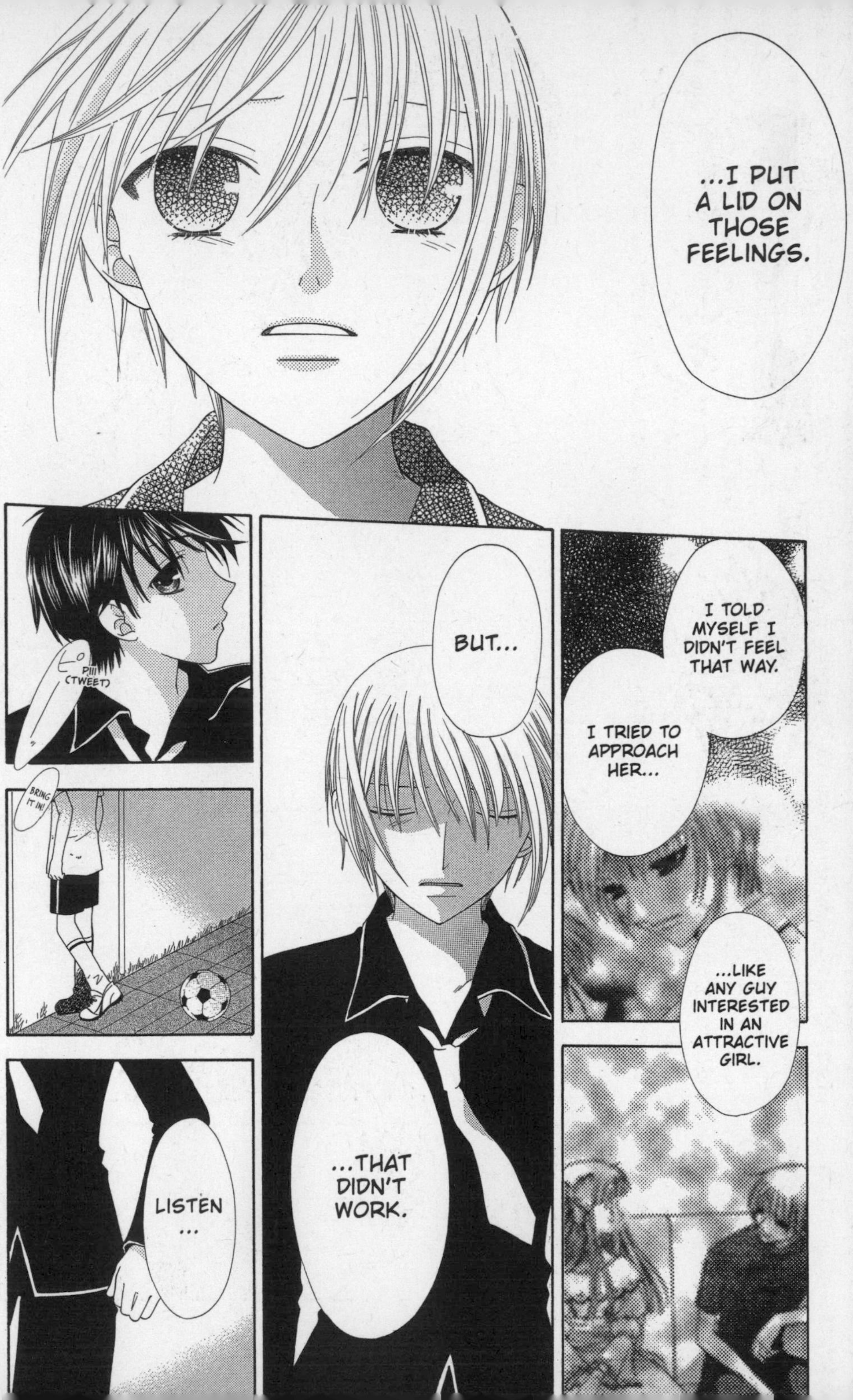
...I PUT A LID ON THOSE FEELINGS.
I TOLD MYSELF I DIDN'T FEEL THAT WAY.
I TRIED TO APPROACH HER...
...LIKE ANY GUY INTERESTED IN AN ATTRACTIVE GIRL.
BUT...
...THAT DIDN'T WORK.
PIII (TWEET)
BRING IT IN!
LISTEN ...

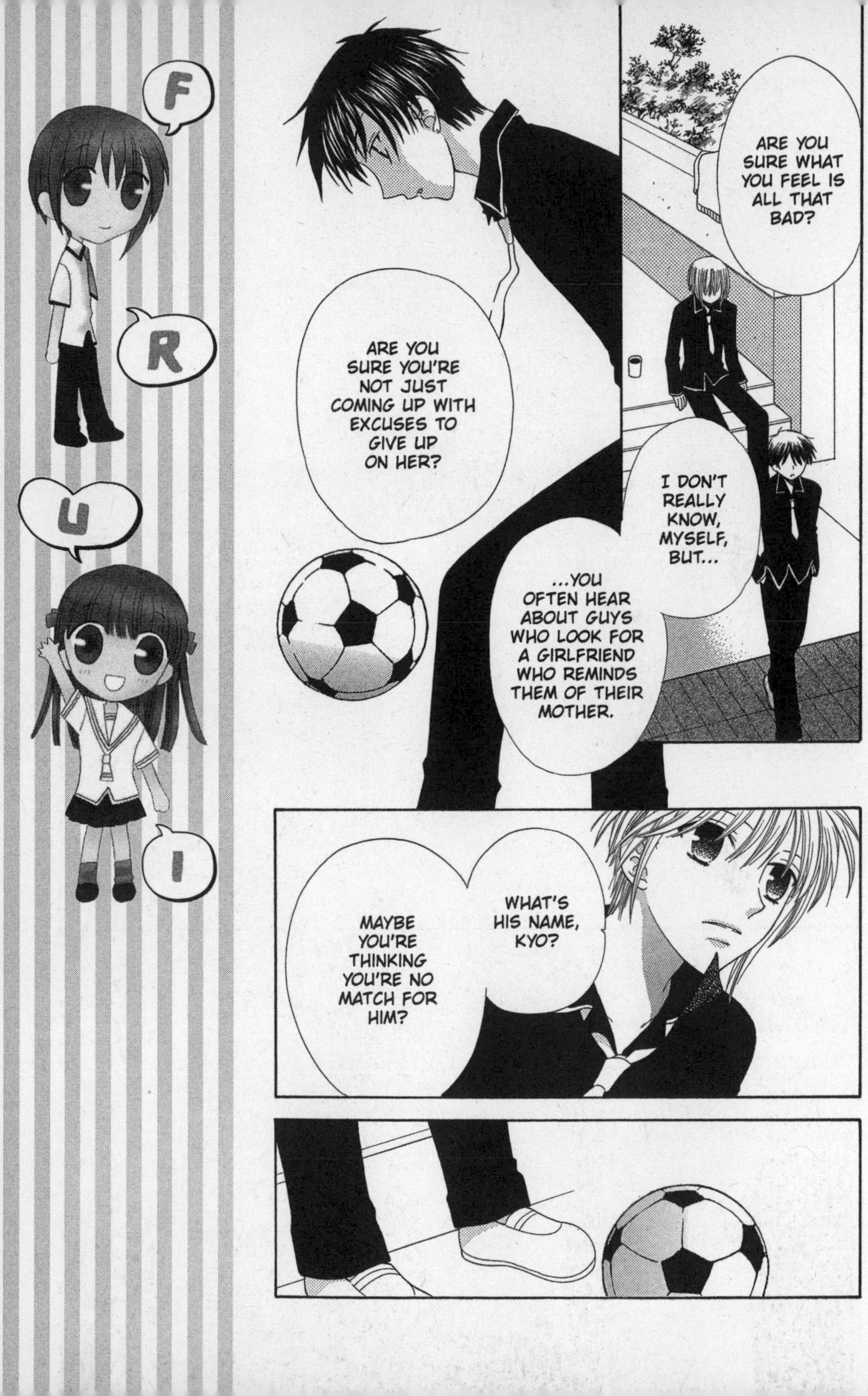
ARE YOU SURE WHAT YOU FEEL IS ALL THAT BAD?
I DON'T REALLY KNOW, MYSELF, BUT...
...YOU OFTEN HEAR ABOUT GUYS WHO LOOK FOR A GIRLFRIEND WHO REMINDS THEM OF THEIR MOTHER.
ARE YOU SURE YOU'RE NOT JUST COMING UP WITH EXCUSES TO GIVE UP ON HER?
WHAT'S HIS NAME, KYO?
MAYBE YOU'RE THINKING YOU'RE NO MATCH FOR HIM?
F
R
U
I

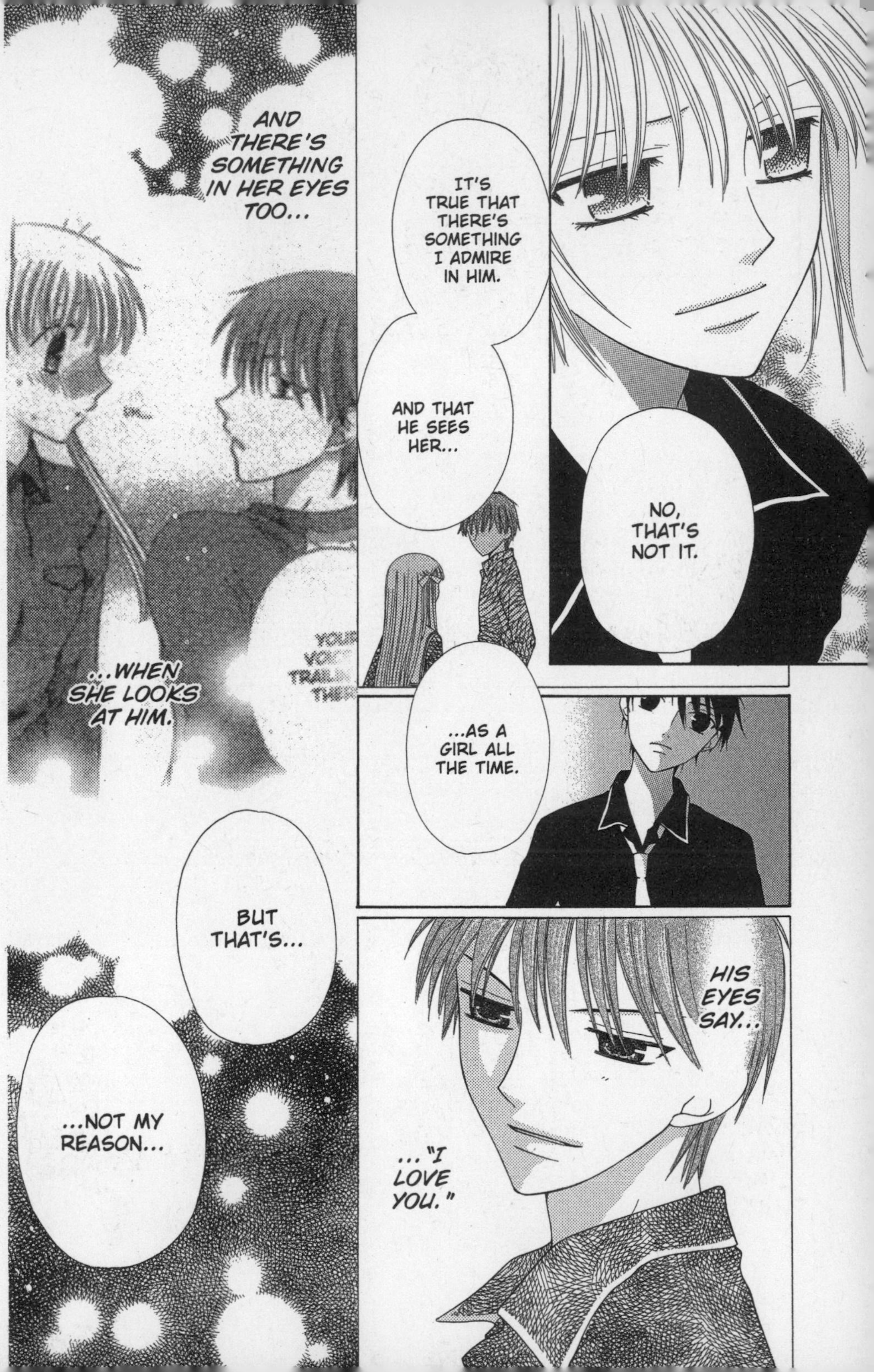
NO, THAT'S NOT IT.
IT'S TRUE THAT THERE'S SOMETHING I ADMIRE IN HIM.
AND THAT HE SEES HER...
...AS A GIRL ALL THE TIME.
HIS EYES SAY...
..."I LOVE YOU."
AND THERE'S SOMETHING IN HER EYES TOO...
...WHEN SHE LOOKS AT HIM.
BUT THAT'S...
...NOT MY REASON...

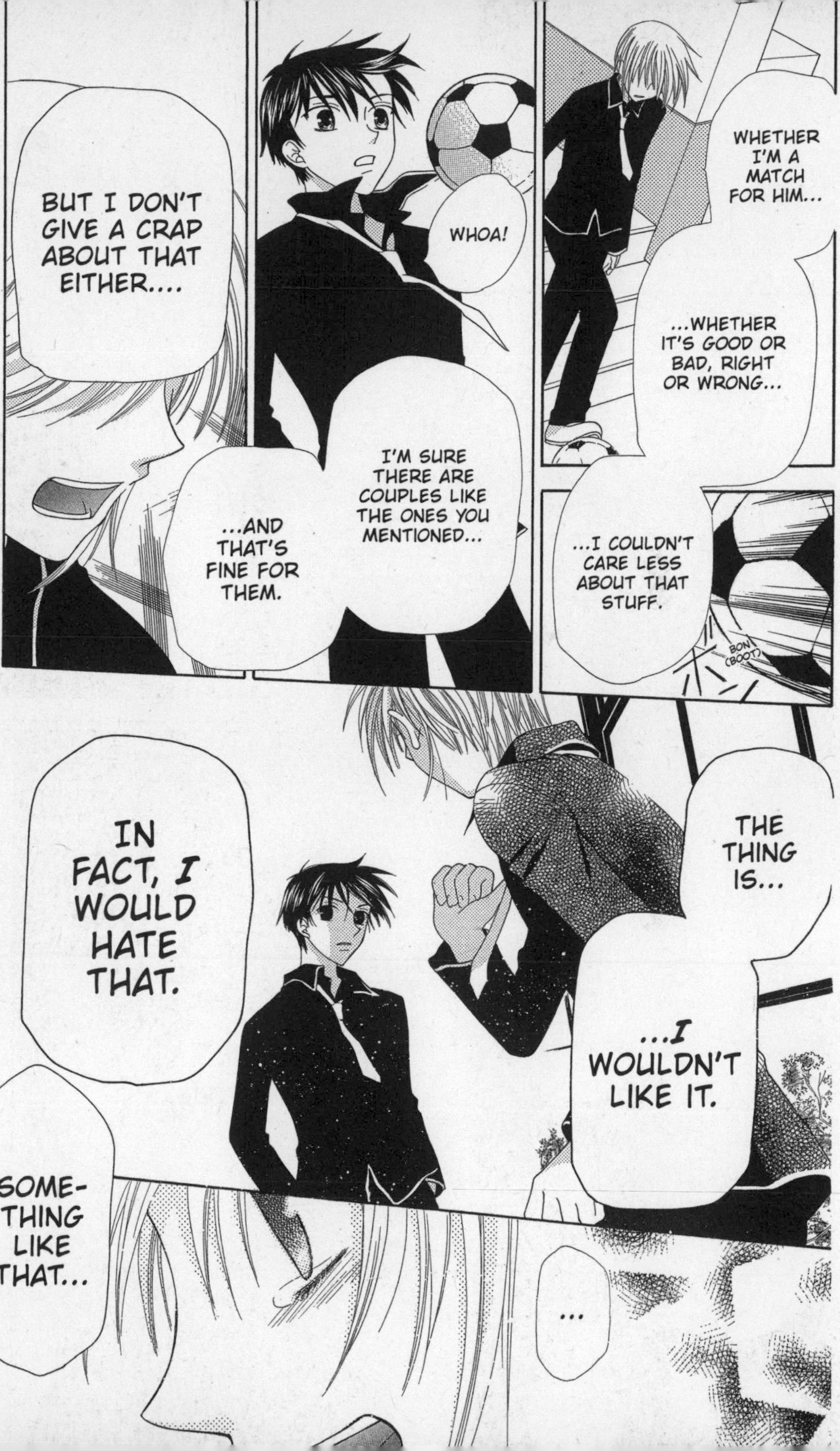
WHETHER I'M A MATCH FOR HIM...
...WHETHER IT'S GOOD OR BAD, RIGHT OR WRONG...
...I COULDN'T CARE LESS ABOUT THAT STUFF.
BON (BOOT)
WHOA!
I'M SURE THERE ARE COUPLES LIKE THE ONES YOU MENTIONED...
...AND THAT'S FINE FOR THEM.
BUT I DON'T GIVE A CRAP ABOUT THAT EITHER....
THE THING IS...
...I WOULDN'T LIKE IT.
IN FACT, I WOULD HATE THAT.
...
SOME-THING LIKE THAT...

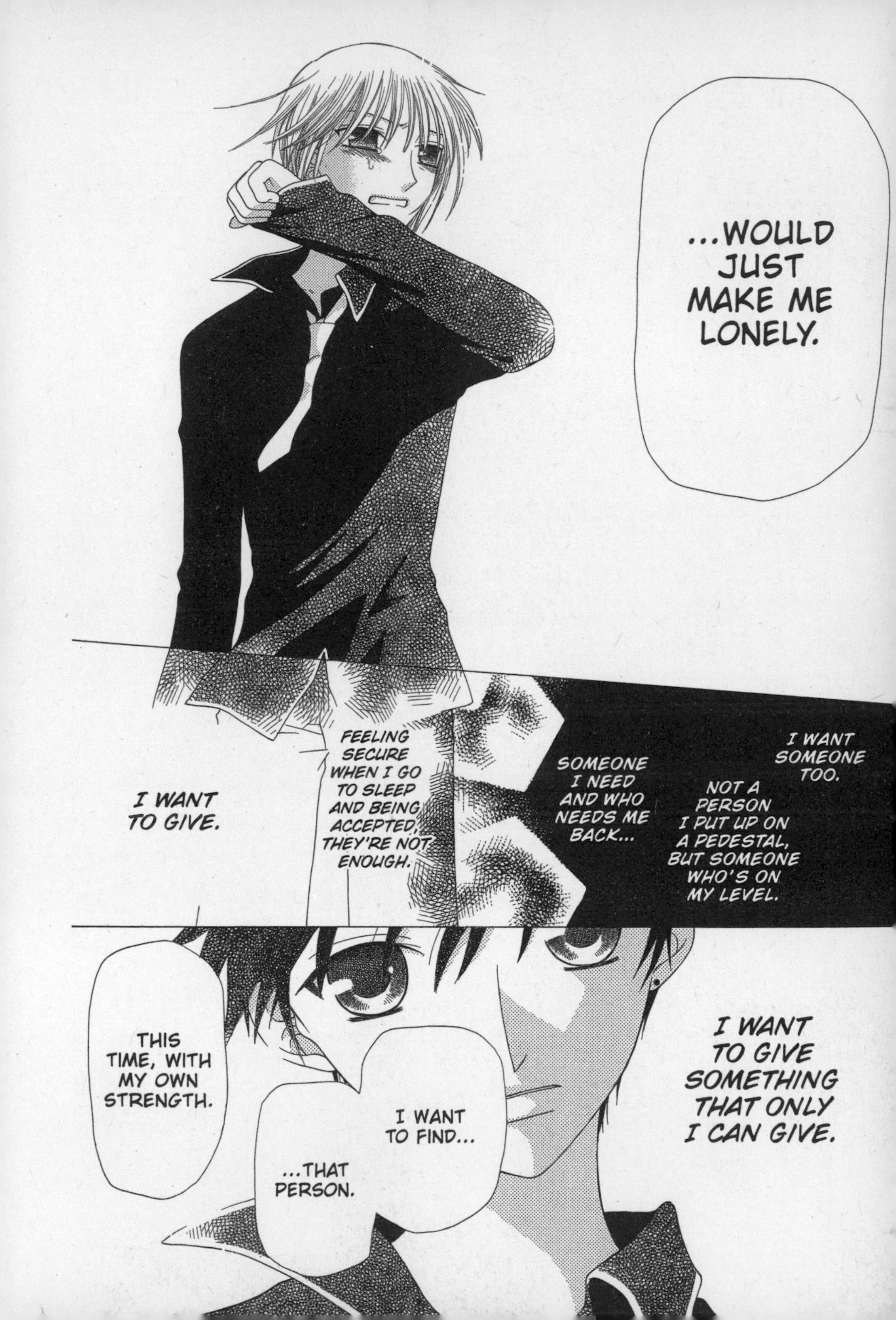
...WOULD JUST MAKE ME LONELY.
I WANT SOMEONE TOO.
NOT A PERSON I PUT UP ON A PEDESTAL, BUT SOMEONE WHO'S ON MY LEVEL.
SOMEONE I NEED AND WHO NEEDS ME BACK...
FEELING SECURE WHEN I GO TO SLEEP AND BEING ACCEPTED, THEY'RE NOT ENOUGH.
I WANT TO GIVE.
I WANT TO GIVE SOMETHING THAT ONLY I CAN GIVE.
I WANT TO FIND...
...THAT PERSON.
THIS TIME, WITH MY OWN STRENGTH.

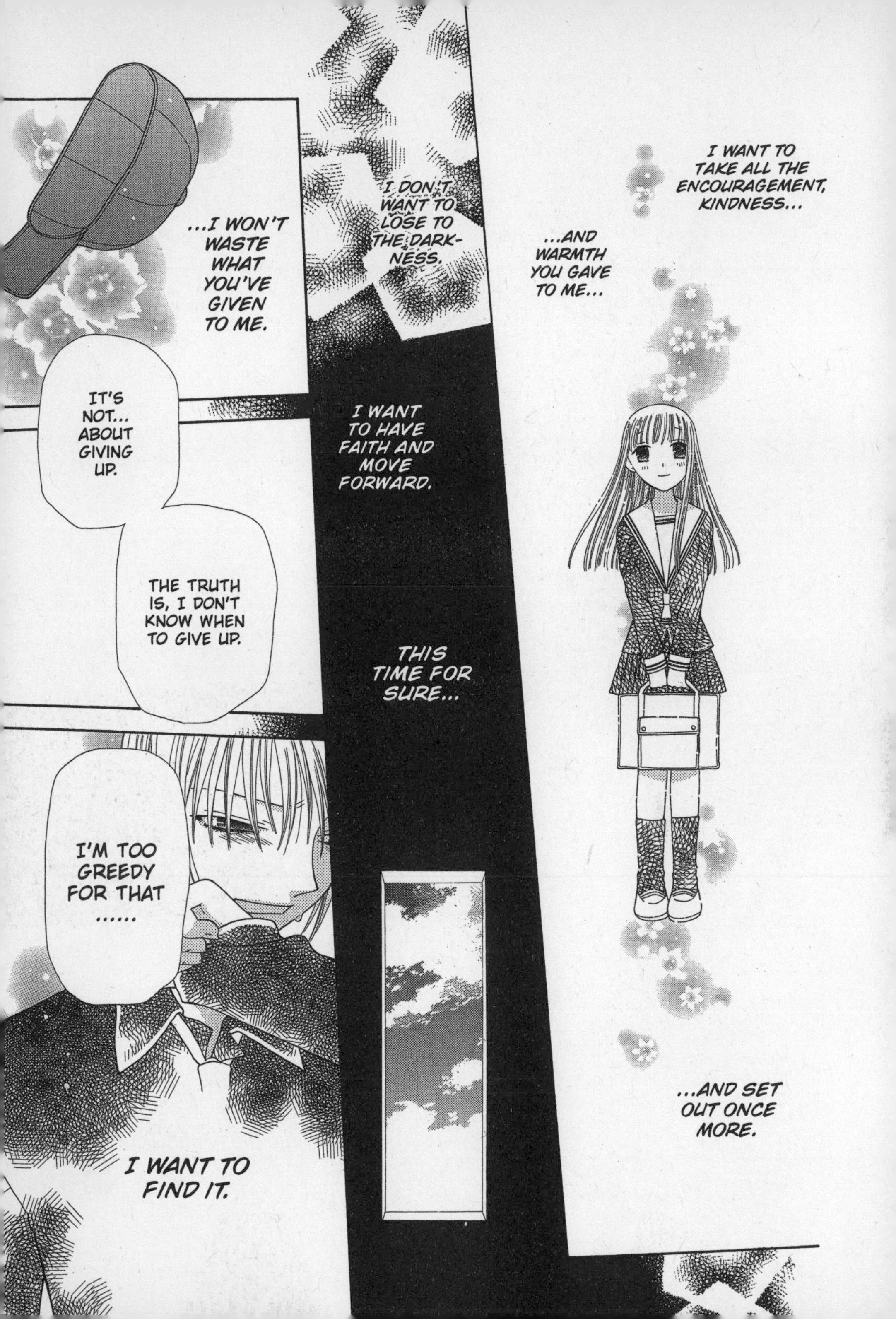
I WANT TO TAKE ALL THE ENCOURAGEMENT, KINDNESS...
...AND WARMTH YOU GAVE TO ME...
...AND SET OUT ONCE MORE.
I DON'T WANT TO LOSE TO THE DARKNESS.
I WANT TO HAVE FAITH AND MOVE FORWARD.
THIS TIME FOR SURE...
...I WON'T WASTE WHAT YOU'VE GIVEN TO ME.
IT'S NOT... ABOUT GIVING UP.
THE TRUTH IS, I DON'T KNOW WHEN TO GIVE UP.
I'M TOO GREEDY FOR THAT ......
I WANT TO FIND IT.

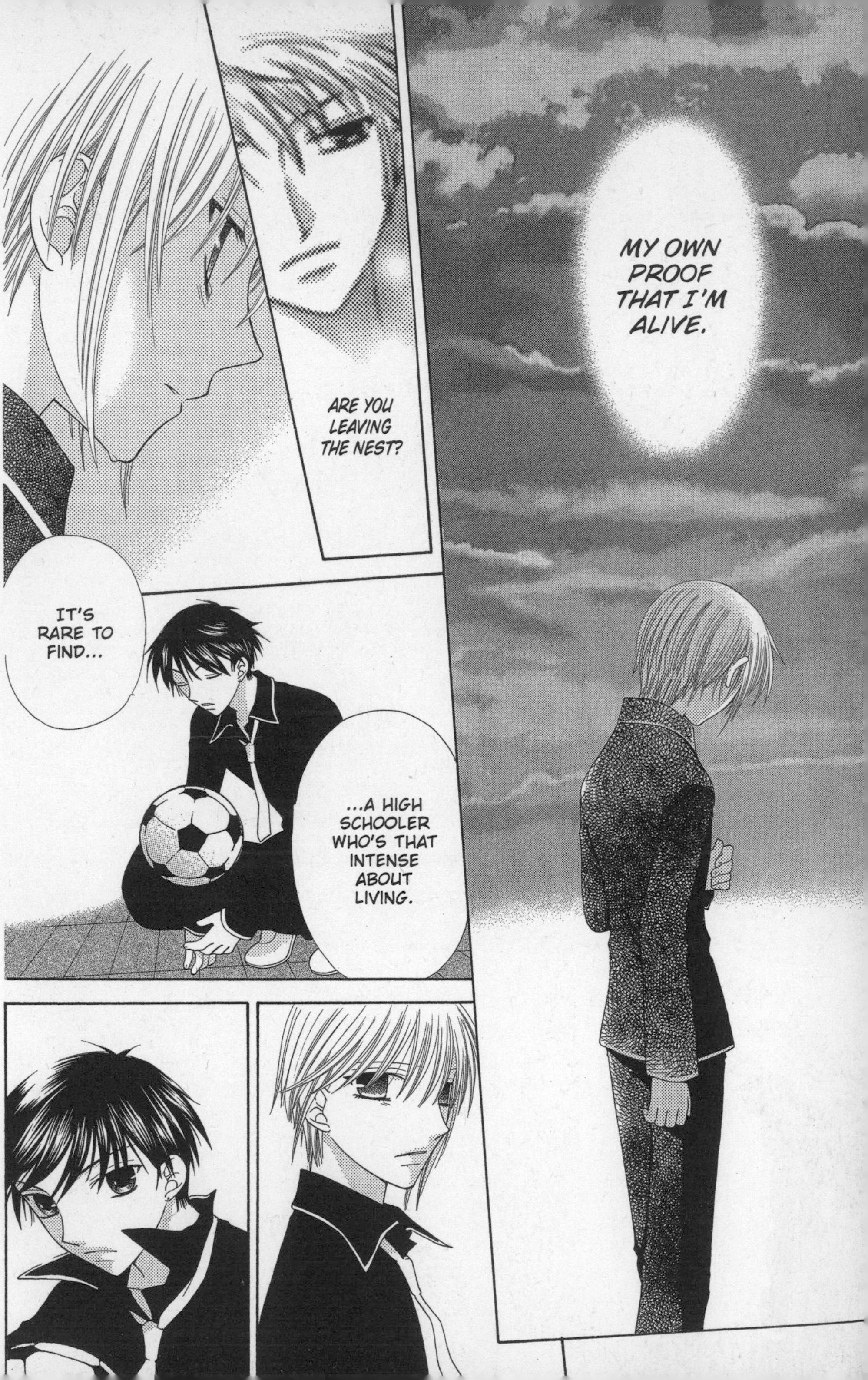
MY OWN PROOF THAT I'M ALIVE.
ARE YOU LEAVING THE NEST?
IT'S RARE TO FIND...
...A HIGH SCHOOLER WHO'S THAT INTENSE ABOUT LIVING.

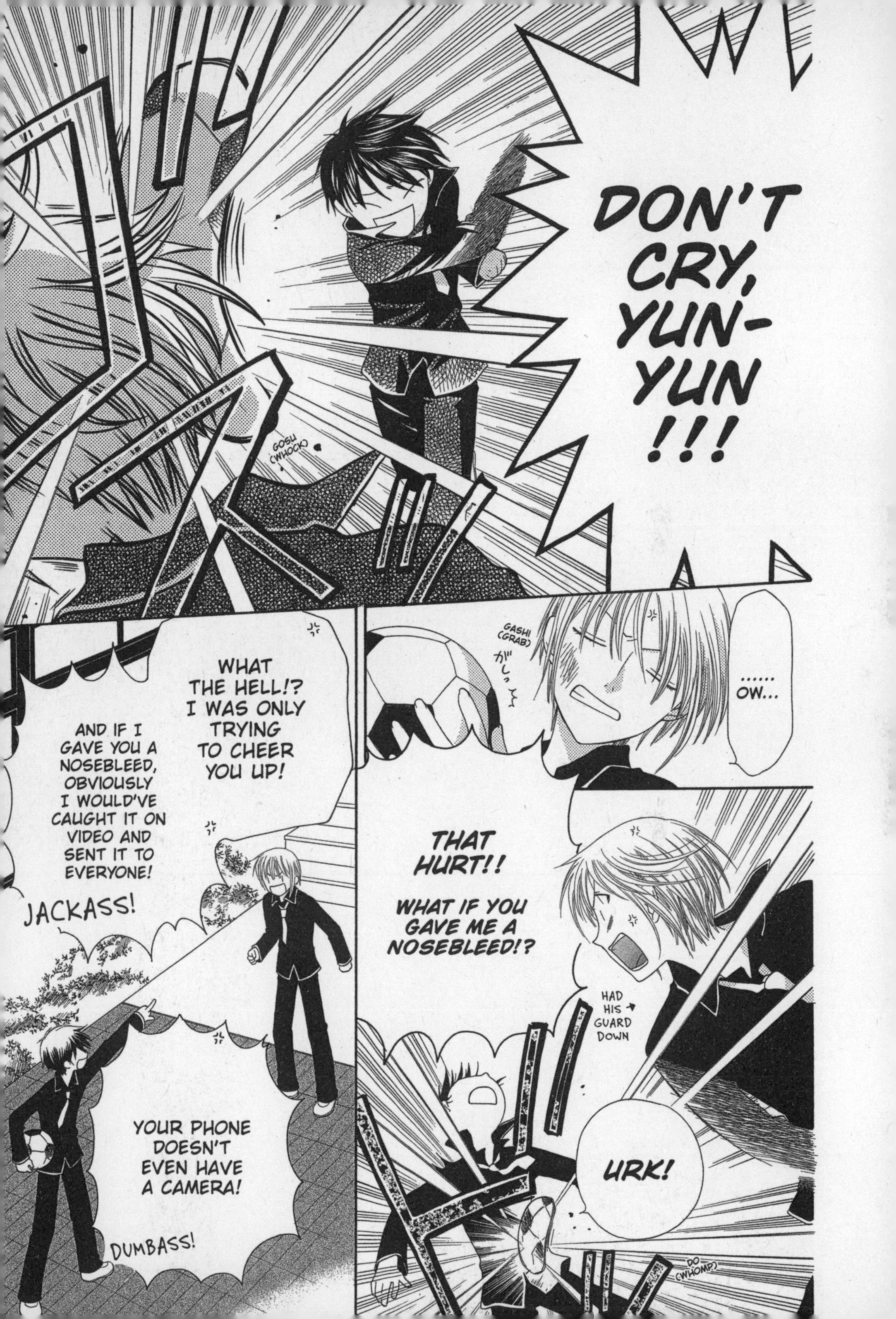
DON'T CRY, YUN-YUN!!!
GOSU (WHOCK)
GASHI (GRAB)
がしっ
......OW...
THAT HURT!!
WHAT IF YOU GAVE ME A NOSEBLEED!?
HAD HIS GUARD DOWN
URK!
DO (WHOMP)
WHAT THE HELL!? I WAS ONLY TRYING TO CHEER YOU UP!
AND IF I GAVE YOU A NOSEBLEED, OBVIOUSLY I WOULD'VE CAUGHT IT ON VIDEO AND SENT IT TO EVERYONE!
JACKASS!
YOUR PHONE DOESN'T EVEN HAVE A CAMERA!
DUMBASS!

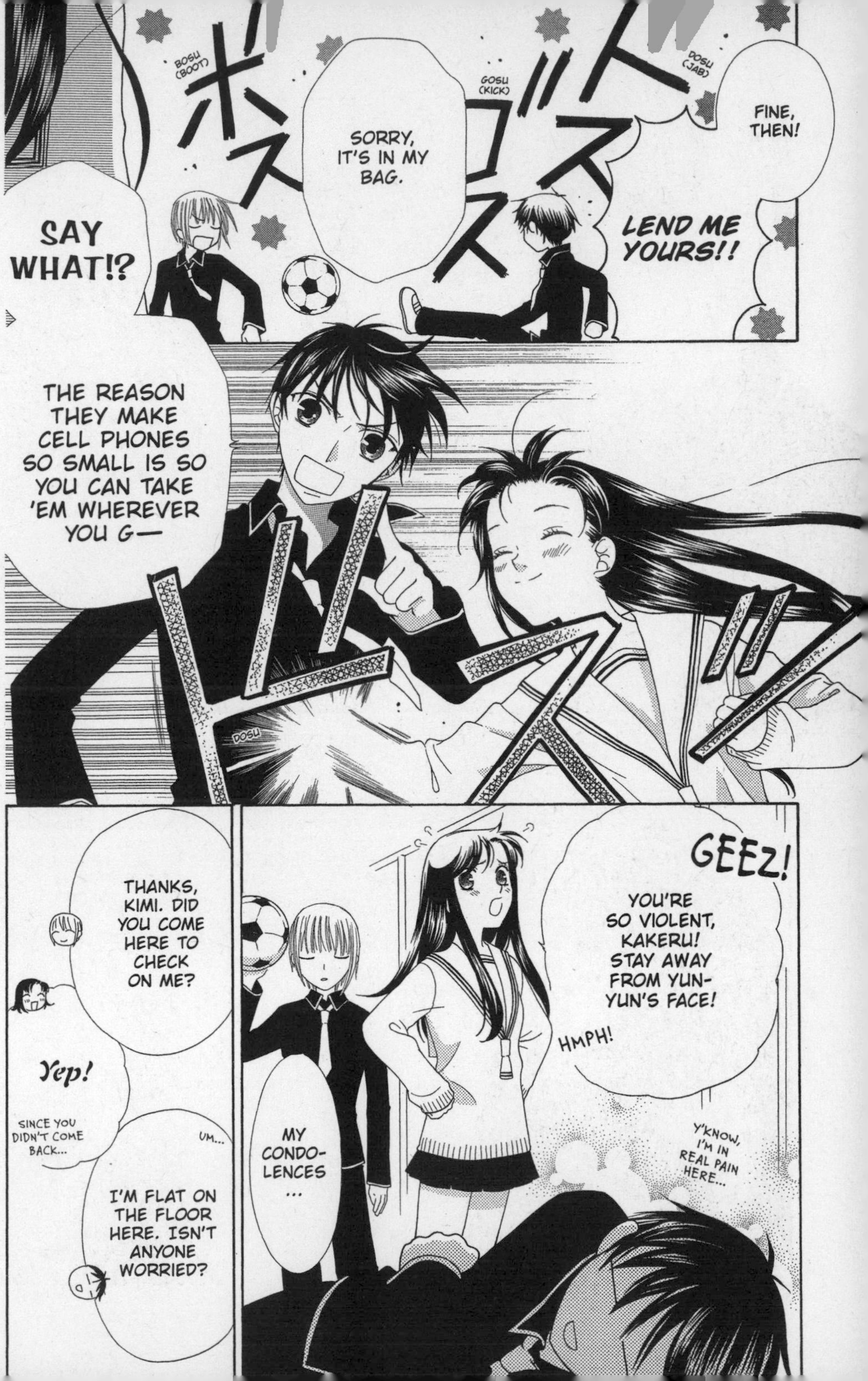
DOSU (JAB)
FINE, THEN!
LEND ME YOURS!!
GOSU (KICK)
SORRY, IT'S IN MY BAG.
BOSU (BOOT)
SAY WHAT!?
THE REASON THEY MAKE CELL PHONES SO SMALL IS SO YOU CAN TAKE 'EM WHEREVER YOU G—
DOSU
GEEZ!
YOU'RE SO VIOLENT, KAKERU! STAY AWAY FROM YUN-YUN'S FACE!
HMPH!
Y'KNOW, I'M IN REAL PAIN HERE...
MY CONDO-LENCES ...
THANKS, KIMI. DID YOU COME HERE TO CHECK ON ME?
Yep!
UM...
SINCE YOU DIDN'T COME BACK...
I'M FLAT ON THE FLOOR HERE. ISN'T ANYONE WORRIED?

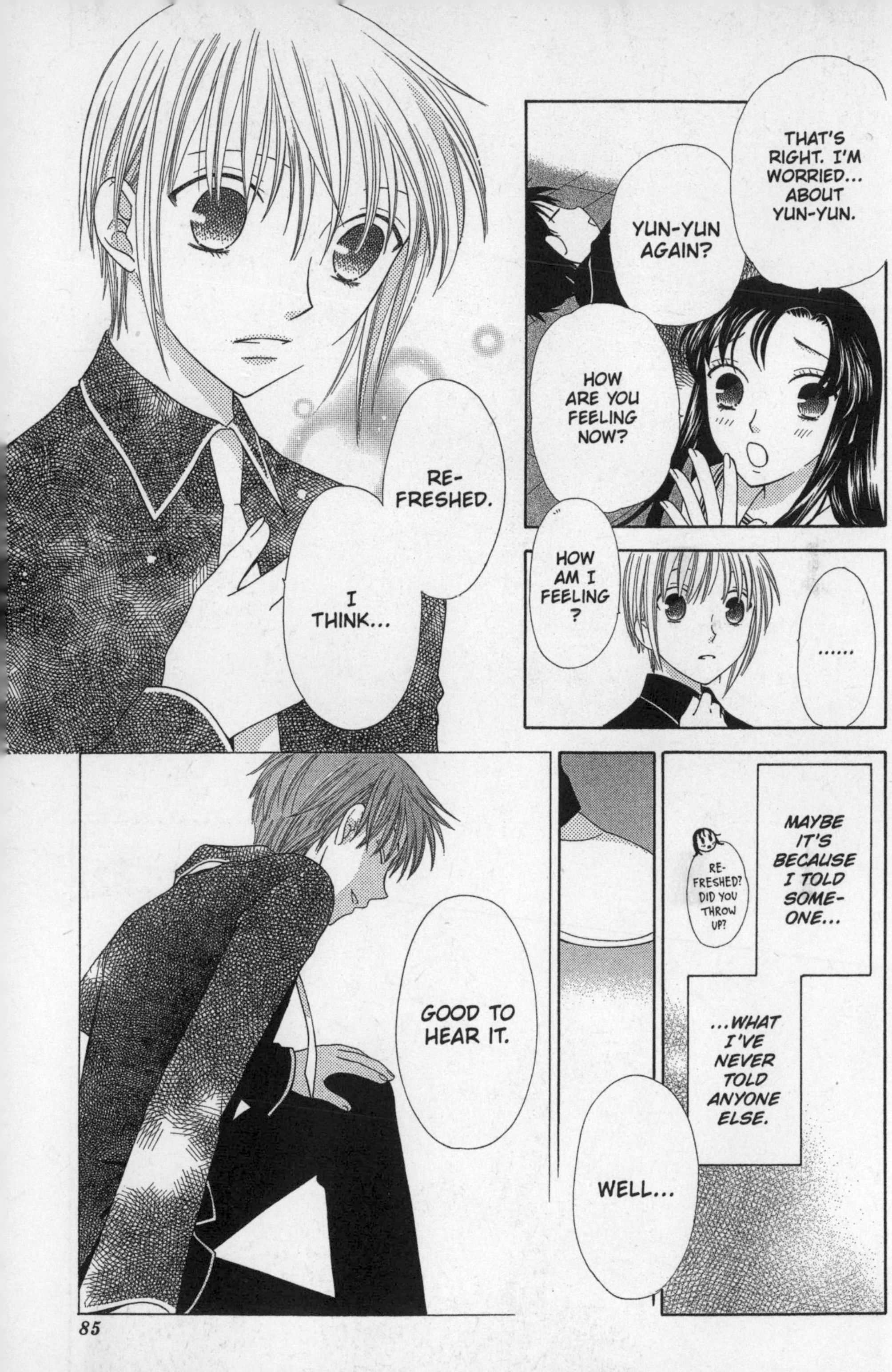
THAT'S RIGHT. I'M WORRIED... ABOUT YUN-YUN.
YUN-YUN AGAIN?
HOW ARE YOU FEELING NOW?
HOW AM I FEELING?
......
RE-FRESHED.
I THINK...
MAYBE IT'S BECAUSE I TOLD SOME-ONE...
RE-FRESHED? DID YOU THROW UP?
...WHAT I'VE NEVER TOLD ANYONE ELSE.
WELL...
GOOD TO HEAR IT.

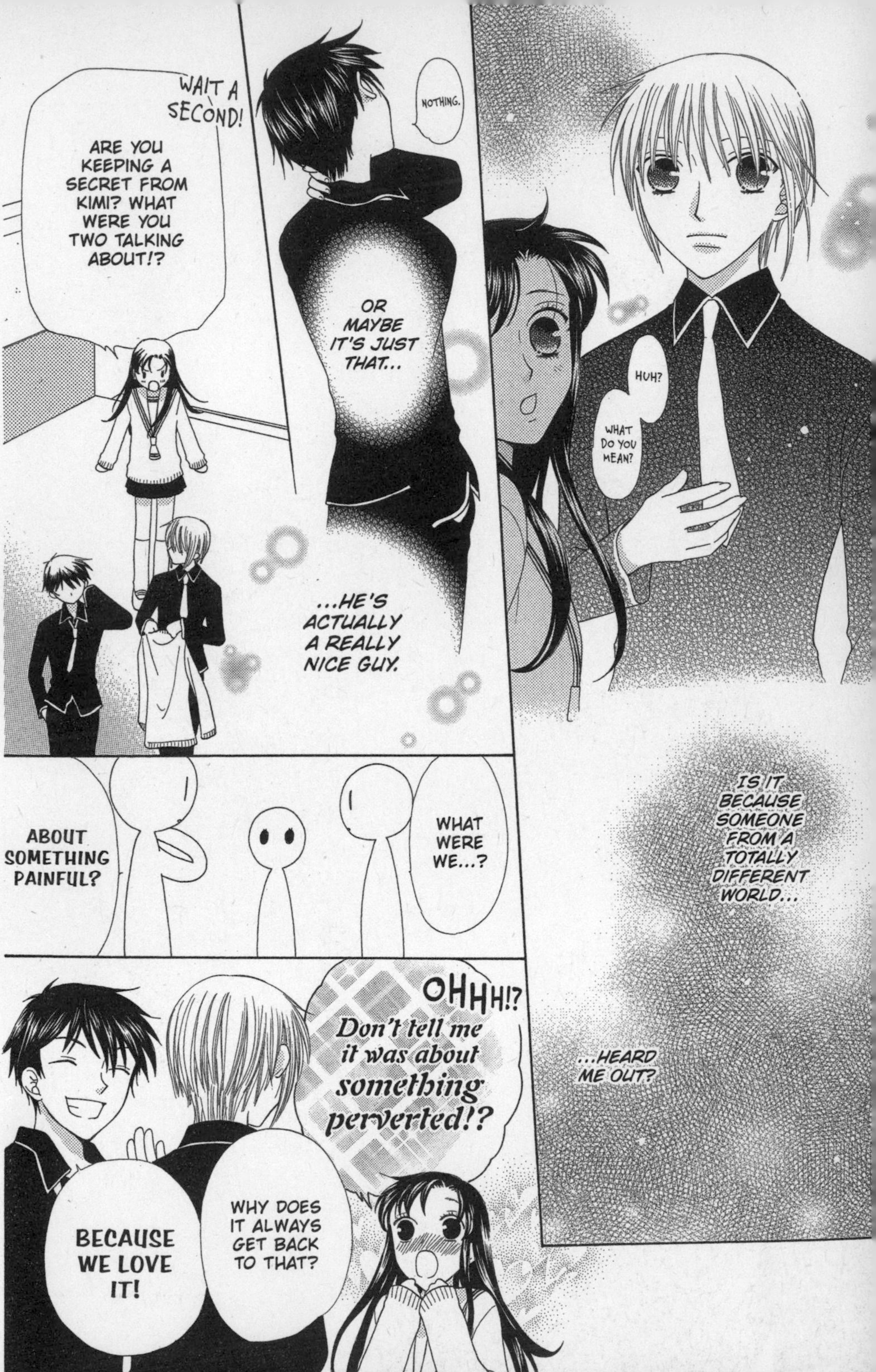
HUH?
WHAT DO YOU MEAN?
IS IT BECAUSE SOMEONE FROM A TOTALLY DIFFERENT WORLD...
...HEARD ME OUT?
NOTHING.
OR MAYBE IT'S JUST THAT...
...HE'S ACTUALLY A REALLY NICE GUY.
WAIT A SECOND!
ARE YOU KEEPING A SECRET FROM KIMI? WHAT WERE YOU TWO TALKING ABOUT!?
WHAT WERE WE...?
ABOUT SOMETHING PAINFUL?
OHHH!? Don't tell me it was about something perverted!?
WHY DOES IT ALWAYS GET BACK TO THAT?
BECAUSE WE LOVE IT!

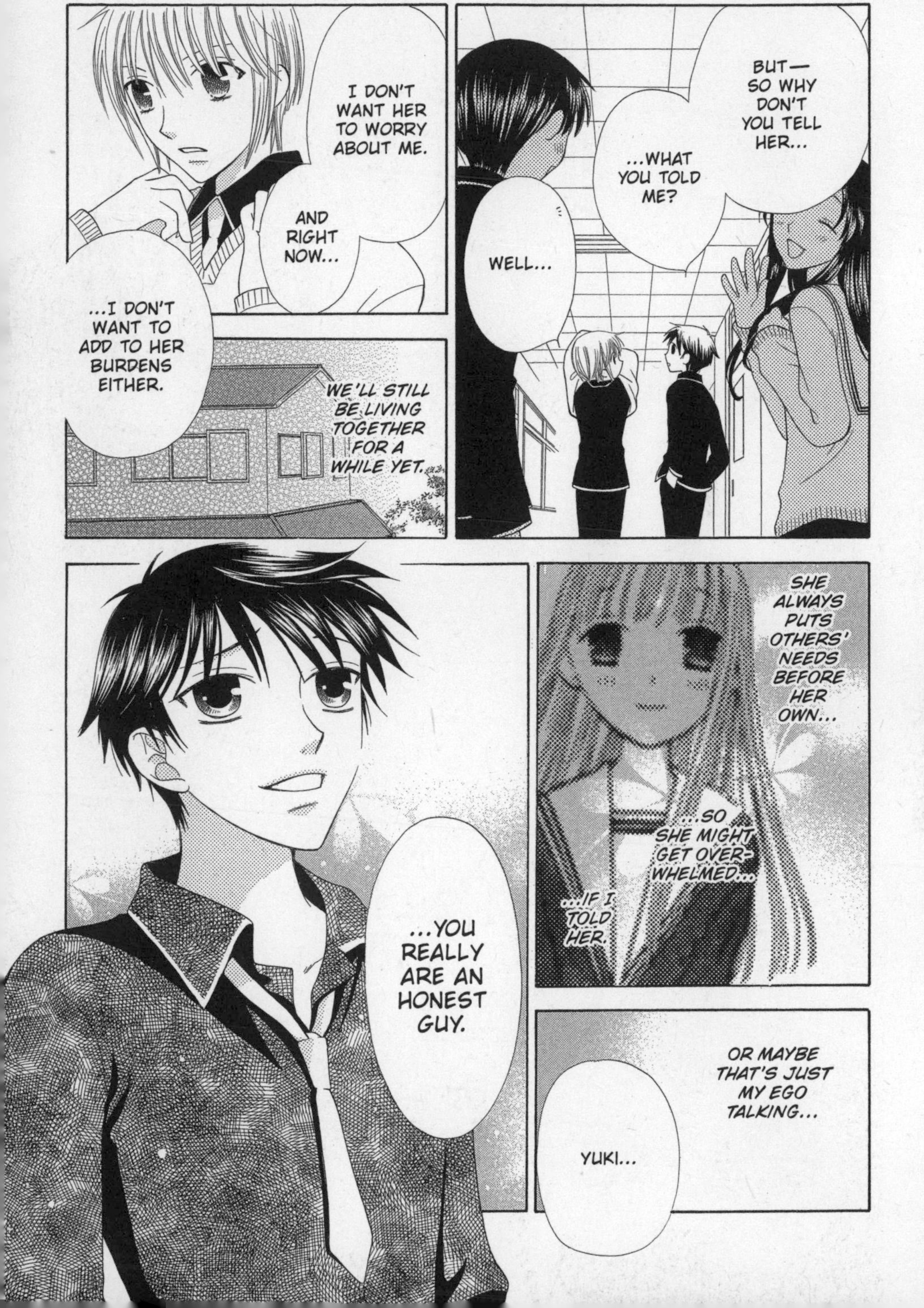
BUT— SO WHY DON'T YOU TELL HER...
...WHAT YOU TOLD ME?
WELL...
I DON'T WANT HER TO WORRY ABOUT ME.
AND RIGHT NOW...
...I DON'T WANT TO ADD TO HER BURDENS EITHER.
WE'LL STILL BE LIVING TOGETHER FOR A WHILE YET.
SHE ALWAYS PUTS OTHERS' NEEDS BEFORE HER OWN...
...SO SHE MIGHT GET OVER-WHELMED...
...IF I TOLD HER.
OR MAYBE THAT'S JUST MY EGO TALKING...
YUKI...
...YOU REALLY ARE AN HONEST GUY.

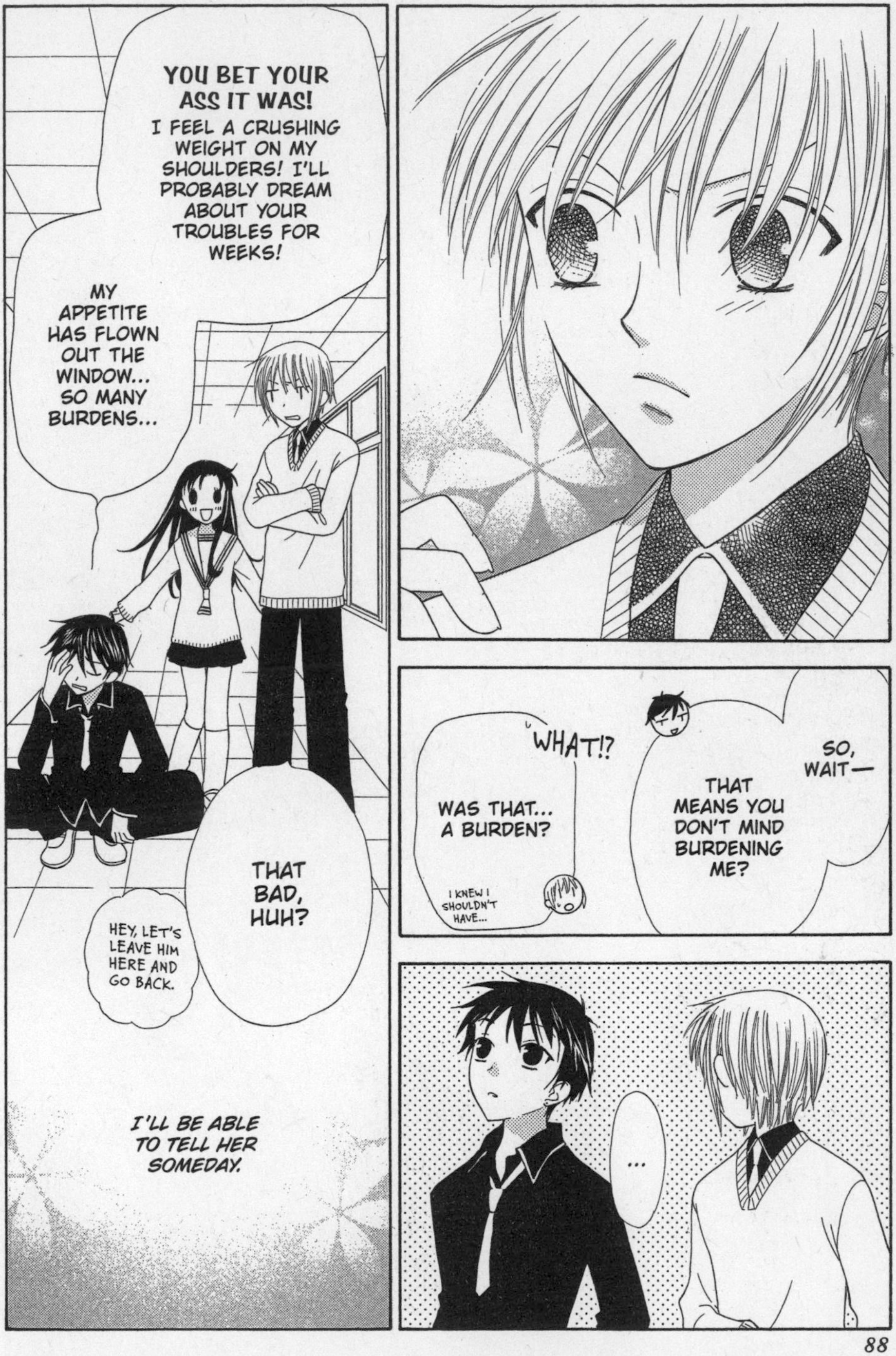
SO, WAIT—
THAT MEANS YOU DON'T MIND BURDENING ME?
WHAT!?
WAS THAT... A BURDEN?
I KNEW I SHOULDN'T HAVE...
...
YOU BET YOUR ASS IT WAS! I FEEL A CRUSHING WEIGHT ON MY SHOULDERS! I'LL PROBABLY DREAM ABOUT YOUR TROUBLES FOR WEEKS!
MY APPETITE HAS FLOWN OUT THE WINDOW... SO MANY BURDENS...
THAT BAD, HUH?
HEY, LET'S LEAVE HIM HERE AND GO BACK.
I'LL BE ABLE TO TELL HER SOMEDAY.

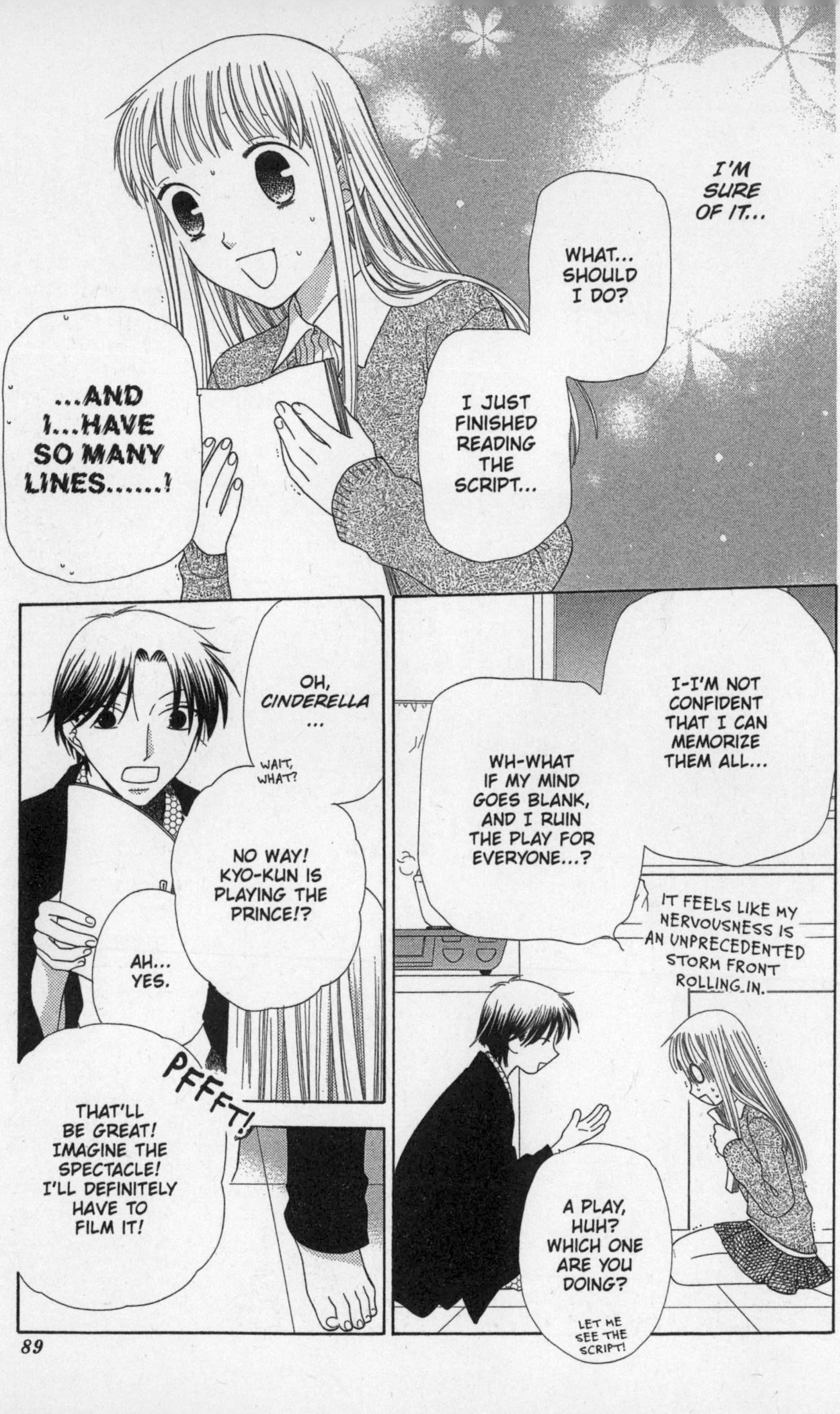
I'M SURE OF IT...
WHAT... SHOULD I DO?
I JUST FINISHED READING THE SCRIPT...
...AND I...HAVE SO MANY LINES......!
I-I'M NOT CONFIDENT THAT I CAN MEMORIZE THEM ALL...
WH-WHAT IF MY MIND GOES BLANK, AND I RUIN THE PLAY FOR EVERYONE...?
IT FEELS LIKE MY NERVOUSNESS IS AN UNPRECEDENTED STORM FRONT ROLLING IN.
A PLAY, HUH? WHICH ONE ARE YOU DOING?
LET ME SEE THE SCRIPT!
OH, CINDERELLA...
WAIT, WHAT?
NO WAY! KYO-KUN IS PLAYING THE PRINCE!?
AH... YES.
PFFFT!
THAT'LL BE GREAT! IMAGINE THE SPECTACLE! I'LL DEFINITELY HAVE TO FILM IT!

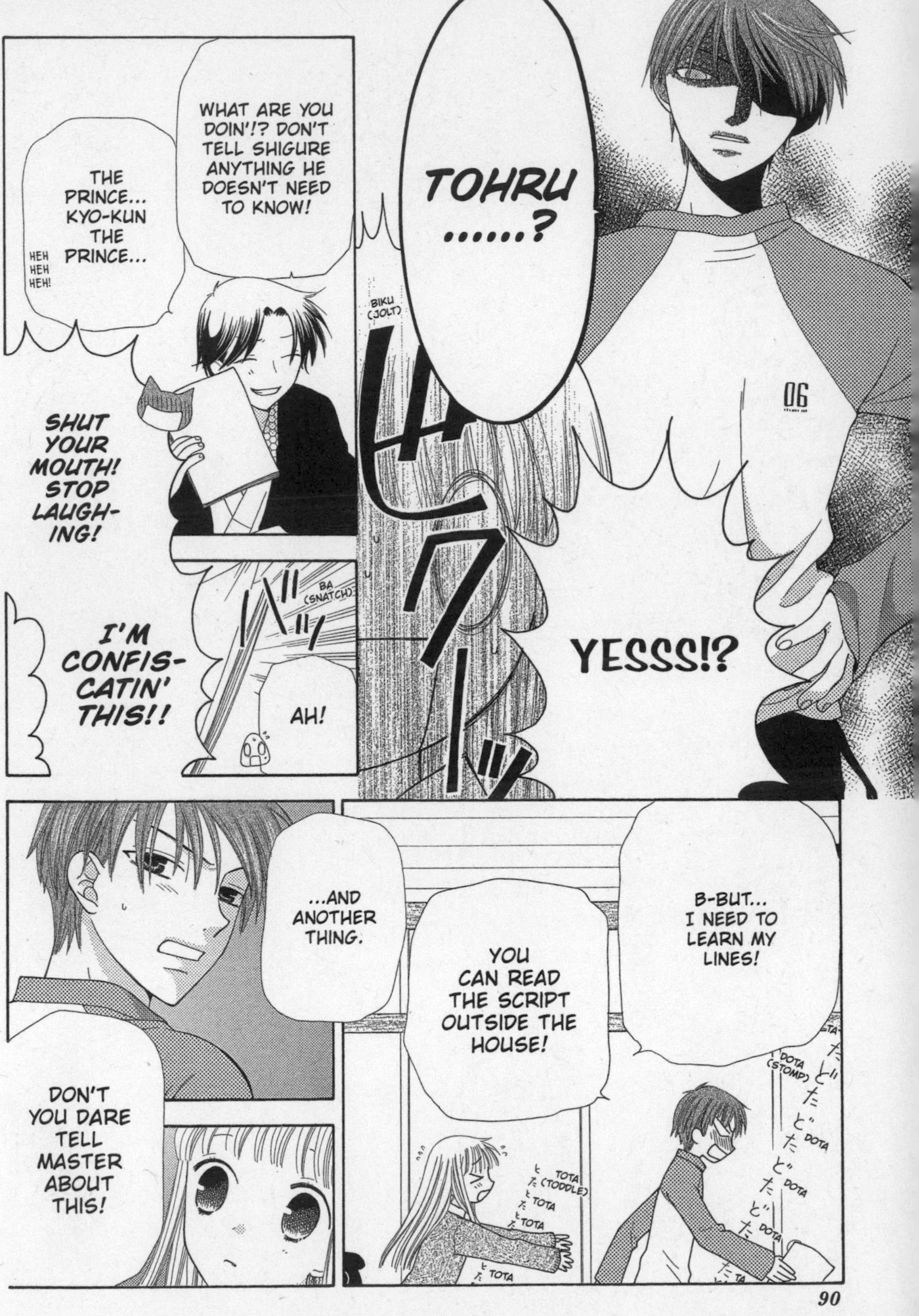
TOHRU......?
BIKU (JOLT)
YESSS!?
WHAT ARE YOU DOIN'!? DON'T TELL SHIGURE ANYTHING HE DOESN'T NEED TO KNOW!
THE PRINCE... KYO-KUN THE PRINCE...
HEH HEH HEH!
SHUT YOUR MOUTH! STOP LAUGH-ING!
BA (SNATCH)
AH!
I'M CONFIS-CATIN' THIS!!
B-BUT... I NEED TO LEARN MY LINES!
YOU CAN READ THE SCRIPT OUTSIDE THE HOUSE!
DOTA (STOMP) DOTA DOTA DOTA
TOTA (TODDLE) TOTA TOTA TOTA
...AND ANOTHER THING.
DON'T YOU DARE TELL MASTER ABOUT THIS!

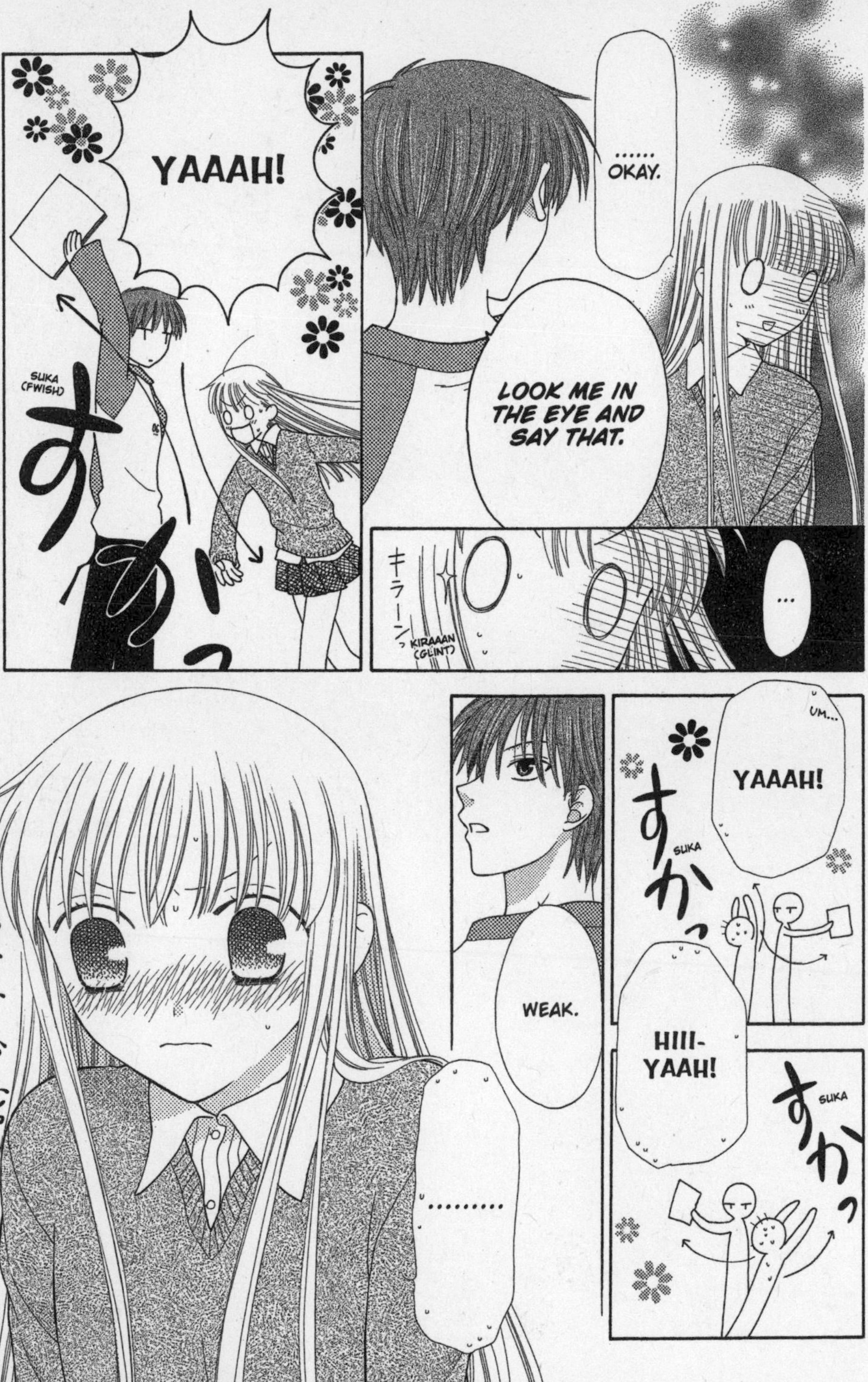

...... OKAY.
LOOK ME IN THE EYE AND SAY THAT.
キラーンッ
KIRAAAN (GLINT)
...
YAAAH!
すかっ
SUKA (FWISH)
UM...
YAAAH!
すかっ
SUKA
HIII-YAAH!
すかっ
SUKA
WEAK.
....
むむむむっ
MU (SULK) MU MU MU

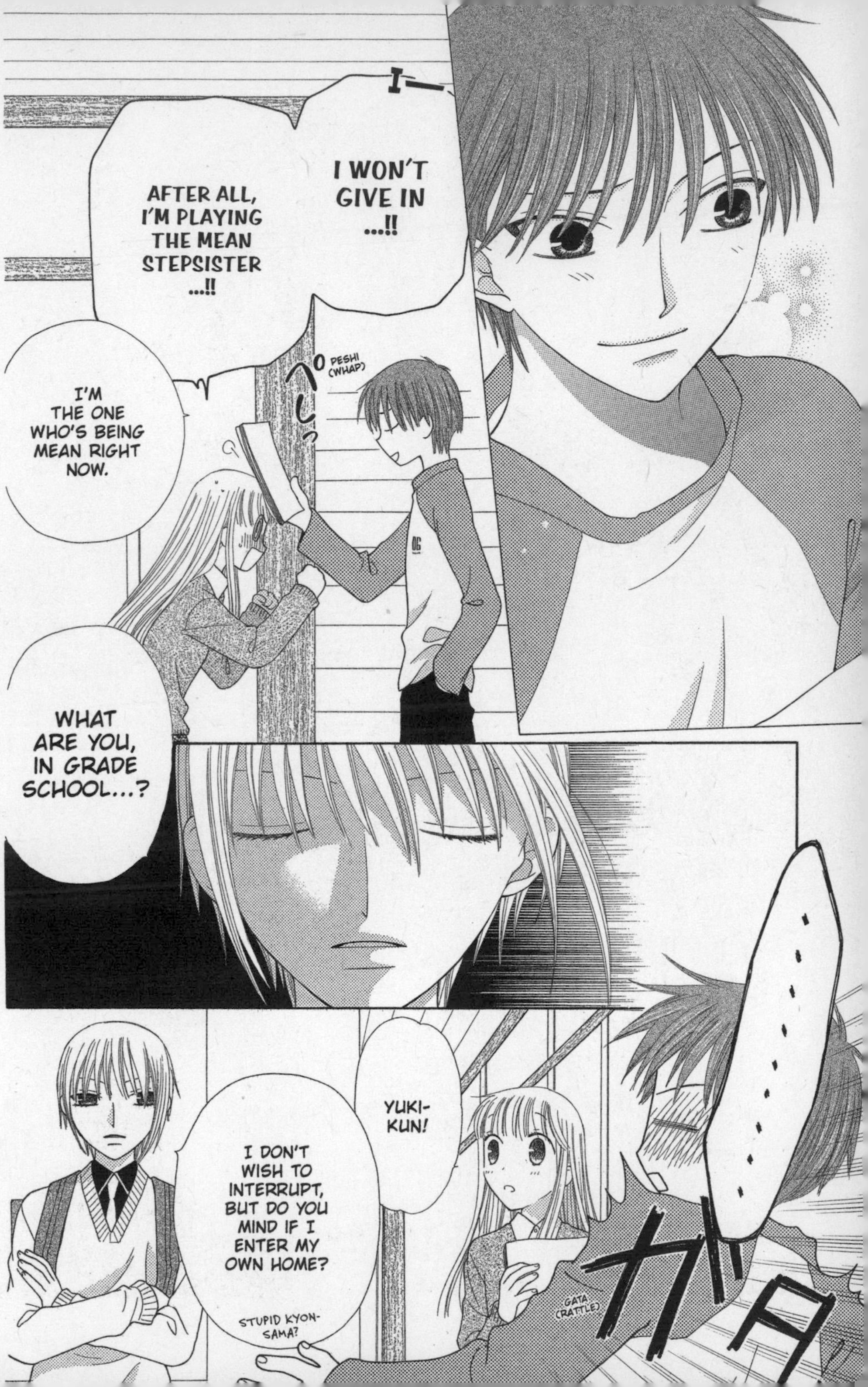
I—
I WON'T GIVE IN ...!!
AFTER ALL, I'M PLAYING THE MEAN STEPSISTER ...!!
PESHI (WHAP)
I'M THE ONE WHO'S BEING MEAN RIGHT NOW.
WHAT ARE YOU, IN GRADE SCHOOL...?
GATA (RATTLE)
YUKI-KUN!
I DON'T WISH TO INTERRUPT, BUT DO YOU MIND IF I ENTER MY OWN HOME?
STUPID KYON-SAMA?

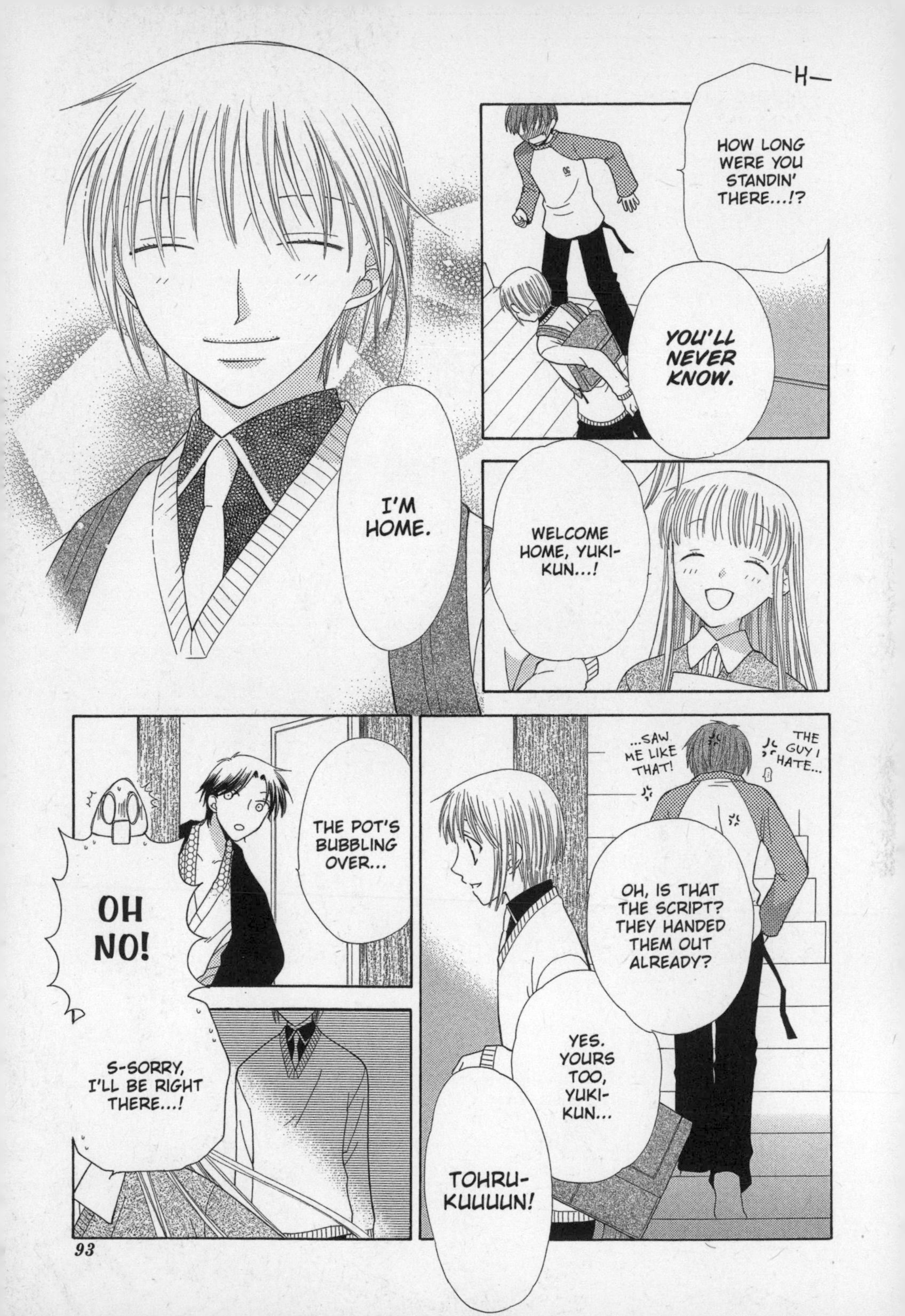
H—
HOW LONG WERE YOU STANDIN' THERE...!?
YOU'LL NEVER KNOW.
WELCOME HOME, YUKI-KUN...!
I'M HOME.
THE GUY I HATE...
...SAW ME LIKE THAT!
OH, IS THAT THE SCRIPT? THEY HANDED THEM OUT ALREADY?
YES. YOURS TOO, YUKI-KUN...
TOHRU-KUUUUN!
THE POT'S BUBBLING OVER...
OH NO!
S-SORRY, I'LL BE RIGHT THERE...!

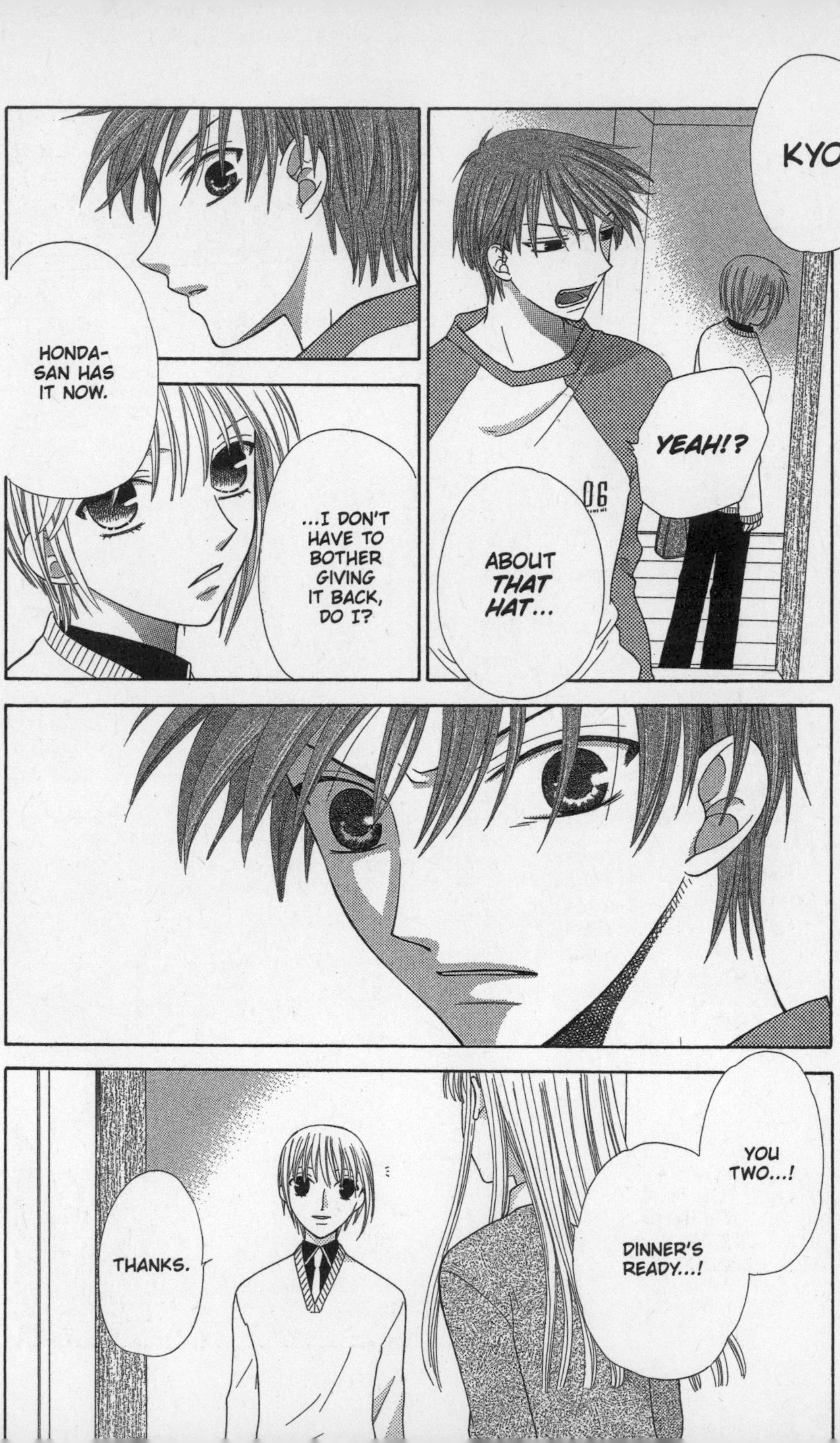
KYO.
YEAH!?
ABOUT THAT HAT...
HONDA-SAN HAS IT NOW.
...I DON'T HAVE TO BOTHER GIVING IT BACK, DO I?
YOU TWO...!
DINNER'S READY...!
THANKS.

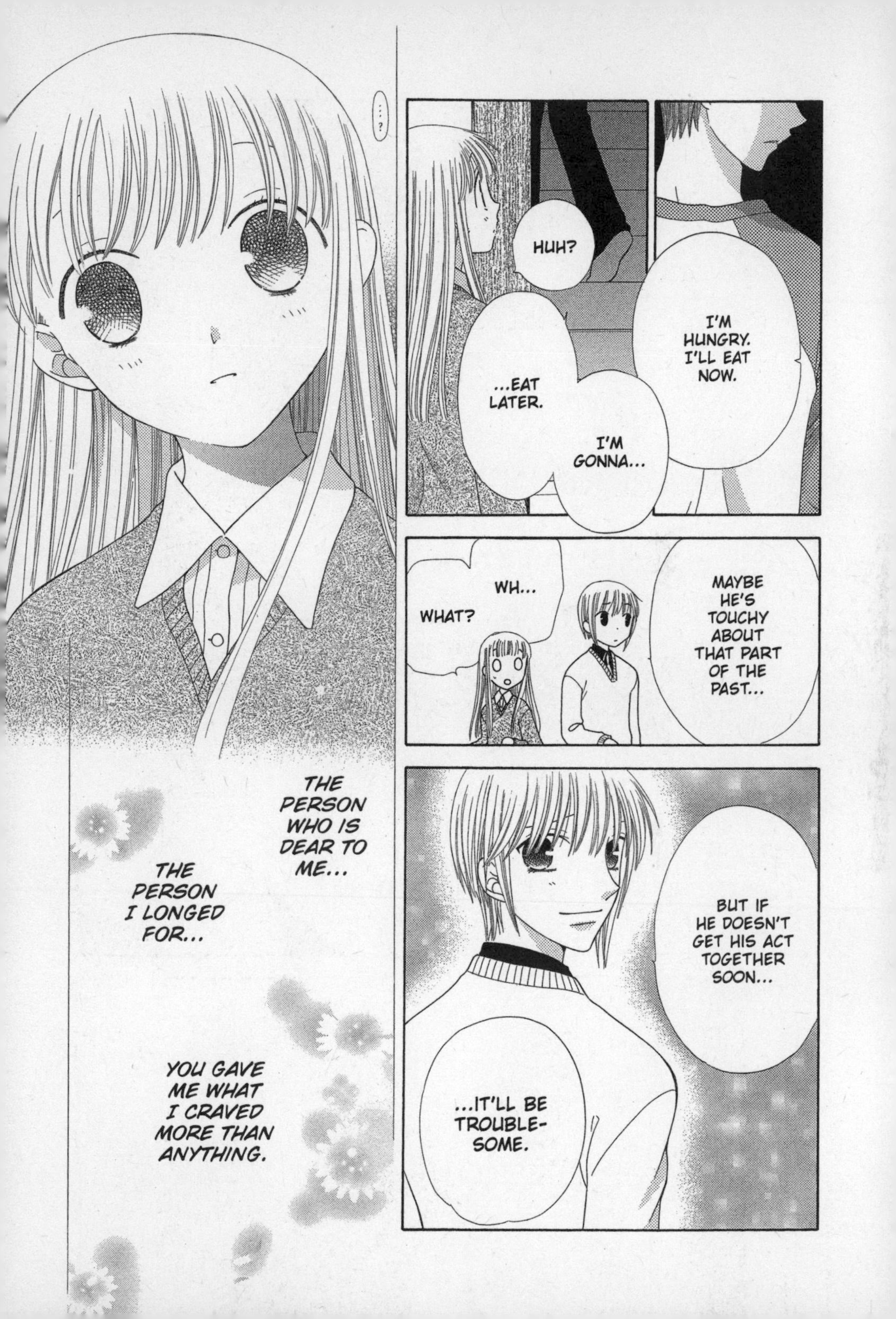
I'M HUNGRY. I'LL EAT NOW.
HUH?
I'M GONNA...
...EAT LATER.
MAYBE HE'S TOUCHY ABOUT THAT PART OF THE PAST...
WH...
WHAT?
BUT IF HE DOESN'T GET HIS ACT TOGETHER SOON...
...IT'LL BE TROUBLE-SOME.
...?
THE PERSON WHO IS DEAR TO ME...
THE PERSON I LONGED FOR...
YOU GAVE ME WHAT I CRAVED MORE THAN ANYTHING.

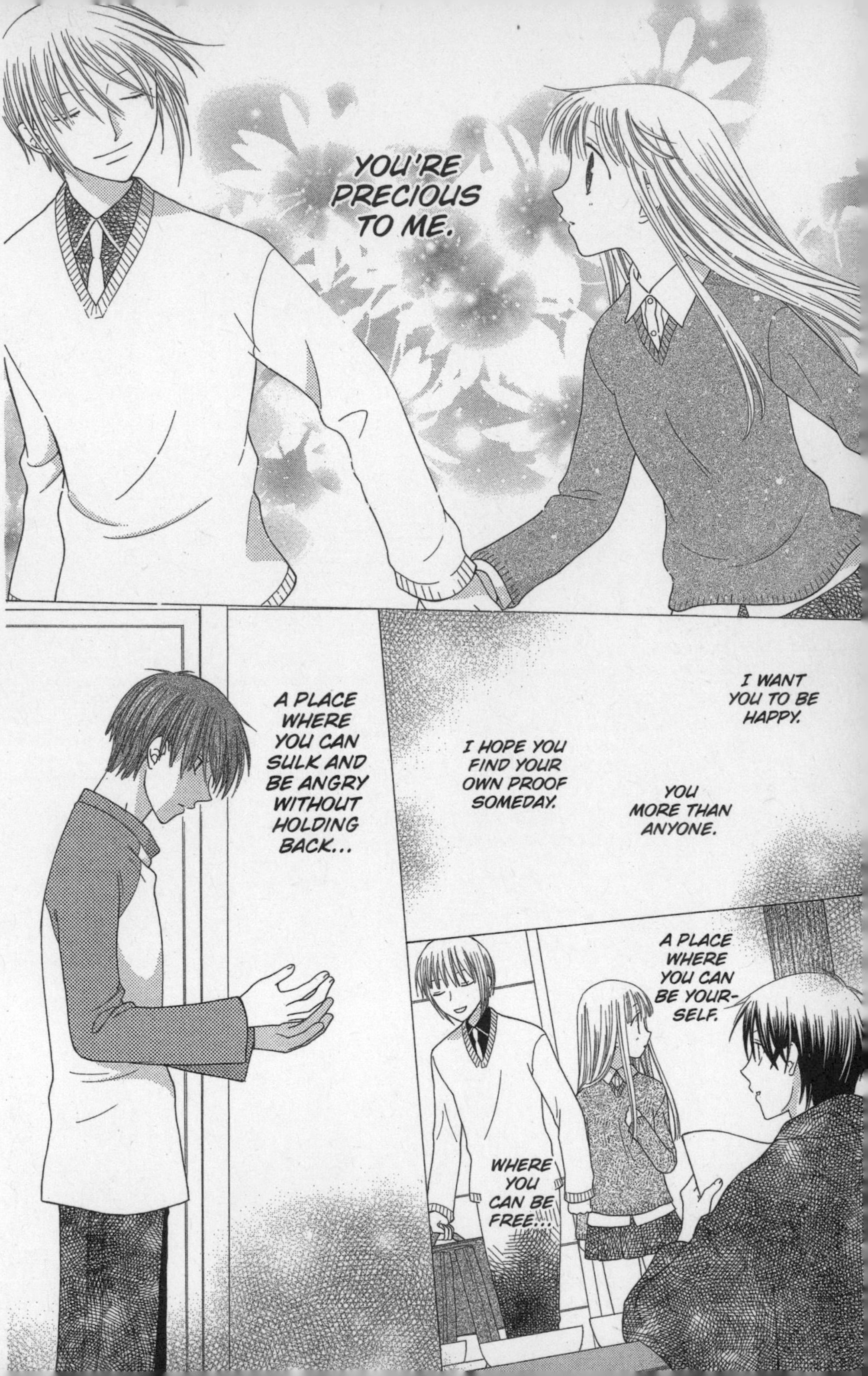
YOU'RE PRECIOUS TO ME.
I WANT YOU TO BE HAPPY.
YOU MORE THAN ANYONE.
I HOPE YOU FIND YOUR OWN PROOF SOMEDAY.
A PLACE WHERE YOU CAN BE YOUR-SELF.
WHERE YOU CAN BE FREE...
A PLACE WHERE YOU CAN SULK AND BE ANGRY WITHOUT HOLDING BACK...

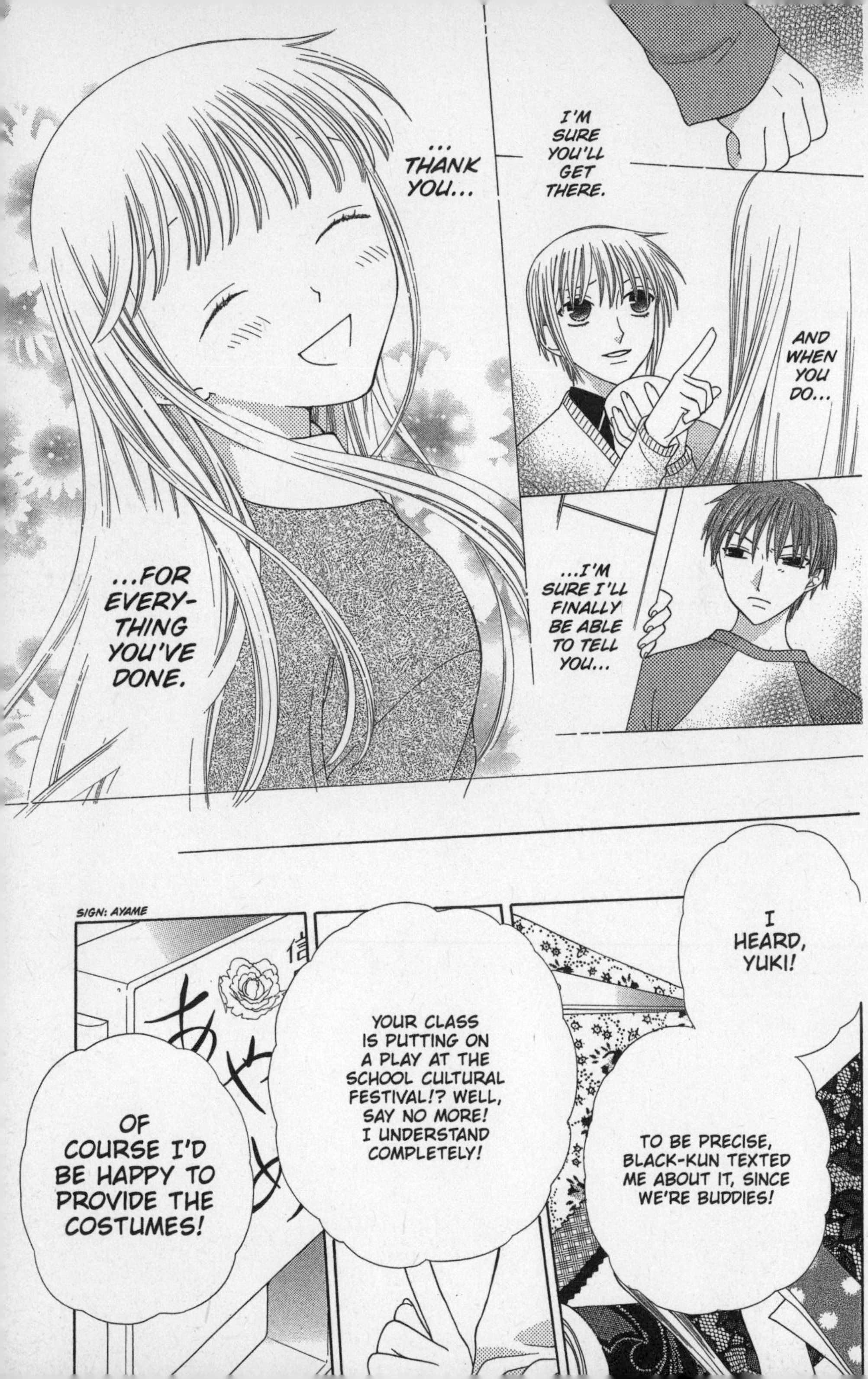
I'M SURE YOU'LL GET THERE.
AND WHEN YOU DO...
...I'M SURE I'LL FINALLY BE ABLE TO TELL YOU...
... THANK YOU...
...FOR EVERY-THING YOU'VE DONE.
SIGN: AYAME
I HEARD, YUKI!
TO BE PRECISE, BLACK-KUN TEXTED ME ABOUT IT, SINCE WE'RE BUDDIES!
YOUR CLASS IS PUTTING ON A PLAY AT THE SCHOOL CULTURAL FESTIVAL!? WELL, SAY NO MORE! I UNDERSTAND COMPLETELY!
OF COURSE I'D BE HAPPY TO PROVIDE THE COSTUMES!

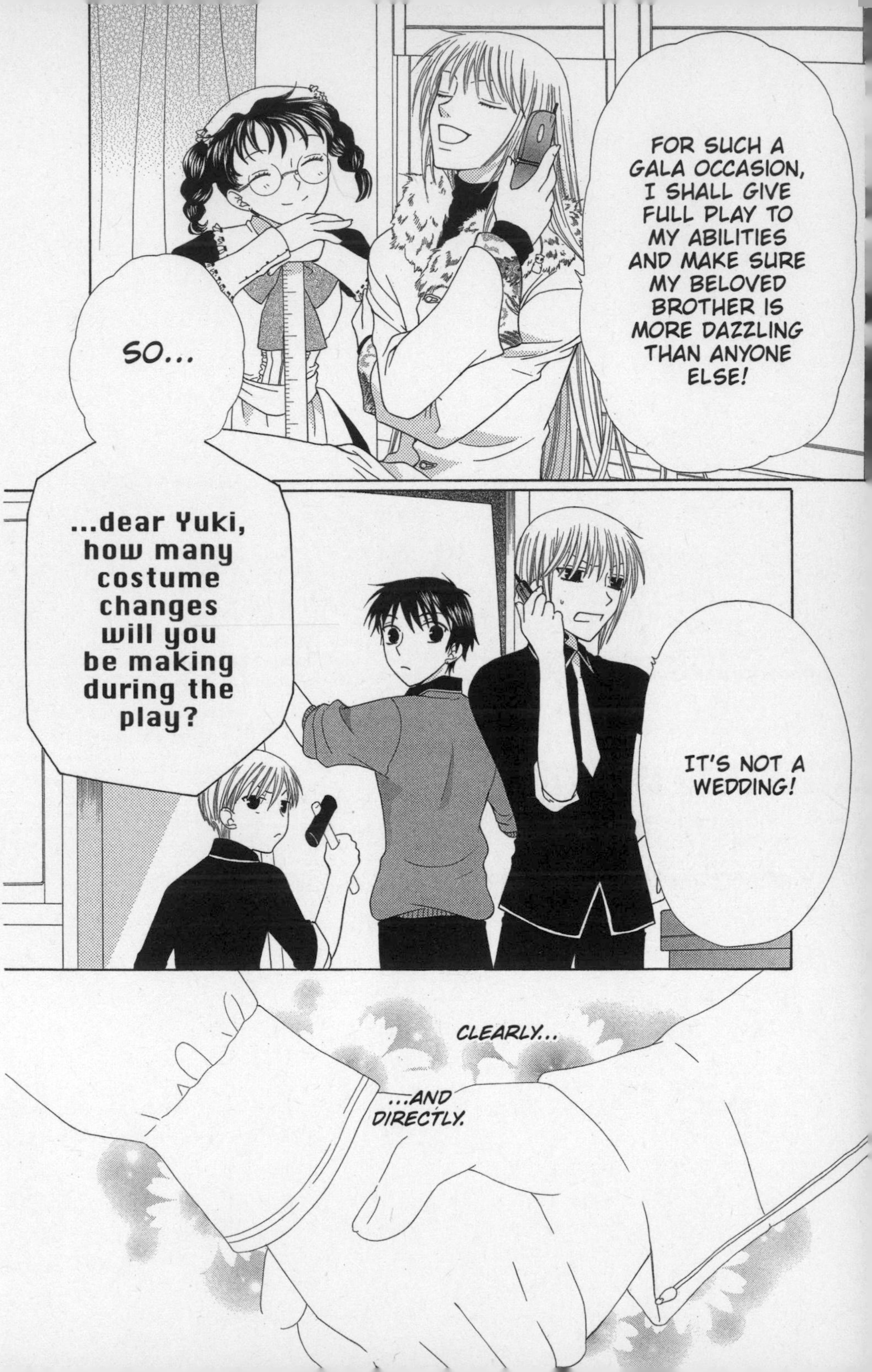
FOR SUCH A GALA OCCASION, I SHALL GIVE FULL PLAY TO MY ABILITIES AND MAKE SURE MY BELOVED BROTHER IS MORE DAZZLING THAN ANYONE ELSE!
SO...
...dear Yuki, how many costume changes will you be making during the play?
IT'S NOT A WEDDING!
CLEARLY...
...AND DIRECTLY.

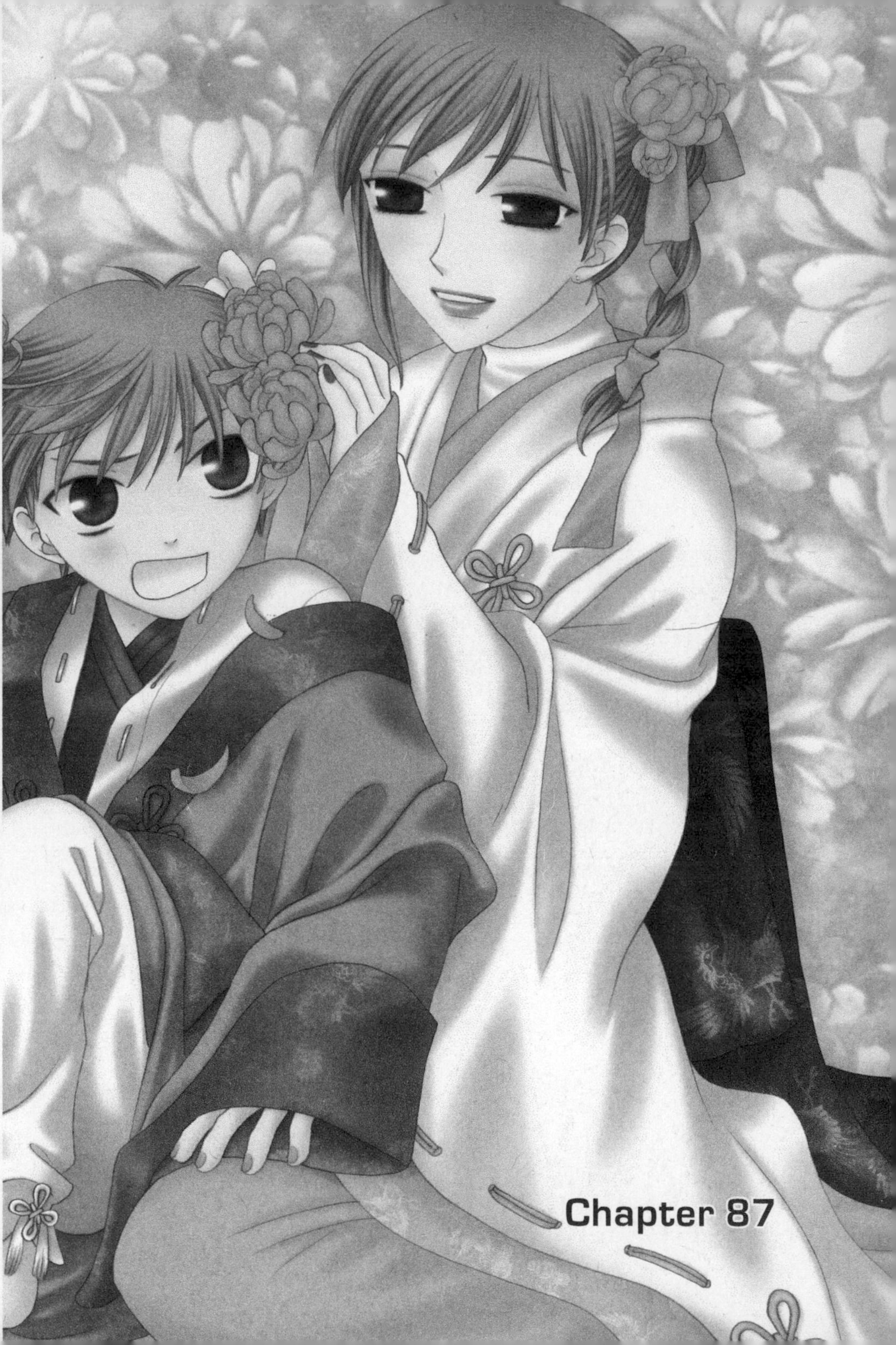

Chapter 87

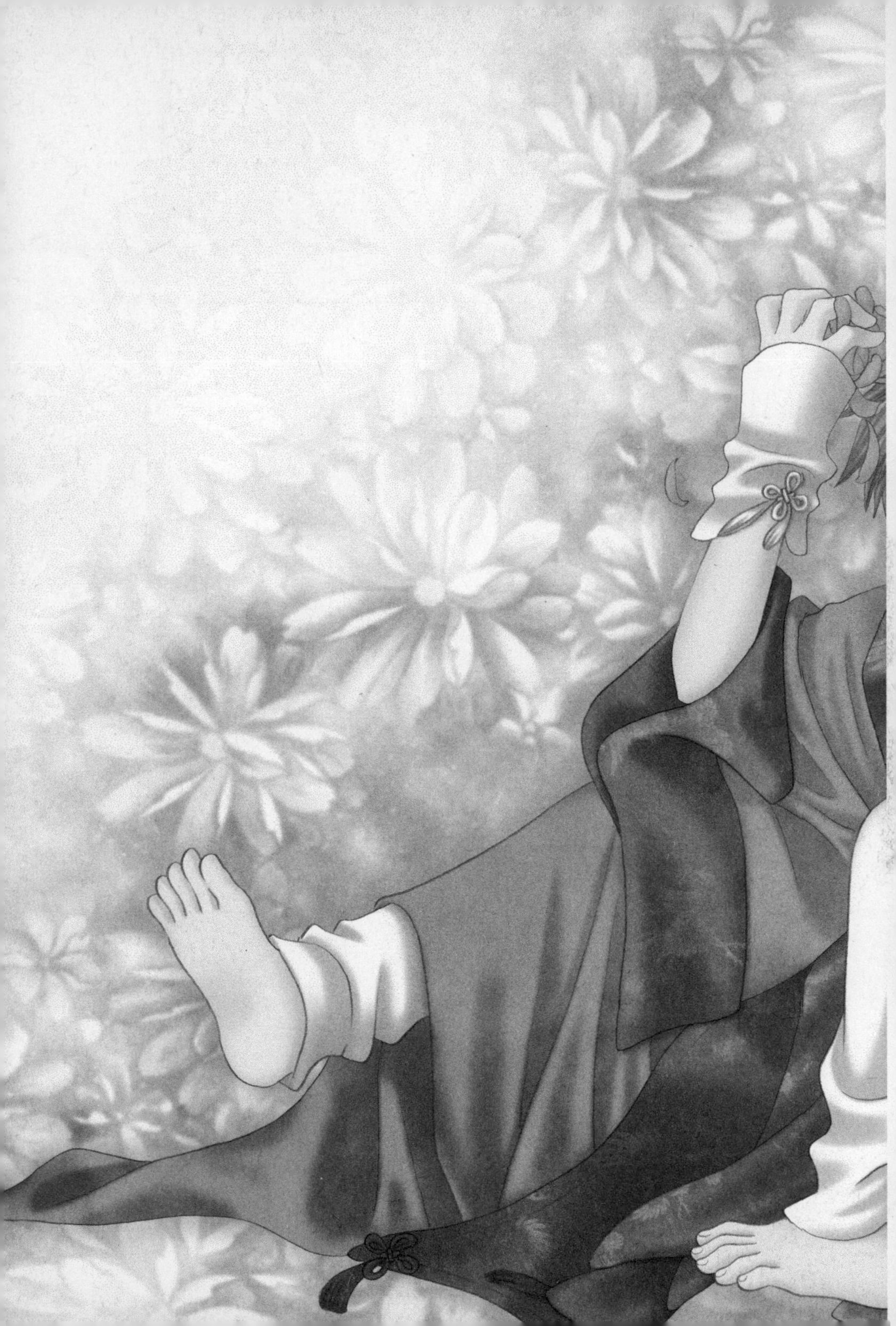

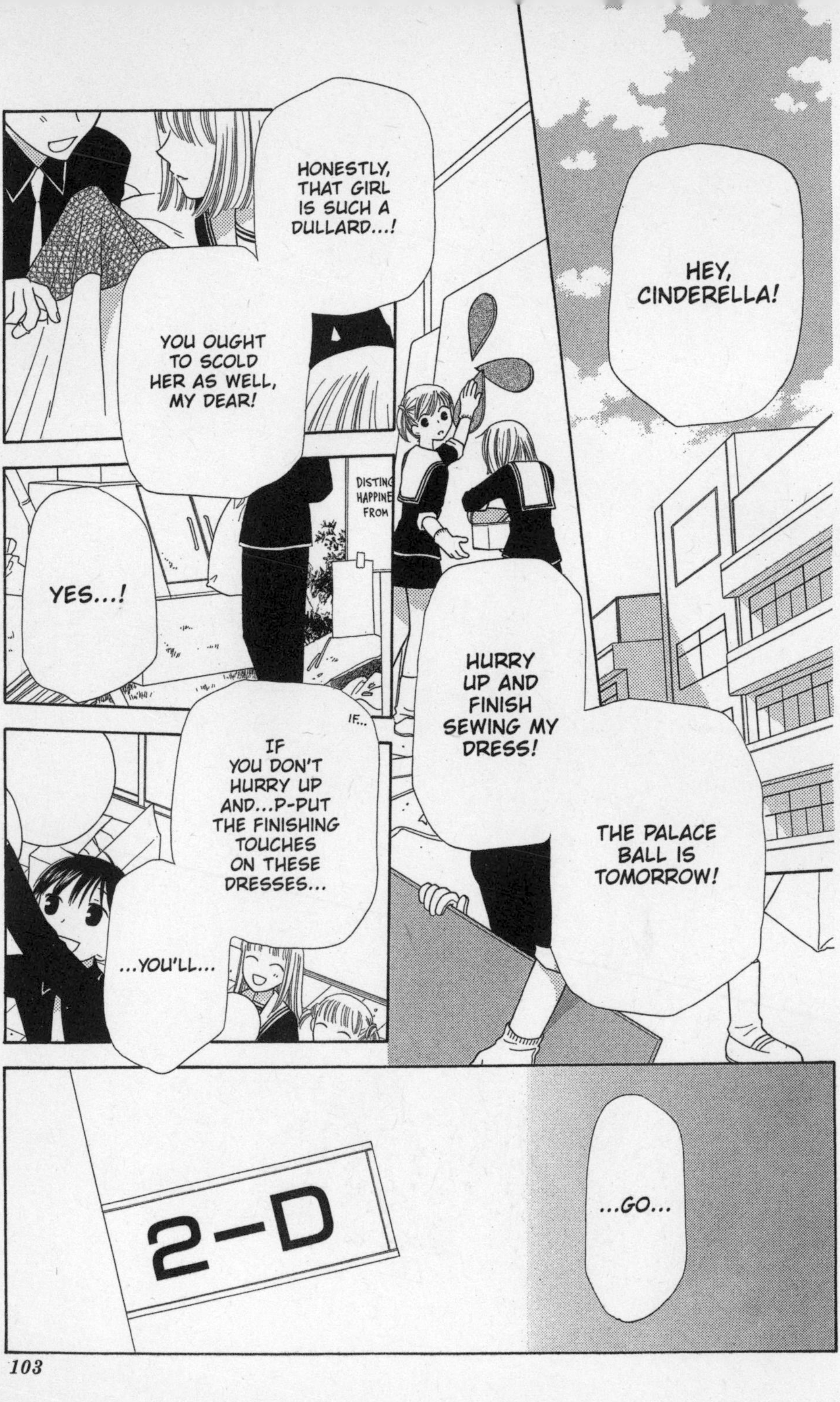
HEY, CINDERELLA!
HURRY UP AND FINISH SEWING MY DRESS!
THE PALACE BALL IS TOMORROW!
HONESTLY, THAT GIRL IS SUCH A DULLARD...!
YOU OUGHT TO SCOLD HER AS WELL, MY DEAR!
YES...!
IF...
IF YOU DON'T HURRY UP AND...P-PUT THE FINISHING TOUCHES ON THESE DRESSES...
...YOU'LL...
2-D
...GO...

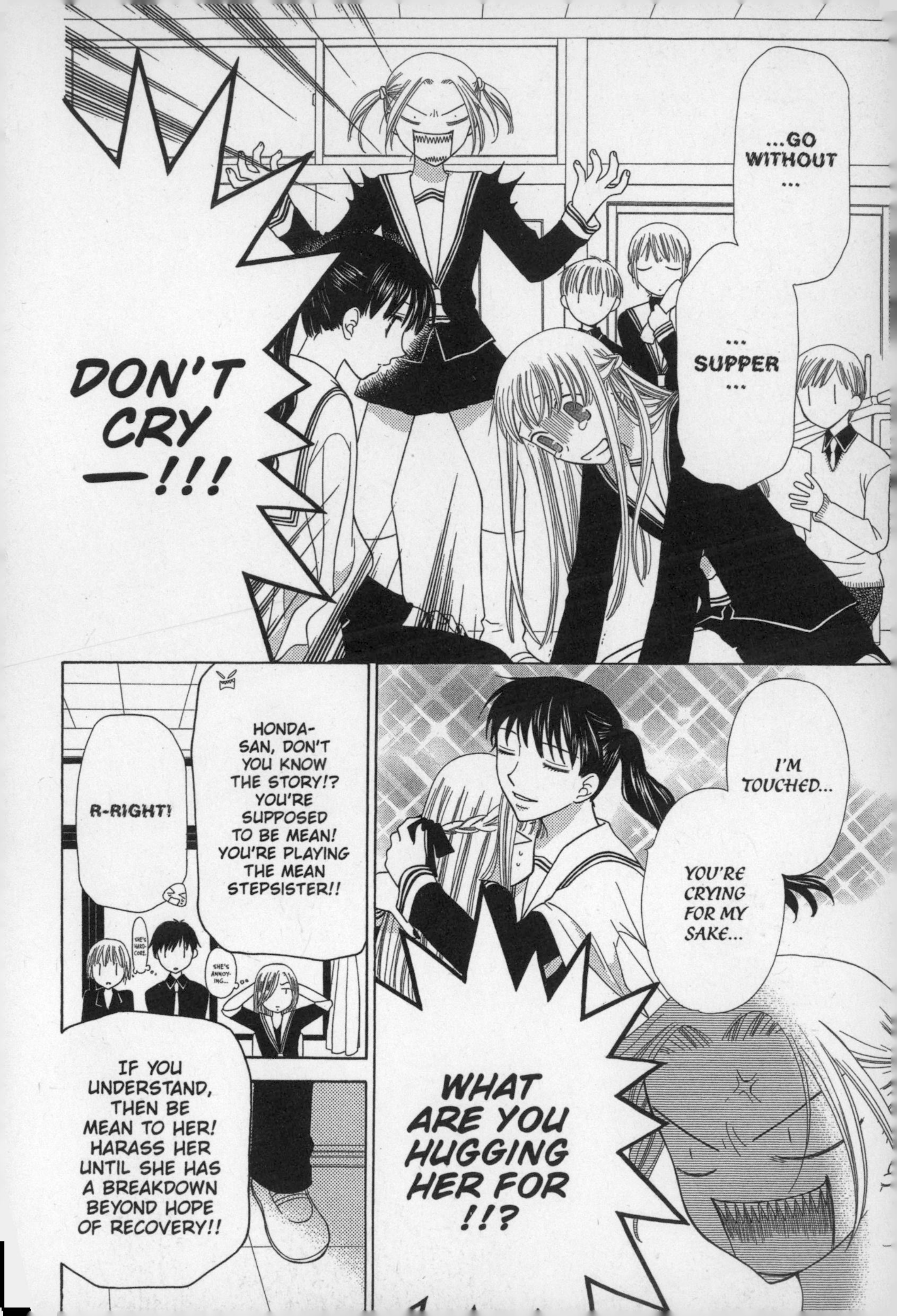
...GO WITHOUT ...
... SUPPER ...
DON'T CRY —!!!
I'M TOUCHED...
YOU'RE CRYING FOR MY SAKE...
WHAT ARE YOU HUGGING HER FOR !!?
HONDA-SAN, DON'T YOU KNOW THE STORY!? YOU'RE SUPPOSED TO BE MEAN! YOU'RE PLAYING THE MEAN STEPSISTER!!
R-RIGHT!
SHE'S ANNOYING...
SHE'S HARDCORE.
IF YOU UNDERSTAND, THEN BE MEAN TO HER! HARASS HER UNTIL SHE HAS A BREAKDOWN BEYOND HOPE OF RECOVERY!!

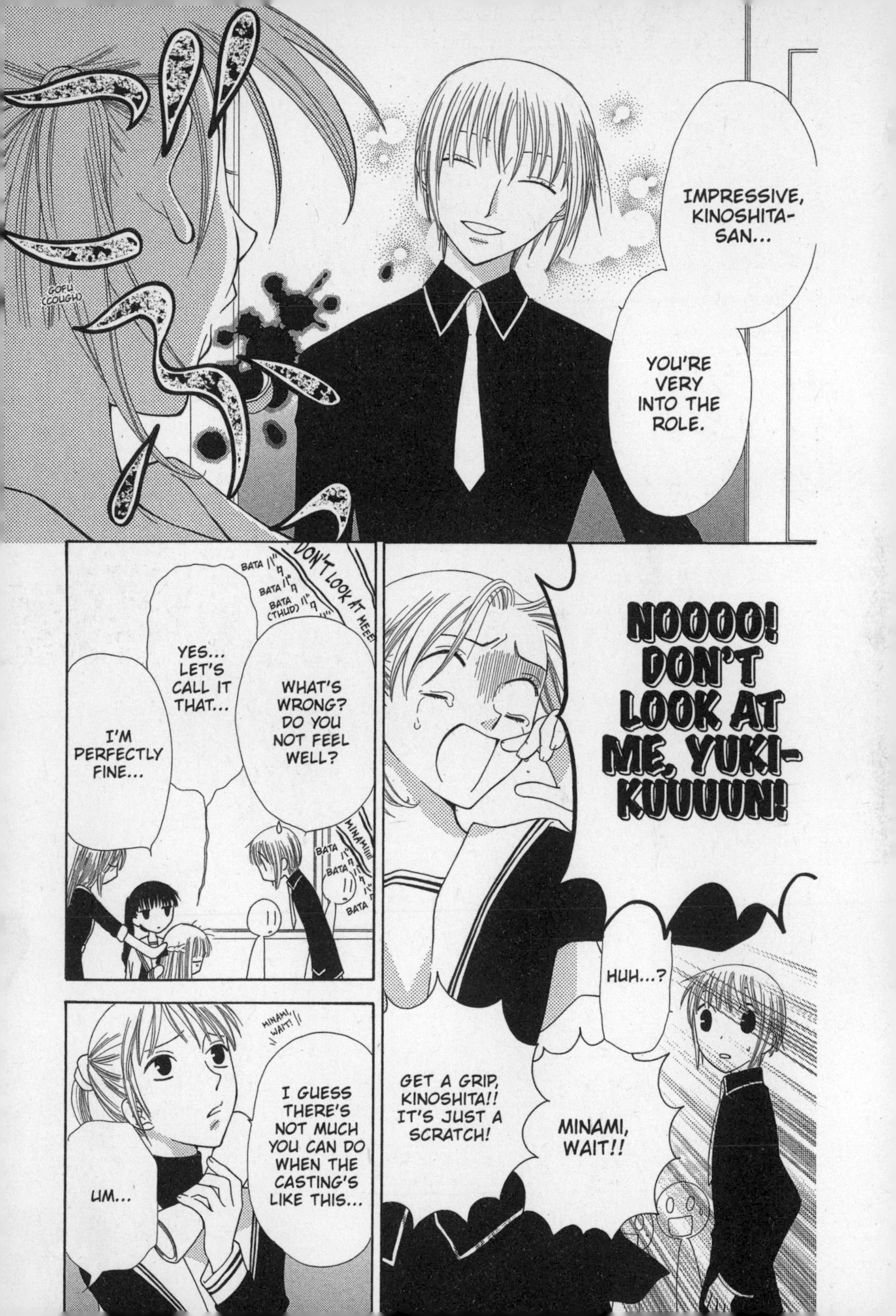
IMPRESSIVE, KINOSHITA-SAN...
YOU'RE VERY INTO THE ROLE.
GOFU (COUGH)
NOOOO! DON'T LOOK AT ME, YUKI-KUUUUN!
HUH...?
MINAMI, WAIT!!
GET A GRIP, KINOSHITA!! IT'S JUST A SCRATCH!
DON'T LOOK AT MEEE
BATA BATA BATA (THUD)
WHAT'S WRONG? DO YOU NOT FEEL WELL?
YES... LET'S CALL IT THAT...
I'M PERFECTLY FINE...
MINAMI!!!!
BATA BATA BATA
MINAMI, WAIT!
I GUESS THERE'S NOT MUCH YOU CAN DO WHEN THE CASTING'S LIKE THIS...
UM...

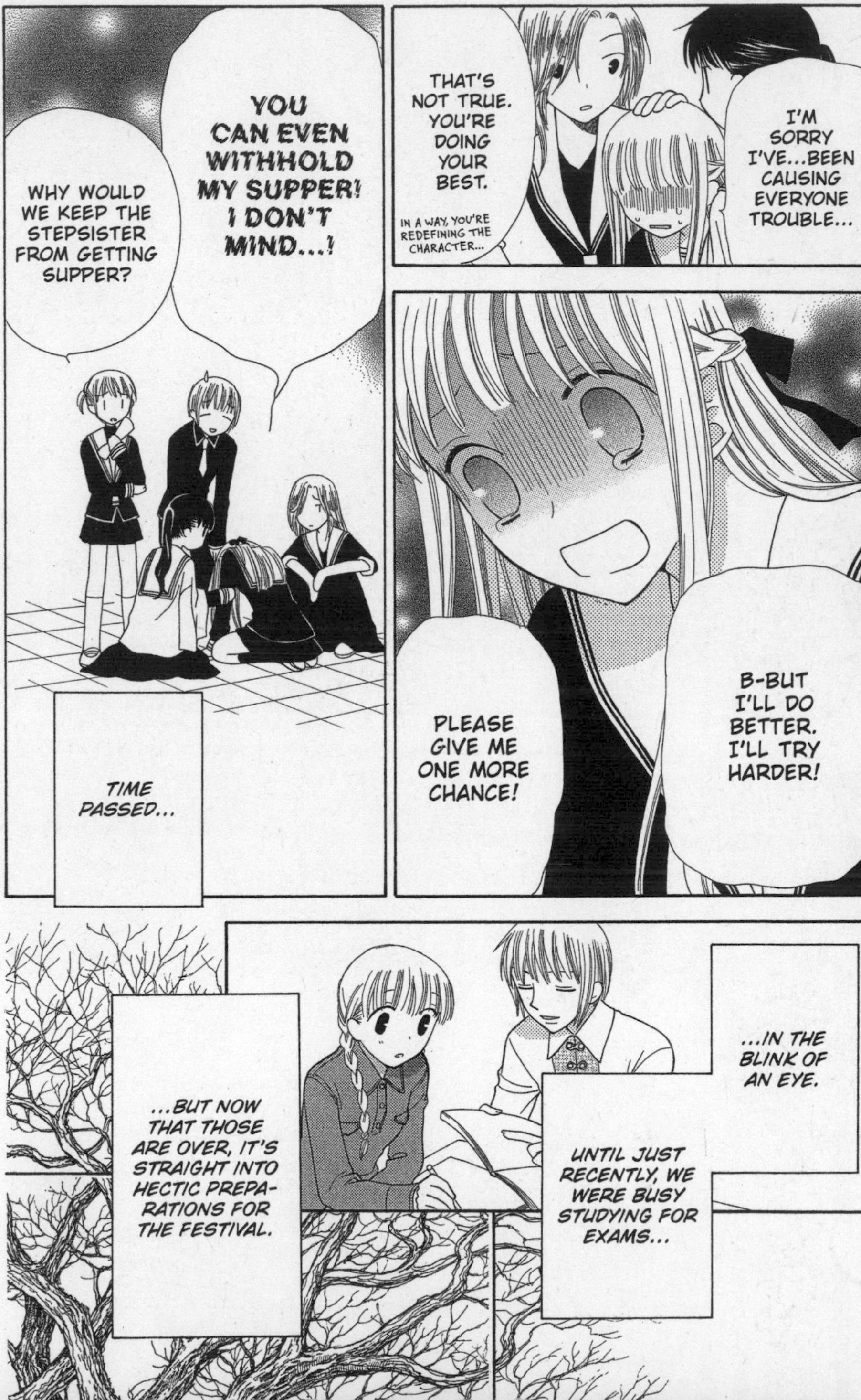
I'M SORRY I'VE...BEEN CAUSING EVERYONE TROUBLE...
THAT'S NOT TRUE. YOU'RE DOING YOUR BEST.
IN A WAY, YOU'RE REDEFINING THE CHARACTER...
B-BUT I'LL DO BETTER. I'LL TRY HARDER!
PLEASE GIVE ME ONE MORE CHANCE!
YOU CAN EVEN WITHHOLD MY SUPPER! I DON'T MIND...!
WHY WOULD WE KEEP THE STEPSISTER FROM GETTING SUPPER?
TIME PASSED...
...IN THE BLINK OF AN EYE.
UNTIL JUST RECENTLY, WE WERE BUSY STUDYING FOR EXAMS...
...BUT NOW THAT THOSE ARE OVER, IT'S STRAIGHT INTO HECTIC PREPARATIONS FOR THE FESTIVAL.

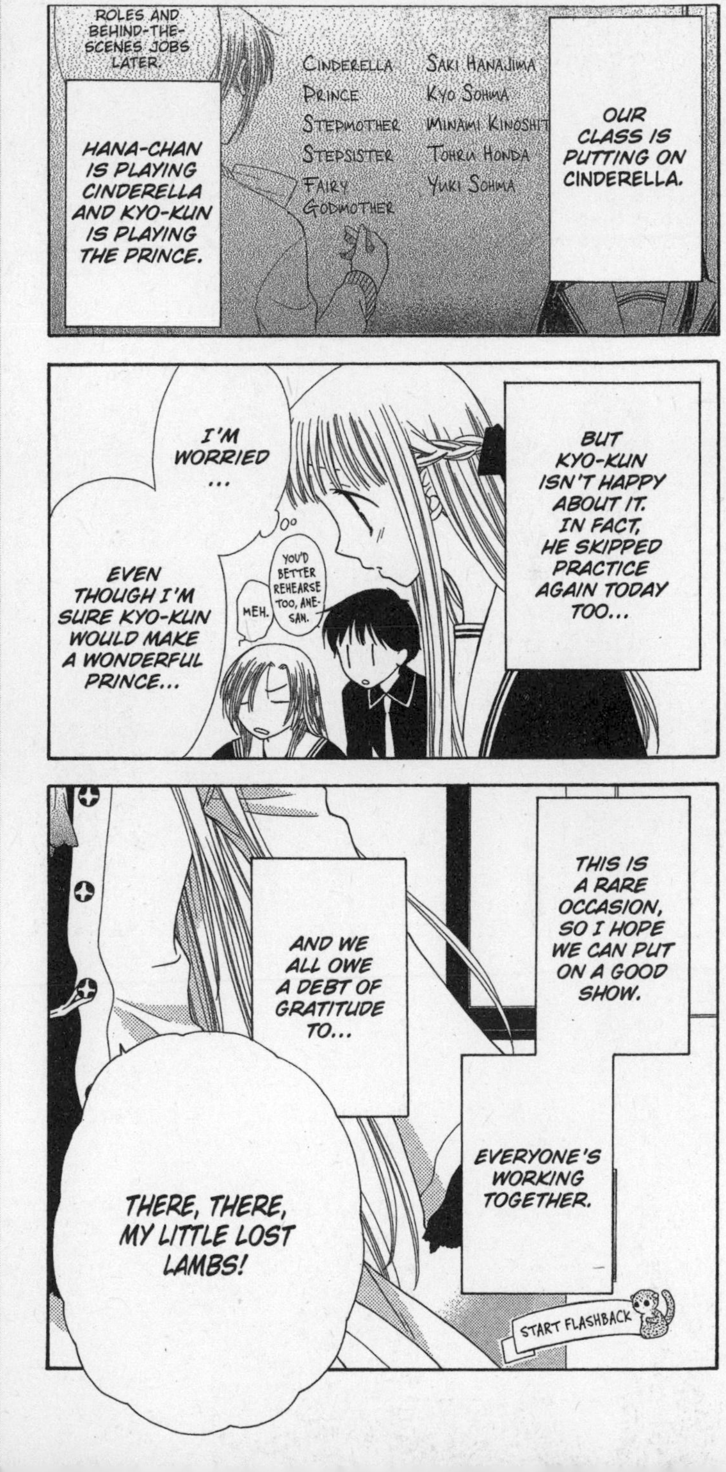
OUR CLASS IS PUTTING ON CINDERELLA.
CINDERELLA SAKI HANAJIMA
PRINCE KYO SOHMA
STEPMOTHER MINAMI KINOSHIT
STEPSISTER TOHRU HONDA
FAIRY GODMOTHER YUKI SOHMA
ROLES AND BEHIND-THE-SCENES JOBS LATER.
HANA-CHAN IS PLAYING CINDERELLA AND KYO-KUN IS PLAYING THE PRINCE.
BUT KYO-KUN ISN'T HAPPY ABOUT IT. IN FACT, HE SKIPPED PRACTICE AGAIN TODAY TOO...
I'M WORRIED...
YOU'D BETTER REHEARSE TOO, ANE-SAN.
MEH.
EVEN THOUGH I'M SURE KYO-KUN WOULD MAKE A WONDERFUL PRINCE...
THIS IS A RARE OCCASION, SO I HOPE WE CAN PUT ON A GOOD SHOW.
AND WE ALL OWE A DEBT OF GRATITUDE TO...
EVERYONE'S WORKING TOGETHER.
THERE, THERE, MY LITTLE LOST LAMBS!
START FLASHBACK
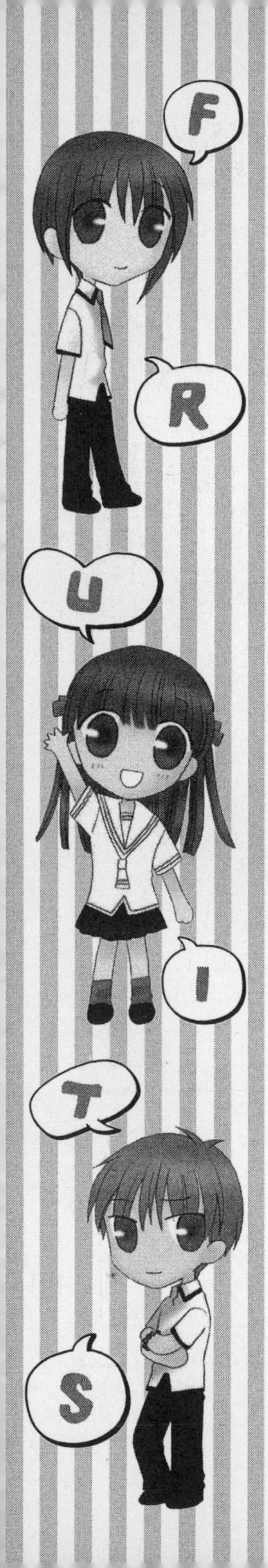
F
R
U
I
T
S

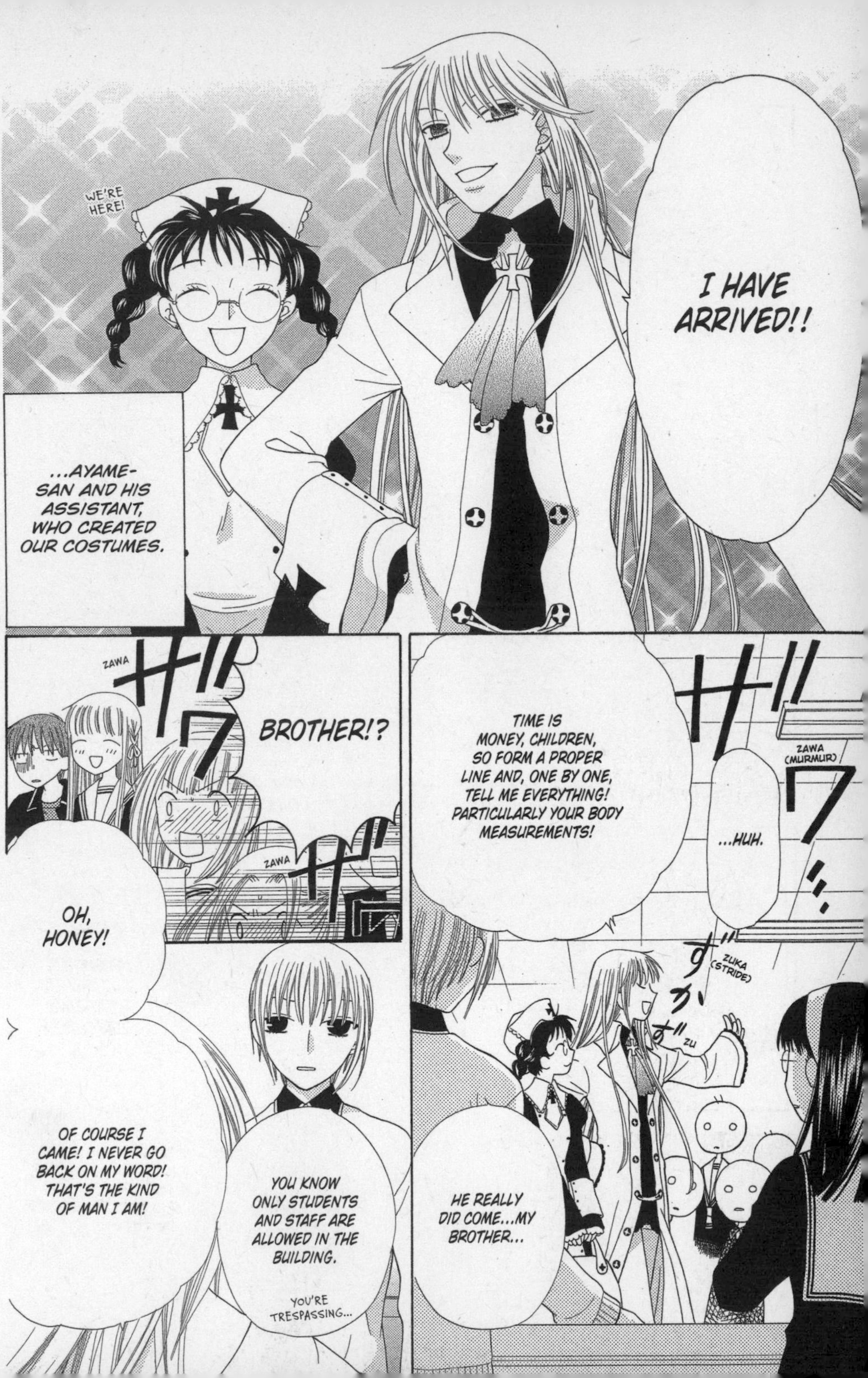
I HAVE ARRIVED!!
WE'RE HERE!
...AYAME-SAN AND HIS ASSISTANT, WHO CREATED OUR COSTUMES.
TIME IS MONEY, CHILDREN, SO FORM A PROPER LINE AND, ONE BY ONE, TELL ME EVERYTHING! PARTICULARLY YOUR BODY MEASUREMENTS!
ZAWA (MURMUR)
...HUH.
ZUKA (STRIDE)
ZU
HE REALLY DID COME...MY BROTHER...
ZAWA
BROTHER!?
ZAWA
OH, HONEY!
OF COURSE I CAME! I NEVER GO BACK ON MY WORD! THAT'S THE KIND OF MAN I AM!
YOU KNOW ONLY STUDENTS AND STAFF ARE ALLOWED IN THE BUILDING.
YOU'RE TRESPASSING...

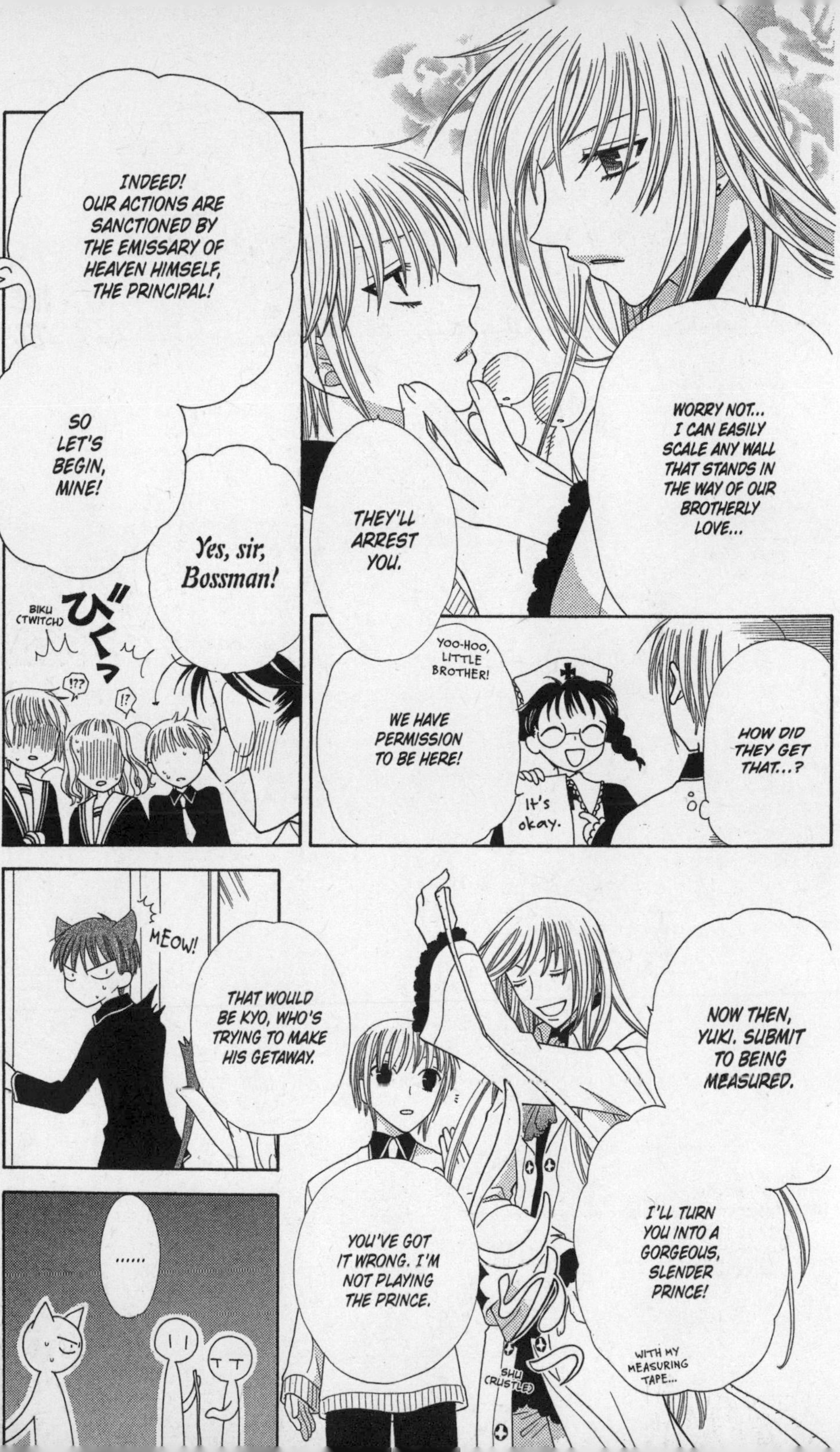
WORRY NOT... I CAN EASILY SCALE ANY WALL THAT STANDS IN THE WAY OF OUR BROTHERLY LOVE...
THEY'LL ARREST YOU.
HOW DID THEY GET THAT...?
YOO-HOO, LITTLE BROTHER!
WE HAVE PERMISSION TO BE HERE!
It's okay.
INDEED! OUR ACTIONS ARE SANCTIONED BY THE EMISSARY OF HEAVEN HIMSELF, THE PRINCIPAL!
SO LET'S BEGIN, MINE!
Yes, sir, Bossman!
ぴくっ
BIKU (TWITCH)
!??
!?
NOW THEN, YUKI. SUBMIT TO BEING MEASURED.
I'LL TURN YOU INTO A GORGEOUS, SLENDER PRINCE!
WITH MY MEASURING TAPE...
SHU (RUSTLE)
YOU'VE GOT IT WRONG. I'M NOT PLAYING THE PRINCE.
MEOW!
THAT WOULD BE KYO, WHO'S TRYING TO MAKE HIS GETAWAY.
......

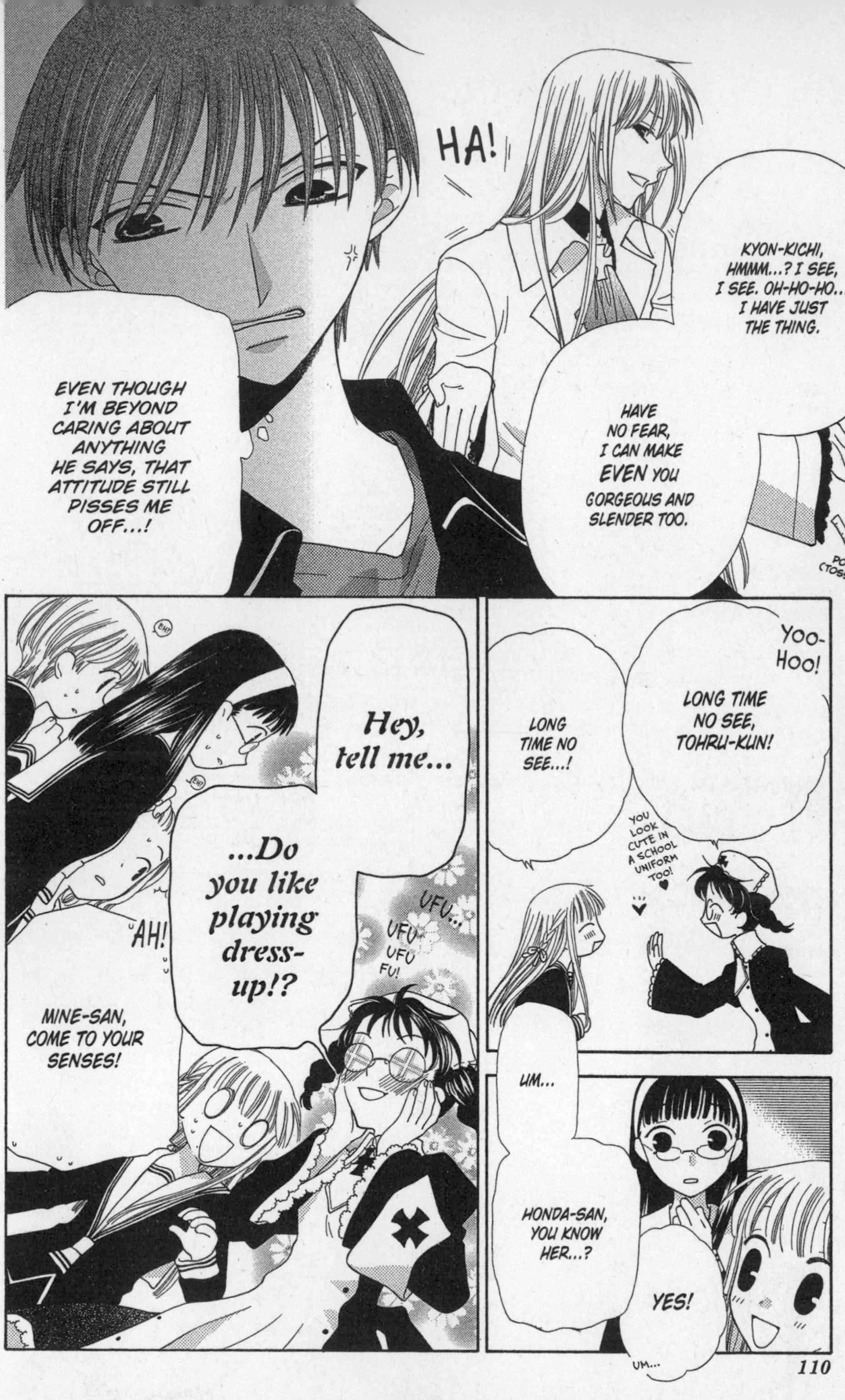
KYON-KICHI, HMMM...? I SEE, I SEE. OH-HO-HO... I HAVE JUST THE THING.
HA!
HAVE NO FEAR, I CAN MAKE EVEN YOU GORGEOUS AND SLENDER TOO.
ポイ
POI (TOSS)
EVEN THOUGH I'M BEYOND CARING ABOUT ANYTHING HE SAYS, THAT ATTITUDE STILL PISSES ME OFF...!
YOO-HOO!
LONG TIME NO SEE, TOHRU-KUN!
LONG TIME NO SEE...!
YOU LOOK CUTE IN A SCHOOL UNIFORM TOO! ♥
UM...
HONDA-SAN, YOU KNOW HER...?
YES!
UM...
Hey, tell me...
...Do you like playing dress-up!?
UFU...
UFU UFU UFU FU!
EH?
EH?
AH!
MINE-SAN, COME TO YOUR SENSES!

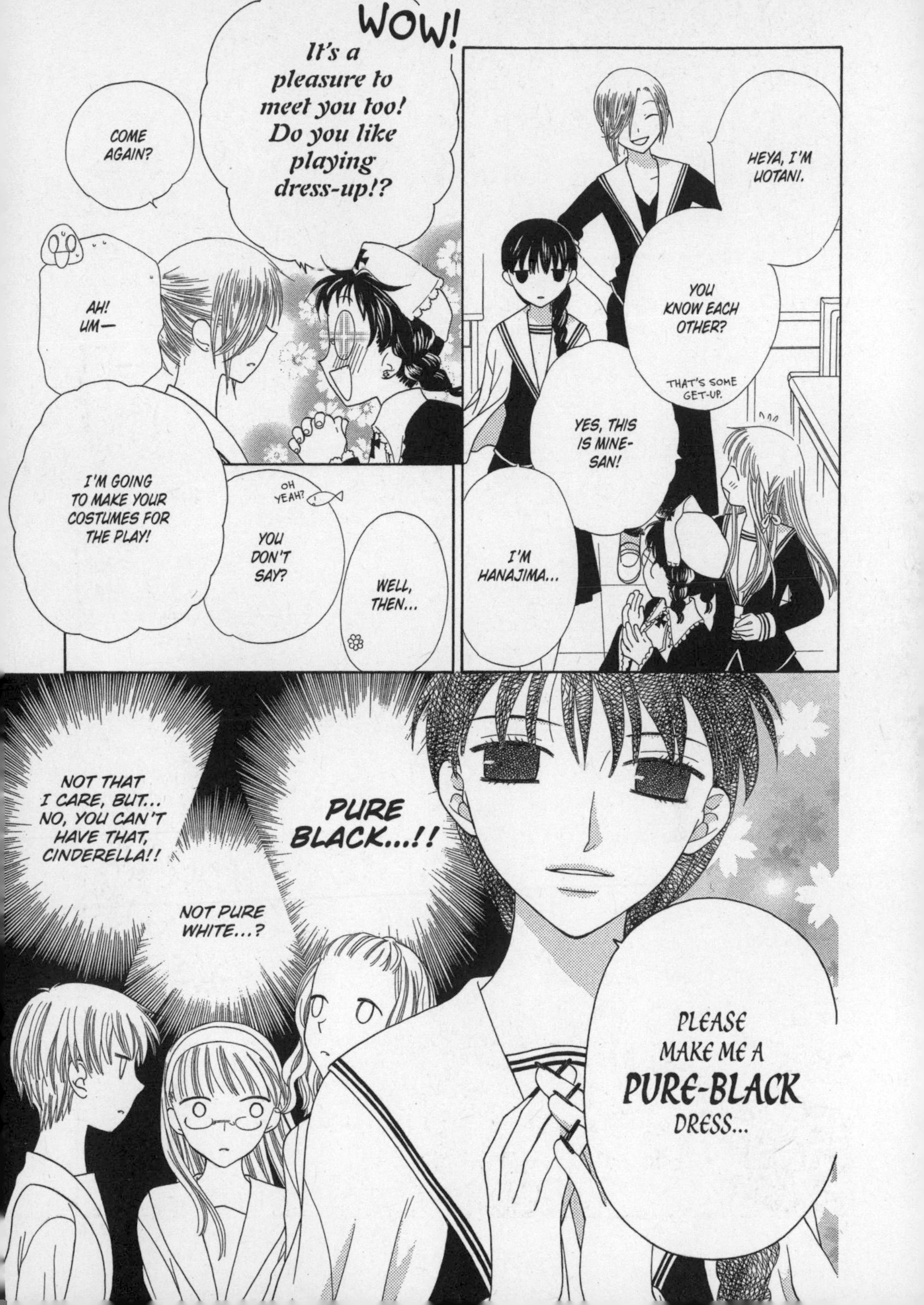
HEYA, I'M UOTANI.
YOU KNOW EACH OTHER?
THAT'S SOME GET-UP.
YES, THIS IS MINE-SAN!
I'M HANAJIMA...
WOW!
It's a pleasure to meet you too! Do you like playing dress-up!?
COME AGAIN?
AH! UM—
I'M GOING TO MAKE YOUR COSTUMES FOR THE PLAY!
WELL, THEN...
OH YEAH?
YOU DON'T SAY?
PLEASE MAKE ME A PURE-BLACK DRESS...
PURE BLACK...!!
NOT PURE WHITE...?
NOT THAT I CARE, BUT... NO, YOU CAN'T HAVE THAT, CINDERELLA!!

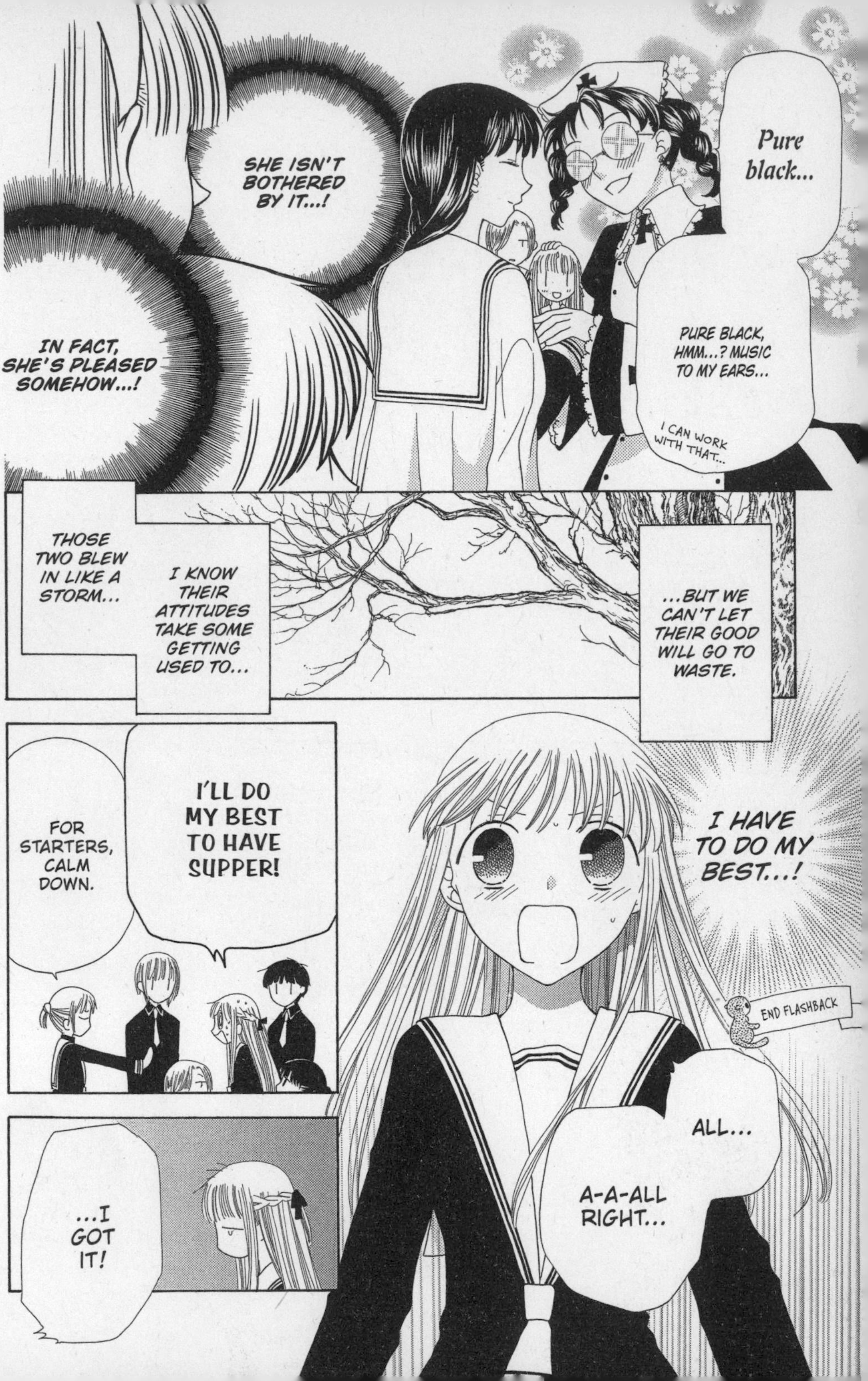
Pure black...
PURE BLACK, HMM...? MUSIC TO MY EARS...
I CAN WORK WITH THAT...
SHE ISN'T BOTHERED BY IT...!
IN FACT, SHE'S PLEASED SOMEHOW...!
THOSE TWO BLEW IN LIKE A STORM...
I KNOW THEIR ATTITUDES TAKE SOME GETTING USED TO...
...BUT WE CAN'T LET THEIR GOOD WILL GO TO WASTE.
I HAVE TO DO MY BEST...!
END FLASHBACK
ALL...
A-A-ALL RIGHT...
I'LL DO MY BEST TO HAVE SUPPER!
FOR STARTERS, CALM DOWN.
...I GOT IT!

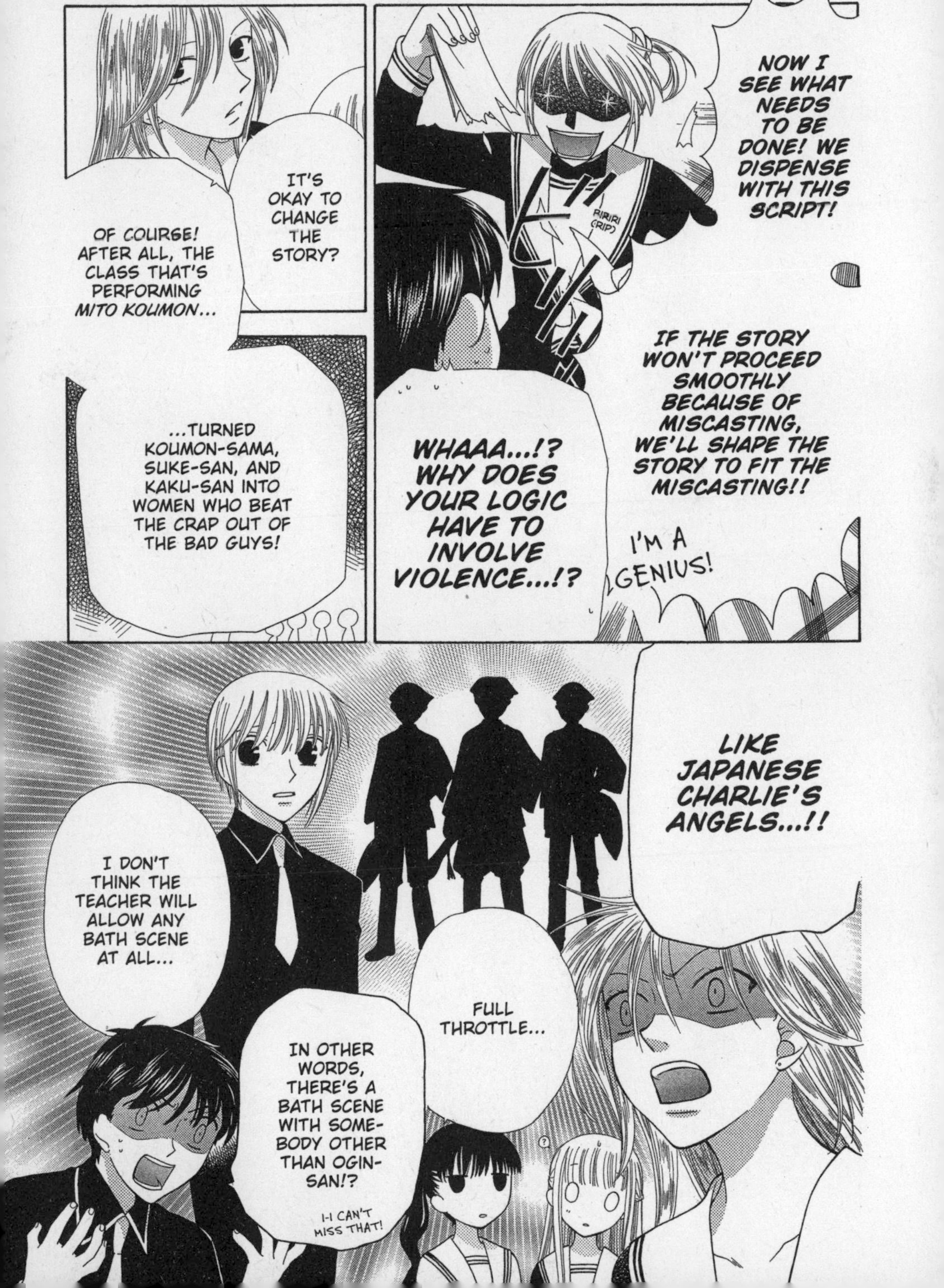

NOW I SEE WHAT NEEDS TO BE DONE! WE DISPENSE WITH THIS SCRIPT!
RIRIRI (RIP)
IF THE STORY WON'T PROCEED SMOOTHLY BECAUSE OF MISCASTING, WE'LL SHAPE THE STORY TO FIT THE MISCASTING!!
I'M A GENIUS!
WHAAA...!? WHY DOES YOUR LOGIC HAVE TO INVOLVE VIOLENCE...!?
IT'S OKAY TO CHANGE THE STORY?
OF COURSE! AFTER ALL, THE CLASS THAT'S PERFORMING *MITO KOUMON*...
...TURNED KOUMON-SAMA, SUKE-SAN, AND KAKU-SAN INTO WOMEN WHO BEAT THE CRAP OUT OF THE BAD GUYS!
LIKE JAPANESE CHARLIE'S ANGELS...!!
FULL THROTTLE...
IN OTHER WORDS, THERE'S A BATH SCENE WITH SOME-BODY OTHER THAN OGIN-SAN!?
I-I CAN'T MISS THAT!
I DON'T THINK THE TEACHER WILL ALLOW ANY BATH SCENE AT ALL...

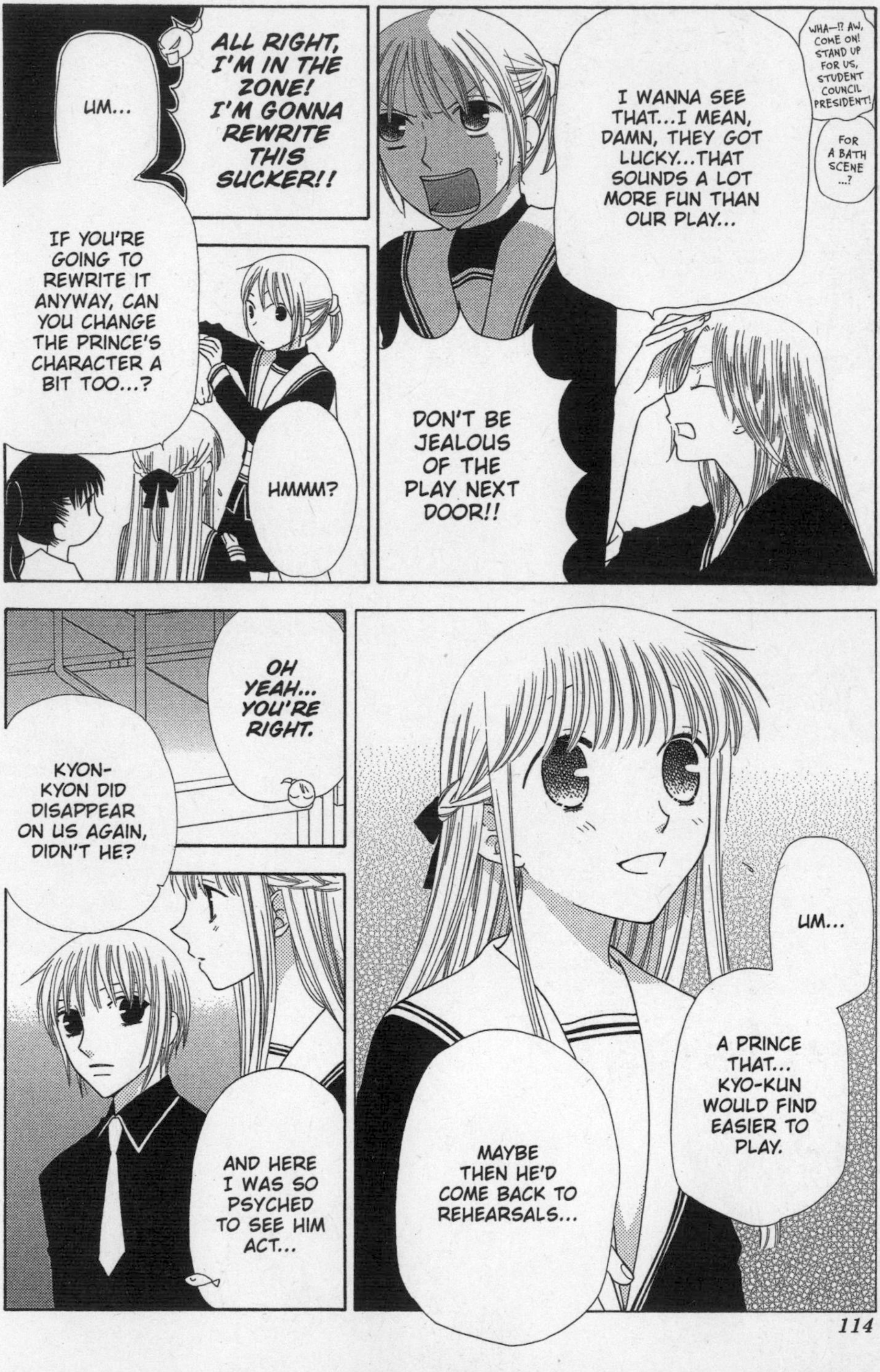
WHA—!? AW, COME ON! STAND UP FOR US, STUDENT COUNCIL PRESIDENT!
FOR A BATH SCENE ...?
I WANNA SEE THAT...I MEAN, DAMN, THEY GOT LUCKY...THAT SOUNDS A LOT MORE FUN THAN OUR PLAY...
DON'T BE JEALOUS OF THE PLAY NEXT DOOR!!
ALL RIGHT, I'M IN THE ZONE! I'M GONNA REWRITE THIS SUCKER!!
UM...
IF YOU'RE GOING TO REWRITE IT ANYWAY, CAN YOU CHANGE THE PRINCE'S CHARACTER A BIT TOO...?
HMMM?
UM...
A PRINCE THAT... KYO-KUN WOULD FIND EASIER TO PLAY.
MAYBE THEN HE'D COME BACK TO REHEARSALS...
OH YEAH... YOU'RE RIGHT.
KYON-KYON DID DISAPPEAR ON US AGAIN, DIDN'T HE?
AND HERE I WAS SO PSYCHED TO SEE HIM ACT...

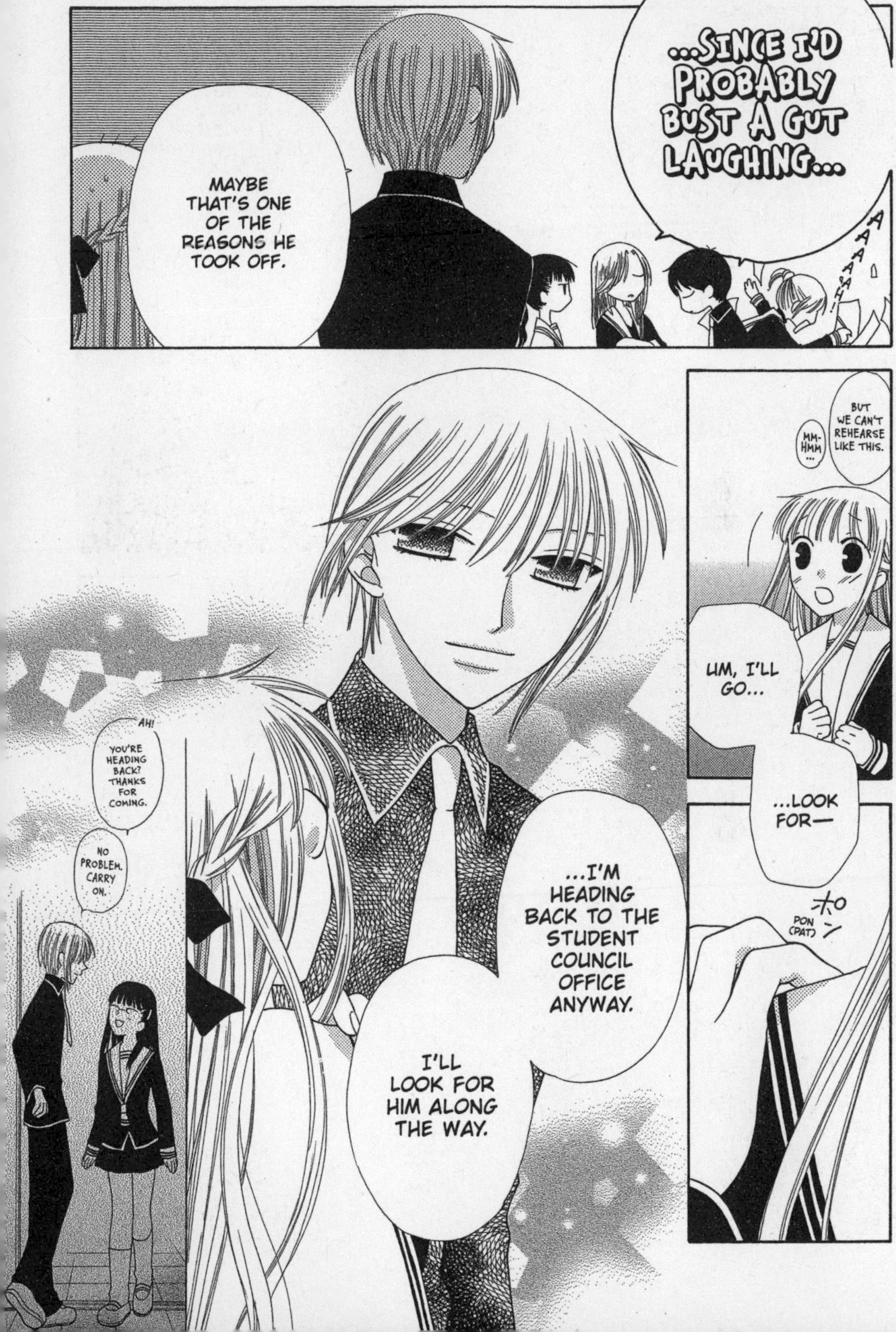
...SINCE I'D PROBABLY BUST A GUT LAUGHING...
AAAAAH!
MAYBE THAT'S ONE OF THE REASONS HE TOOK OFF.
BUT WE CAN'T REHEARSE LIKE THIS.
MM-HMM...
UM, I'LL GO...
...LOOK FOR—
ポン
PON (PAT)
...I'M HEADING BACK TO THE STUDENT COUNCIL OFFICE ANYWAY.
I'LL LOOK FOR HIM ALONG THE WAY.
AH!
YOU'RE HEADING BACK? THANKS FOR COMING.
NO PROBLEM. CARRY ON.

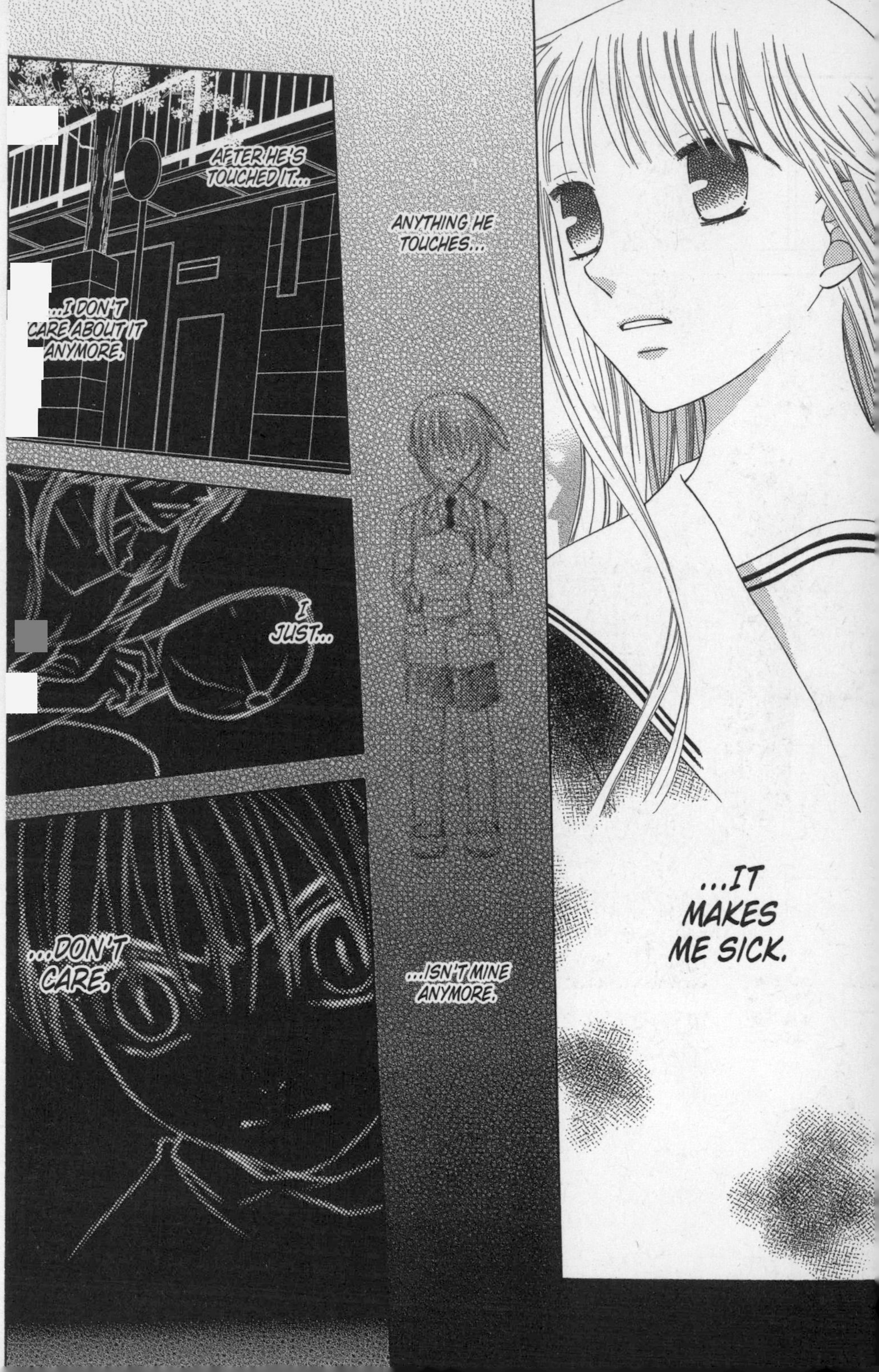
...IT MAKES ME SICK.
ANYTHING HE TOUCHES...
...ISN'T MINE ANYMORE.
AFTER HE'S TOUCHED IT...
...I DON'T CARE ABOUT IT ANYMORE.
I JUST...
...DON'T CARE.

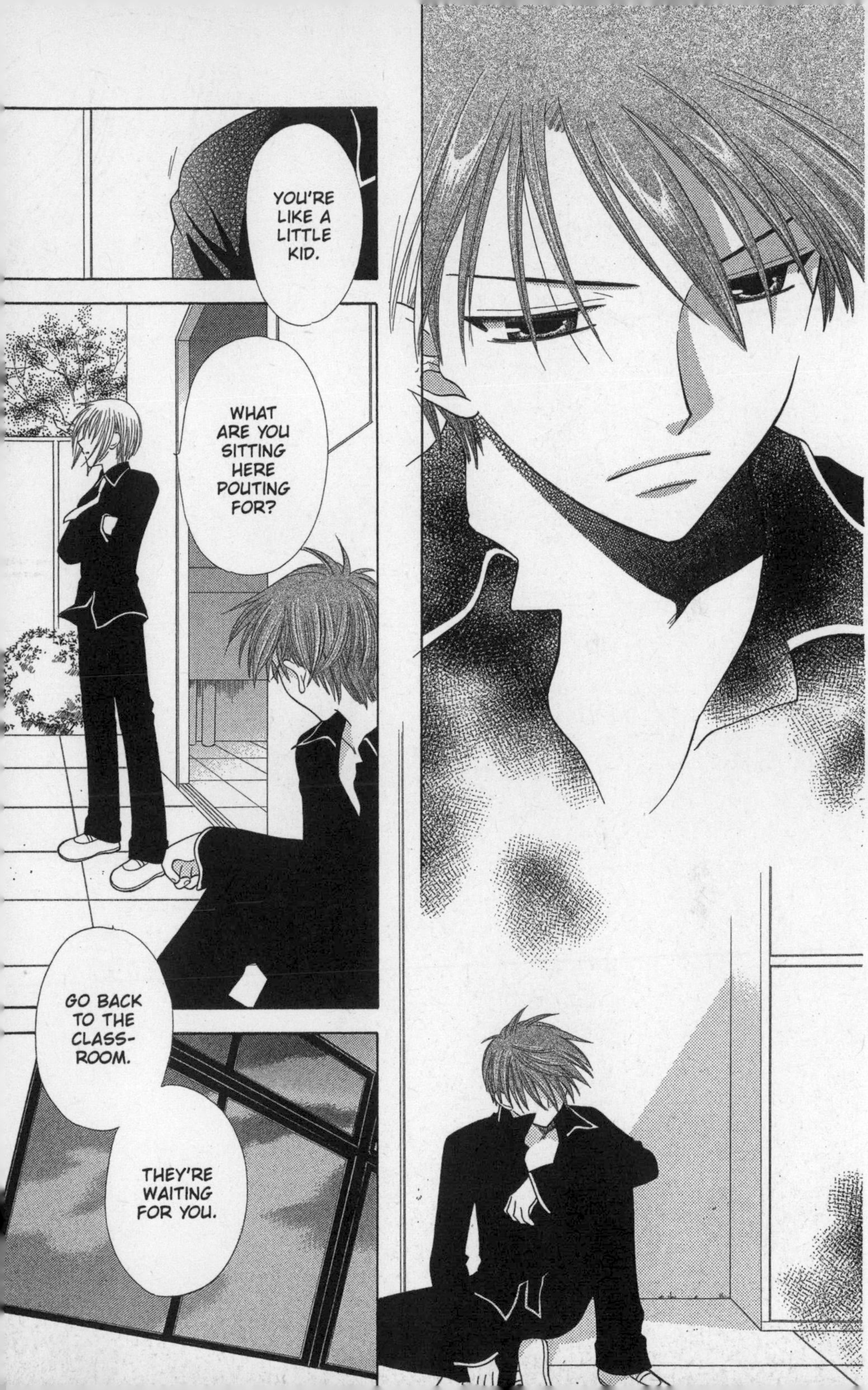
YOU'RE LIKE A LITTLE KID.
WHAT ARE YOU SITTING HERE POUTING FOR?
GO BACK TO THE CLASS-ROOM.
THEY'RE WAITING FOR YOU.

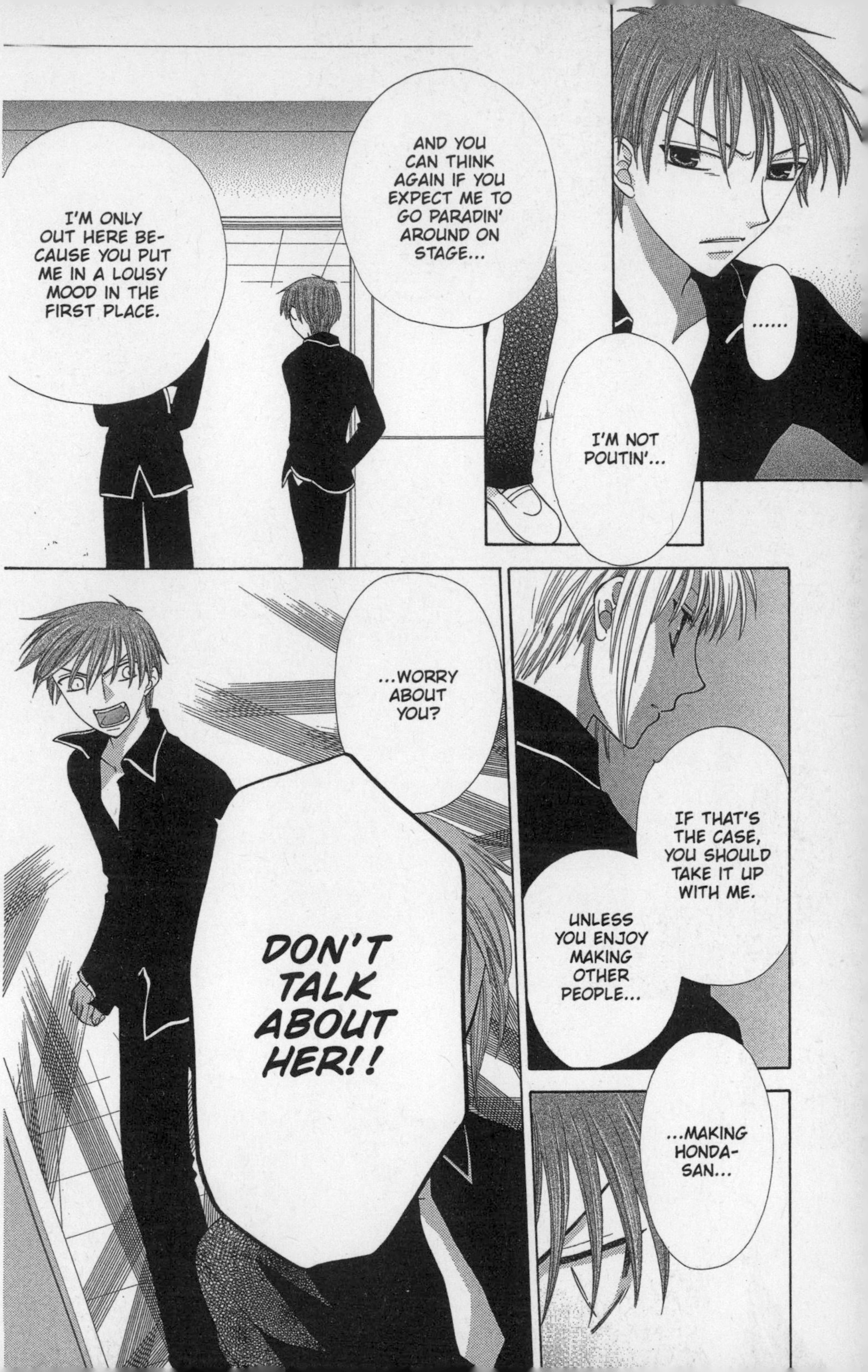
......
I'M NOT POUTIN'...
AND YOU CAN THINK AGAIN IF YOU EXPECT ME TO GO PARADIN' AROUND ON STAGE...
I'M ONLY OUT HERE BE-CAUSE YOU PUT ME IN A LOUSY MOOD IN THE FIRST PLACE.
IF THAT'S THE CASE, YOU SHOULD TAKE IT UP WITH ME.
UNLESS YOU ENJOY MAKING OTHER PEOPLE...
...MAKING HONDA-SAN...
...WORRY ABOUT YOU?
DON'T TALK ABOUT HER!!

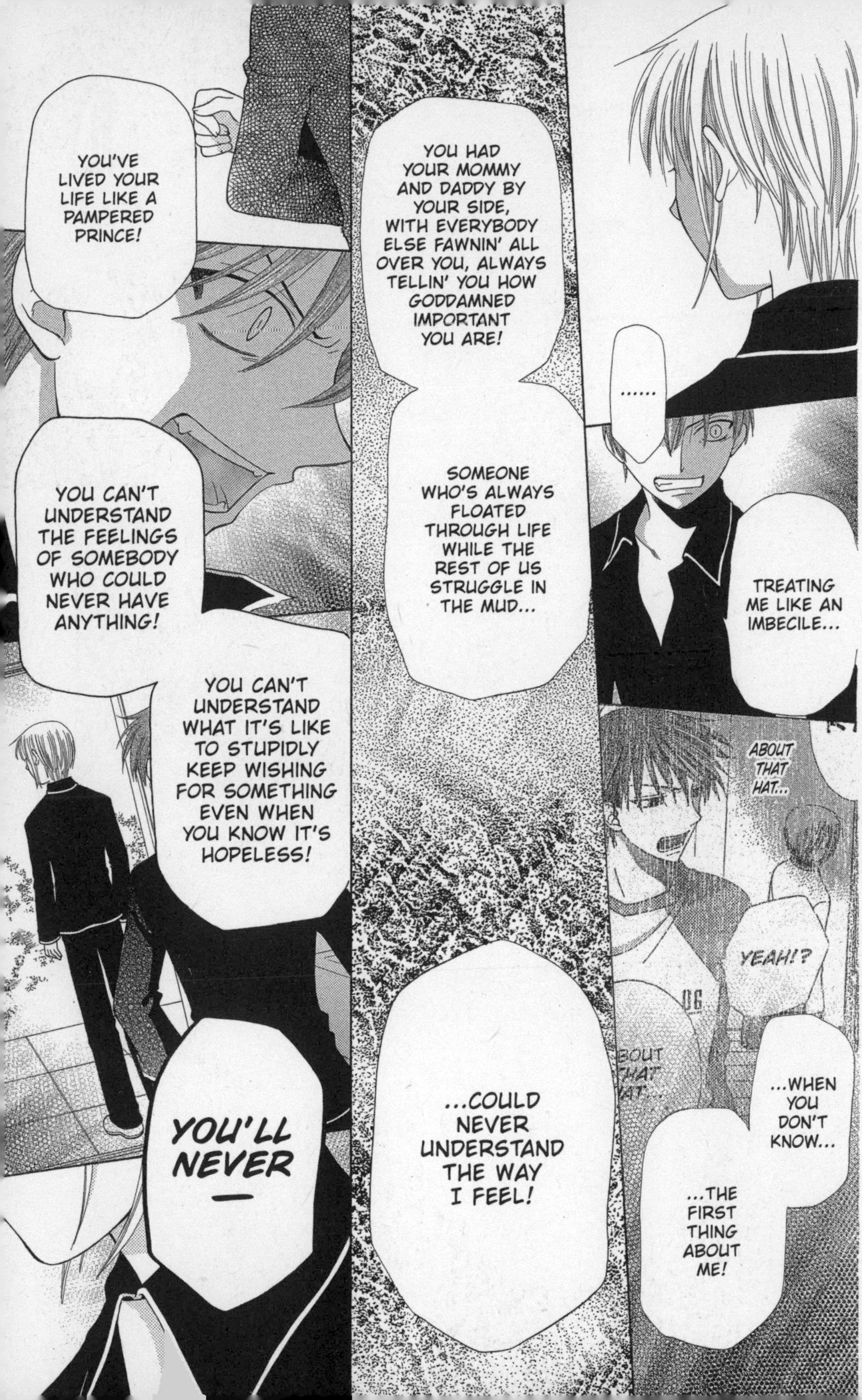
......
TREATING ME LIKE AN IMBECILE...
ABOUT THAT HAT...
YEAH!?
...WHEN YOU DON'T KNOW...
...THE FIRST THING ABOUT ME!
YOU HAD YOUR MOMMY AND DADDY BY YOUR SIDE, WITH EVERYBODY ELSE FAWNIN' ALL OVER YOU, ALWAYS TELLIN' YOU HOW GODDAMNED IMPORTANT YOU ARE!
SOMEONE WHO'S ALWAYS FLOATED THROUGH LIFE WHILE THE REST OF US STRUGGLE IN THE MUD...
...COULD NEVER UNDERSTAND THE WAY I FEEL!
YOU'VE LIVED YOUR LIFE LIKE A PAMPERED PRINCE!
YOU CAN'T UNDERSTAND THE FEELINGS OF SOMEBODY WHO COULD NEVER HAVE ANYTHING!
YOU CAN'T UNDERSTAND WHAT IT'S LIKE TO STUPIDLY KEEP WISHING FOR SOMETHING EVEN WHEN YOU KNOW IT'S HOPELESS!
YOU'LL NEVER —

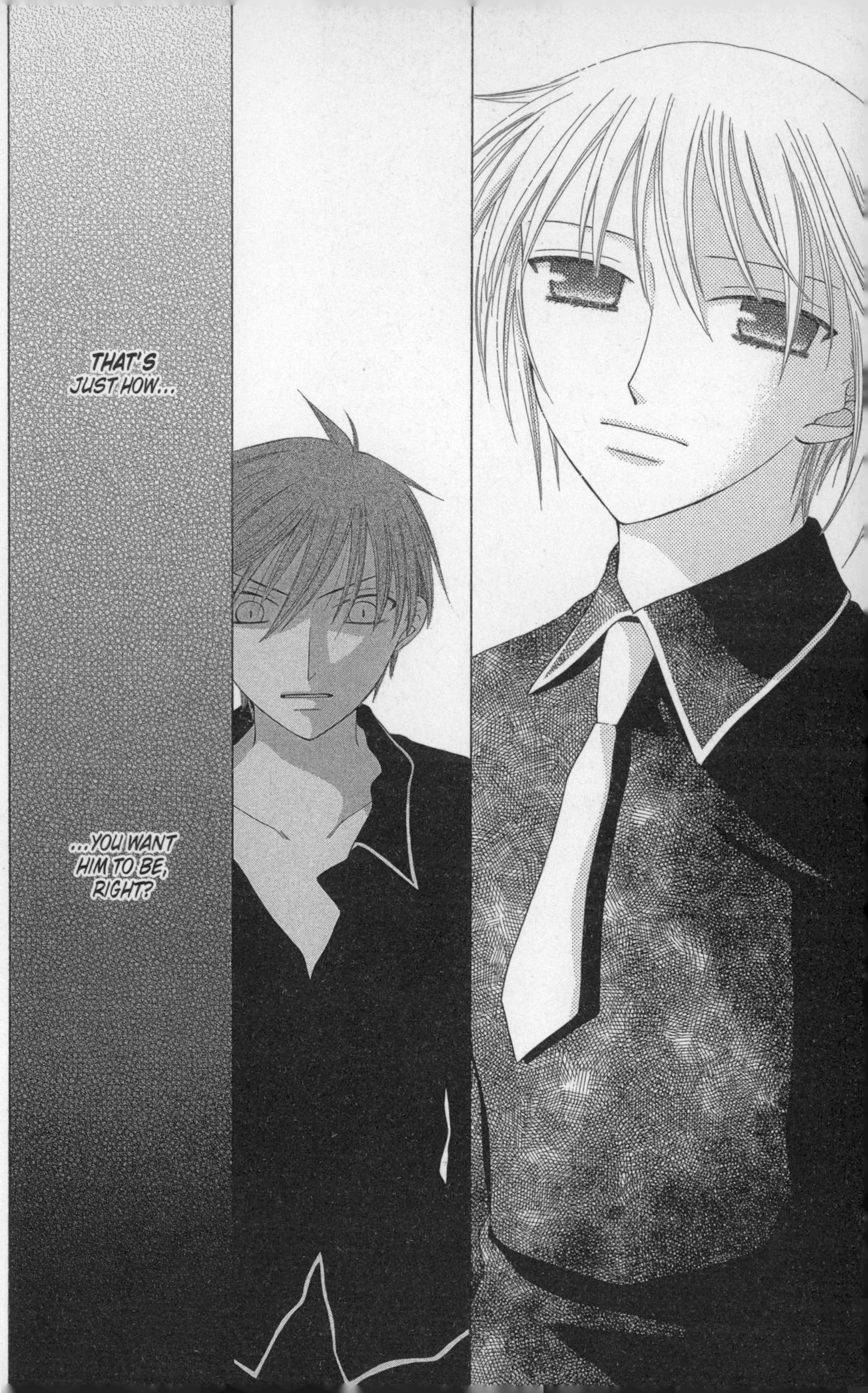
THAT'S JUST HOW...
...YOU WANT HIM TO BE, RIGHT?

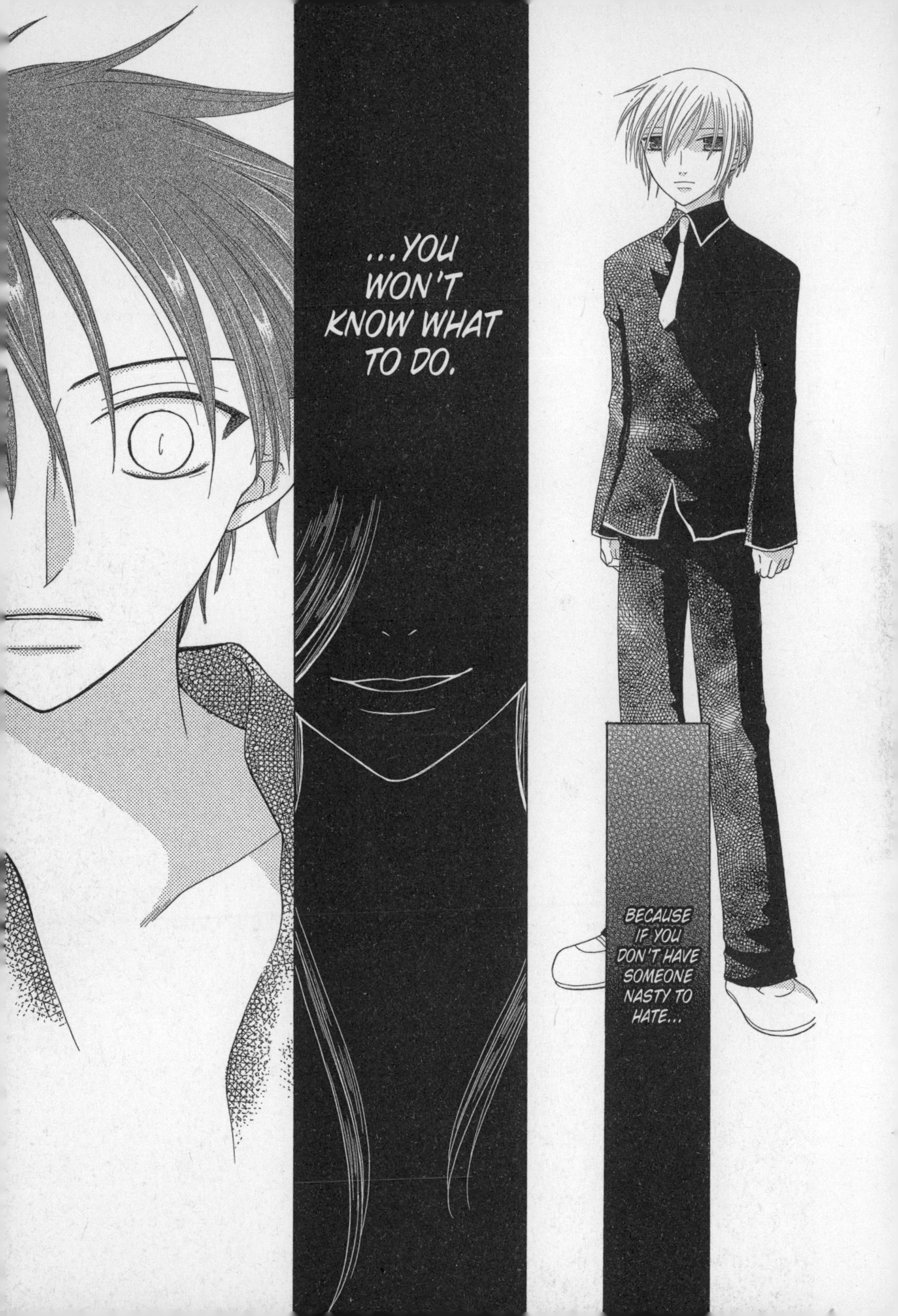
BECAUSE IF YOU DON'T HAVE SOMEONE NASTY TO HATE...
...YOU WON'T KNOW WHAT TO DO.

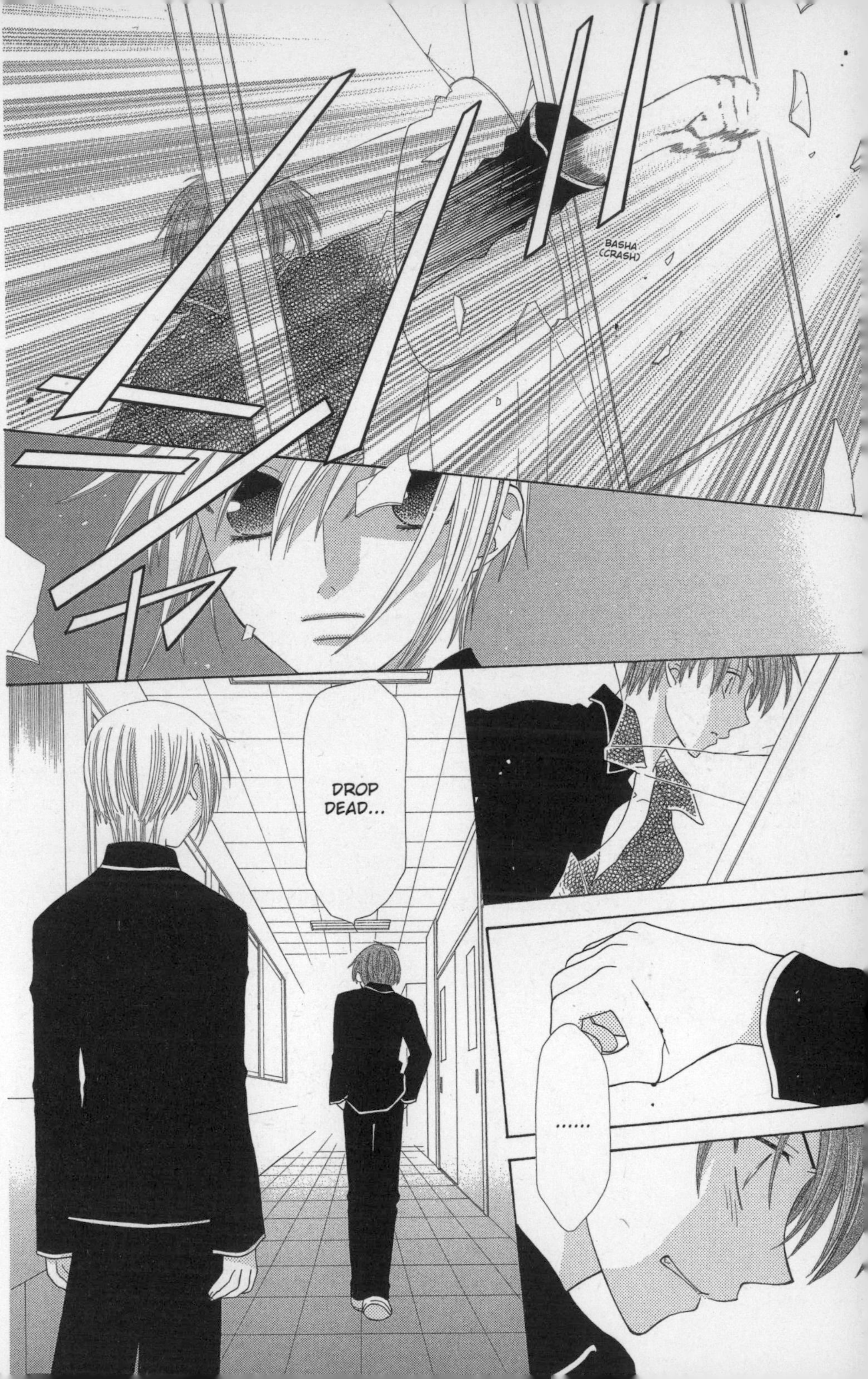
BASHA (CRASH)
DROP DEAD...
......

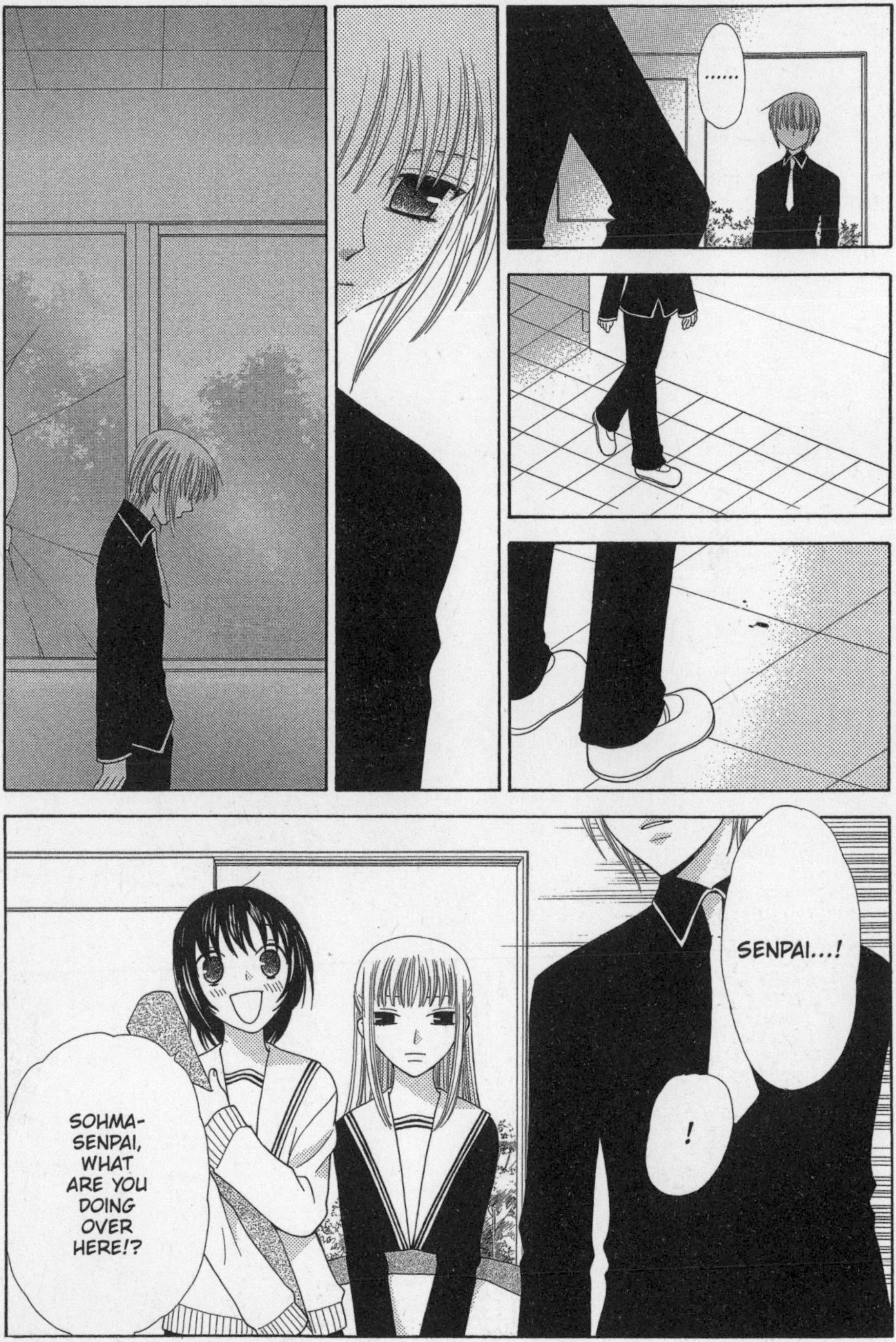
......
SENPAI...!
!
SOHMA-SENPAI, WHAT ARE YOU DOING OVER HERE!?

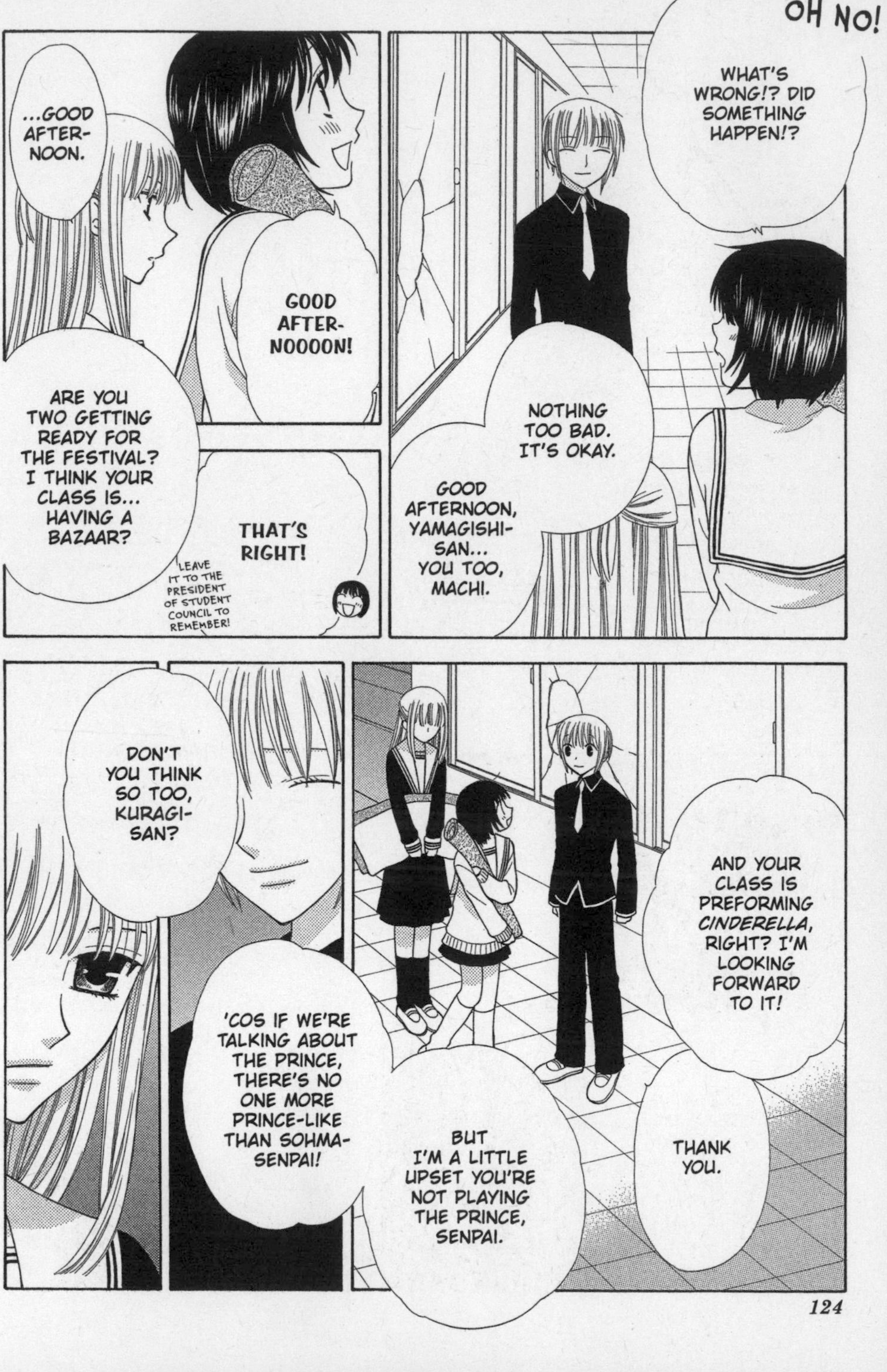
OH NO!
WHAT'S WRONG!? DID SOMETHING HAPPEN!?
NOTHING TOO BAD. IT'S OKAY.
GOOD AFTERNOON, YAMAGISHI-SAN... YOU TOO, MACHI.
GOOD AFTER-NOOOON!
...GOOD AFTER-NOON.
ARE YOU TWO GETTING READY FOR THE FESTIVAL? I THINK YOUR CLASS IS... HAVING A BAZAAR?
THAT'S RIGHT!
LEAVE IT TO THE PRESIDENT OF STUDENT COUNCIL TO REMEMBER!
AND YOUR CLASS IS PREFORMING *CINDERELLA*, RIGHT? I'M LOOKING FORWARD TO IT!
THANK YOU.
BUT I'M A LITTLE UPSET YOU'RE NOT PLAYING THE PRINCE, SENPAI.
'COS IF WE'RE TALKING ABOUT THE PRINCE, THERE'S NO ONE MORE PRINCE-LIKE THAN SOHMA-SENPAI!
DON'T YOU THINK SO TOO, KURAGI-SAN?

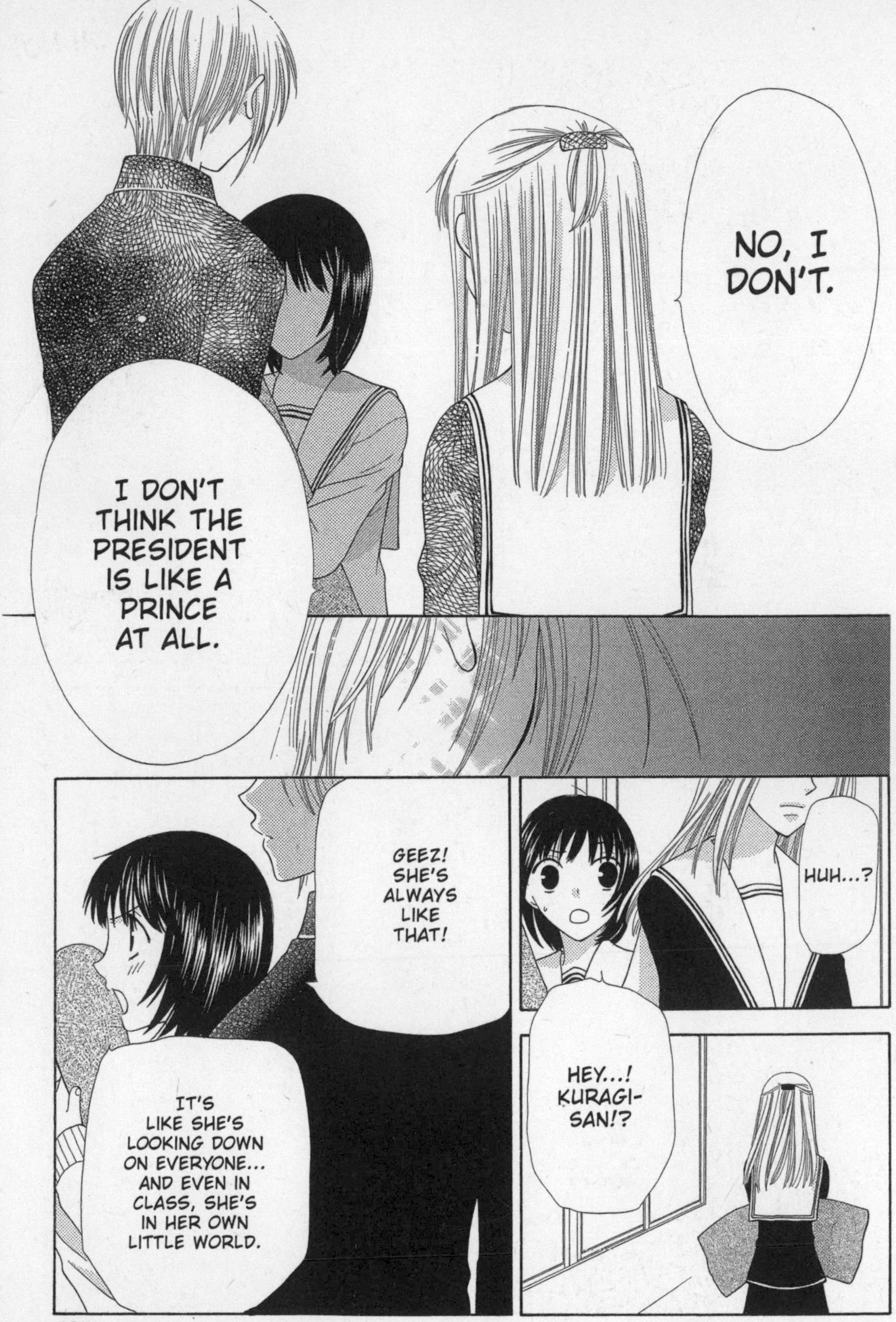
NO, I DON'T.
I DON'T THINK THE PRESIDENT IS LIKE A PRINCE AT ALL.
HUH...?
HEY...! KURAGI-SAN!?
GEEZ! SHE'S ALWAYS LIKE THAT!
IT'S LIKE SHE'S LOOKING DOWN ON EVERYONE... AND EVEN IN CLASS, SHE'S IN HER OWN LITTLE WORLD.

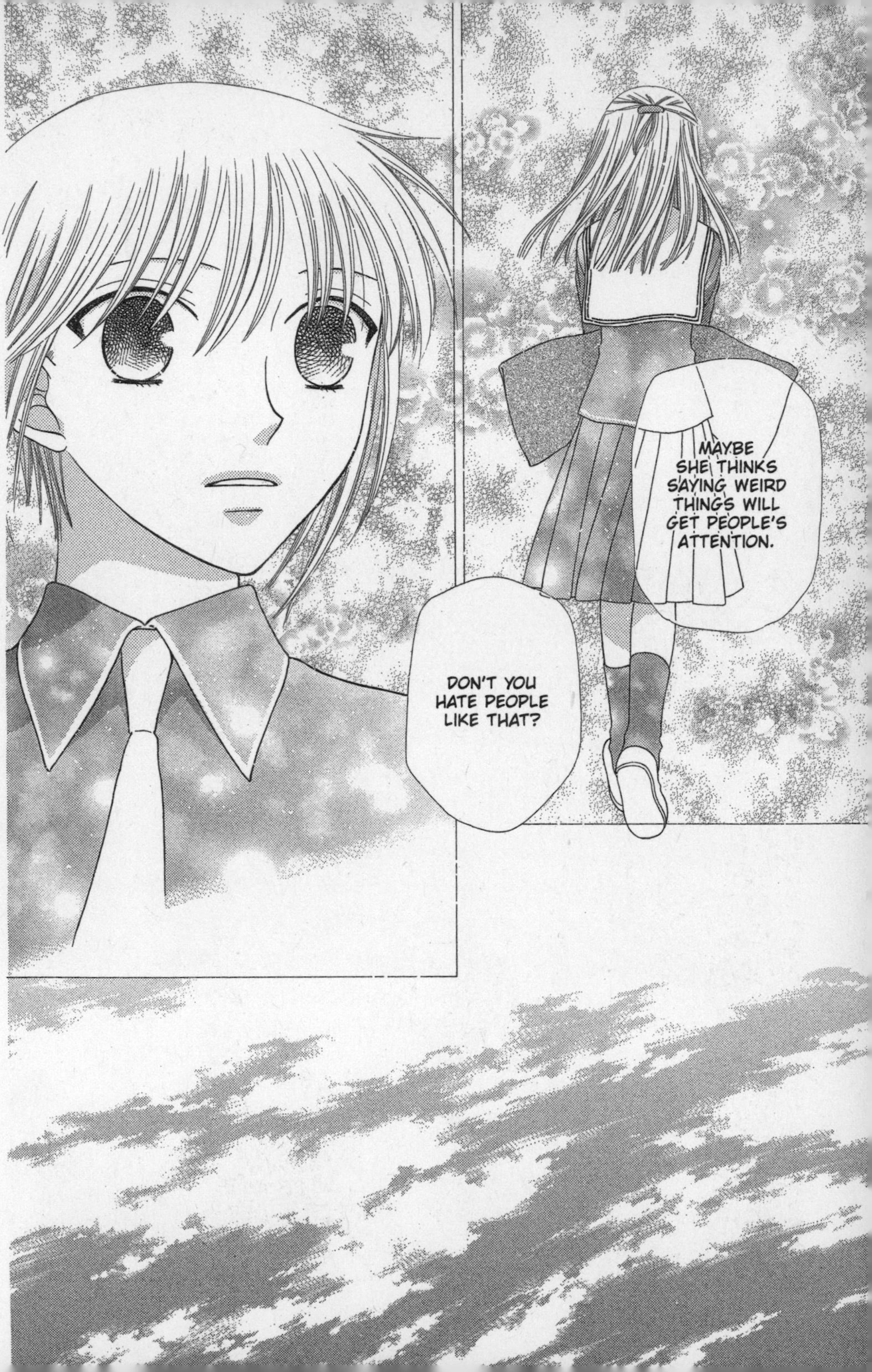
MAYBE SHE THINKS SAYING WEIRD THINGS WILL GET PEOPLE'S ATTENTION.
DON'T YOU HATE PEOPLE LIKE THAT?

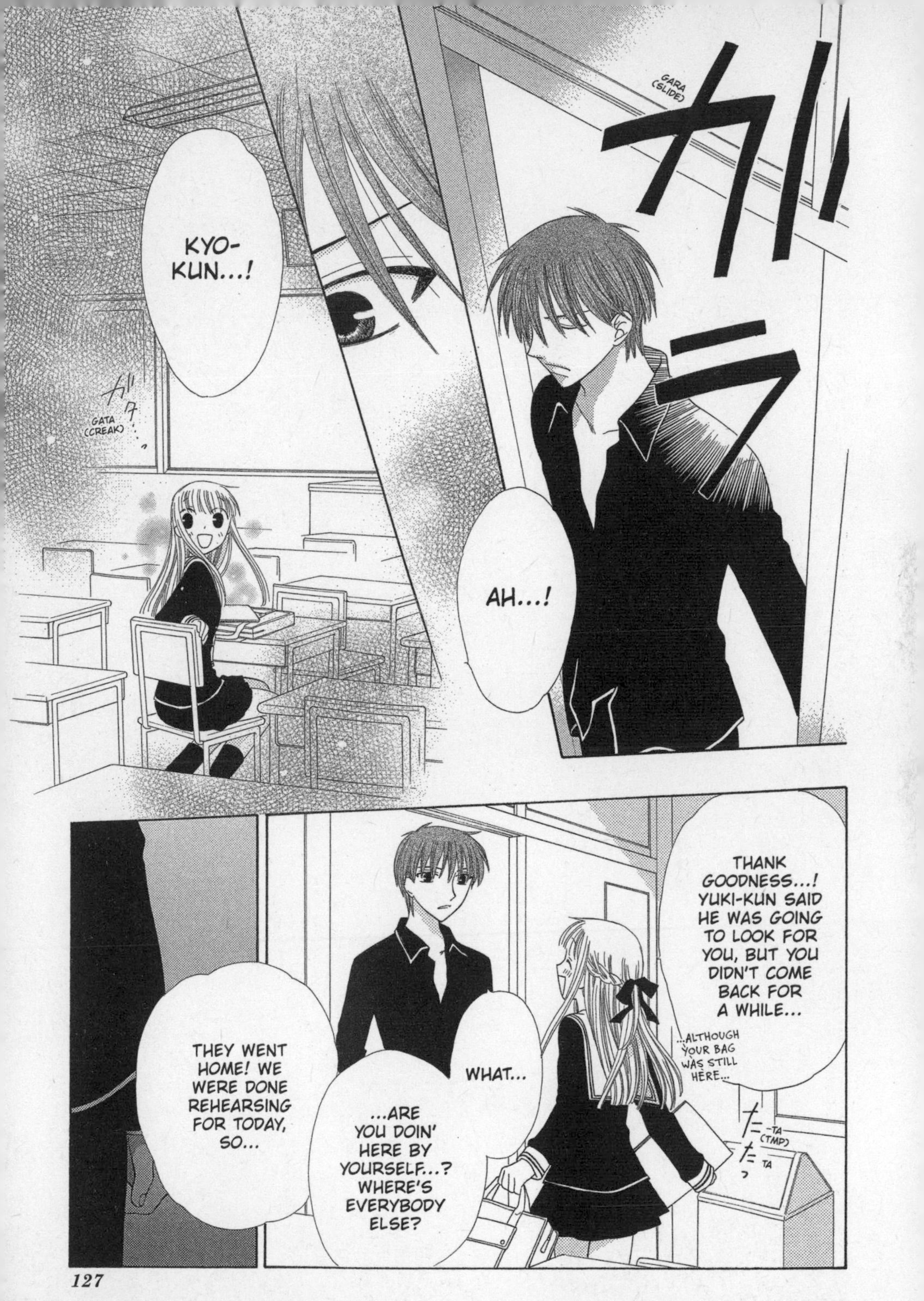
GARA (SLIDE)
AH...!
GATA (CREAK)
KYO-KUN...!
THANK GOODNESS...! YUKI-KUN SAID HE WAS GOING TO LOOK FOR YOU, BUT YOU DIDN'T COME BACK FOR A WHILE...
...ALTHOUGH YOUR BAG WAS STILL HERE...
-TA (TMP) TA
WHAT...
...ARE YOU DOIN' HERE BY YOURSELF...? WHERE'S EVERYBODY ELSE?
THEY WENT HOME! WE WERE DONE REHEARSING FOR TODAY, SO...

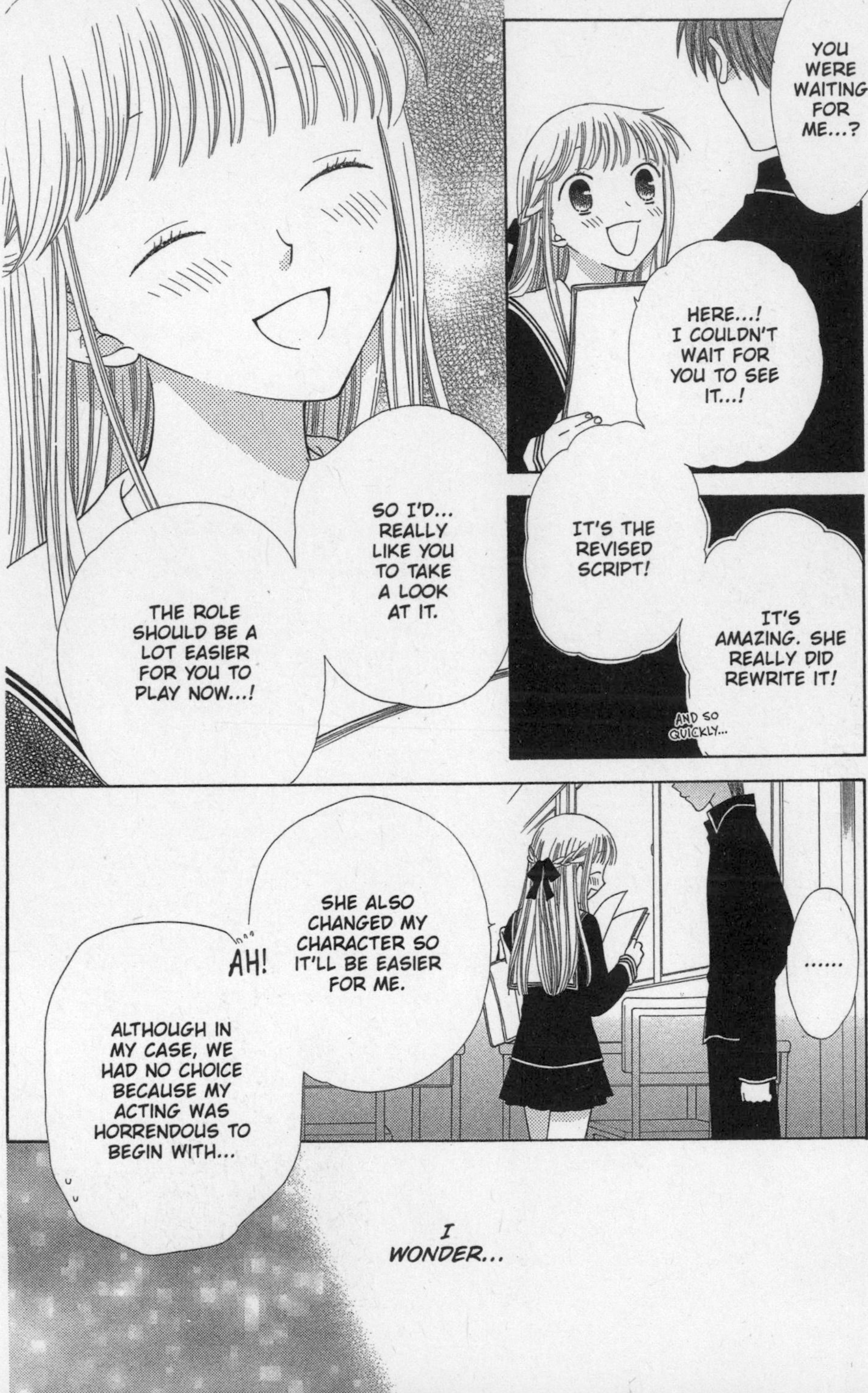
YOU WERE WAITING FOR ME...?
HERE...! I COULDN'T WAIT FOR YOU TO SEE IT...!
IT'S THE REVISED SCRIPT!
IT'S AMAZING. SHE REALLY DID REWRITE IT!
AND SO QUICKLY...
SO I'D... REALLY LIKE YOU TO TAKE A LOOK AT IT.
THE ROLE SHOULD BE A LOT EASIER FOR YOU TO PLAY NOW...!
......
SHE ALSO CHANGED MY CHARACTER SO IT'LL BE EASIER FOR ME.
AH!
ALTHOUGH IN MY CASE, WE HAD NO CHOICE BECAUSE MY ACTING WAS HORRENDOUS TO BEGIN WITH...
I WONDER...

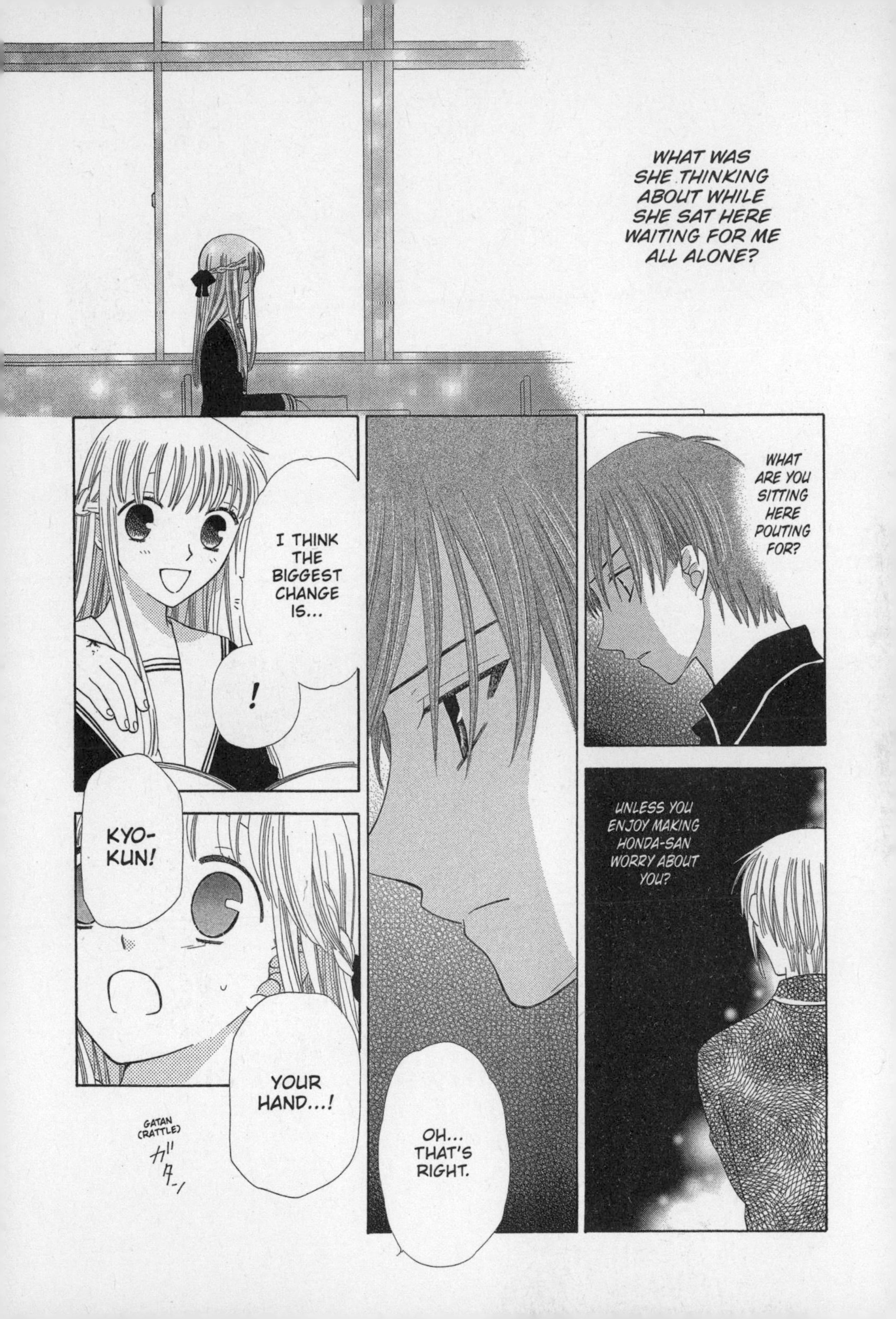
WHAT WAS SHE THINKING ABOUT WHILE SHE SAT HERE WAITING FOR ME ALL ALONE?
WHAT ARE YOU SITTING HERE POUTING FOR?
UNLESS YOU ENJOY MAKING HONDA-SAN WORRY ABOUT YOU?
OH... THAT'S RIGHT.
I THINK THE BIGGEST CHANGE IS...
!
KYO-KUN!
YOUR HAND...!
GATAN (RATTLE)

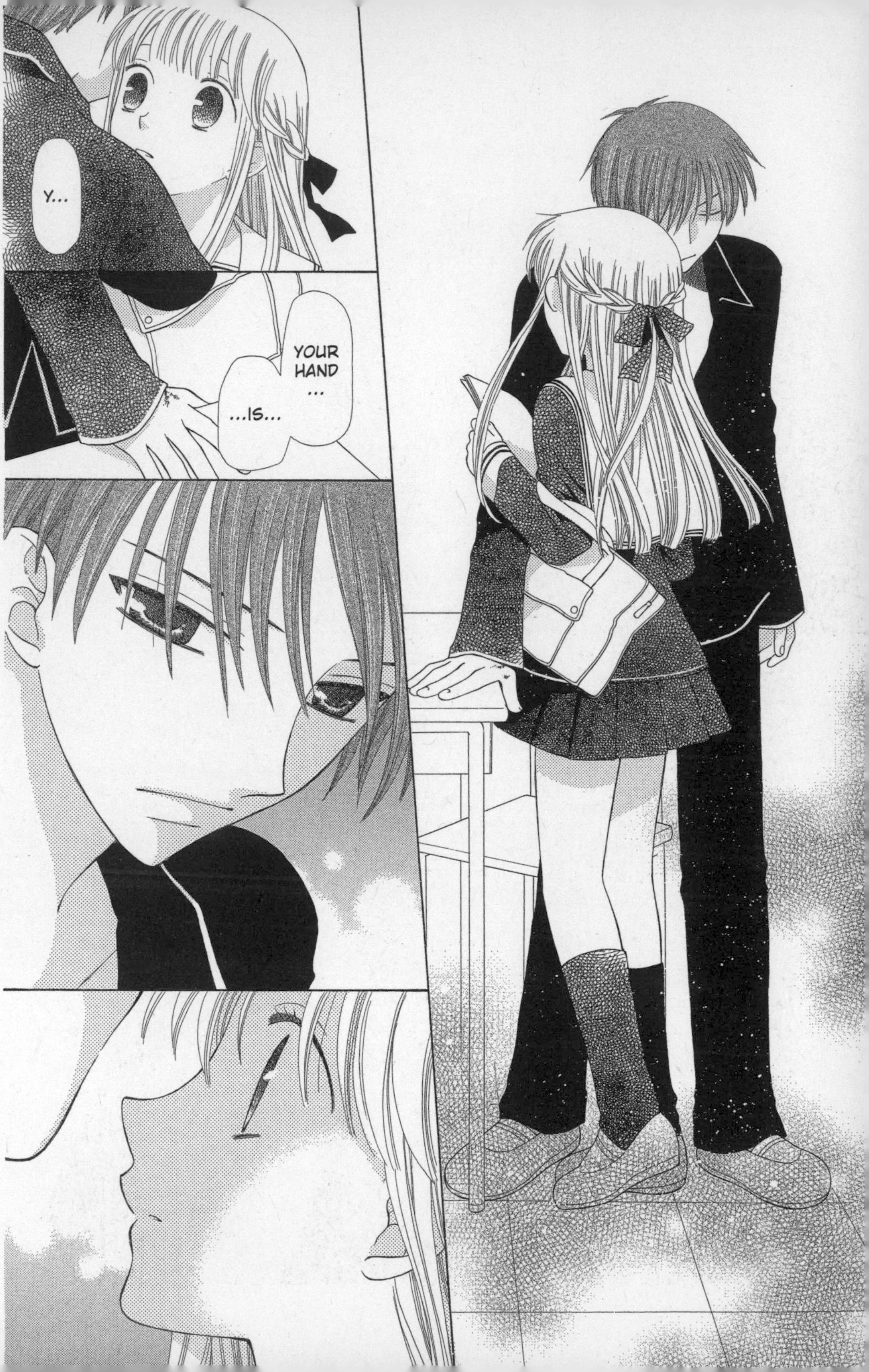
Y...
YOUR HAND ...
...IS...

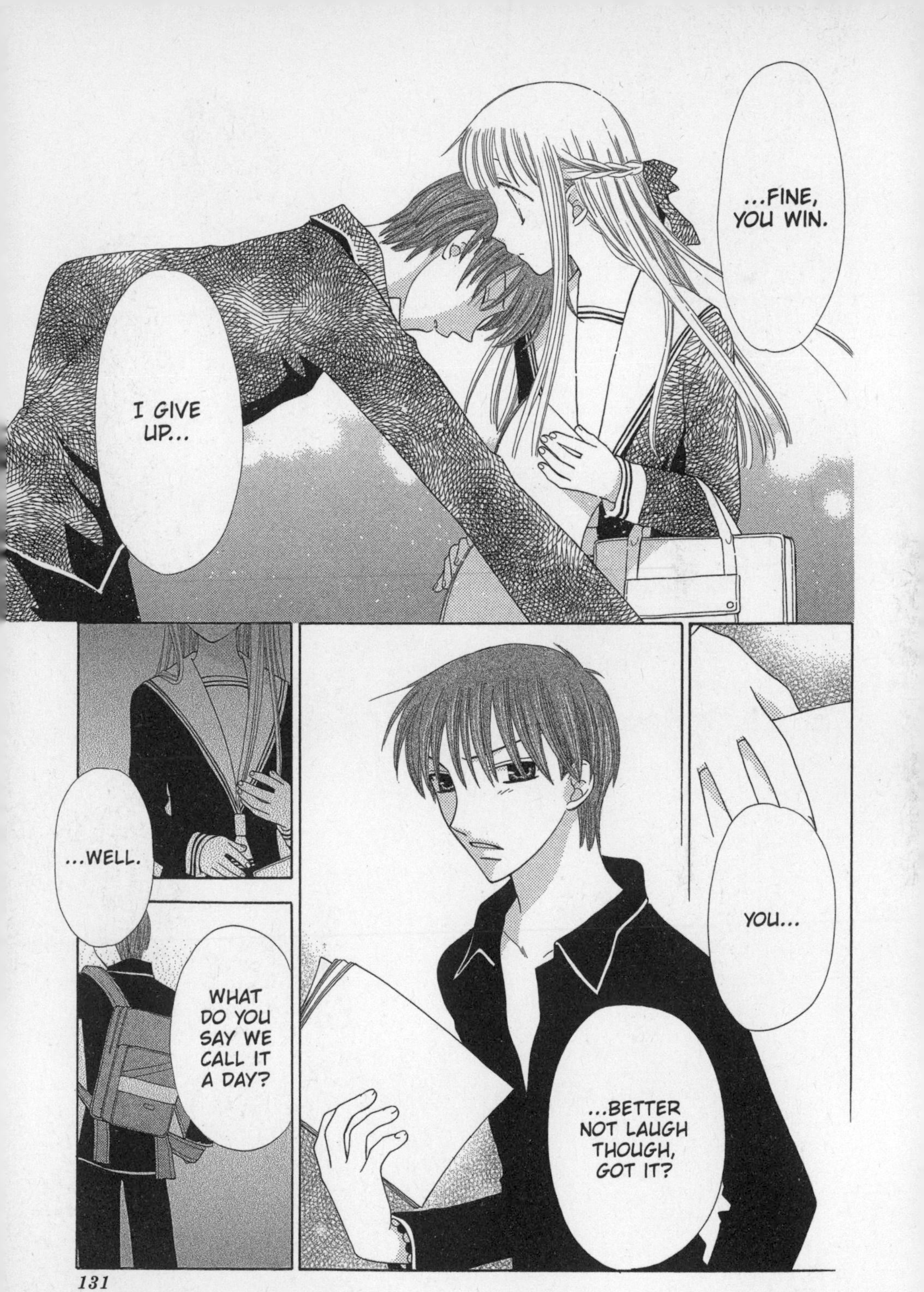
...FINE, YOU WIN.
I GIVE UP...
YOU...
...BETTER NOT LAUGH THOUGH, GOT IT?
...WELL.
WHAT DO YOU SAY WE CALL IT A DAY?

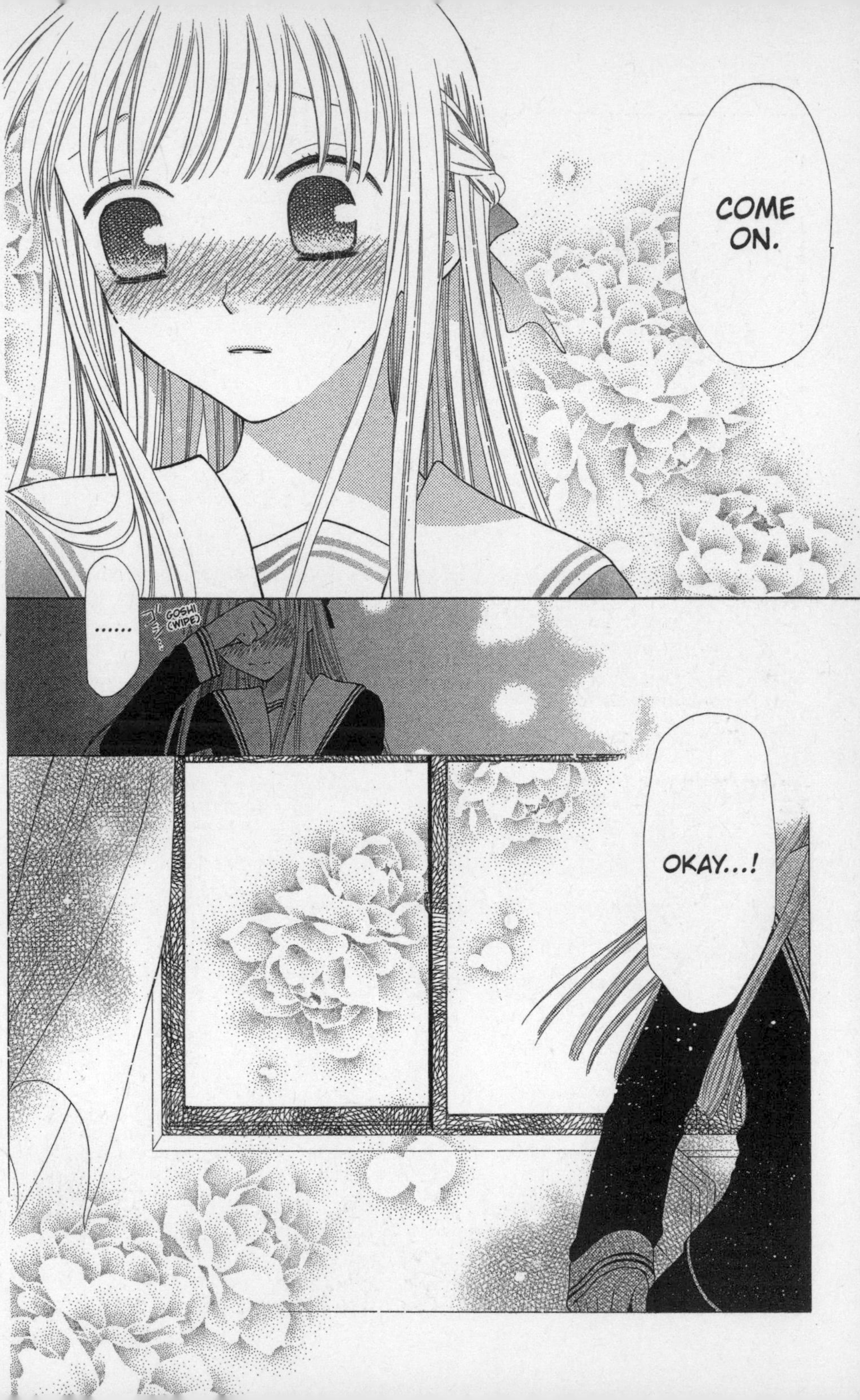
COME ON.
......
GOSHI (WIPE)
OKAY...!

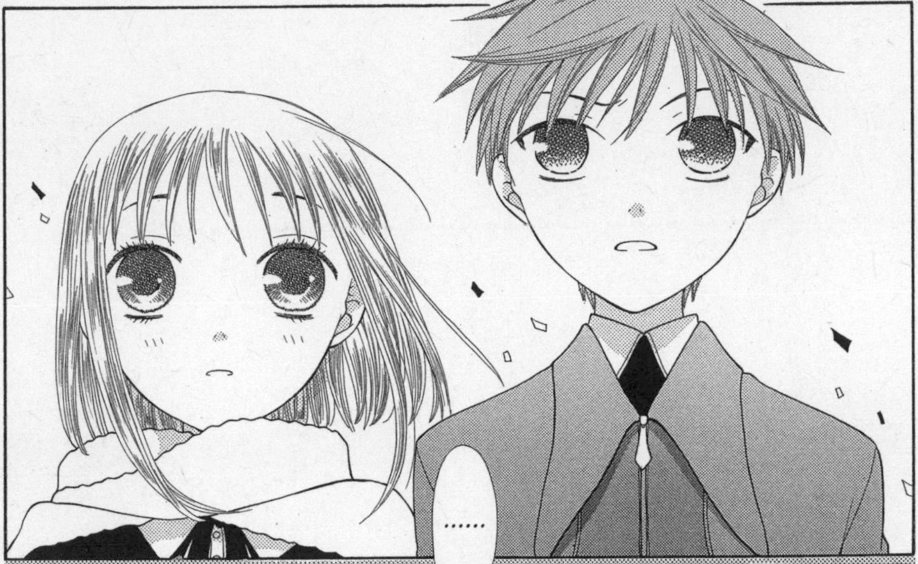
......

KAIBARA High School CULTURAL FESTIVAL

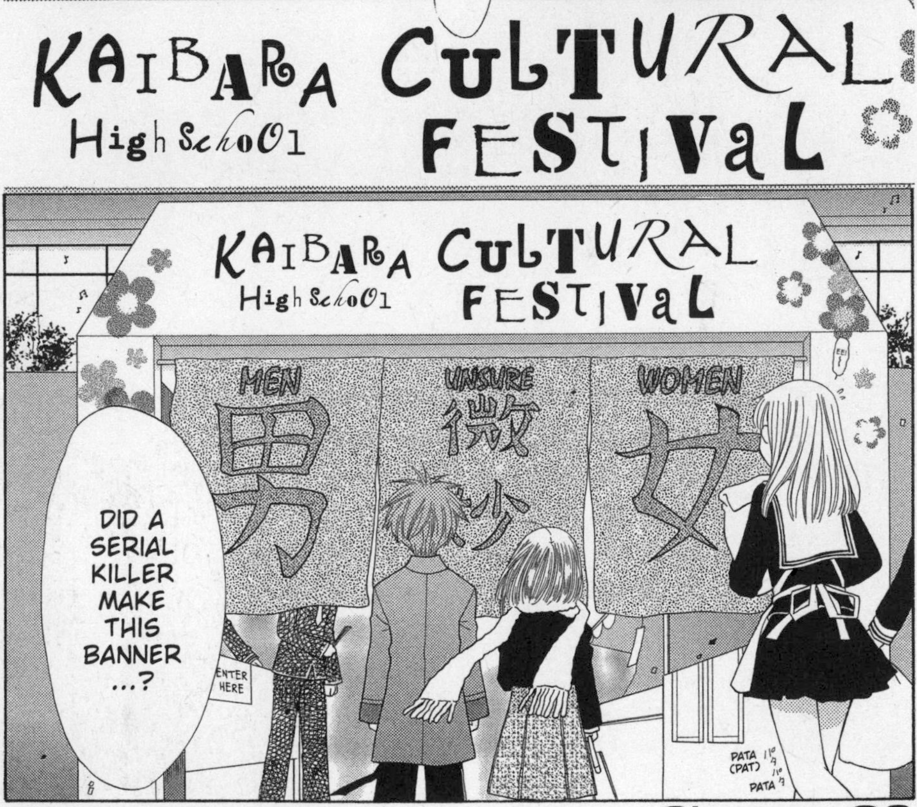
KAIBARA High School CULTURAL FESTIVAL
WOMEN
女
UNSURE
微妙
MEN
男
PATA (PAT) パタ パタ PATA
ENTER HERE
DID A SERIAL KILLER MAKE THIS BANNER ...?

Chapter 88

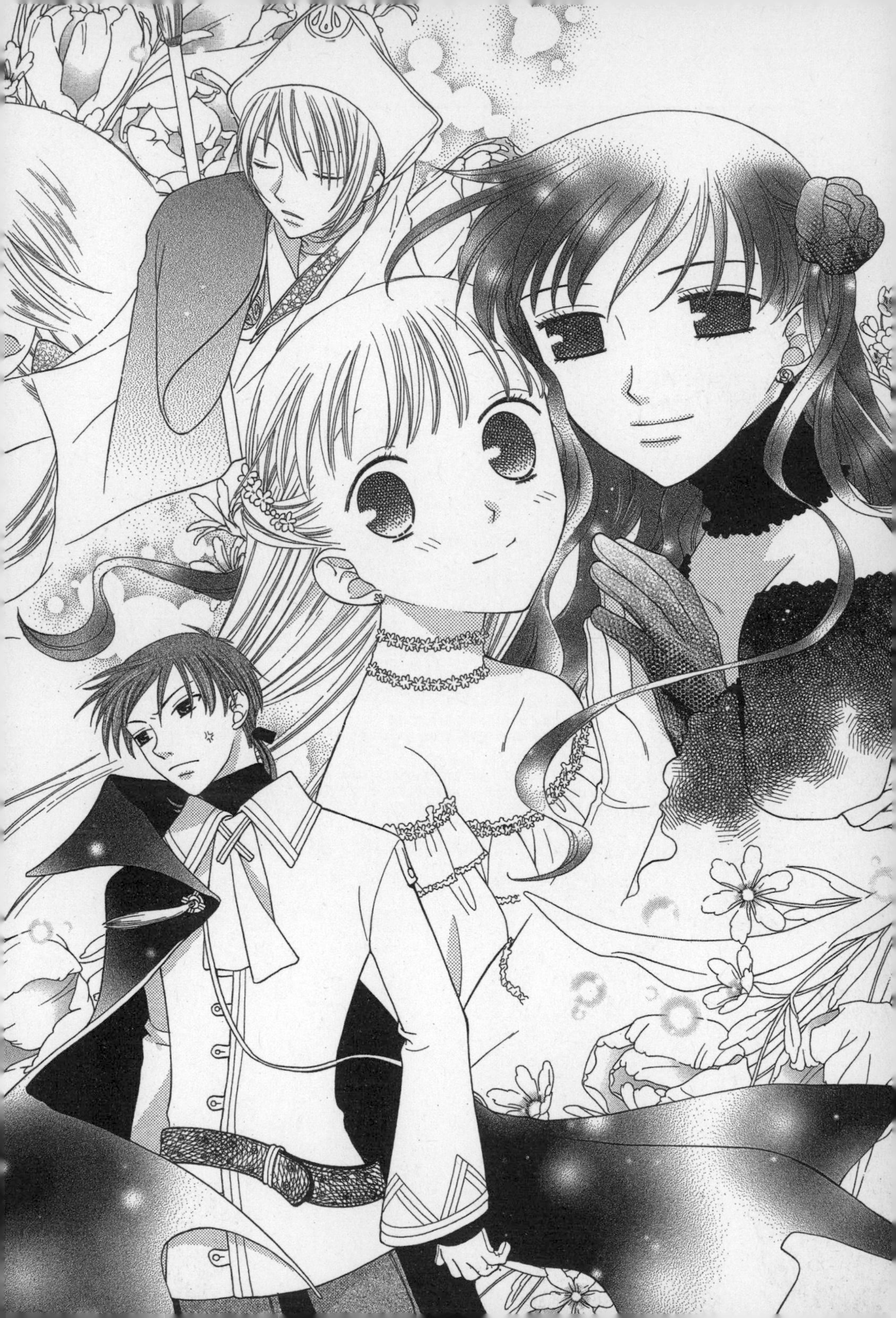

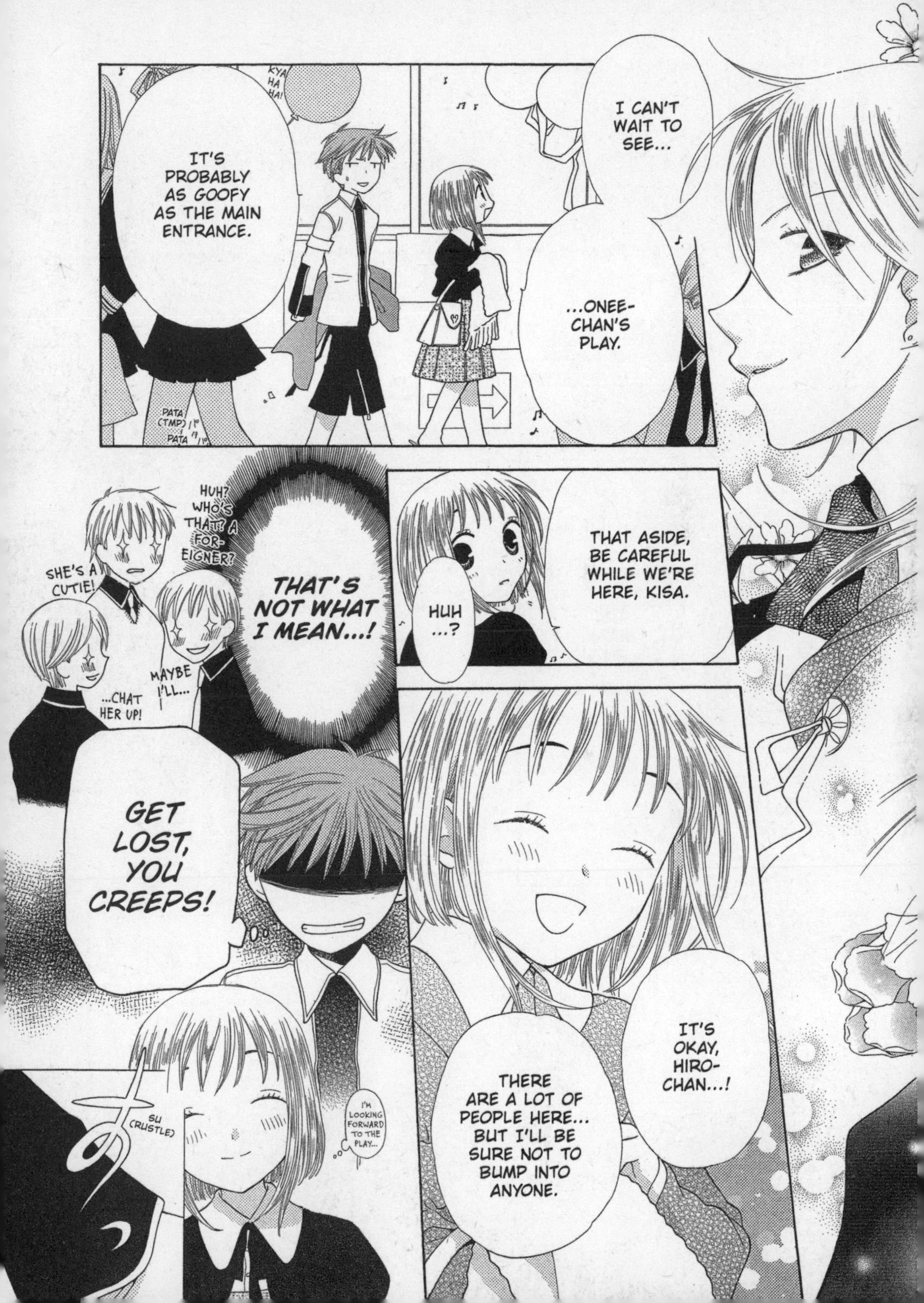
I CAN'T WAIT TO SEE...
...ONEE-CHAN'S PLAY.
KYA HA HA!
IT'S PROBABLY AS GOOFY AS THE MAIN ENTRANCE.
PATA (TMP) PATA
THAT ASIDE, BE CAREFUL WHILE WE'RE HERE, KISA.
HUH ...?
HUH? WHO'S THAT? A FOREIGNER?
SHE'S A CUTIE!
MAYBE I'LL...
...CHAT HER UP!
THAT'S NOT WHAT I MEAN...!
IT'S OKAY, HIRO-CHAN...!
THERE ARE A LOT OF PEOPLE HERE... BUT I'LL BE SURE NOT TO BUMP INTO ANYONE.
GET LOST, YOU CREEPS!
SU (RUSTLE)
I'M LOOKING FORWARD TO THE PLAY...

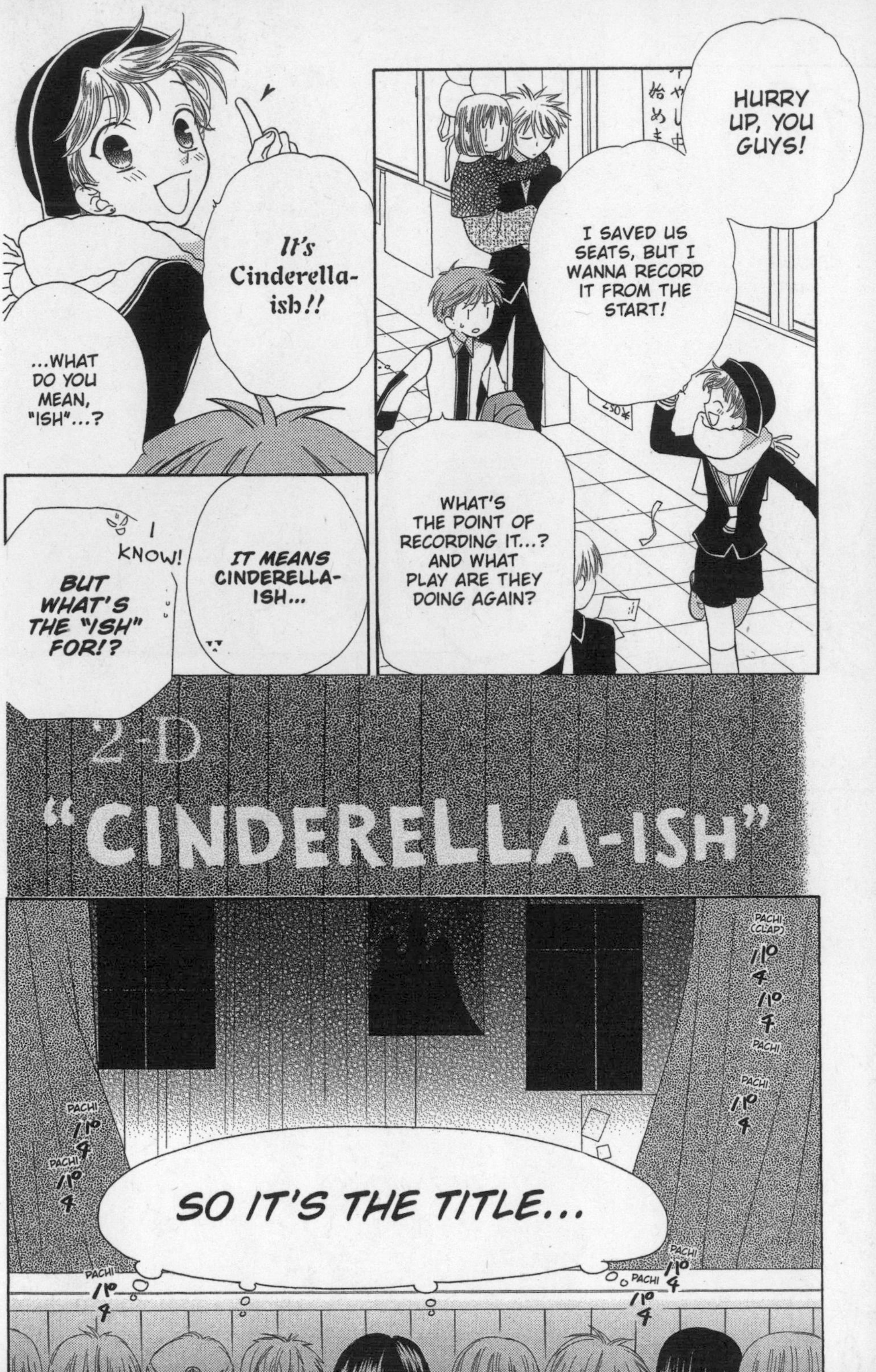
HURRY UP, YOU GUYS!
I SAVED US SEATS, BUT I WANNA RECORD IT FROM THE START!
WHAT'S THE POINT OF RECORDING IT...? AND WHAT PLAY ARE THEY DOING AGAIN?
It's Cinderella-ish!!
...WHAT DO YOU MEAN, "ISH"...?
IT MEANS CINDERELLA-ISH...
I KNOW!
BUT WHAT'S THE "ISH" FOR!?
2-D
"CINDERELLA-ISH"
PACHI (CLAP)
PACHI
PACHI
PACHI
PACHI
SO IT'S THE TITLE...
PACHI
PACHI
PACHI

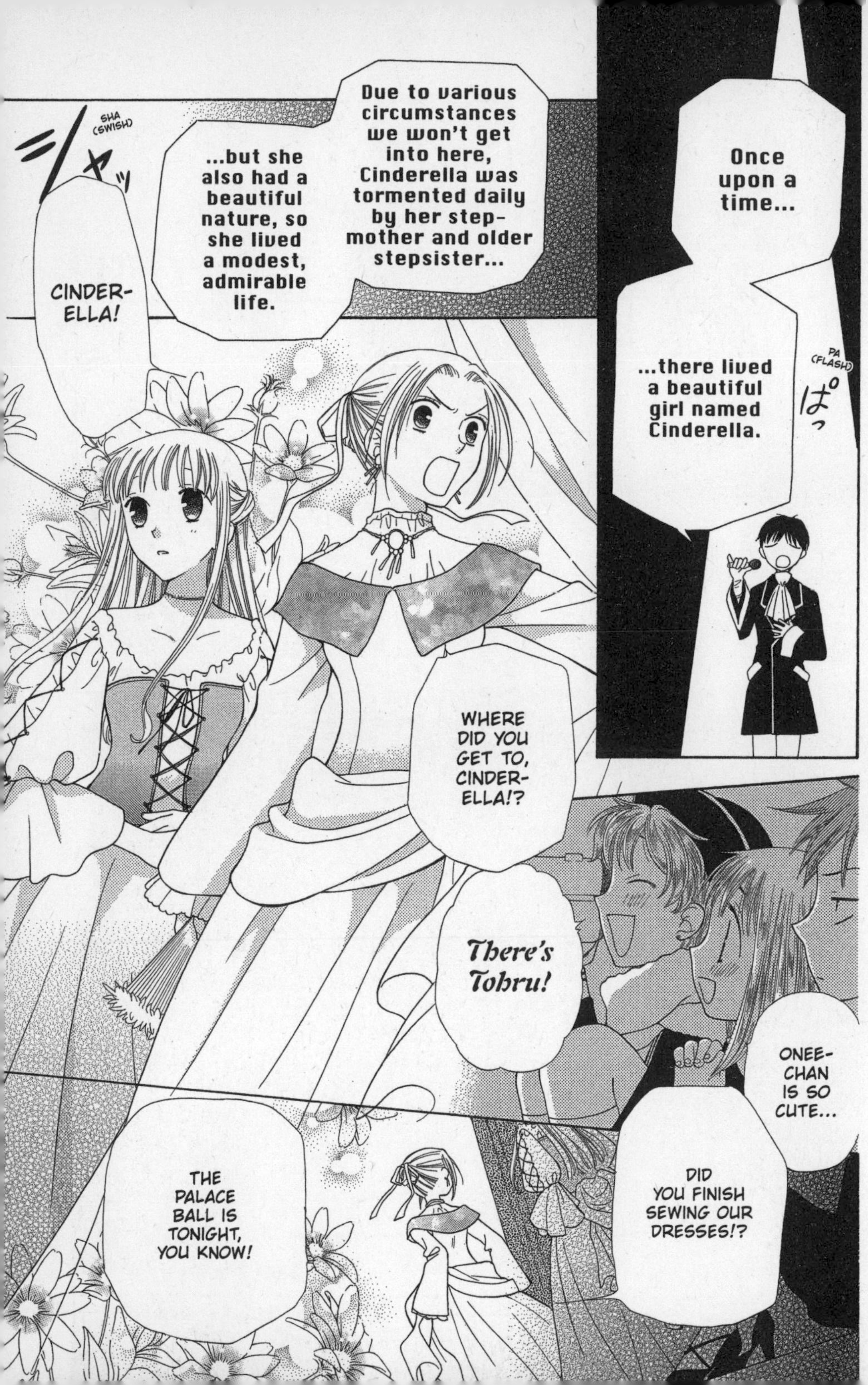
Once upon a time...
...there lived a beautiful girl named Cinderella.
PA (FLASH)
ぱっ
Due to various circumstances we won't get into here, Cinderella was tormented daily by her stepmother and older stepsister...
...but she also had a beautiful nature, so she lived a modest, admirable life.
SHA (SWISH)
シャッ
CINDERELLA!
WHERE DID YOU GET TO, CINDERELLA!?
There's Tohru!
ONEE-CHAN IS SO CUTE...
DID YOU FINISH SEWING OUR DRESSES!?
THE PALACE BALL IS TONIGHT, YOU KNOW!

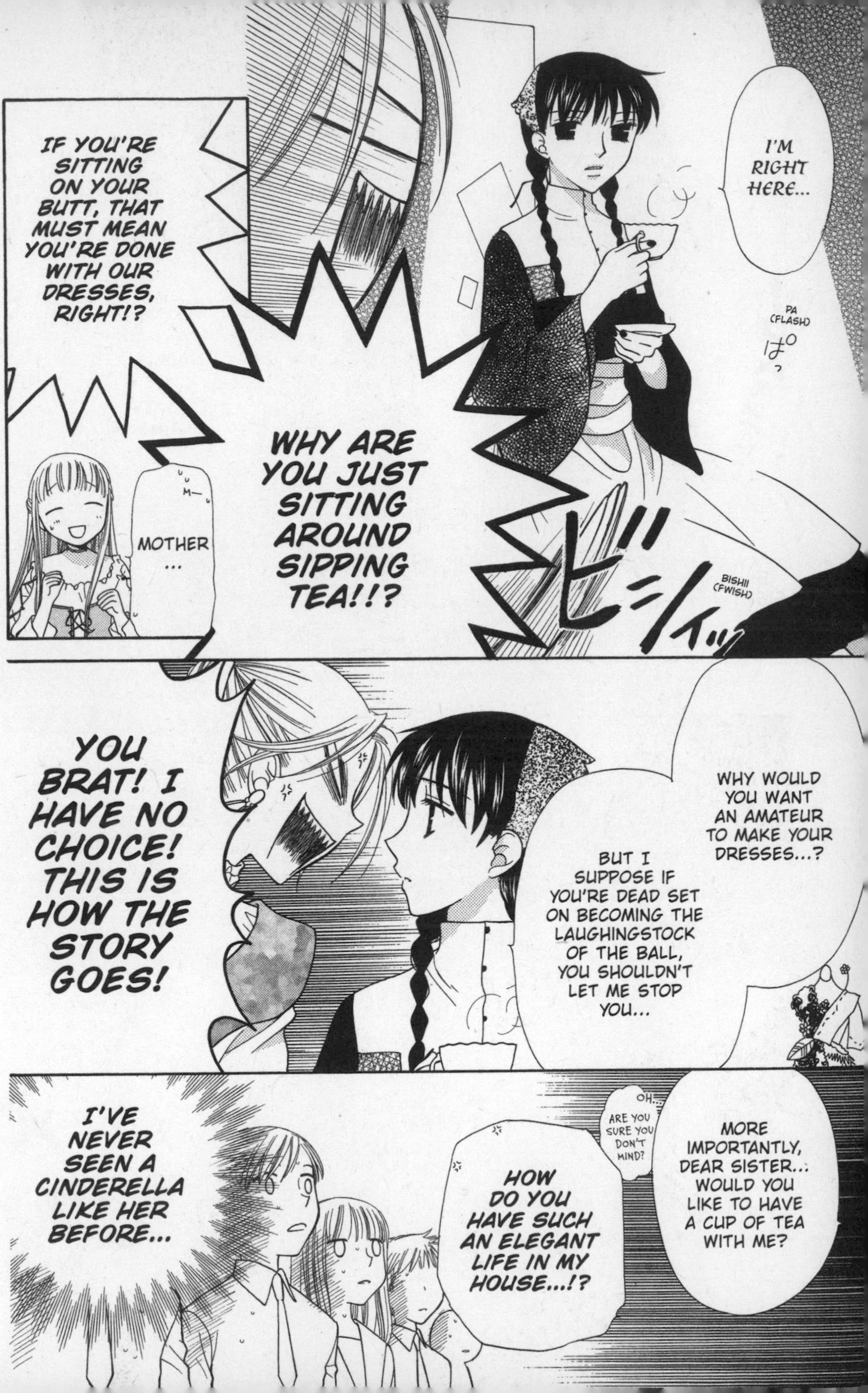

I'M RIGHT HERE...
PA (FLASH)
ぱっ
IF YOU'RE SITTING ON YOUR BUTT, THAT MUST MEAN YOU'RE DONE WITH OUR DRESSES, RIGHT!?
WHY ARE YOU JUST SITTING AROUND SIPPING TEA!!?
BISHII (FWISH)
ビシッ
U U M— MOTHER...
WHY WOULD YOU WANT AN AMATEUR TO MAKE YOUR DRESSES...?
BUT I SUPPOSE IF YOU'RE DEAD SET ON BECOMING THE LAUGHINGSTOCK OF THE BALL, YOU SHOULDN'T LET ME STOP YOU...
YOU BRAT! I HAVE NO CHOICE! THIS IS HOW THE STORY GOES!
MORE IMPORTANTLY, DEAR SISTER... WOULD YOU LIKE TO HAVE A CUP OF TEA WITH ME?
OH... ARE YOU SURE YOU DON'T MIND?
HOW DO YOU HAVE SUCH AN ELEGANT LIFE IN MY HOUSE...!?
I'VE NEVER SEEN A CINDERELLA LIKE HER BEFORE...

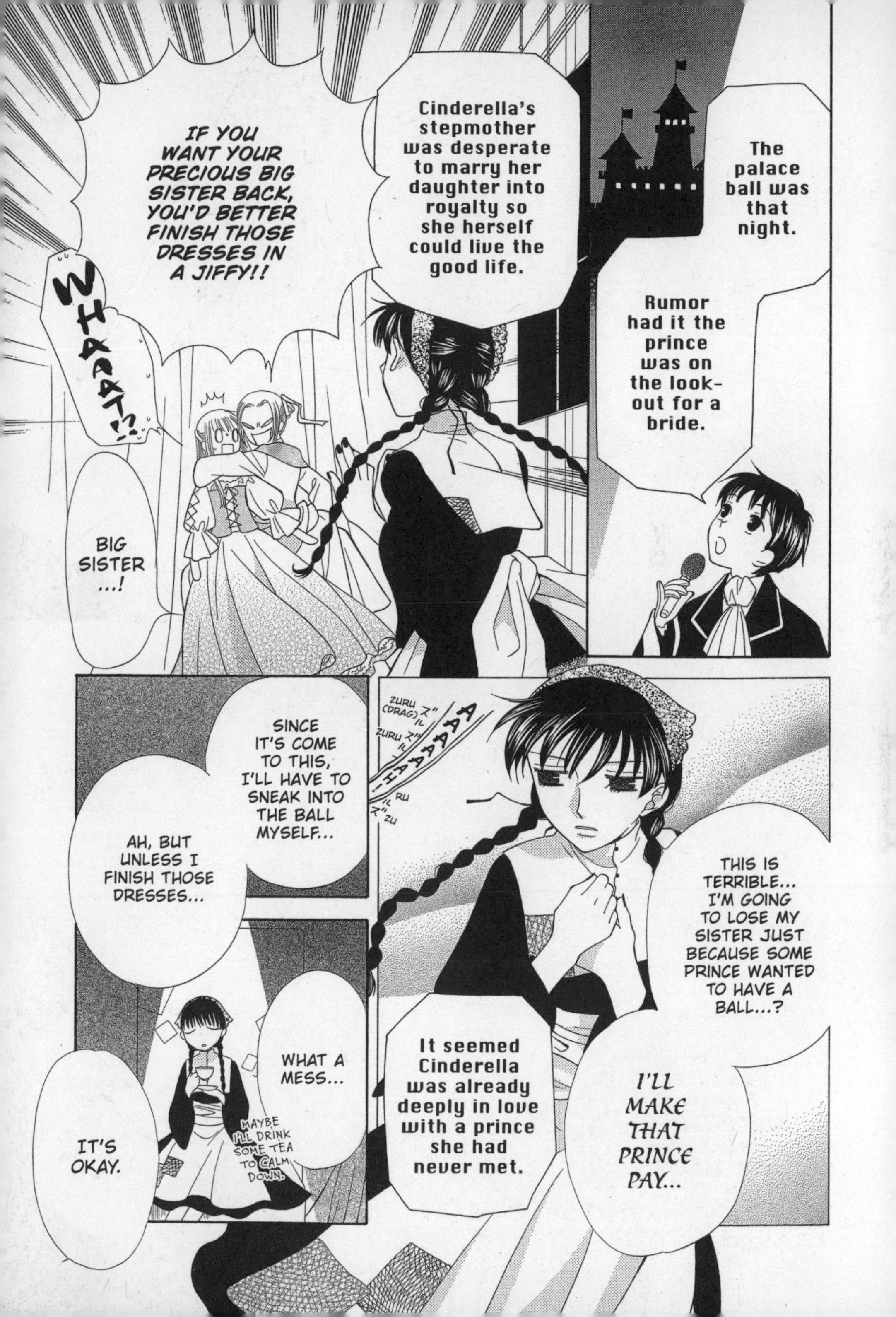
The palace ball was that night.
Rumor had it the prince was on the look-out for a bride.
Cinderella's stepmother was desperate to marry her daughter into royalty so she herself could live the good life.
IF YOU WANT YOUR PRECIOUS BIG SISTER BACK, YOU'D BETTER FINISH THOSE DRESSES IN A JIFFY!!
WHAAAT!?
BIG SISTER ...!
AAAAAH!
ZURU (DRAG) ZURU ZURU ZURU
THIS IS TERRIBLE... I'M GOING TO LOSE MY SISTER JUST BECAUSE SOME PRINCE WANTED TO HAVE A BALL...?
I'LL MAKE THAT PRINCE PAY...
It seemed Cinderella was already deeply in love with a prince she had never met.
SINCE IT'S COME TO THIS, I'LL HAVE TO SNEAK INTO THE BALL MYSELF...
AH, BUT UNLESS I FINISH THOSE DRESSES...
WHAT A MESS...
MAYBE I'LL DRINK SOME TEA TO CALM DOWN.
IT'S OKAY.

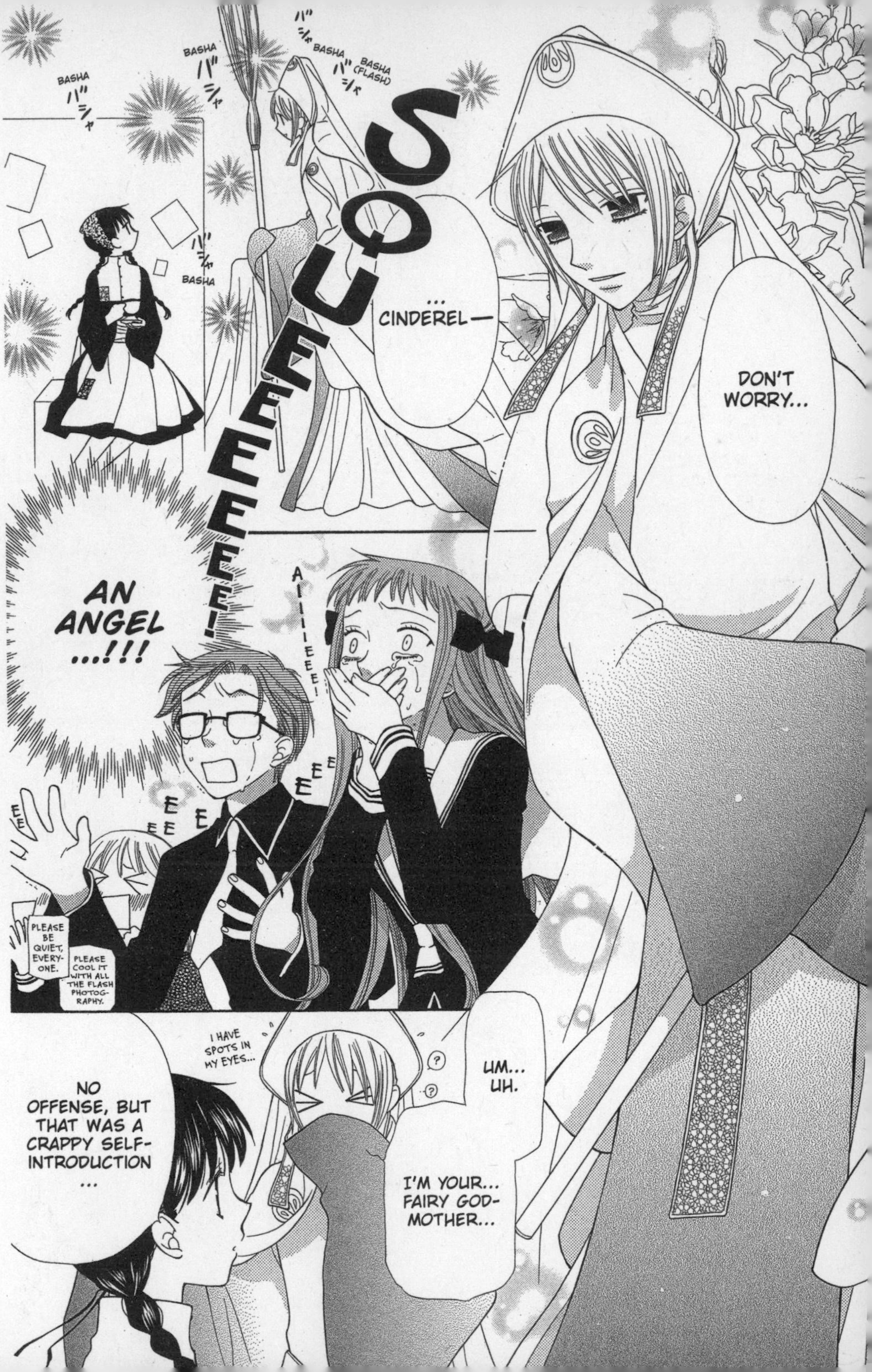

DON'T WORRY...
...CINDEREL—
BASHA
BASHA (FLASH)
BASHA
BASHA
BASHA
SQUEEEEEEEE!
AIIIEEE!
AN ANGEL ...!!!
EEE
EEE
EE
PLEASE COOL IT WITH ALL THE FLASH PHOTOGRAPHY.
PLEASE BE QUIET, EVERY-ONE.
I'M YOUR... FAIRY GOD-MOTHER...
UM... UH.
I HAVE SPOTS IN MY EYES...
NO OFFENSE, BUT THAT WAS A CRAPPY SELF-INTRODUCTION ...

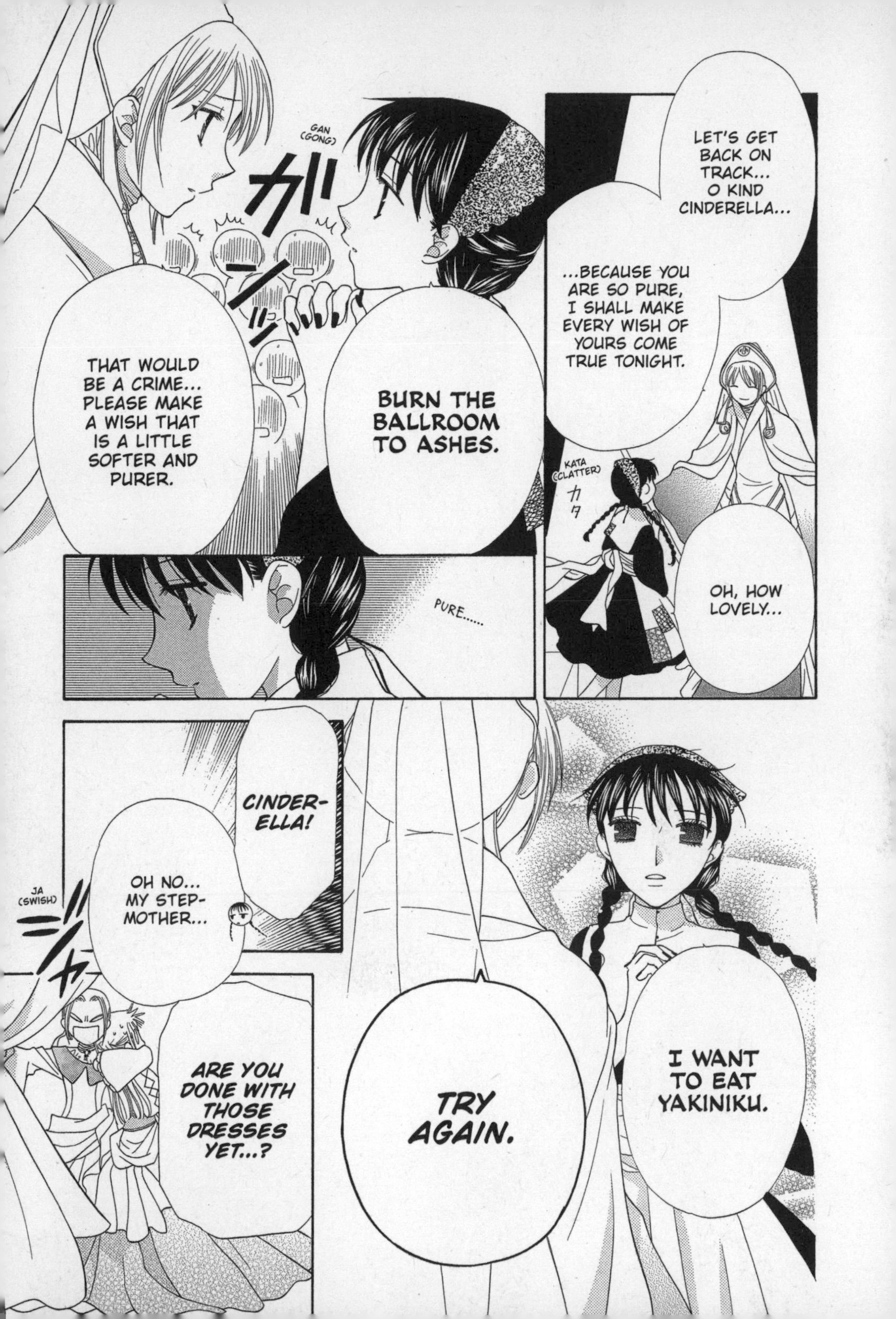
LET'S GET BACK ON TRACK... O KIND CINDERELLA...
...BECAUSE YOU ARE SO PURE, I SHALL MAKE EVERY WISH OF YOURS COME TRUE TONIGHT.
KATA (CLATTER)
OH, HOW LOVELY...
GAN (GONG)
BURN THE BALLROOM TO ASHES.
THAT WOULD BE A CRIME... PLEASE MAKE A WISH THAT IS A LITTLE SOFTER AND PURER.
PURE......
I WANT TO EAT YAKINIKU.
TRY AGAIN.
CINDER-ELLA!
OH NO... MY STEP-MOTHER...
JA (SWISH)
ARE YOU DONE WITH THOSE DRESSES YET...?

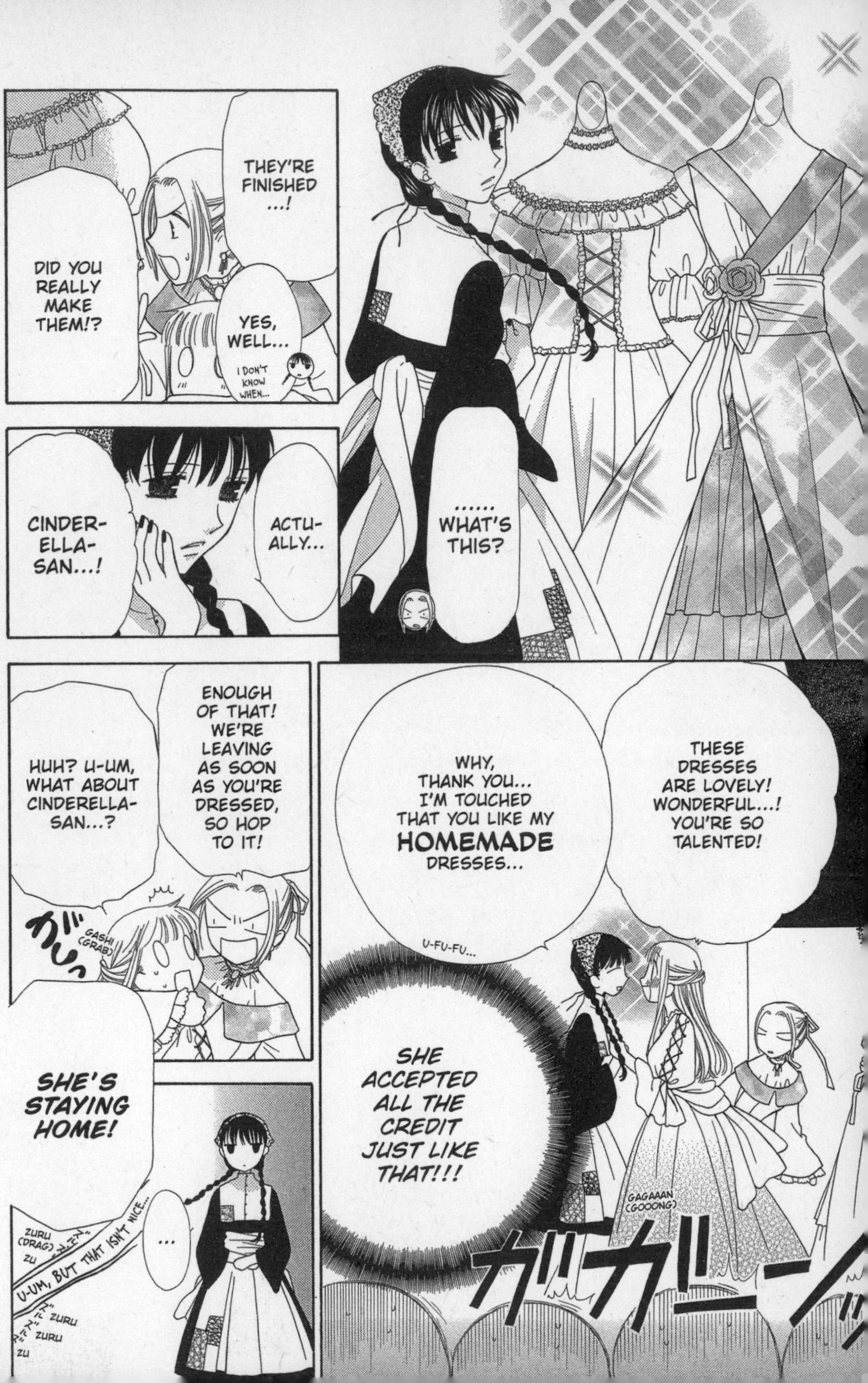
......
WHAT'S THIS?
THEY'RE FINISHED ...!
DID YOU REALLY MAKE THEM!?
YES, WELL...
I DON'T KNOW WHEN...
ACTUALLY...
CINDERELLA-SAN...!
THESE DRESSES ARE LOVELY! WONDERFUL...! YOU'RE SO TALENTED!
WHY, THANK YOU... I'M TOUCHED THAT YOU LIKE MY HOMEMADE DRESSES...
U-FU-FU...
SHE ACCEPTED ALL THE CREDIT JUST LIKE THAT!!!
GAGAAAN (GOOONG)
ENOUGH OF THAT! WE'RE LEAVING AS SOON AS YOU'RE DRESSED, SO HOP TO IT!
HUH? U-UM, WHAT ABOUT CINDERELLA-SAN...?
GASHI (GRAB)
SHE'S STAYING HOME!
...
U-UM, BUT THAT ISN'T NICE...
ZURU (DRAG) ZU
ZURU ZURU ZU

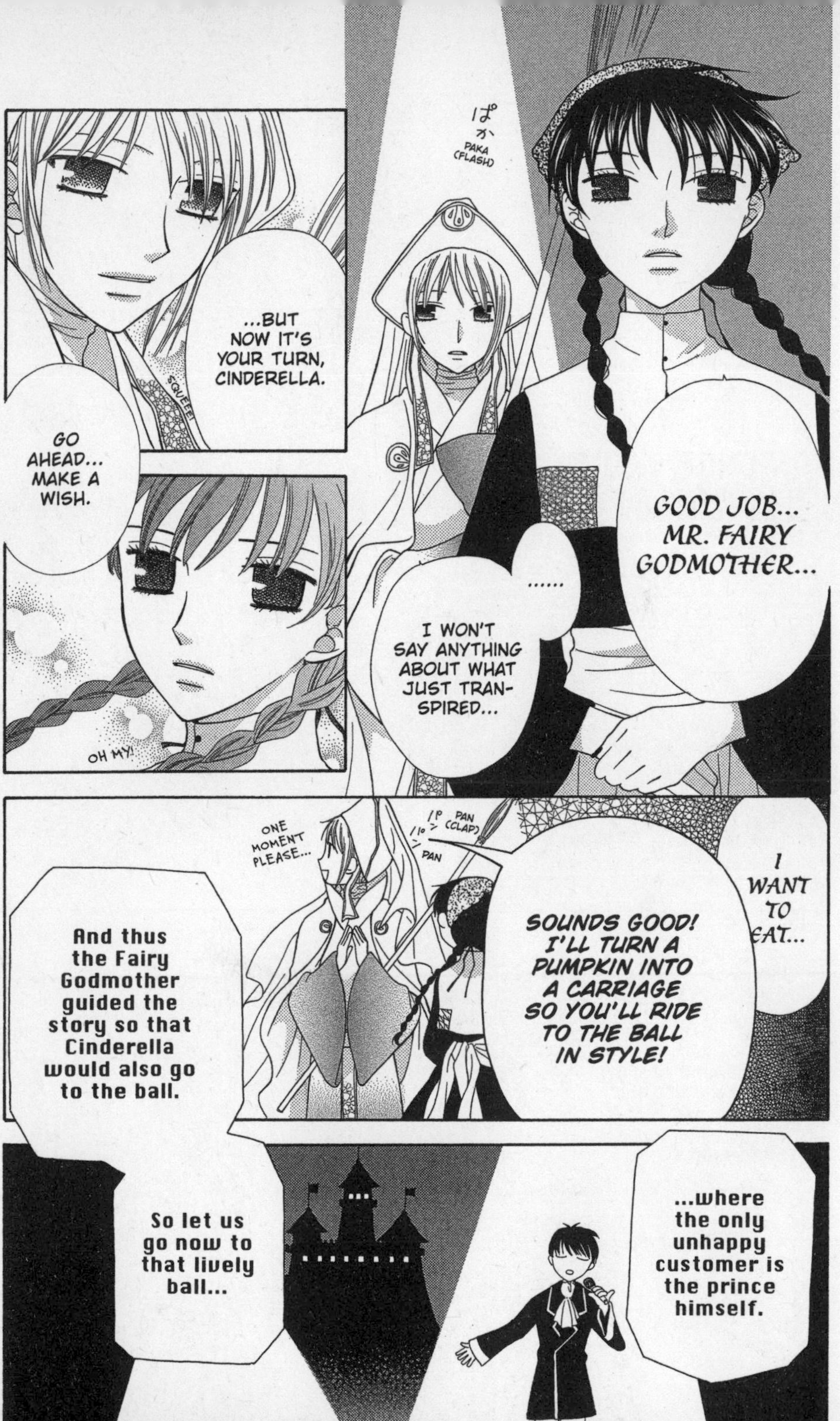
ぱか
PAKA (FLASH)
GOOD JOB... MR. FAIRY GODMOTHER...
......
I WON'T SAY ANYTHING ABOUT WHAT JUST TRANSPIRED...
...BUT NOW IT'S YOUR TURN, CINDERELLA.
SQUEE!
GO AHEAD... MAKE A WISH.
OH MY!
I WANT TO EAT...
SOUNDS GOOD! I'LL TURN A PUMPKIN INTO A CARRIAGE SO YOU'LL RIDE TO THE BALL IN STYLE!
ぱん PAN (CLAP)
ぱん PAN
ONE MOMENT PLEASE...
And thus the Fairy Godmother guided the story so that Cinderella would also go to the ball.
So let us go now to that lively ball...
...where the only unhappy customer is the prince himself.

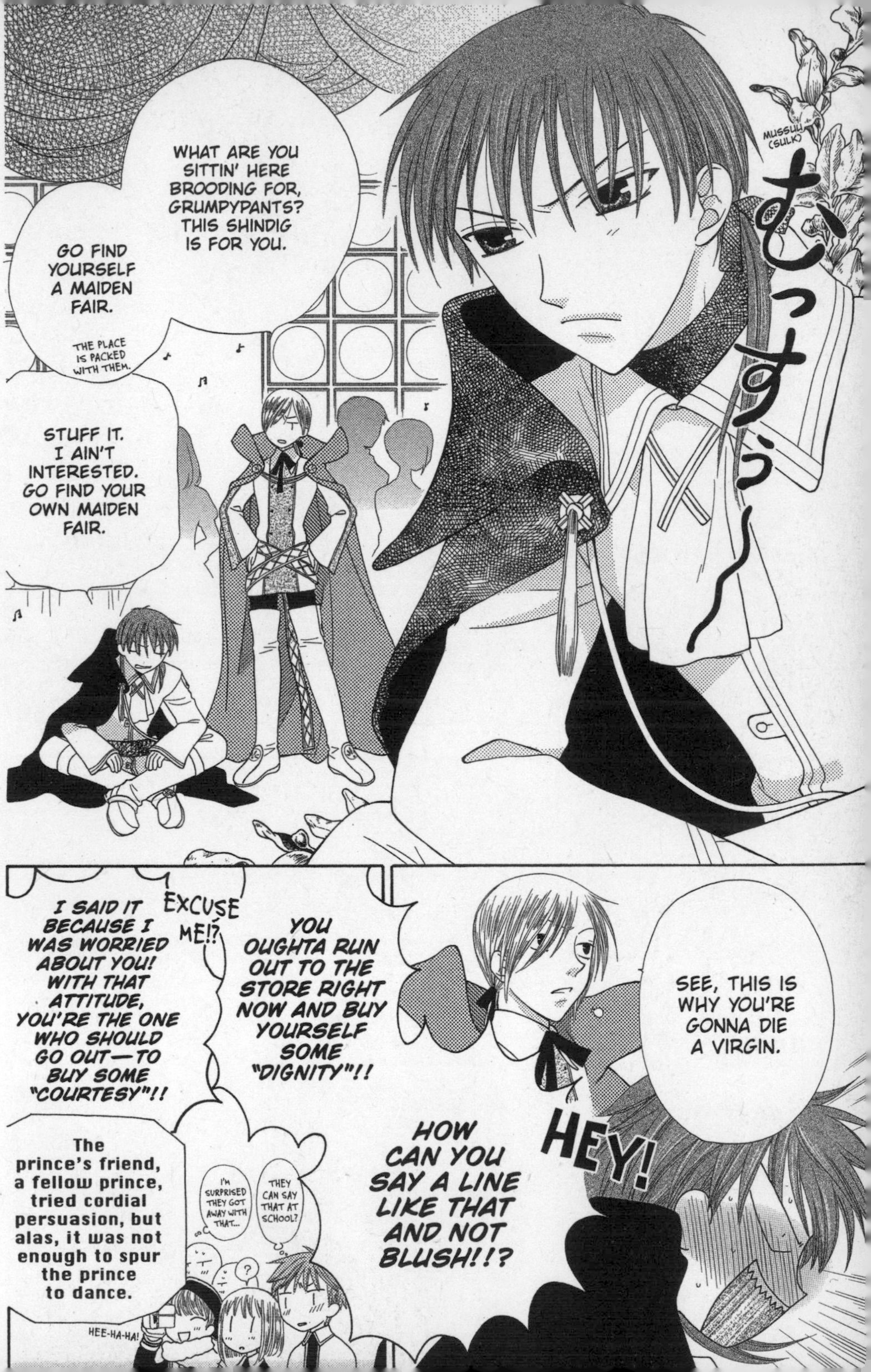
MUSSUU (SULK)
むっすぅ~
WHAT ARE YOU SITTIN' HERE BROODING FOR, GRUMPYPANTS? THIS SHINDIG IS FOR YOU.
GO FIND YOURSELF A MAIDEN FAIR.
THE PLACE IS PACKED WITH THEM.
STUFF IT. I AIN'T INTERESTED. GO FIND YOUR OWN MAIDEN FAIR.
SEE, THIS IS WHY YOU'RE GONNA DIE A VIRGIN.
HEY!
HOW CAN YOU SAY A LINE LIKE THAT AND NOT BLUSH!!?
YOU OUGHTA RUN OUT TO THE STORE RIGHT NOW AND BUY YOURSELF SOME "DIGNITY"!!
EXCUSE ME!?
I SAID IT BECAUSE I WAS WORRIED ABOUT YOU! WITH THAT ATTITUDE, YOU'RE THE ONE WHO SHOULD GO OUT—TO BUY SOME "COURTESY"!!
The prince's friend, a fellow prince, tried cordial persuasion, but alas, it was not enough to spur the prince to dance.
THEY CAN SAY THAT AT SCHOOL?
I'M SURPRISED THEY GOT AWAY WITH THAT...
HEE-HA-HA!

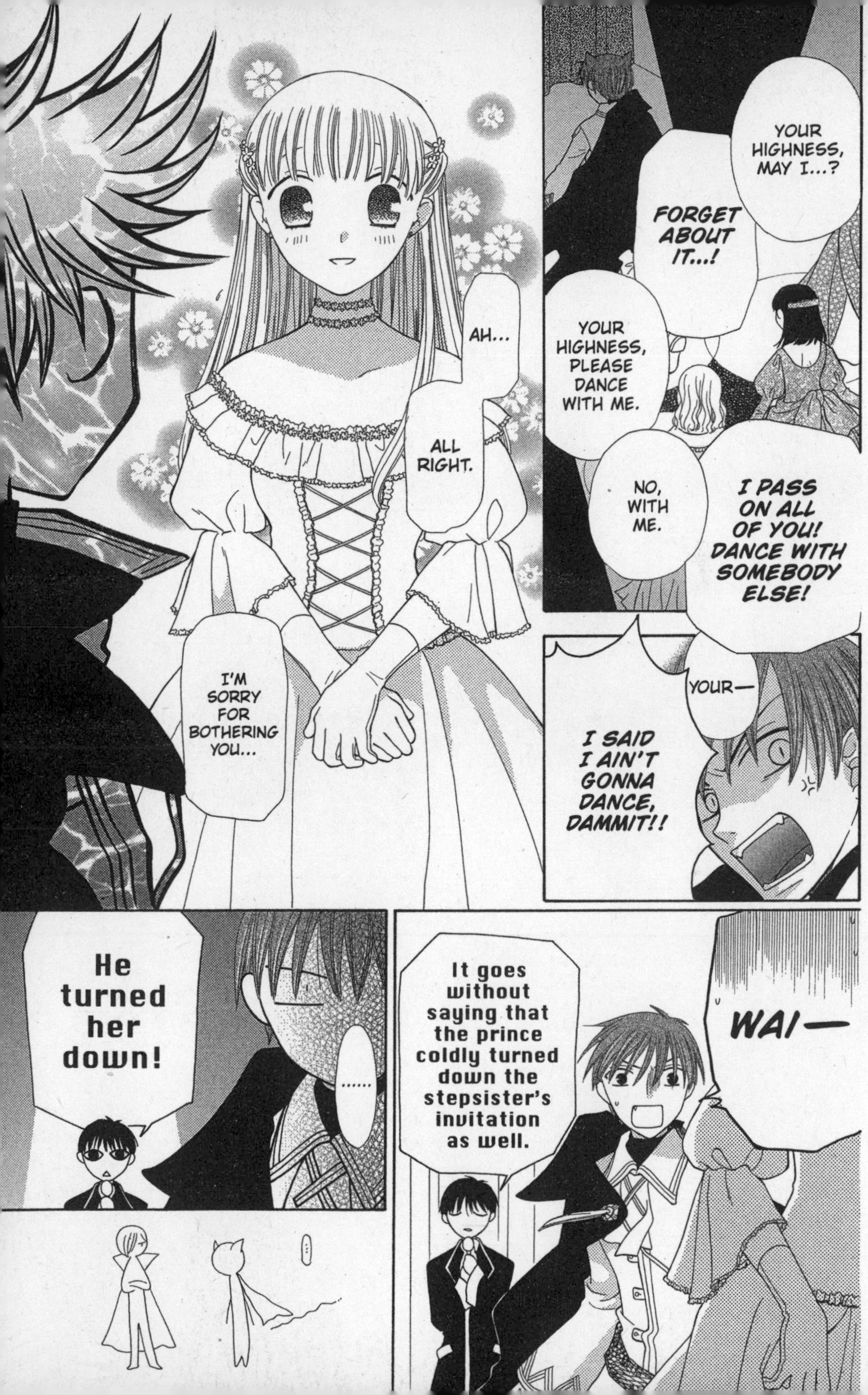
YOUR HIGHNESS, MAY I...?
FORGET ABOUT IT...!
YOUR HIGHNESS, PLEASE DANCE WITH ME.
NO, WITH ME.
I PASS ON ALL OF YOU! DANCE WITH SOMEBODY ELSE!
YOUR—
I SAID I AIN'T GONNA DANCE, DAMMIT!!
AH...
ALL RIGHT.
I'M SORRY FOR BOTHERING YOU...
WAI—
It goes without saying that the prince coldly turned down the stepsister's invitation as well.
He turned her down!
......

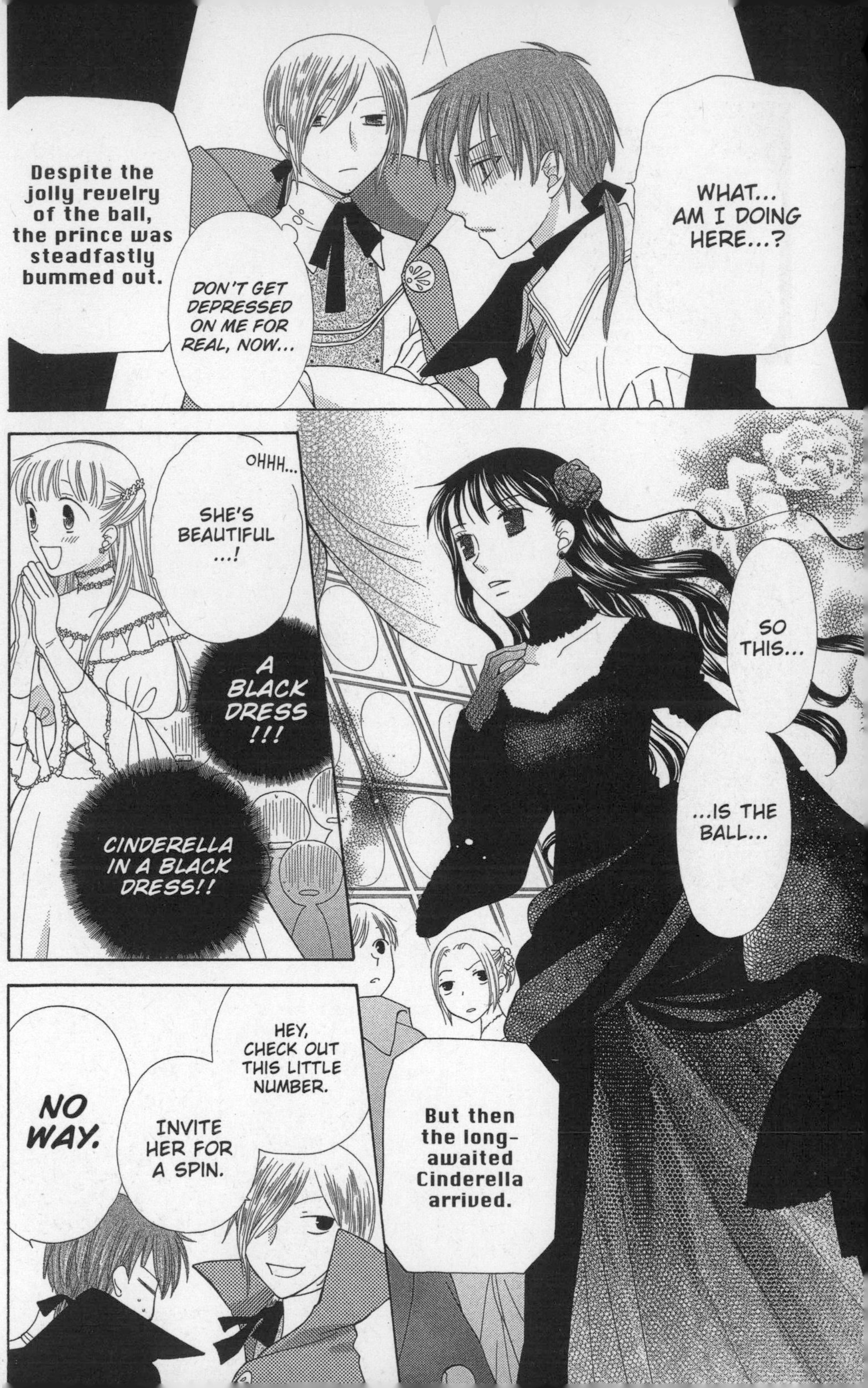
WHAT... AM I DOING HERE...?
Despite the jolly revelry of the ball, the prince was steadfastly bummed out.
DON'T GET DEPRESSED ON ME FOR REAL, NOW...
SO THIS...
...IS THE BALL...
OHHH...
SHE'S BEAUTIFUL ...!
A BLACK DRESS !!!
CINDERELLA IN A BLACK DRESS!!
But then the long-awaited Cinderella arrived.
HEY, CHECK OUT THIS LITTLE NUMBER.
INVITE HER FOR A SPIN.
NO WAY.

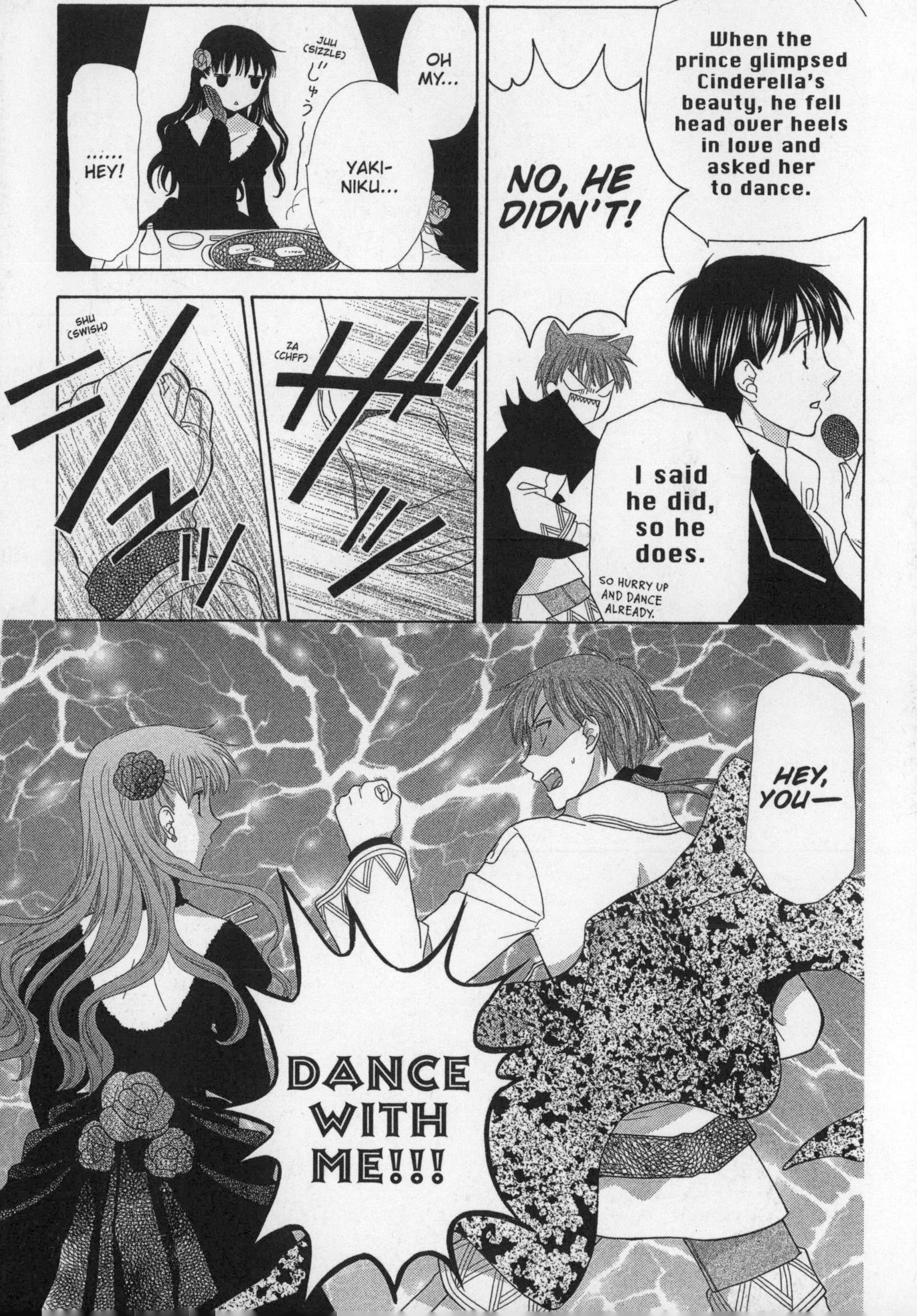
When the prince glimpsed Cinderella's beauty, he fell head over heels in love and asked her to dance.
NO, HE DIDN'T!
I said he did, so he does.
SO HURRY UP AND DANCE ALREADY.
OH MY...
JUU (SIZZLE)
じゅう~
YAKI-NIKU...
......HEY!
ZA (CHFF)
SHU (SWISH)
HEY, YOU—
DANCE WITH ME!!!

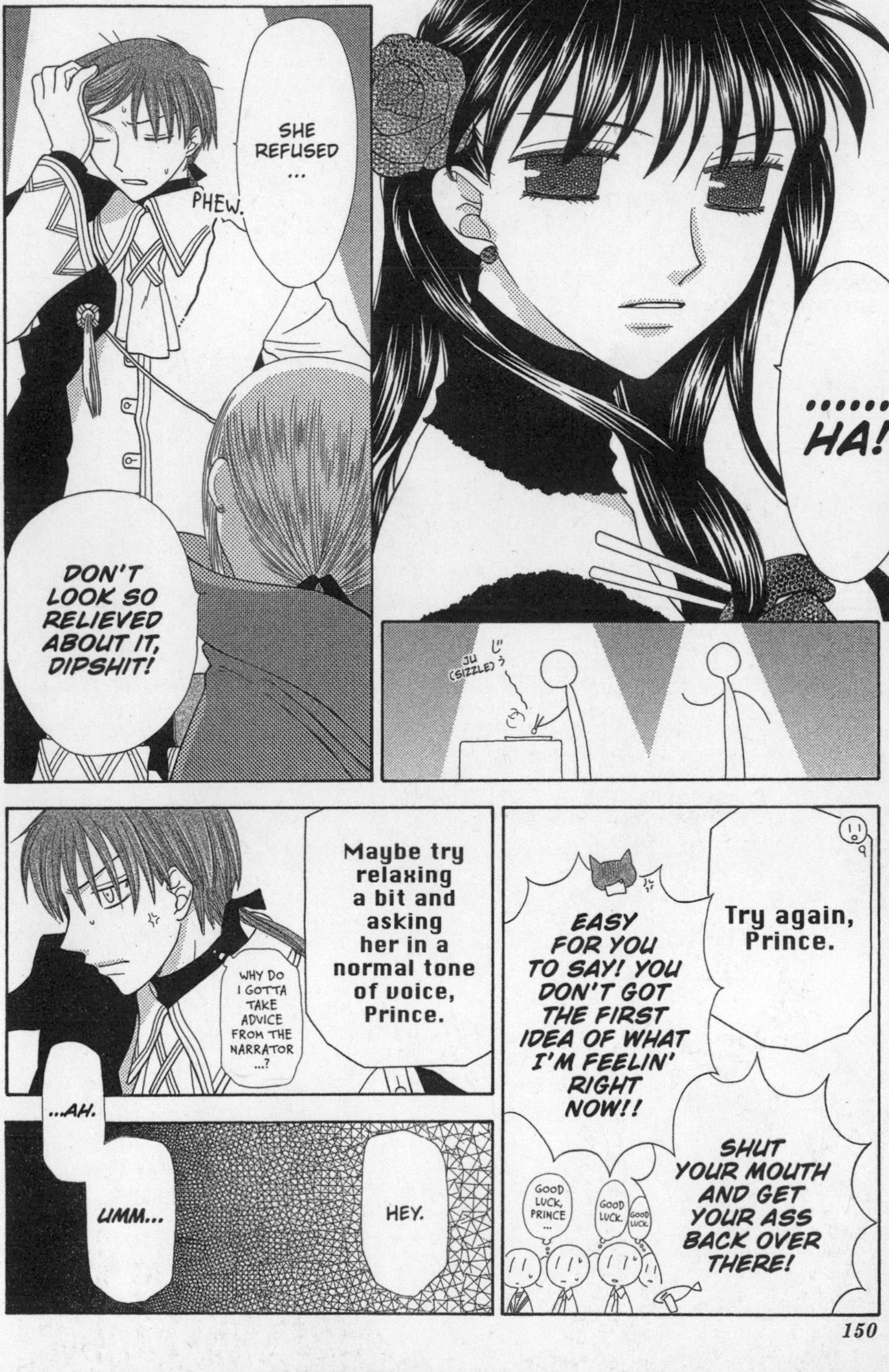
......HA!
JU (SIZZLE)
SHE REFUSED...
PHEW.
DON'T LOOK SO RELIEVED ABOUT IT, DIPSHIT!
Try again, Prince.
EASY FOR YOU TO SAY! YOU DON'T GOT THE FIRST IDEA OF WHAT I'M FEELIN' RIGHT NOW!!
SHUT YOUR MOUTH AND GET YOUR ASS BACK OVER THERE!
GOOD LUCK.
GOOD LUCK.
GOOD LUCK, PRINCE...
Maybe try relaxing a bit and asking her in a normal tone of voice, Prince.
WHY DO I GOTTA TAKE ADVICE FROM THE NARRATOR...?
HEY.
UMM...
...AH.

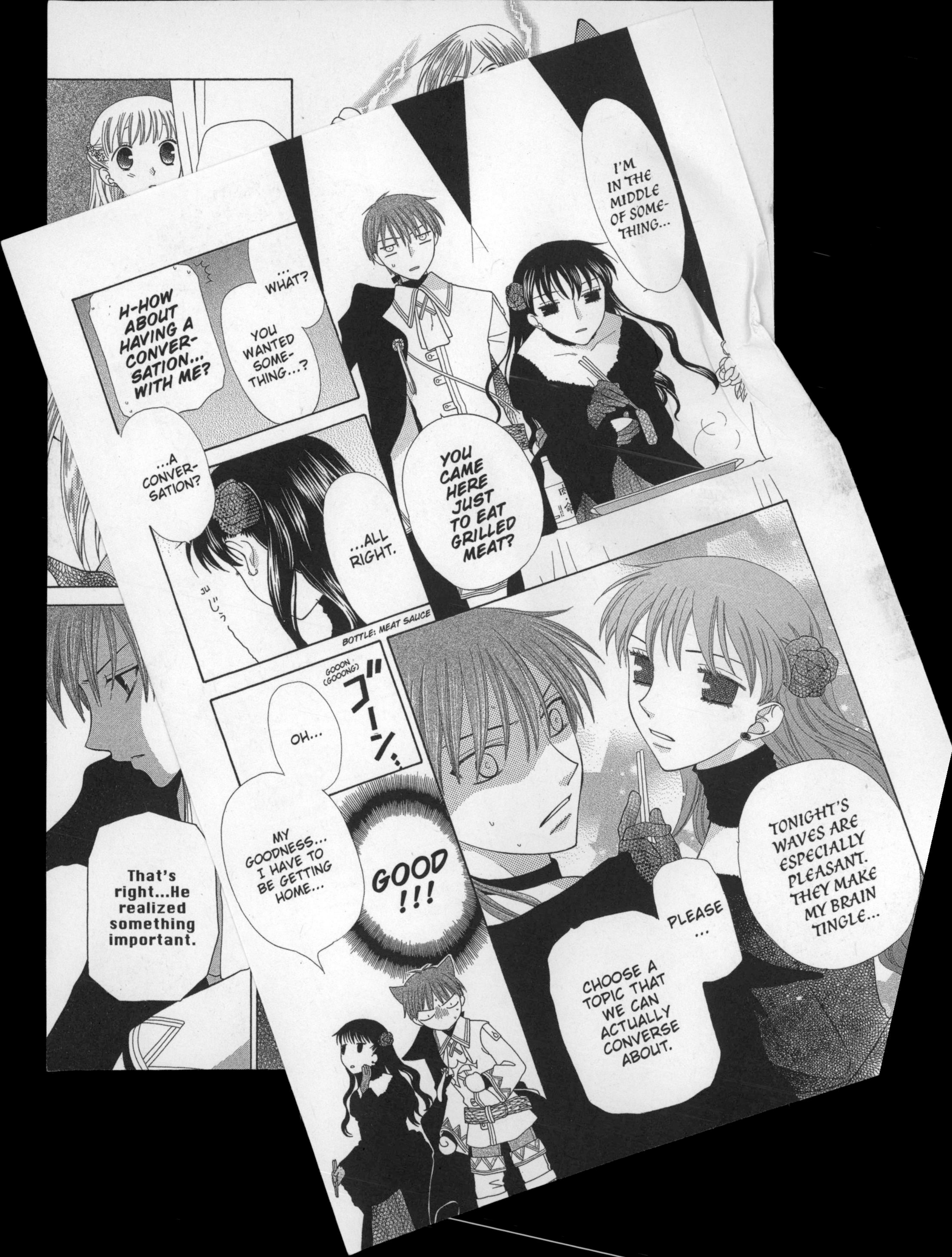
I'M IN THE MIDDLE OF SOME-THING...
...WHAT?
YOU WANTED SOME-THING...?
H-HOW ABOUT HAVING A CONVER-SATION... WITH ME?
YOU CAME HERE JUST TO EAT GRILLED MEAT?
...ALL RIGHT.
...A CONVER-SATION?
JU じゅう
BOTTLE: MEAT SAUCE
TONIGHT'S WAVES ARE ESPECIALLY PLEASANT. THEY MAKE MY BRAIN TINGLE...
GOOON (GOOONG)
ゴーン
OH...
MY GOODNESS... I HAVE TO BE GETTING HOME...
GOOD !!!
PLEASE ...
CHOOSE A TOPIC THAT WE CAN ACTUALLY CONVERSE ABOUT.
That's right...He realized something important.

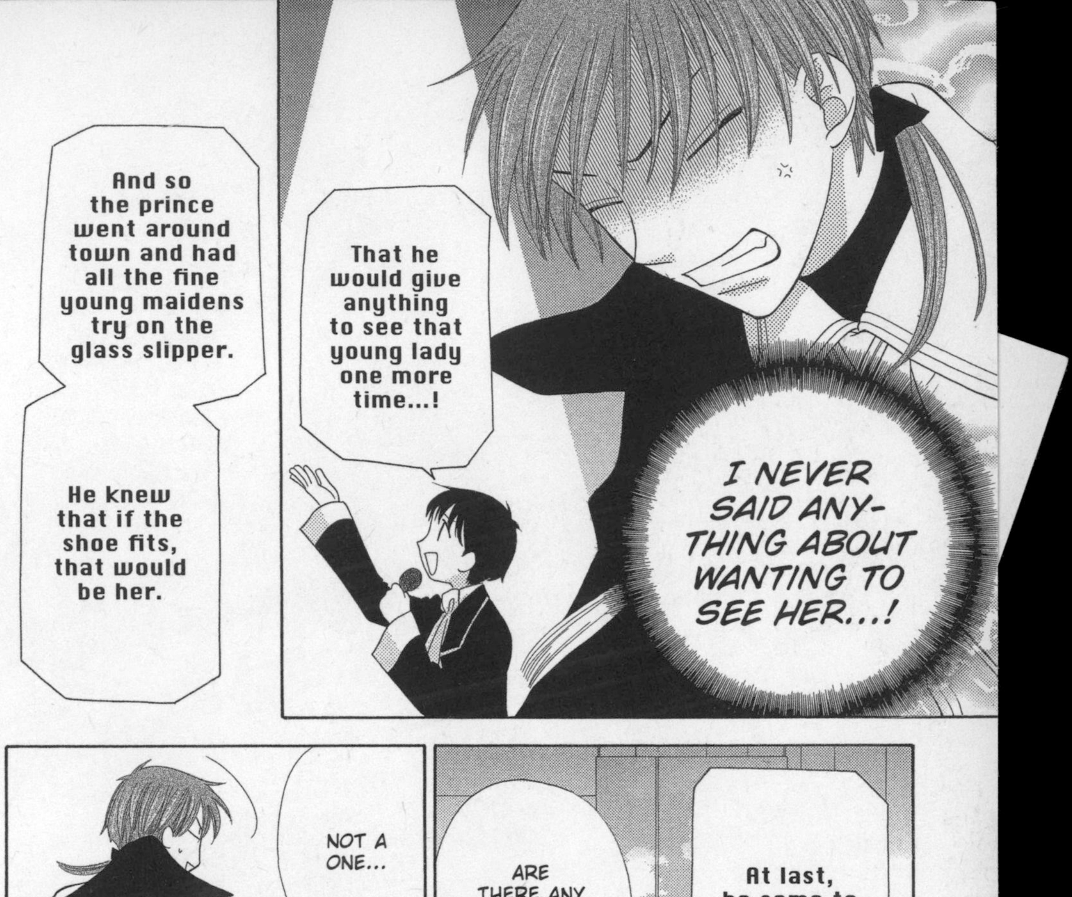
That he would give anything to see that young lady one more time...!
I NEVER SAID ANY-THING ABOUT WANTING TO SEE HER...!
And so the prince went around town and had all the fine young maidens try on the glass slipper.
He knew that if the shoe fits, that would be her.
At last, he came to Cinderella's house.
ARE THERE ANY OTHER FAIR MAIDENS IN THIS HOME?
THAT'S NOT MY SHOE...
NOT A ONE...
OH-HO-HO!
I SEE. THEN WE'RE OUTTA HERE.
UM...?
PLEASE WAIT. THERE IS ONE MORE... CINDERELLA-SAN...

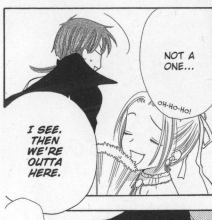

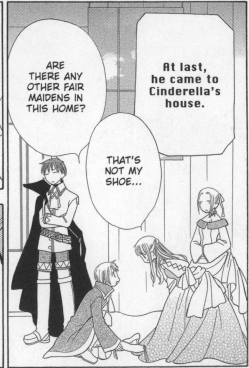

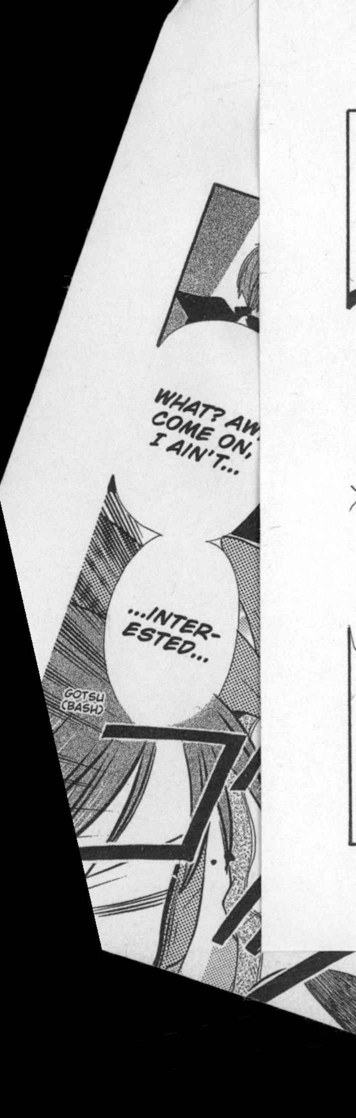
WHAT? AW COME ON, I AIN'T...
...INTER-ESTED...
GOTSU (BASH)

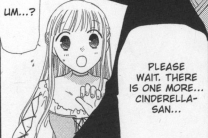

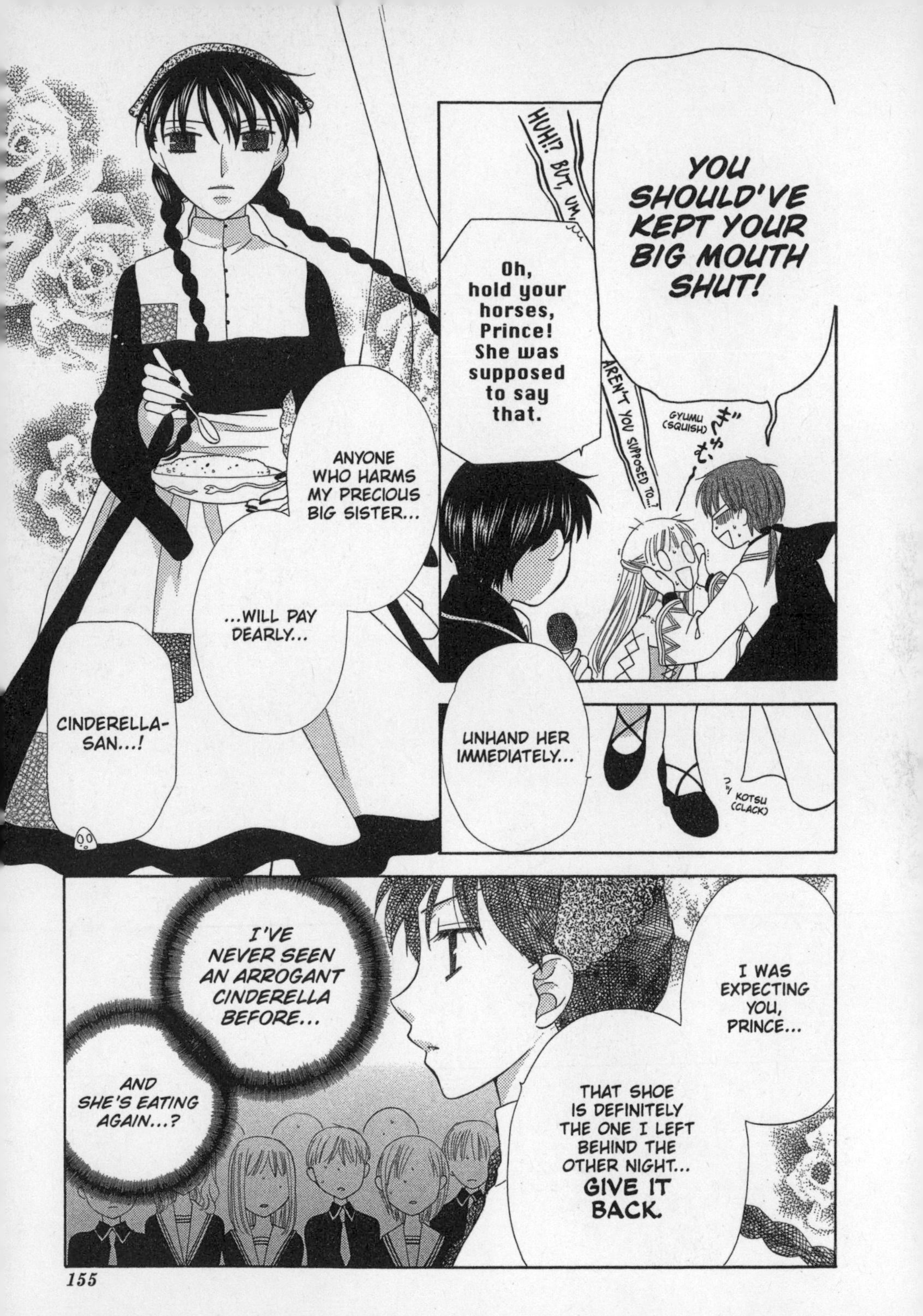
YOU SHOULD'VE KEPT YOUR BIG MOUTH SHUT!
HUH!? BUT, UM...
Oh, hold your horses, Prince! She was supposed to say that.
AREN'T YOU SUPPOSED TO...?
ぎゅむ
GYUMU (SQUISH)
UNHAND HER IMMEDIATELY...
KOTSU (CLACK)
ANYONE WHO HARMS MY PRECIOUS BIG SISTER...
...WILL PAY DEARLY...
CINDERELLA-SAN...!
I WAS EXPECTING YOU, PRINCE...
THAT SHOE IS DEFINITELY THE ONE I LEFT BEHIND THE OTHER NIGHT... GIVE IT BACK.
I'VE NEVER SEEN AN ARROGANT CINDERELLA BEFORE...
AND SHE'S EATING AGAIN...?

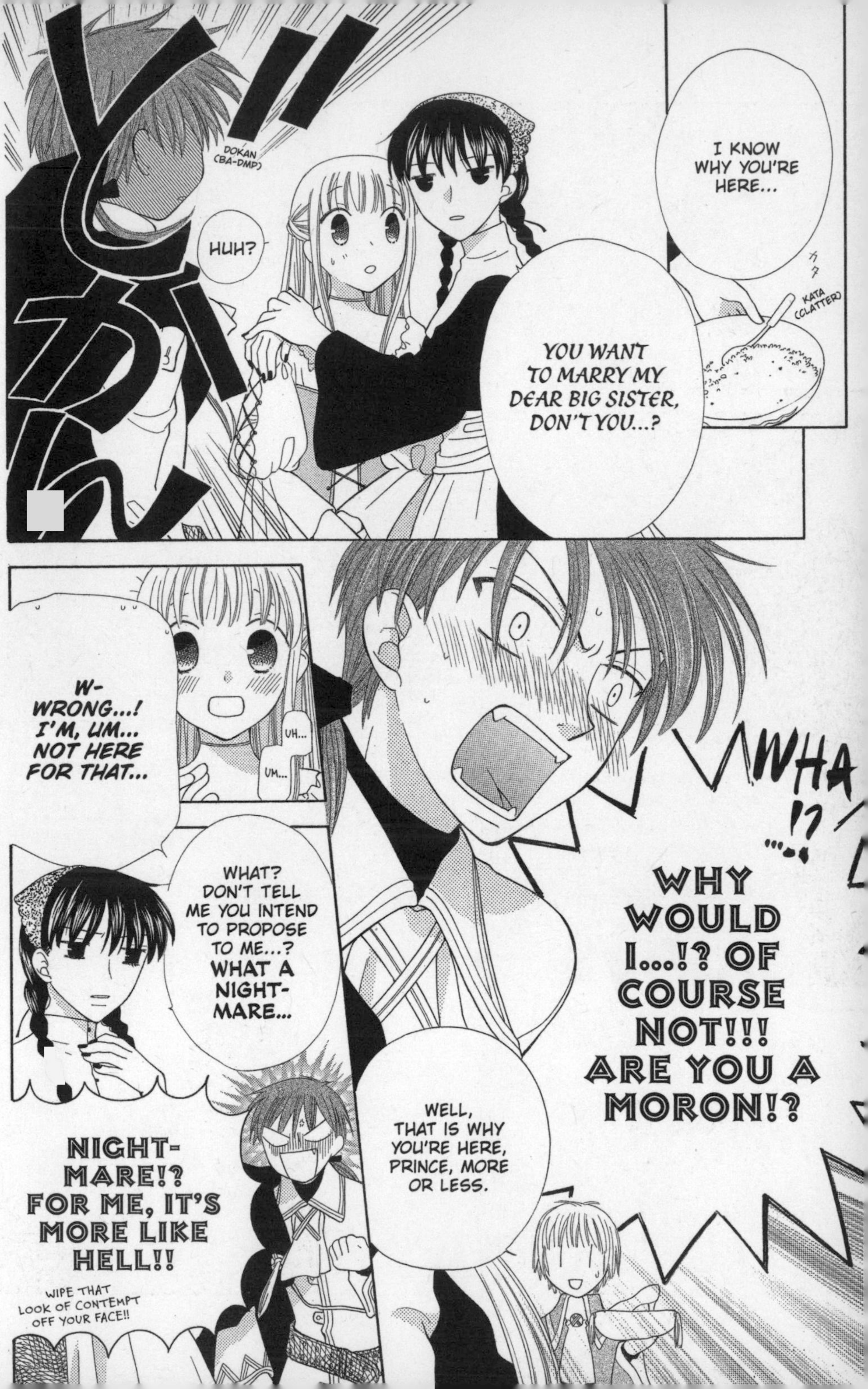

I KNOW WHY YOU'RE HERE...
KATA (CLATTER)
YOU WANT TO MARRY MY DEAR BIG SISTER, DON'T YOU...?
DOKAN (BA-DMP)
HUH?
WHA!?
WHY WOULD I...!? OF COURSE NOT!!! ARE YOU A MORON!?
W-WRONG...! I'M, UM... NOT HERE FOR THAT...
UH...
UM...
WHAT? DON'T TELL ME YOU INTEND TO PROPOSE TO ME...? WHAT A NIGHT-MARE...
WELL, THAT IS WHY YOU'RE HERE, PRINCE, MORE OR LESS.
NIGHT-MARE!? FOR ME, IT'S MORE LIKE HELL!!
WIPE THAT LOOK OF CONTEMPT OFF YOUR FACE!!

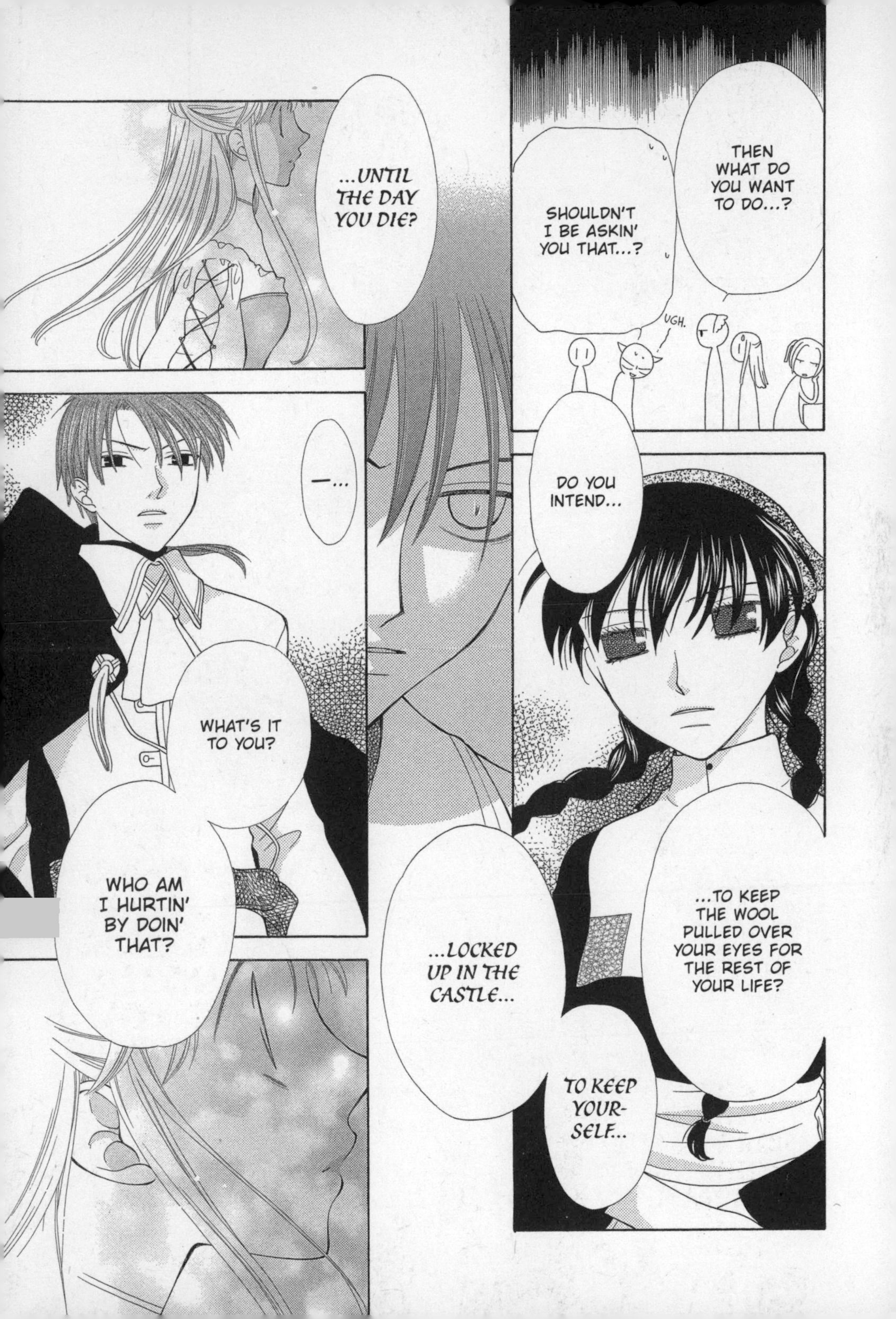
THEN WHAT DO YOU WANT TO DO...?
SHOULDN'T I BE ASKIN' YOU THAT...?
UGH.
DO YOU INTEND...
...TO KEEP THE WOOL PULLED OVER YOUR EYES FOR THE REST OF YOUR LIFE?
TO KEEP YOURSELF...
...LOCKED UP IN THE CASTLE...
...UNTIL THE DAY YOU DIE?
—...
WHAT'S IT TO YOU?
WHO AM I HURTIN' BY DOIN' THAT?

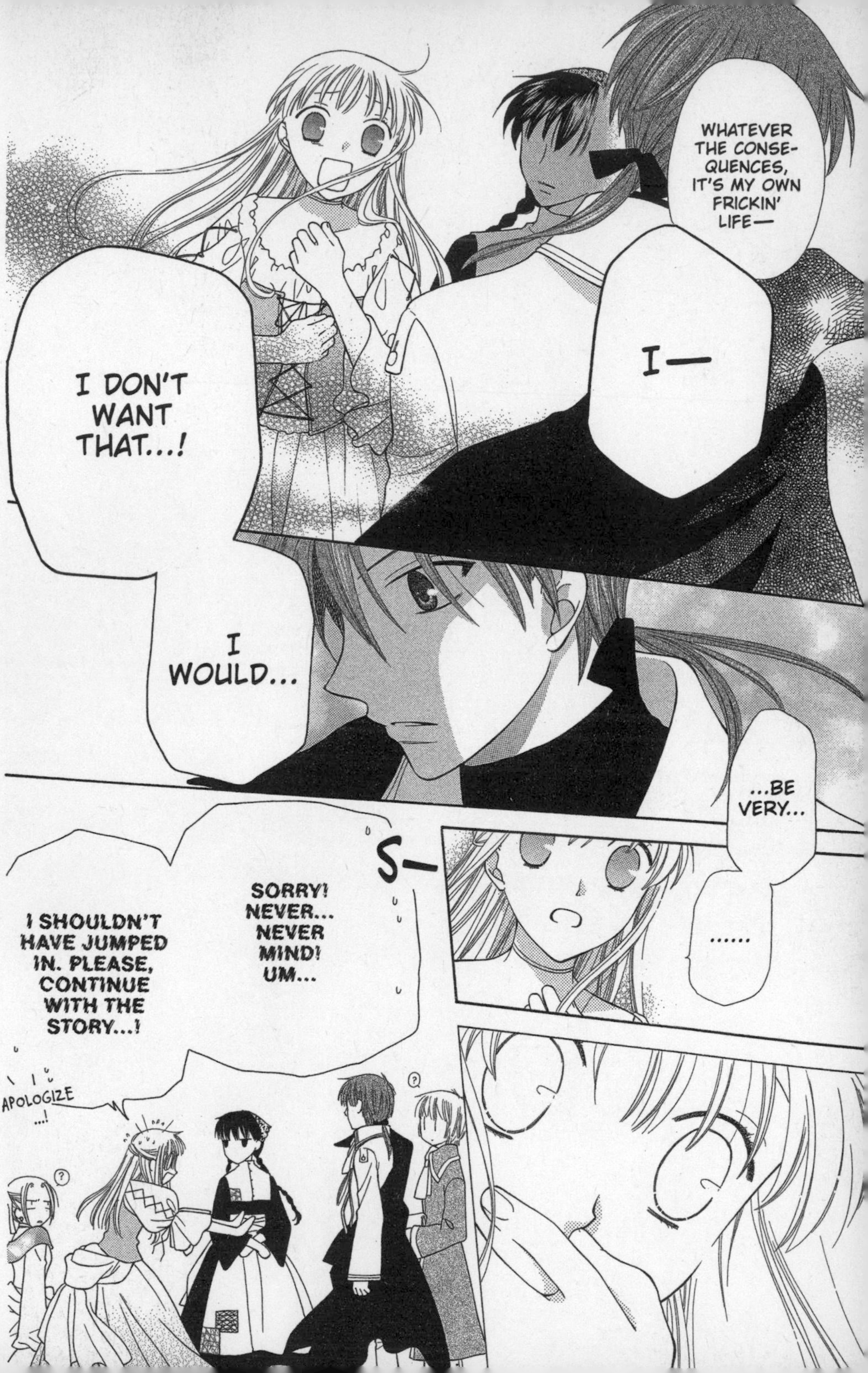
WHATEVER THE CONSE-QUENCES, IT'S MY OWN FRICKIN' LIFE—
I—
I DON'T WANT THAT...!
I WOULD...
...BE VERY...
......
S—
SORRY! NEVER... NEVER MIND! UM...
I SHOULDN'T HAVE JUMPED IN. PLEASE, CONTINUE WITH THE STORY...!
APOLOGIZE ...!

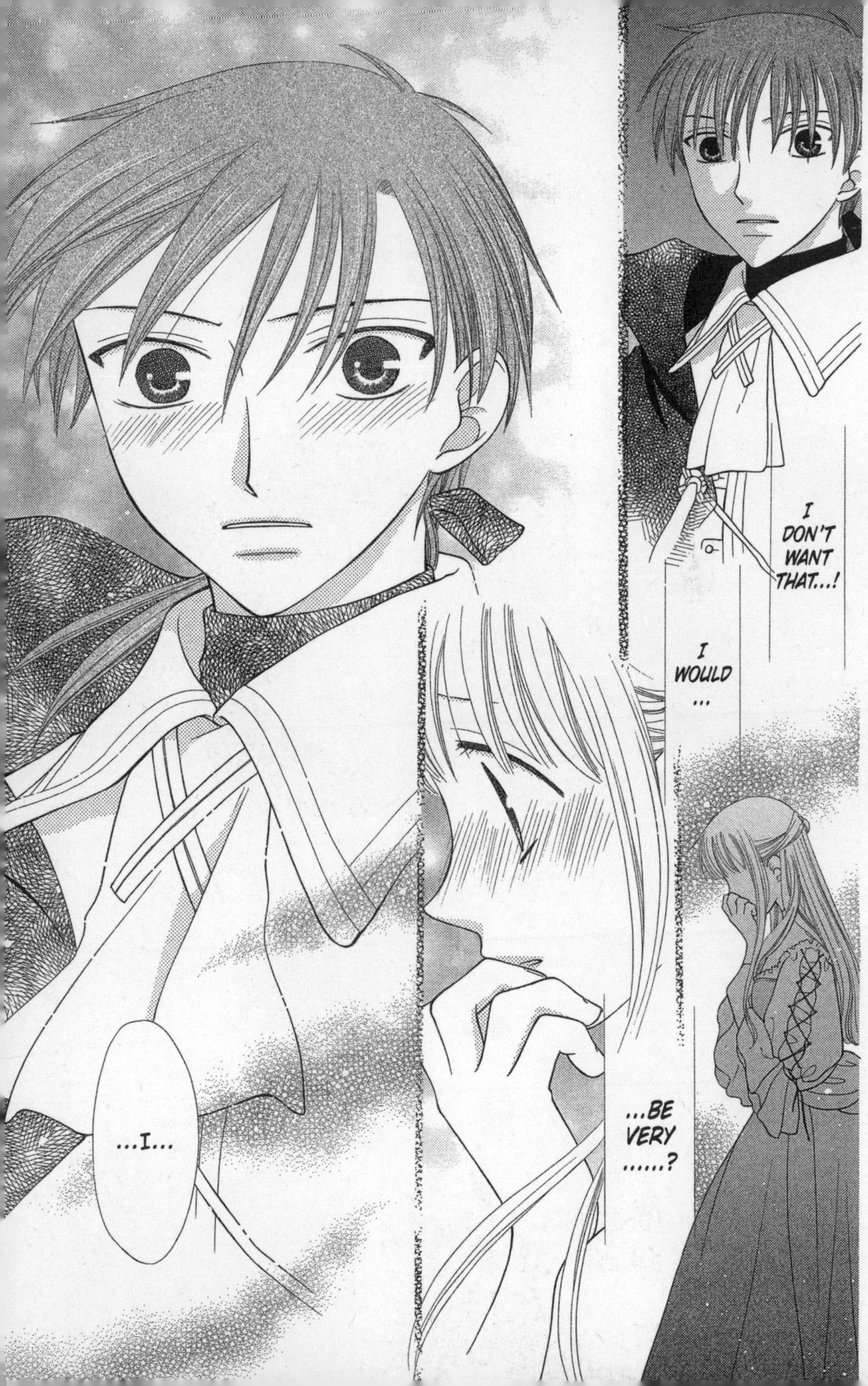
I DON'T WANT THAT...!
I WOULD ...
...BE VERY ......?
...I...

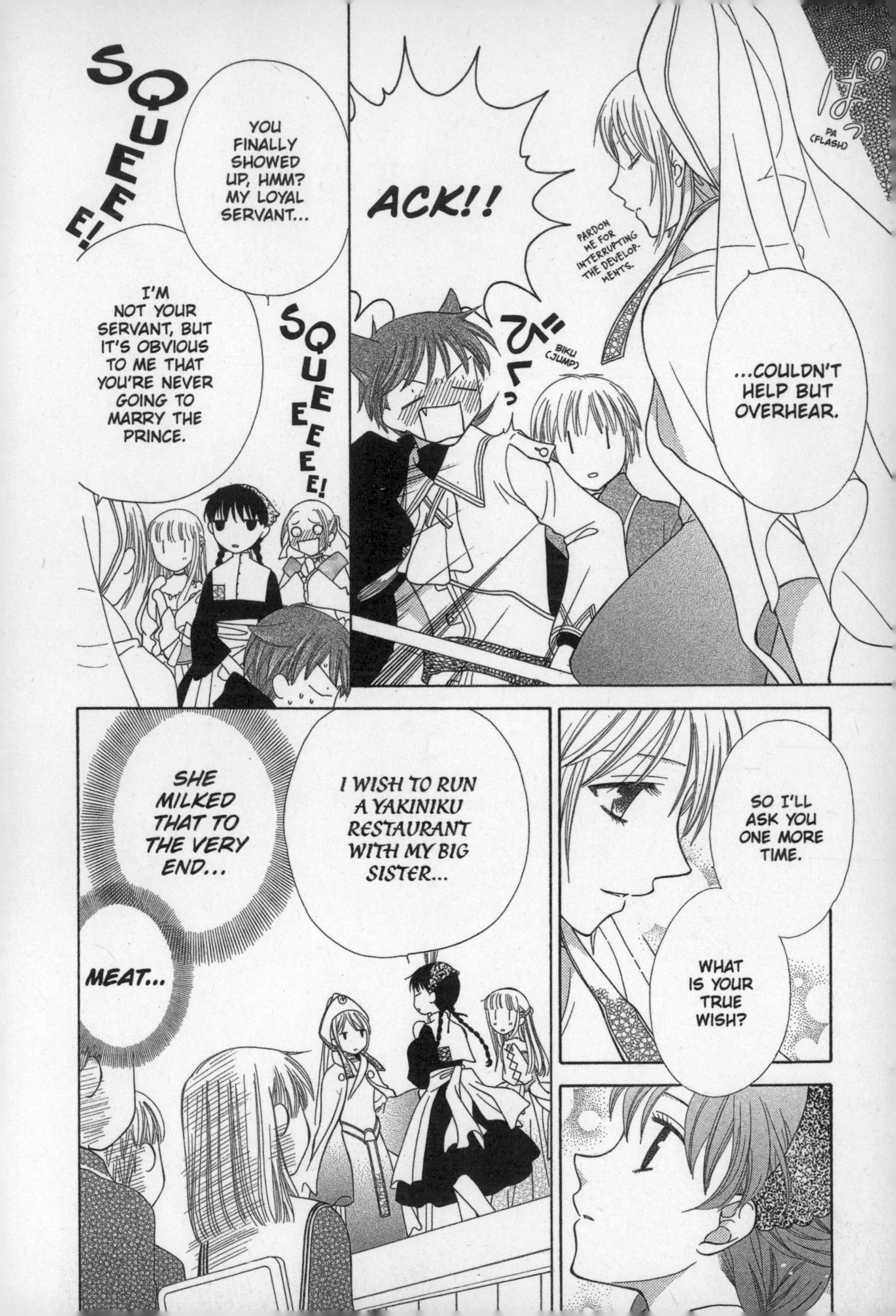
ぱっ
PA (FLASH)
PARDON ME FOR INTERRUPTING THE DEVELOPMENTS.
...COULDN'T HELP BUT OVERHEAR.
ACK!!
びくっ
BIKU (JUMP)
YOU FINALLY SHOWED UP, HMM? MY LOYAL SERVANT...
SQUEEE!
I'M NOT YOUR SERVANT, BUT IT'S OBVIOUS TO ME THAT YOU'RE NEVER GOING TO MARRY THE PRINCE.
SQUEEEEEE!
SO I'LL ASK YOU ONE MORE TIME.
WHAT IS YOUR TRUE WISH?
I WISH TO RUN A YAKINIKU RESTAURANT WITH MY BIG SISTER...
SHE MILKED THAT TO THE VERY END...
MEAT...

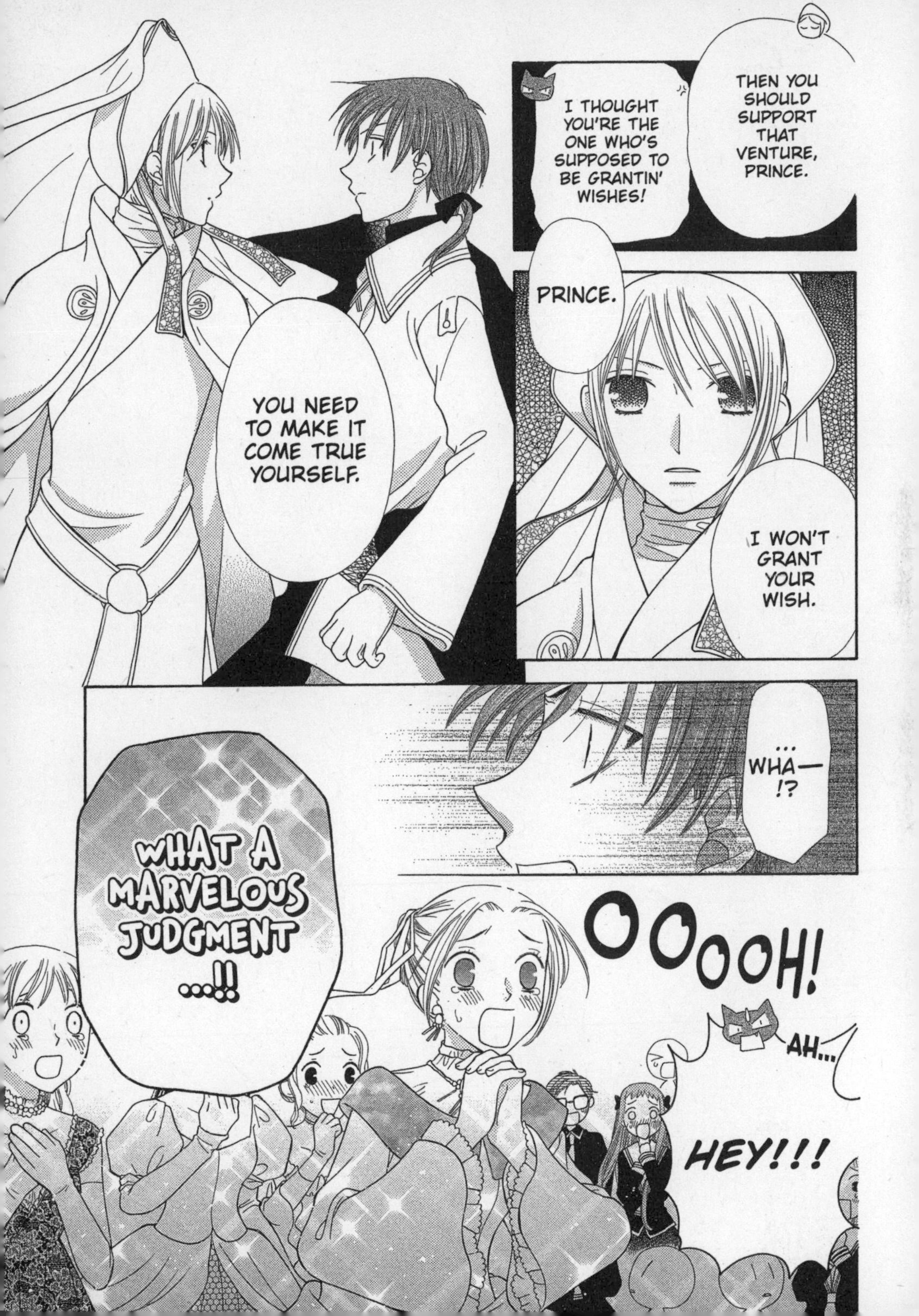
THEN YOU SHOULD SUPPORT THAT VENTURE, PRINCE.
I THOUGHT YOU'RE THE ONE WHO'S SUPPOSED TO BE GRANTIN' WISHES!
PRINCE.
I WON'T GRANT YOUR WISH.
YOU NEED TO MAKE IT COME TRUE YOURSELF.
...WHA—!?
OOOOOH!
WHAT A MARVELOUS JUDGMENT ...!!
AH...
HEY!!!

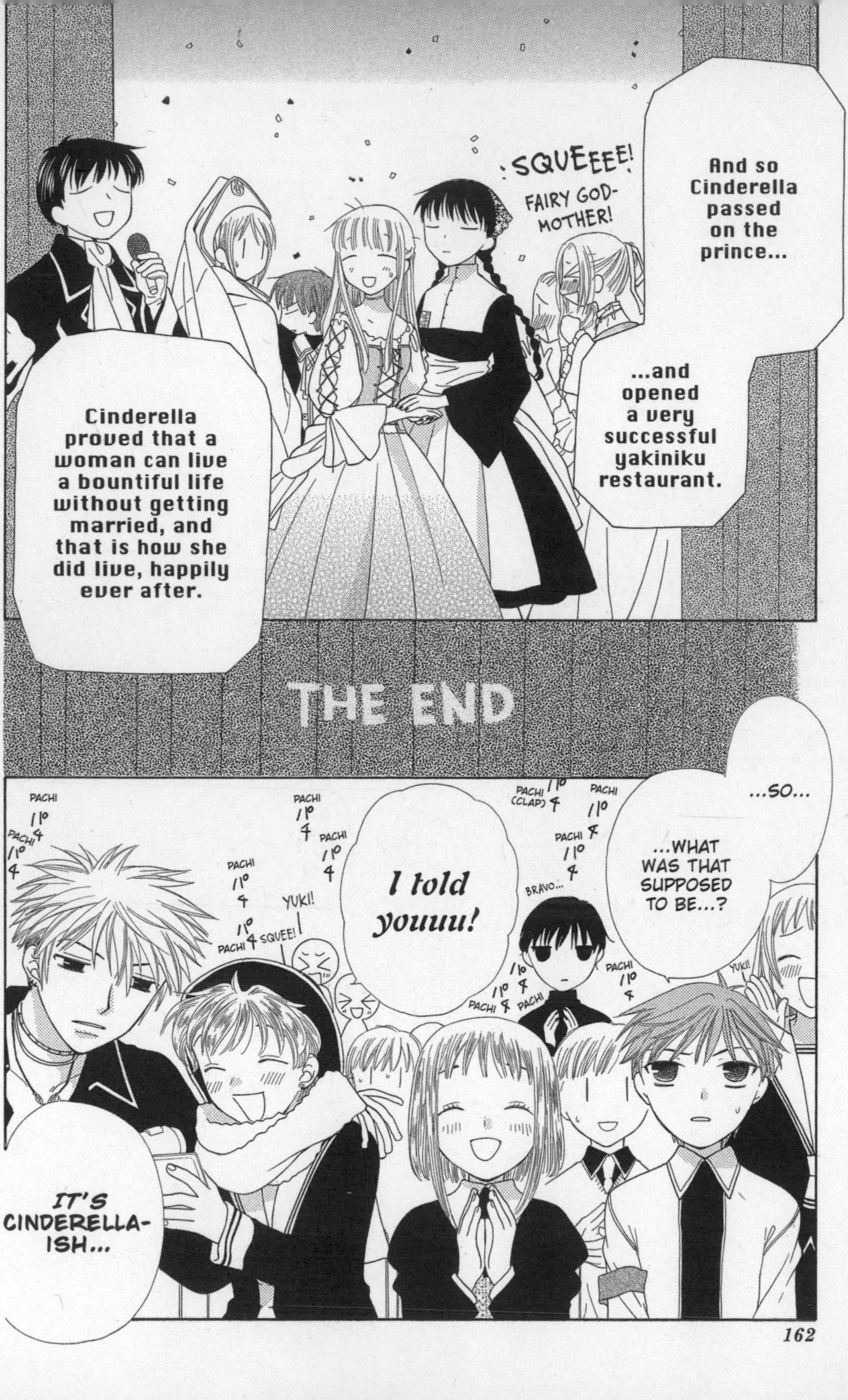
And so Cinderella passed on the prince...
SQUEEEE!
FAIRY GOD-MOTHER!
...and opened a very successful yakiniku restaurant.
Cinderella proved that a woman can live a bountiful life without getting married, and that is how she did live, happily ever after.
THE END
...SO...
...WHAT WAS THAT SUPPOSED TO BE...?
YUKI!
PACHI PACHI (CLAP)
BRAVO...
I told youuu!
YUKI!
SQUEE!
IT'S CINDERELLA-ISH...

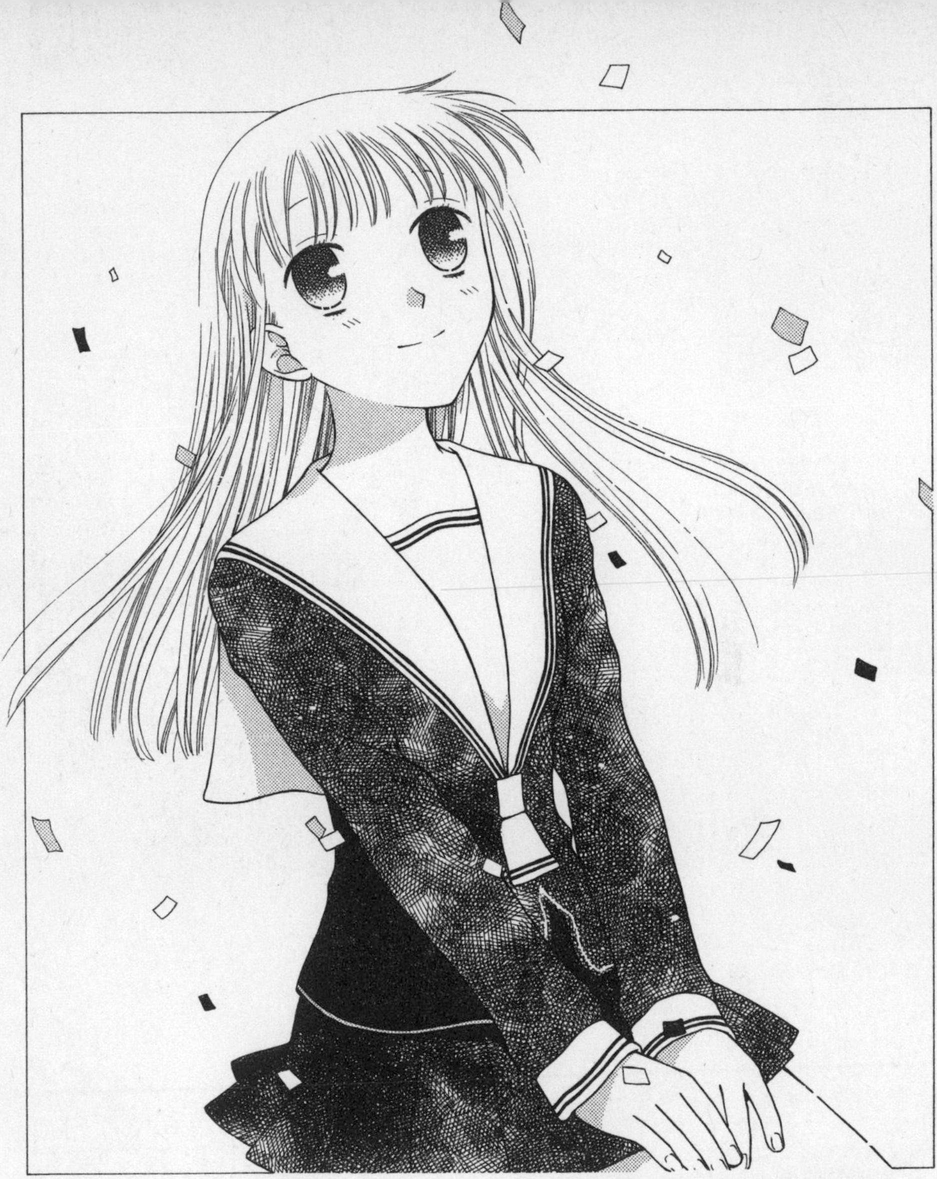

Chapter 89

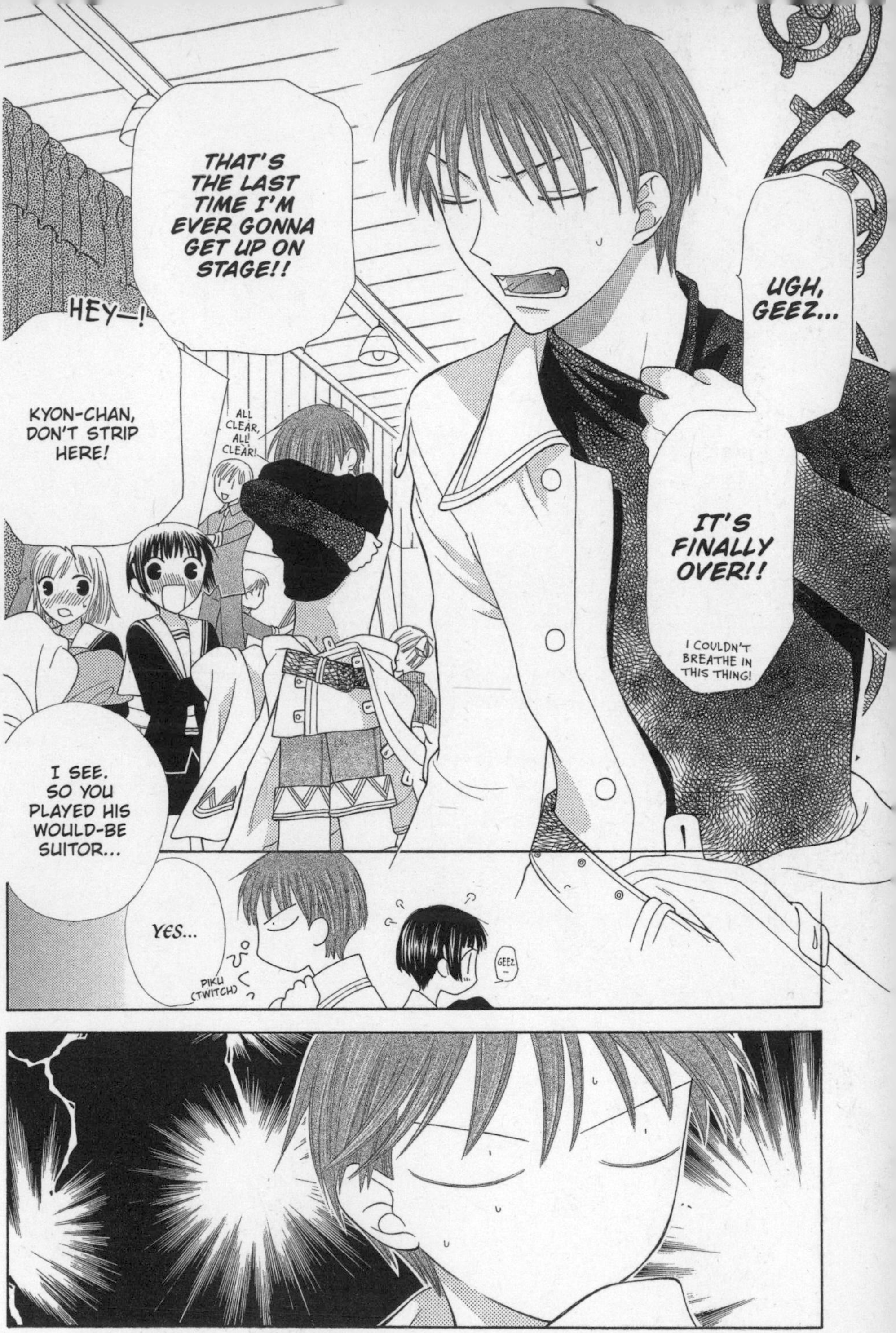
UGH, GEEZ...
IT'S FINALLY OVER!!
I COULDN'T BREATHE IN THIS THING!
THAT'S THE LAST TIME I'M EVER GONNA GET UP ON STAGE!!
HEY—!
ALL CLEAR, ALL CLEAR!
KYON-CHAN, DON'T STRIP HERE!
I SEE. SO YOU PLAYED HIS WOULD-BE SUITOR...
GEEZ...
PIKU (TWITCH)
YES...

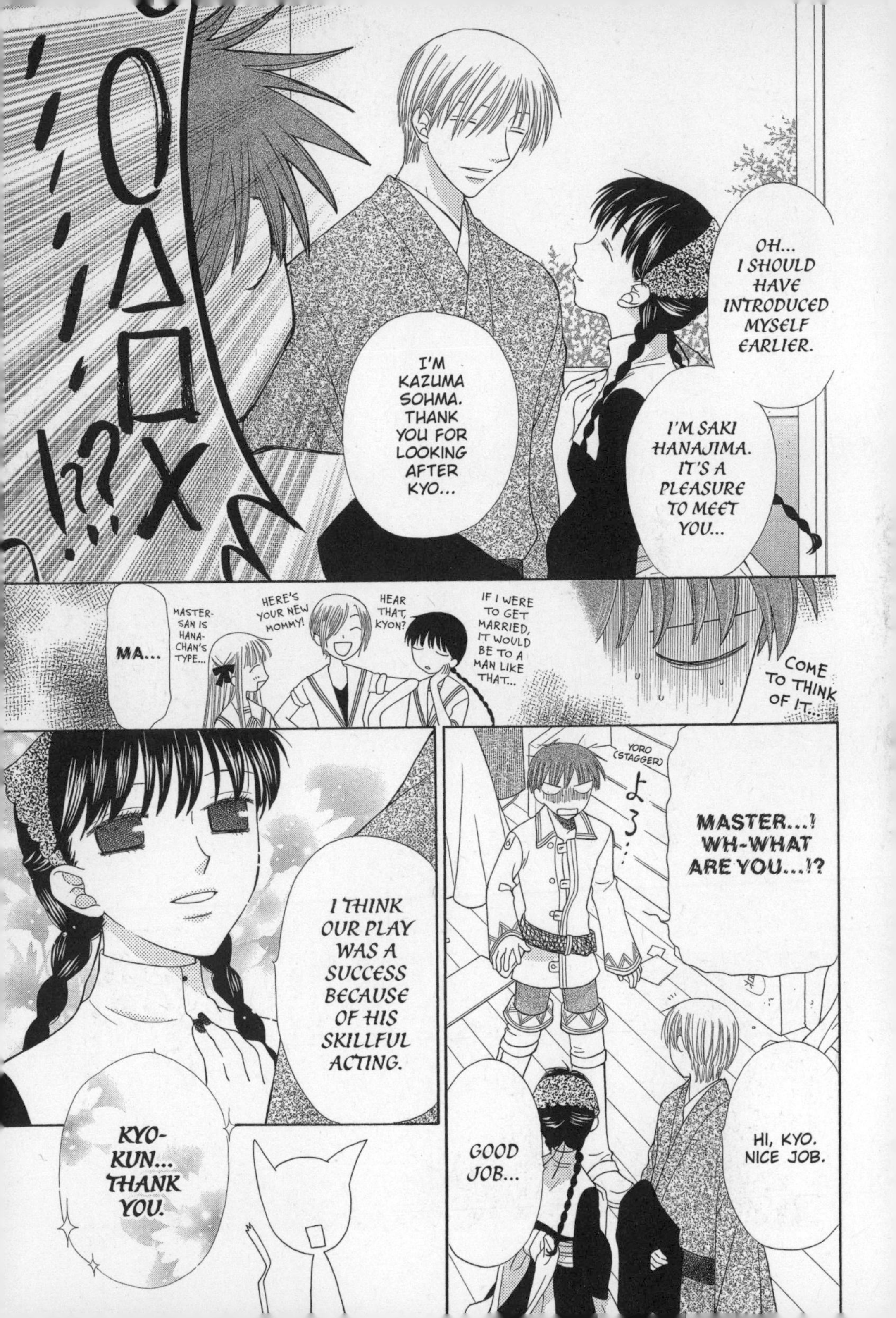
OH... I SHOULD HAVE INTRODUCED MYSELF EARLIER.
I'M SAKI HANAJIMA. IT'S A PLEASURE TO MEET YOU...
I'M KAZUMA SOHMA. THANK YOU FOR LOOKING AFTER KYO...
O△□X!?
COME TO THINK OF IT...
IF I WERE TO GET MARRIED, IT WOULD BE TO A MAN LIKE THAT...
HEAR THAT, KYON?
HERE'S YOUR NEW MOMMY!
MASTER-SAN IS HANA-CHAN'S TYPE...
MA...
MASTER...! WH-WHAT ARE YOU...!?
YORO (STAGGER)
HI, KYO. NICE JOB.
GOOD JOB...
I THINK OUR PLAY WAS A SUCCESS BECAUSE OF HIS SKILLFUL ACTING.
KYO-KUN... THANK YOU.

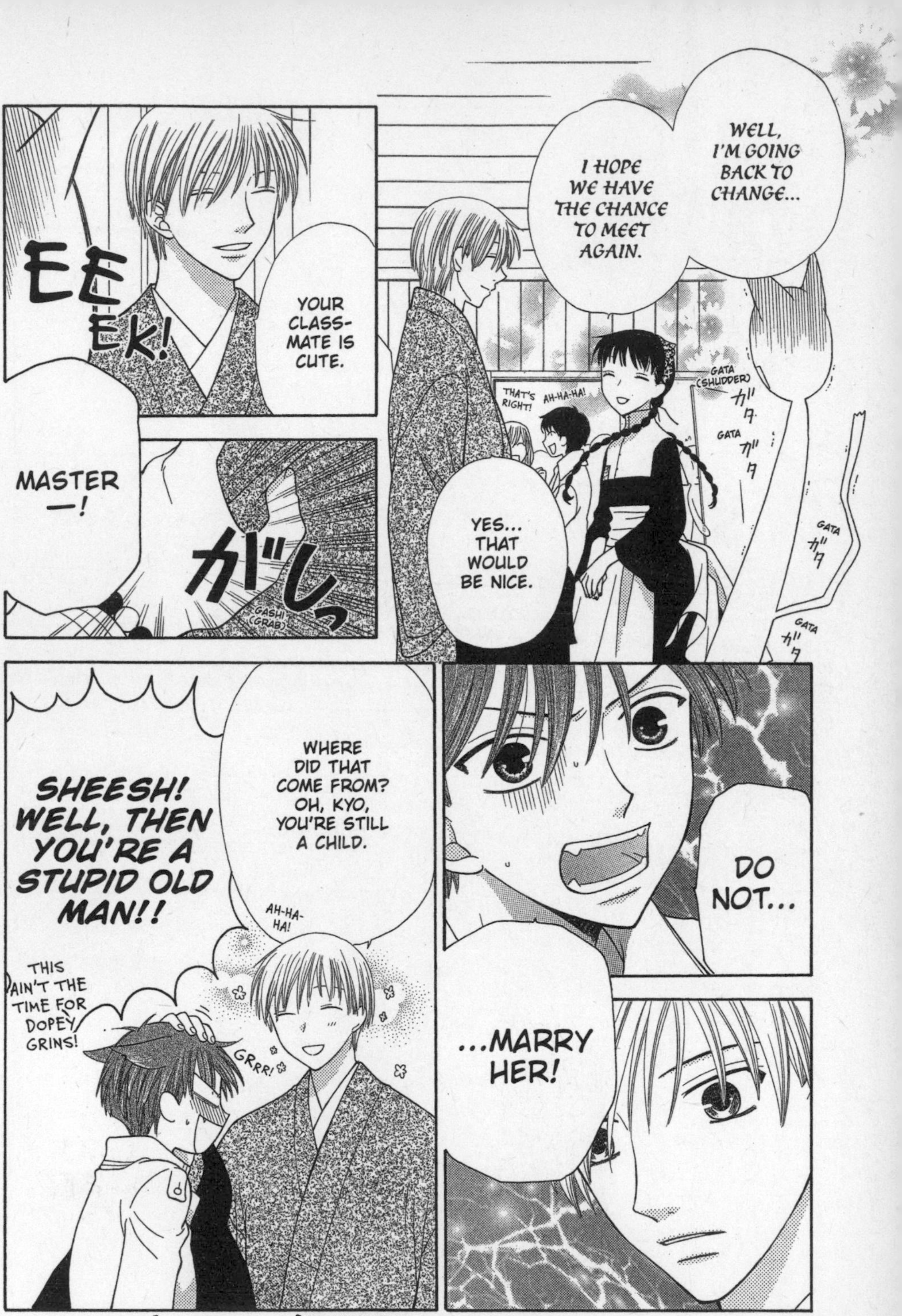
WELL, I'M GOING BACK TO CHANGE...
I HOPE WE HAVE THE CHANCE TO MEET AGAIN.
GATA (SHUDDER) ガタ
GATA ガタ
THAT'S RIGHT!
AH-HA-HA!
YES... THAT WOULD BE NICE.
GATA ガタ
GATA ガタ
YOUR CLASSMATE IS CUTE.
EEEK!
MASTER—!
がしっ
GASHI (GRAB)
DO NOT...
...MARRY HER!
WHERE DID THAT COME FROM? OH, KYO, YOU'RE STILL A CHILD.
SHEESH! WELL, THEN YOU'RE A STUPID OLD MAN!!
AH-HA-HA!
THIS AIN'T THE TIME FOR DOPEY GRINS!
GRRR!

DOTING CHILD↗ ↖DOTING PARENT

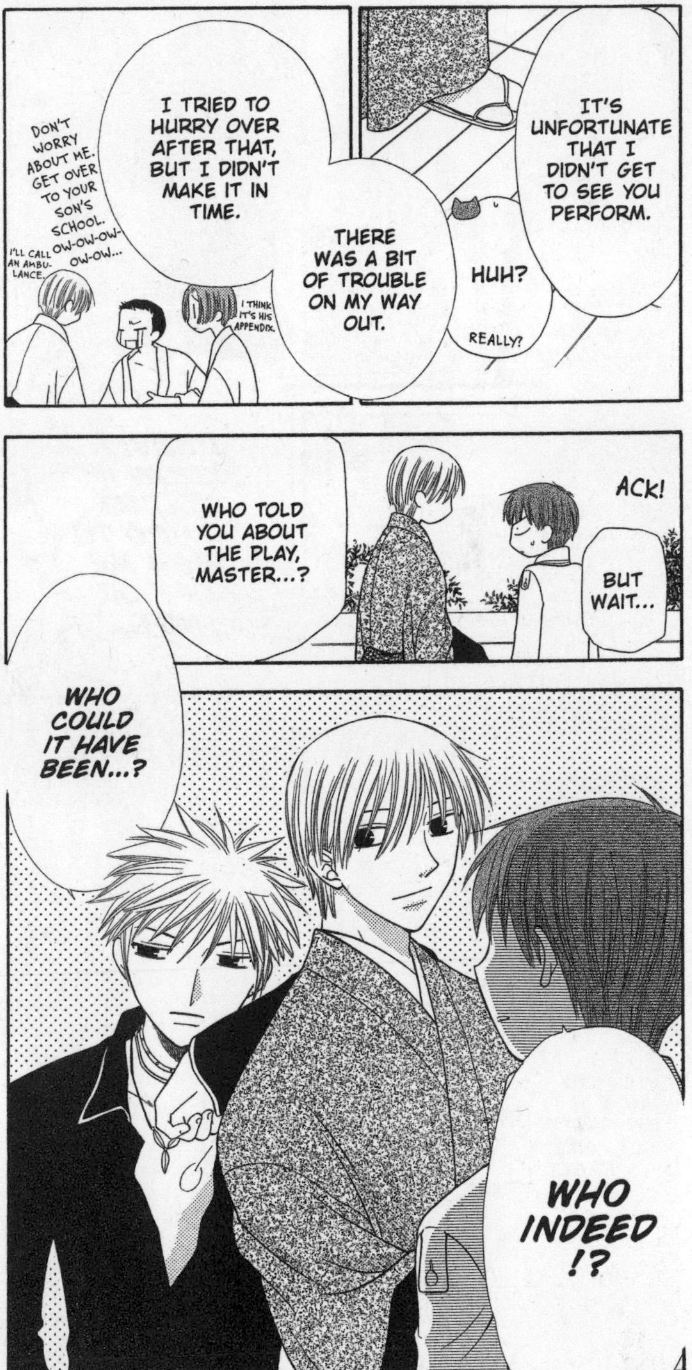
IT'S UNFORTUNATE THAT I DIDN'T GET TO SEE YOU PERFORM.
HUH?
REALLY?
THERE WAS A BIT OF TROUBLE ON MY WAY OUT.
I TRIED TO HURRY OVER AFTER THAT, BUT I DIDN'T MAKE IT IN TIME.
DON'T WORRY ABOUT ME. GET OVER TO YOUR SON'S SCHOOL. OW-OW-OW-OW-OW...
I THINK IT'S HIS APPENDIX.
I'LL CALL AN AMBULANCE.
ACK!
BUT WAIT...
WHO TOLD YOU ABOUT THE PLAY, MASTER...?
WHO COULD IT HAVE BEEN...?
WHO INDEED !?

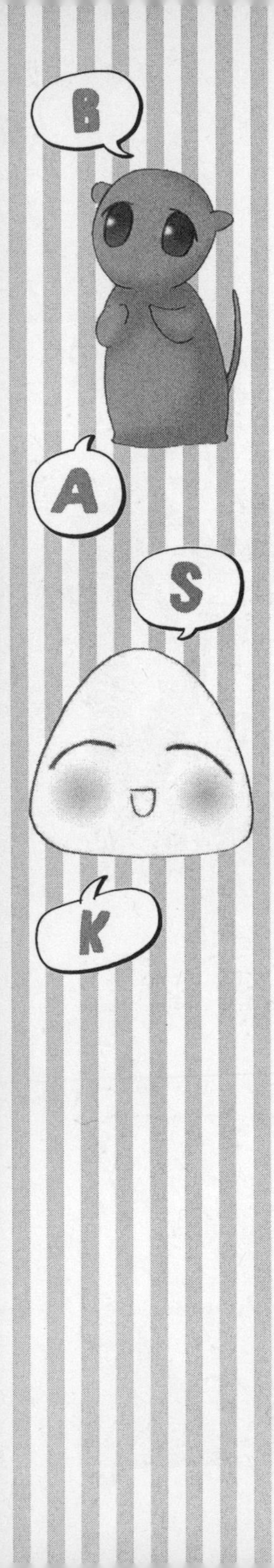
B
A
S
K

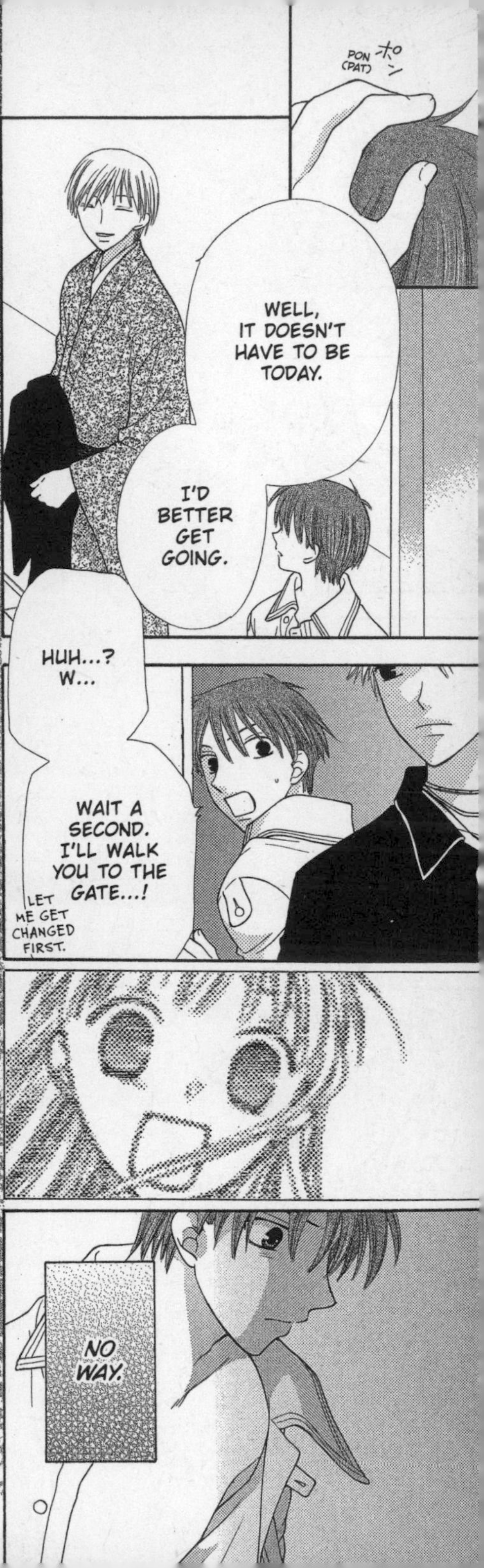
PON (PAT)
WELL, IT DOESN'T HAVE TO BE TODAY.
I'D BETTER GET GOING.
HUH...? W...
WAIT A SECOND. I'LL WALK YOU TO THE GATE...!
LET ME GET CHANGED FIRST.
NO WAY.
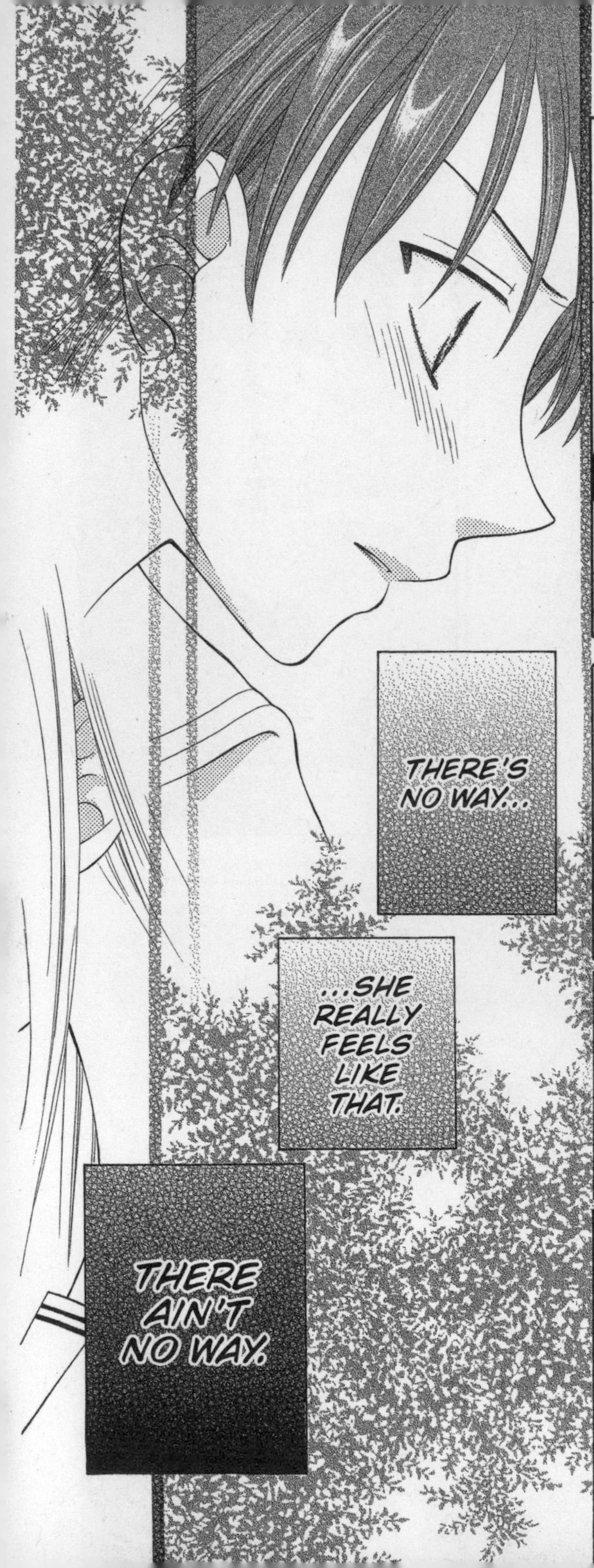
THERE'S NO WAY...
...SHE REALLY FEELS LIKE THAT.
THERE AIN'T NO WAY.

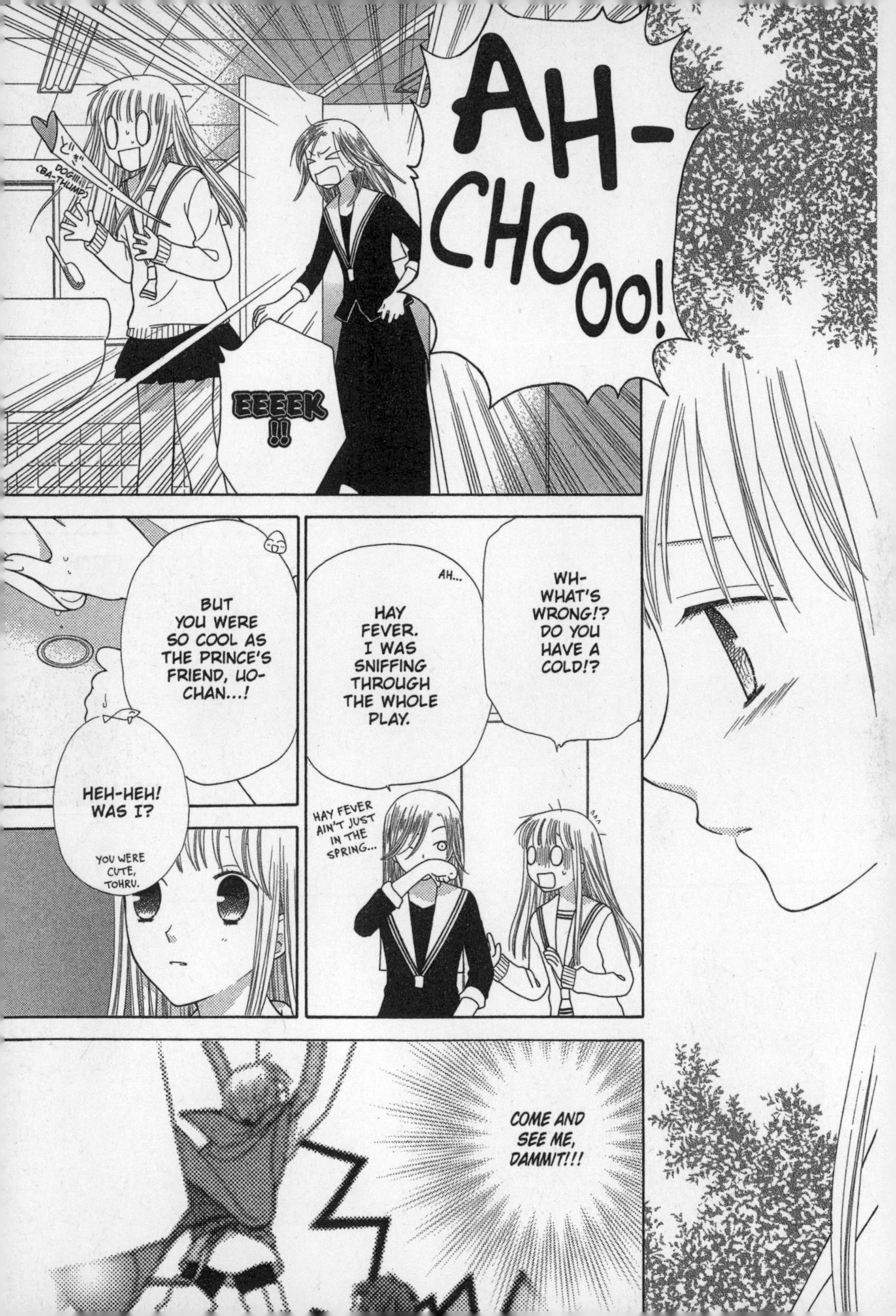
AH-CHOOO!
EEEEK!!
DOGI!! (BA-THUMP)
WH-WHAT'S WRONG!? DO YOU HAVE A COLD!?
AH...
HAY FEVER. I WAS SNIFFING THROUGH THE WHOLE PLAY.
HAY FEVER AIN'T JUST IN THE SPRING...
BUT YOU WERE SO COOL AS THE PRINCE'S FRIEND, UO-CHAN...!
HEH-HEH! WAS I?
YOU WERE CUTE, TOHRU.
COME AND SEE ME, DAMMIT!!!

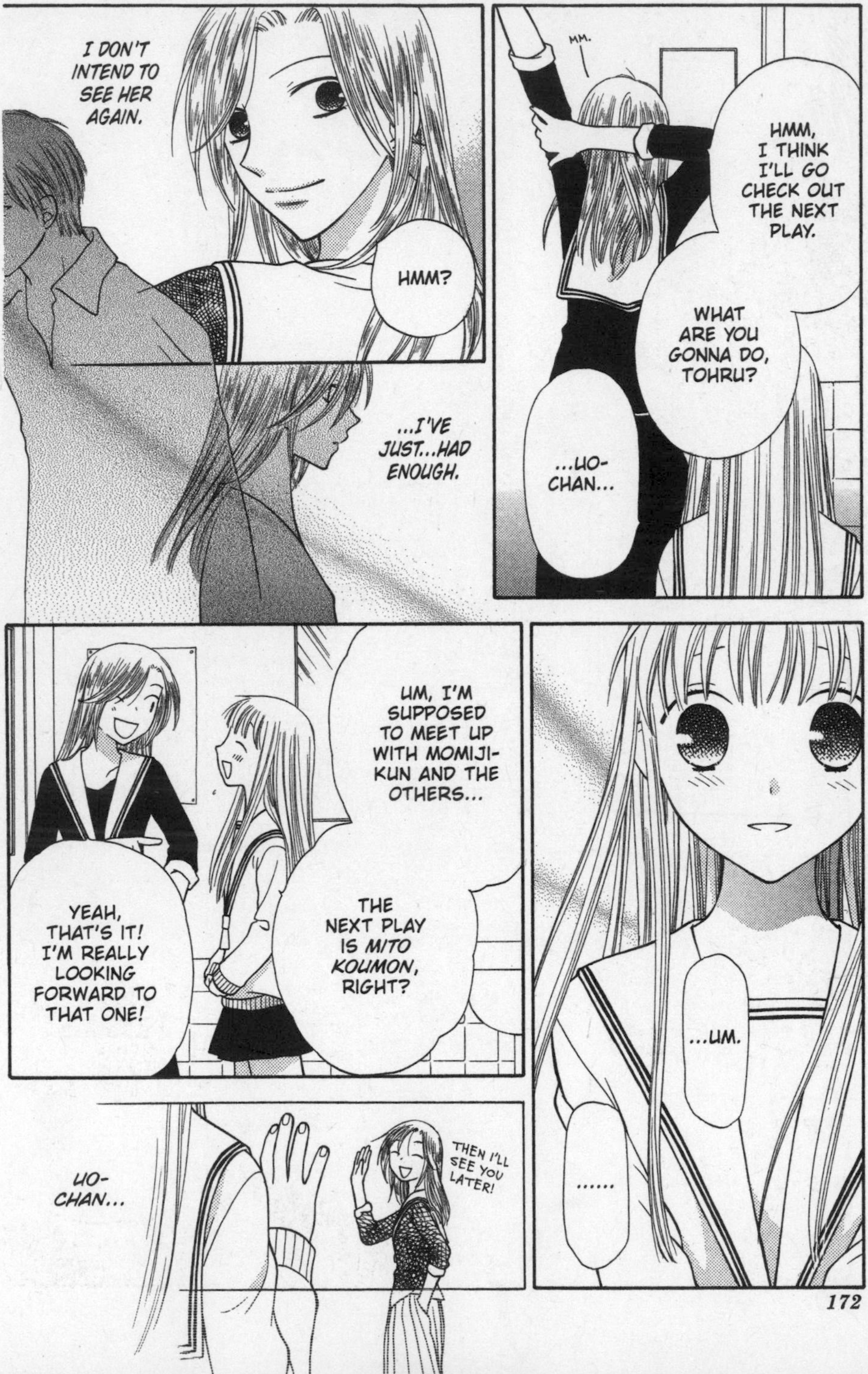
MM.
HMM, I THINK I'LL GO CHECK OUT THE NEXT PLAY.
WHAT ARE YOU GONNA DO, TOHRU?
...UO-CHAN...
I DON'T INTEND TO SEE HER AGAIN.
HMM?
...I'VE JUST...HAD ENOUGH.
...UM.
......
UM, I'M SUPPOSED TO MEET UP WITH MOMIJI-KUN AND THE OTHERS...
THE NEXT PLAY IS *MITO KOUMON*, RIGHT?
YEAH, THAT'S IT! I'M REALLY LOOKING FORWARD TO THAT ONE!
THEN I'LL SEE YOU LATER!
UO-CHAN...

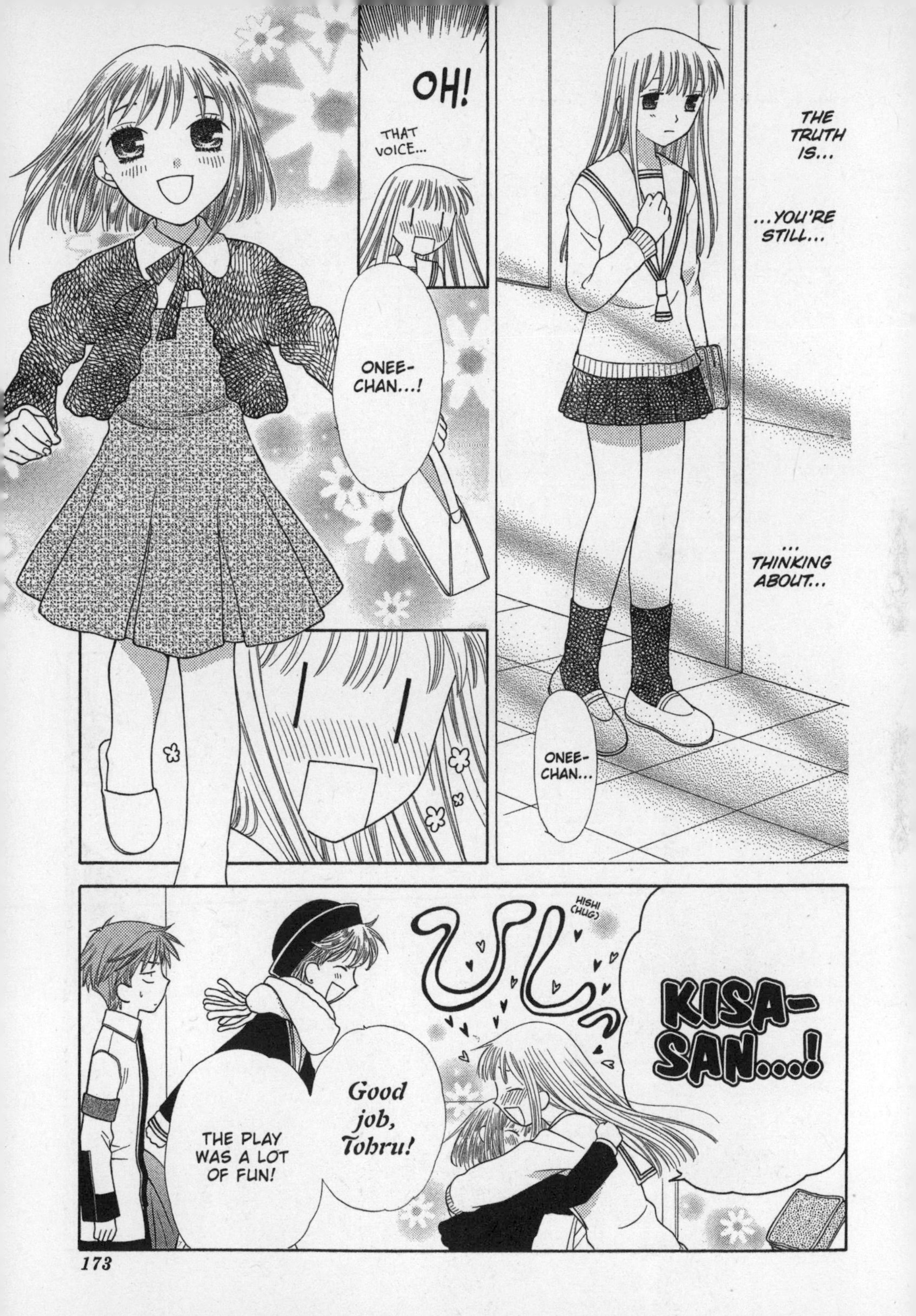
THE TRUTH IS...
...YOU'RE STILL...
...THINKING ABOUT...
ONEE-CHAN...
OH!
THAT VOICE...
ONEE-CHAN...!
KISA-SAN...!
HISHI (HUG)
Good job, Tohru!
THE PLAY WAS A LOT OF FUN!

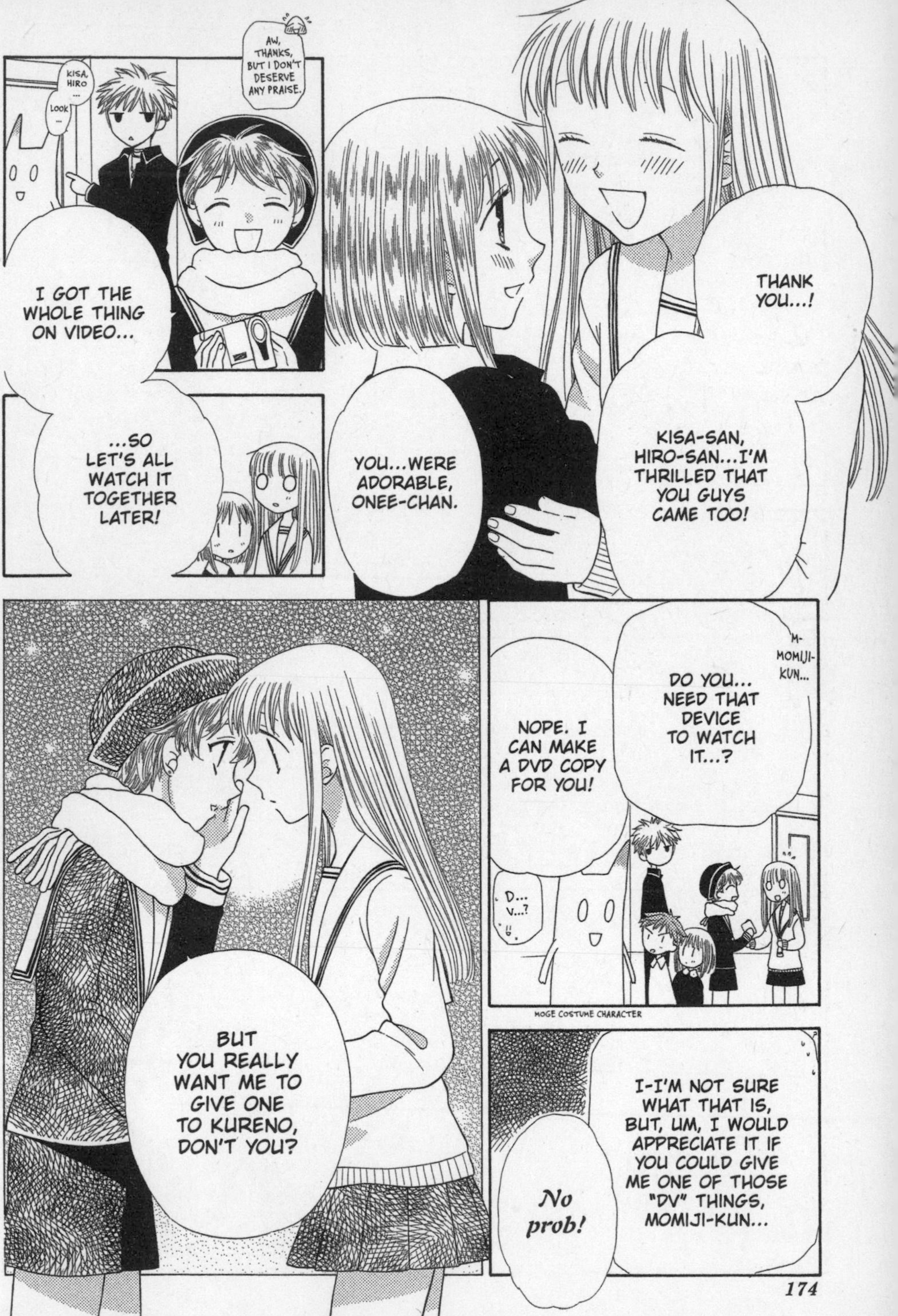
THANK YOU...!
KISA-SAN, HIRO-SAN...I'M THRILLED THAT YOU GUYS CAME TOO!
YOU...WERE ADORABLE, ONEE-CHAN.
AW, THANKS, BUT I DON'T DESERVE ANY PRAISE.
KISA, HIRO ... LOOK ...
I GOT THE WHOLE THING ON VIDEO...
...SO LET'S ALL WATCH IT TOGETHER LATER!
M-MOMIJI-KUN...
DO YOU... NEED THAT DEVICE TO WATCH IT...?
NOPE. I CAN MAKE A DVD COPY FOR YOU!
D... V...?
MOGE COSTUME CHARACTER
I-I'M NOT SURE WHAT THAT IS, BUT, UM, I WOULD APPRECIATE IT IF YOU COULD GIVE ME ONE OF THOSE "DV" THINGS, MOMIJI-KUN...
No prob!
BUT YOU REALLY WANT ME TO GIVE ONE TO KURENO, DON'T YOU?

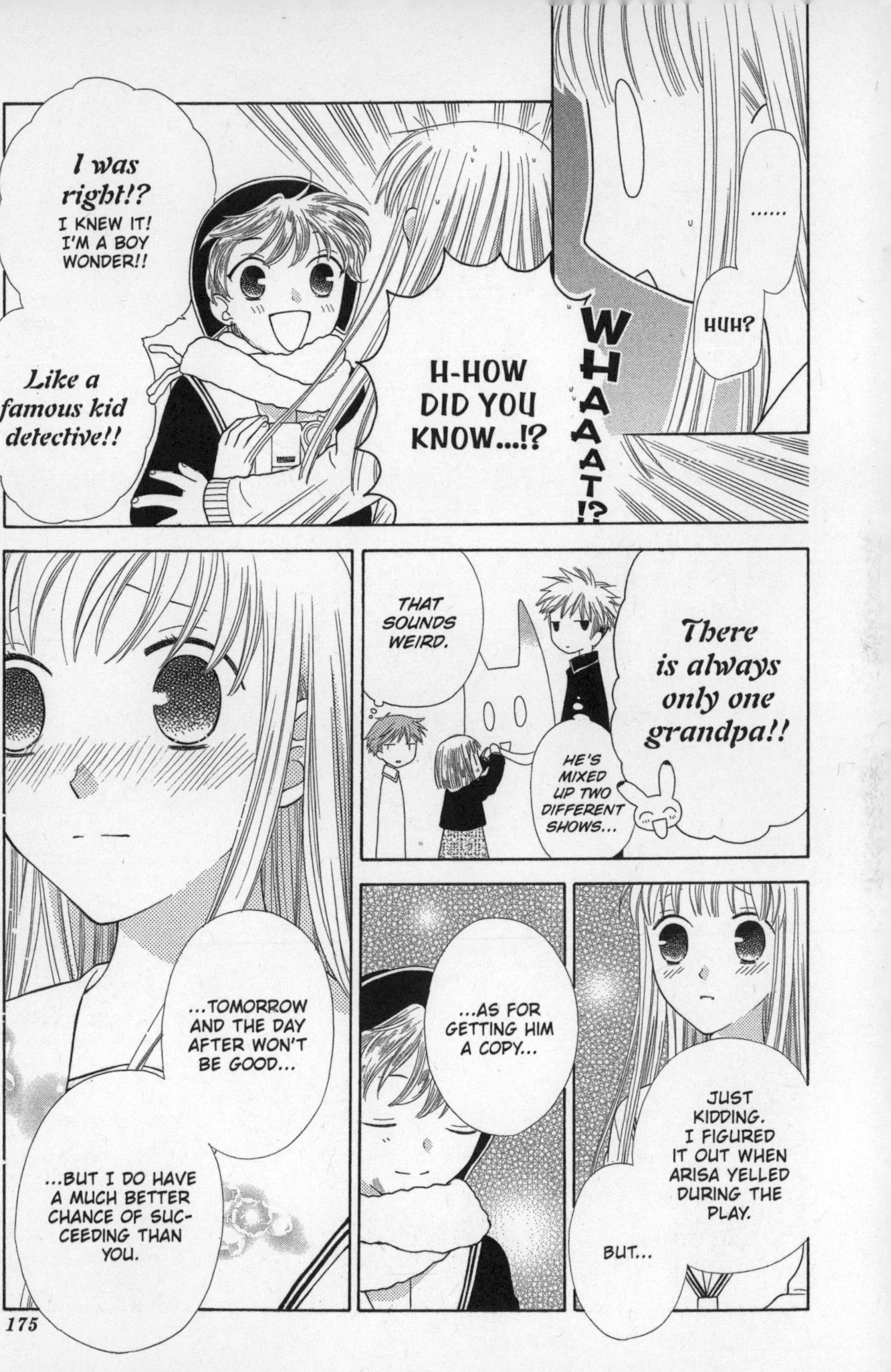
......
HUH?
WHAAAT!?
H-HOW DID YOU KNOW...!?
I was right!? I KNEW IT! I'M A BOY WONDER!!
Like a famous kid detective!!
There is always only one grandpa!!
HE'S MIXED UP TWO DIFFERENT SHOWS...
THAT SOUNDS WEIRD.
JUST KIDDING. I FIGURED IT OUT WHEN ARISA YELLED DURING THE PLAY.
BUT...
...AS FOR GETTING HIM A COPY...
...TOMORROW AND THE DAY AFTER WON'T BE GOOD...
...BUT I DO HAVE A MUCH BETTER CHANCE OF SUC-CEEDING THAN YOU.

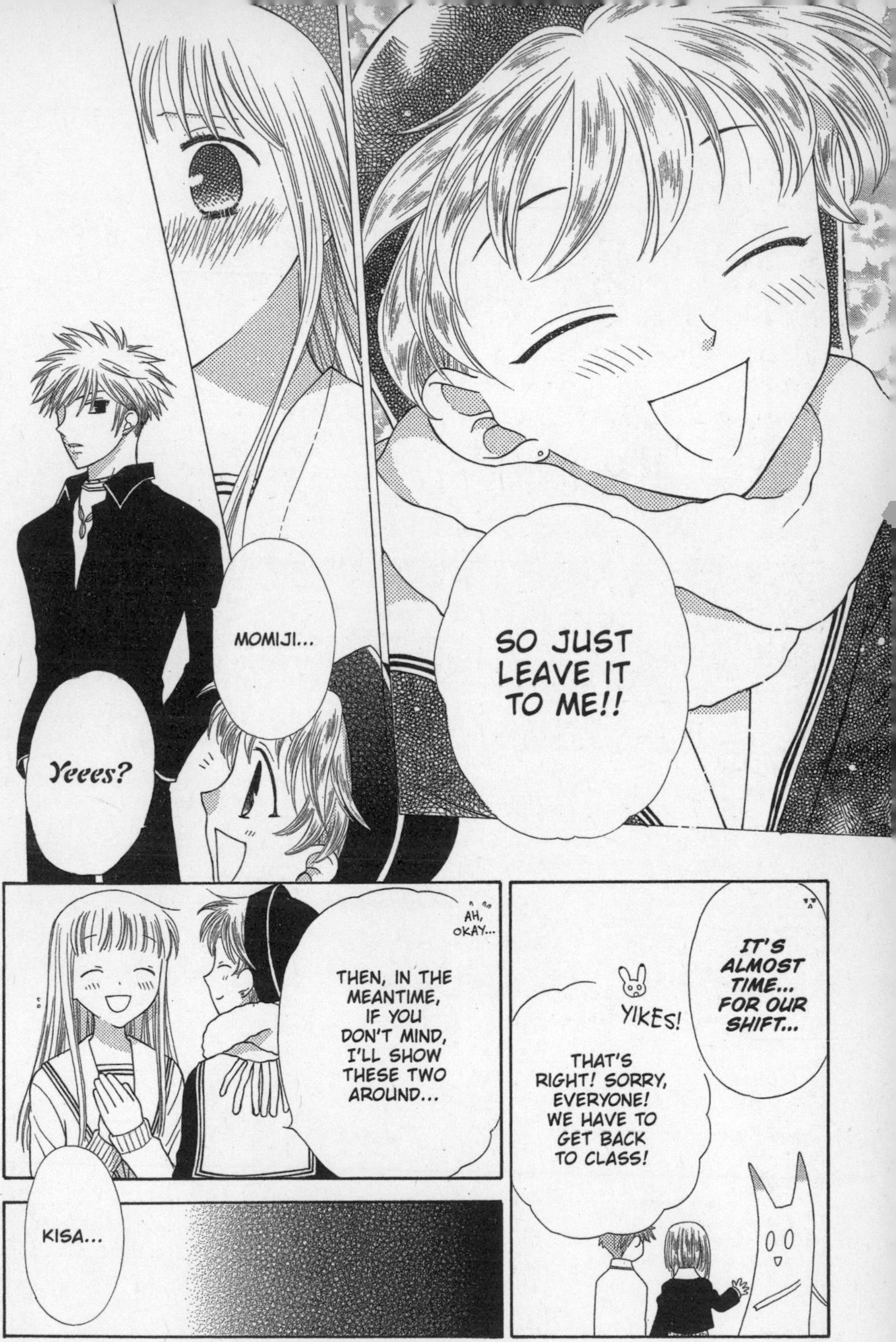
SO JUST LEAVE IT TO ME!!
MOMIJI...
Yeees?
IT'S ALMOST TIME... FOR OUR SHIFT...
YIKES!
THAT'S RIGHT! SORRY, EVERYONE! WE HAVE TO GET BACK TO CLASS!
AH, OKAY...
THEN, IN THE MEANTIME, IF YOU DON'T MIND, I'LL SHOW THESE TWO AROUND...
KISA...

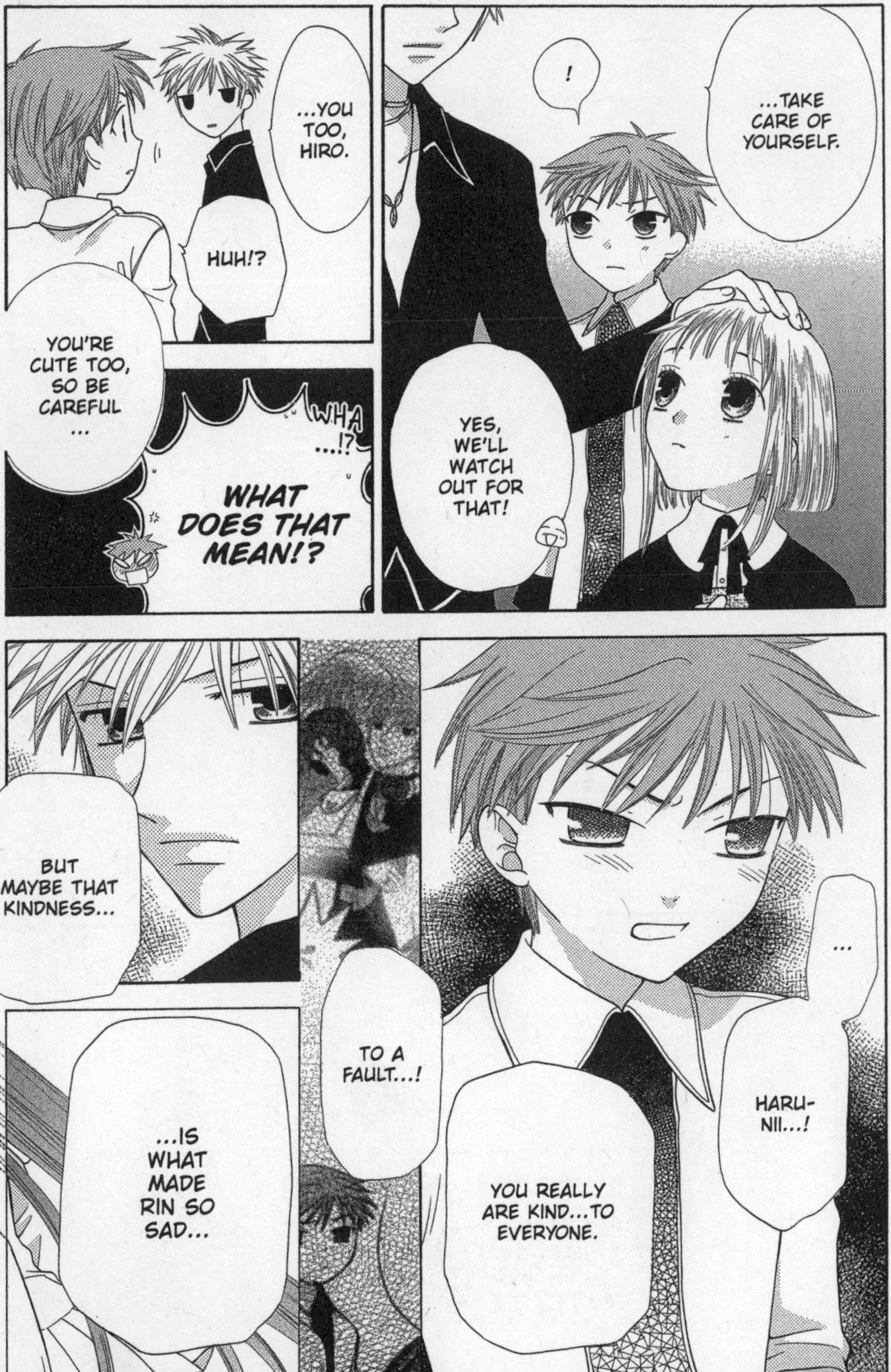
!
...TAKE CARE OF YOURSELF.
YES, WE'LL WATCH OUT FOR THAT!
...YOU TOO, HIRO.
HUH!?
YOU'RE CUTE TOO, SO BE CAREFUL ...
WHA ...!?
WHAT DOES THAT MEAN!?
...
HARU-NII...!
YOU REALLY ARE KIND...TO EVERYONE.
TO A FAULT...!
BUT MAYBE THAT KINDNESS...
...IS WHAT MADE RIN SO SAD...

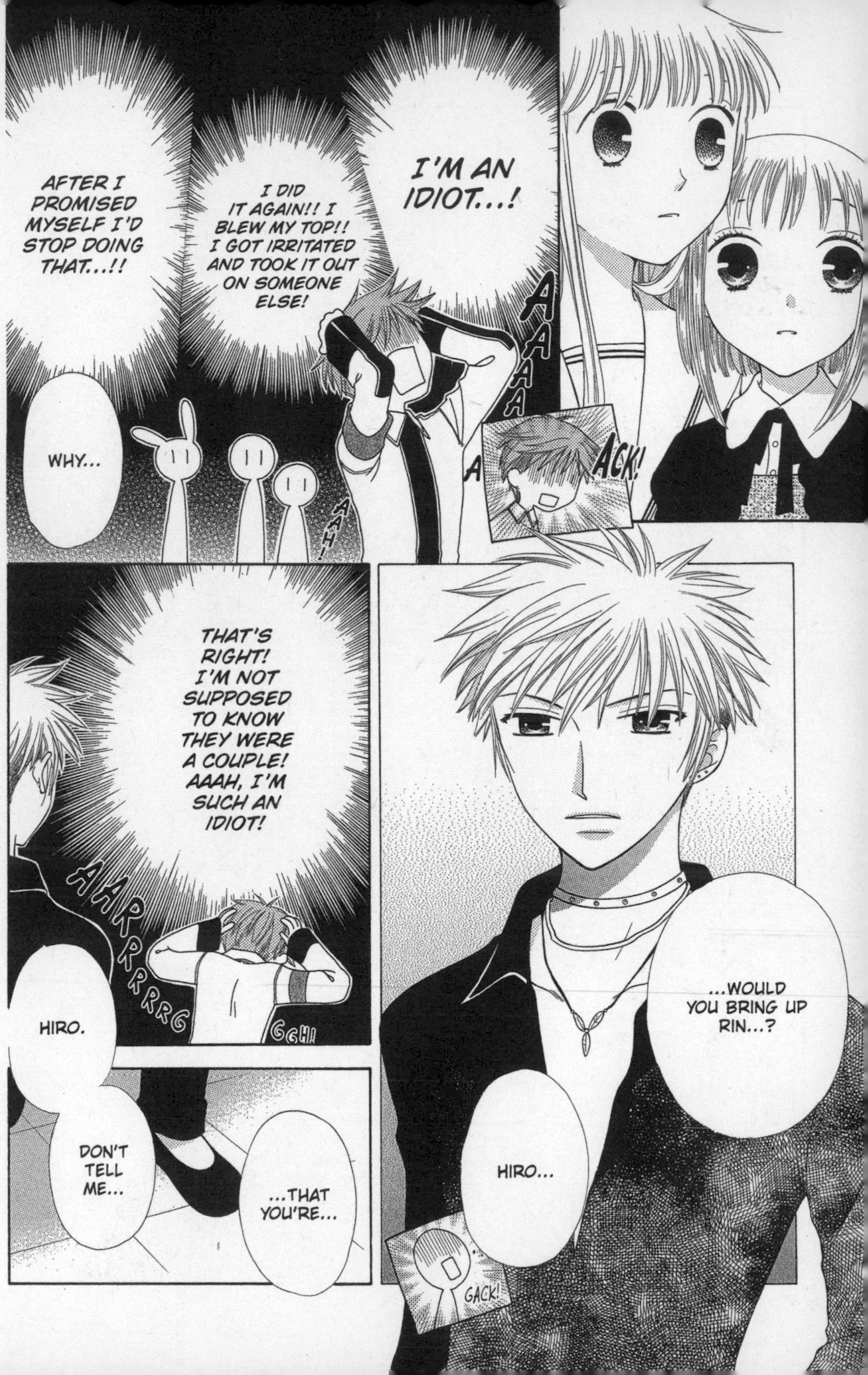
AAAAAAA
ACK!
I'M AN IDIOT...!
I DID IT AGAIN!! I BLEW MY TOP!! I GOT IRRITATED AND TOOK IT OUT ON SOMEONE ELSE!
AFTER I PROMISED MYSELF I'D STOP DOING THAT...!!
AAH!
WHY...
...WOULD YOU BRING UP RIN...?
HIRO...
GACK!
THAT'S RIGHT! I'M NOT SUPPOSED TO KNOW THEY WERE A COUPLE! AAAH, I'M SUCH AN IDIOT!
AARRRRRG
GGH!
HIRO.
DON'T TELL ME...
...THAT YOU'RE...

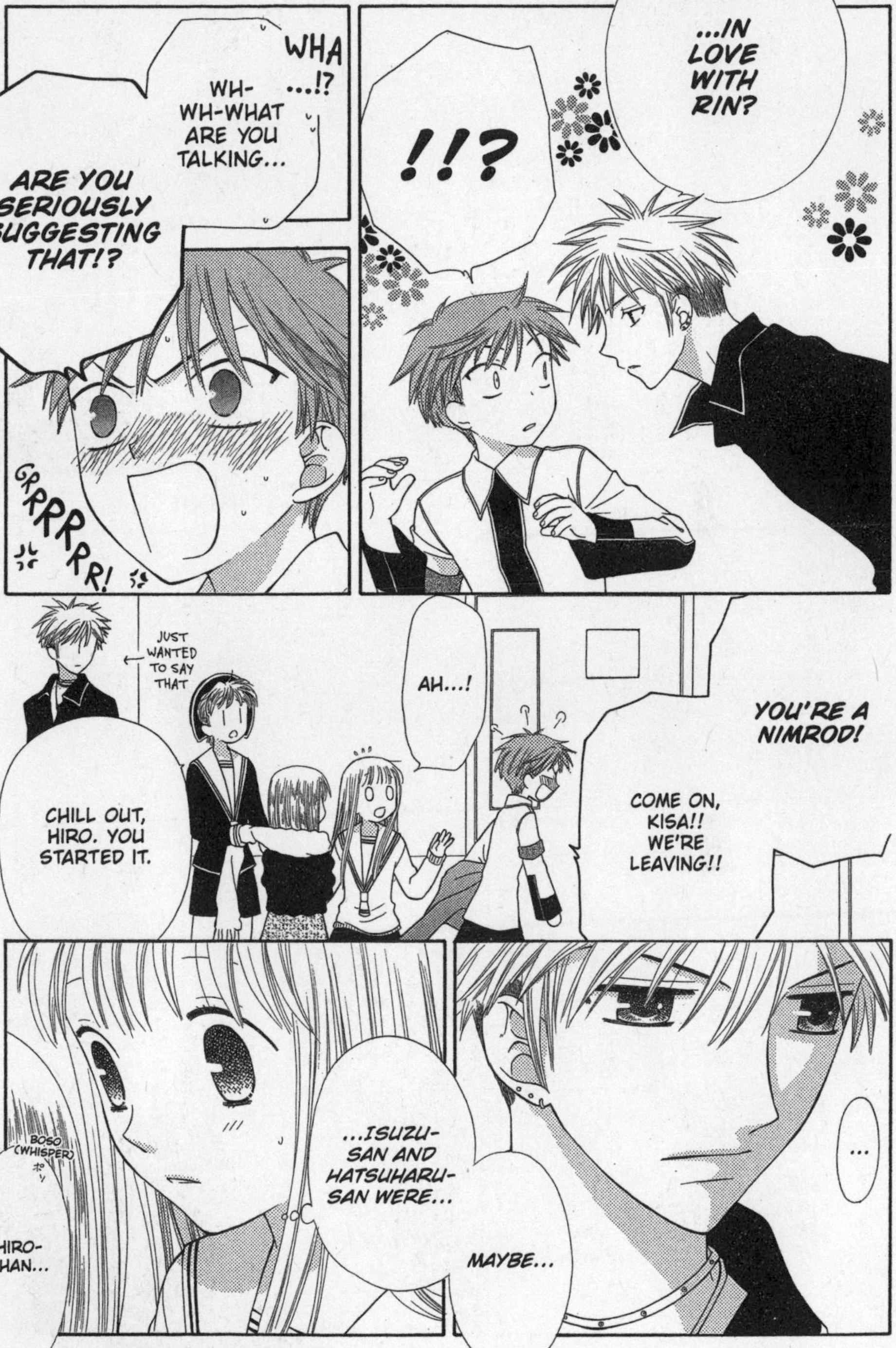
...IN LOVE WITH RIN?
!!?
WHA ...!?
WH- WH-WHAT ARE YOU TALKING...
ARE YOU SERIOUSLY SUGGESTING THAT!?
GRRRRRR!
YOU'RE A NIMROD!
COME ON, KISA!! WE'RE LEAVING!!
AH...!
JUST WANTED TO SAY THAT
CHILL OUT, HIRO. YOU STARTED IT.
...
...ISUZU-SAN AND HATSUHARU-SAN WERE...
MAYBE...
BOSO (WHISPER)
HIRO-CHAN...

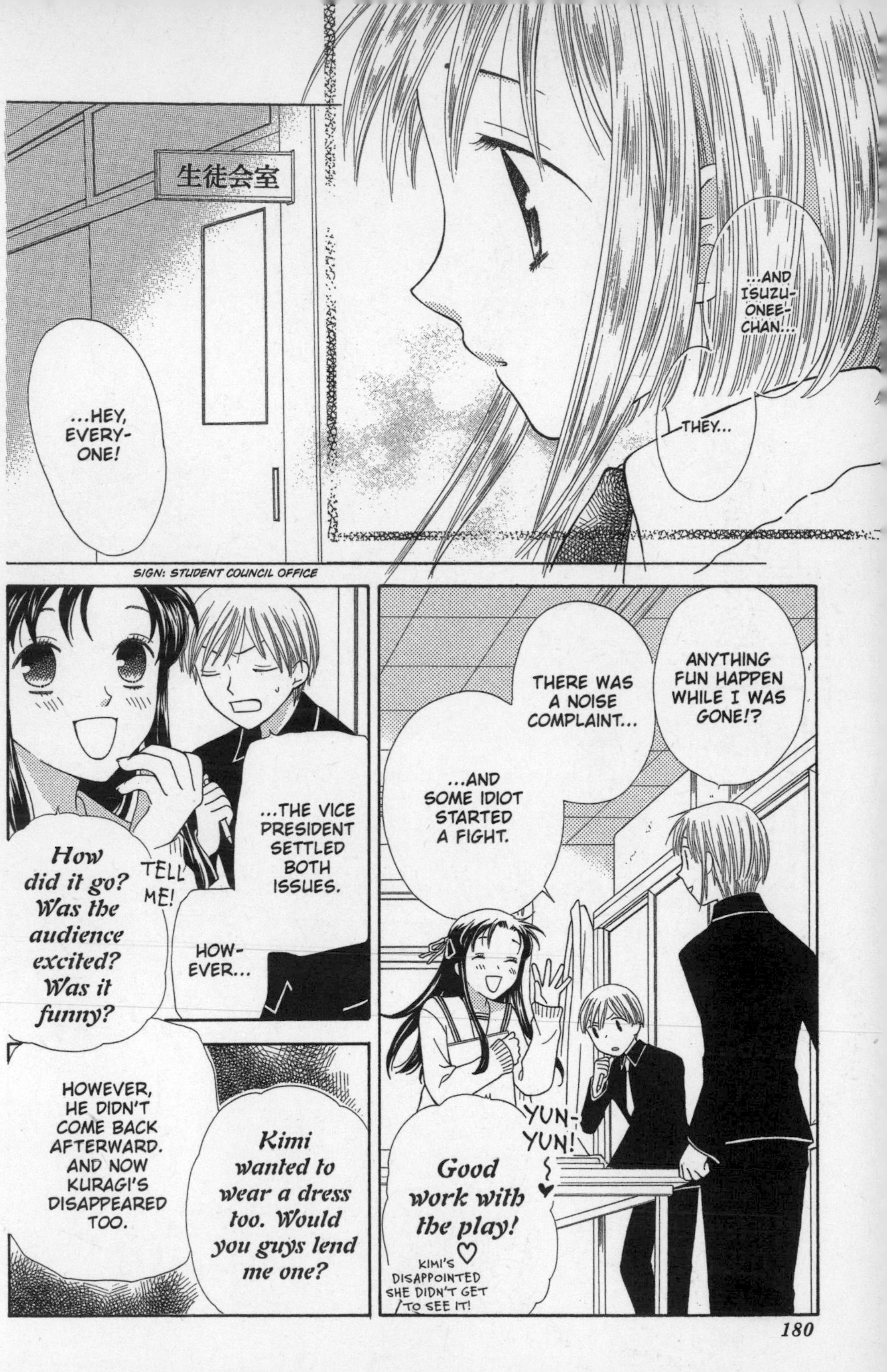
...AND ISUZU-ONEE-CHAN...
THEY...
生徒会室
...HEY, EVERY-ONE!
SIGN: STUDENT COUNCIL OFFICE
ANYTHING FUN HAPPEN WHILE I WAS GONE!?
THERE WAS A NOISE COMPLAINT...
...AND SOME IDIOT STARTED A FIGHT.
YUN-YUN!
Good work with the play! ♡
KIMI'S DISAPPOINTED SHE DIDN'T GET TO SEE IT!
...THE VICE PRESIDENT SETTLED BOTH ISSUES.
TELL ME!
How did it go? Was the audience excited? Was it funny?
HOW-EVER...
Kimi wanted to wear a dress too. Would you guys lend me one?
HOWEVER, HE DIDN'T COME BACK AFTERWARD. AND NOW KURAGI'S DISAPPEARED TOO.

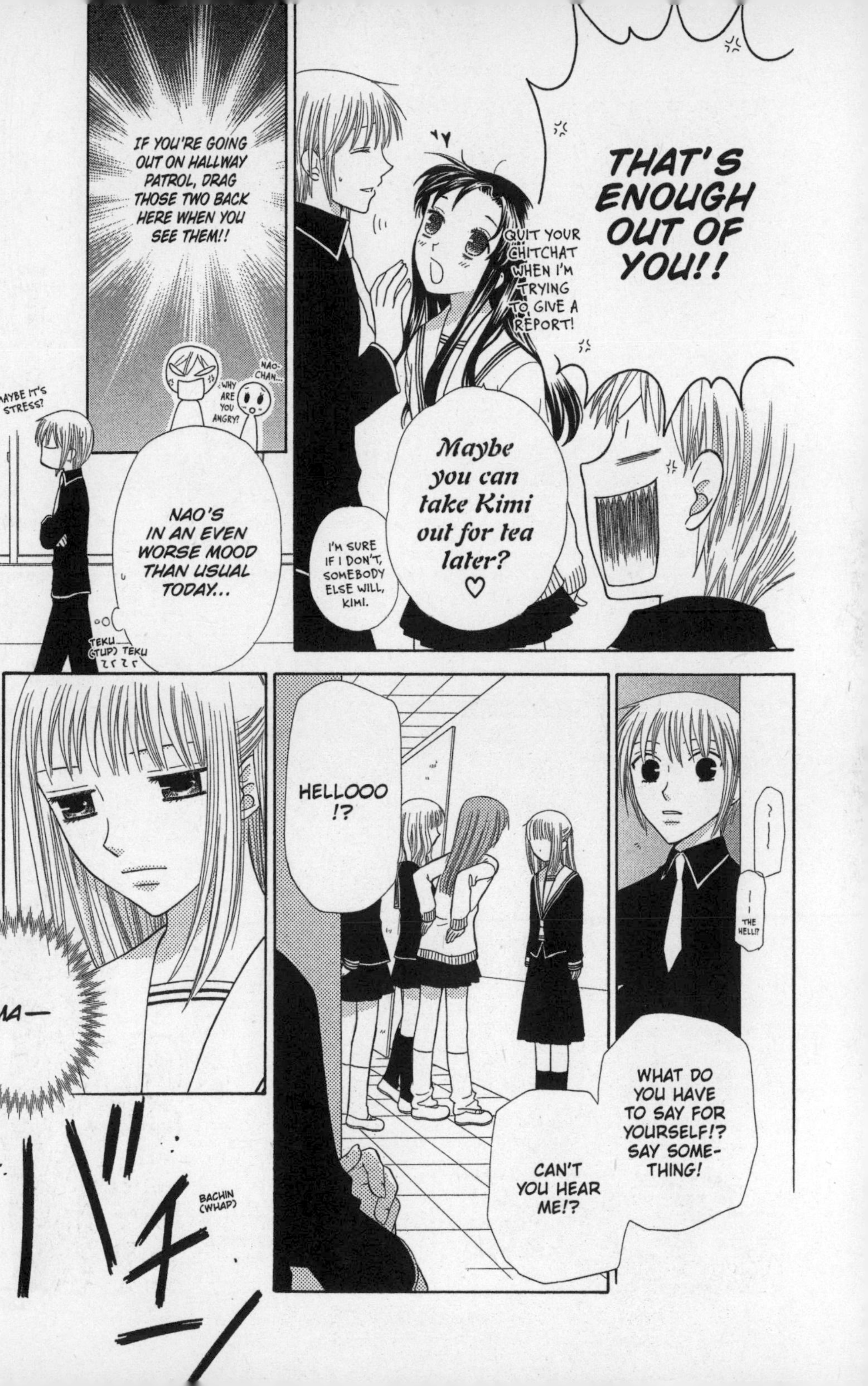
THAT'S ENOUGH OUT OF YOU!!
QUIT YOUR CHITCHAT WHEN I'M TRYING TO GIVE A REPORT!
Maybe you can take Kimi out for tea later? ♡
I'M SURE IF I DON'T, SOMEBODY ELSE WILL, KIMI.
IF YOU'RE GOING OUT ON HALLWAY PATROL, DRAG THOSE TWO BACK HERE WHEN YOU SEE THEM!!
NAO-CHAN...
WHY ARE YOU ANGRY?
NAO'S IN AN EVEN WORSE MOOD THAN USUAL TODAY...
MAYBE IT'S STRESS?
TEKU (STUP) TEKU
THE HELL!?
HELLOOO !?
WHAT DO YOU HAVE TO SAY FOR YOURSELF!? SAY SOME-THING!
CAN'T YOU HEAR ME!?
MA—
BACHIN (WHAP)

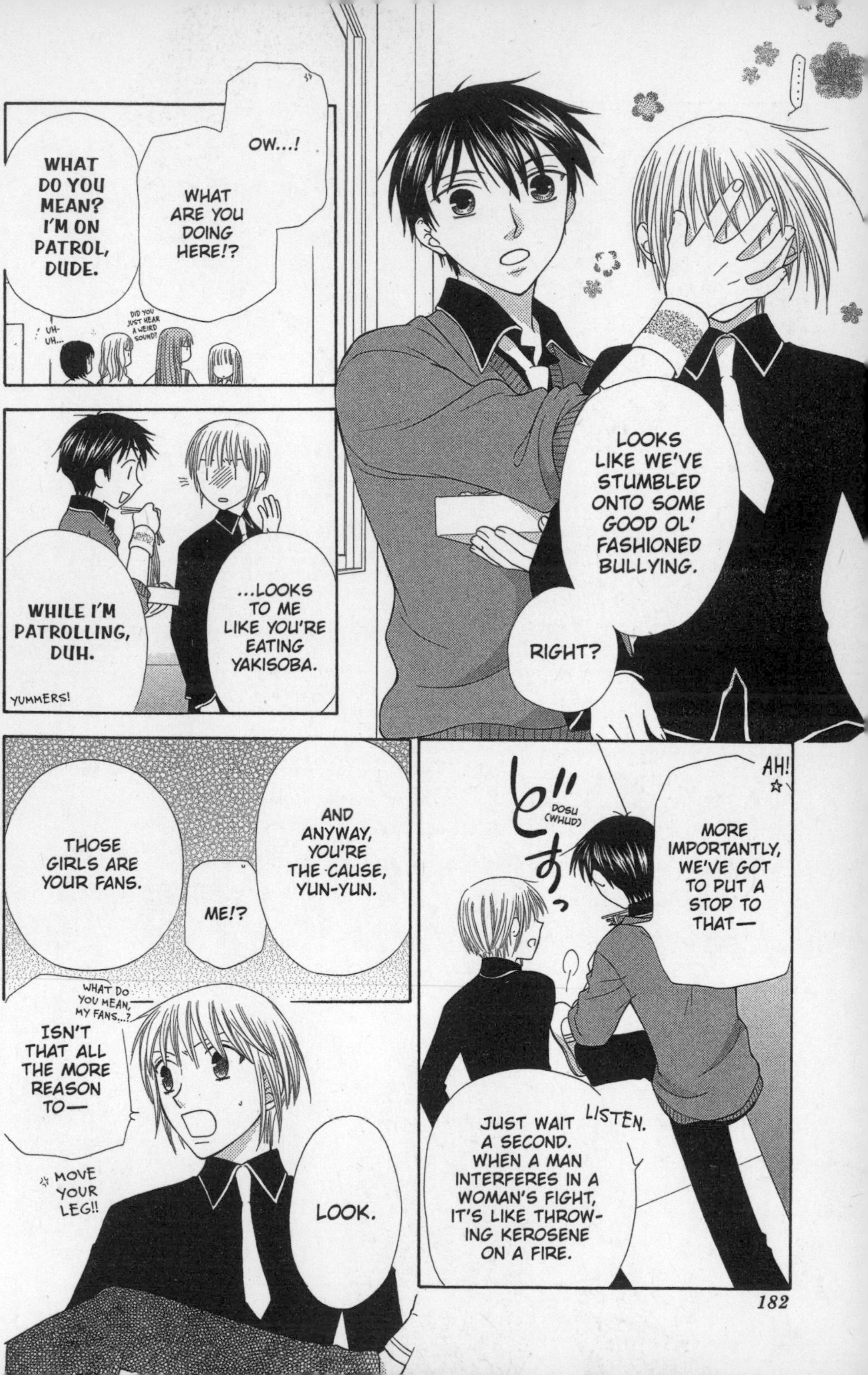
...
LOOKS LIKE WE'VE STUMBLED ONTO SOME GOOD OL' FASHIONED BULLYING.
RIGHT?
OW...!
WHAT ARE YOU DOING HERE!?
WHAT DO YOU MEAN? I'M ON PATROL, DUDE.
DID YOU JUST HEAR A WEIRD SOUND?
UH-UH...
...LOOKS TO ME LIKE YOU'RE EATING YAKISOBA.
WHILE I'M PATROLLING, DUH.
YUMMERS!
AH!
DOSU (WHUD)
MORE IMPORTANTLY, WE'VE GOT TO PUT A STOP TO THAT—
LISTEN.
JUST WAIT A SECOND. WHEN A MAN INTERFERES IN A WOMAN'S FIGHT, IT'S LIKE THROWING KEROSENE ON A FIRE.
AND ANYWAY, YOU'RE THE CAUSE, YUN-YUN.
ME!?
THOSE GIRLS ARE YOUR FANS.
LOOK.
WHAT DO YOU MEAN, MY FANS...?
ISN'T THAT ALL THE MORE REASON TO—
MOVE YOUR LEG!!

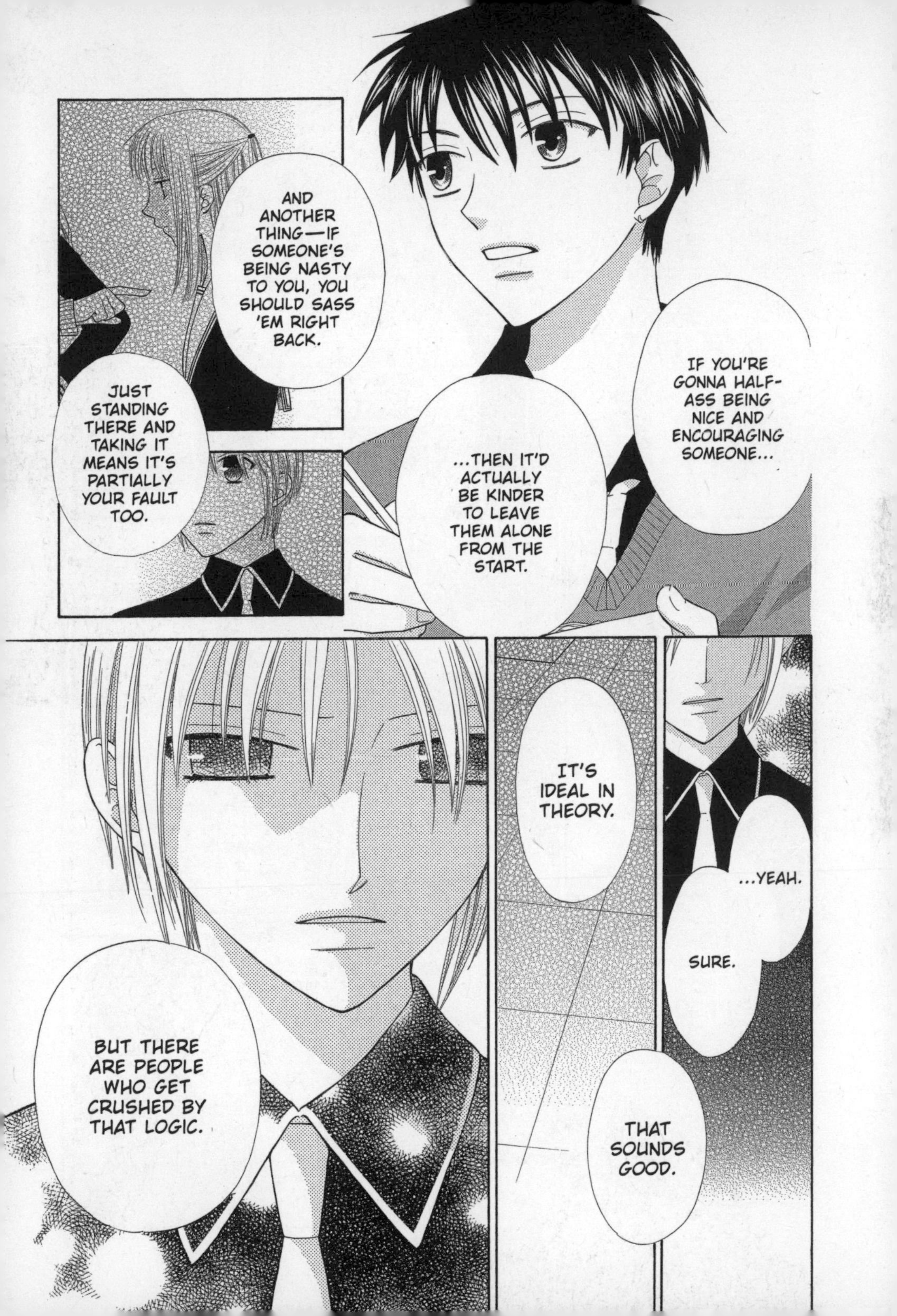
IF YOU'RE GONNA HALF-ASS BEING NICE AND ENCOURAGING SOMEONE...
...THEN IT'D ACTUALLY BE KINDER TO LEAVE THEM ALONE FROM THE START.
AND ANOTHER THING—IF SOMEONE'S BEING NASTY TO YOU, YOU SHOULD SASS 'EM RIGHT BACK.
JUST STANDING THERE AND TAKING IT MEANS IT'S PARTIALLY YOUR FAULT TOO.
...YEAH.
SURE.
THAT SOUNDS GOOD.
IT'S IDEAL IN THEORY.
BUT THERE ARE PEOPLE WHO GET CRUSHED BY THAT LOGIC.

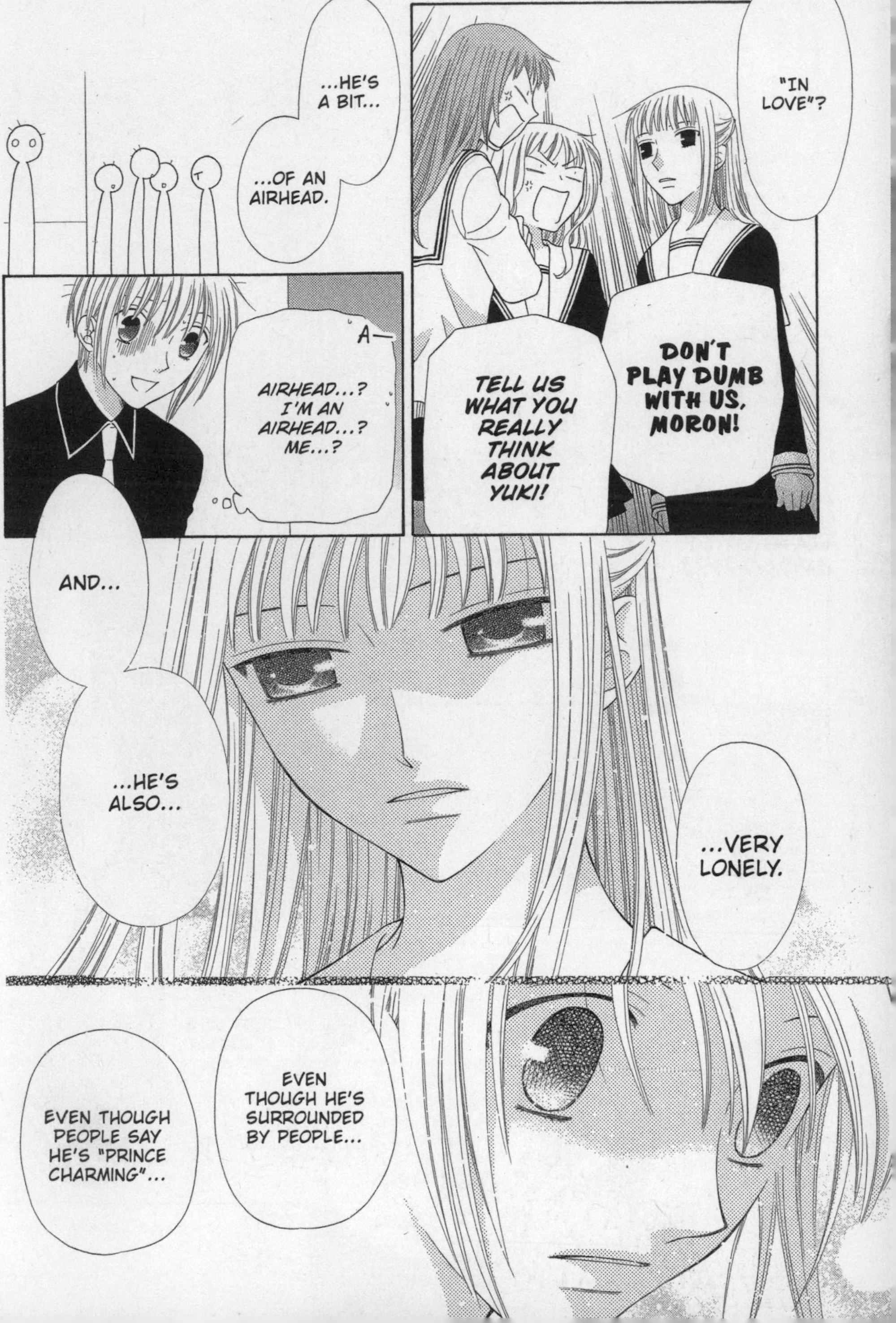
"IN LOVE"?
DON'T PLAY DUMB WITH US, MORON!
TELL US WHAT YOU REALLY THINK ABOUT YUKI!
...HE'S A BIT...
...OF AN AIRHEAD.
A—
AIRHEAD...? I'M AN AIRHEAD...? ME...?
AND...
...HE'S ALSO...
...VERY LONELY.
EVEN THOUGH HE'S SURROUNDED BY PEOPLE...
EVEN THOUGH PEOPLE SAY HE'S "PRINCE CHARMING"...

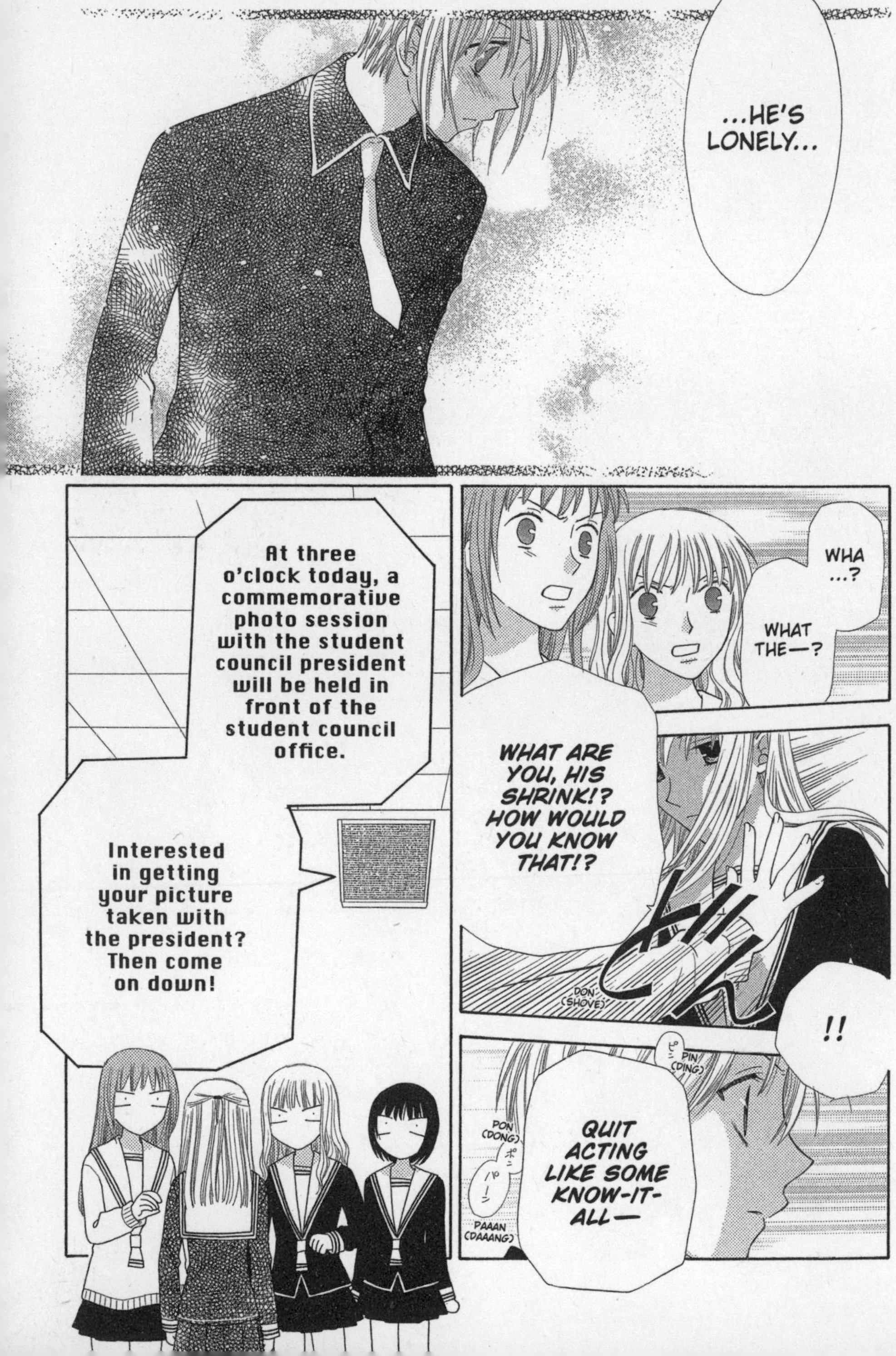
...HE'S LONELY...
WHA ...?
WHAT THE—?
WHAT ARE YOU, HIS SHRINK!? HOW WOULD YOU KNOW THAT!?
DON (SHOVE)
!!
PIN (DING)
PON (DONG)
PAAAN (DAAANG)
QUIT ACTING LIKE SOME KNOW-IT-ALL—
At three o'clock today, a commemorative photo session with the student council president will be held in front of the student council office.
Interested in getting your picture taken with the president? Then come on down!

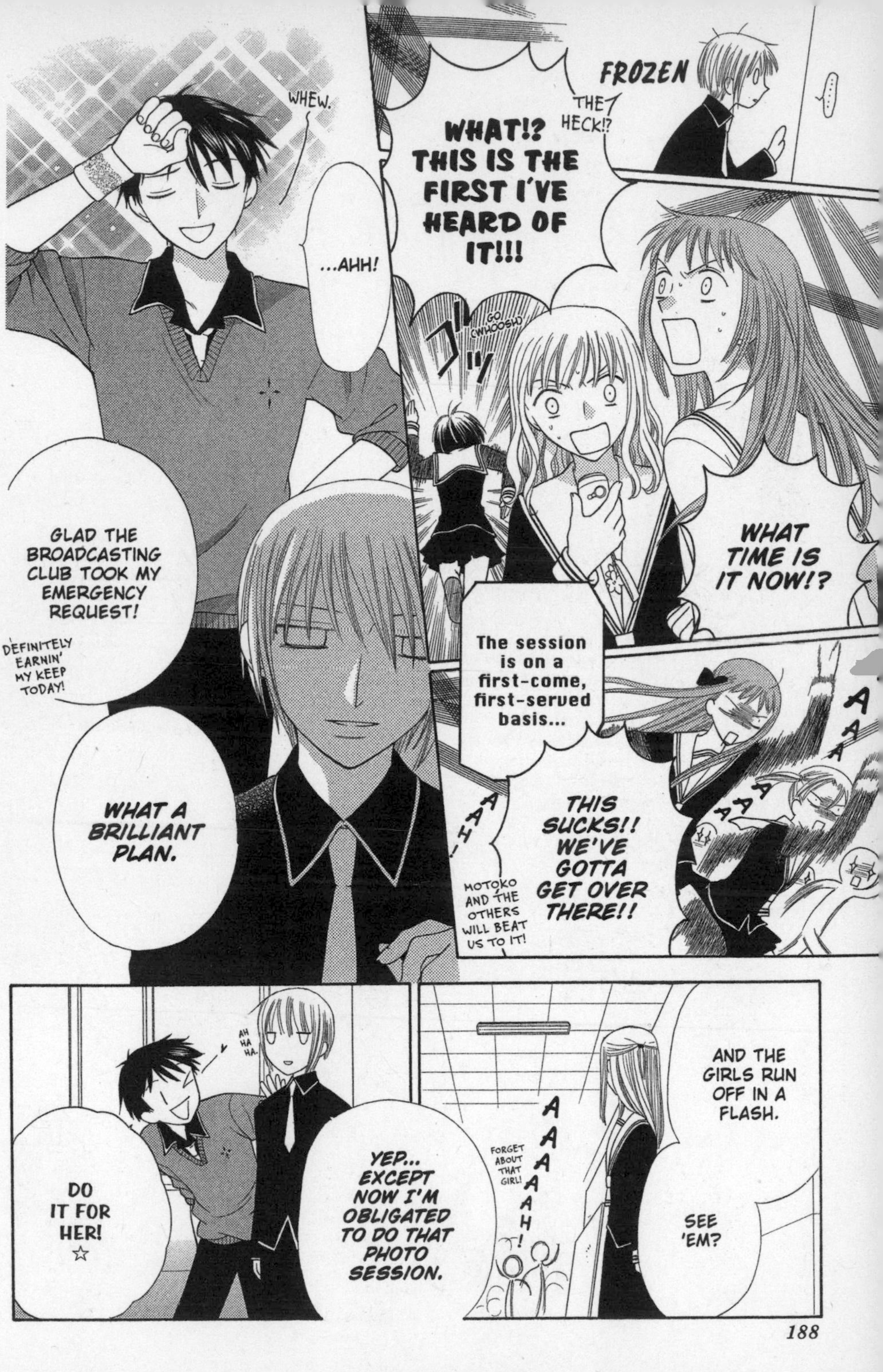
......
FROZEN
THE HECK!?
WHAT!? THIS IS THE FIRST I'VE HEARD OF IT!!!
GO (WHOOSH)
WHAT TIME IS IT NOW!?
The session is on a first-come, first-served basis...
AAAAAA
THIS SUCKS!! WE'VE GOTTA GET OVER THERE!!
AAAH!
MOTOKO AND THE OTHERS WILL BEAT US TO IT!
WHEW.
...AHH!
GLAD THE BROADCASTING CLUB TOOK MY EMERGENCY REQUEST!
DEFINITELY EARNIN' MY KEEP TODAY!
WHAT A BRILLIANT PLAN.
AND THE GIRLS RUN OFF IN A FLASH.
SEE 'EM?
AAAAAAH!
FORGET ABOUT THAT GIRL!
YEP... EXCEPT NOW I'M OBLIGATED TO DO THAT PHOTO SESSION.
AH HA HA.
DO IT FOR HER! ☆

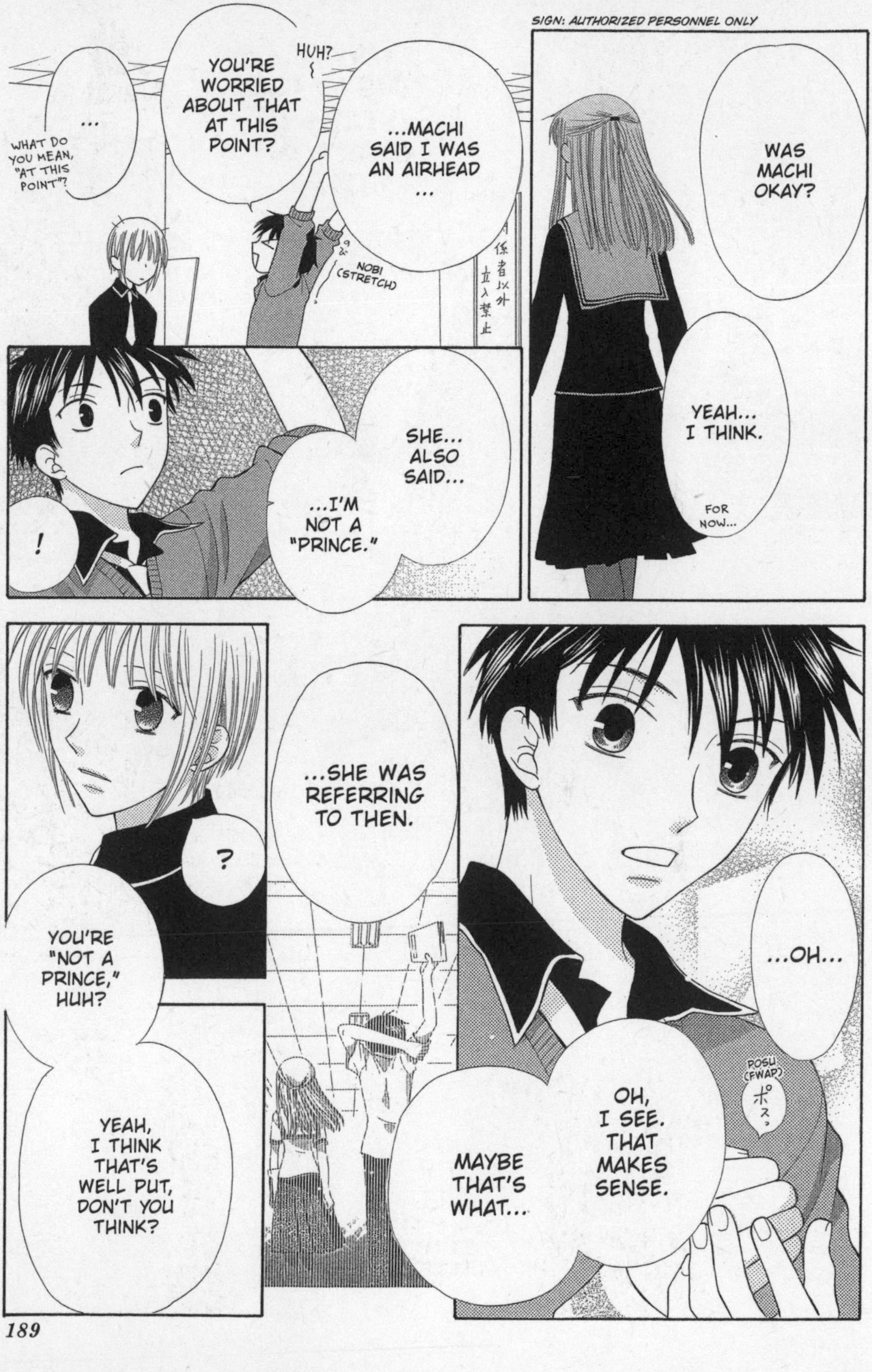
SIGN: AUTHORIZED PERSONNEL ONLY
WAS MACHI OKAY?
YEAH... I THINK.
FOR NOW...
...MACHI SAID I WAS AN AIRHEAD ...
HUH?
NOBI (STRETCH)
関係者以外立入禁止
YOU'RE WORRIED ABOUT THAT AT THIS POINT?
...
WHAT DO YOU MEAN, "AT THIS POINT"?
SHE... ALSO SAID...
...I'M NOT A "PRINCE."
!
...OH...
POSU (FWAP)
ポスッ
OH, I SEE. THAT MAKES SENSE.
MAYBE THAT'S WHAT...
...SHE WAS REFERRING TO THEN.
?
YOU'RE "NOT A PRINCE," HUH?
YEAH, I THINK THAT'S WELL PUT, DON'T YOU THINK?

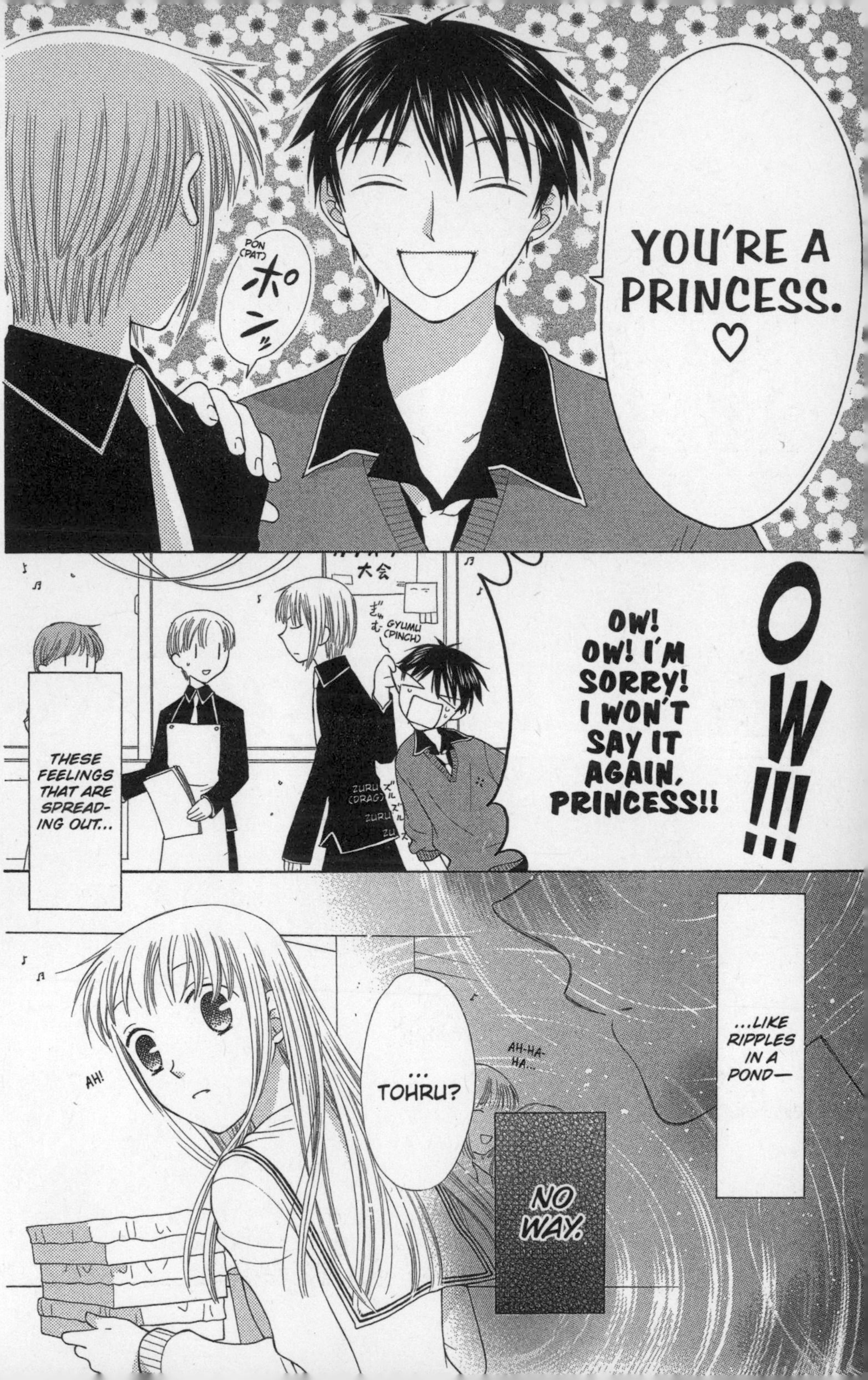
YOU'RE A PRINCESS. ♡
PON (PAT)
ポンッ
OW!!!
OW! OW! I'M SORRY! I WON'T SAY IT AGAIN, PRINCESS!!
ぎゅむ GYUMU (PINCH)
ズルズルズル ZURU (DRAG) ZURU ZURU
THESE FEELINGS THAT ARE SPREADING OUT...
...LIKE RIPPLES IN A POND—
AH-HA-HA...
NO WAY.
... TOHRU?
AH!

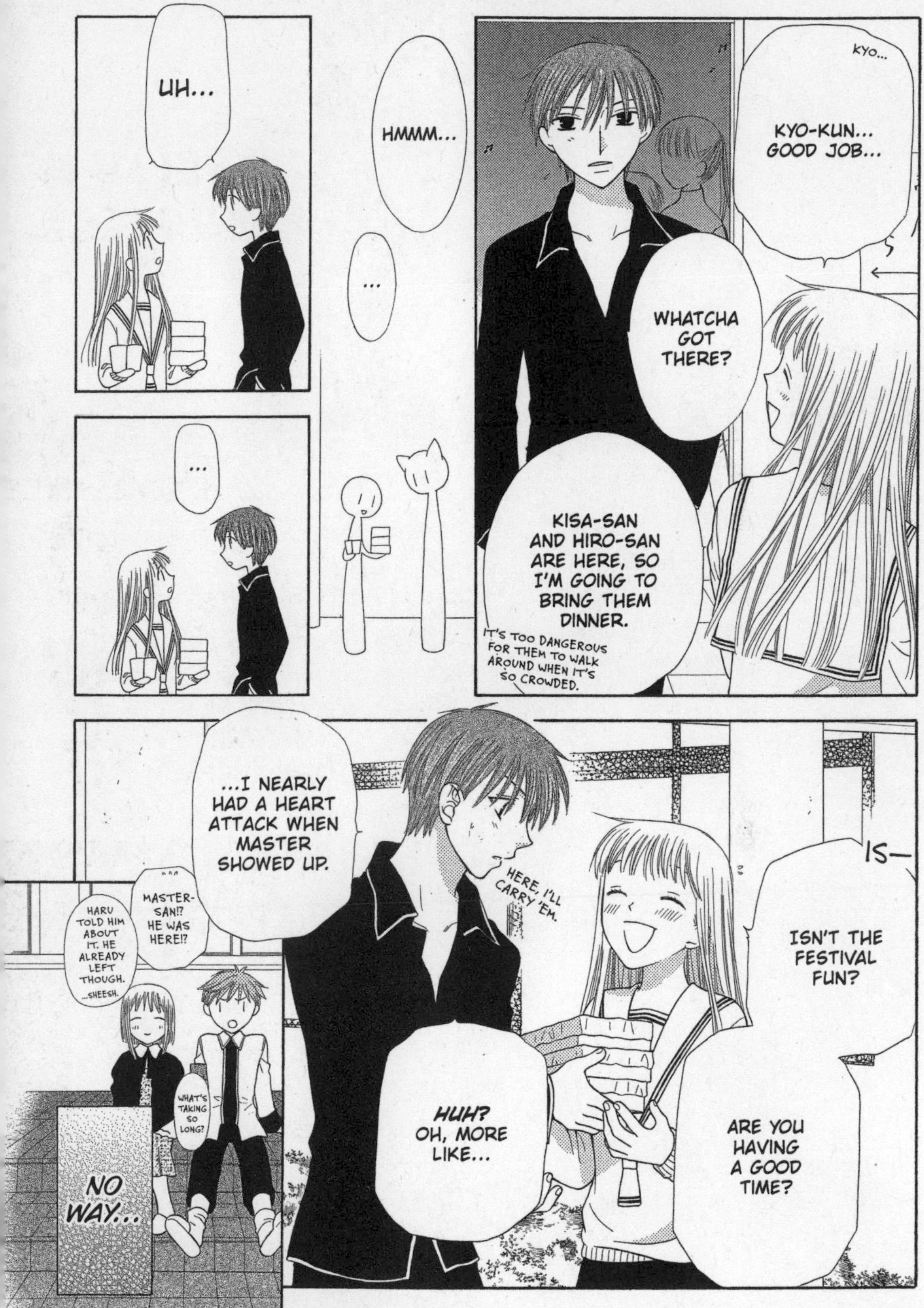
KYO...
KYO-KUN... GOOD JOB...
WHATCHA GOT THERE?
KISA-SAN AND HIRO-SAN ARE HERE, SO I'M GOING TO BRING THEM DINNER.
IT'S TOO DANGEROUS FOR THEM TO WALK AROUND WHEN IT'S SO CROWDED.
HMMM...
...
UH...
...
IS—
ISN'T THE FESTIVAL FUN?
ARE YOU HAVING A GOOD TIME?
HERE, I'LL CARRY 'EM.
HUH? OH, MORE LIKE...
...I NEARLY HAD A HEART ATTACK WHEN MASTER SHOWED UP.
MASTER-SAN!? HE WAS HERE!?
HARU TOLD HIM ABOUT IT. HE ALREADY LEFT THOUGH. ...SHEESH.
WHAT'S TAKING SO LONG?
NO WAY...

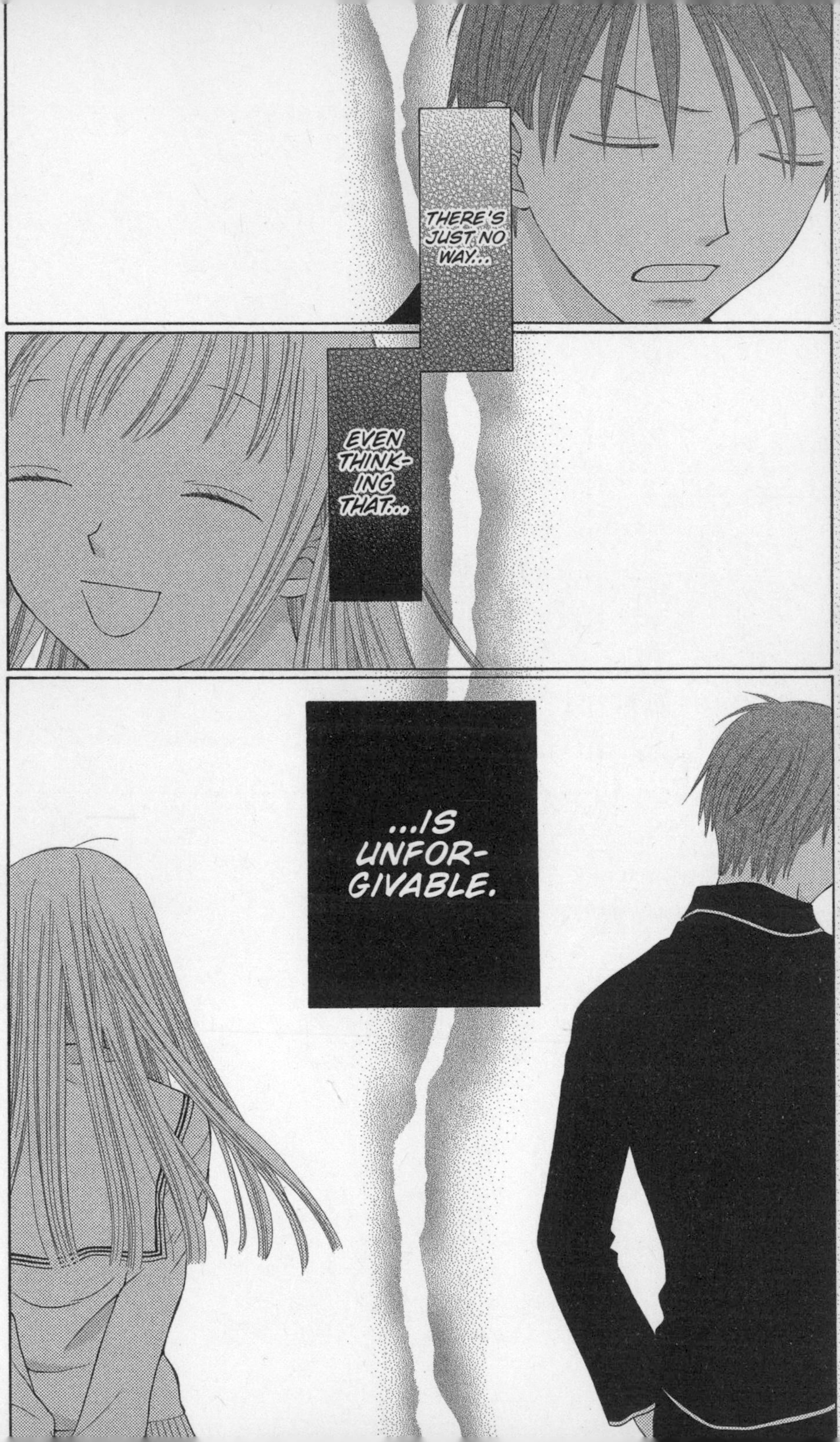
THERE'S JUST NO WAY...
EVEN THINK-ING THAT...
...IS UNFOR-GIVABLE.

COLLECTOR'S EDITION

Fruits Basket

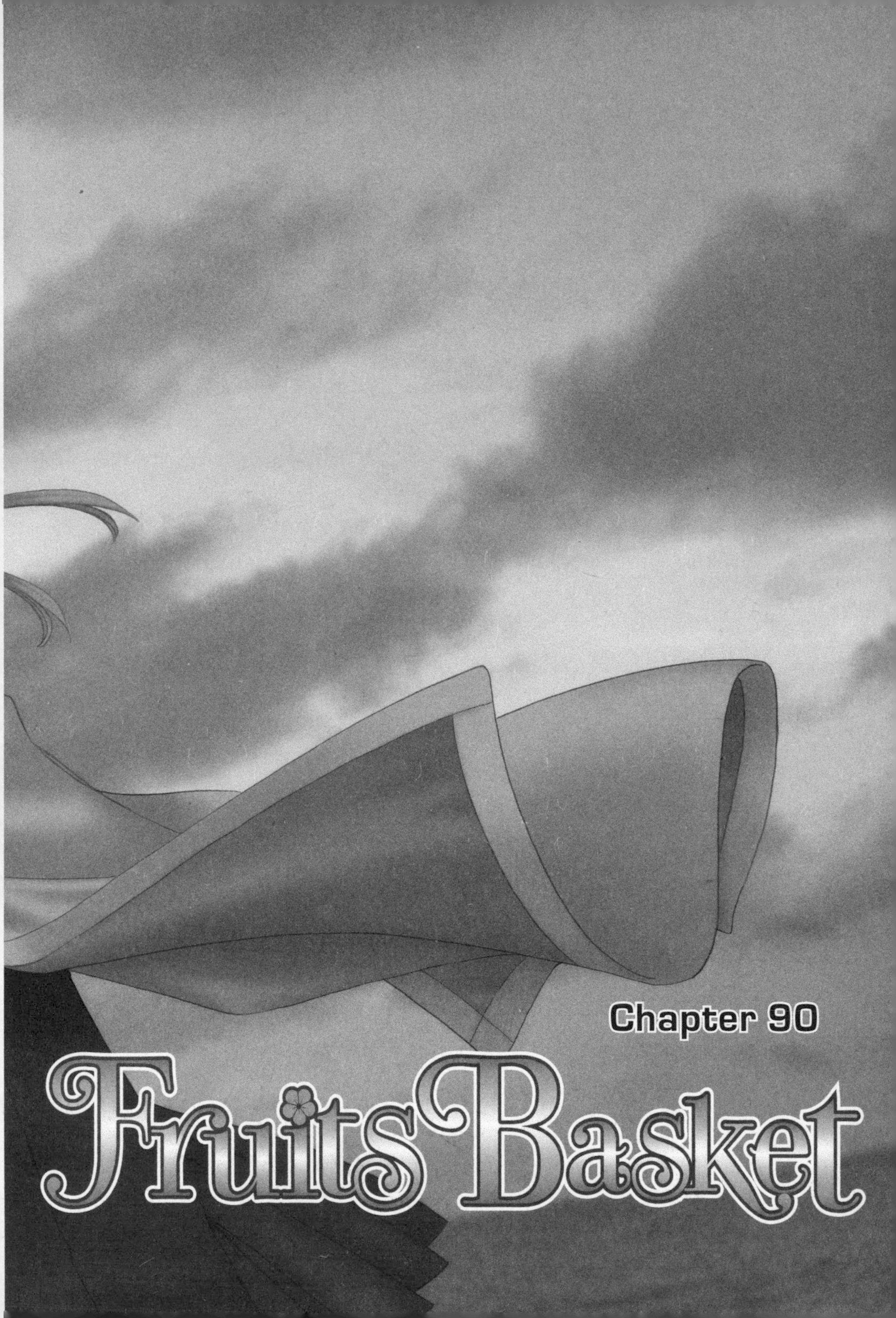
Chapter 90
Fruits Basket

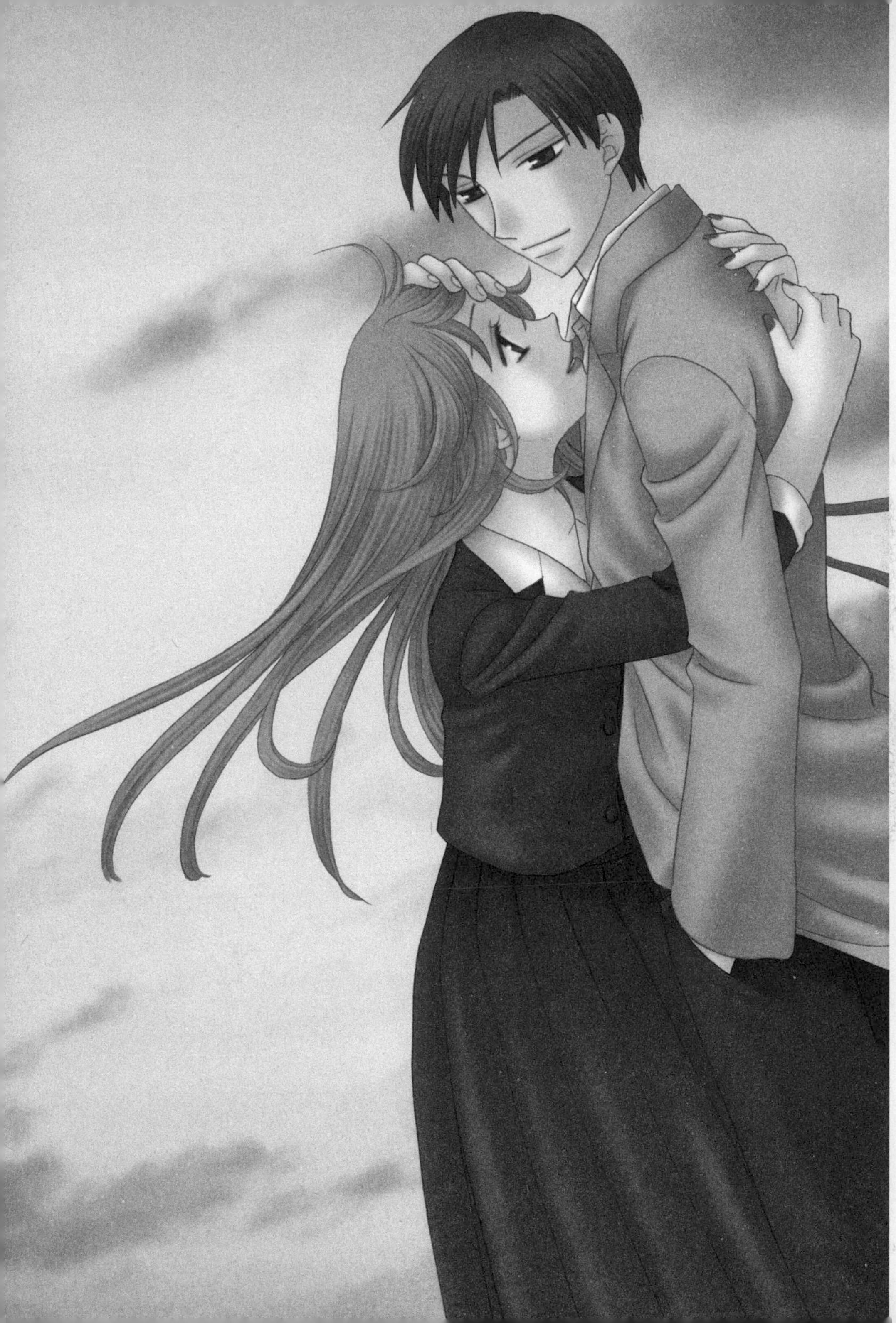

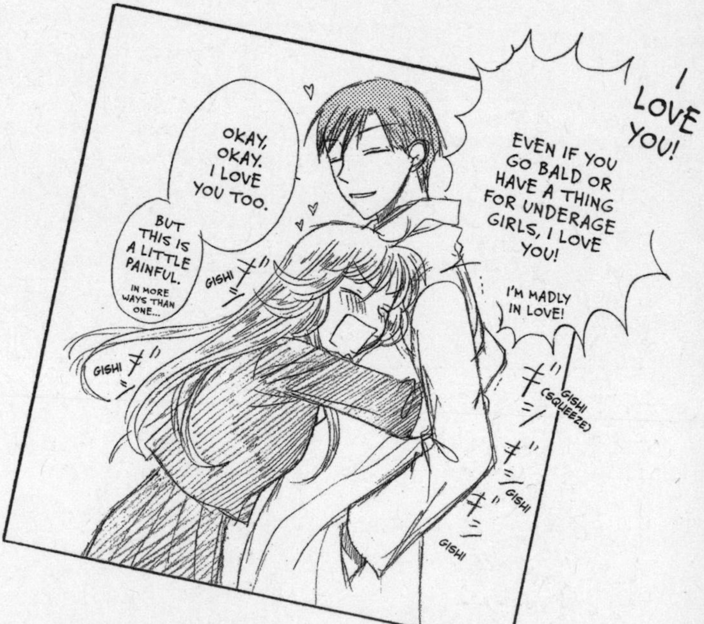
I LOVE YOU!
EVEN IF YOU GO BALD OR HAVE A THING FOR UNDERAGE GIRLS, I LOVE YOU!
I'M MADLY IN LOVE!
OKAY, OKAY. I LOVE YOU TOO.
BUT THIS IS A LITTLE PAINFUL.
IN MORE WAYS THAN ONE...
GISHI (SQUEEZE)
GISHI
GISHI
GISHI!
GISHI!

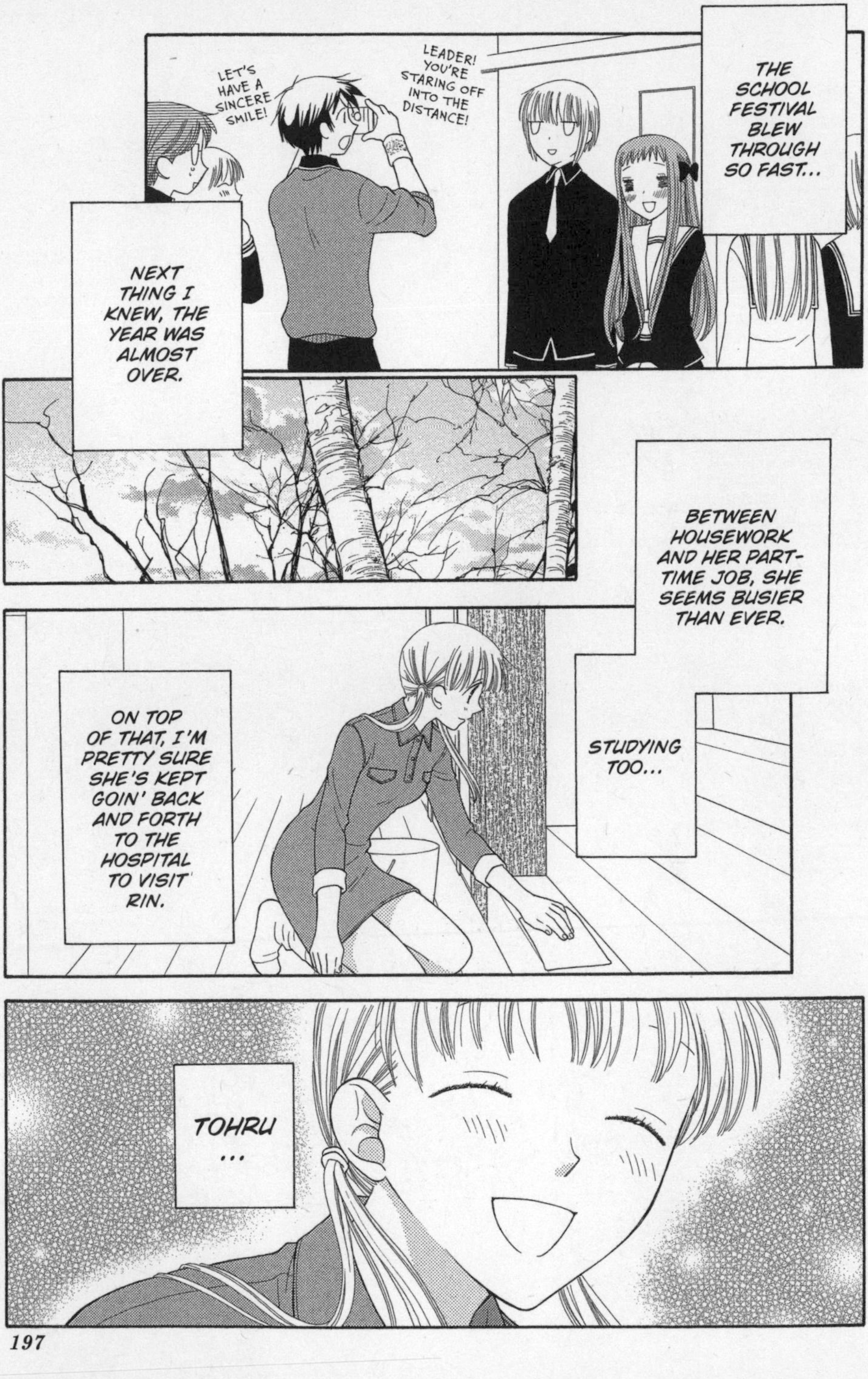
THE SCHOOL FESTIVAL BLEW THROUGH SO FAST...
LEADER! YOU'RE STARING OFF INTO THE DISTANCE!
LET'S HAVE A SINCERE SMILE!
NEXT THING I KNEW, THE YEAR WAS ALMOST OVER.
BETWEEN HOUSEWORK AND HER PART-TIME JOB, SHE SEEMS BUSIER THAN EVER.
STUDYING TOO...
ON TOP OF THAT, I'M PRETTY SURE SHE'S KEPT GOIN' BACK AND FORTH TO THE HOSPITAL TO VISIT RIN.
TOHRU
...

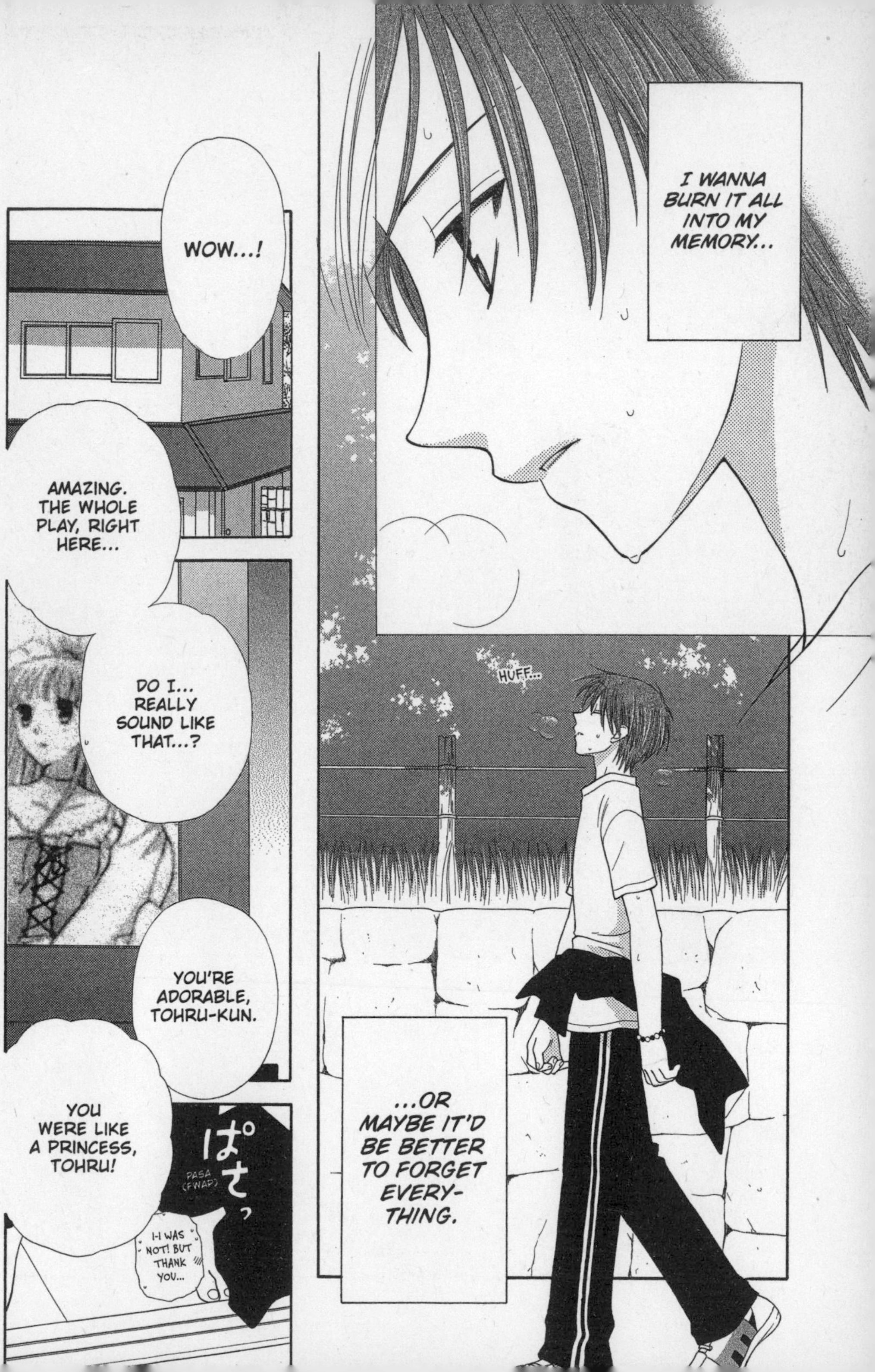
I WANNA BURN IT ALL INTO MY MEMORY...
HUFF...
...OR MAYBE IT'D BE BETTER TO FORGET EVERY-THING.
WOW...!
AMAZING. THE WHOLE PLAY, RIGHT HERE...
DO I... REALLY SOUND LIKE THAT...?
YOU'RE ADORABLE, TOHRU-KUN.
YOU WERE LIKE A PRINCESS, TOHRU!
ぱさっ
PASA (FWAP)
I-I WAS NOT! BUT THANK YOU...

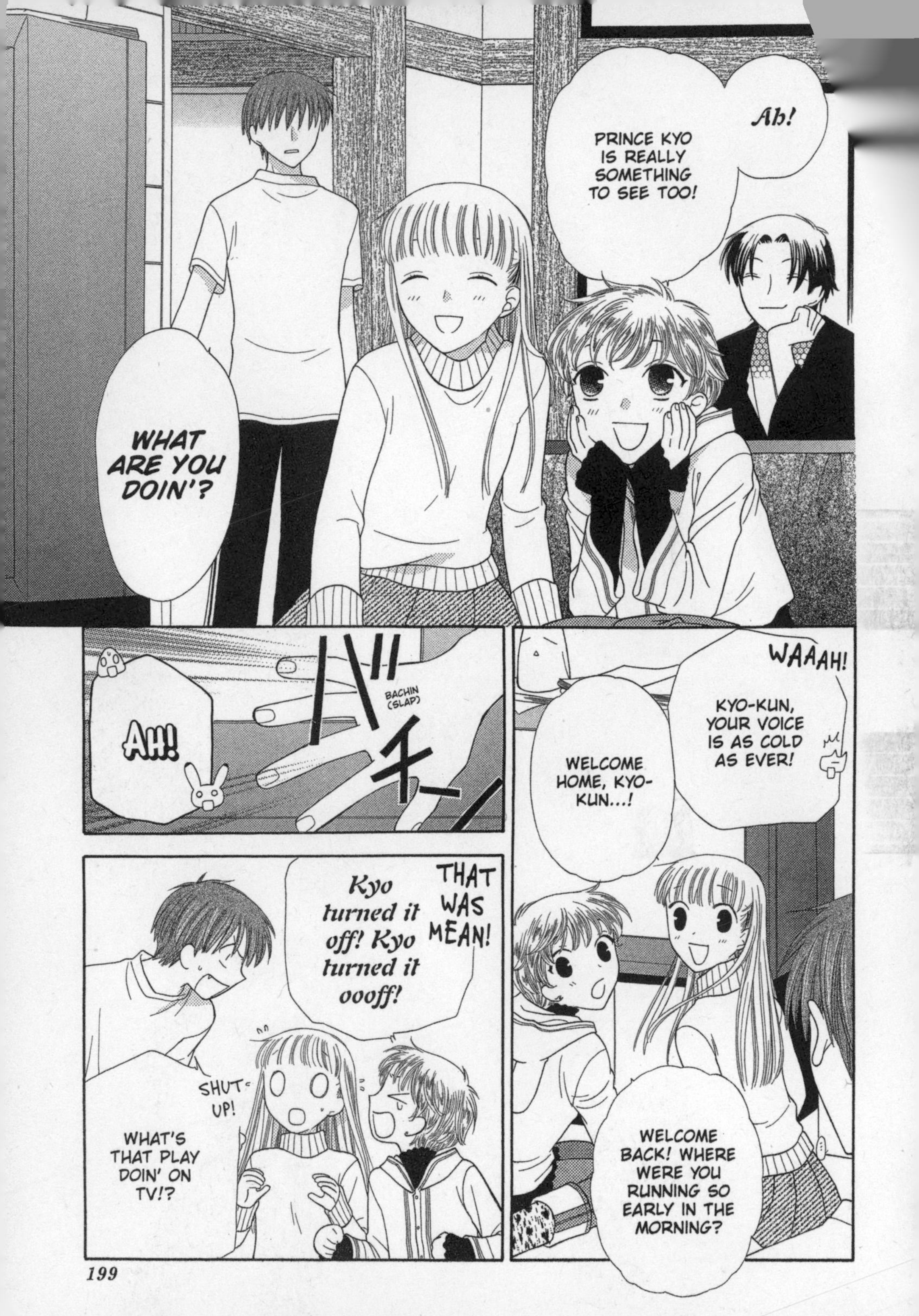
Ah!
PRINCE KYO IS REALLY SOMETHING TO SEE TOO!
WHAT ARE YOU DOIN'?
WAAAH!
KYO-KUN, YOUR VOICE IS AS COLD AS EVER!
WELCOME HOME, KYO-KUN...!
WELCOME BACK! WHERE WERE YOU RUNNING SO EARLY IN THE MORNING?
バチーン
BACHIN (SLAP)
AH!
THAT WAS MEAN!
Kyo turned it off! Kyo turned it oooff!
SHUT-UP!
WHAT'S THAT PLAY DOIN' ON TV!?

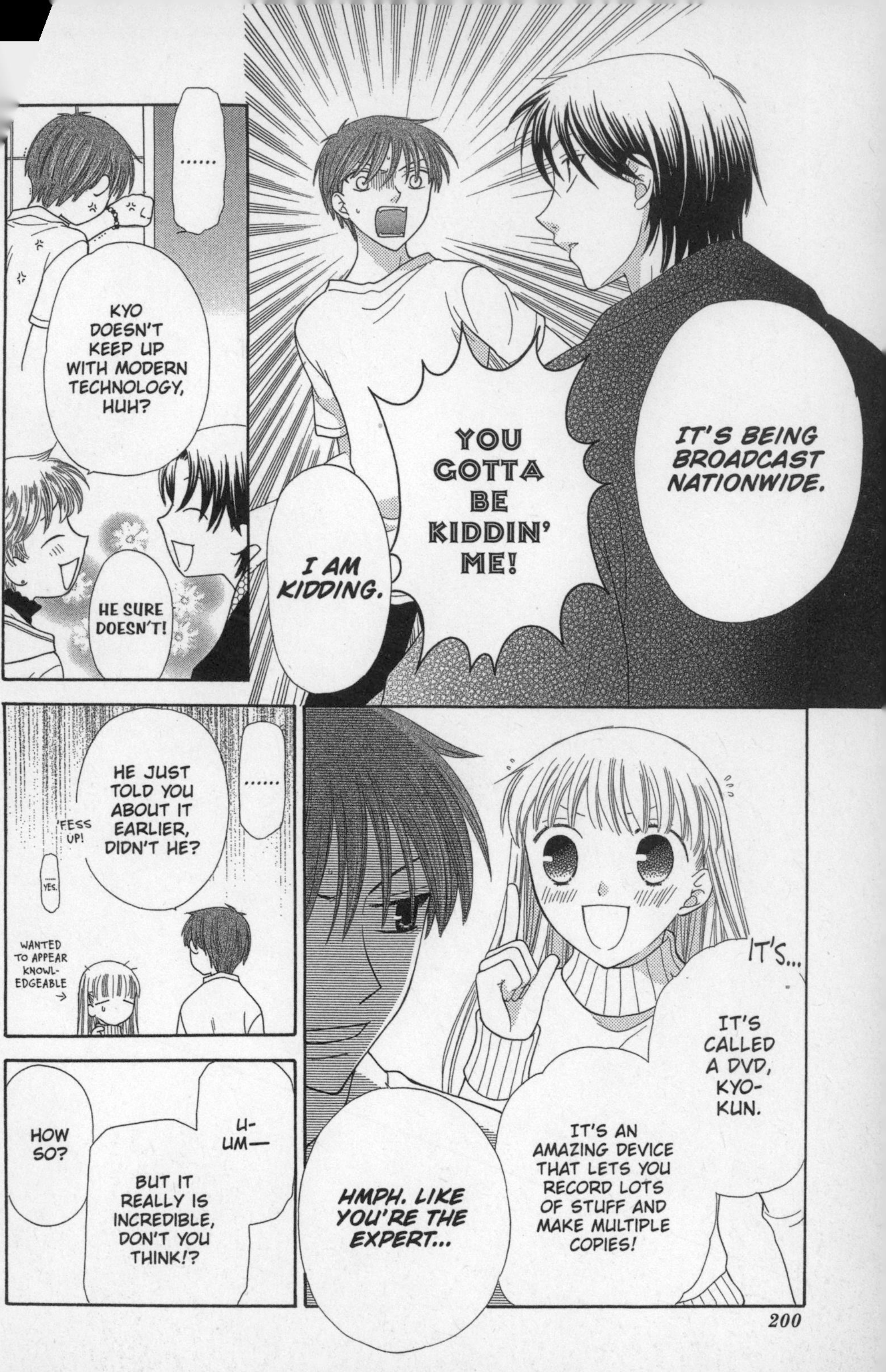
IT'S BEING BROADCAST NATIONWIDE.
YOU GOTTA BE KIDDIN' ME!
I AM KIDDING.
......
KYO DOESN'T KEEP UP WITH MODERN TECHNOLOGY, HUH?
HE SURE DOESN'T!
IT'S...
IT'S CALLED A DVD, KYO-KUN.
IT'S AN AMAZING DEVICE THAT LETS YOU RECORD LOTS OF STUFF AND MAKE MULTIPLE COPIES!
HMPH. LIKE YOU'RE THE EXPERT...
......
HE JUST TOLD YOU ABOUT IT EARLIER, DIDN'T HE?
'FESS UP!
......YES.
WANTED TO APPEAR KNOWL-EDGEABLE →
U-UM—
BUT IT REALLY IS INCREDIBLE, DON'T YOU THINK!?
HOW SO?

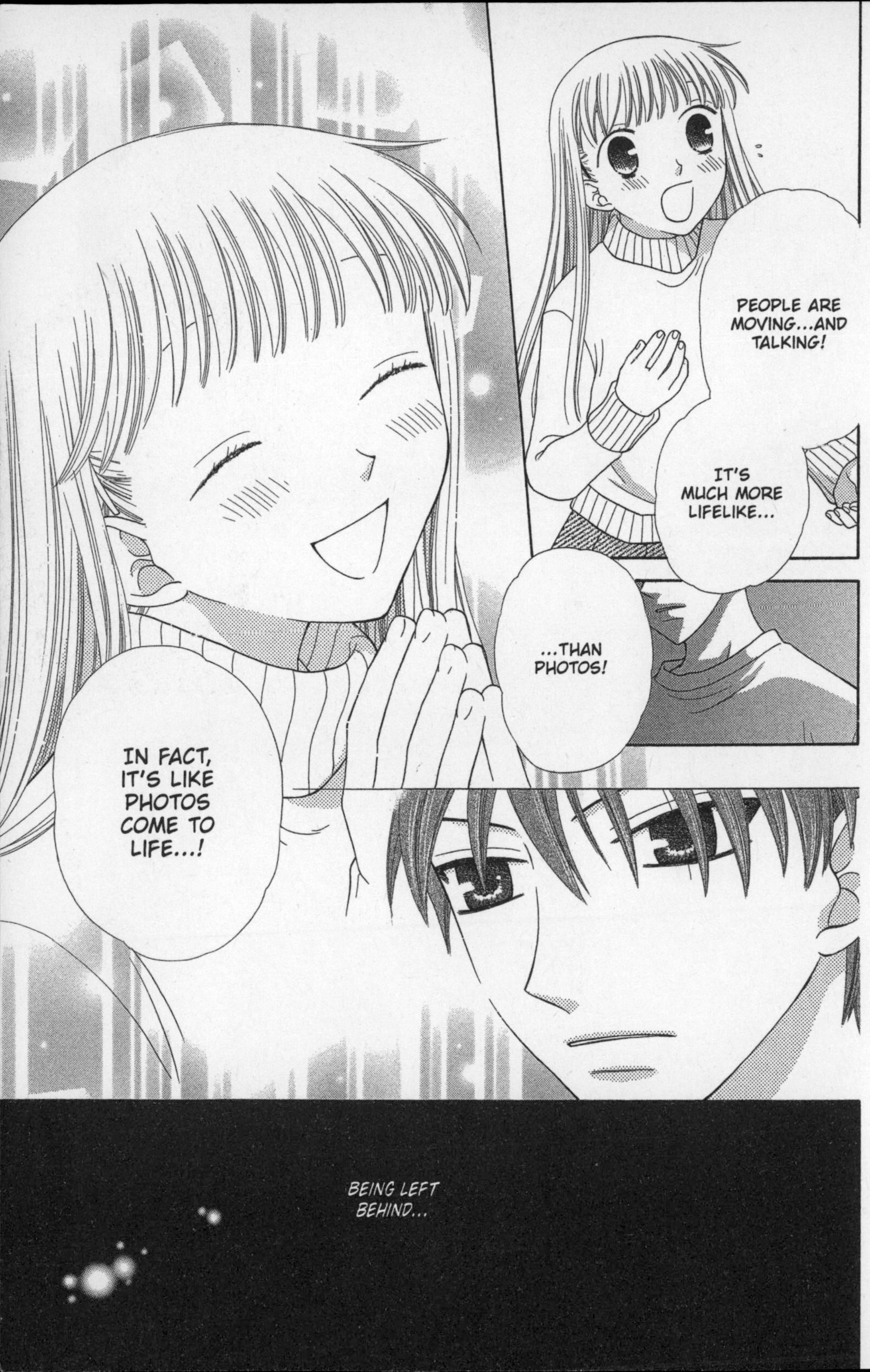
PEOPLE ARE MOVING...AND TALKING!
IT'S MUCH MORE LIFELIKE...
...THAN PHOTOS!
IN FACT, IT'S LIKE PHOTOS COME TO LIFE...!
BEING LEFT BEHIND...

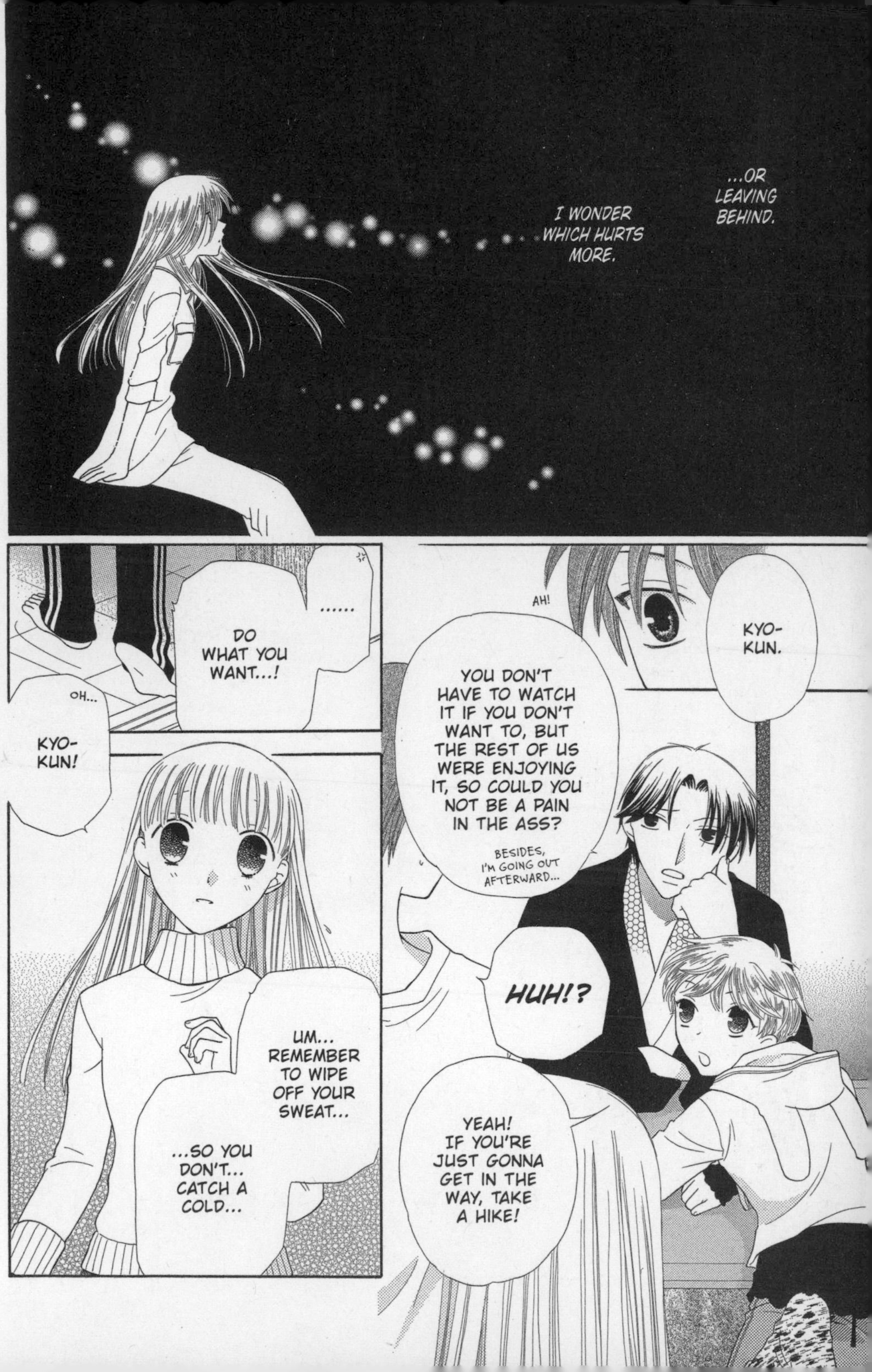

...OR LEAVING BEHIND.
I WONDER WHICH HURTS MORE.
KYO-KUN.
AH!
YOU DON'T HAVE TO WATCH IT IF YOU DON'T WANT TO, BUT THE REST OF US WERE ENJOYING IT, SO COULD YOU NOT BE A PAIN IN THE ASS?
BESIDES, I'M GOING OUT AFTERWARD...
HUH!?
YEAH! IF YOU'RE JUST GONNA GET IN THE WAY, TAKE A HIKE!
......
DO WHAT YOU WANT...!
OH...
KYO-KUN!
UM... REMEMBER TO WIPE OFF YOUR SWEAT...
...SO YOU DON'T... CATCH A COLD...

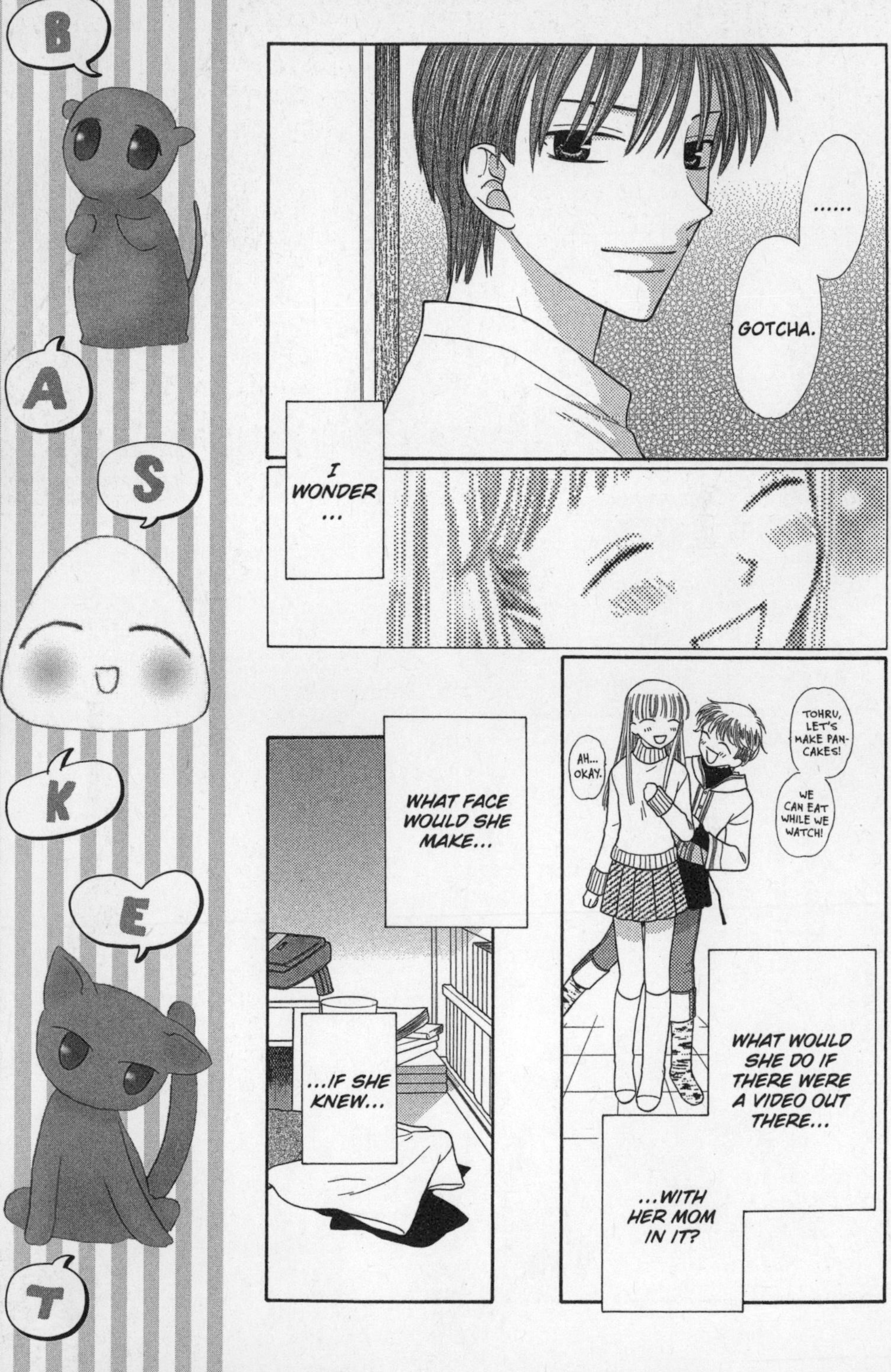

B
A
S
K
E
T
......
GOTCHA.
I WONDER...
TOHRU, LET'S MAKE PAN-CAKES!
AH... OKAY.
WE CAN EAT WHILE WE WATCH!
WHAT WOULD SHE DO IF THERE WERE A VIDEO OUT THERE...
...WITH HER MOM IN IT?
WHAT FACE WOULD SHE MAKE...
...IF SHE KNEW...

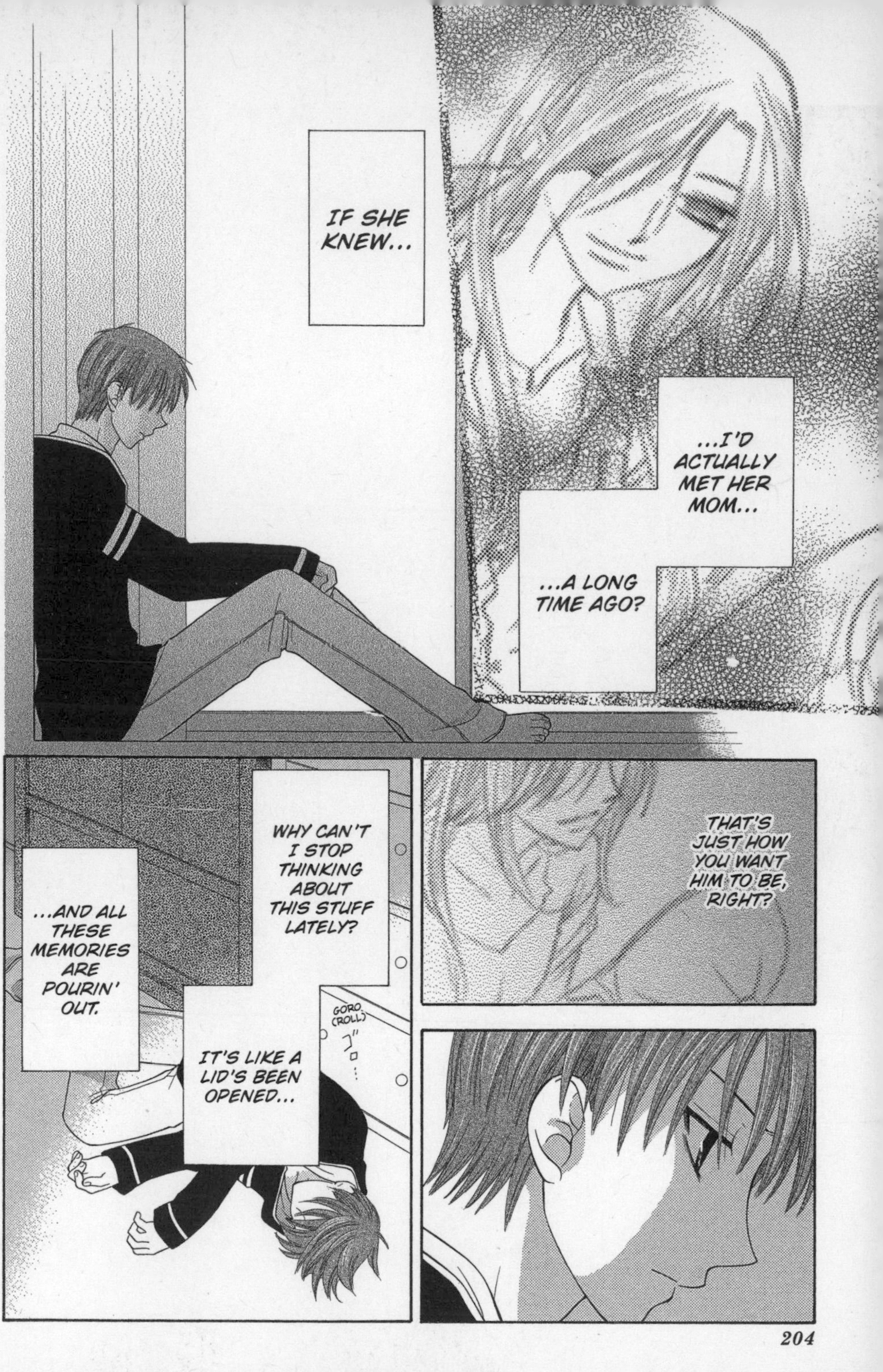
IF SHE KNEW...
...I'D ACTUALLY MET HER MOM...
...A LONG TIME AGO?
THAT'S JUST HOW YOU WANT HIM TO BE, RIGHT?
WHY CAN'T I STOP THINKING ABOUT THIS STUFF LATELY?
...AND ALL THESE MEMORIES ARE POURIN' OUT.
IT'S LIKE A LID'S BEEN OPENED...
GORO (ROLL)
ゴロ...

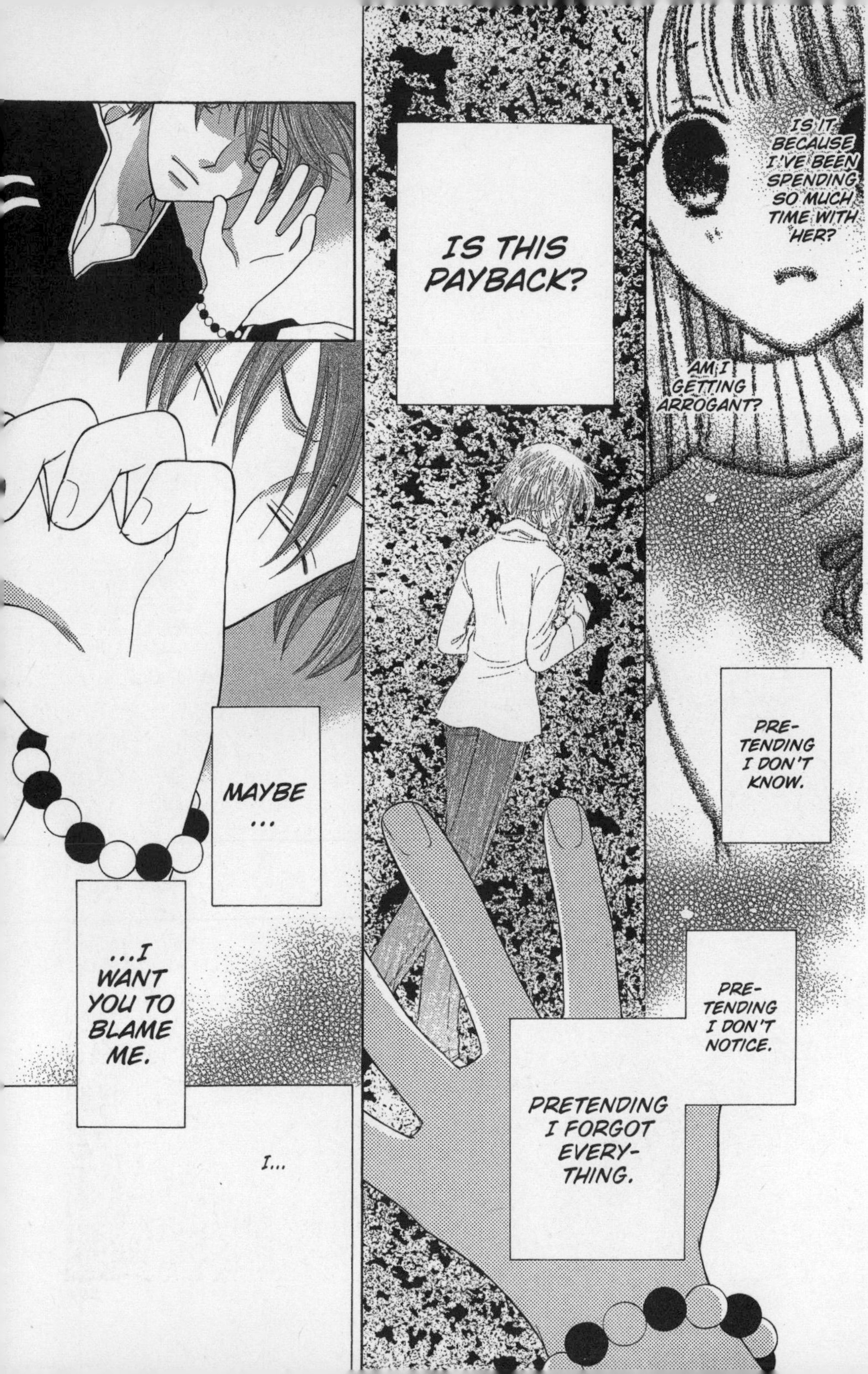
IS IT BECAUSE I'VE BEEN SPENDING SO MUCH TIME WITH HER?
AM I GETTING ARROGANT?
PRE-TENDING I DON'T KNOW.
PRE-TENDING I DON'T NOTICE.
PRETENDING I FORGOT EVERY-THING.
IS THIS PAYBACK?
MAYBE ...
...I WANT YOU TO BLAME ME.
I...

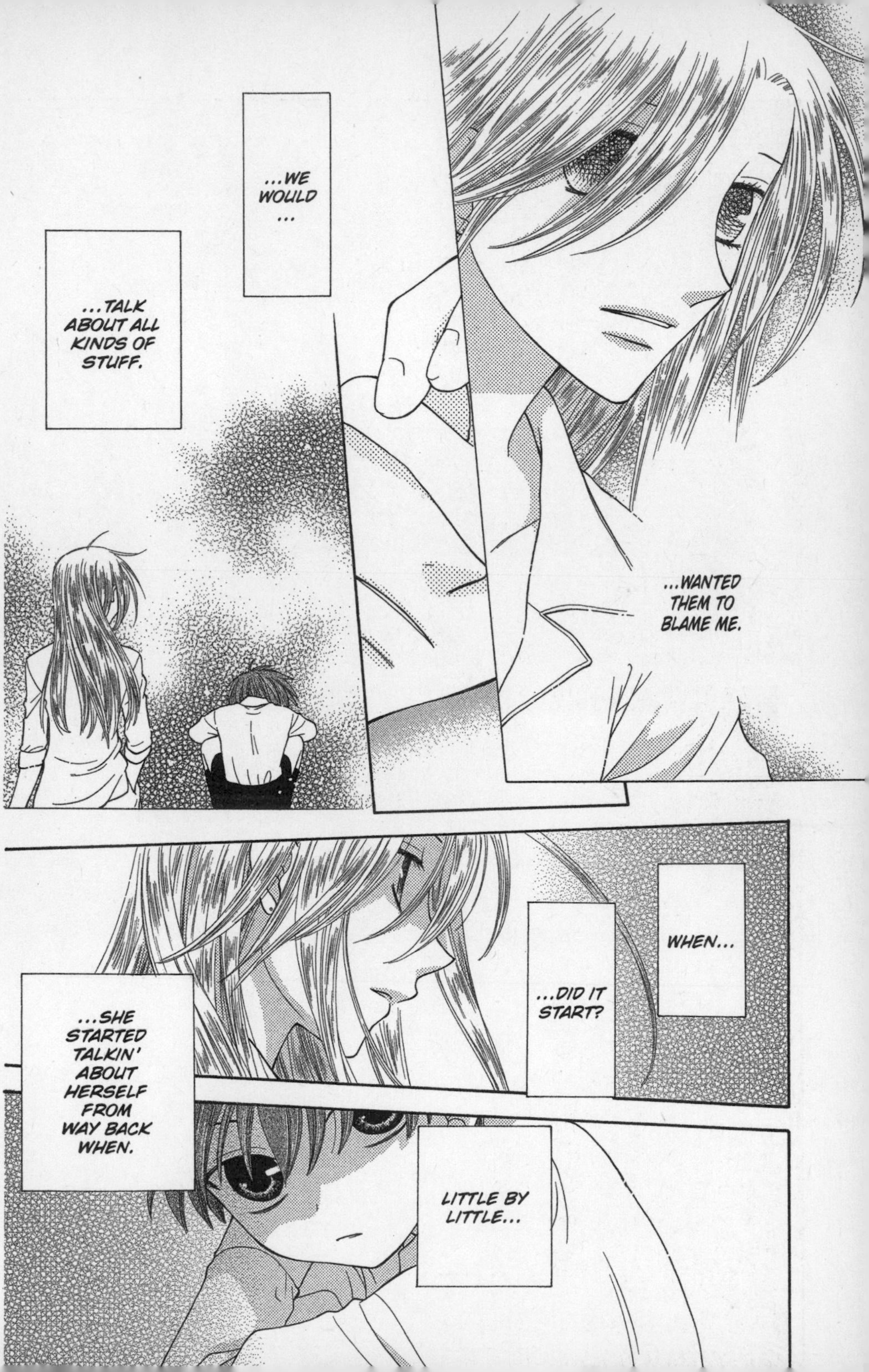
...WANTED THEM TO BLAME ME.
...WE WOULD...
...TALK ABOUT ALL KINDS OF STUFF.
WHEN...
...DID IT START?
...SHE STARTED TALKIN' ABOUT HERSELF FROM WAY BACK WHEN.
LITTLE BY LITTLE...

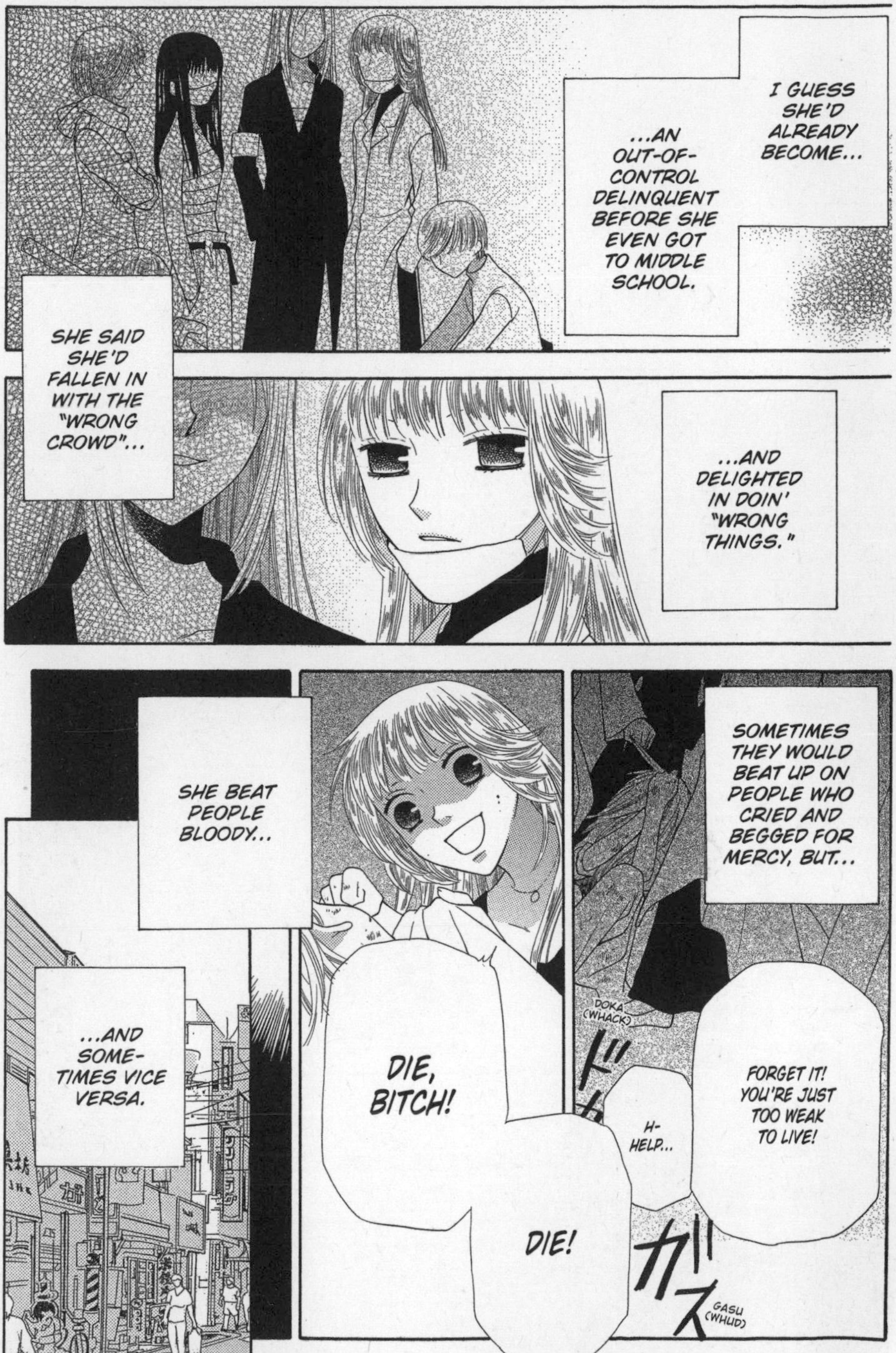
I GUESS SHE'D ALREADY BECOME...
...AN OUT-OF-CONTROL DELINQUENT BEFORE SHE EVEN GOT TO MIDDLE SCHOOL.
SHE SAID SHE'D FALLEN IN WITH THE "WRONG CROWD"...
...AND DELIGHTED IN DOIN' "WRONG THINGS."
SOMETIMES THEY WOULD BEAT UP ON PEOPLE WHO CRIED AND BEGGED FOR MERCY, BUT...
DOKA (WHACK)
FORGET IT! YOU'RE JUST TOO WEAK TO LIVE!
H-HELP...
GASU (WHUD)
SHE BEAT PEOPLE BLOODY...
DIE, BITCH!
DIE!
...AND SOME-TIMES VICE VERSA.

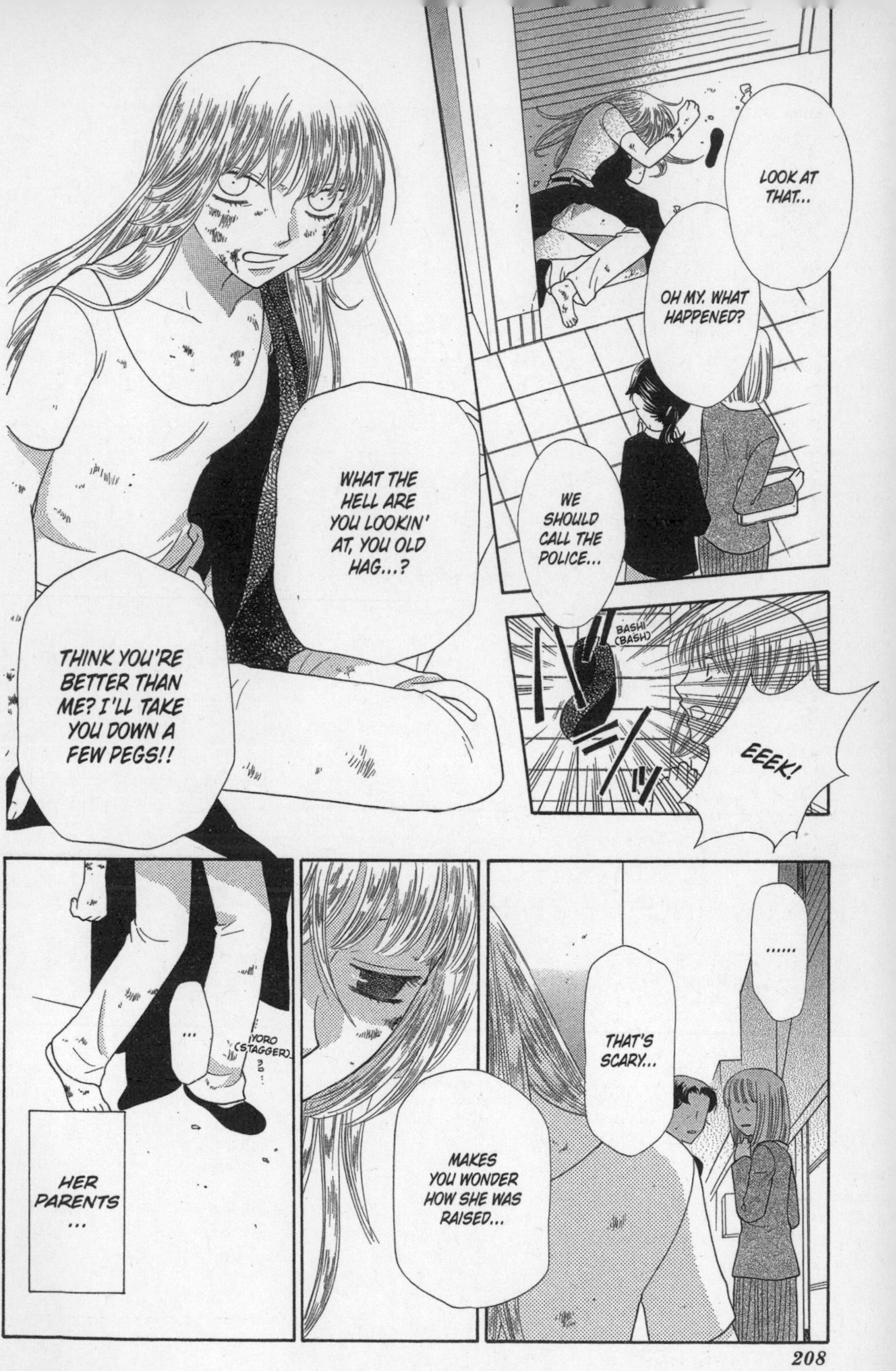
LOOK AT THAT...
OH MY. WHAT HAPPENED?
WE SHOULD CALL THE POLICE...
BASHI (BASH)
EEEK!
WHAT THE HELL ARE YOU LOOKIN' AT, YOU OLD HAG...?
THINK YOU'RE BETTER THAN ME? I'LL TAKE YOU DOWN A FEW PEGS!!
......
THAT'S SCARY...
MAKES YOU WONDER HOW SHE WAS RAISED...
...
YORO (STAGGER)
HER PARENTS ...

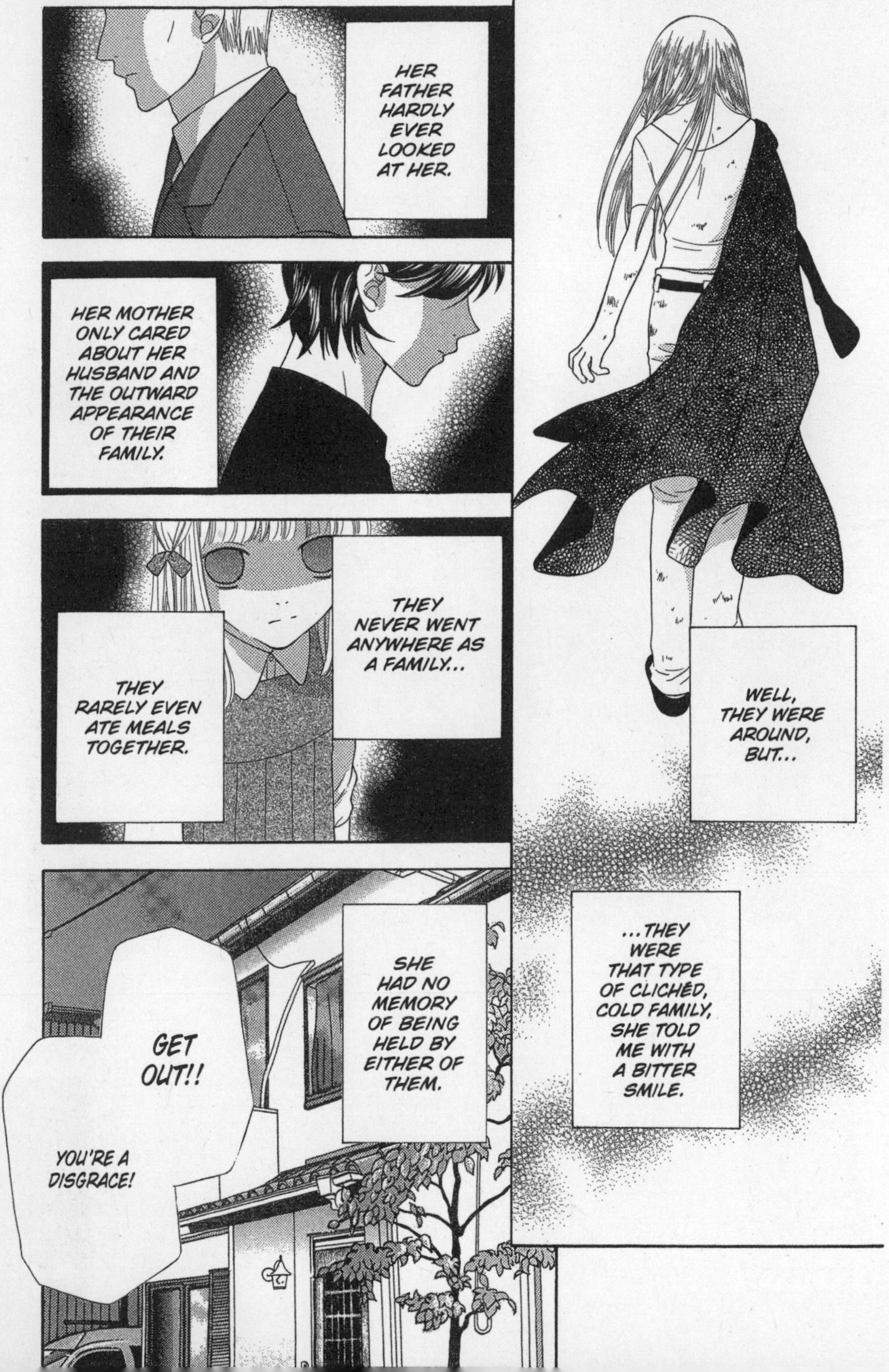
WELL, THEY WERE AROUND, BUT...
...THEY WERE THAT TYPE OF CLICHED, COLD FAMILY, SHE TOLD ME WITH A BITTER SMILE.
HER FATHER HARDLY EVER LOOKED AT HER.
HER MOTHER ONLY CARED ABOUT HER HUSBAND AND THE OUTWARD APPEARANCE OF THEIR FAMILY.
THEY NEVER WENT ANYWHERE AS A FAMILY...
THEY RARELY EVEN ATE MEALS TOGETHER.
SHE HAD NO MEMORY OF BEING HELD BY EITHER OF THEM.
GET OUT!!
YOU'RE A DISGRACE!

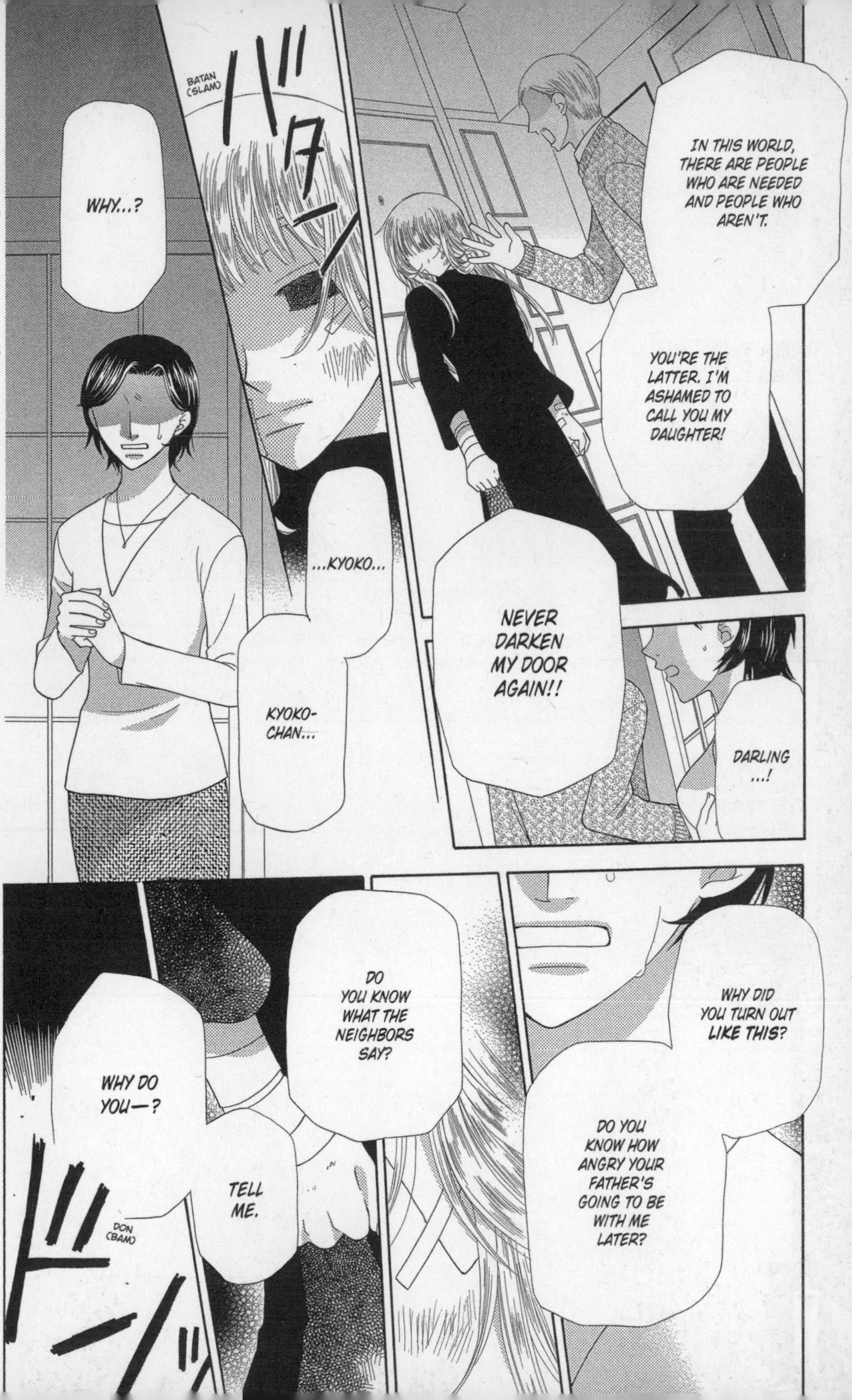
IN THIS WORLD, THERE ARE PEOPLE WHO ARE NEEDED AND PEOPLE WHO AREN'T.
YOU'RE THE LATTER. I'M ASHAMED TO CALL YOU MY DAUGHTER!
NEVER DARKEN MY DOOR AGAIN!!
BATAN (SLAM)
DARLING ...!
WHY...?
...KYOKO...
KYOKO-CHAN...
WHY DID YOU TURN OUT LIKE THIS?
DO YOU KNOW HOW ANGRY YOUR FATHER'S GOING TO BE WITH ME LATER?
DO YOU KNOW WHAT THE NEIGHBORS SAY?
WHY DO YOU—?
TELL ME.
DON (BAM)

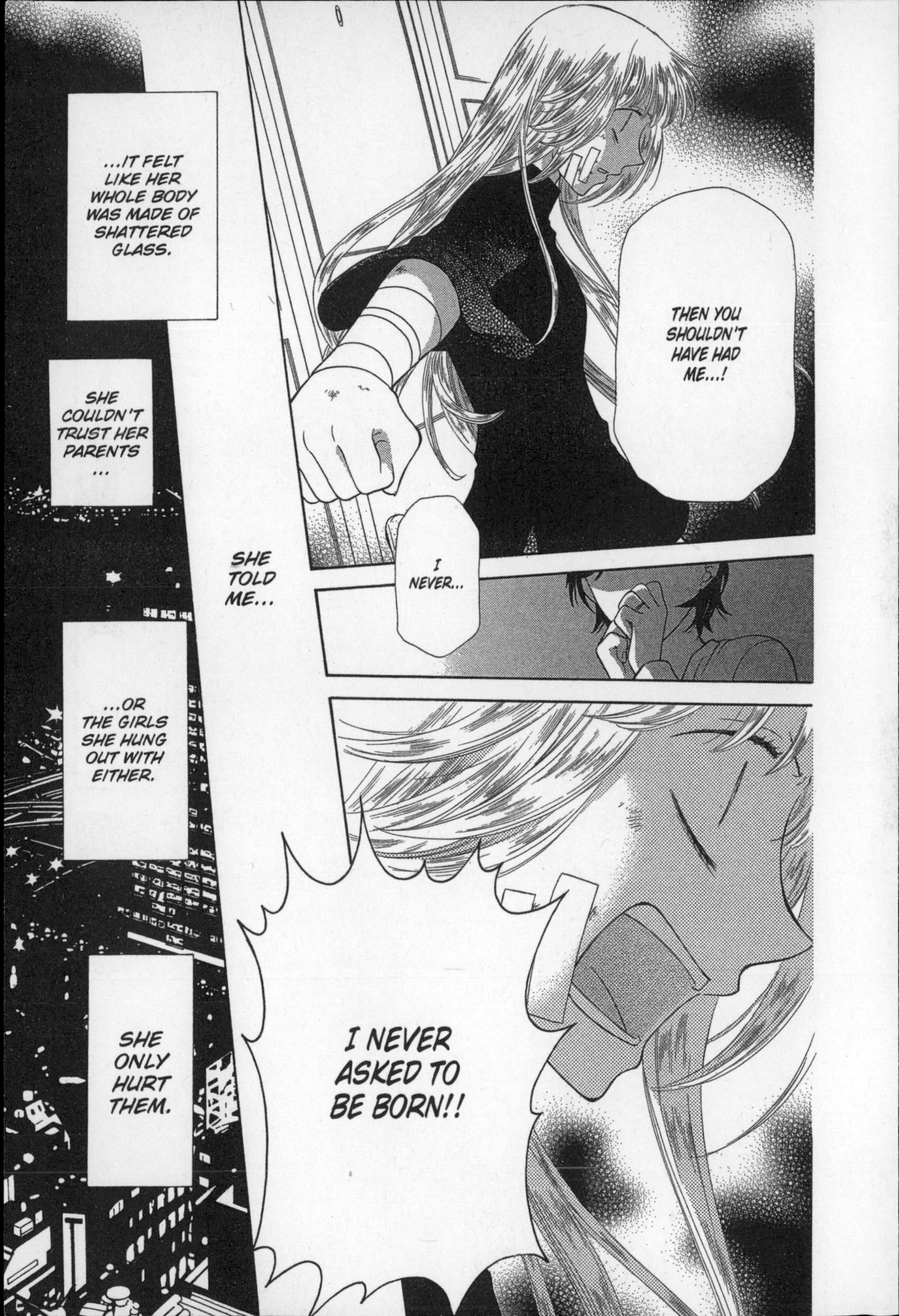
THEN YOU SHOULDN'T HAVE HAD ME...!
I NEVER...
SHE TOLD ME...
I NEVER ASKED TO BE BORN!!
...IT FELT LIKE HER WHOLE BODY WAS MADE OF SHATTERED GLASS.
SHE COULDN'T TRUST HER PARENTS ...
...OR THE GIRLS SHE HUNG OUT WITH EITHER.
SHE ONLY HURT THEM.

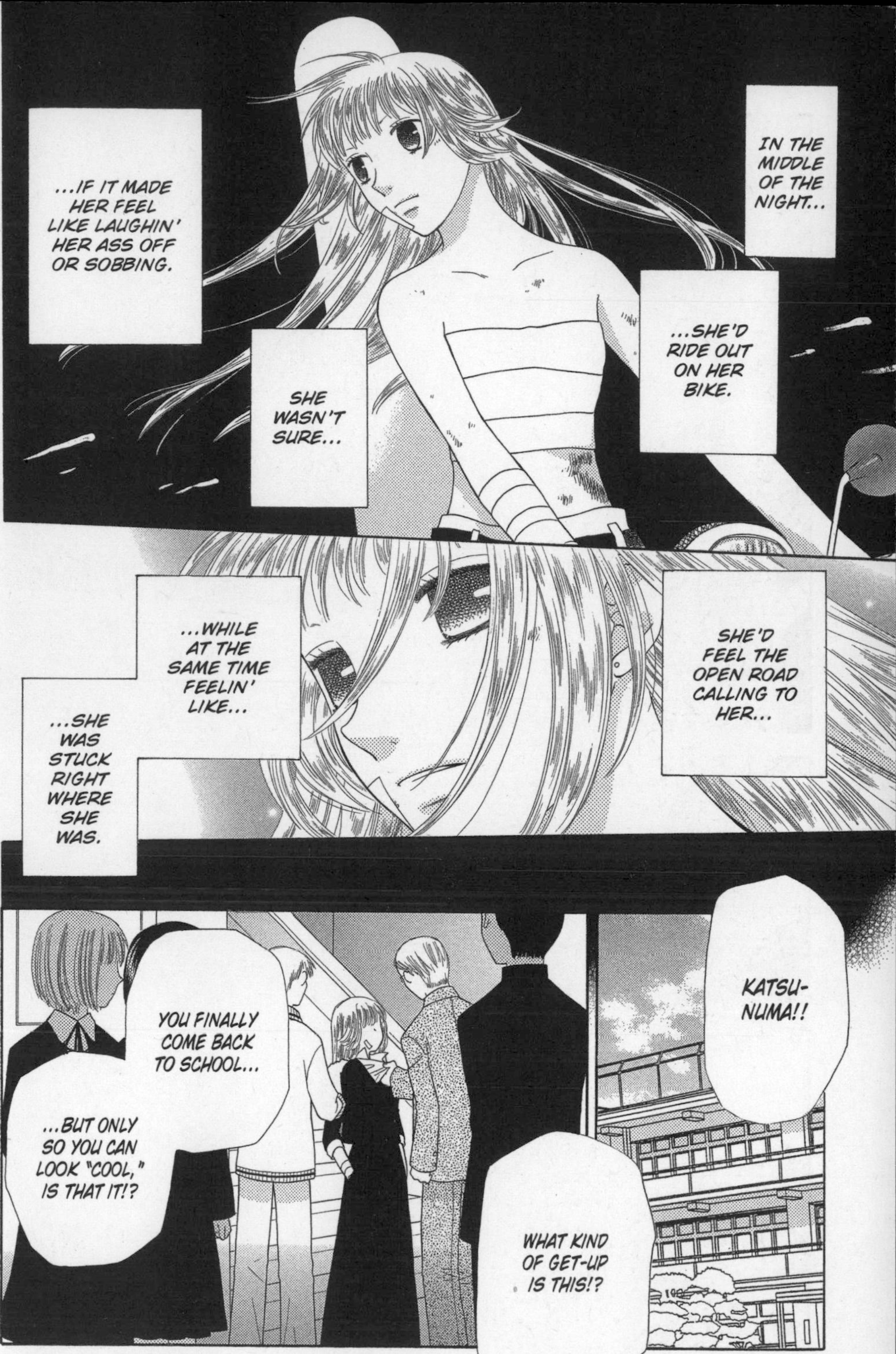
IN THE MIDDLE OF THE NIGHT...
...SHE'D RIDE OUT ON HER BIKE.
SHE WASN'T SURE...
...IF IT MADE HER FEEL LIKE LAUGHIN' HER ASS OFF OR SOBBING.
SHE'D FEEL THE OPEN ROAD CALLING TO HER...
...WHILE AT THE SAME TIME FEELIN' LIKE...
...SHE WAS STUCK RIGHT WHERE SHE WAS.
KATSU-NUMA!!
YOU FINALLY COME BACK TO SCHOOL...
...BUT ONLY SO YOU CAN LOOK "COOL," IS THAT IT!?
WHAT KIND OF GET-UP IS THIS!?

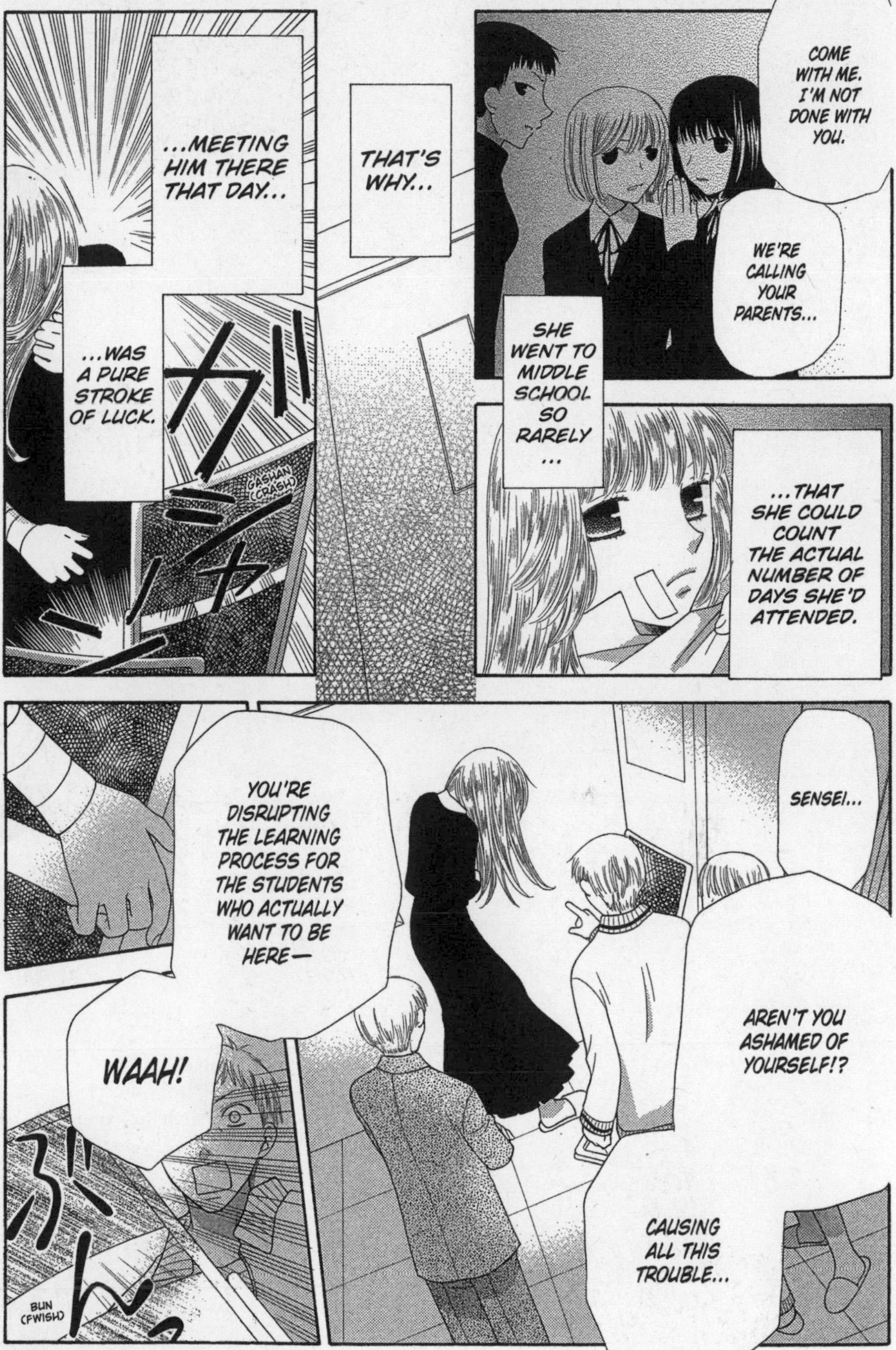
COME WITH ME. I'M NOT DONE WITH YOU.
WE'RE CALLING YOUR PARENTS...
SHE WENT TO MIDDLE SCHOOL SO RARELY...
...THAT SHE COULD COUNT THE ACTUAL NUMBER OF DAYS SHE'D ATTENDED.
THAT'S WHY...
...MEETING HIM THERE THAT DAY...
...WAS A PURE STROKE OF LUCK.
GASHAN (CRASH)
SENSEI...
YOU'RE DISRUPTING THE LEARNING PROCESS FOR THE STUDENTS WHO ACTUALLY WANT TO BE HERE—
AREN'T YOU ASHAMED OF YOURSELF!?
CAUSING ALL THIS TROUBLE...
WAAH!
BUN (FWISH)

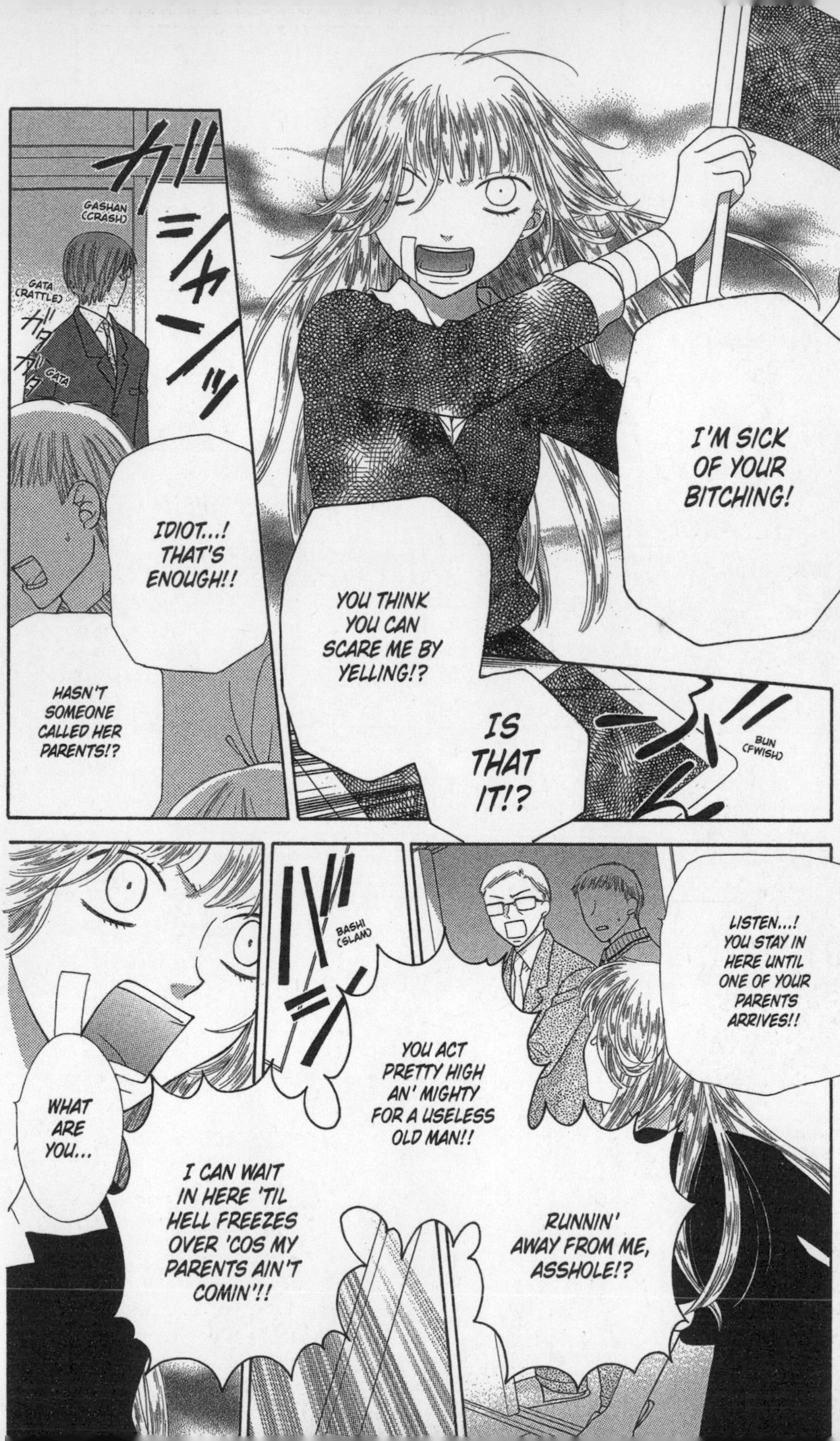
I'M SICK OF YOUR BITCHING!
YOU THINK YOU CAN SCARE ME BY YELLING!?
IS THAT IT!?
BUN (FWISH)
GASHAN (CRASH)
GATA (RATTLE)
GATA
IDIOT...! THAT'S ENOUGH!!
HASN'T SOMEONE CALLED HER PARENTS!?
L...
LISTEN...! YOU STAY IN HERE UNTIL ONE OF YOUR PARENTS ARRIVES!!
BASHI (SLAM)
YOU ACT PRETTY HIGH AN' MIGHTY FOR A USELESS OLD MAN!!
RUNNIN' AWAY FROM ME, ASSHOLE!?
I CAN WAIT IN HERE 'TIL HELL FREEZES OVER 'COS MY PARENTS AIN'T COMIN'!!
WHAT ARE YOU...

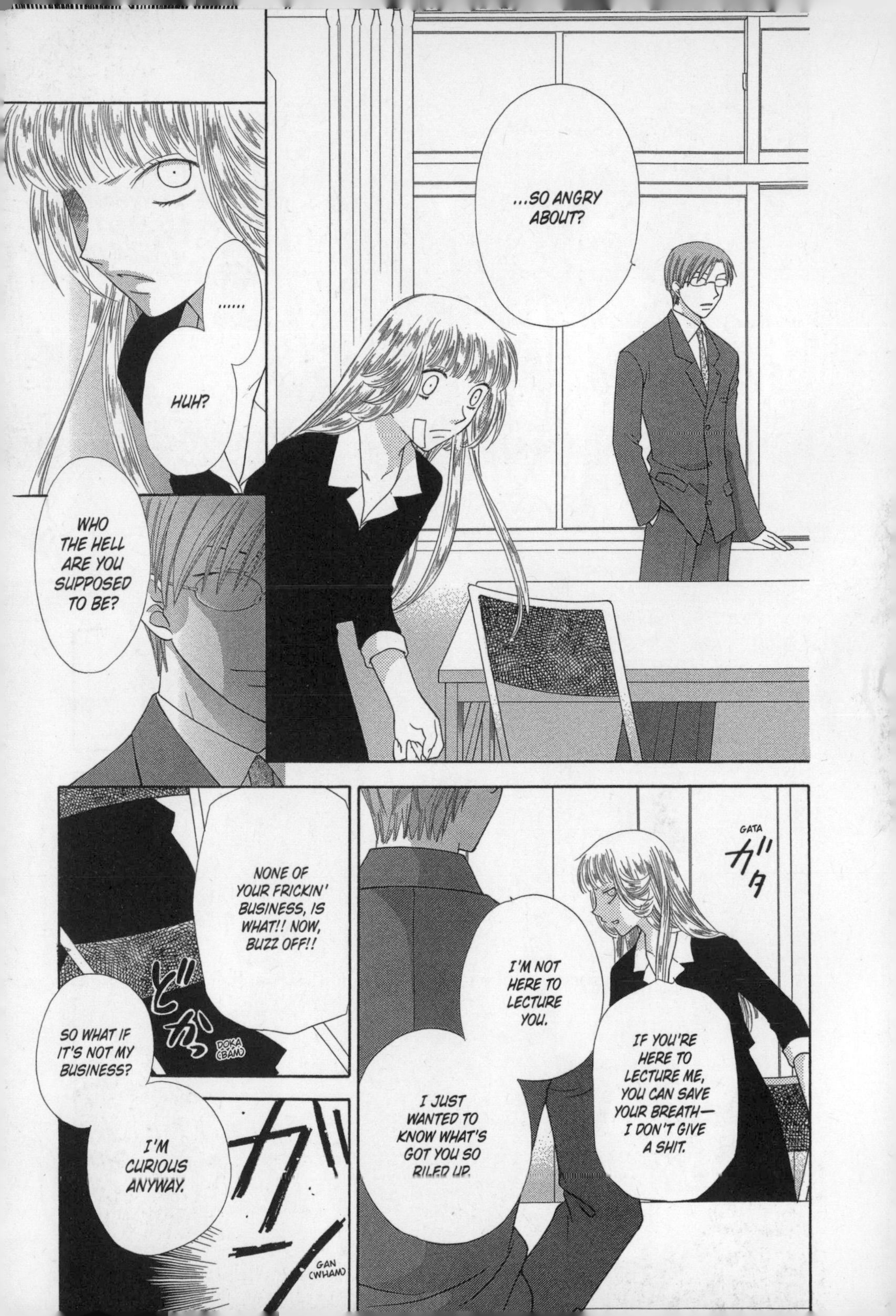
...SO ANGRY ABOUT?
......
HUH?
WHO THE HELL ARE YOU SUPPOSED TO BE?
GATA
IF YOU'RE HERE TO LECTURE ME, YOU CAN SAVE YOUR BREATH—I DON'T GIVE A SHIT.
I'M NOT HERE TO LECTURE YOU.
I JUST WANTED TO KNOW WHAT'S GOT YOU SO RILED UP.
NONE OF YOUR FRICKIN' BUSINESS, IS WHAT!! NOW, BUZZ OFF!!
DOKA (BAM)
SO WHAT IF IT'S NOT MY BUSINESS?
I'M CURIOUS ANYWAY.
GAN (WHAM)

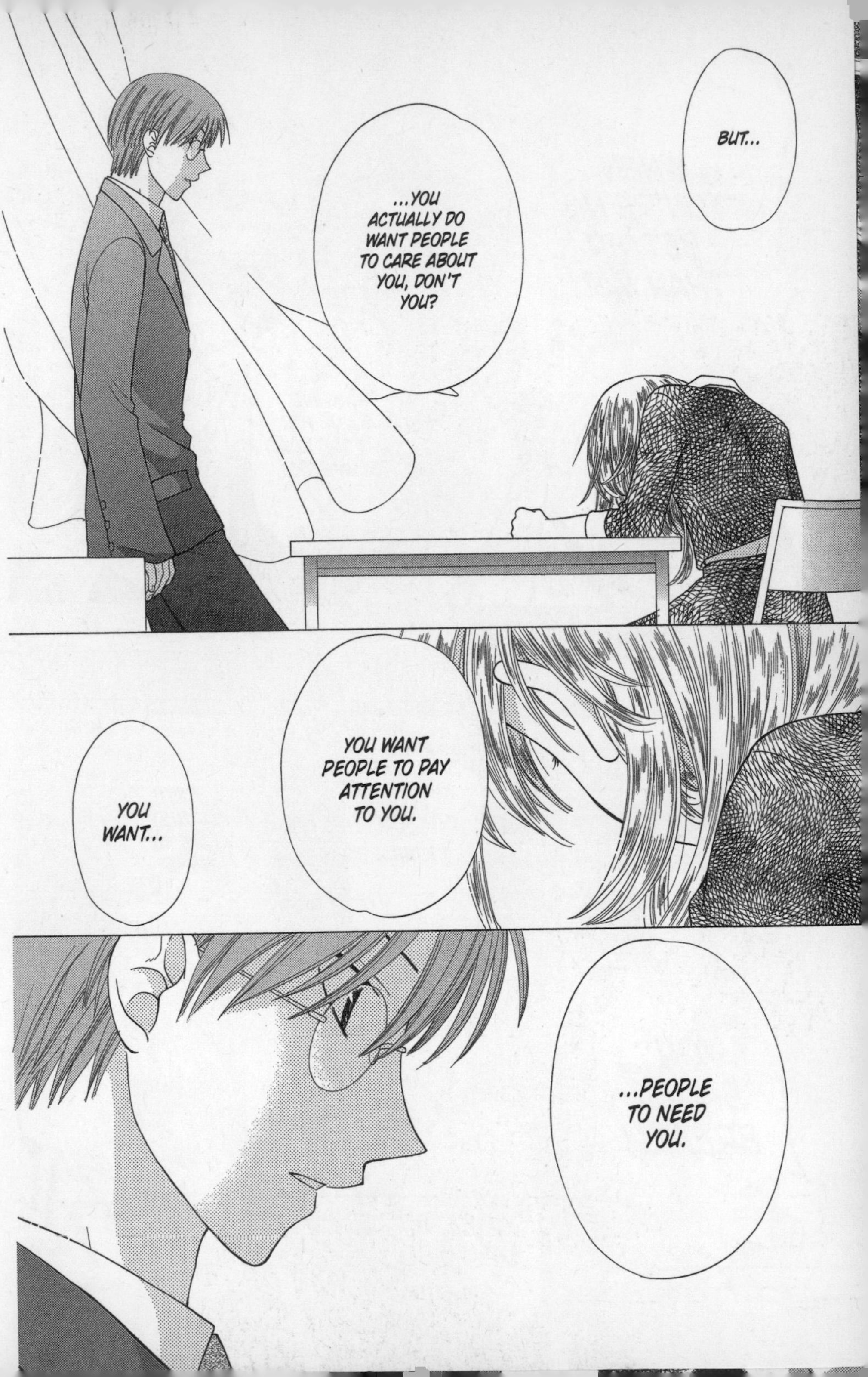
BUT...
...YOU ACTUALLY DO WANT PEOPLE TO CARE ABOUT YOU, DON'T YOU?
YOU WANT PEOPLE TO PAY ATTENTION TO YOU.
YOU WANT...
...PEOPLE TO NEED YOU.

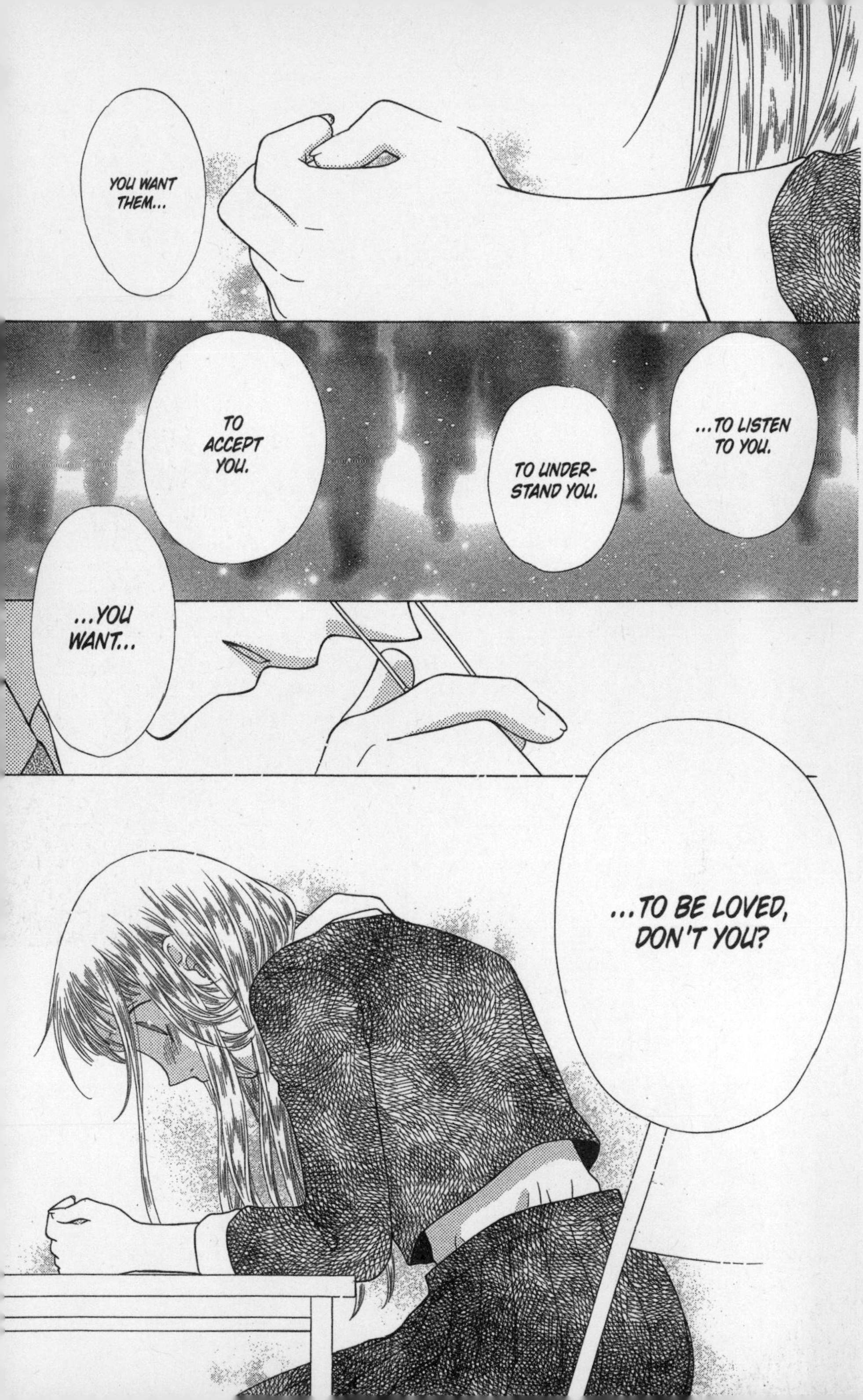
YOU WANT THEM...
...TO LISTEN TO YOU.
TO UNDER-STAND YOU.
TO ACCEPT YOU.
...YOU WANT...
...TO BE LOVED, DON'T YOU?

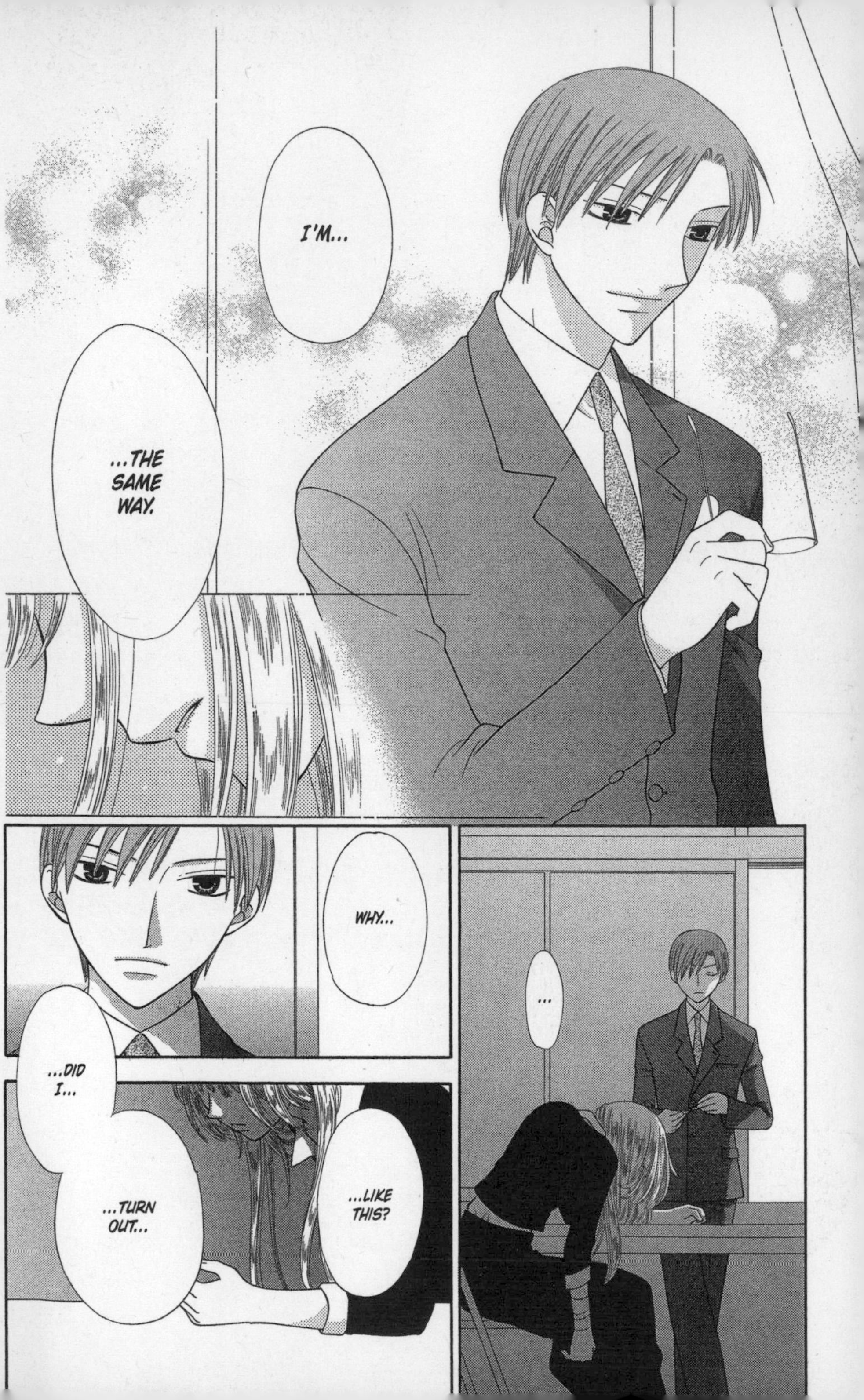
I'M...
...THE SAME WAY.
...
WHY...
...DID I...
...TURN OUT...
...LIKE THIS?

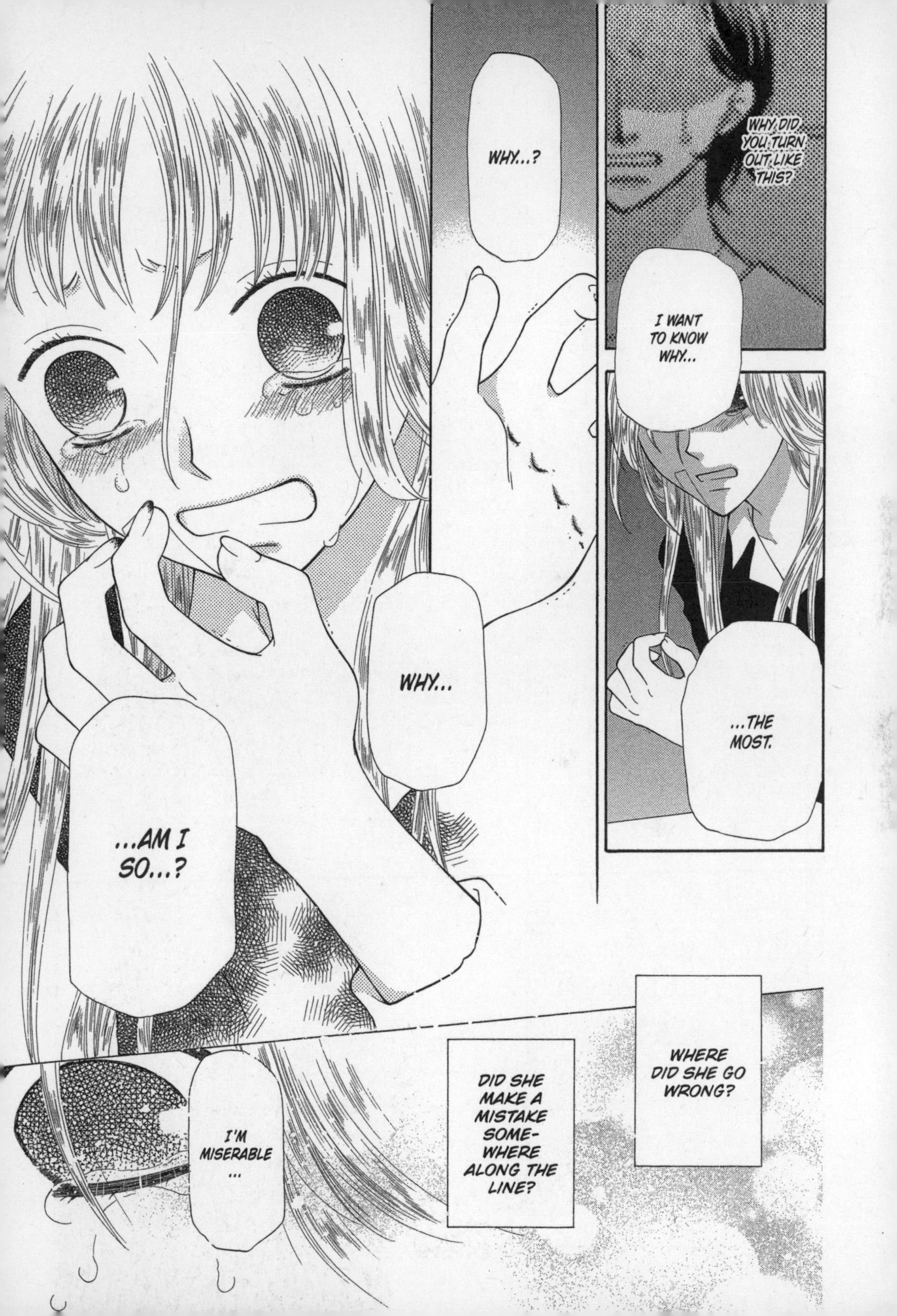
WHY DID YOU TURN OUT LIKE THIS?
I WANT TO KNOW WHY...
...THE MOST.
WHY...?
WHY...
...AM I SO...?
WHERE DID SHE GO WRONG?
DID SHE MAKE A MISTAKE SOME-WHERE ALONG THE LINE?
I'M MISERABLE...

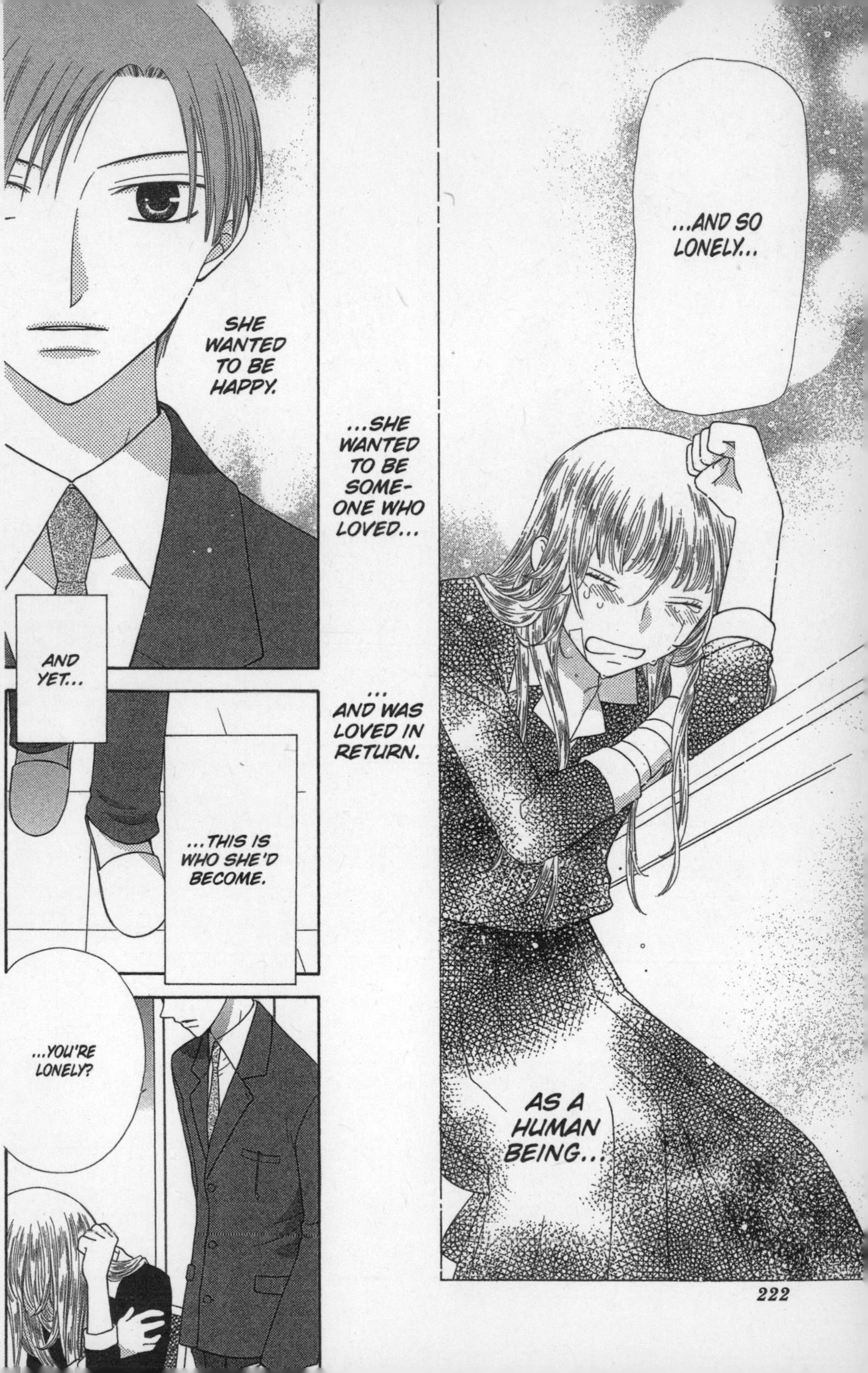
...AND SO LONELY...
AS A HUMAN BEING...
SHE WANTED TO BE HAPPY.
...SHE WANTED TO BE SOME-ONE WHO LOVED...
... ...AND WAS LOVED IN RETURN.
AND YET...
...THIS IS WHO SHE'D BECOME.
...YOU'RE LONELY?

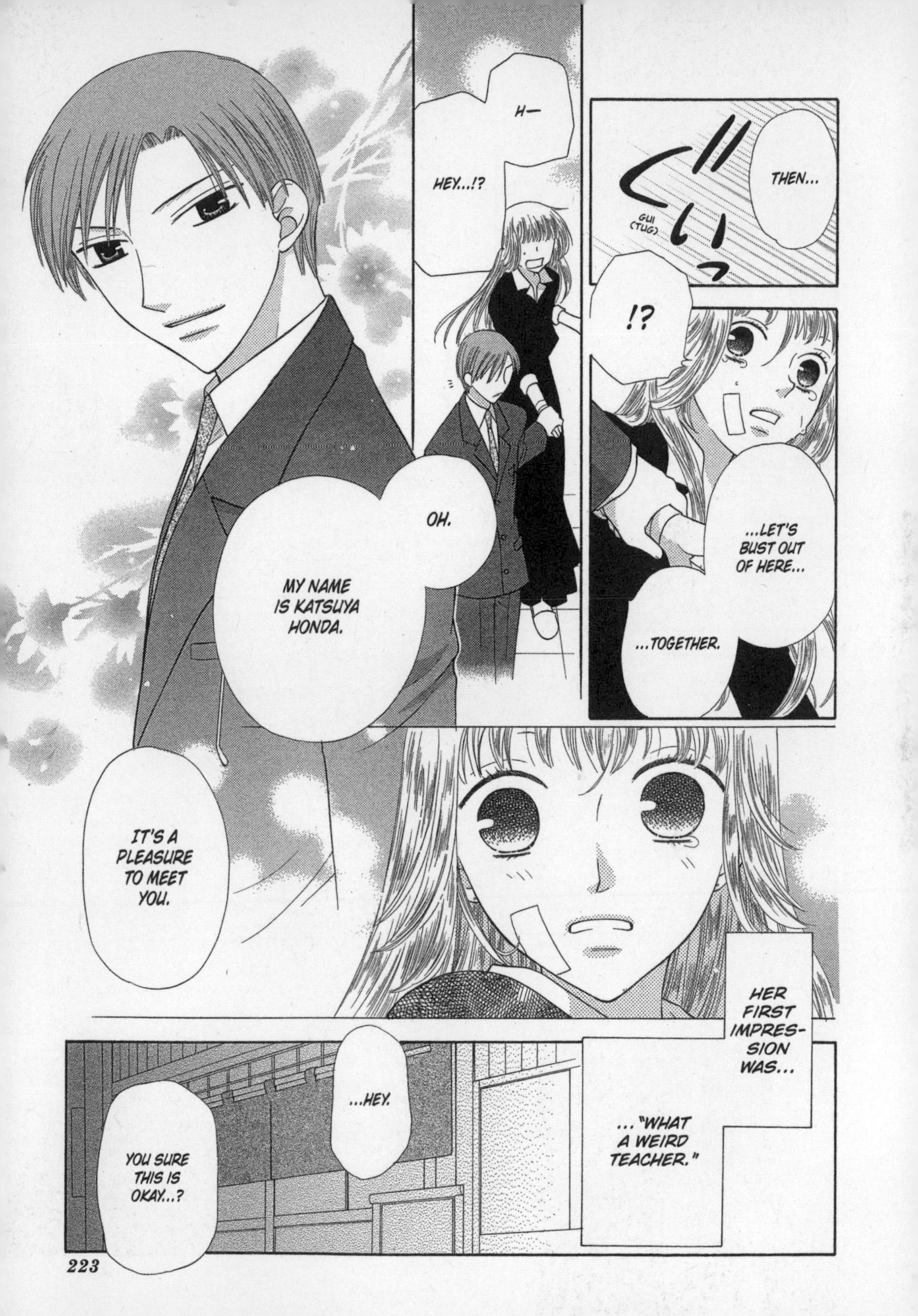
THEN...
GUI (TUG)
!?
...LET'S BUST OUT OF HERE...
...TOGETHER.
H—
HEY...!?
OH.
MY NAME IS KATSUYA HONDA.
IT'S A PLEASURE TO MEET YOU.
HER FIRST IMPRESSION WAS...
..."WHAT A WEIRD TEACHER."
...HEY.
YOU SURE THIS IS OKAY...?

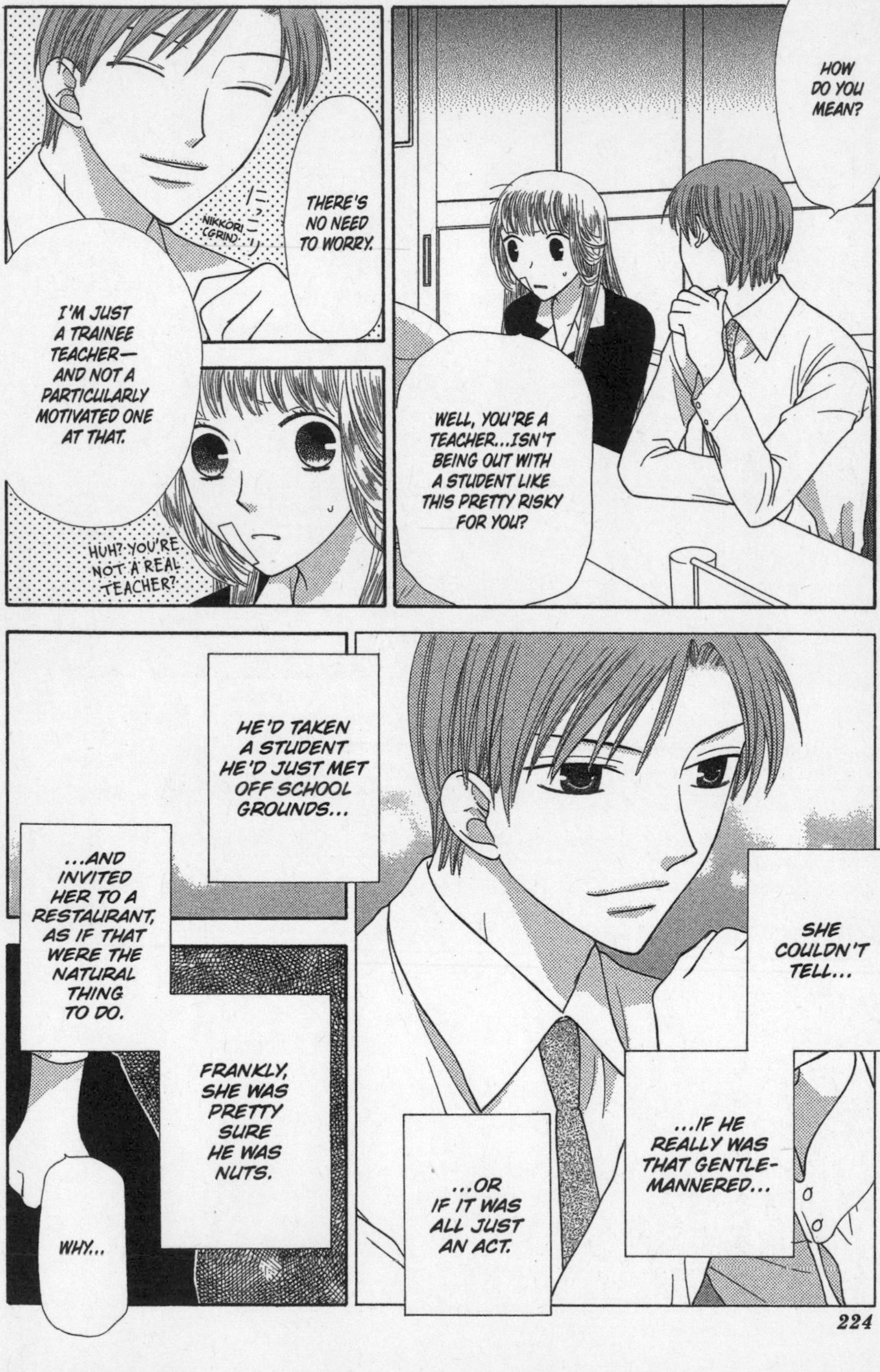
HOW DO YOU MEAN?
WELL, YOU'RE A TEACHER...ISN'T BEING OUT WITH A STUDENT LIKE THIS PRETTY RISKY FOR YOU?
THERE'S NO NEED TO WORRY.
NIKKORI (GRIN)
I'M JUST A TRAINEE TEACHER— AND NOT A PARTICULARLY MOTIVATED ONE AT THAT.
HUH? YOU'RE NOT A REAL TEACHER?
SHE COULDN'T TELL...
...IF HE REALLY WAS THAT GENTLE-MANNERED...
...OR IF IT WAS ALL JUST AN ACT.
HE'D TAKEN A STUDENT HE'D JUST MET OFF SCHOOL GROUNDS...
...AND INVITED HER TO A RESTAURANT, AS IF THAT WERE THE NATURAL THING TO DO.
FRANKLY, SHE WAS PRETTY SURE HE WAS NUTS.
WHY...

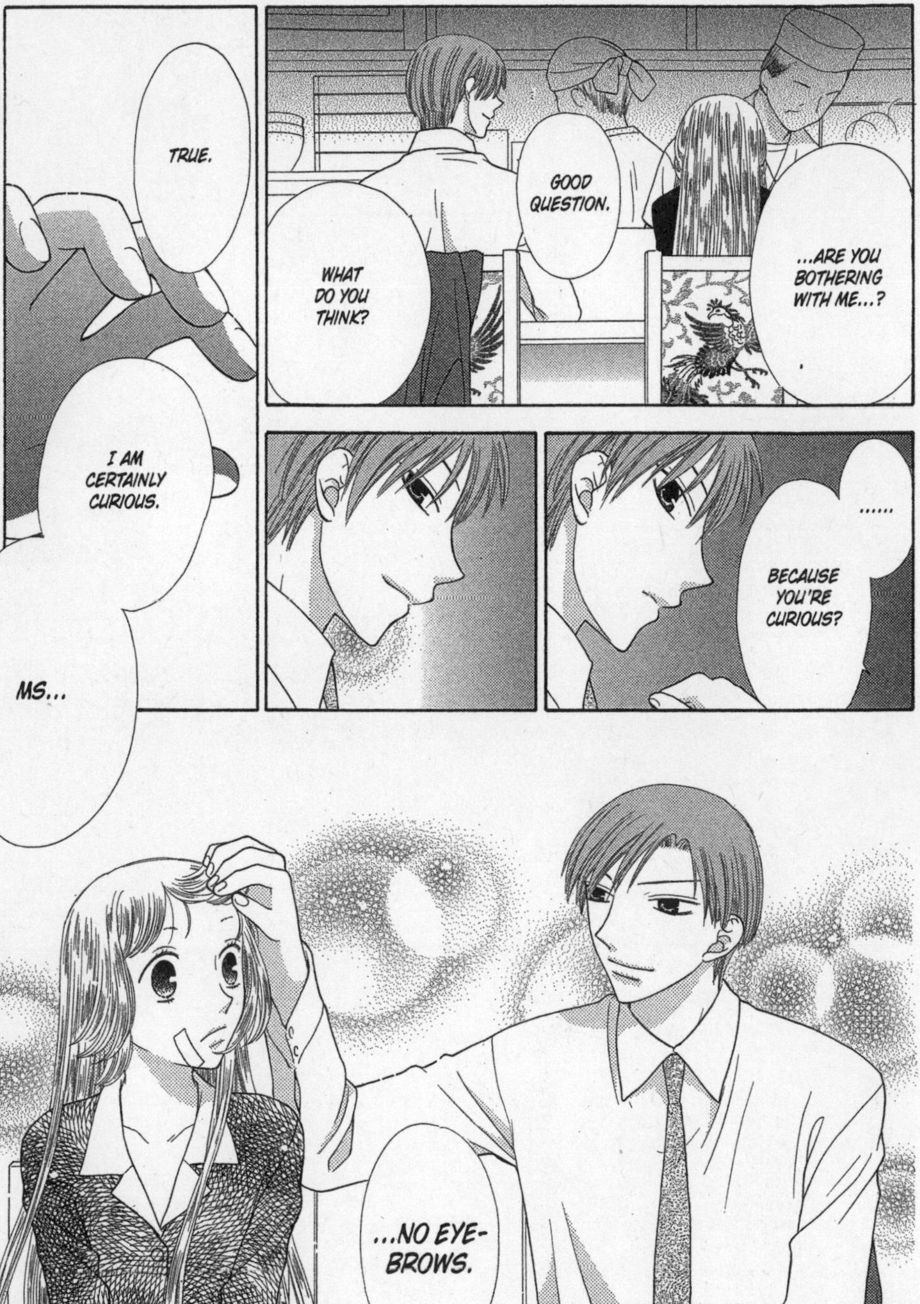
...ARE YOU BOTHERING WITH ME...?
GOOD QUESTION.
WHAT DO YOU THINK?
......
BECAUSE YOU'RE CURIOUS?
TRUE.
I AM CERTAINLY CURIOUS.
MS...
...NO EYE-BROWS.

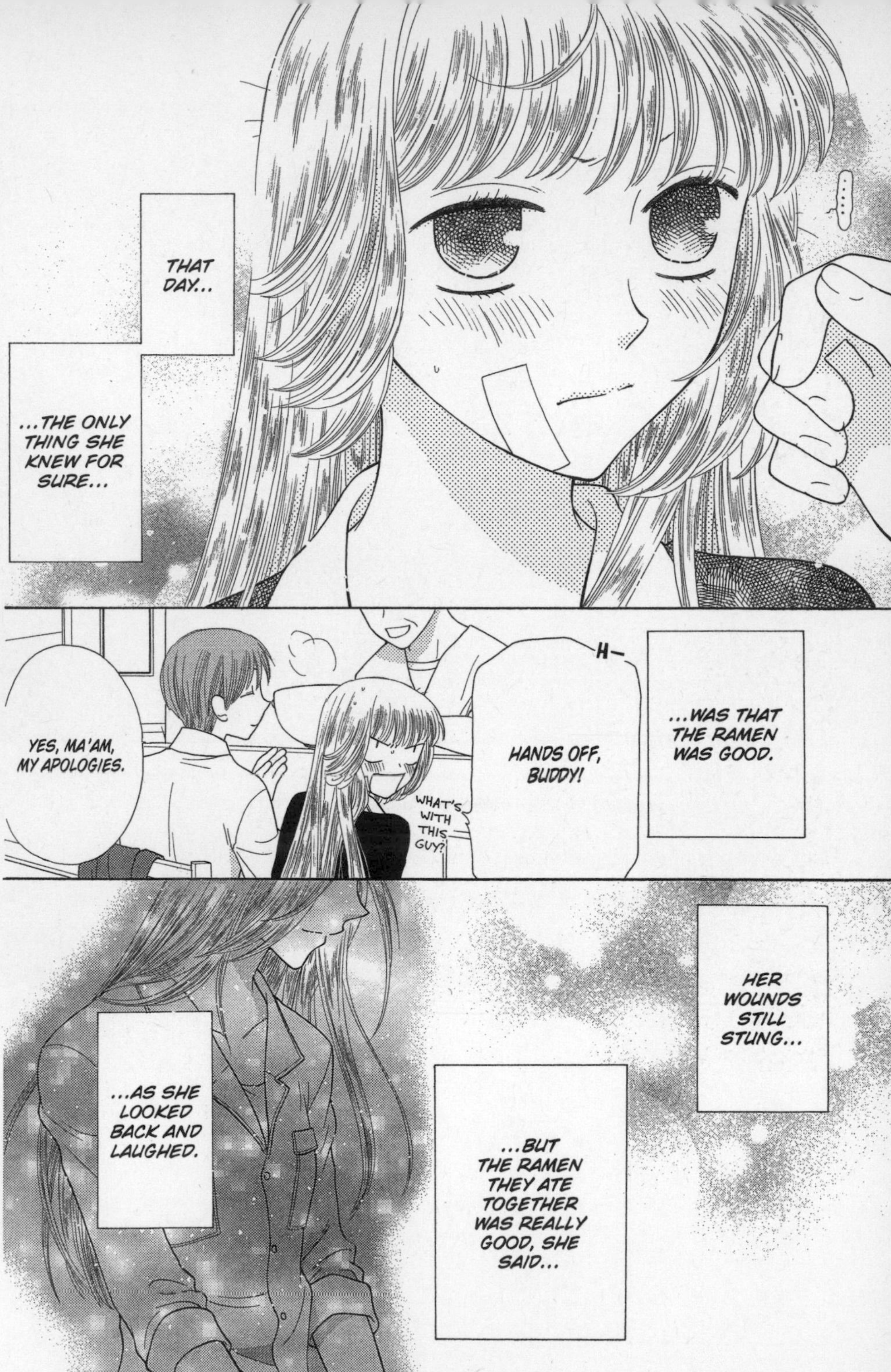
......
THAT DAY...
...THE ONLY THING SHE KNEW FOR SURE...
...WAS THAT THE RAMEN WAS GOOD.
H—
HANDS OFF, BUDDY!
WHAT'S WITH THIS GUY?
YES, MA'AM, MY APOLOGIES.
HER WOUNDS STILL STUNG...
...BUT THE RAMEN THEY ATE TOGETHER WAS REALLY GOOD, SHE SAID...
...AS SHE LOOKED BACK AND LAUGHED.

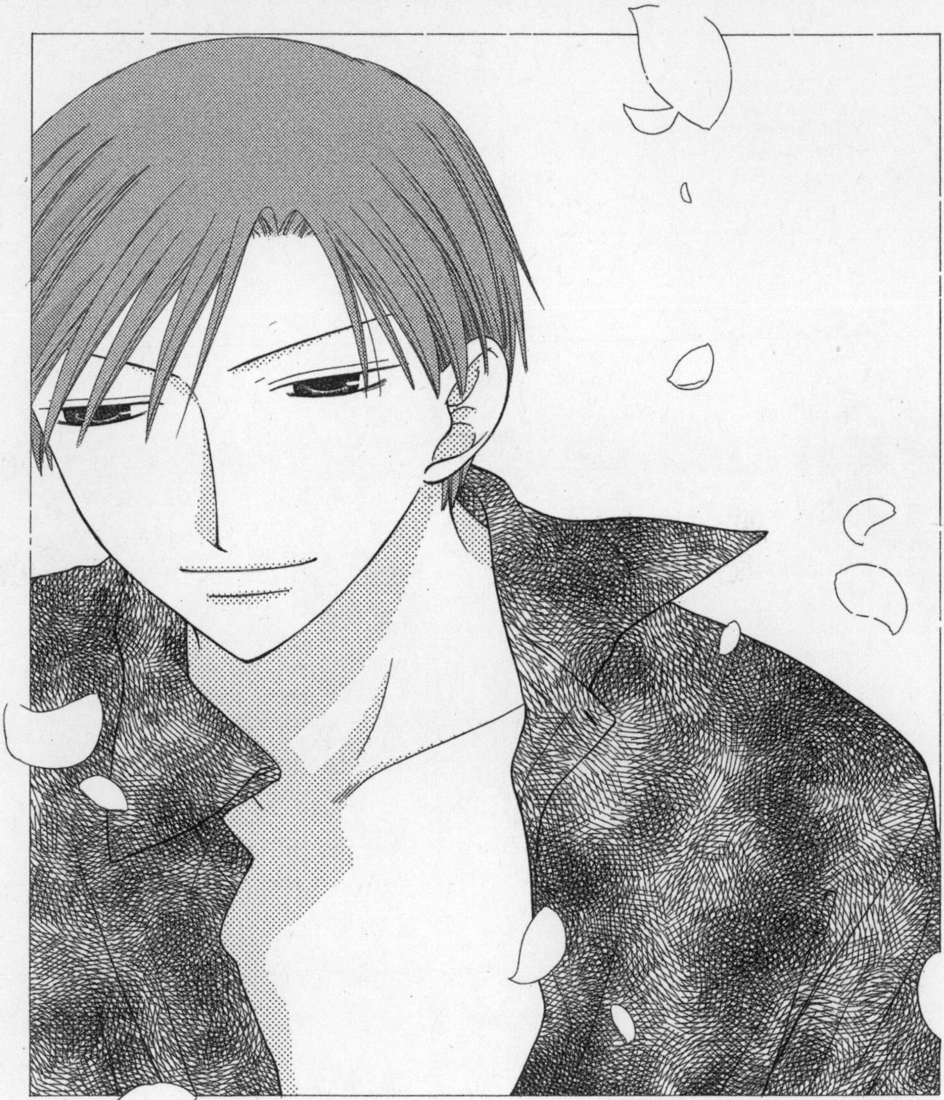

Chapter 91

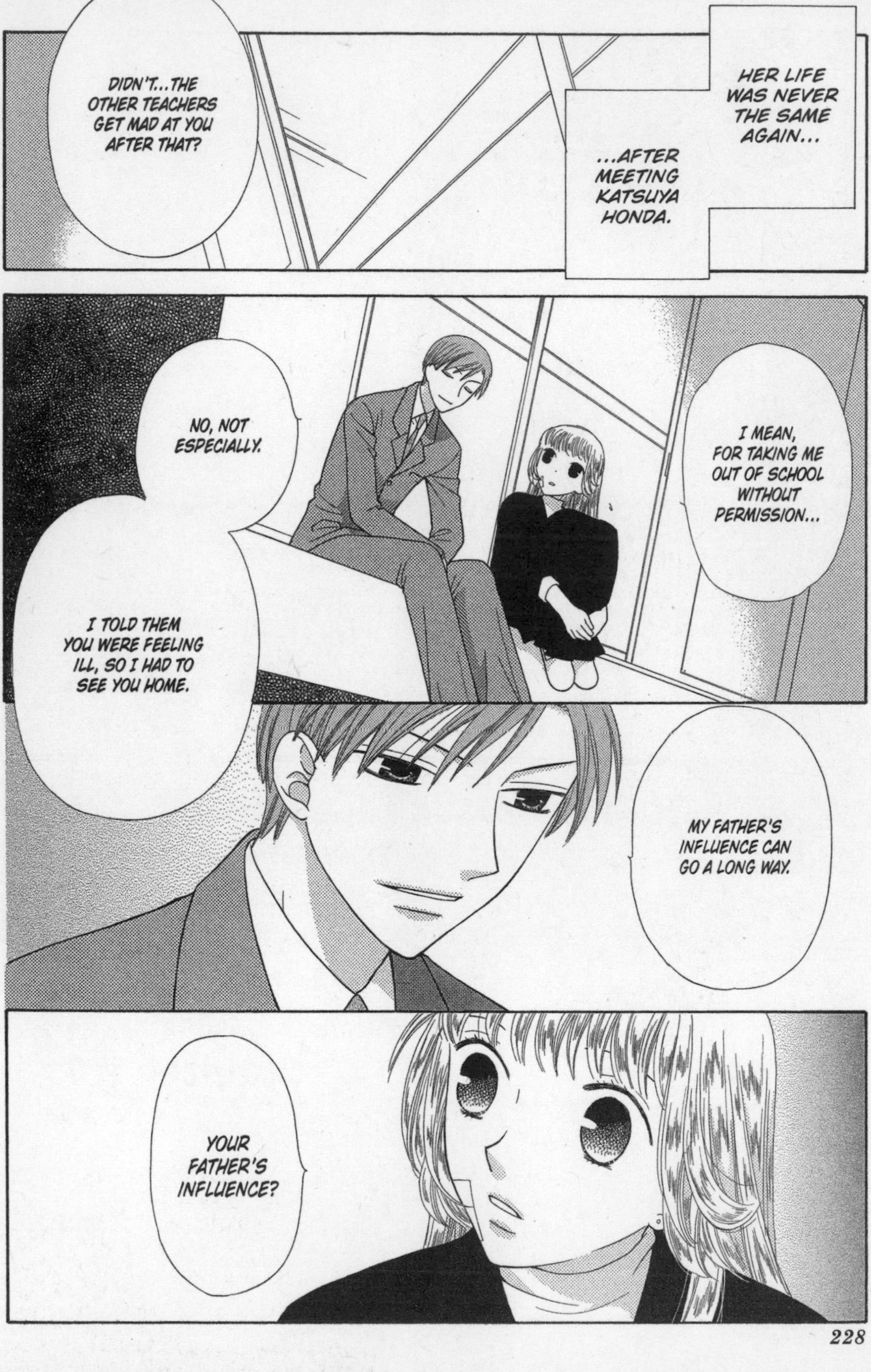
HER LIFE WAS NEVER THE SAME AGAIN...
...AFTER MEETING KATSUYA HONDA.
DIDN'T...THE OTHER TEACHERS GET MAD AT YOU AFTER THAT?
I MEAN, FOR TAKING ME OUT OF SCHOOL WITHOUT PERMISSION...
NO, NOT ESPECIALLY.
I TOLD THEM YOU WERE FEELING ILL, SO I HAD TO SEE YOU HOME.
MY FATHER'S INFLUENCE CAN GO A LONG WAY.
YOUR FATHER'S INFLUENCE?

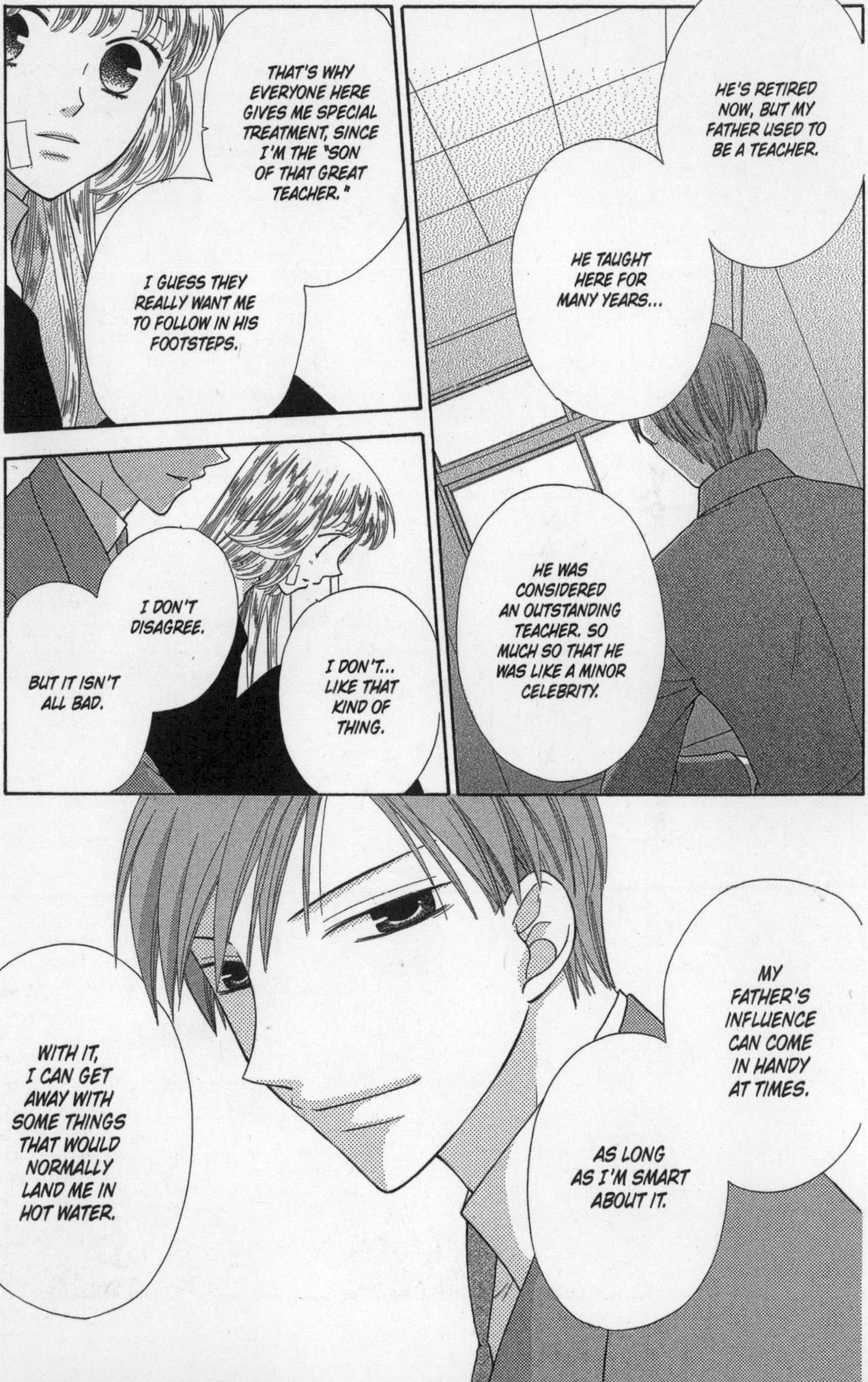
HE'S RETIRED NOW, BUT MY FATHER USED TO BE A TEACHER.
HE TAUGHT HERE FOR MANY YEARS...
HE WAS CONSIDERED AN OUTSTANDING TEACHER. SO MUCH SO THAT HE WAS LIKE A MINOR CELEBRITY.
THAT'S WHY EVERYONE HERE GIVES ME SPECIAL TREATMENT, SINCE I'M THE "SON OF THAT GREAT TEACHER."
I GUESS THEY REALLY WANT ME TO FOLLOW IN HIS FOOTSTEPS.
I DON'T... LIKE THAT KIND OF THING.
I DON'T DISAGREE.
BUT IT ISN'T ALL BAD.
MY FATHER'S INFLUENCE CAN COME IN HANDY AT TIMES.
AS LONG AS I'M SMART ABOUT IT.
WITH IT, I CAN GET AWAY WITH SOME THINGS THAT WOULD NORMALLY LAND ME IN HOT WATER.

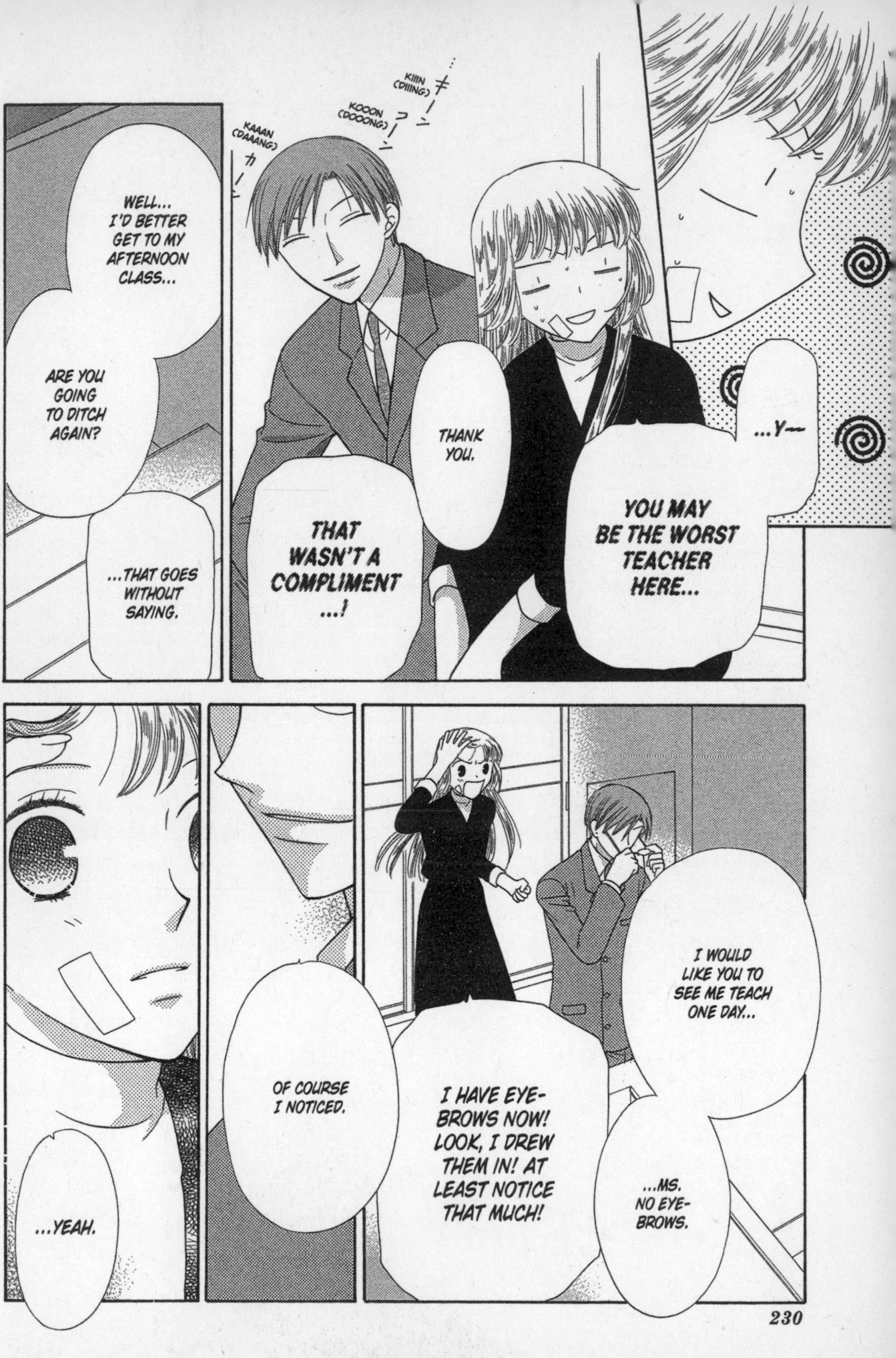
KIIIN (DIIING)
KOOON (DOOONG)
KAAAN (DAAANG)
...Y—
YOU MAY BE THE WORST TEACHER HERE...
THANK YOU.
THAT WASN'T A COMPLIMENT ...!
WELL... I'D BETTER GET TO MY AFTERNOON CLASS...
ARE YOU GOING TO DITCH AGAIN?
...THAT GOES WITHOUT SAYING.
I WOULD LIKE YOU TO SEE ME TEACH ONE DAY...
...MS. NO EYE-BROWS.
I HAVE EYE-BROWS NOW! LOOK, I DREW THEM IN! AT LEAST NOTICE THAT MUCH!
OF COURSE I NOTICED.
...YEAH.

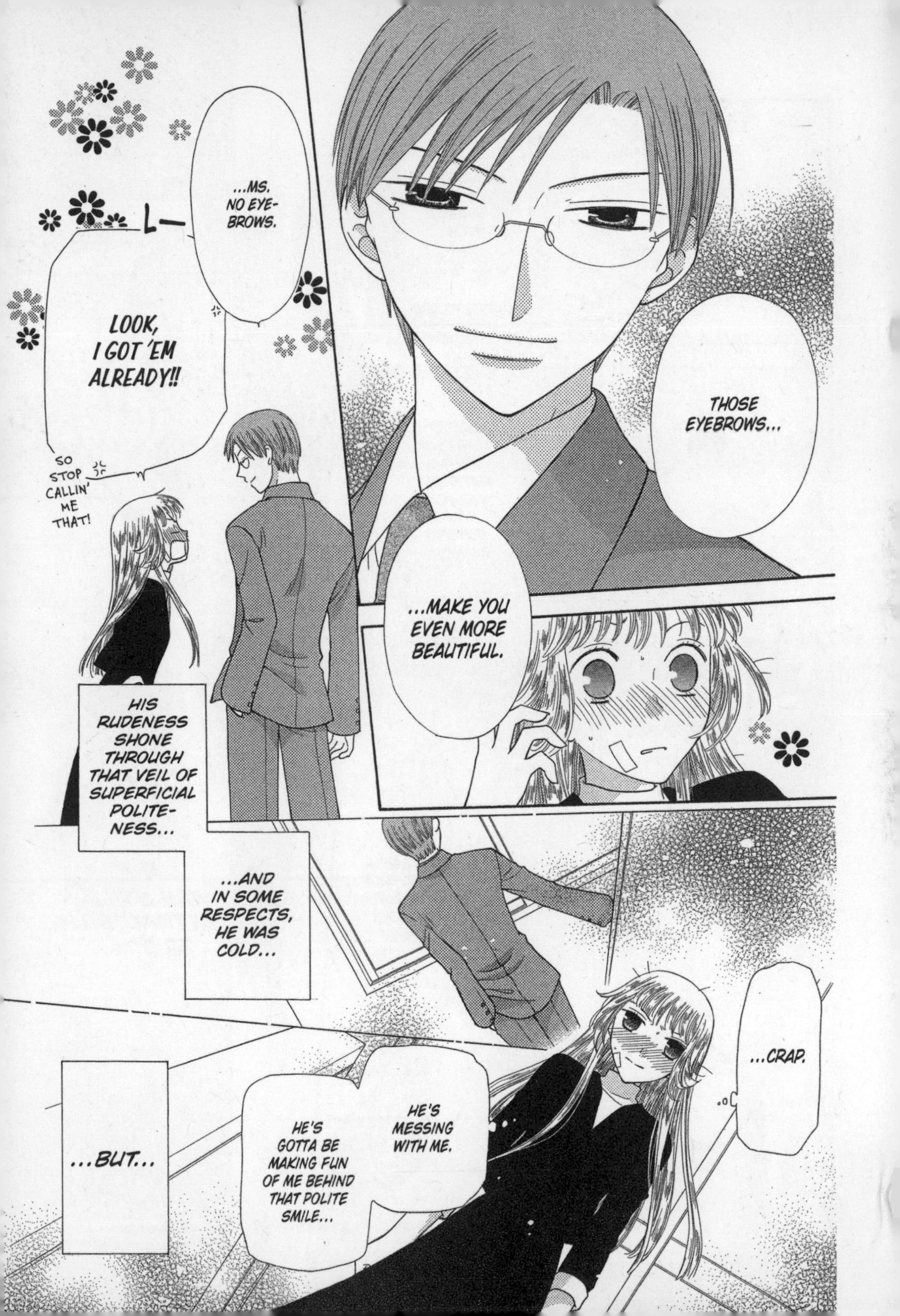
THOSE EYEBROWS...
...MAKE YOU EVEN MORE BEAUTIFUL.
...MS. NO EYE-BROWS.
L—
LOOK, I GOT 'EM ALREADY!!
SO STOP CALLIN' ME THAT!
HIS RUDENESS SHONE THROUGH THAT VEIL OF SUPERFICIAL POLITE-NESS...
...AND IN SOME RESPECTS, HE WAS COLD...
...CRAP.
HE'S MESSING WITH ME.
HE'S GOTTA BE MAKING FUN OF ME BEHIND THAT POLITE SMILE...
...BUT...

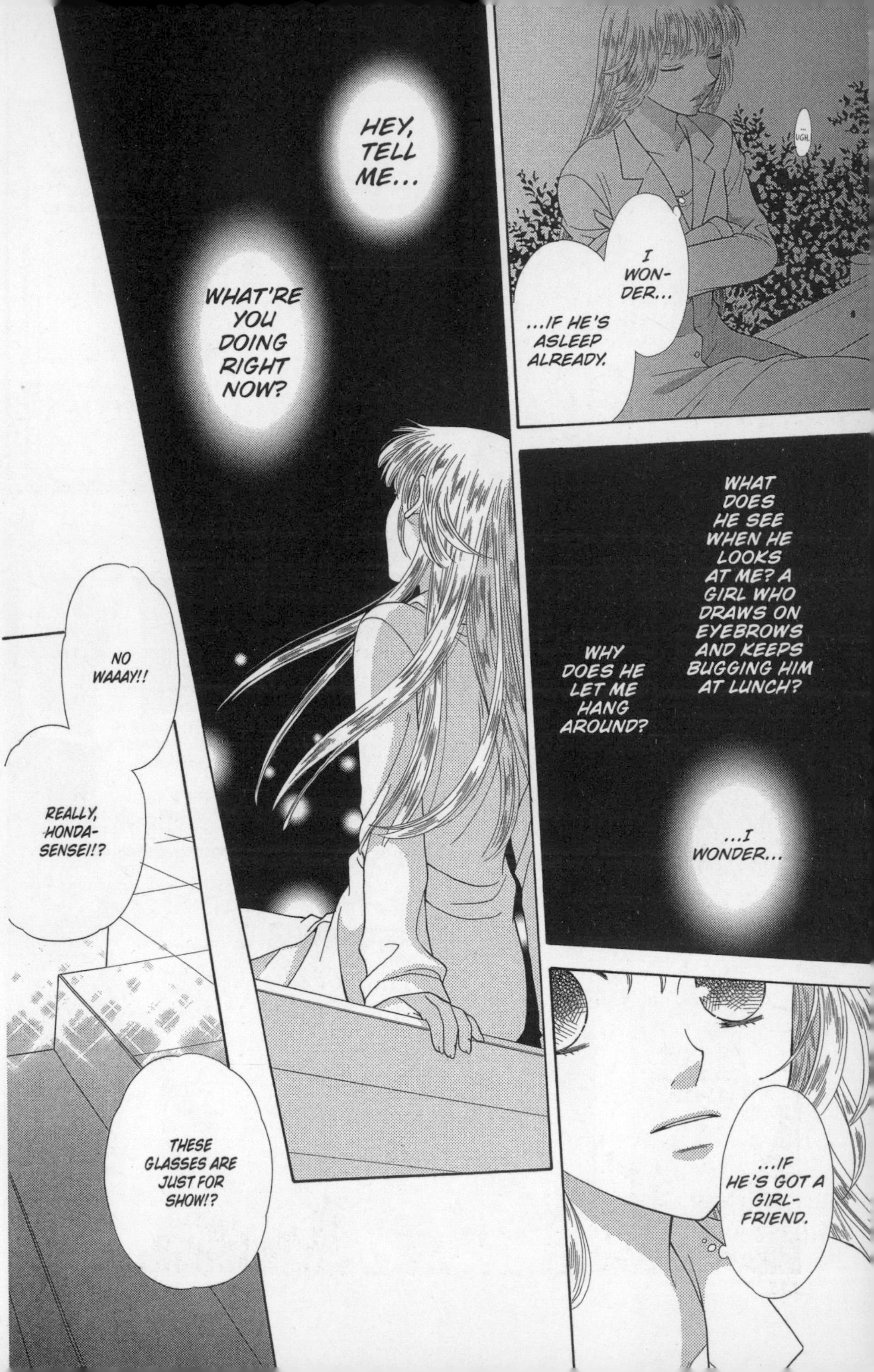
...UGH.
I WONDER...
...IF HE'S ASLEEP ALREADY.
WHAT DOES HE SEE WHEN HE LOOKS AT ME? A GIRL WHO DRAWS ON EYEBROWS AND KEEPS BUGGING HIM AT LUNCH?
WHY DOES HE LET ME HANG AROUND?
...I WONDER...
...IF HE'S GOT A GIRLFRIEND.
HEY, TELL ME...
WHAT'RE YOU DOING RIGHT NOW?
NO WAAAY!!
REALLY, HONDA-SENSEI!?
THESE GLASSES ARE JUST FOR SHOW!?

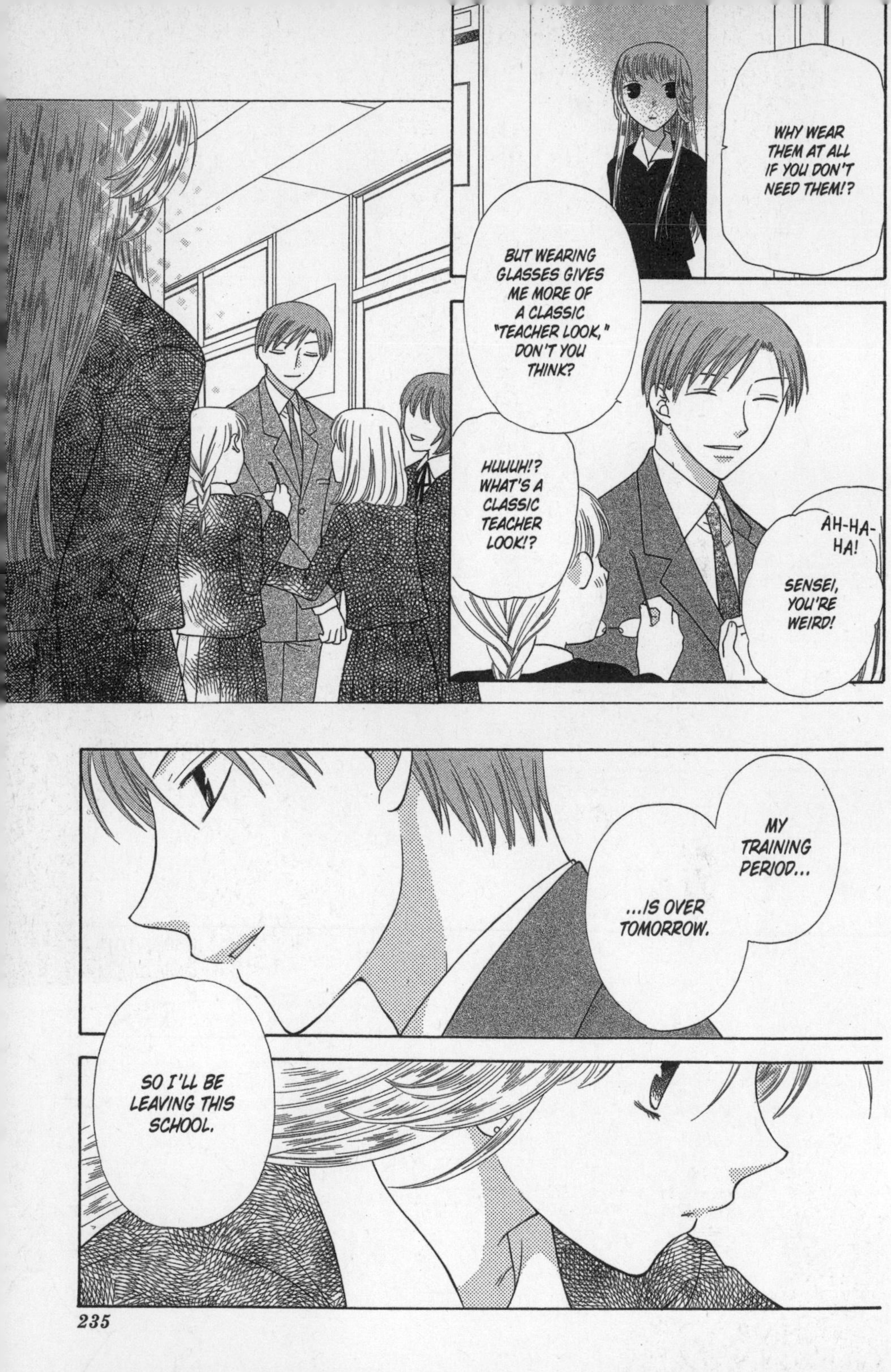
WHY WEAR THEM AT ALL IF YOU DON'T NEED THEM!?
BUT WEARING GLASSES GIVES ME MORE OF A CLASSIC "TEACHER LOOK," DON'T YOU THINK?
HUUUH!? WHAT'S A CLASSIC TEACHER LOOK!?
AH-HA-HA! SENSEI, YOU'RE WEIRD!
MY TRAINING PERIOD...
...IS OVER TOMORROW.
SO I'LL BE LEAVING THIS SCHOOL.

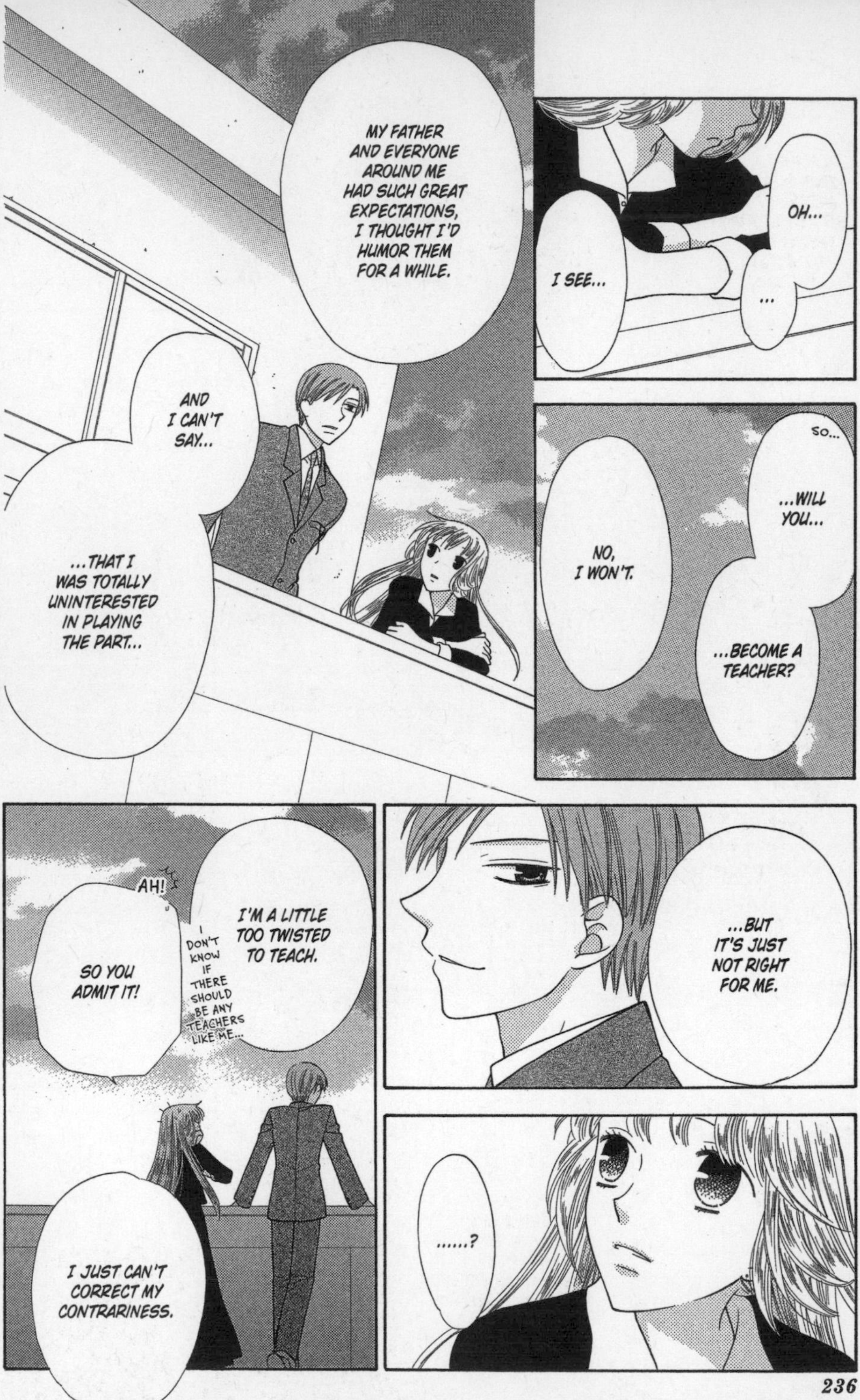
OH...
...
I SEE...
SO...
...WILL YOU...
...BECOME A TEACHER?
NO, I WON'T.
MY FATHER AND EVERYONE AROUND ME HAD SUCH GREAT EXPECTATIONS, I THOUGHT I'D HUMOR THEM FOR A WHILE.
AND I CAN'T SAY...
...THAT I WAS TOTALLY UNINTERESTED IN PLAYING THE PART...
...BUT IT'S JUST NOT RIGHT FOR ME.
......?
I'M A LITTLE TOO TWISTED TO TEACH.
I DON'T KNOW IF THERE SHOULD BE ANY TEACHERS LIKE ME...
AH!
SO YOU ADMIT IT!
I JUST CAN'T CORRECT MY CONTRARINESS.

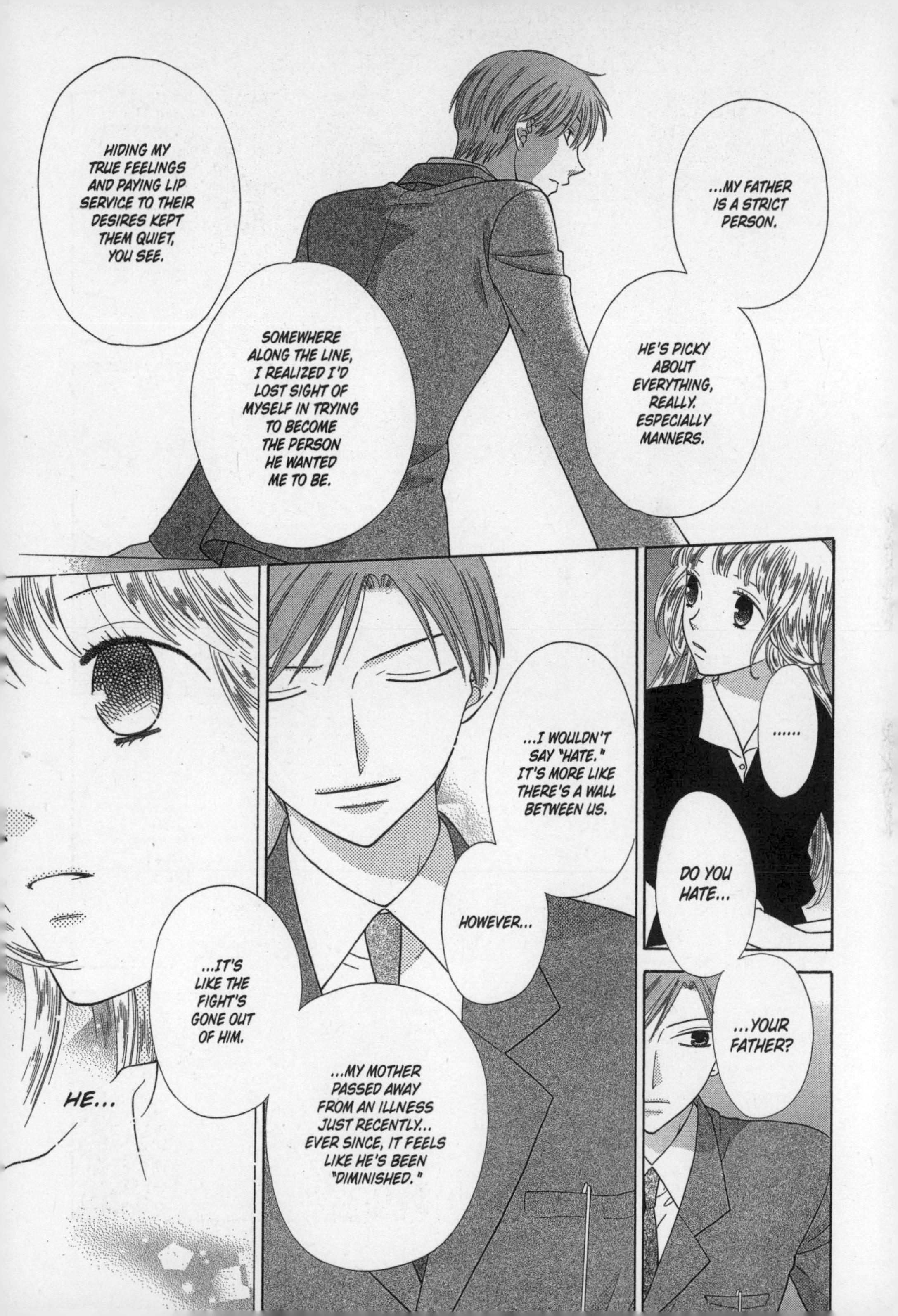
...MY FATHER IS A STRICT PERSON.
HE'S PICKY ABOUT EVERYTHING, REALLY. ESPECIALLY MANNERS.
SOMEWHERE ALONG THE LINE, I REALIZED I'D LOST SIGHT OF MYSELF IN TRYING TO BECOME THE PERSON HE WANTED ME TO BE.
HIDING MY TRUE FEELINGS AND PAYING LIP SERVICE TO THEIR DESIRES KEPT THEM QUIET, YOU SEE.
......
DO YOU HATE...
...YOUR FATHER?
...I WOULDN'T SAY "HATE." IT'S MORE LIKE THERE'S A WALL BETWEEN US.
HOWEVER...
...MY MOTHER PASSED AWAY FROM AN ILLNESS JUST RECENTLY... EVER SINCE, IT FEELS LIKE HE'S BEEN "DIMINISHED."
HE...
...IT'S LIKE THE FIGHT'S GONE OUT OF HIM.

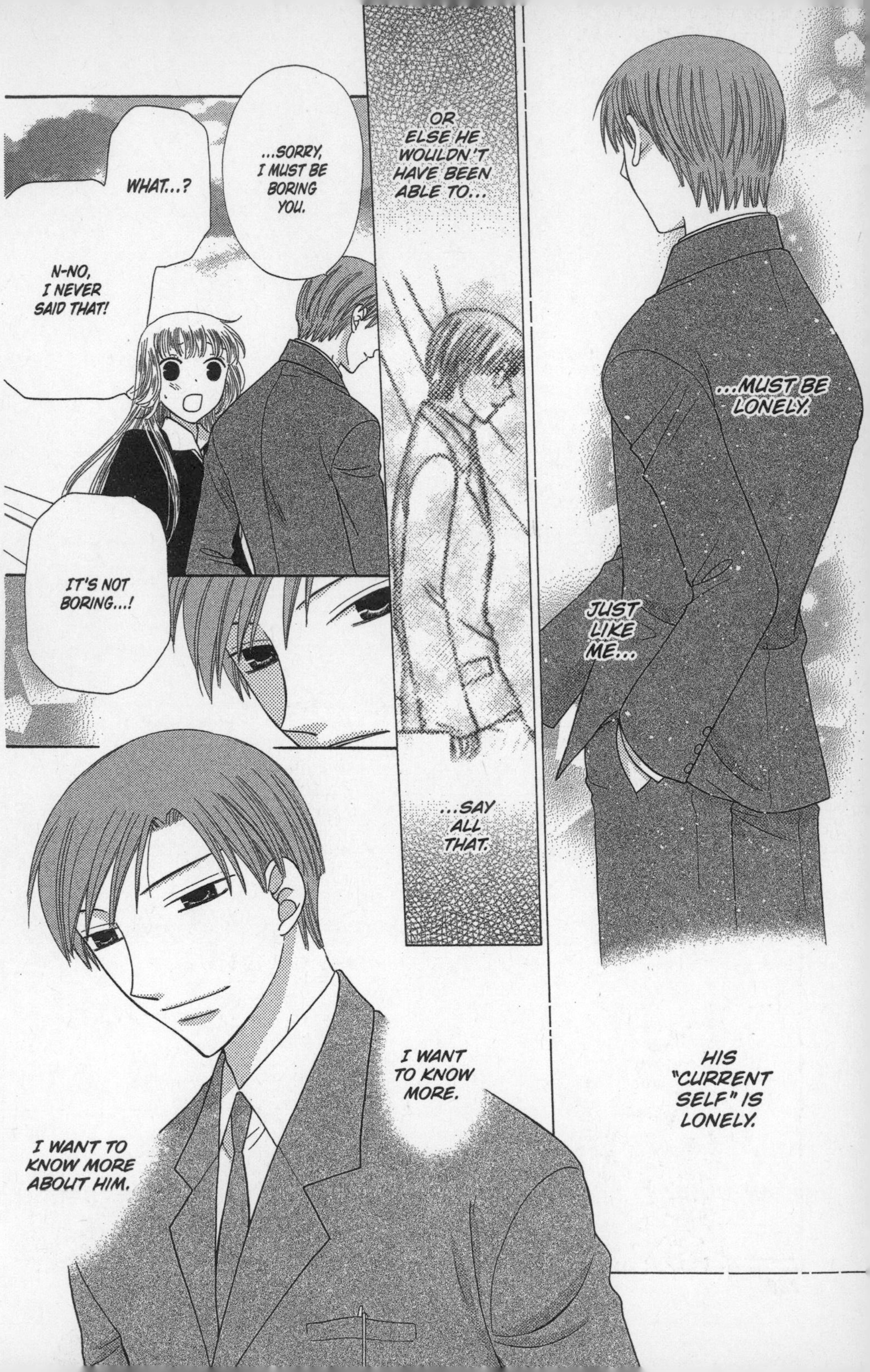
...MUST BE LONELY.
JUST LIKE ME...
HIS "CURRENT SELF" IS LONELY.
OR ELSE HE WOULDN'T HAVE BEEN ABLE TO...
...SAY ALL THAT.
...SORRY, I MUST BE BORING YOU.
WHAT...?
N-NO, I NEVER SAID THAT!
IT'S NOT BORING...!
I WANT TO KNOW MORE.
I WANT TO KNOW MORE ABOUT HIM.

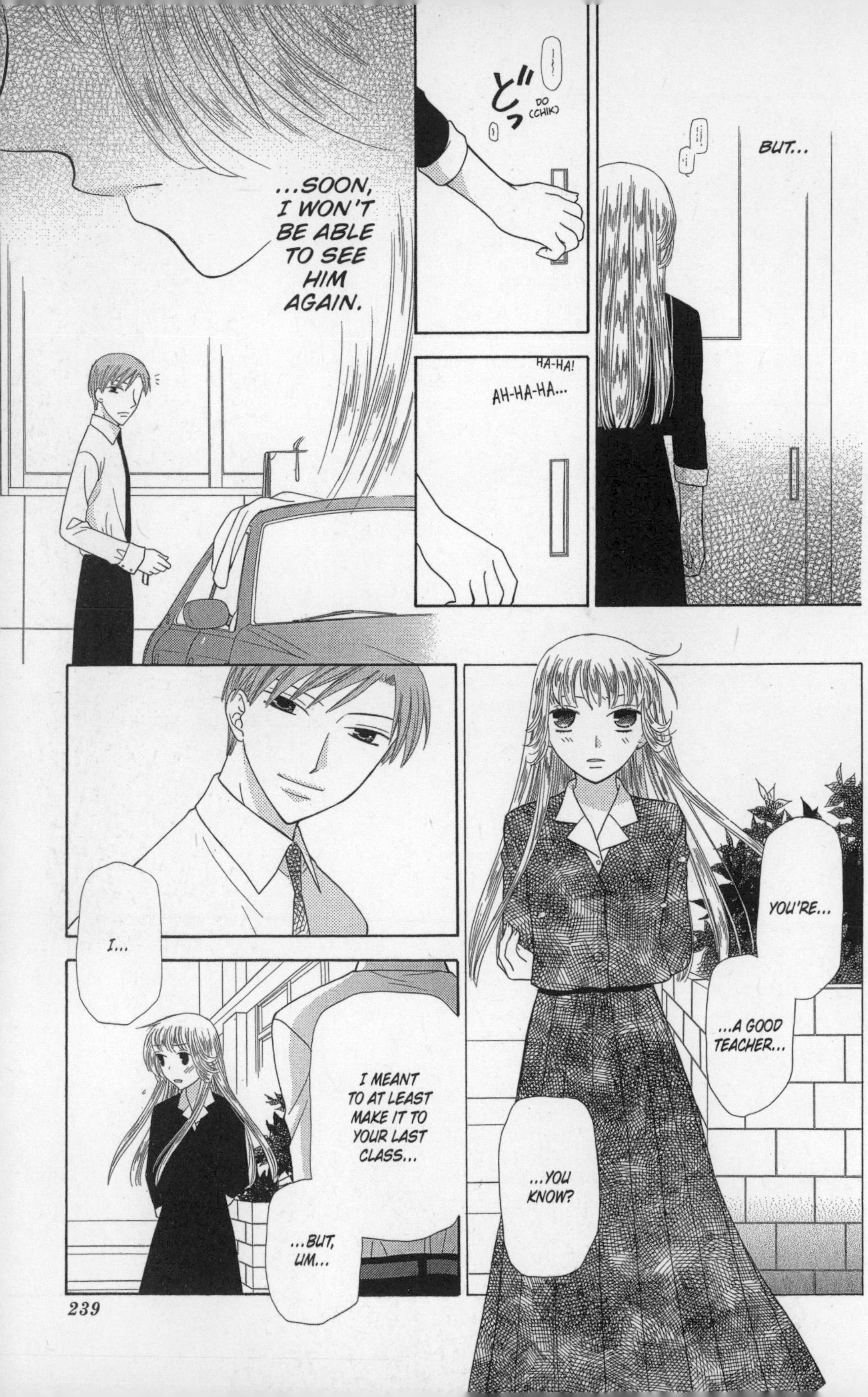

BUT...
どっ
DO (CHIK)
HA-HA!
AH-HA-HA...
...SOON, I WON'T BE ABLE TO SEE HIM AGAIN.
YOU'RE...
...A GOOD TEACHER...
...YOU KNOW?
I...
I MEANT TO AT LEAST MAKE IT TO YOUR LAST CLASS...
...BUT, UM...

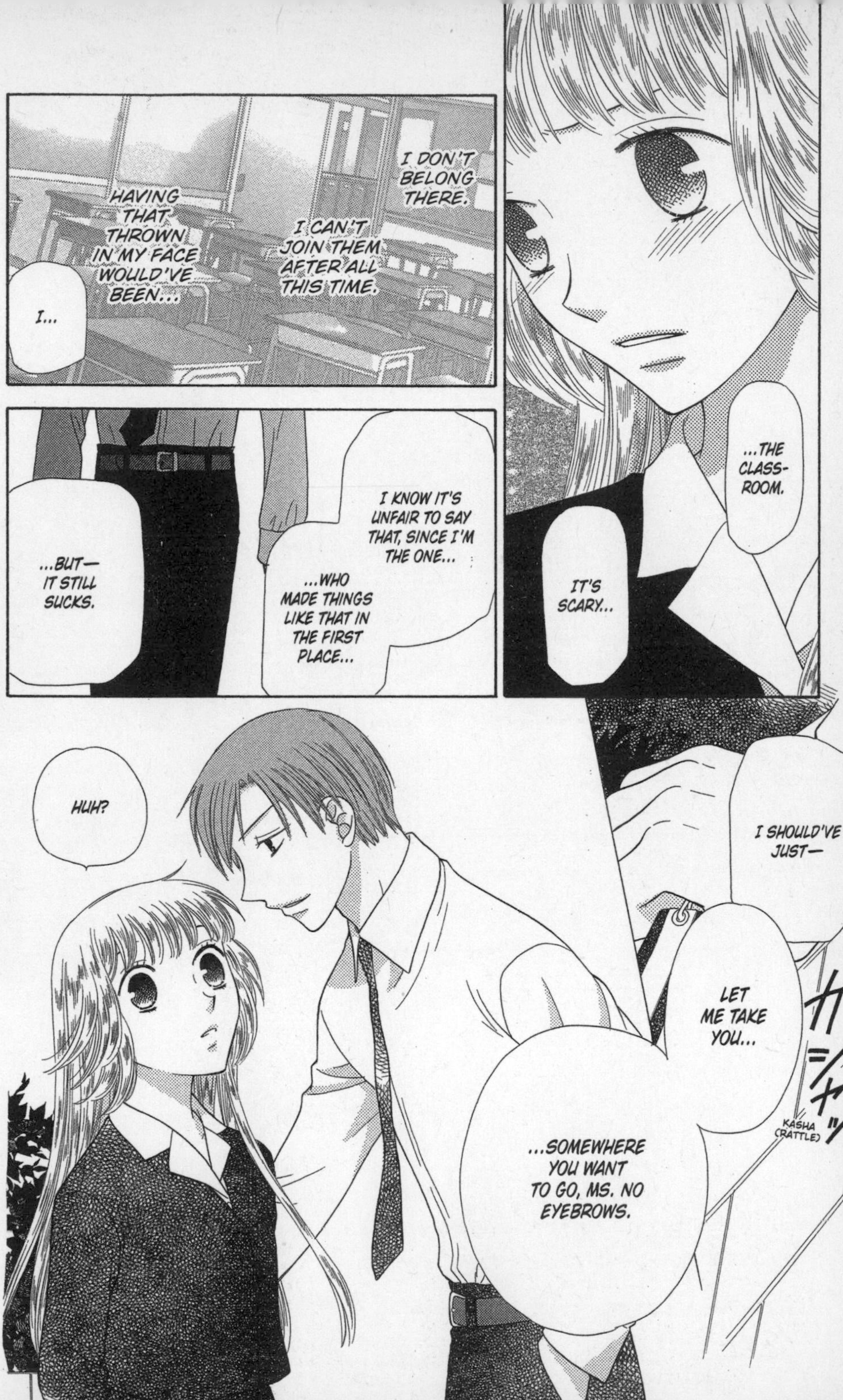
...THE CLASSROOM.
IT'S SCARY...
I DON'T BELONG THERE.
I CAN'T JOIN THEM AFTER ALL THIS TIME.
HAVING THAT THROWN IN MY FACE WOULD'VE BEEN...
I...
I KNOW IT'S UNFAIR TO SAY THAT, SINCE I'M THE ONE...
...WHO MADE THINGS LIKE THAT IN THE FIRST PLACE...
...BUT— IT STILL SUCKS.
I SHOULD'VE JUST—
LET ME TAKE YOU...
KASHA (RATTLE)
...SOMEWHERE YOU WANT TO GO, MS. NO EYEBROWS.
HUH?

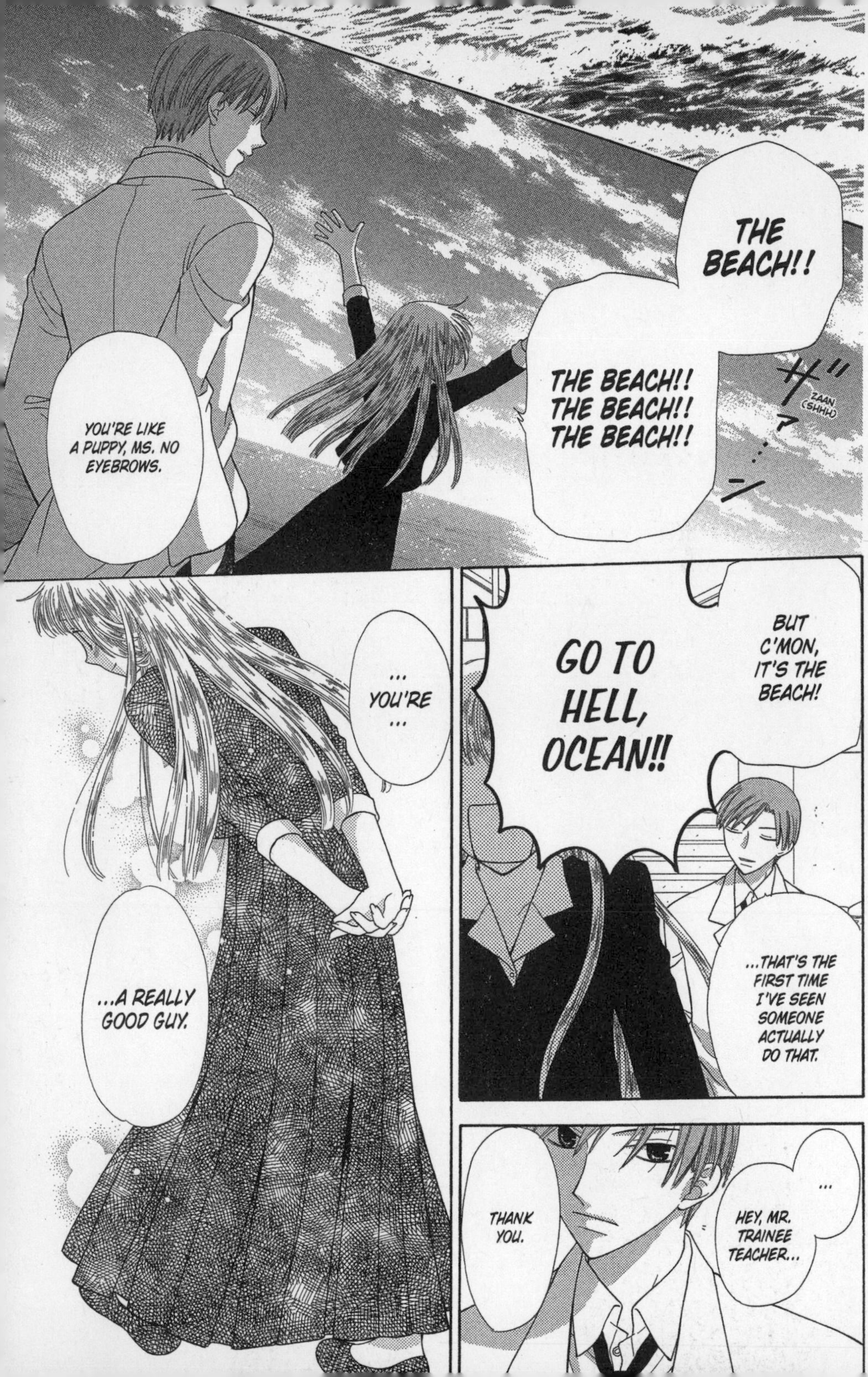
THE BEACH!!
THE BEACH!! THE BEACH!! THE BEACH!!
ZAAN (SHHH)
YOU'RE LIKE A PUPPY, MS. NO EYEBROWS.
BUT C'MON, IT'S THE BEACH!
GO TO HELL, OCEAN!!
...THAT'S THE FIRST TIME I'VE SEEN SOMEONE ACTUALLY DO THAT.
...
HEY, MR. TRAINEE TEACHER...
THANK YOU.
... YOU'RE ...
...A REALLY GOOD GUY.

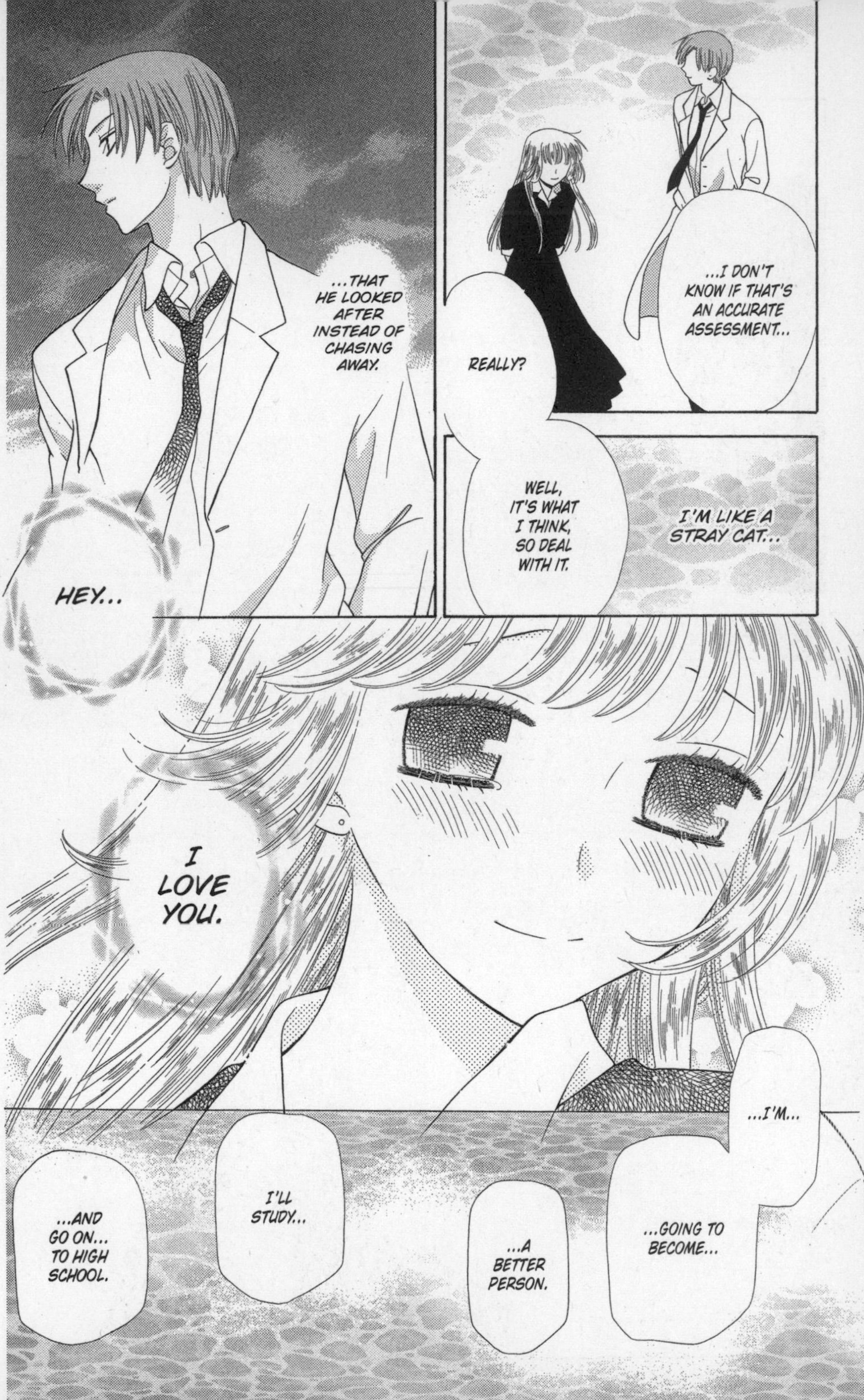
...I DON'T KNOW IF THAT'S AN ACCURATE ASSESSMENT...
REALLY?
I'M LIKE A STRAY CAT...
WELL, IT'S WHAT I THINK, SO DEAL WITH IT.
...THAT HE LOOKED AFTER INSTEAD OF CHASING AWAY.
HEY...
I LOVE YOU.
...I'M...
...GOING TO BECOME...
...A BETTER PERSON.
I'LL STUDY...
...AND GO ON... TO HIGH SCHOOL.

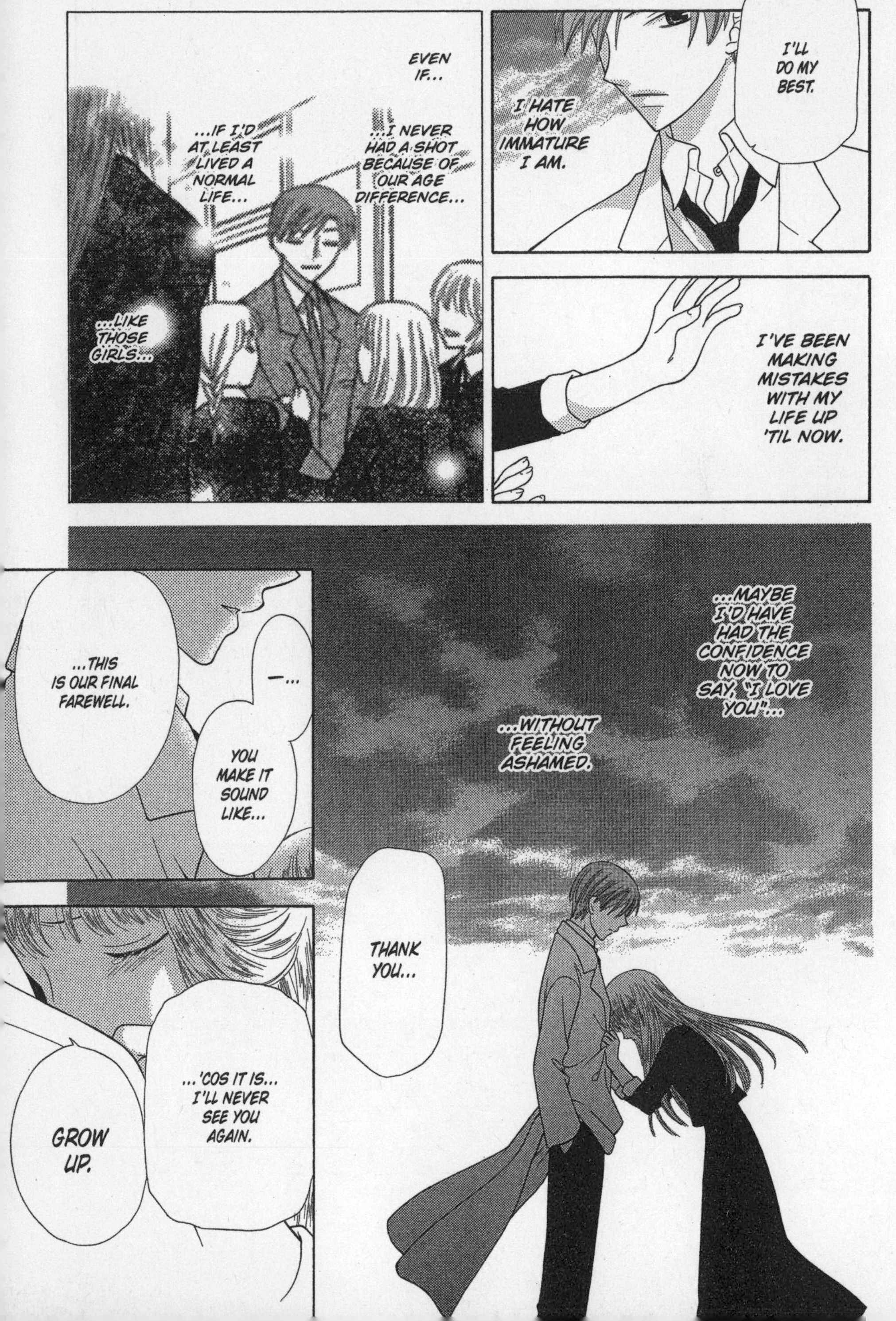
I'LL DO MY BEST.
I HATE HOW IMMATURE I AM.
I'VE BEEN MAKING MISTAKES WITH MY LIFE UP 'TIL NOW.
EVEN IF...
...I NEVER HAD A SHOT BECAUSE OF OUR AGE DIFFERENCE...
...IF I'D AT LEAST LIVED A NORMAL LIFE...
...LIKE THOSE GIRLS...
...MAYBE I'D HAVE HAD THE CONFIDENCE NOW TO SAY, "I LOVE YOU"...
...WITHOUT FEELING ASHAMED.
THANK YOU...
...THIS IS OUR FINAL FAREWELL.
—...
YOU MAKE IT SOUND LIKE...
...'COS IT IS... I'LL NEVER SEE YOU AGAIN.
GROW UP.

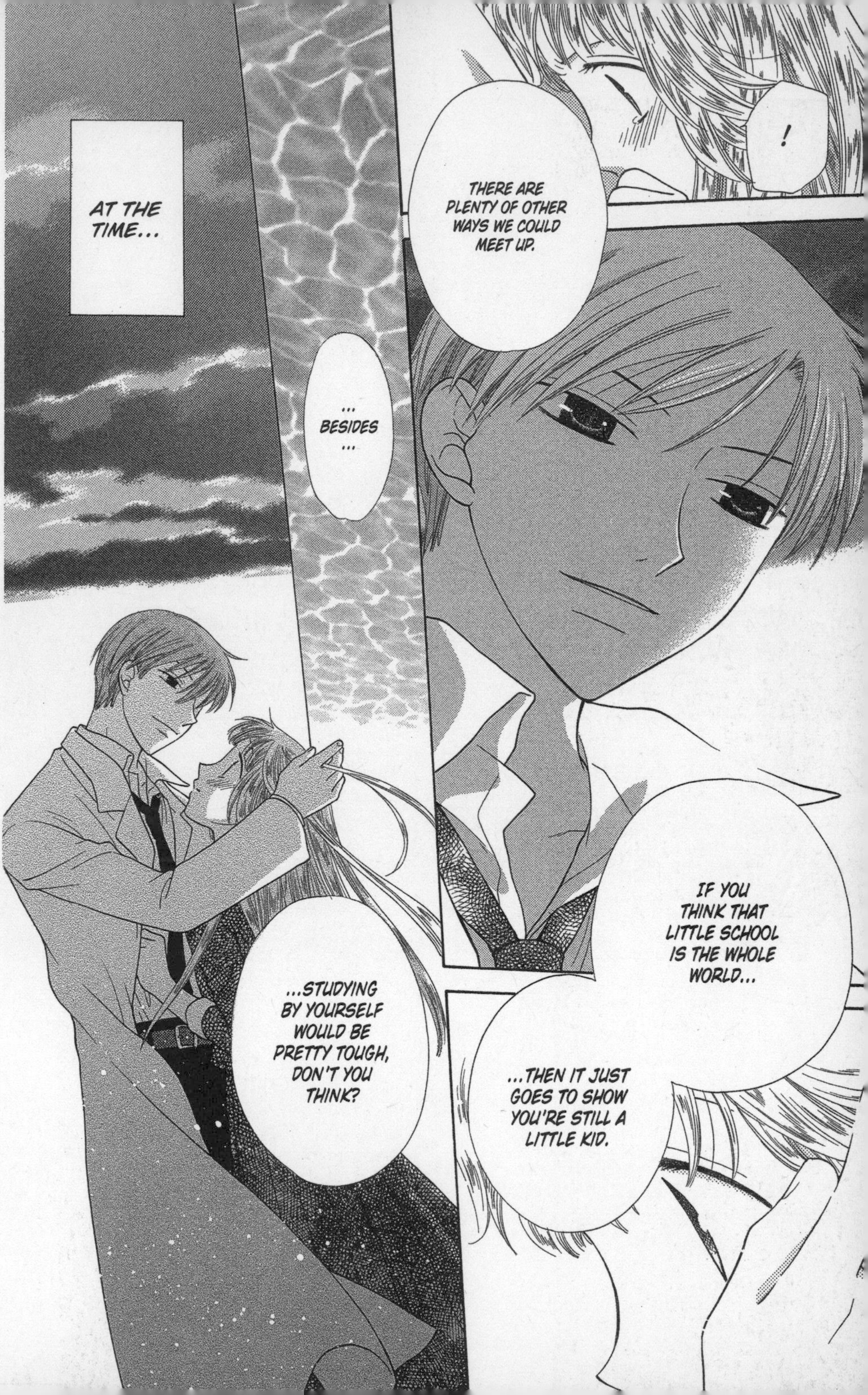
!
THERE ARE PLENTY OF OTHER WAYS WE COULD MEET UP.
...BESIDES...
...STUDYING BY YOURSELF WOULD BE PRETTY TOUGH, DON'T YOU THINK?
IF YOU THINK THAT LITTLE SCHOOL IS THE WHOLE WORLD...
...THEN IT JUST GOES TO SHOW YOU'RE STILL A LITTLE KID.
AT THE TIME...

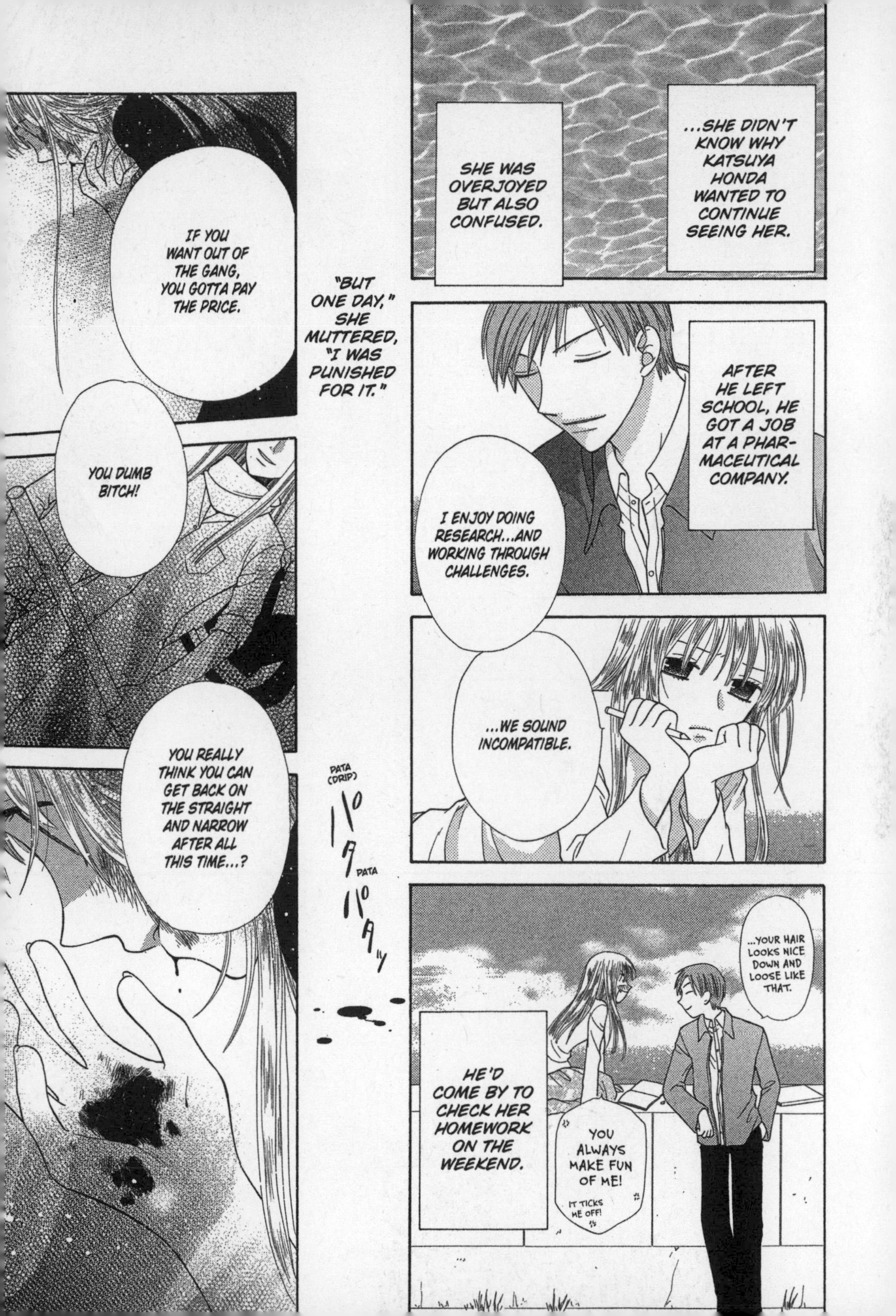
...SHE DIDN'T KNOW WHY KATSUYA HONDA WANTED TO CONTINUE SEEING HER.
SHE WAS OVERJOYED BUT ALSO CONFUSED.
AFTER HE LEFT SCHOOL, HE GOT A JOB AT A PHARMACEUTICAL COMPANY.
I ENJOY DOING RESEARCH...AND WORKING THROUGH CHALLENGES.
...WE SOUND INCOMPATIBLE.
...YOUR HAIR LOOKS NICE DOWN AND LOOSE LIKE THAT.
HE'D COME BY TO CHECK HER HOMEWORK ON THE WEEKEND.
YOU ALWAYS MAKE FUN OF ME!
IT TICKS ME OFF!
"BUT ONE DAY," SHE MUTTERED, "I WAS PUNISHED FOR IT."
IF YOU WANT OUT OF THE GANG, YOU GOTTA PAY THE PRICE.
YOU DUMB BITCH!
YOU REALLY THINK YOU CAN GET BACK ON THE STRAIGHT AND NARROW AFTER ALL THIS TIME...?
PATA (DRIP)
PATA

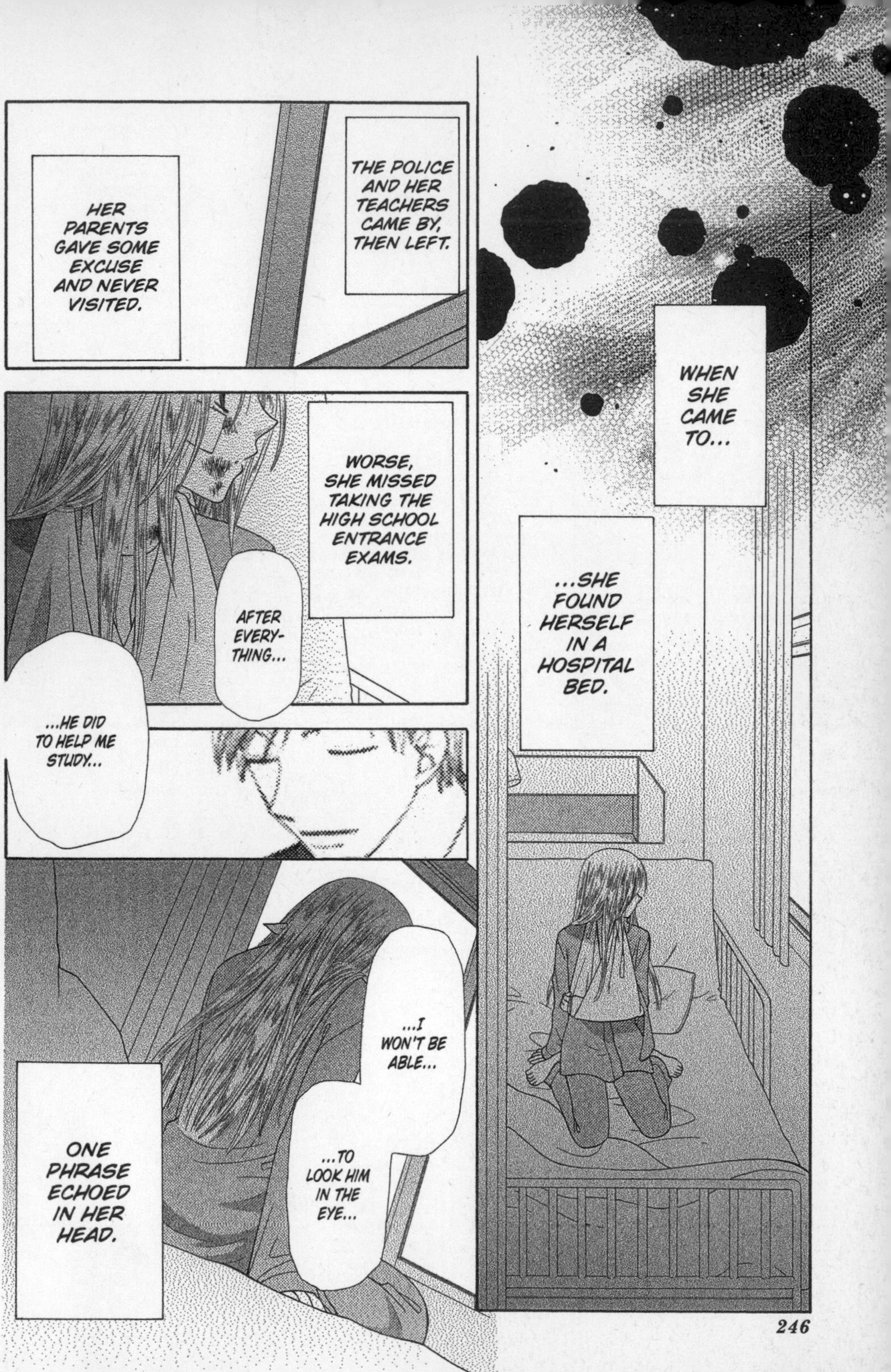
WHEN SHE CAME TO...
...SHE FOUND HERSELF IN A HOSPITAL BED.
THE POLICE AND HER TEACHERS CAME BY, THEN LEFT.
HER PARENTS GAVE SOME EXCUSE AND NEVER VISITED.
WORSE, SHE MISSED TAKING THE HIGH SCHOOL ENTRANCE EXAMS.
AFTER EVERY-THING...
...HE DID TO HELP ME STUDY...
...I WON'T BE ABLE...
...TO LOOK HIM IN THE EYE...
ONE PHRASE ECHOED IN HER HEAD.

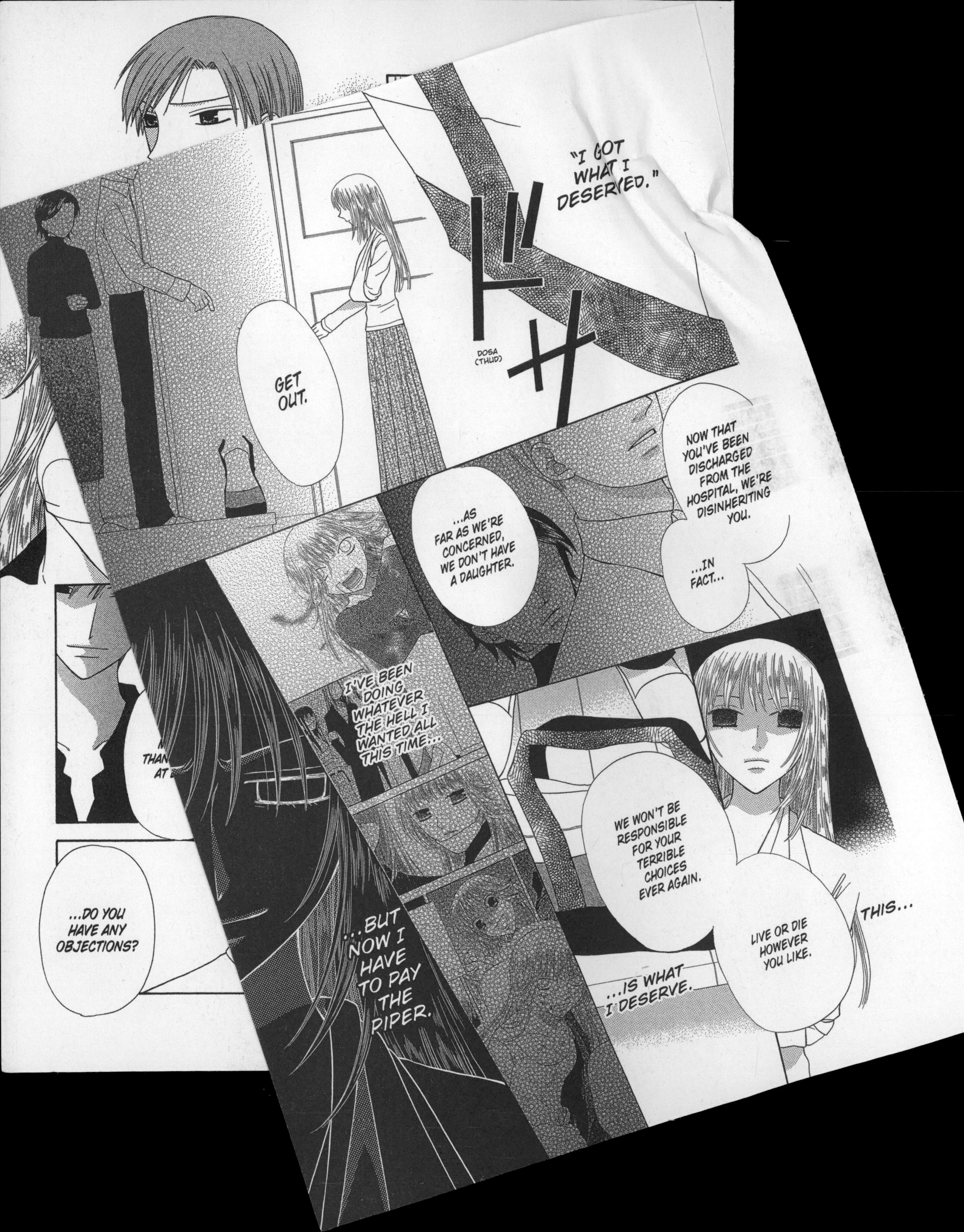
"I GOT WHAT I DESERVED."
DOSA (THUD)
GET OUT.
NOW THAT YOU'VE BEEN DISCHARGED FROM THE HOSPITAL, WE'RE DISINHERITING YOU.
...IN FACT...
...AS FAR AS WE'RE CONCERNED, WE DON'T HAVE A DAUGHTER.
WE WON'T BE RESPONSIBLE FOR YOUR TERRIBLE CHOICES EVER AGAIN.
LIVE OR DIE HOWEVER YOU LIKE.
THIS...
...IS WHAT I DESERVE.
I'VE BEEN DOING WHATEVER THE HELL I WANTED ALL THIS TIME...
...BUT NOW I HAVE TO PAY THE PIPER.
...DO YOU HAVE ANY OBJECTIONS?

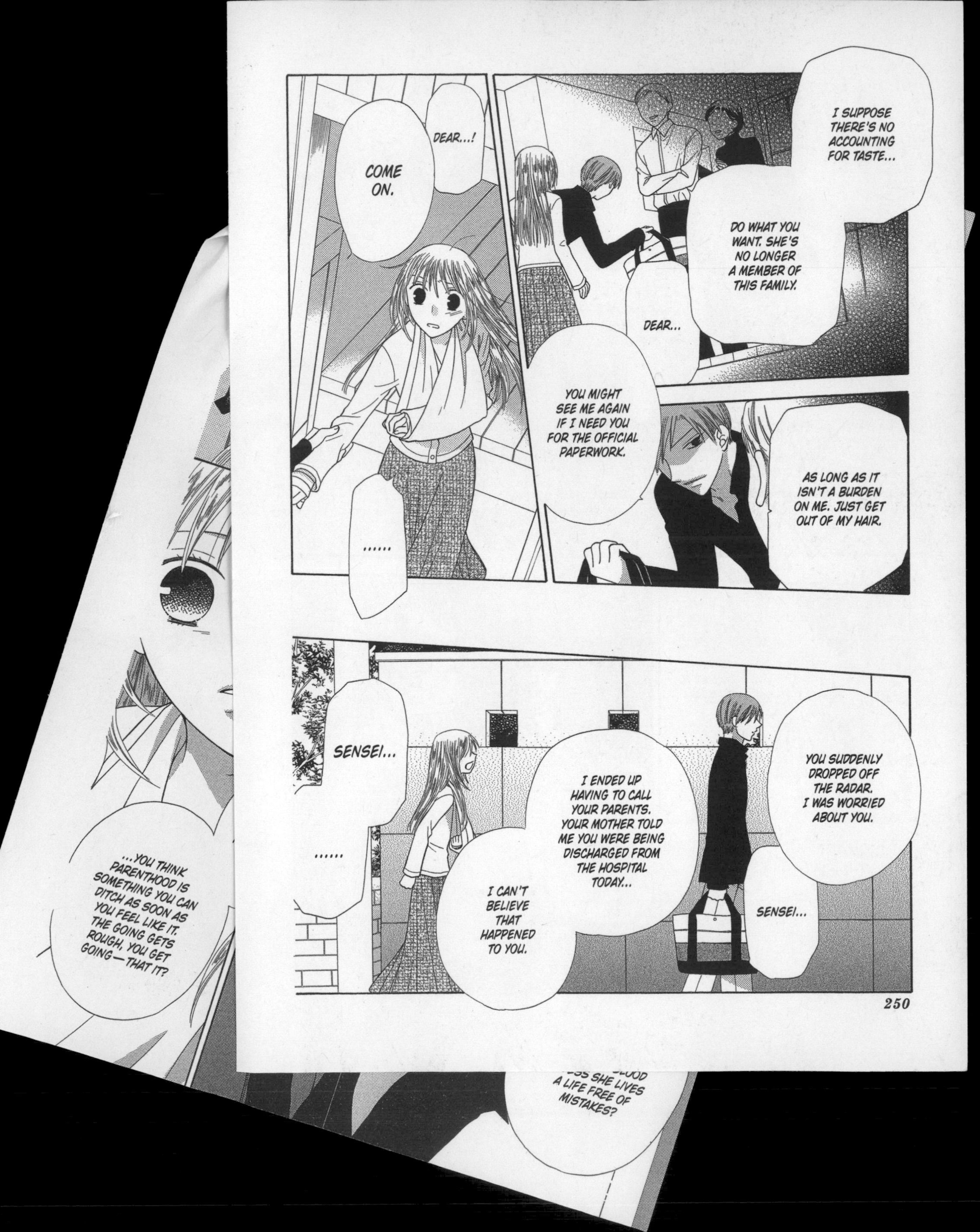
I SUPPOSE THERE'S NO ACCOUNTING FOR TASTE...
DO WHAT YOU WANT. SHE'S NO LONGER A MEMBER OF THIS FAMILY.
DEAR...
AS LONG AS IT ISN'T A BURDEN ON ME. JUST GET OUT OF MY HAIR.
YOU MIGHT SEE ME AGAIN IF I NEED YOU FOR THE OFFICIAL PAPERWORK.
DEAR...!
COME ON.
......
YOU SUDDENLY DROPPED OFF THE RADAR. I WAS WORRIED ABOUT YOU.
SENSEI...
I ENDED UP HAVING TO CALL YOUR PARENTS. YOUR MOTHER TOLD ME YOU WERE BEING DISCHARGED FROM THE HOSPITAL TODAY...
I CAN'T BELIEVE THAT HAPPENED TO YOU.
SENSEI...
......

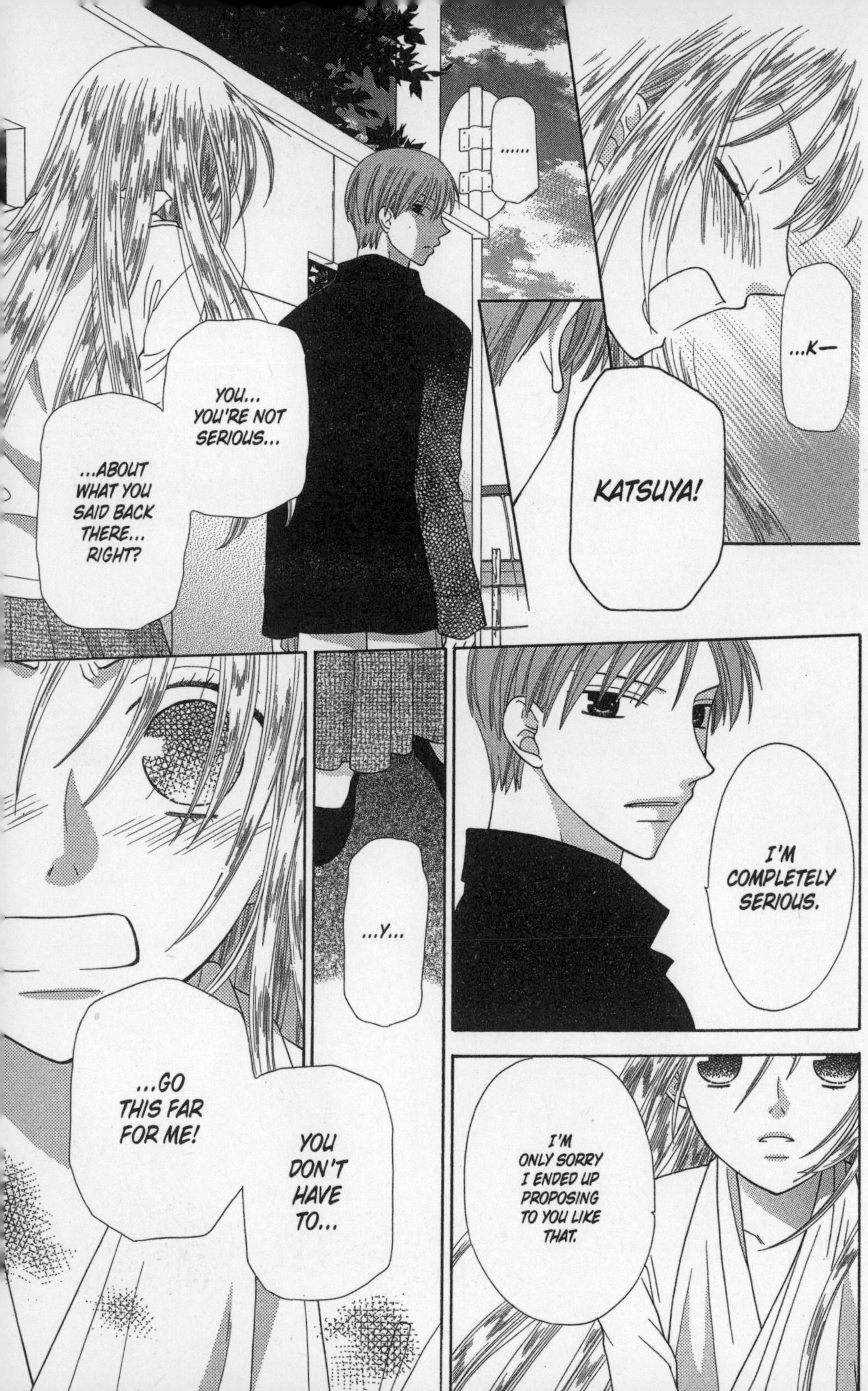
...K—
KATSUYA!
......
YOU... YOU'RE NOT SERIOUS...
...ABOUT WHAT YOU SAID BACK THERE... RIGHT?
I'M COMPLETELY SERIOUS.
...Y...
YOU DON'T HAVE TO...
...GO THIS FAR FOR ME!
I'M ONLY SORRY I ENDED UP PROPOSING TO YOU LIKE THAT.

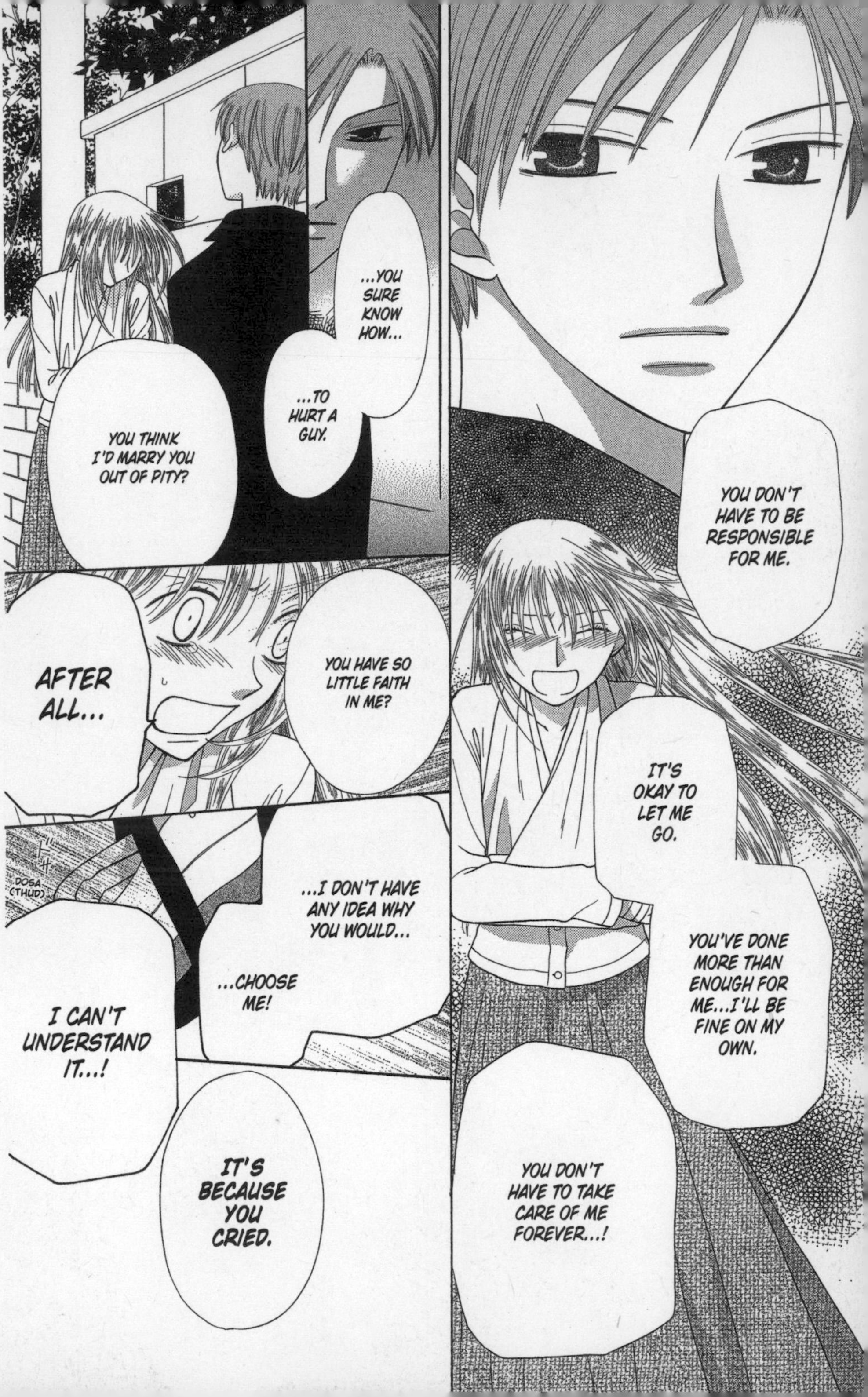
YOU DON'T HAVE TO BE RESPONSIBLE FOR ME.
IT'S OKAY TO LET ME GO.
YOU'VE DONE MORE THAN ENOUGH FOR ME...I'LL BE FINE ON MY OWN.
YOU DON'T HAVE TO TAKE CARE OF ME FOREVER...!
...YOU SURE KNOW HOW...
...TO HURT A GUY.
YOU THINK I'D MARRY YOU OUT OF PITY?
YOU HAVE SO LITTLE FAITH IN ME?
AFTER ALL...
DOSA (THUD)
...I DON'T HAVE ANY IDEA WHY YOU WOULD...
...CHOOSE ME!
I CAN'T UNDERSTAND IT...!
IT'S BECAUSE YOU CRIED.

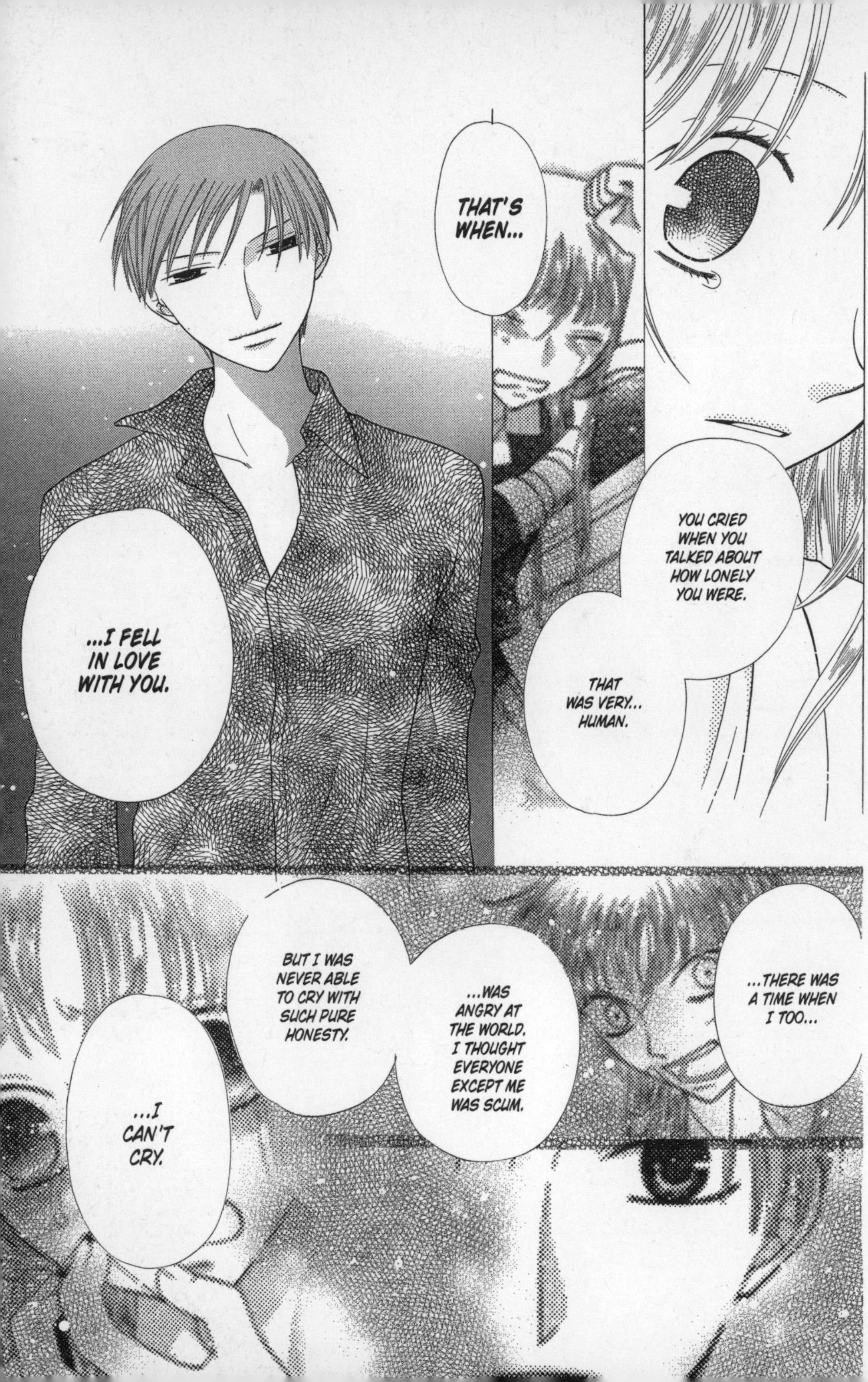
YOU CRIED WHEN YOU TALKED ABOUT HOW LONELY YOU WERE.
THAT WAS VERY... HUMAN.
THAT'S WHEN...
...I FELL IN LOVE WITH YOU.
...THERE WAS A TIME WHEN I TOO...
...WAS ANGRY AT THE WORLD. I THOUGHT EVERYONE EXCEPT ME WAS SCUM.
BUT I WAS NEVER ABLE TO CRY WITH SUCH PURE HONESTY.
...I CAN'T CRY.

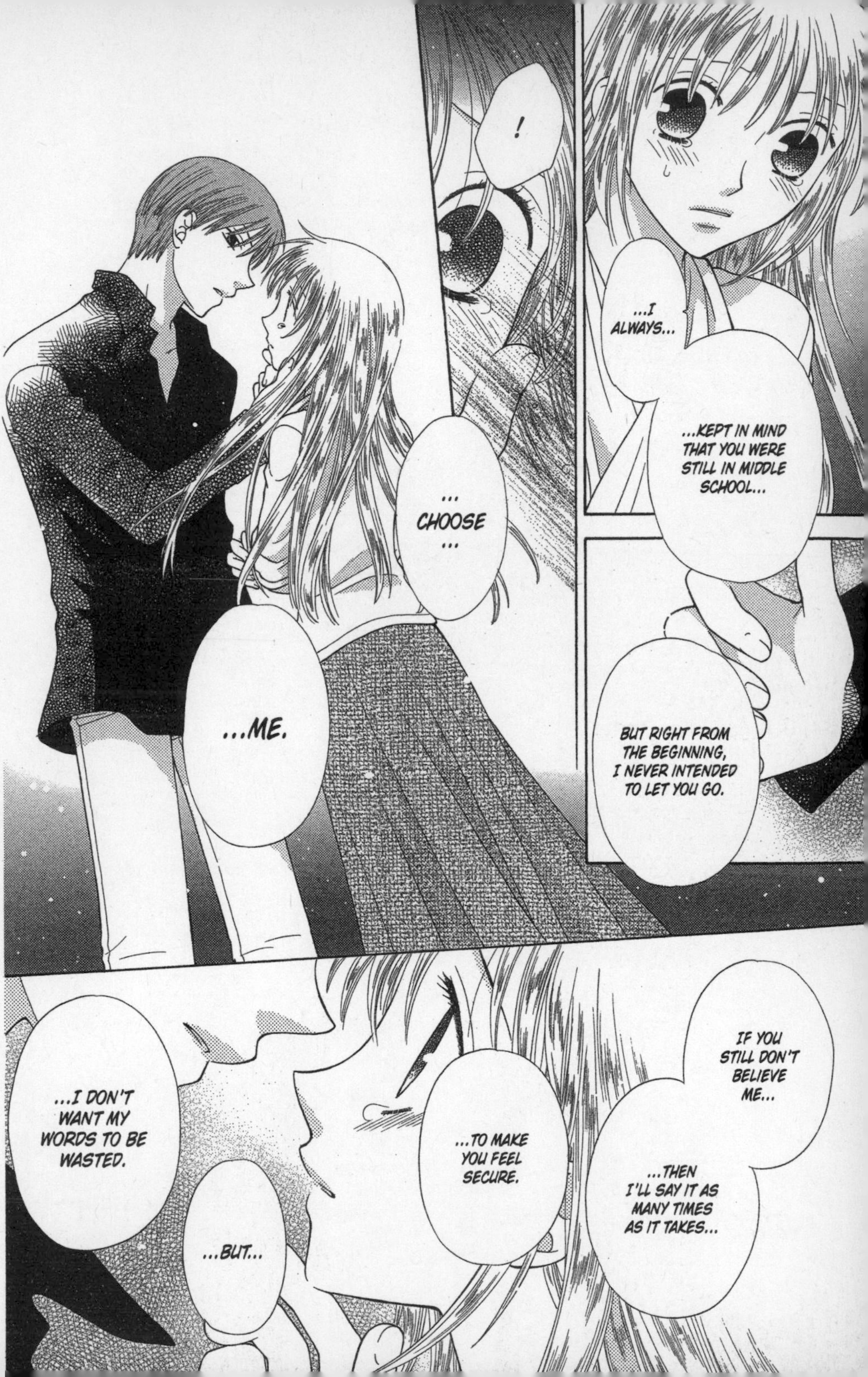
...I ALWAYS...
...KEPT IN MIND THAT YOU WERE STILL IN MIDDLE SCHOOL...
BUT RIGHT FROM THE BEGINNING, I NEVER INTENDED TO LET YOU GO.
!
...CHOOSE...
...ME.
IF YOU STILL DON'T BELIEVE ME...
...THEN I'LL SAY IT AS MANY TIMES AS IT TAKES...
...TO MAKE YOU FEEL SECURE.
...BUT...
...I DON'T WANT MY WORDS TO BE WASTED.

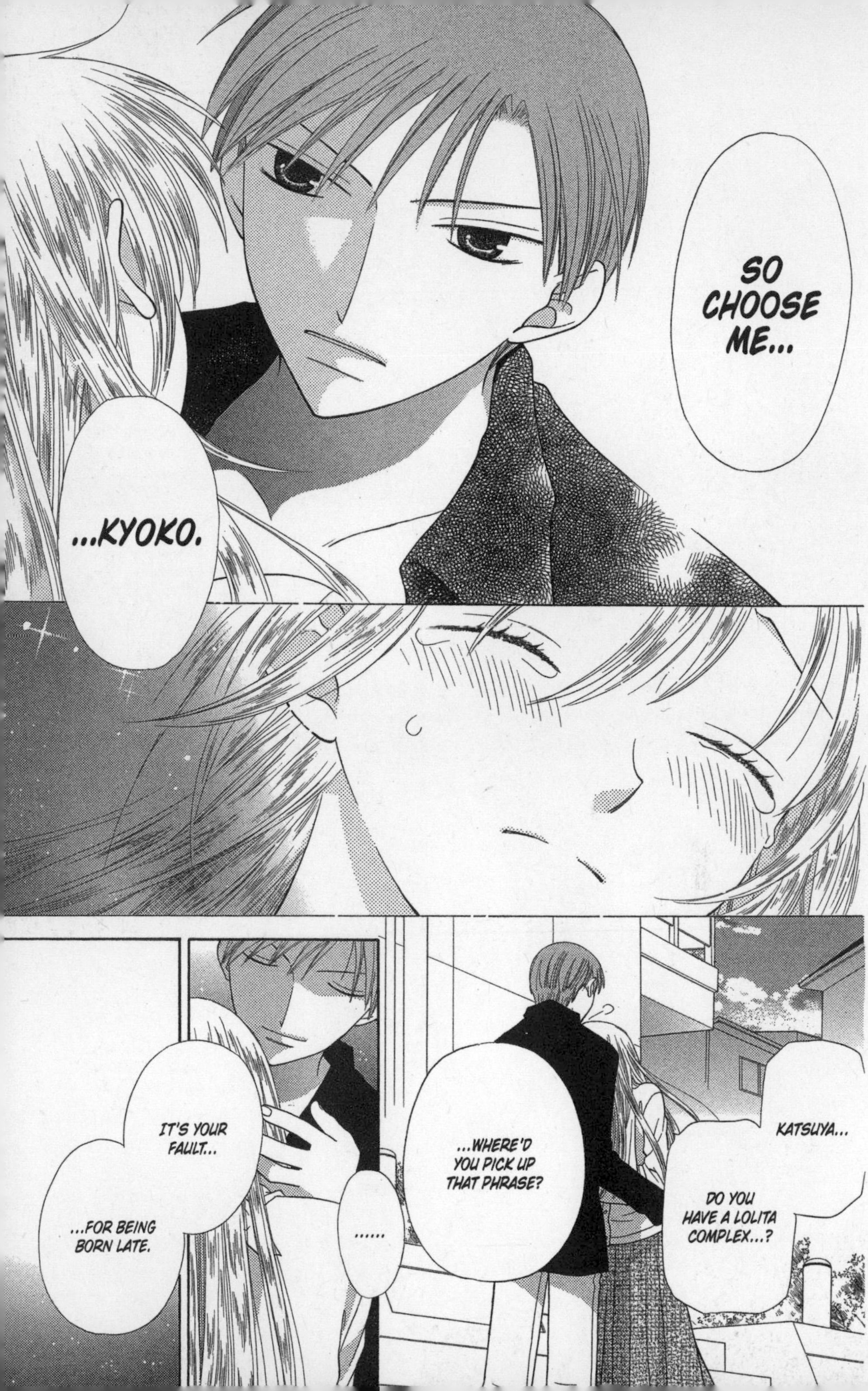
SO CHOOSE ME...
...KYOKO.
KATSUYA...
DO YOU HAVE A LOLITA COMPLEX...?
...WHERE'D YOU PICK UP THAT PHRASE?
......
IT'S YOUR FAULT...
...FOR BEING BORN LATE.

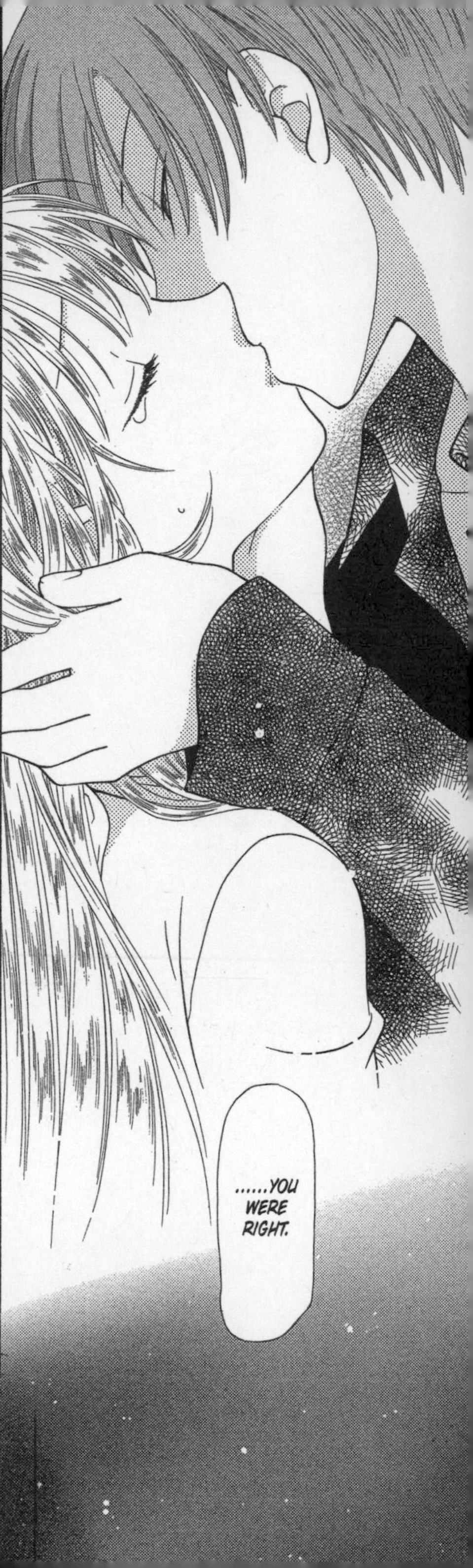
......YOU WERE RIGHT.
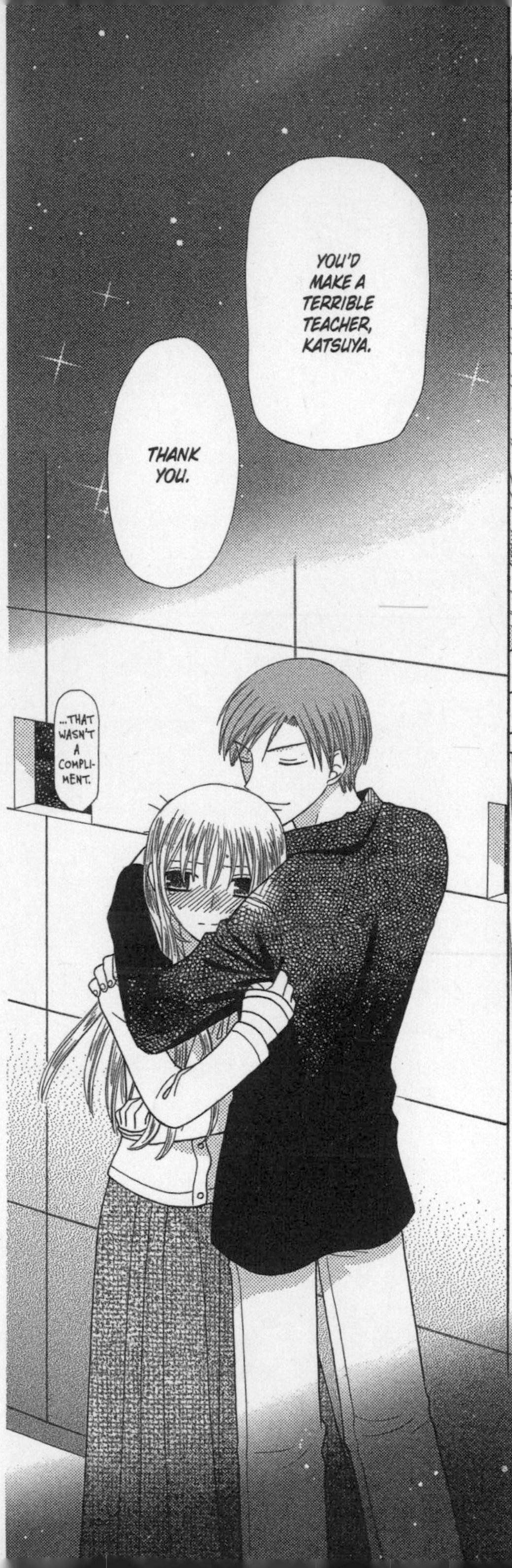
YOU'D MAKE A TERRIBLE TEACHER, KATSUYA.
THANK YOU.
...THAT WASN'T A COMPLI-MENT.

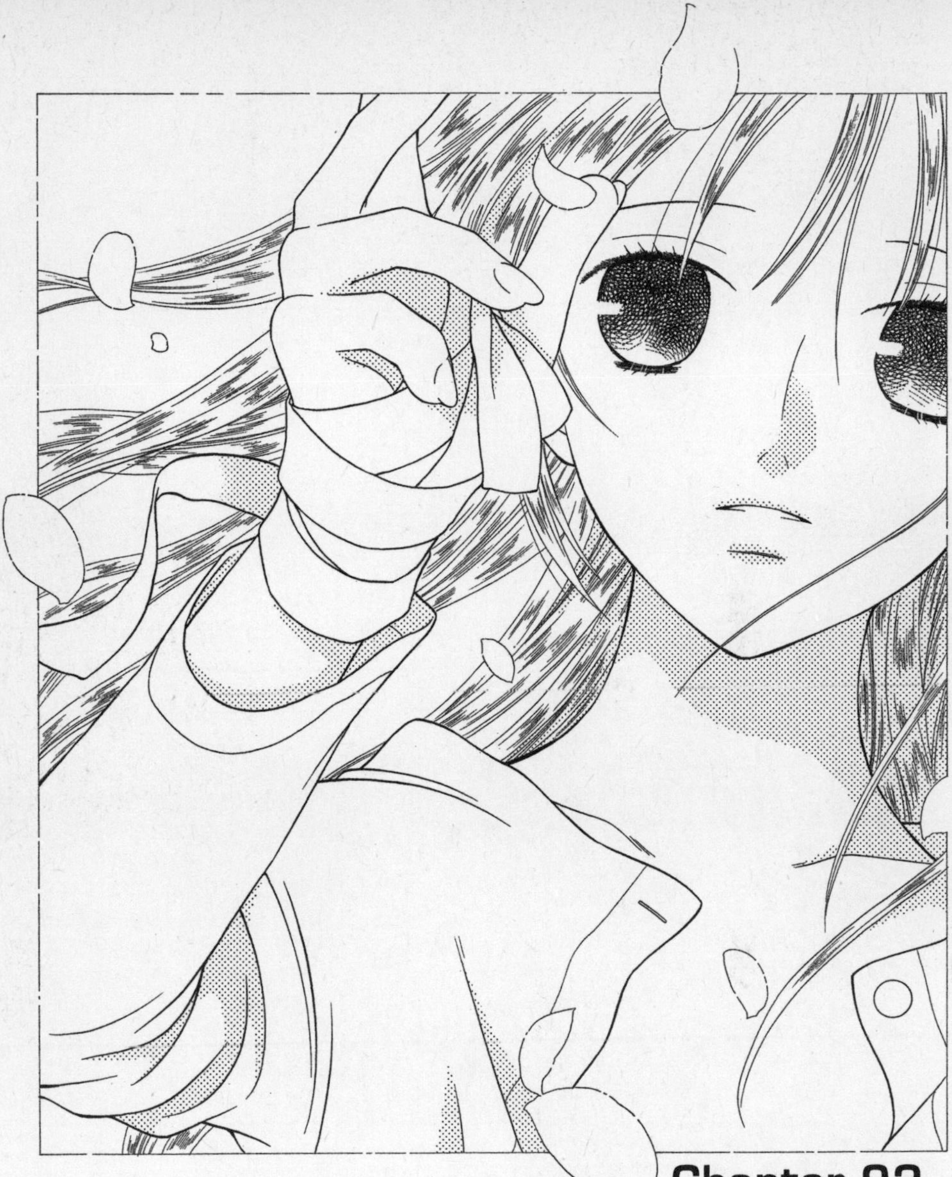

Chapter 92

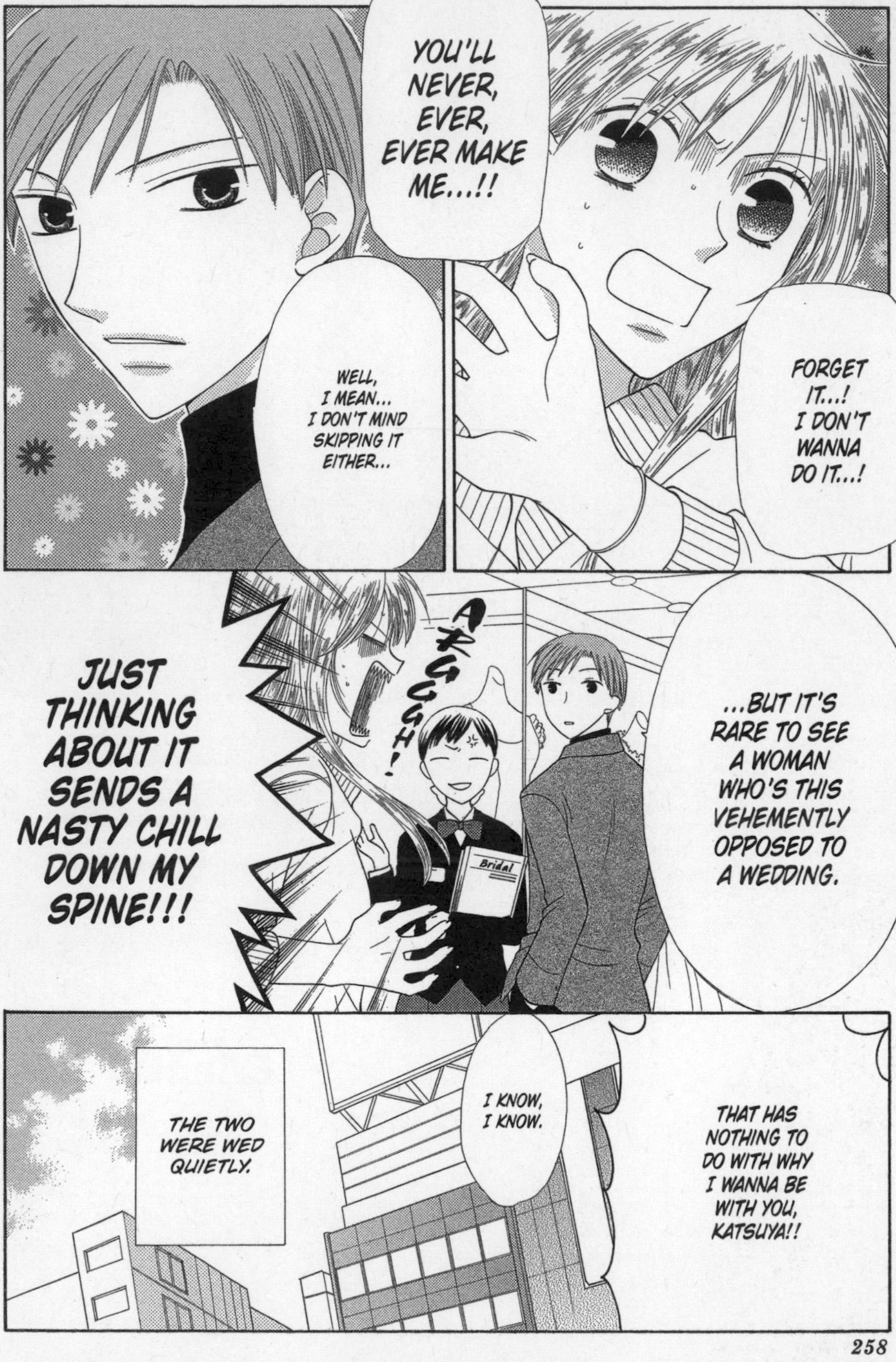
FORGET IT...! I DON'T WANNA DO IT...!
YOU'LL NEVER, EVER, EVER MAKE ME...!!
WELL, I MEAN... I DON'T MIND SKIPPING IT EITHER...
...BUT IT'S RARE TO SEE A WOMAN WHO'S THIS VEHEMENTLY OPPOSED TO A WEDDING.
ARGGGH!
Bridal
JUST THINKING ABOUT IT SENDS A NASTY CHILL DOWN MY SPINE!!!
THAT HAS NOTHING TO DO WITH WHY I WANNA BE WITH YOU, KATSUYA!!
I KNOW, I KNOW.
THE TWO WERE WED QUIETLY.

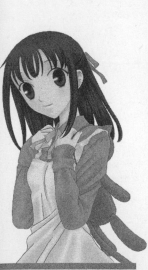

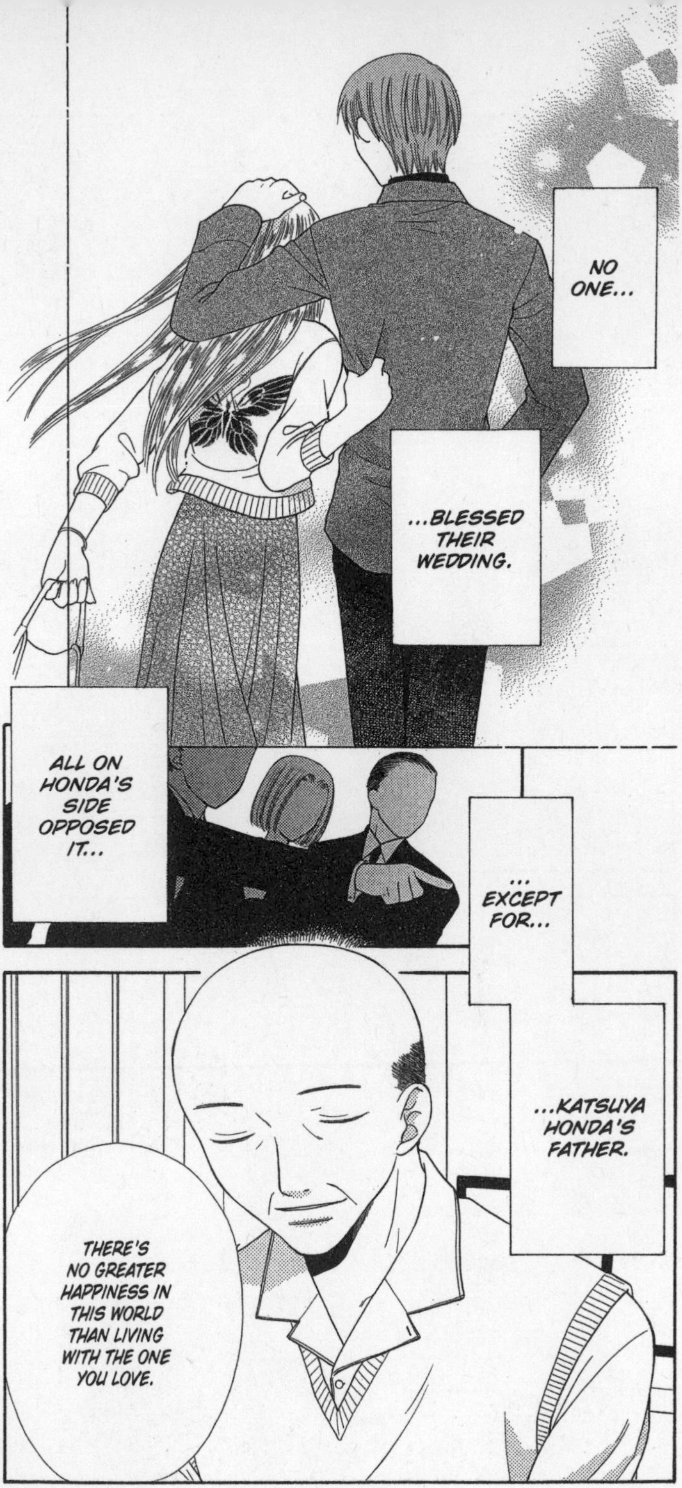
NO ONE...
...BLESSED THEIR WEDDING.
ALL ON HONDA'S SIDE OPPOSED IT...
...EXCEPT FOR...
...KATSUYA HONDA'S FATHER.
THERE'S NO GREATER HAPPINESS IN THIS WORLD THAN LIVING WITH THE ONE YOU LOVE.

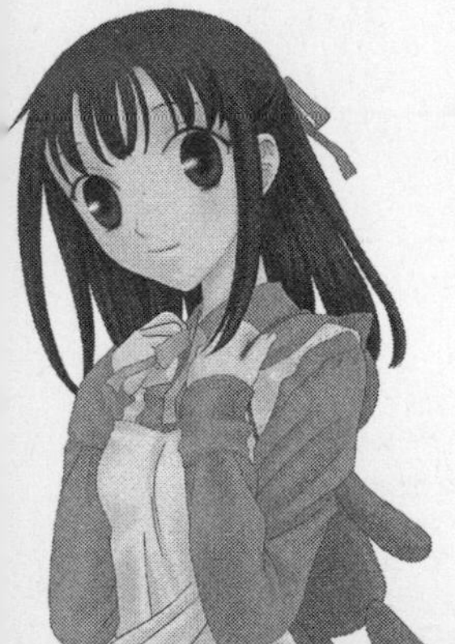

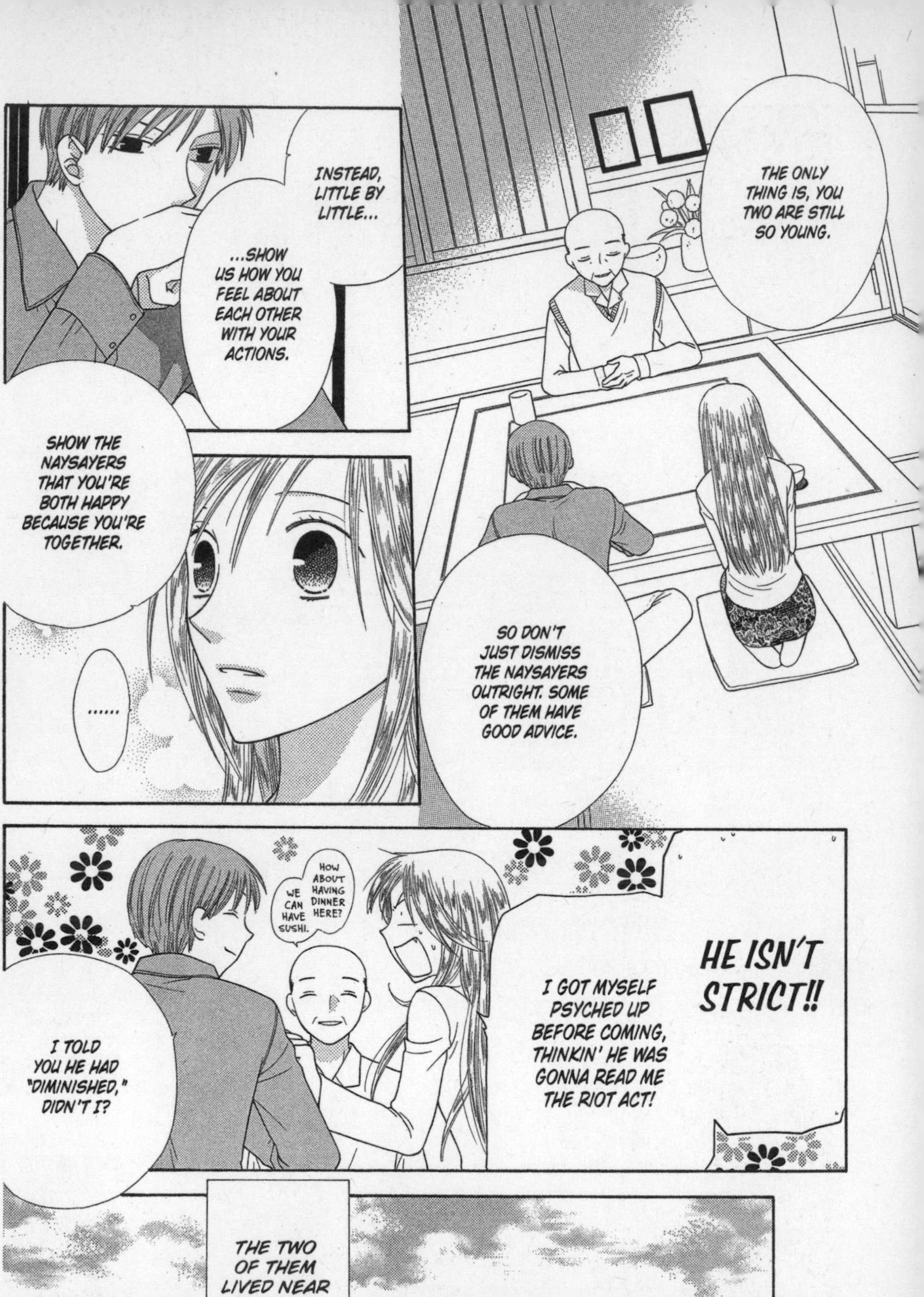
THE ONLY THING IS, YOU TWO ARE STILL SO YOUNG.
SO DON'T JUST DISMISS THE NAYSAYERS OUTRIGHT. SOME OF THEM HAVE GOOD ADVICE.
INSTEAD, LITTLE BY LITTLE...
...SHOW US HOW YOU FEEL ABOUT EACH OTHER WITH YOUR ACTIONS.
SHOW THE NAYSAYERS THAT YOU'RE BOTH HAPPY BECAUSE YOU'RE TOGETHER.
......
HE ISN'T STRICT!!
I GOT MYSELF PSYCHED UP BEFORE COMING, THINKIN' HE WAS GONNA READ ME THE RIOT ACT!
HOW ABOUT HAVING DINNER HERE?
WE CAN HAVE SUSHI.
I TOLD YOU HE HAD "DIMINISHED," DIDN'T I?
THE TWO OF THEM LIVED NEAR THE SEA.

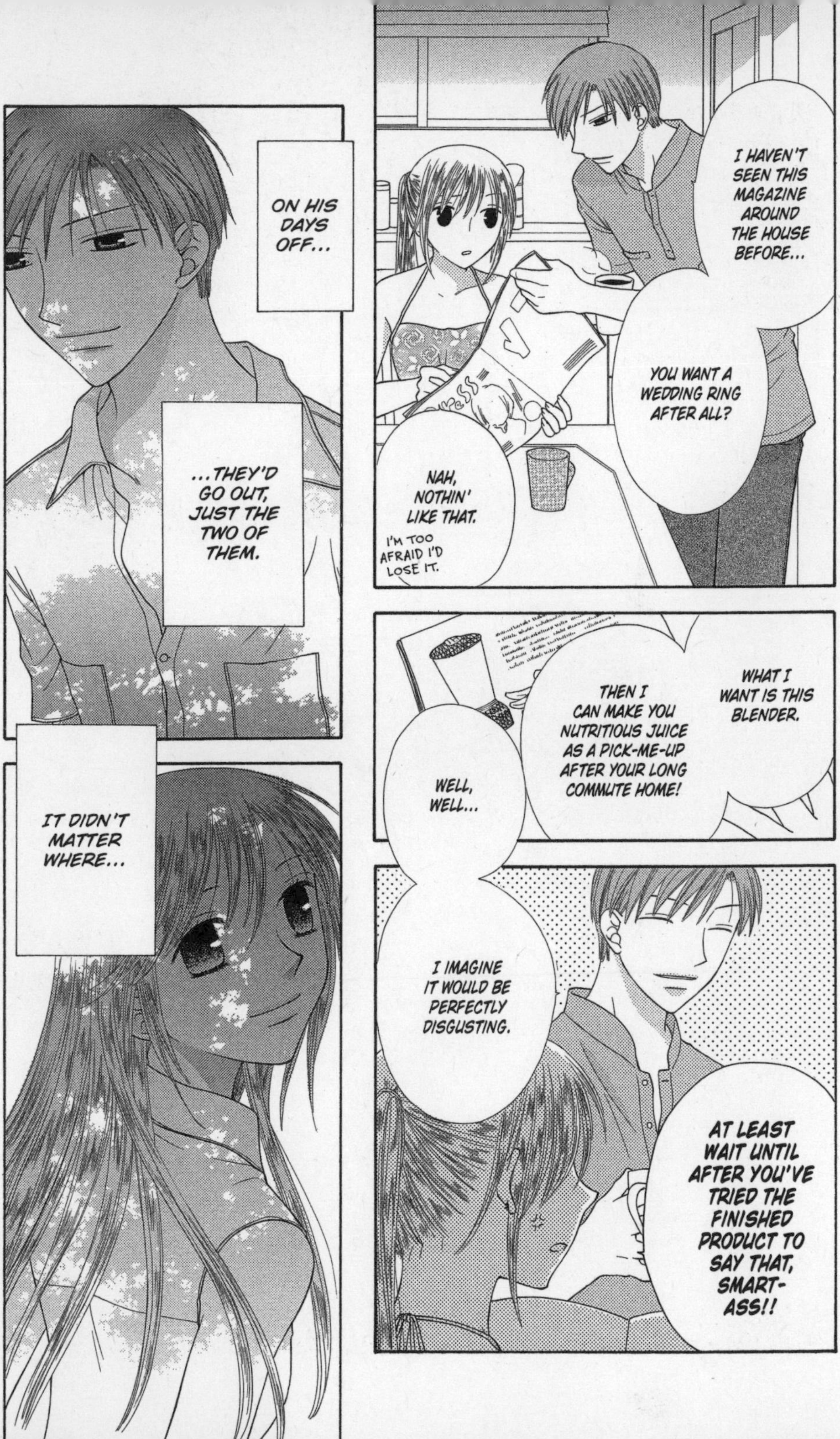
I HAVEN'T SEEN THIS MAGAZINE AROUND THE HOUSE BEFORE...
YOU WANT A WEDDING RING AFTER ALL?
NAH, NOTHIN' LIKE THAT.
I'M TOO AFRAID I'D LOSE IT.
WHAT I WANT IS THIS BLENDER.
THEN I CAN MAKE YOU NUTRITIOUS JUICE AS A PICK-ME-UP AFTER YOUR LONG COMMUTE HOME!
WELL, WELL...
I IMAGINE IT WOULD BE PERFECTLY DISGUSTING.
AT LEAST WAIT UNTIL AFTER YOU'VE TRIED THE FINISHED PRODUCT TO SAY THAT, SMART-ASS!!
ON HIS DAYS OFF...
...THEY'D GO OUT, JUST THE TWO OF THEM.
IT DIDN'T MATTER WHERE...

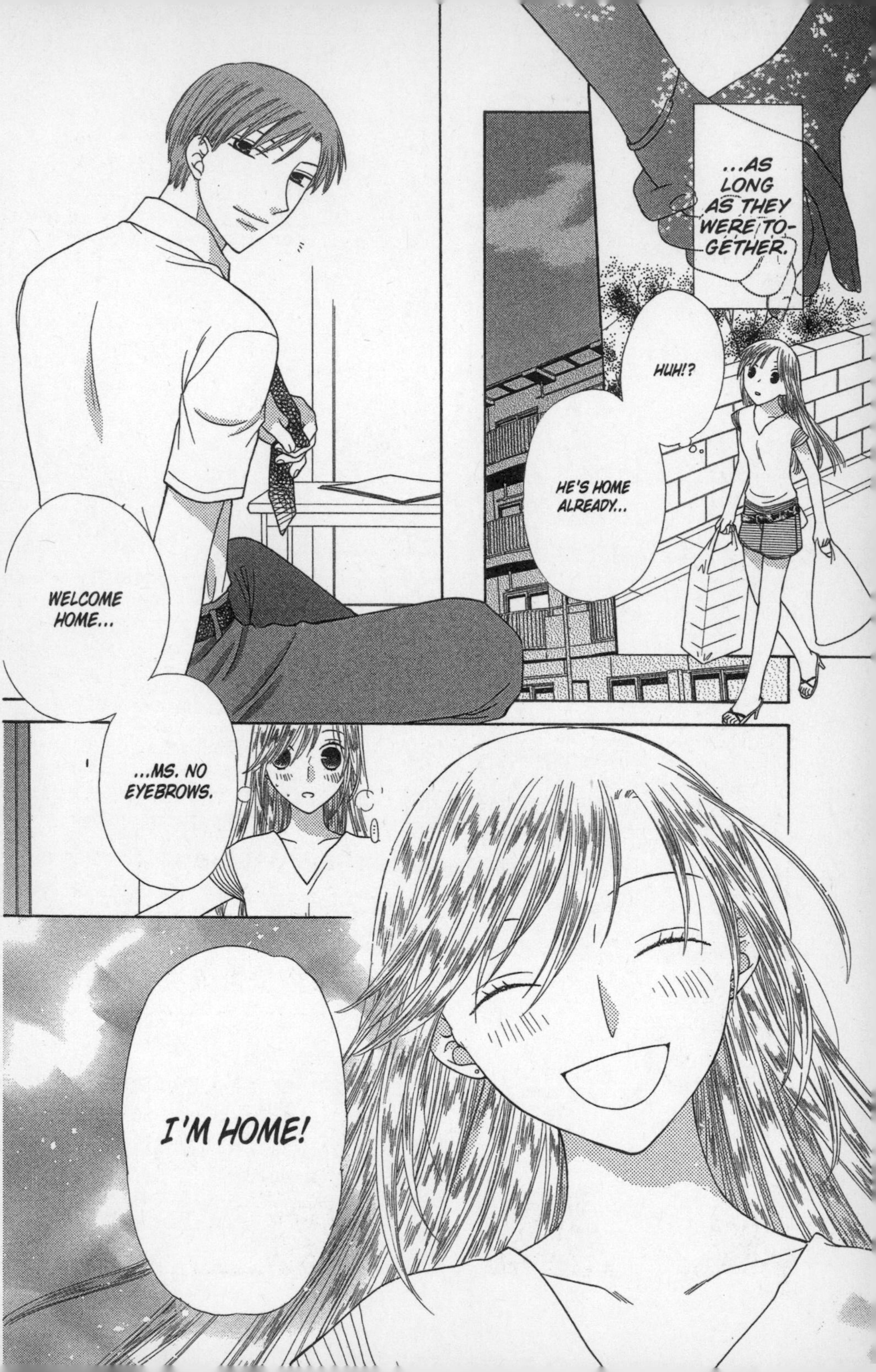

...AS LONG AS THEY WERE TO-GETHER.
HUH!?
HE'S HOME ALREADY...
WELCOME HOME...
...MS. NO EYEBROWS.
I'M HOME!

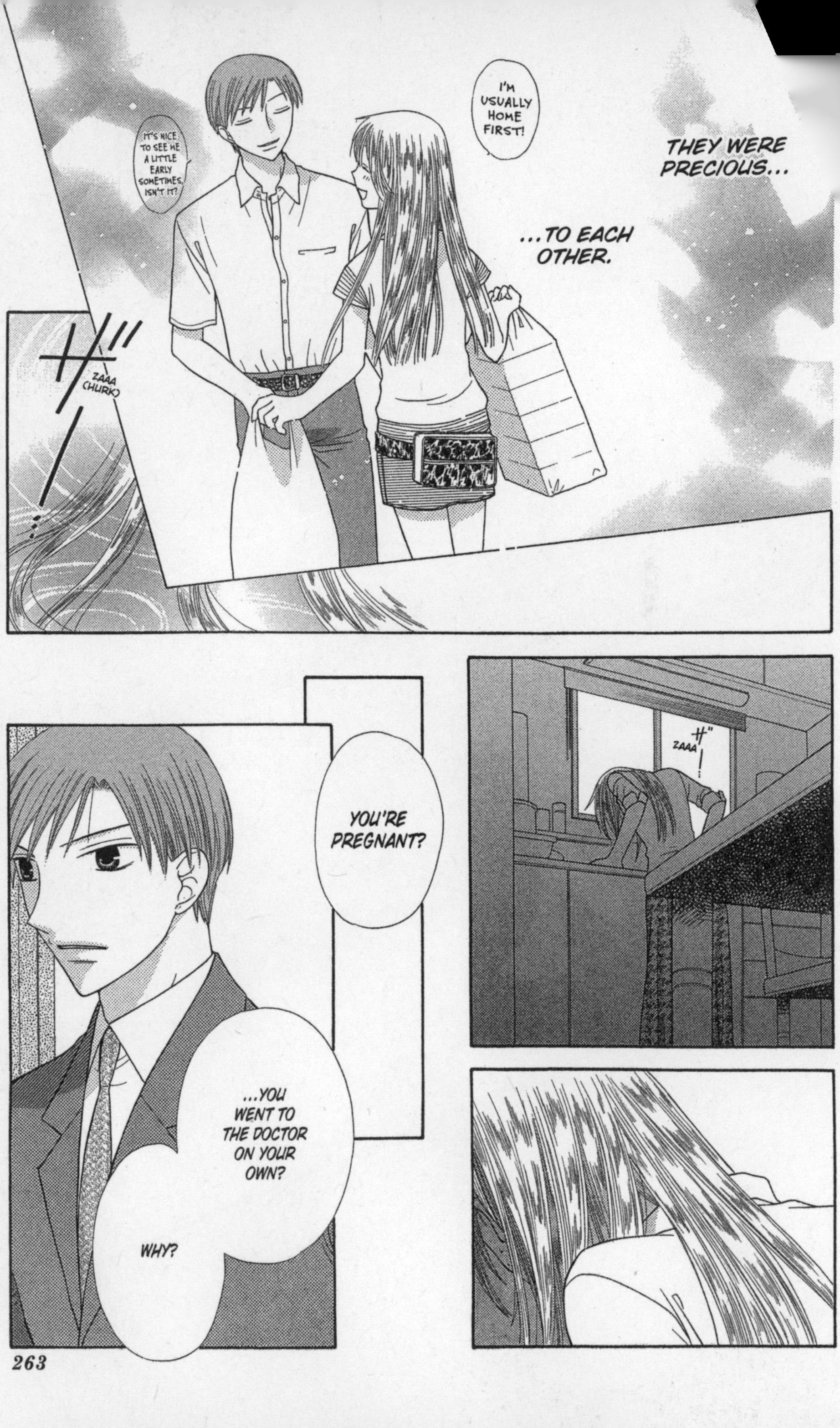
THEY WERE PRECIOUS...
...TO EACH OTHER.
I'M USUALLY HOME FIRST!
IT'S NICE TO SEE ME A LITTLE EARLY SOMETIMES, ISN'T IT?
ZAAA (CHURK)
ZAAA
YOU'RE PREGNANT?
...YOU WENT TO THE DOCTOR ON YOUR OWN?
WHY?

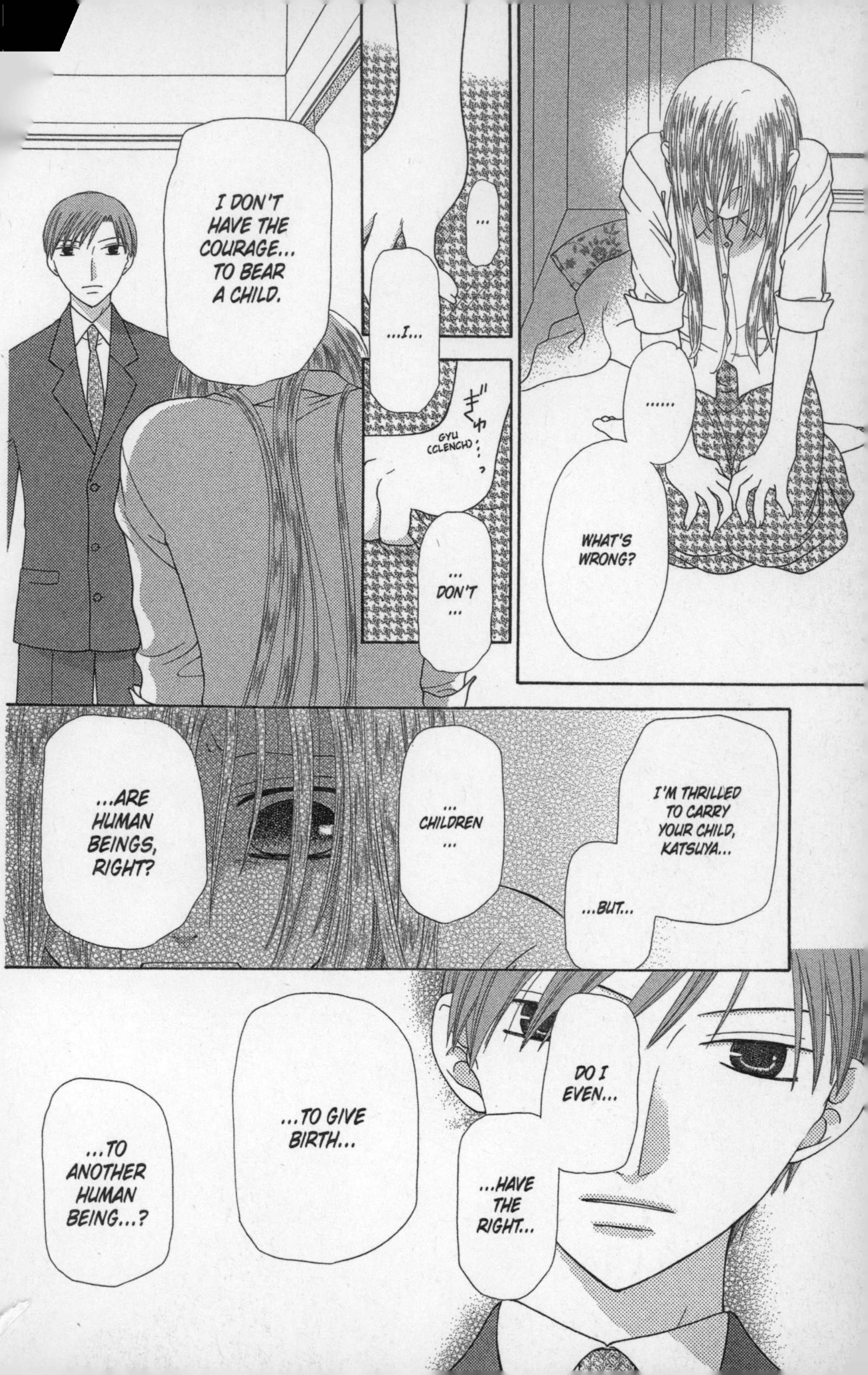
......
WHAT'S WRONG?
...
...I...
GYU (CLENCH)
... DON'T ...
I DON'T HAVE THE COURAGE... TO BEAR A CHILD.
I'M THRILLED TO CARRY YOUR CHILD, KATSUYA...
...BUT...
... CHILDREN ...
...ARE HUMAN BEINGS, RIGHT?
DO I EVEN...
...HAVE THE RIGHT...
...TO GIVE BIRTH...
...TO ANOTHER HUMAN BEING...?

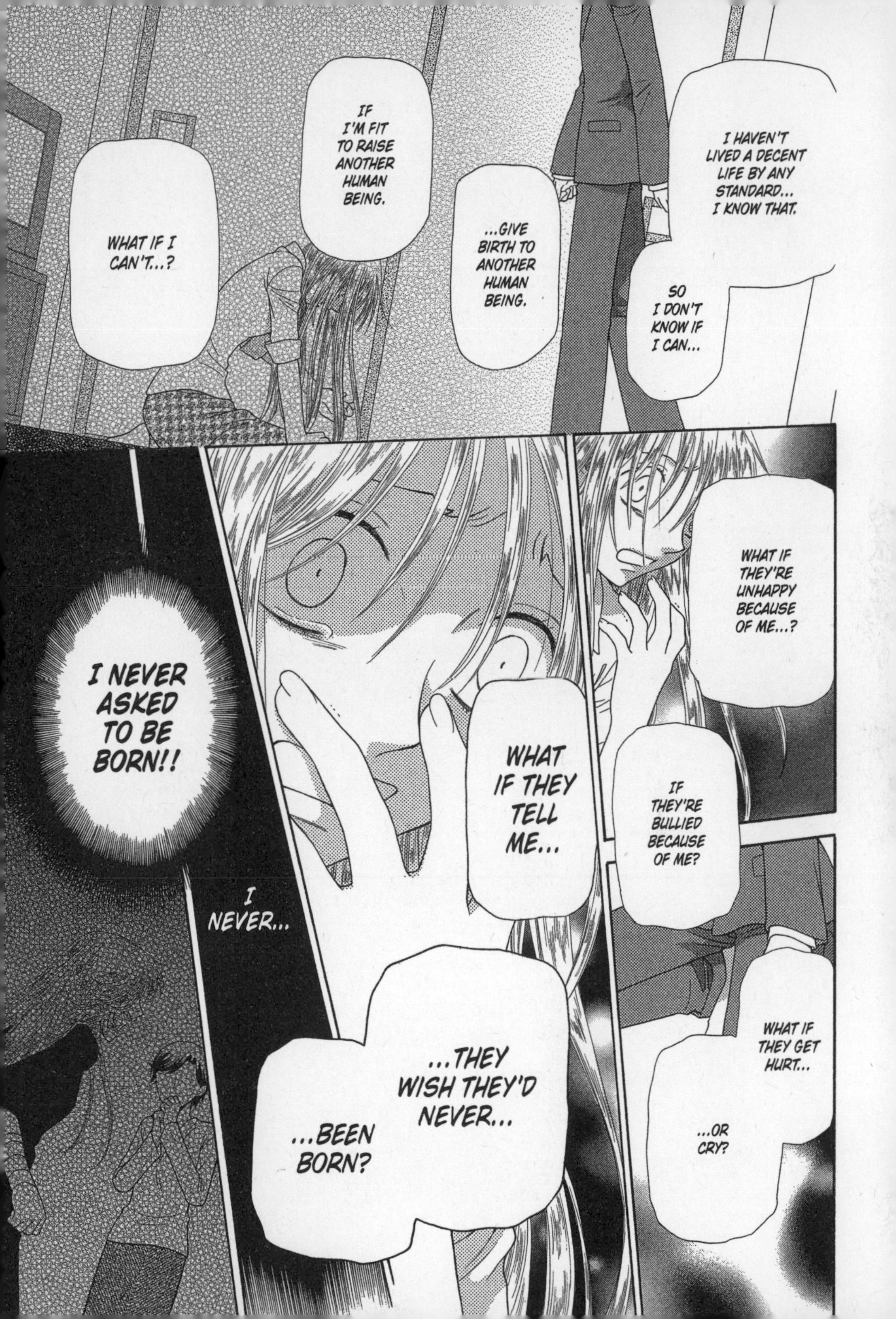
I HAVEN'T LIVED A DECENT LIFE BY ANY STANDARD... I KNOW THAT.
SO I DON'T KNOW IF I CAN...
...GIVE BIRTH TO ANOTHER HUMAN BEING.
IF I'M FIT TO RAISE ANOTHER HUMAN BEING.
WHAT IF I CAN'T...?
WHAT IF THEY'RE UNHAPPY BECAUSE OF ME...?
IF THEY'RE BULLIED BECAUSE OF ME?
WHAT IF THEY GET HURT...
...OR CRY?
WHAT IF THEY TELL ME...
...THEY WISH THEY'D NEVER...
...BEEN BORN?
I NEVER ASKED TO BE BORN!!
I NEVER...

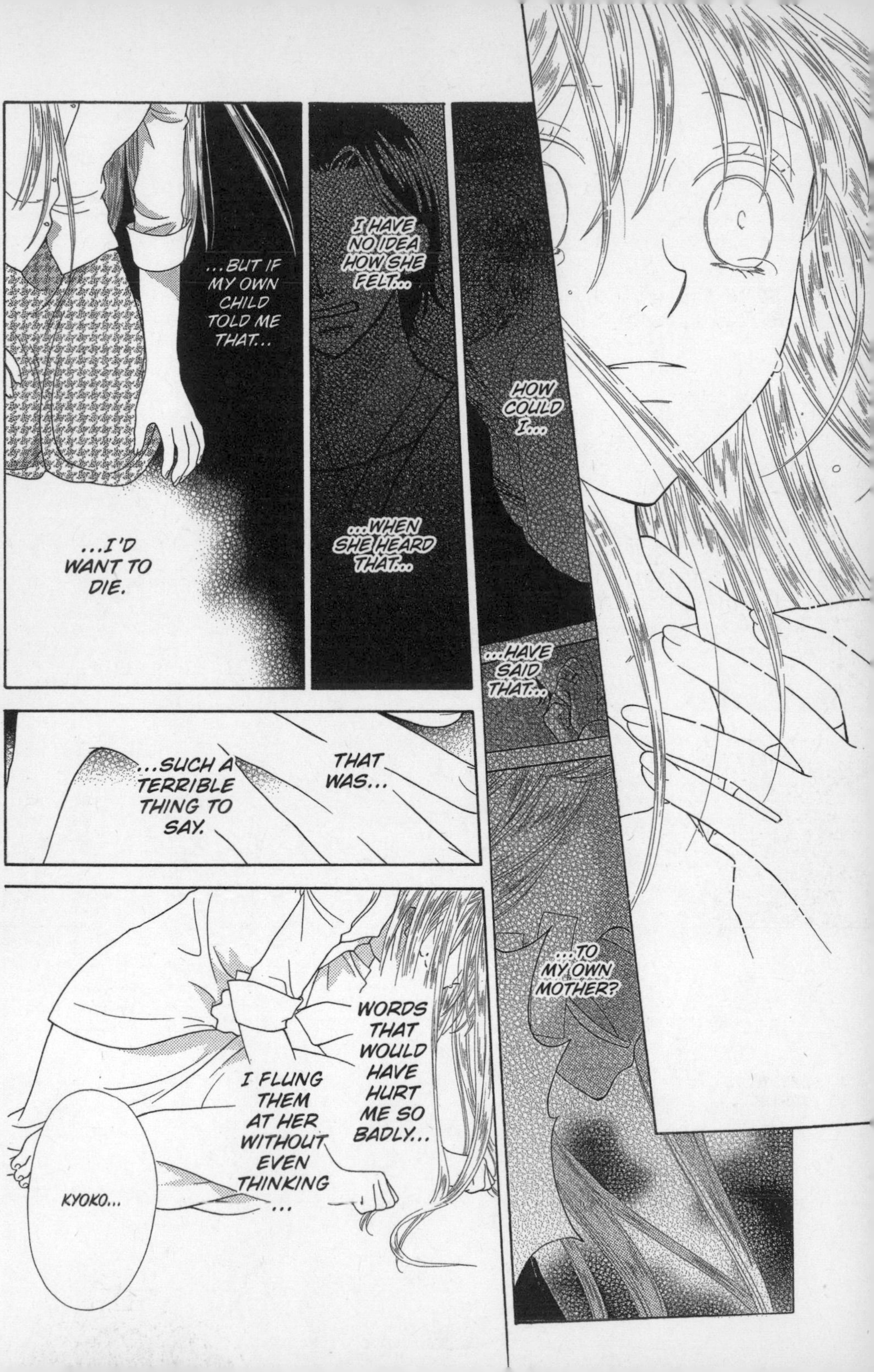
HOW COULD I...
...HAVE SAID THAT...
...TO MY OWN MOTHER?
I HAVE NO IDEA HOW SHE FELT...
...WHEN SHE HEARD THAT...
...BUT IF MY OWN CHILD TOLD ME THAT...
...I'D WANT TO DIE.
THAT WAS...
...SUCH A TERRIBLE THING TO SAY.
WORDS THAT WOULD HAVE HURT ME SO BADLY...
I FLUNG THEM AT HER WITHOUT EVEN THINKING...
KYOKO...

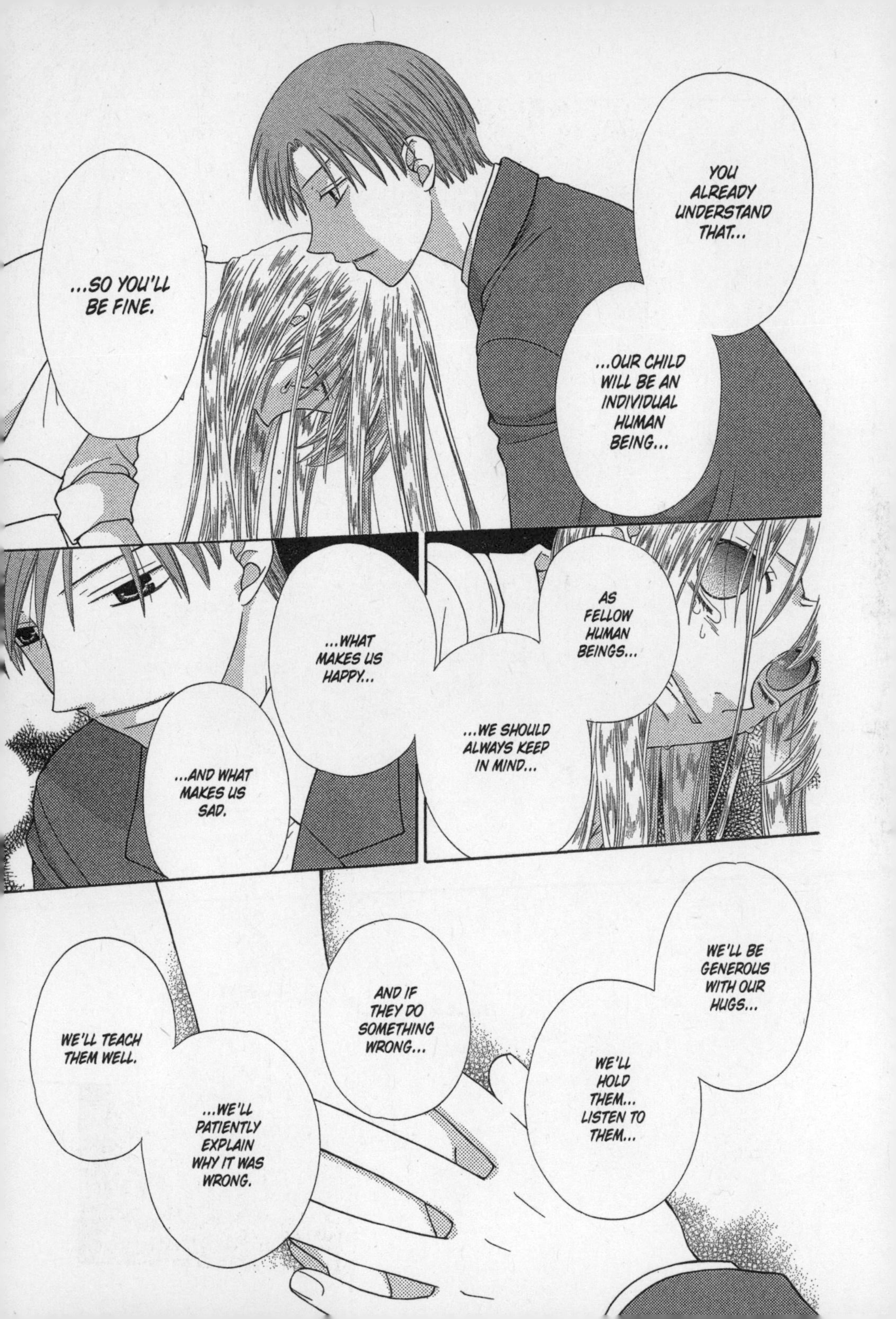
YOU ALREADY UNDERSTAND THAT...
...OUR CHILD WILL BE AN INDIVIDUAL HUMAN BEING...
...SO YOU'LL BE FINE.
AS FELLOW HUMAN BEINGS...
...WE SHOULD ALWAYS KEEP IN MIND...
...WHAT MAKES US HAPPY...
...AND WHAT MAKES US SAD.
WE'LL BE GENEROUS WITH OUR HUGS...
WE'LL HOLD THEM... LISTEN TO THEM...
AND IF THEY DO SOMETHING WRONG...
...WE'LL PATIENTLY EXPLAIN WHY IT WAS WRONG.
WE'LL TEACH THEM WELL.

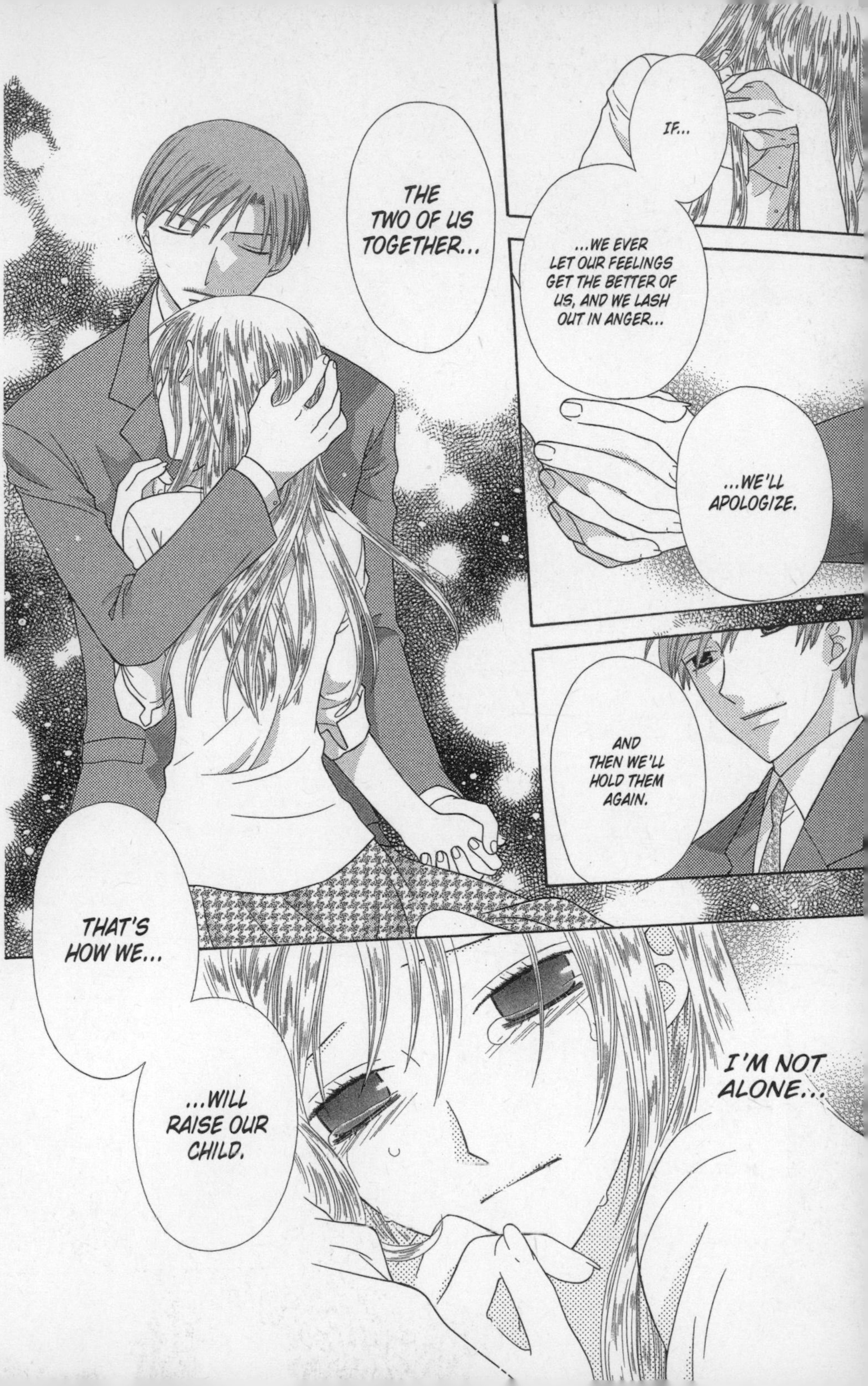
IF...
...WE EVER LET OUR FEELINGS GET THE BETTER OF US, AND WE LASH OUT IN ANGER...
...WE'LL APOLOGIZE.
AND THEN WE'LL HOLD THEM AGAIN.
THE TWO OF US TOGETHER...
I'M NOT ALONE...
THAT'S HOW WE...
...WILL RAISE OUR CHILD.

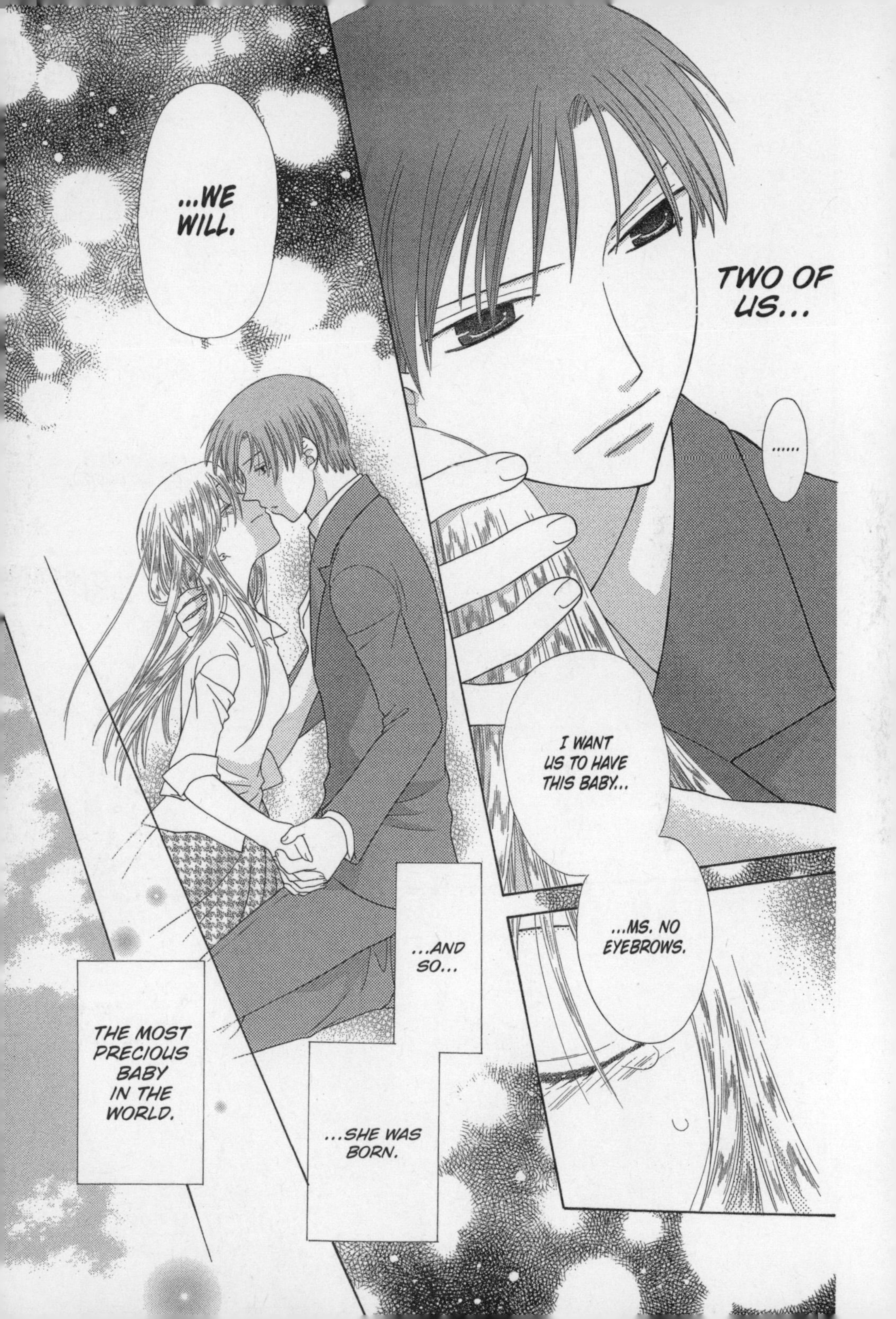
TWO OF US...
......
I WANT US TO HAVE THIS BABY...
...MS. NO EYEBROWS.
...WE WILL.
...AND SO...
...SHE WAS BORN.
THE MOST PRECIOUS BABY IN THE WORLD.

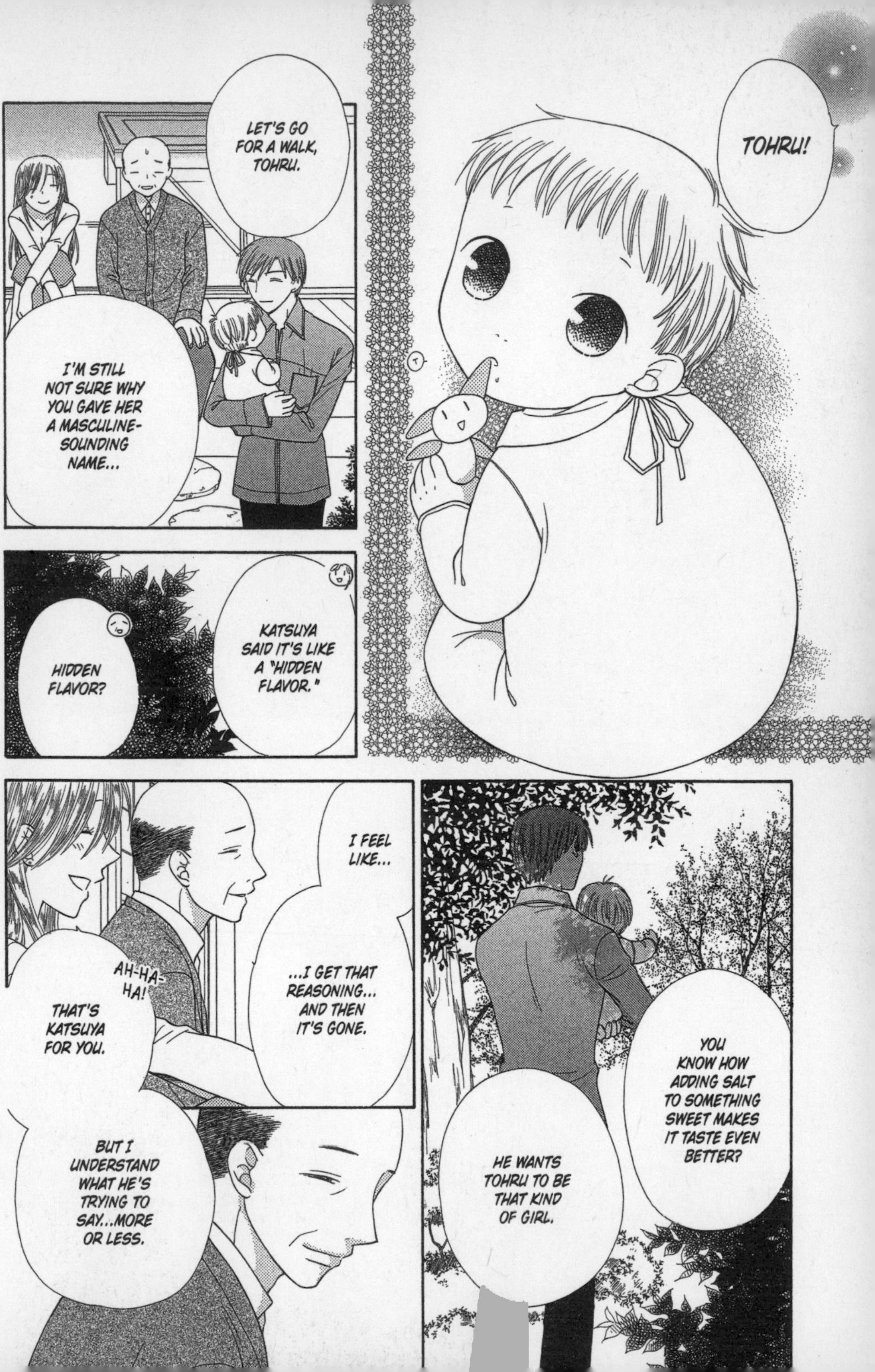
TOHRU!
LET'S GO FOR A WALK, TOHRU.
I'M STILL NOT SURE WHY YOU GAVE HER A MASCULINE-SOUNDING NAME...
KATSUYA SAID IT'S LIKE A "HIDDEN FLAVOR."
HIDDEN FLAVOR?
YOU KNOW HOW ADDING SALT TO SOMETHING SWEET MAKES IT TASTE EVEN BETTER?
HE WANTS TOHRU TO BE THAT KIND OF GIRL.
I FEEL LIKE...
...I GET THAT REASONING... AND THEN IT'S GONE.
AH-HA-HA!
THAT'S KATSUYA FOR YOU.
BUT I UNDERSTAND WHAT HE'S TRYING TO SAY...MORE OR LESS.

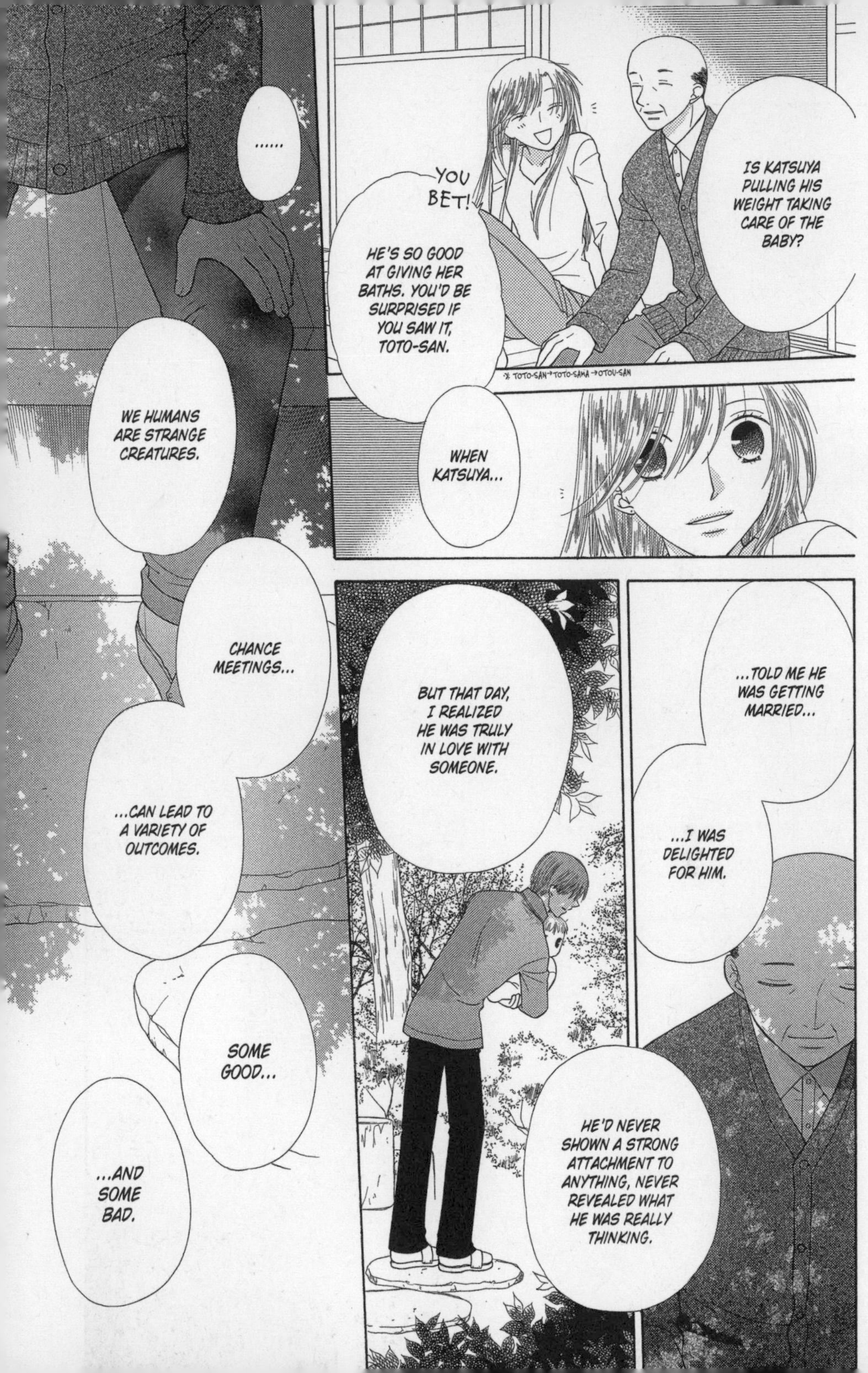
IS KATSUYA PULLING HIS WEIGHT TAKING CARE OF THE BABY?
YOU BET!
HE'S SO GOOD AT GIVING HER BATHS. YOU'D BE SURPRISED IF YOU SAW IT, TOTO-SAN.
※ TOTO-SAN→TOTO-SAMA→OTOU-SAN
WHEN KATSUYA...
...TOLD ME HE WAS GETTING MARRIED...
...I WAS DELIGHTED FOR HIM.
HE'D NEVER SHOWN A STRONG ATTACHMENT TO ANYTHING, NEVER REVEALED WHAT HE WAS REALLY THINKING.
BUT THAT DAY, I REALIZED HE WAS TRULY IN LOVE WITH SOMEONE.
......
WE HUMANS ARE STRANGE CREATURES.
CHANCE MEETINGS...
...CAN LEAD TO A VARIETY OF OUTCOMES.
SOME GOOD...
...AND SOME BAD.

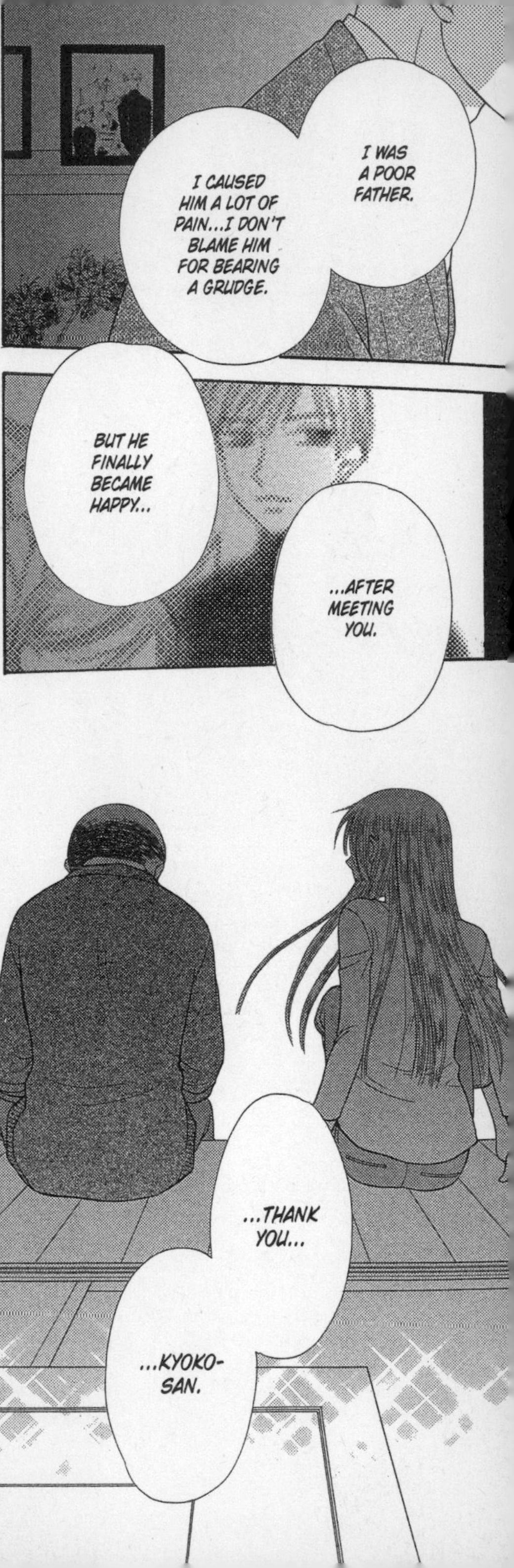
I WAS A POOR FATHER.
I CAUSED HIM A LOT OF PAIN...I DON'T BLAME HIM FOR BEARING A GRUDGE.
BUT HE FINALLY BECAME HAPPY...
...AFTER MEETING YOU.
...THANK YOU...
...KYOKO-SAN.
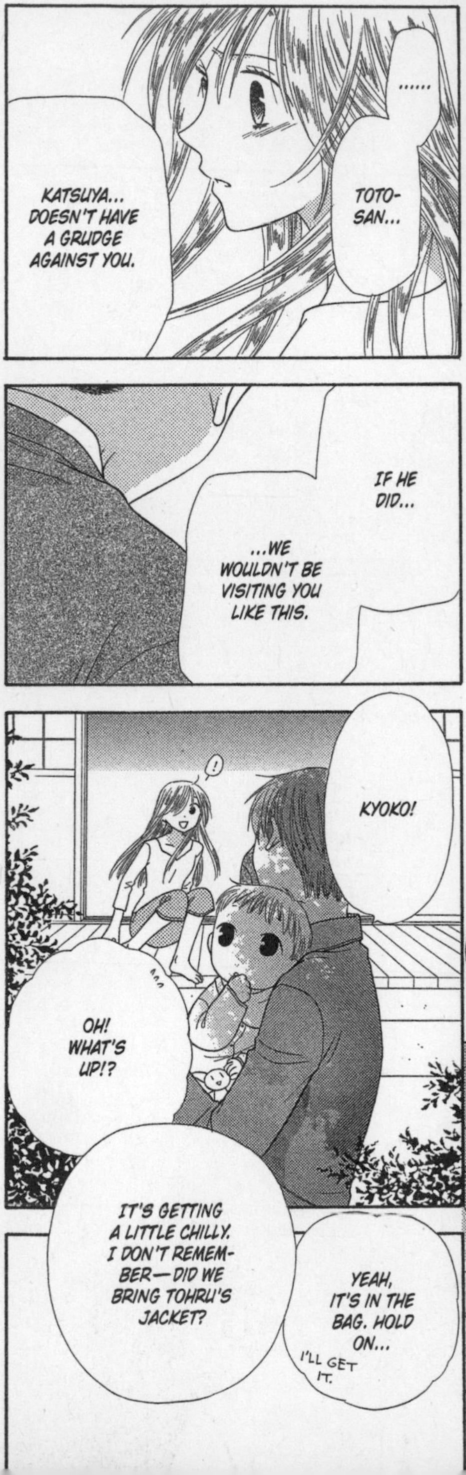
......
TOTO-SAN...
KATSUYA... DOESN'T HAVE A GRUDGE AGAINST YOU.
IF HE DID...
...WE WOULDN'T BE VISITING YOU LIKE THIS.
KYOKO!
!
OH! WHAT'S UP!?
IT'S GETTING A LITTLE CHILLY. I DON'T REMEMBER—DID WE BRING TOHRU'S JACKET?
YEAH, IT'S IN THE BAG. HOLD ON...
I'LL GET IT.

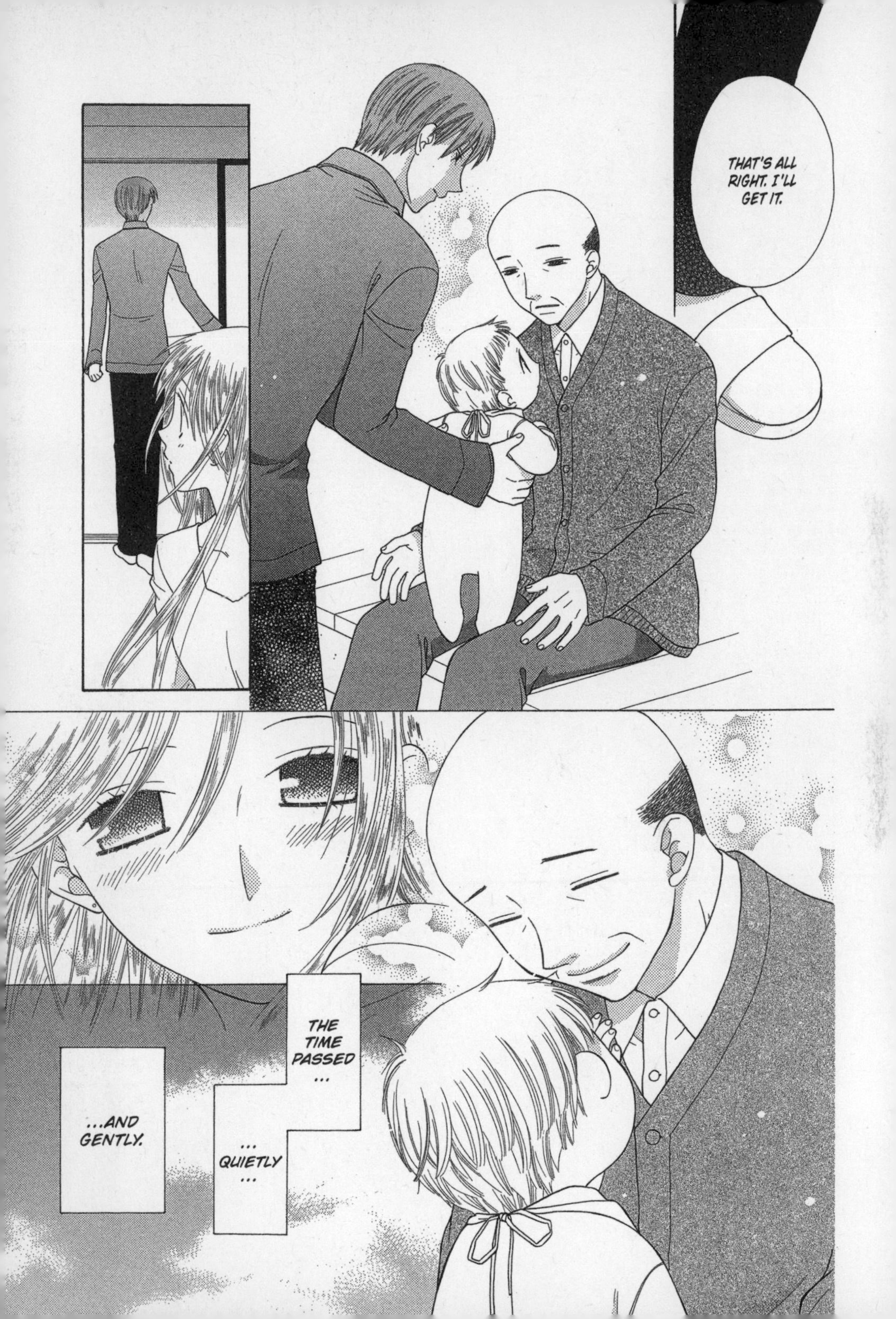
THAT'S ALL RIGHT. I'LL GET IT.
THE TIME PASSED ...
... QUIETLY ...
...AND GENTLY.

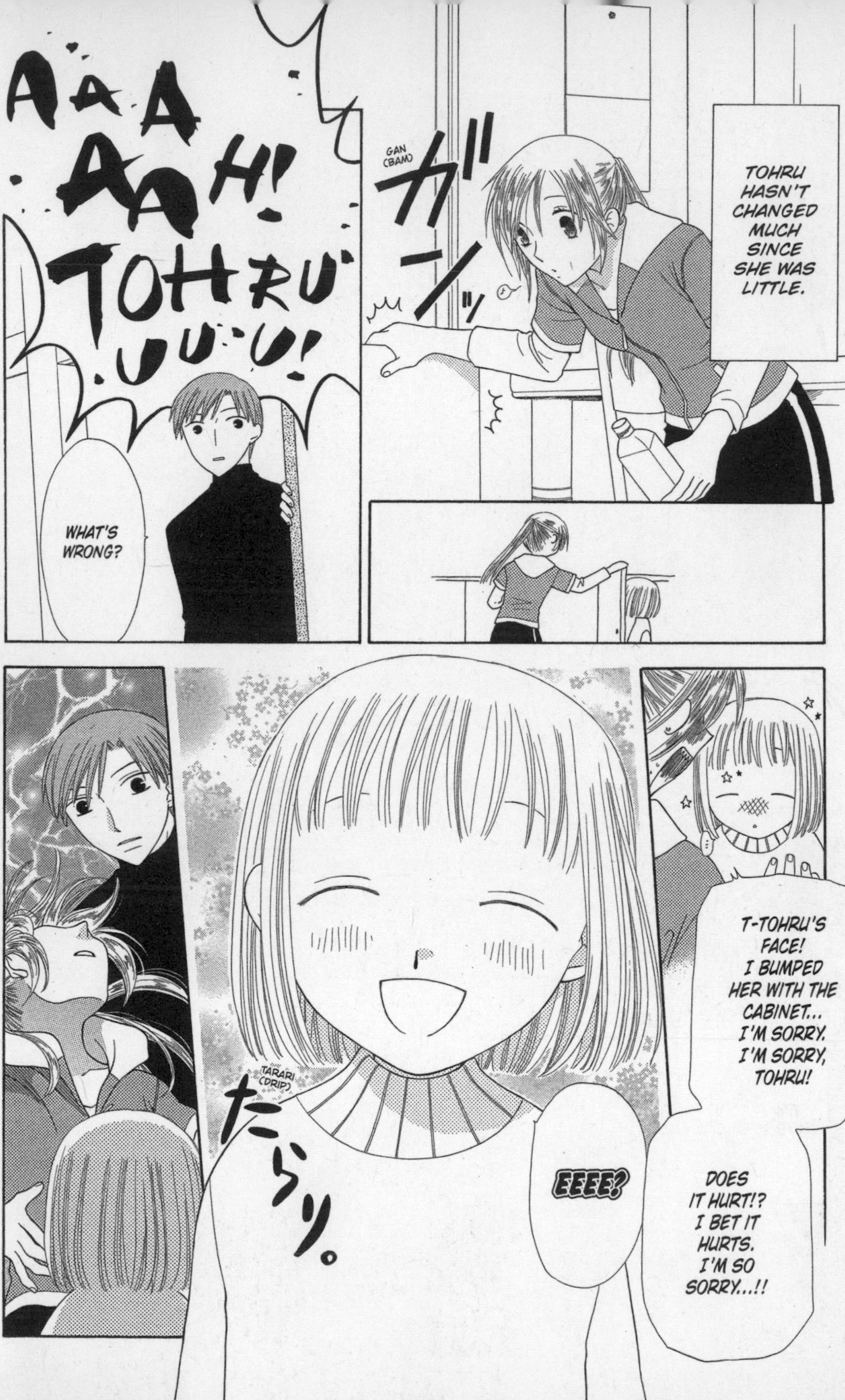
GAN (BAM)
ガーン
TOHRU HASN'T CHANGED MUCH SINCE SHE WAS LITTLE.
AAAAAH! TOHRUUUU!
WHAT'S WRONG?
T-TOHRU'S FACE! I BUMPED HER WITH THE CABINET... I'M SORRY. I'M SORRY, TOHRU!
TARARI (DRIP)
たらり。
EEEE?
DOES IT HURT!? I BET IT HURTS. I'M SO SORRY...!!

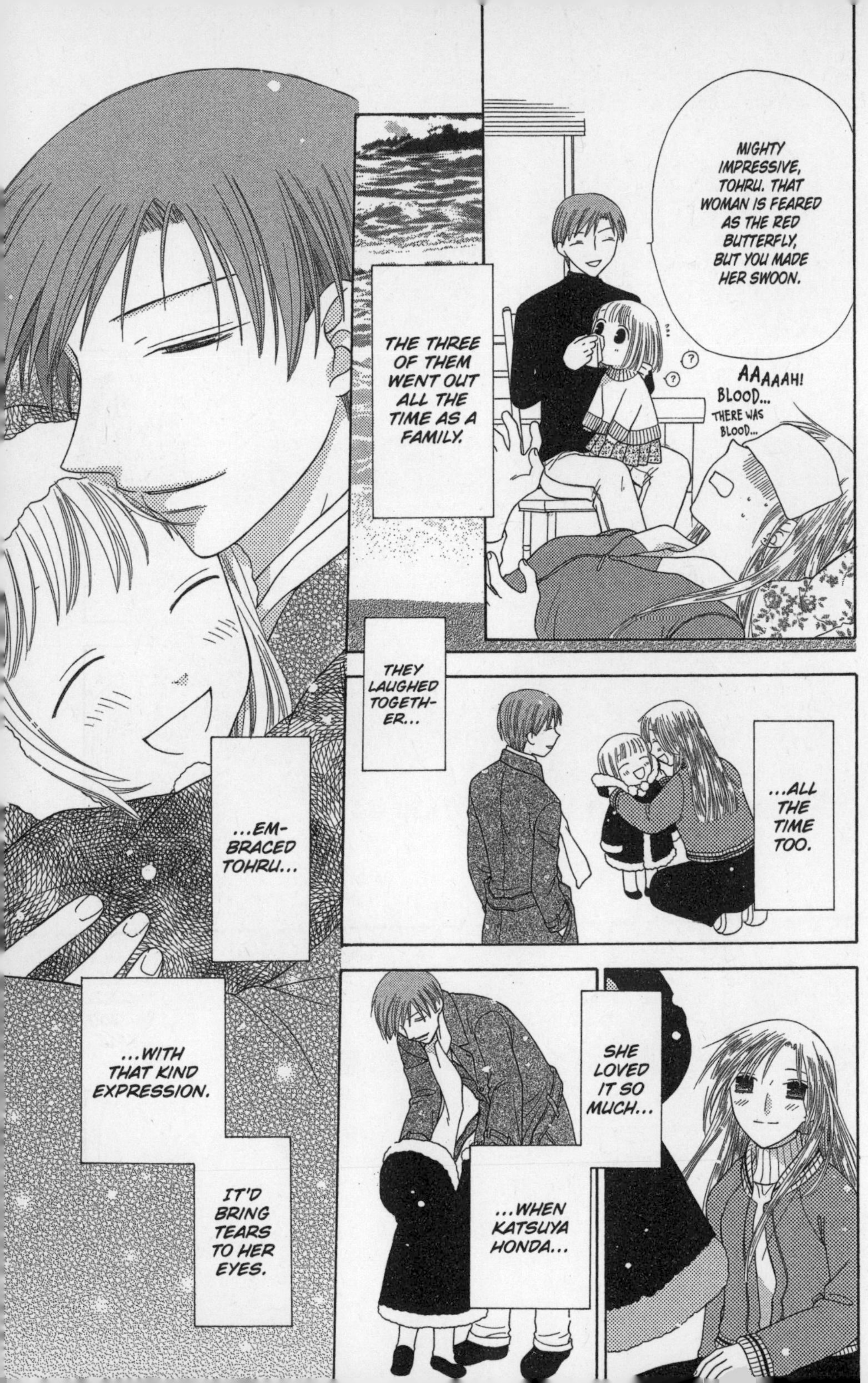
MIGHTY IMPRESSIVE, TOHRU. THAT WOMAN IS FEARED AS THE RED BUTTERFLY, BUT YOU MADE HER SWOON.
AAAAAAH! BLOOD...
THERE WAS BLOOD...
THE THREE OF THEM WENT OUT ALL THE TIME AS A FAMILY.
THEY LAUGHED TOGETH-ER...
...ALL THE TIME TOO.
SHE LOVED IT SO MUCH...
...WHEN KATSUYA HONDA...
...EM-BRACED TOHRU...
...WITH THAT KIND EXPRESSION.
IT'D BRING TEARS TO HER EYES.

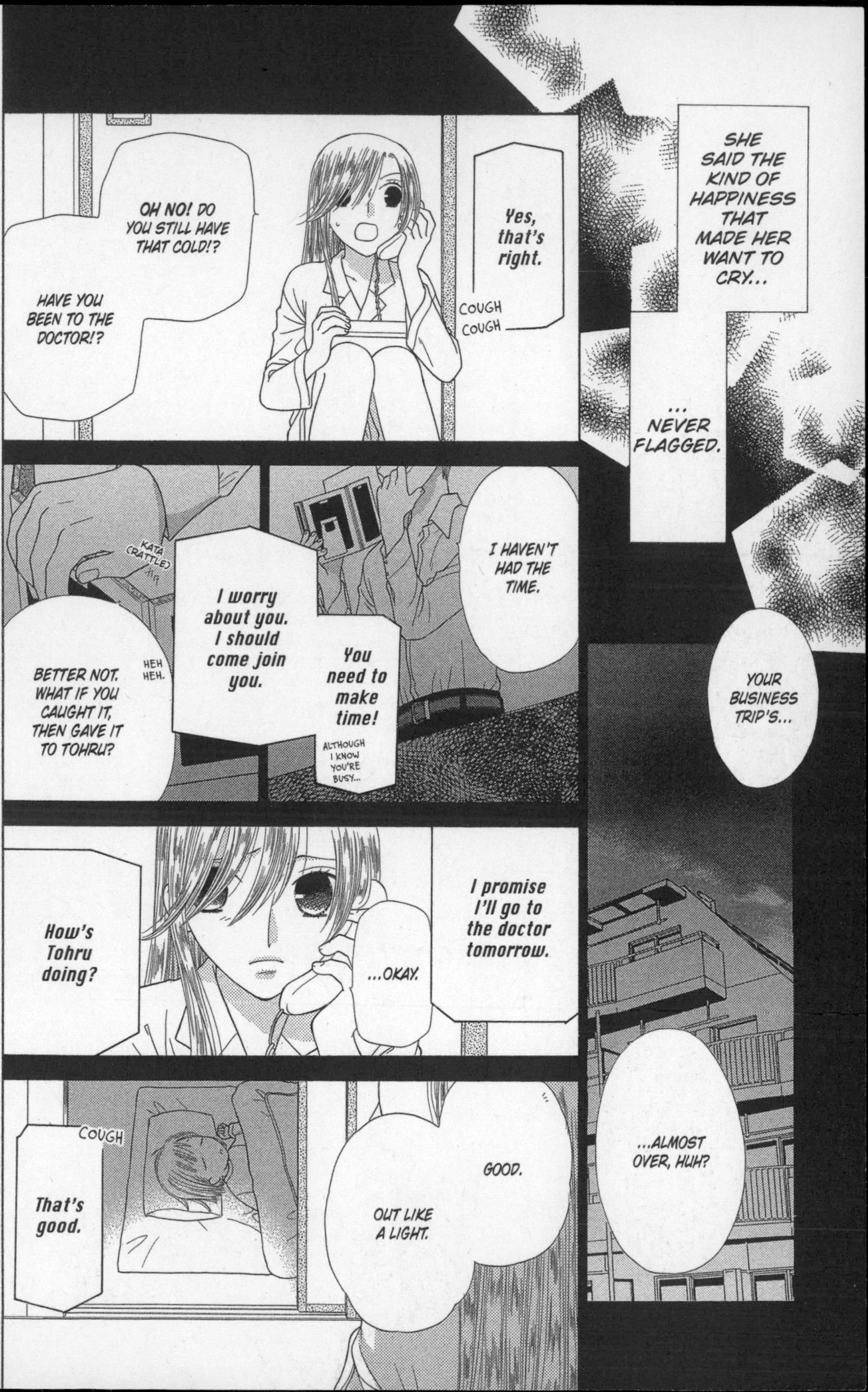
SHE SAID THE KIND OF HAPPINESS THAT MADE HER WANT TO CRY...
...NEVER FLAGGED.
YOUR BUSINESS TRIP'S...
...ALMOST OVER, HUH?
Yes, that's right.
COUGH COUGH
OH NO! DO YOU STILL HAVE THAT COLD!?
HAVE YOU BEEN TO THE DOCTOR!?
I HAVEN'T HAD THE TIME.
You need to make time!
ALTHOUGH I KNOW YOU'RE BUSY...
I worry about you. I should come join you.
KATA (RATTLE)
HEH HEH.
BETTER NOT. WHAT IF YOU CAUGHT IT, THEN GAVE IT TO TOHRU?
I promise I'll go to the doctor tomorrow.
...OKAY.
How's Tohru doing?
GOOD.
OUT LIKE A LIGHT.
COUGH
That's good.

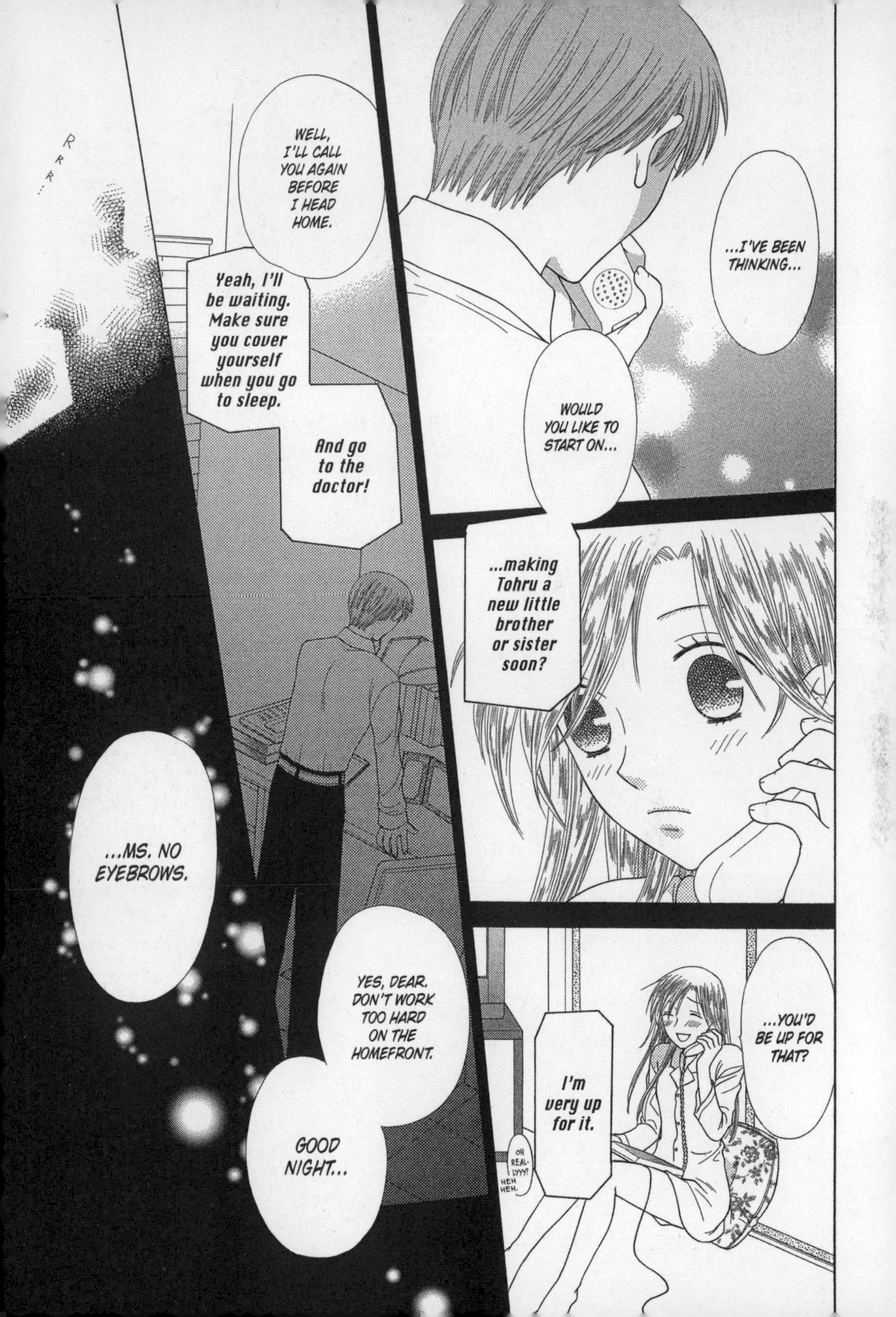

...I'VE BEEN THINKING...
WOULD YOU LIKE TO START ON...
...making Tohru a new little brother or sister soon?
...YOU'D BE UP FOR THAT?
I'm very up for it.
OH REAL-LYYY? HEH HEH.
WELL, I'LL CALL YOU AGAIN BEFORE I HEAD HOME.
Yeah, I'll be waiting. Make sure you cover yourself when you go to sleep.
And go to the doctor!
YES, DEAR. DON'T WORK TOO HARD ON THE HOMEFRONT.
GOOD NIGHT...
R R R...
...MS. NO EYEBROWS.

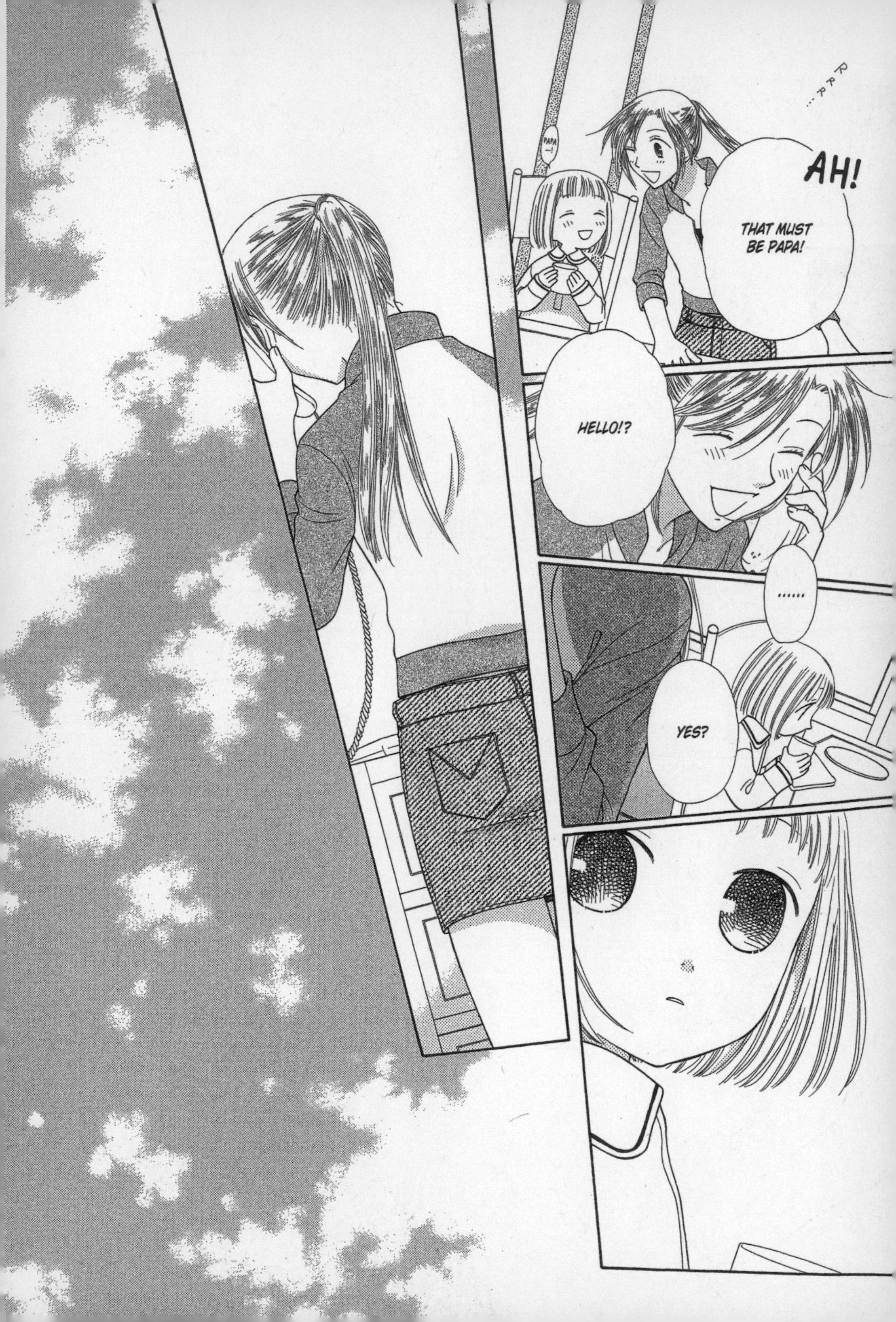

...RRR
AH!
THAT MUST BE PAPA!
PAPA—!
HELLO!?
......
YES?

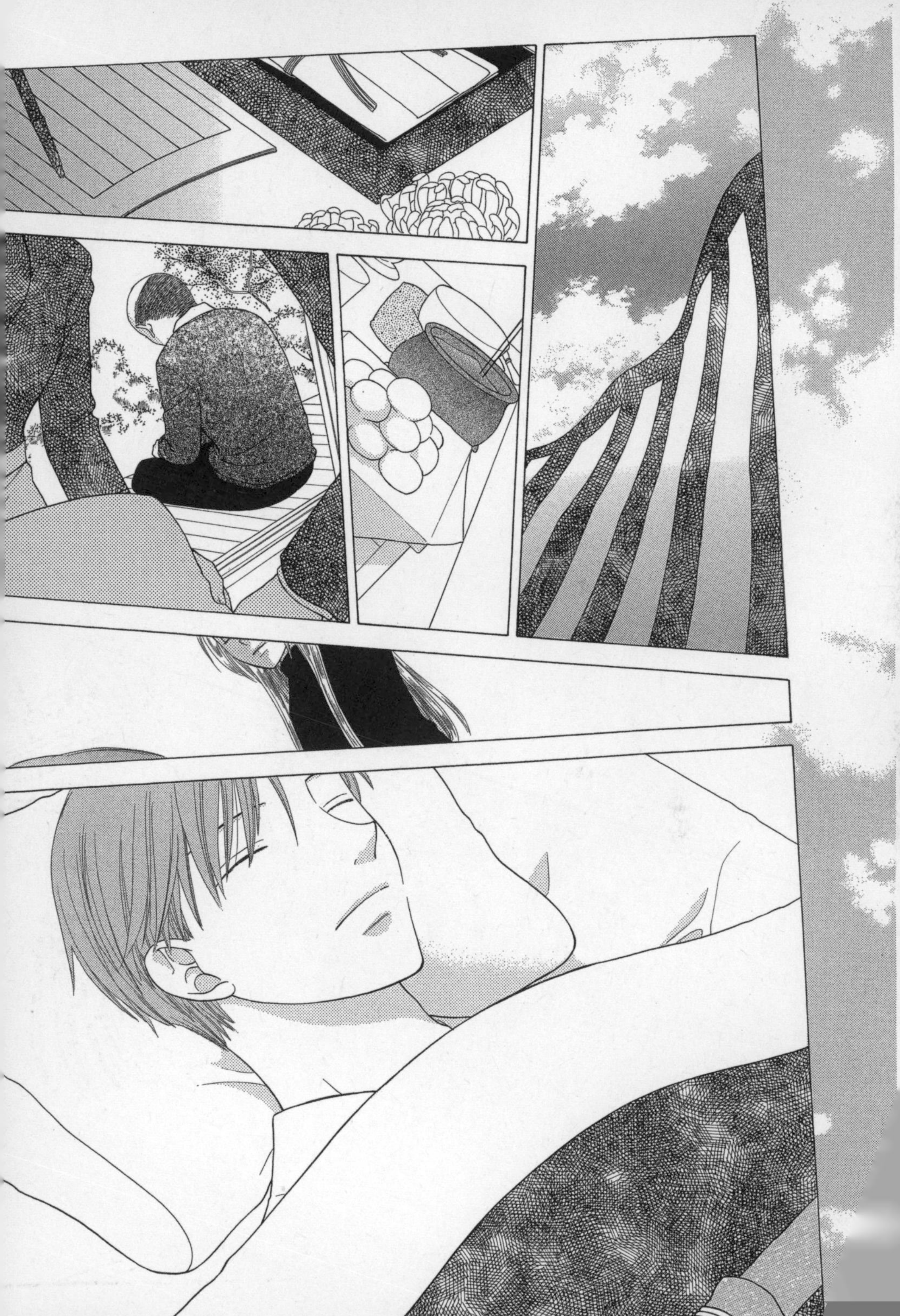

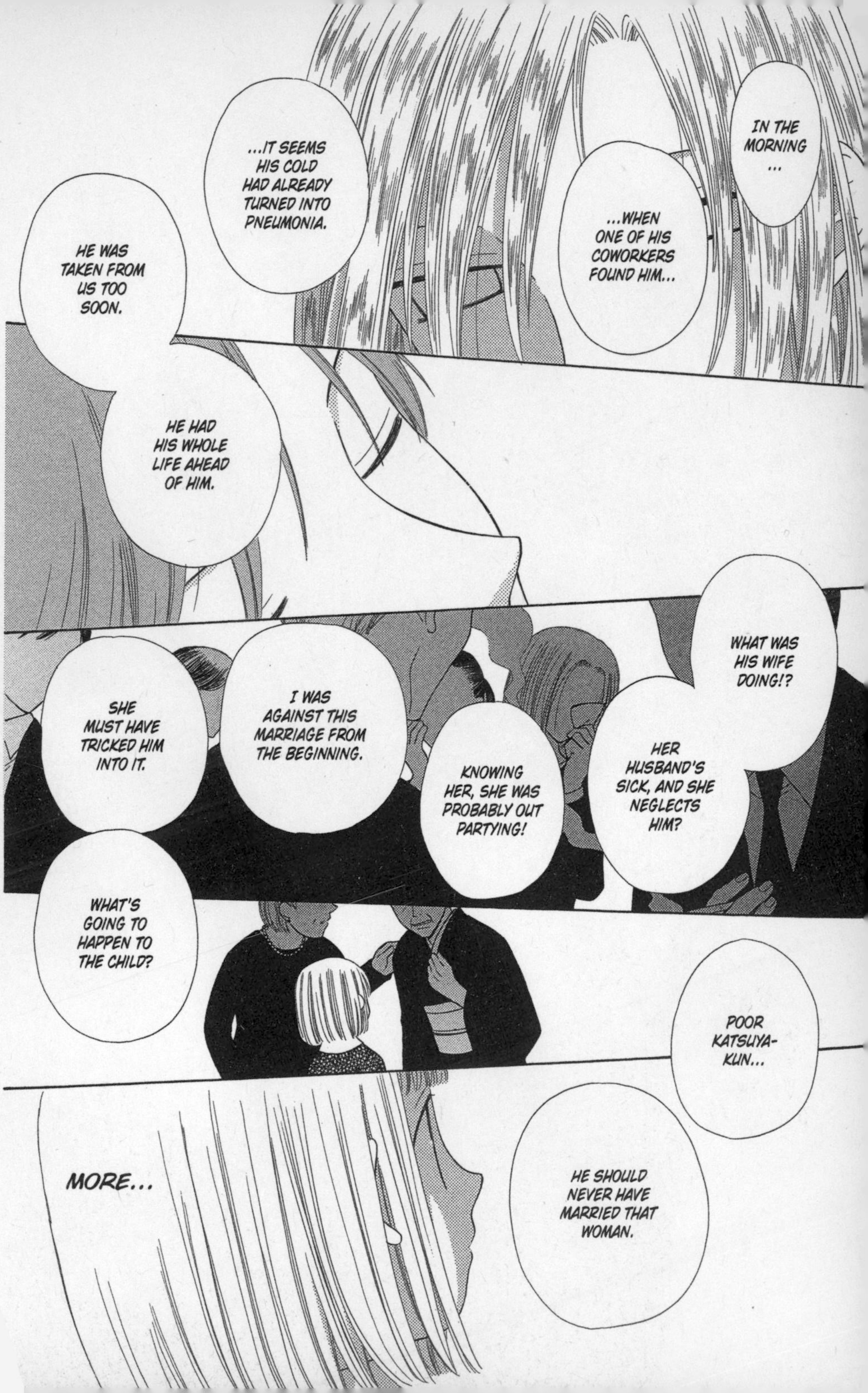
IN THE MORNING ...
...WHEN ONE OF HIS COWORKERS FOUND HIM...
...IT SEEMS HIS COLD HAD ALREADY TURNED INTO PNEUMONIA.
HE WAS TAKEN FROM US TOO SOON.
HE HAD HIS WHOLE LIFE AHEAD OF HIM.
WHAT WAS HIS WIFE DOING!?
HER HUSBAND'S SICK, AND SHE NEGLECTS HIM?
KNOWING HER, SHE WAS PROBABLY OUT PARTYING!
I WAS AGAINST THIS MARRIAGE FROM THE BEGINNING.
SHE MUST HAVE TRICKED HIM INTO IT.
POOR KATSUYA-KUN...
WHAT'S GOING TO HAPPEN TO THE CHILD?
HE SHOULD NEVER HAVE MARRIED THAT WOMAN.
MORE...

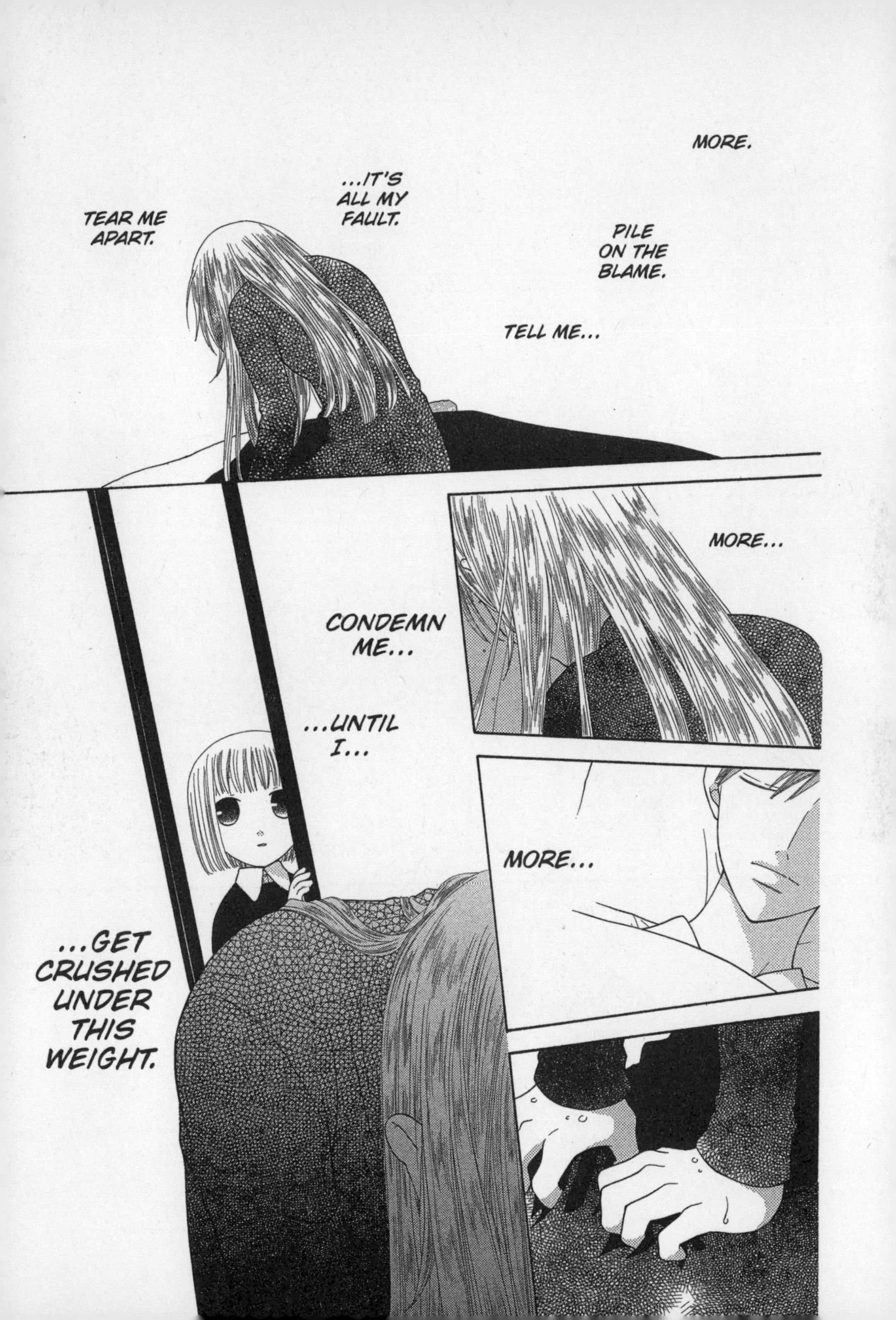
MORE.
PILE ON THE BLAME.
TELL ME...
...IT'S ALL MY FAULT.
TEAR ME APART.
MORE...
CONDEMN ME...
MORE...
...UNTIL I...
...GET CRUSHED UNDER THIS WEIGHT.

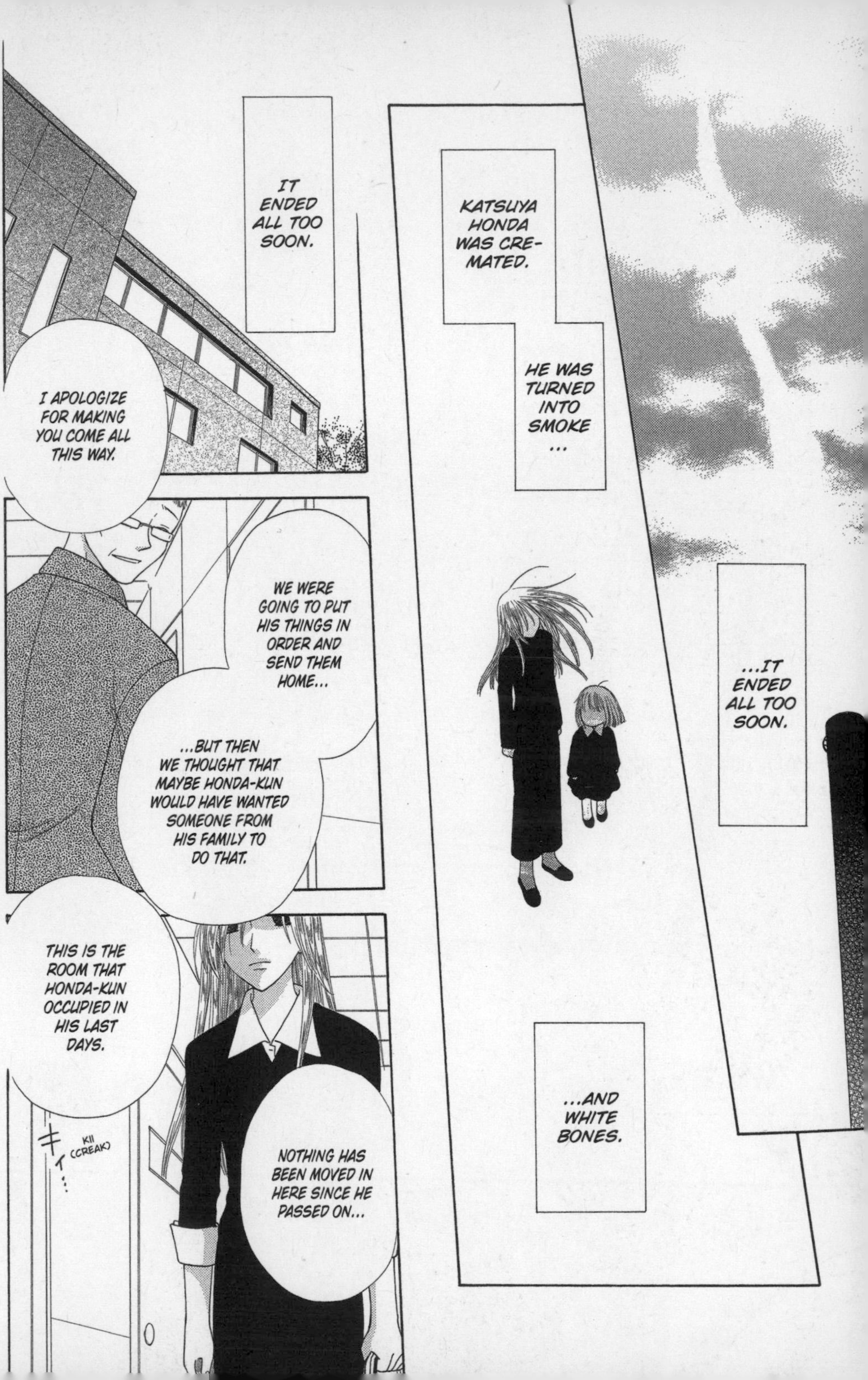
KATSUYA HONDA WAS CRE-MATED.
HE WAS TURNED INTO SMOKE ...
...AND WHITE BONES.
...IT ENDED ALL TOO SOON.
IT ENDED ALL TOO SOON.
I APOLOGIZE FOR MAKING YOU COME ALL THIS WAY.
WE WERE GOING TO PUT HIS THINGS IN ORDER AND SEND THEM HOME...
...BUT THEN WE THOUGHT THAT MAYBE HONDA-KUN WOULD HAVE WANTED SOMEONE FROM HIS FAMILY TO DO THAT.
THIS IS THE ROOM THAT HONDA-KUN OCCUPIED IN HIS LAST DAYS.
KII (CREAK)
NOTHING HAS BEEN MOVED IN HERE SINCE HE PASSED ON...

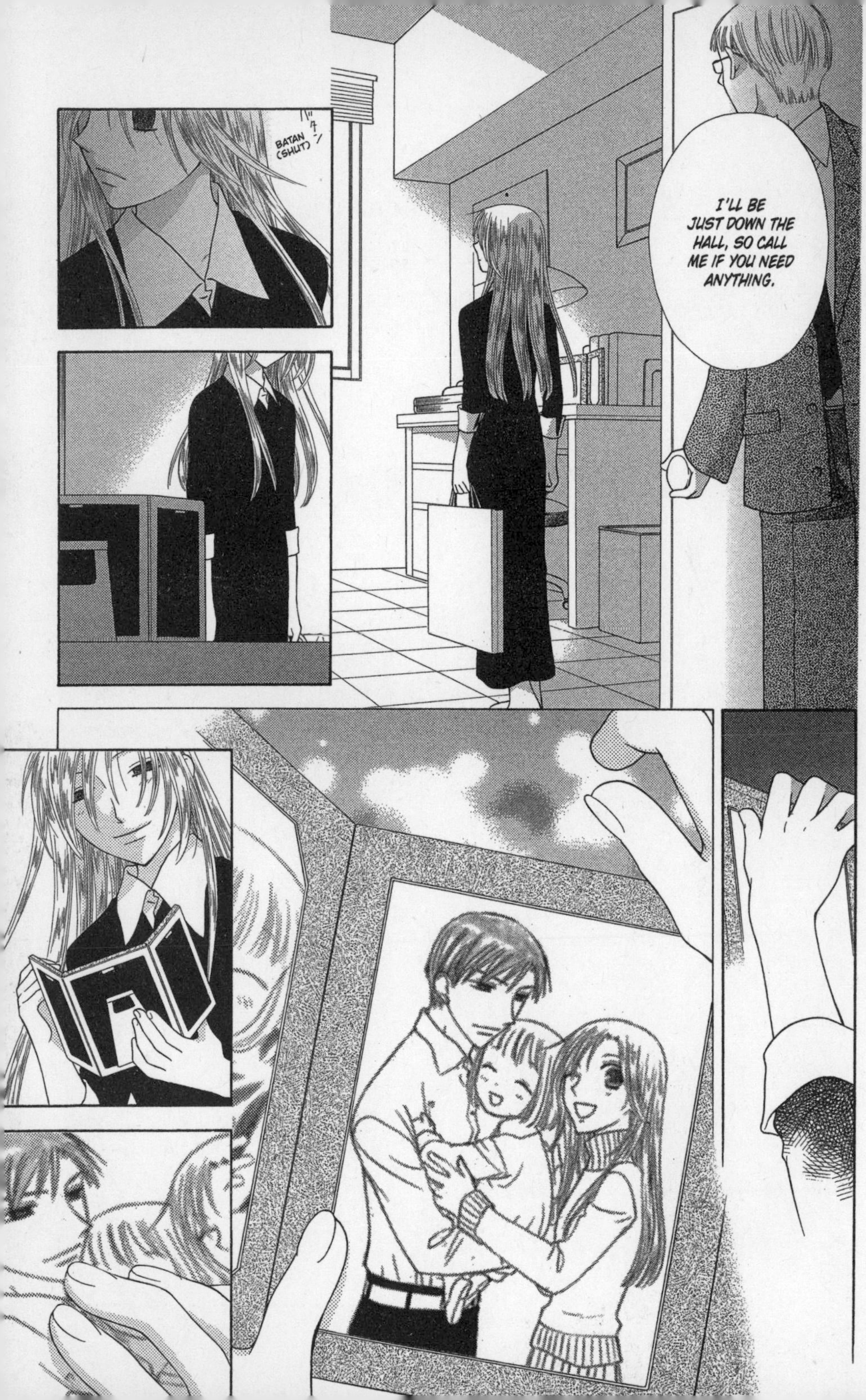
I'LL BE JUST DOWN THE HALL, SO CALL ME IF YOU NEED ANYTHING.
BATAN (SHUT)

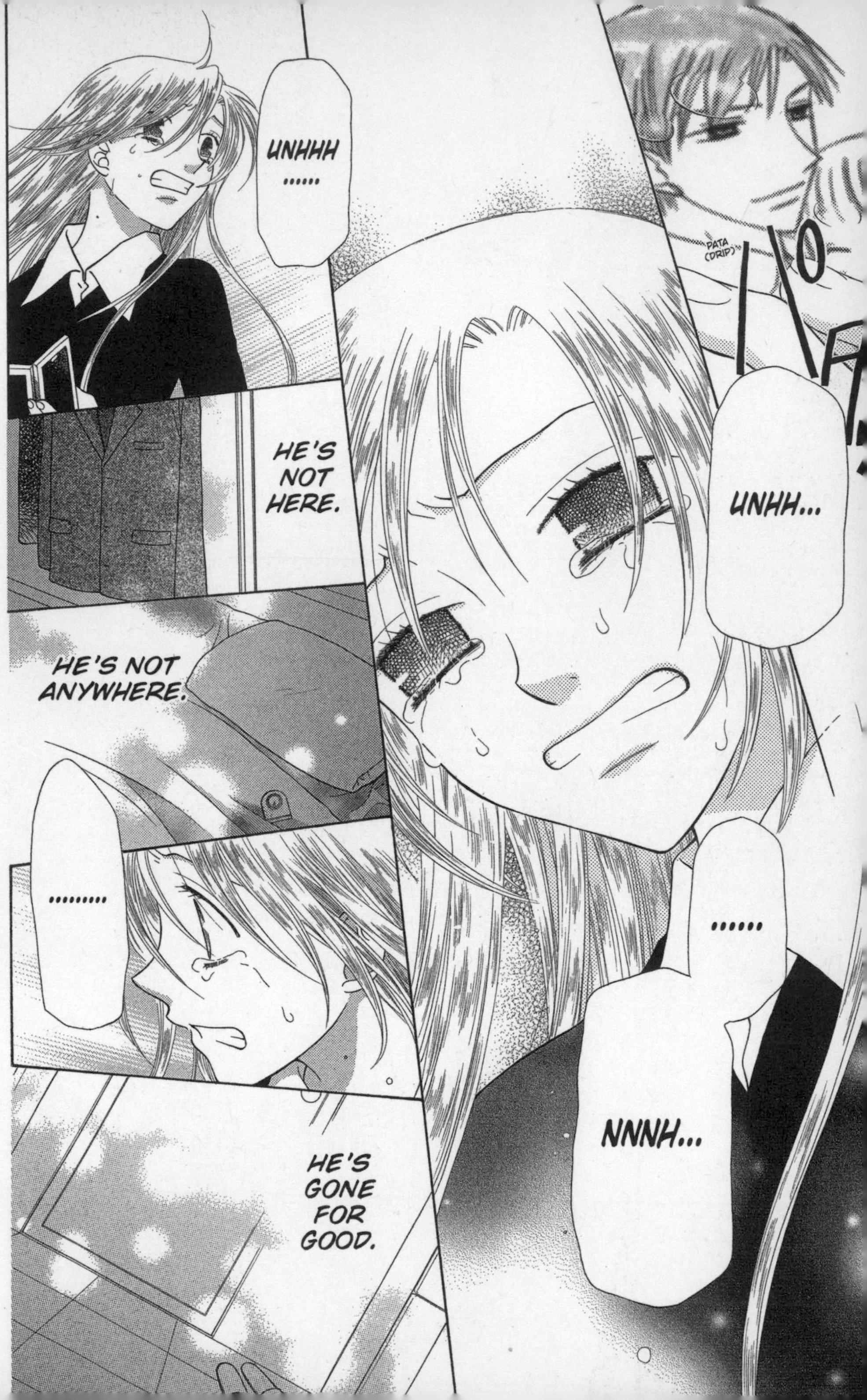
PATA (DRIP)
UNHH...
......
NNNH...
UNHHH ......
HE'S NOT HERE.
HE'S NOT ANYWHERE.
....
HE'S GONE FOR GOOD.

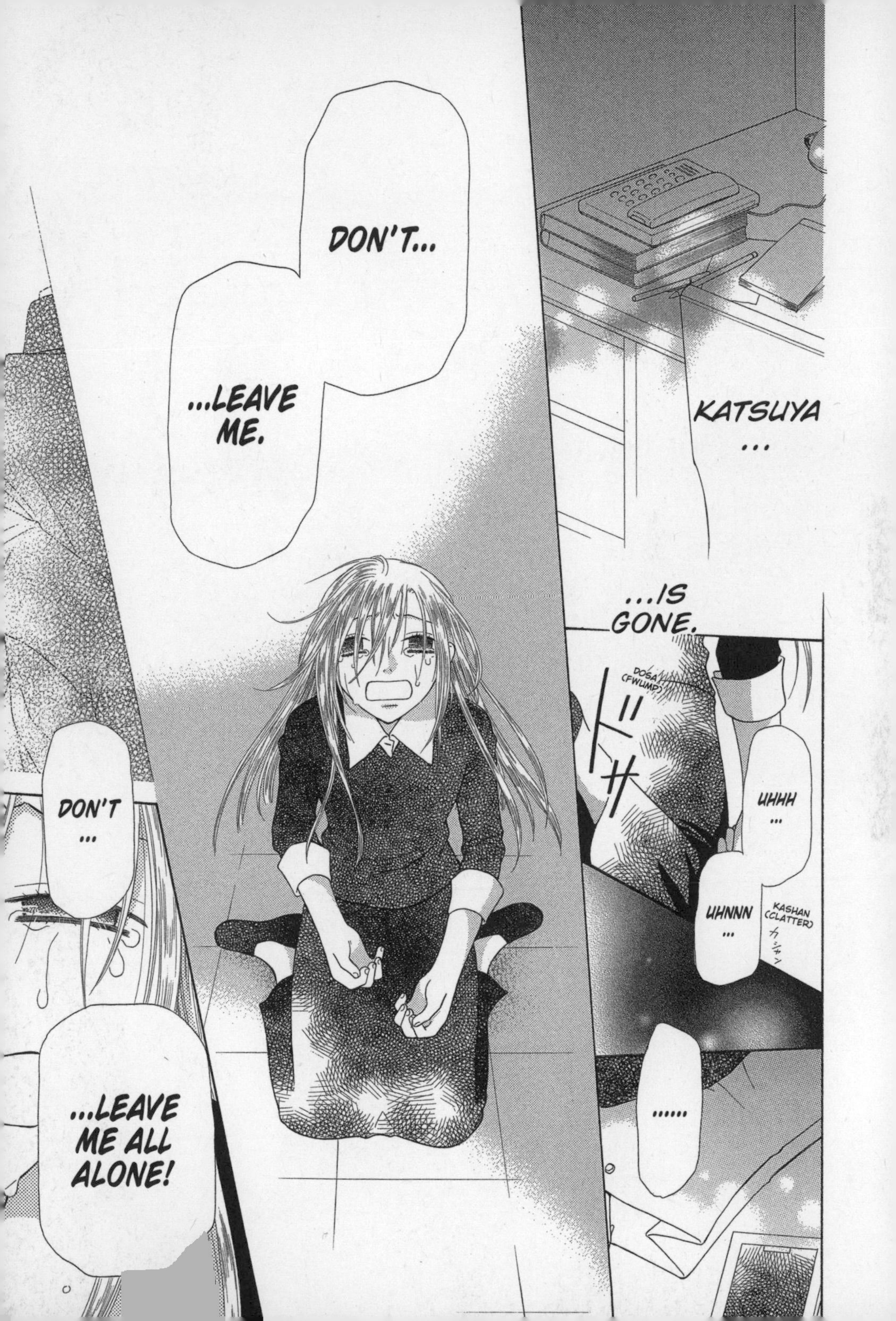
KATSUYA ...
...IS GONE.
DOSA (FWUMP)
UHHH ...
UHNNN ...
KASHAN (CLATTER)
......
DON'T...
...LEAVE ME.
DON'T ...
...LEAVE ME ALL ALONE!

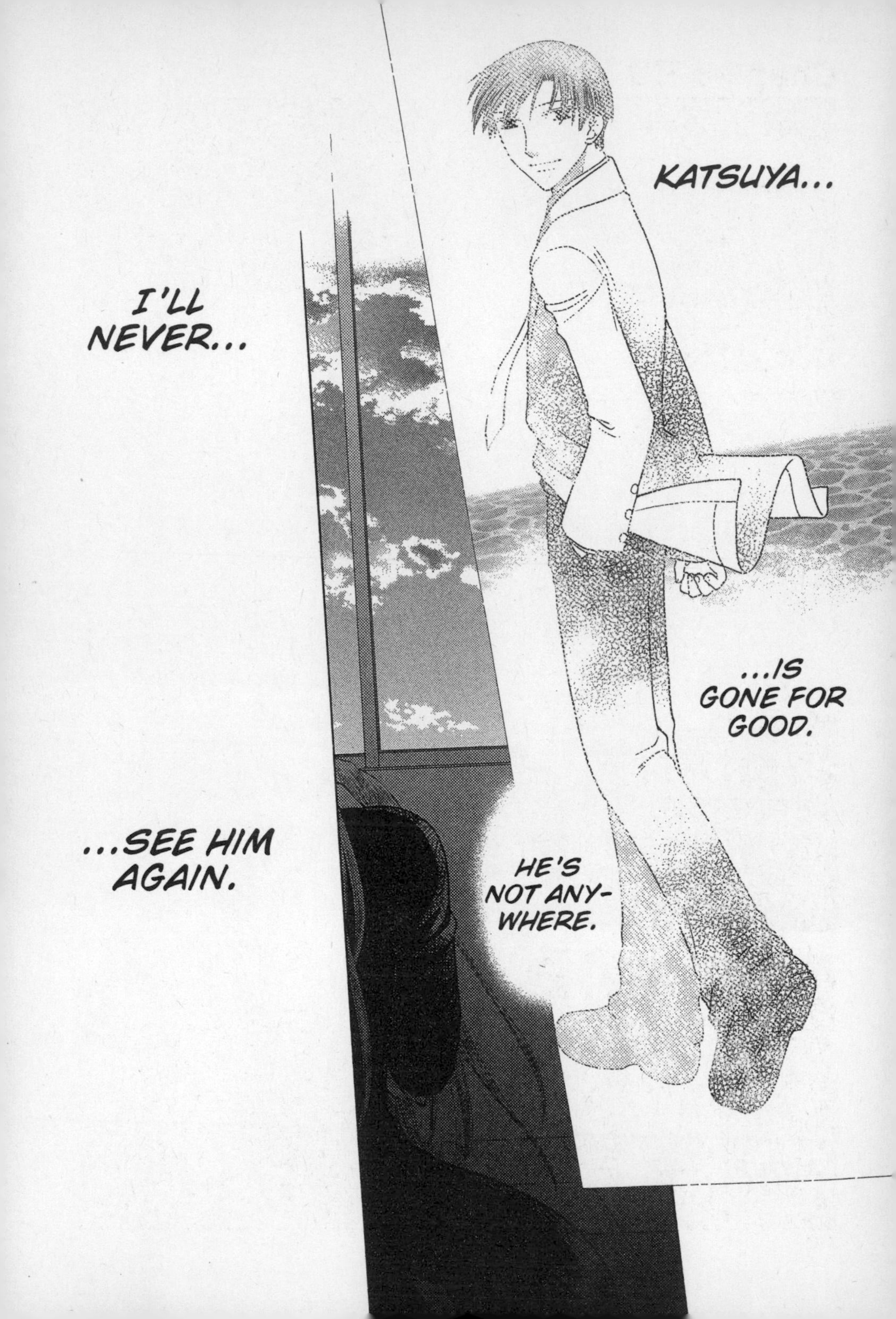
KATSUYA...
...IS GONE FOR GOOD.
HE'S NOT ANY-WHERE.
I'LL NEVER...
...SEE HIM AGAIN.

Chapter 93

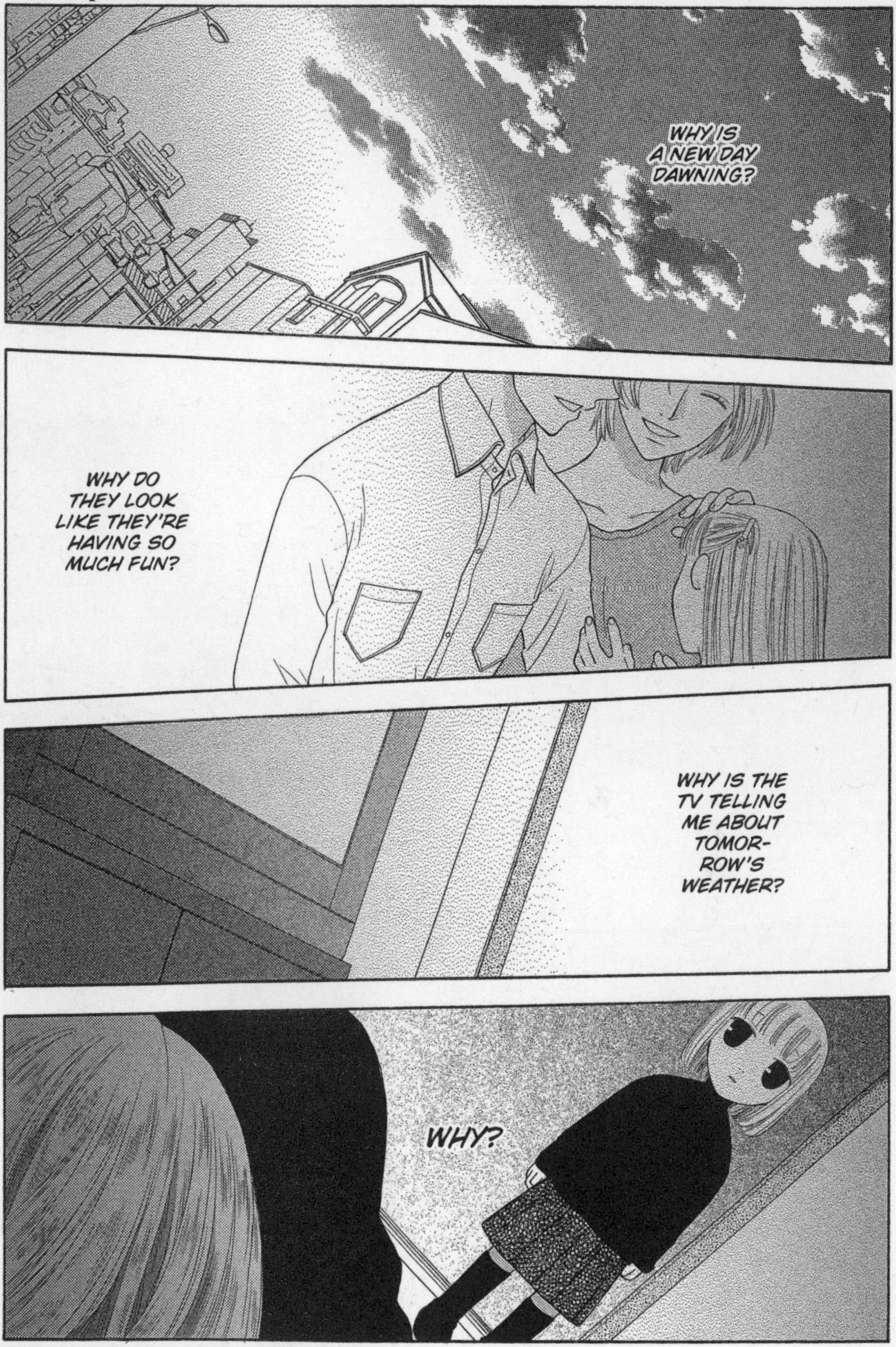
WHY IS A NEW DAY DAWNING?
WHY DO THEY LOOK LIKE THEY'RE HAVING SO MUCH FUN?
WHY IS THE TV TELLING ME ABOUT TOMOR-ROW'S WEATHER?
WHY?

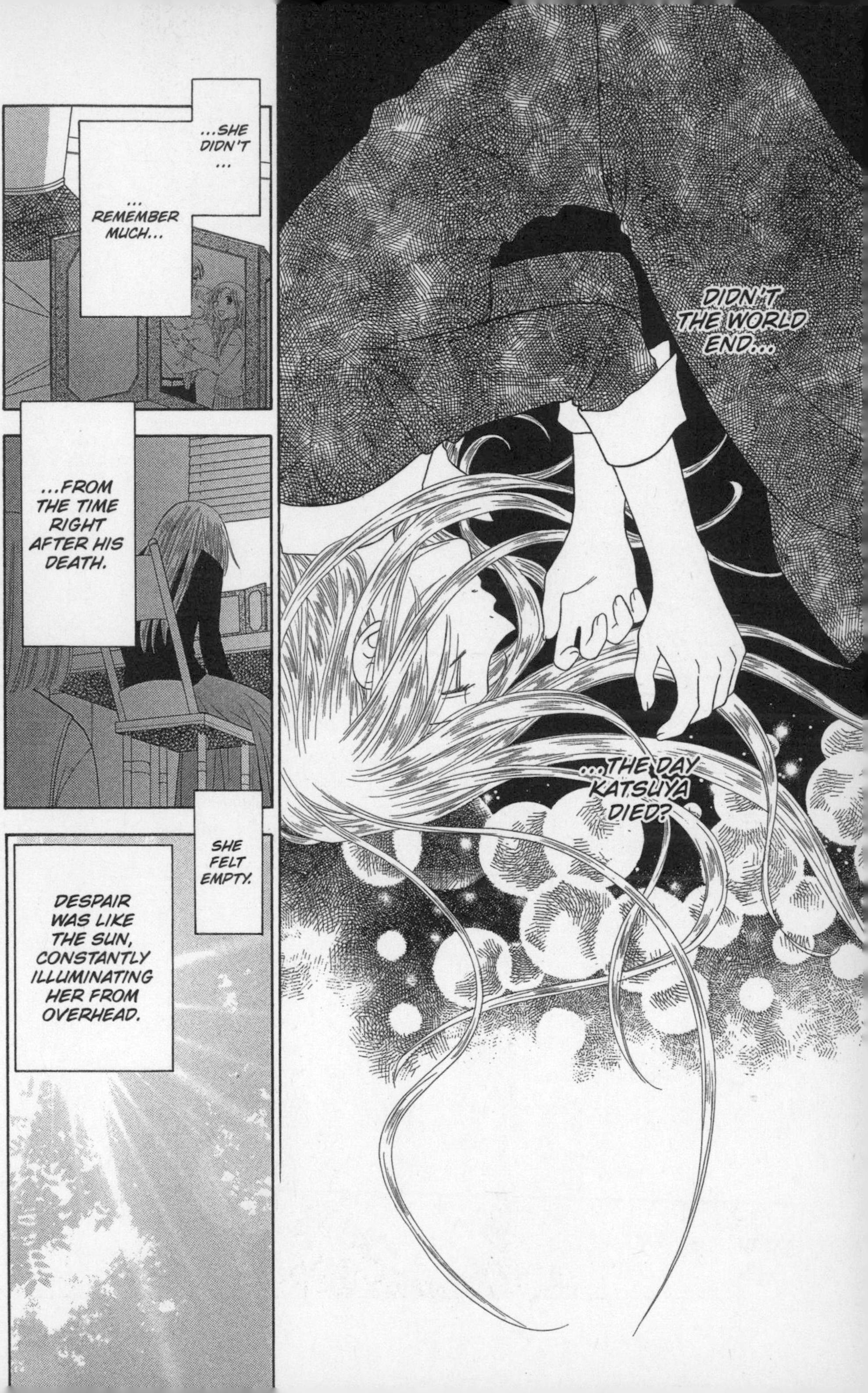
DIDN'T THE WORLD END...
...THE DAY KATSUYA DIED?
...SHE DIDN'T ...
... REMEMBER MUCH...
...FROM THE TIME RIGHT AFTER HIS DEATH.
SHE FELT EMPTY.
DESPAIR WAS LIKE THE SUN, CONSTANTLY ILLUMINATING HER FROM OVERHEAD.

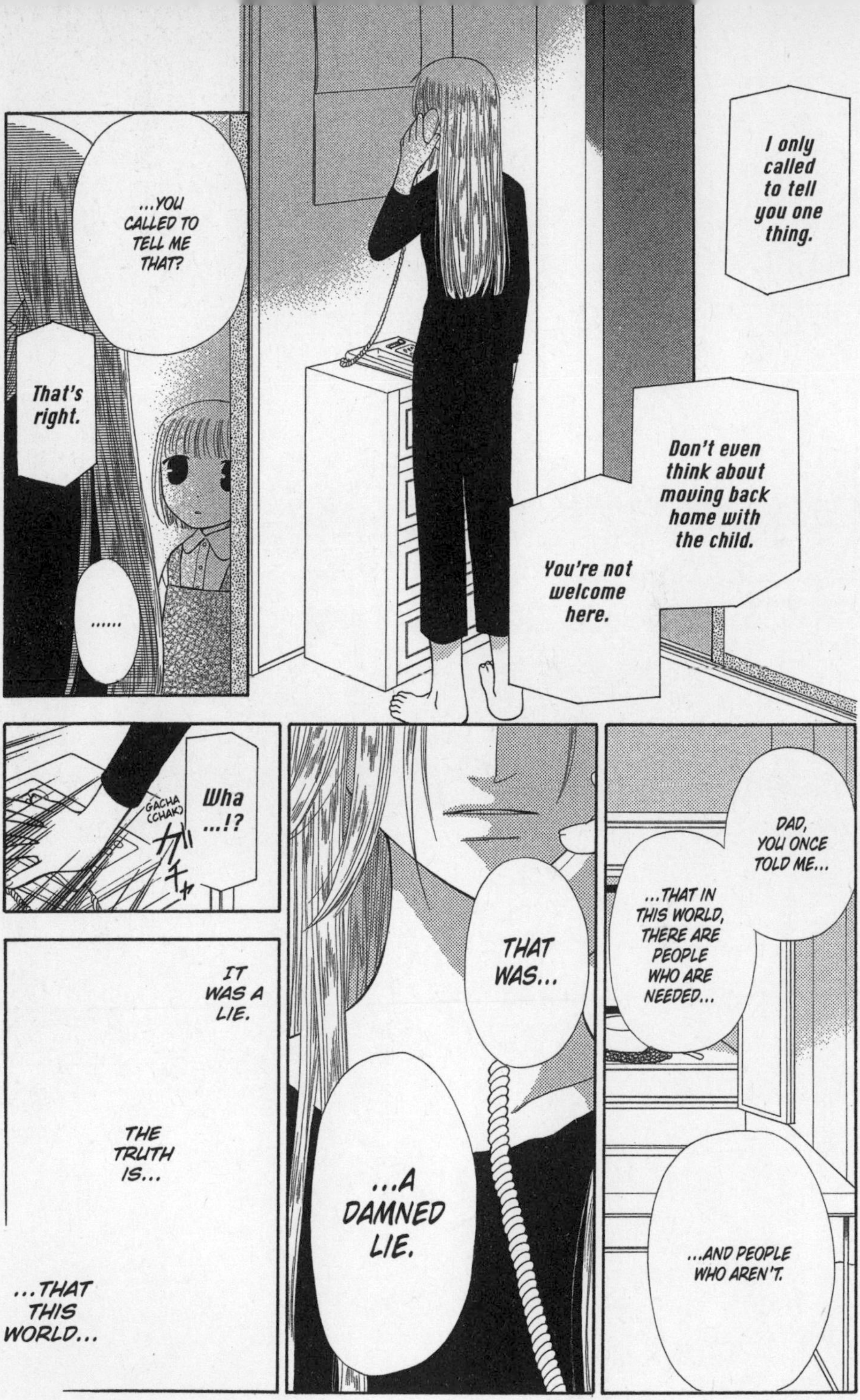
I only called to tell you one thing.
Don't even think about moving back home with the child.
You're not welcome here.
...YOU CALLED TO TELL ME THAT?
That's right.
......
DAD, YOU ONCE TOLD ME...
...THAT IN THIS WORLD, THERE ARE PEOPLE WHO ARE NEEDED...
...AND PEOPLE WHO AREN'T.
THAT WAS...
...A DAMNED LIE.
GACHA (CHAK)
ガチャ
Wha ...!?
IT WAS A LIE.
THE TRUTH IS...
...THAT THIS WORLD...

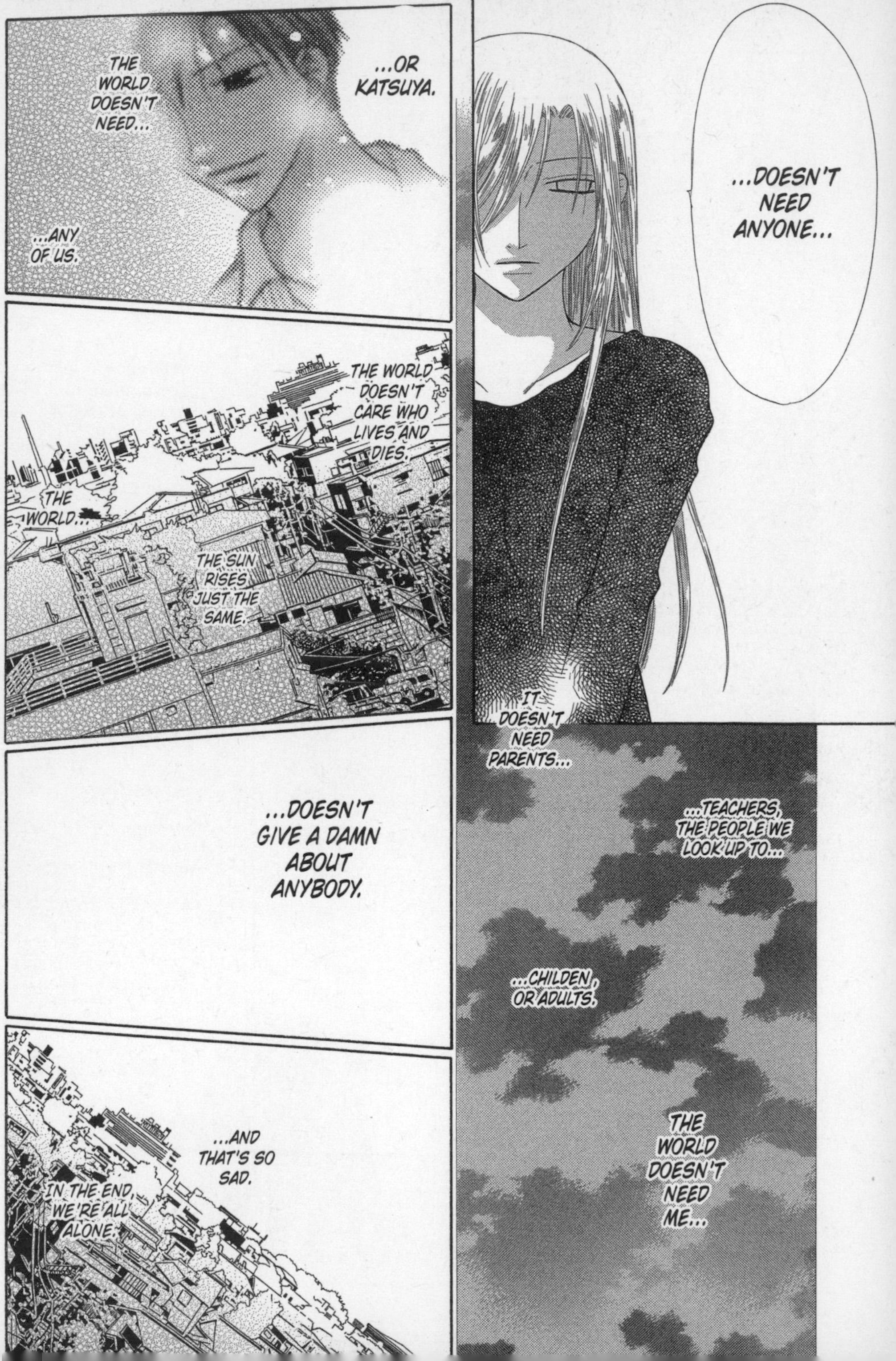
...DOESN'T NEED ANYONE...
IT DOESN'T NEED PARENTS...
...TEACHERS, THE PEOPLE WE LOOK UP TO...
...CHILDEN, OR ADULTS.
THE WORLD DOESN'T NEED ME...
...OR KATSUYA.
THE WORLD DOESN'T NEED...
...ANY OF US.
THE WORLD DOESN'T CARE WHO LIVES AND DIES.
THE WORLD...
THE SUN RISES JUST THE SAME.
...DOESN'T GIVE A DAMN ABOUT ANYBODY.
...AND THAT'S SO SAD.
IN THE END, WE'RE ALL ALONE.

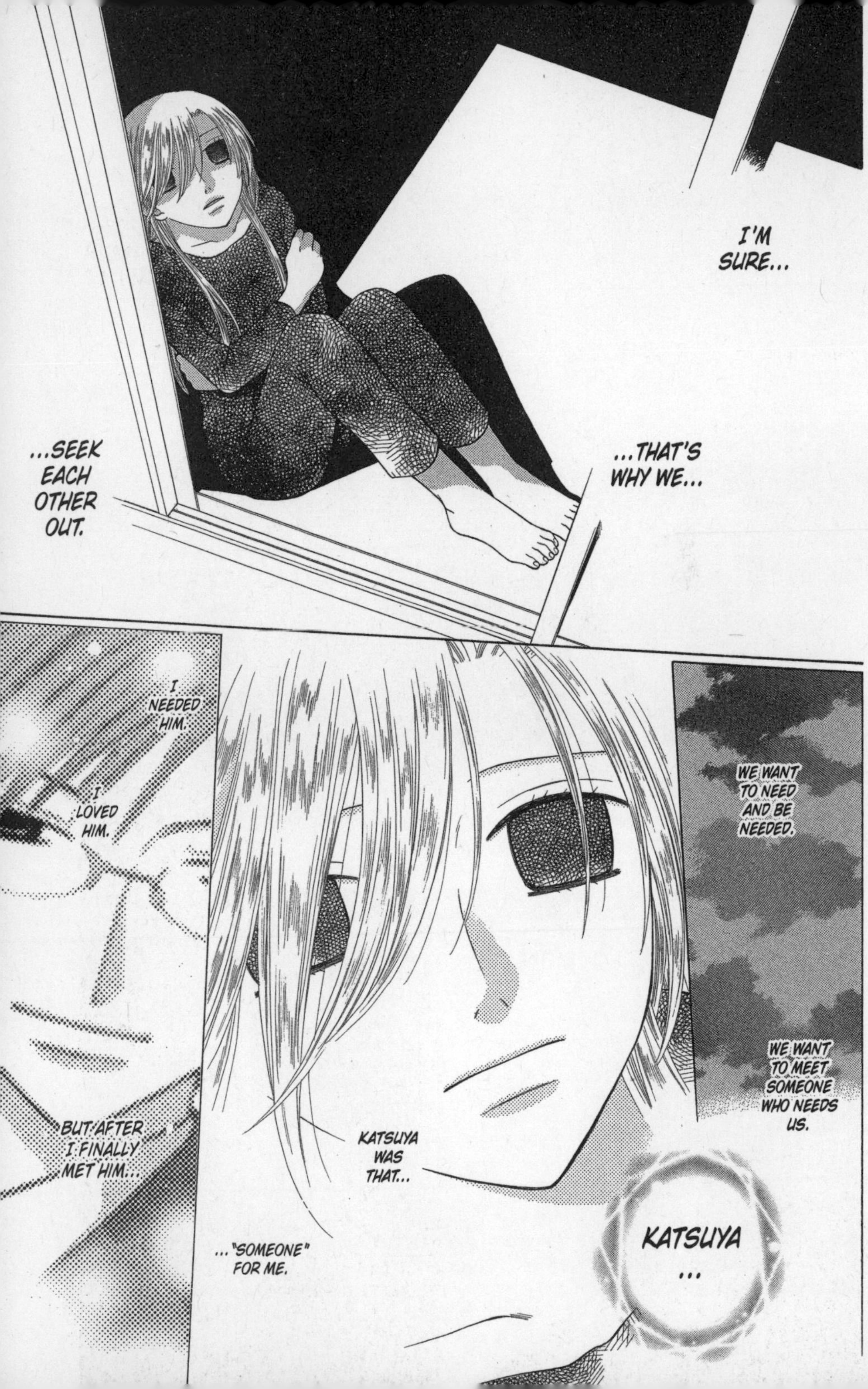

I'M SURE...
...THAT'S WHY WE...
...SEEK EACH OTHER OUT.
WE WANT TO NEED AND BE NEEDED.
WE WANT TO MEET SOMEONE WHO NEEDS US.
KATSUYA WAS THAT...
..."SOMEONE" FOR ME.
KATSUYA...
I NEEDED HIM.
I LOVED HIM.
BUT AFTER I FINALLY MET HIM...

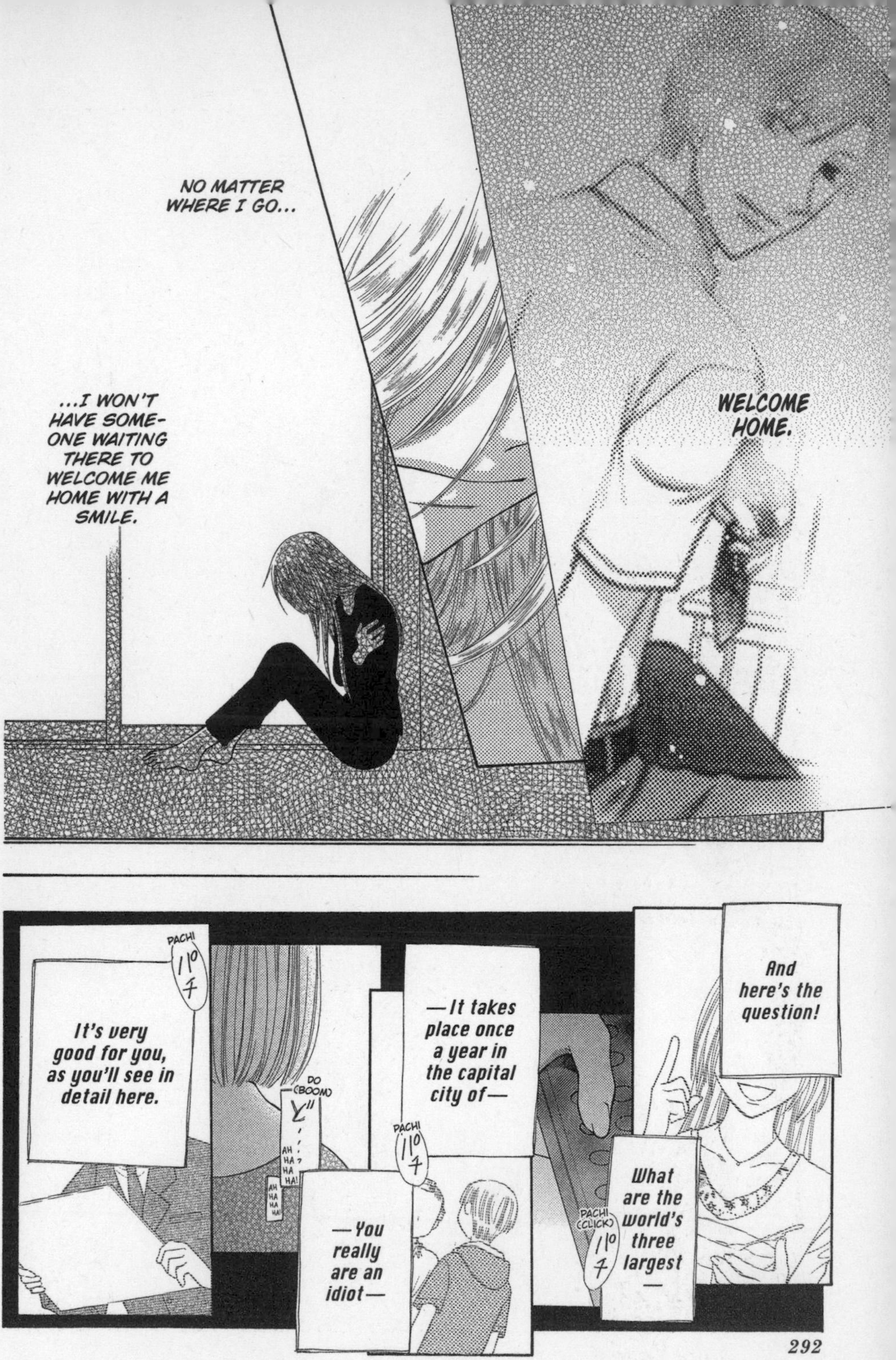
WELCOME HOME.
NO MATTER WHERE I GO...
...I WON'T HAVE SOME-ONE WAITING THERE TO WELCOME ME HOME WITH A SMILE.
And here's the question!
PACHI (CLICK)
What are the world's three largest—
—It takes place once a year in the capital city of—
PACHI
—You really are an idiot—
DO (BOOM)
AH HA HA HA!
AH HA HA HA!
PACHI
It's very good for you, as you'll see in detail here.

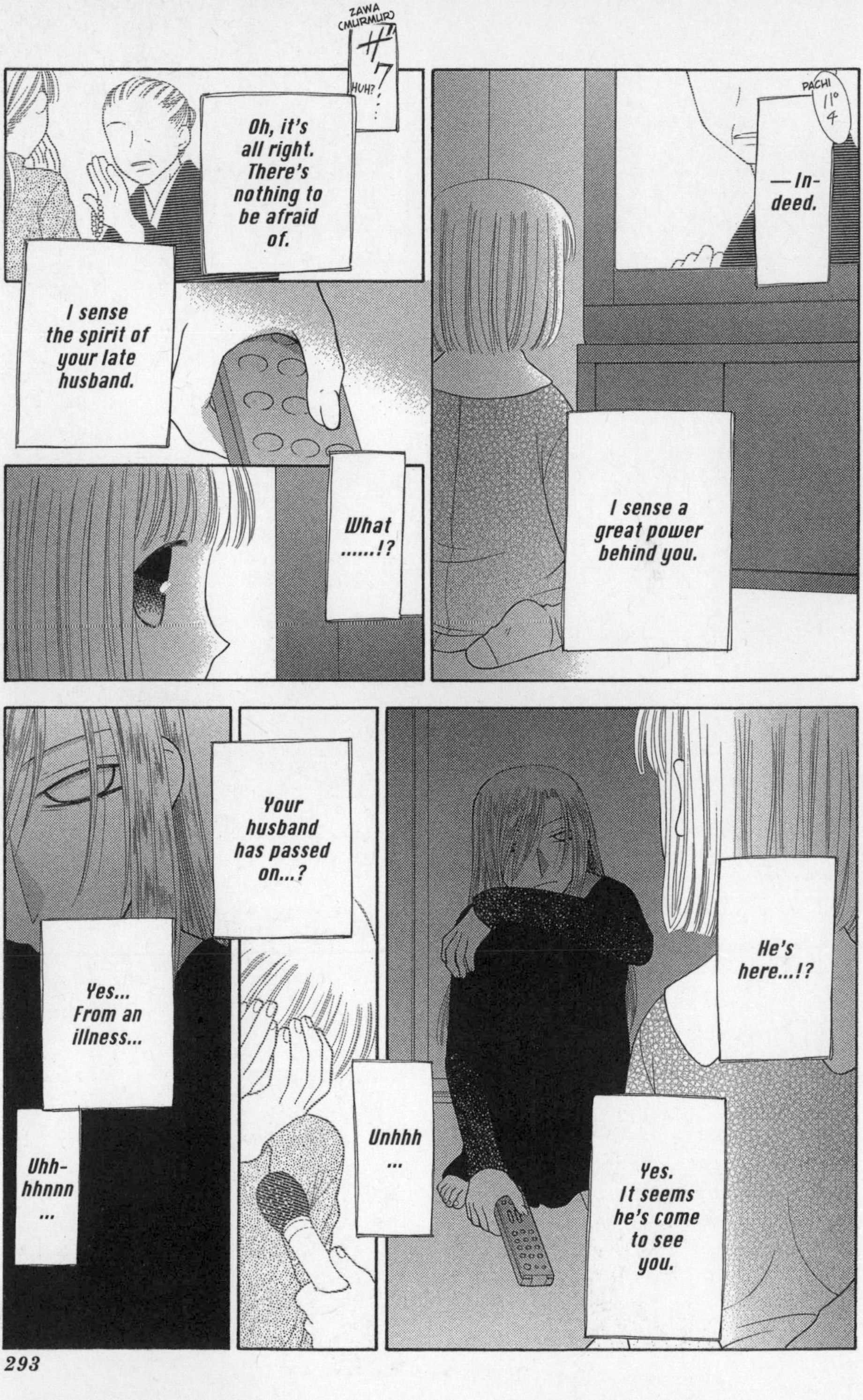

PACHI
—In-deed.
I sense a great power behind you.
ZAWA (MURMUR)
HUH? ...
Oh, it's all right. There's nothing to be afraid of.
I sense the spirit of your late husband.
What ......!?
He's here...!?
Yes. It seems he's come to see you.
Your husband has passed on...?
Unhhh ...
Yes... From an illness...
Uhh-hhnnn ...

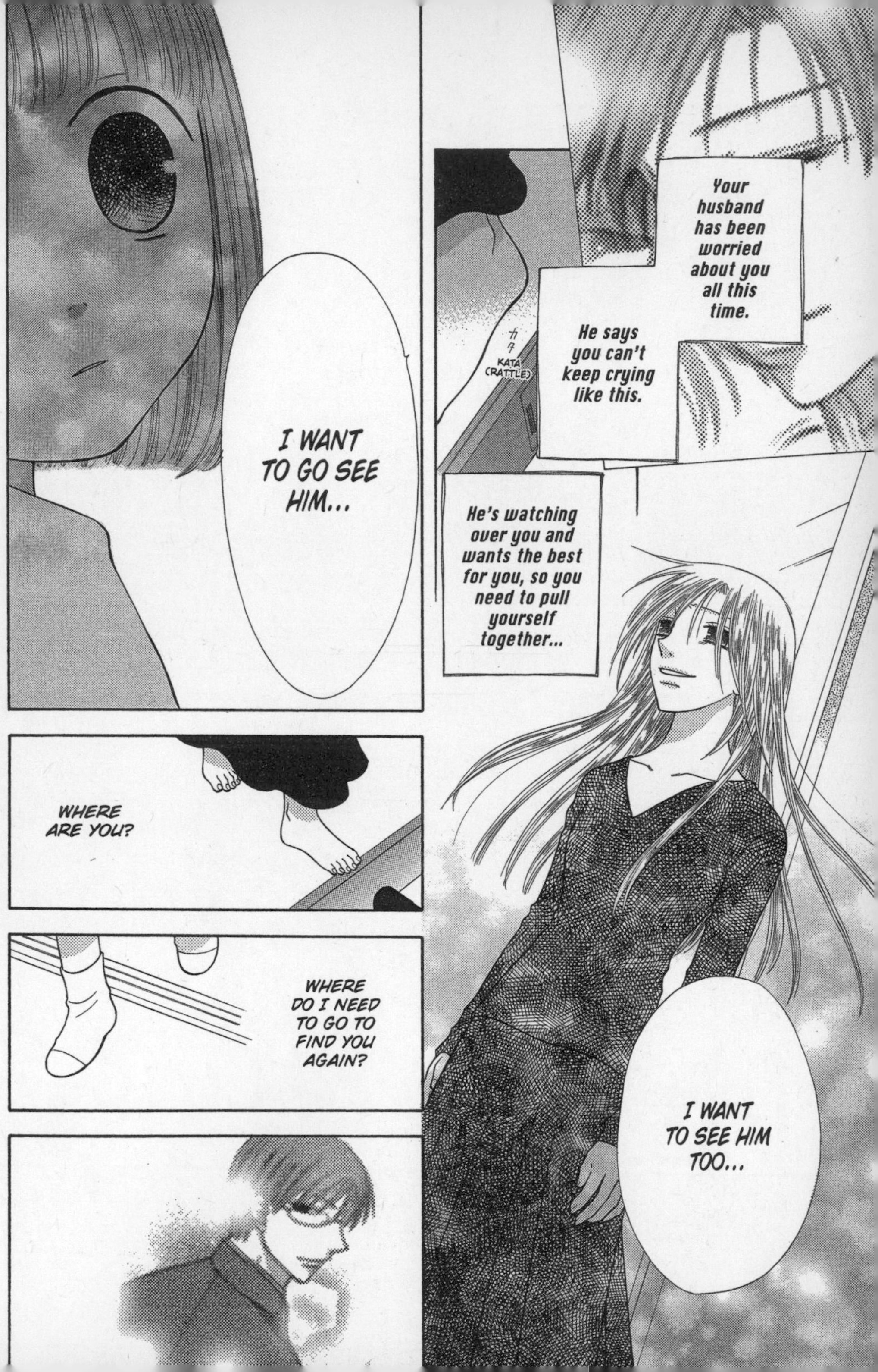
Your husband has been worried about you all this time.
He says you can't keep crying like this.
KATA (RATTLE)
He's watching over you and wants the best for you, so you need to pull yourself together...
I WANT TO SEE HIM TOO...
I WANT TO GO SEE HIM...
WHERE ARE YOU?
WHERE DO I NEED TO GO TO FIND YOU AGAIN?

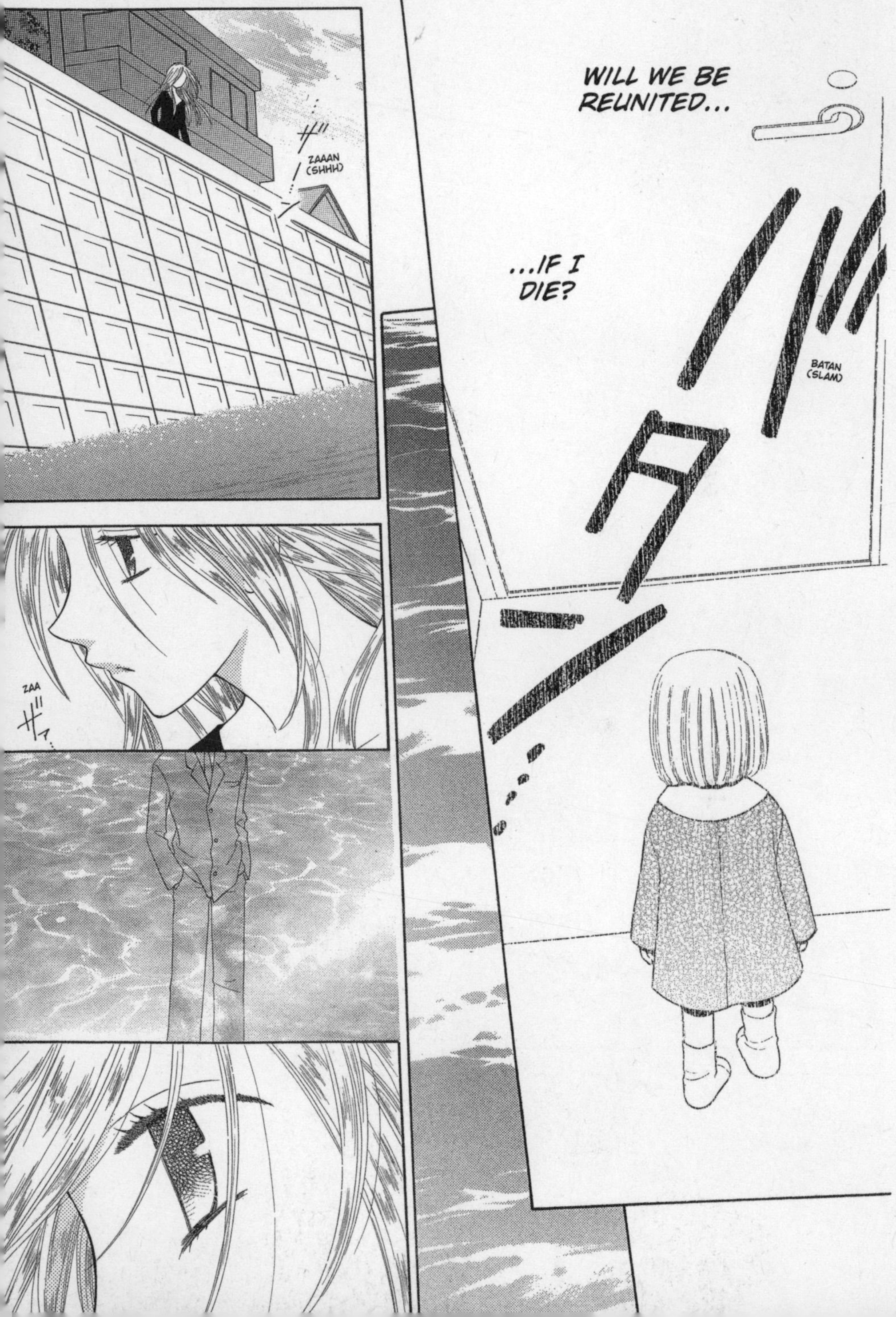
WILL WE BE REUNITED...
...IF I DIE?
BATAN (SLAM)
ZAAAN (SHHH)
ZAA

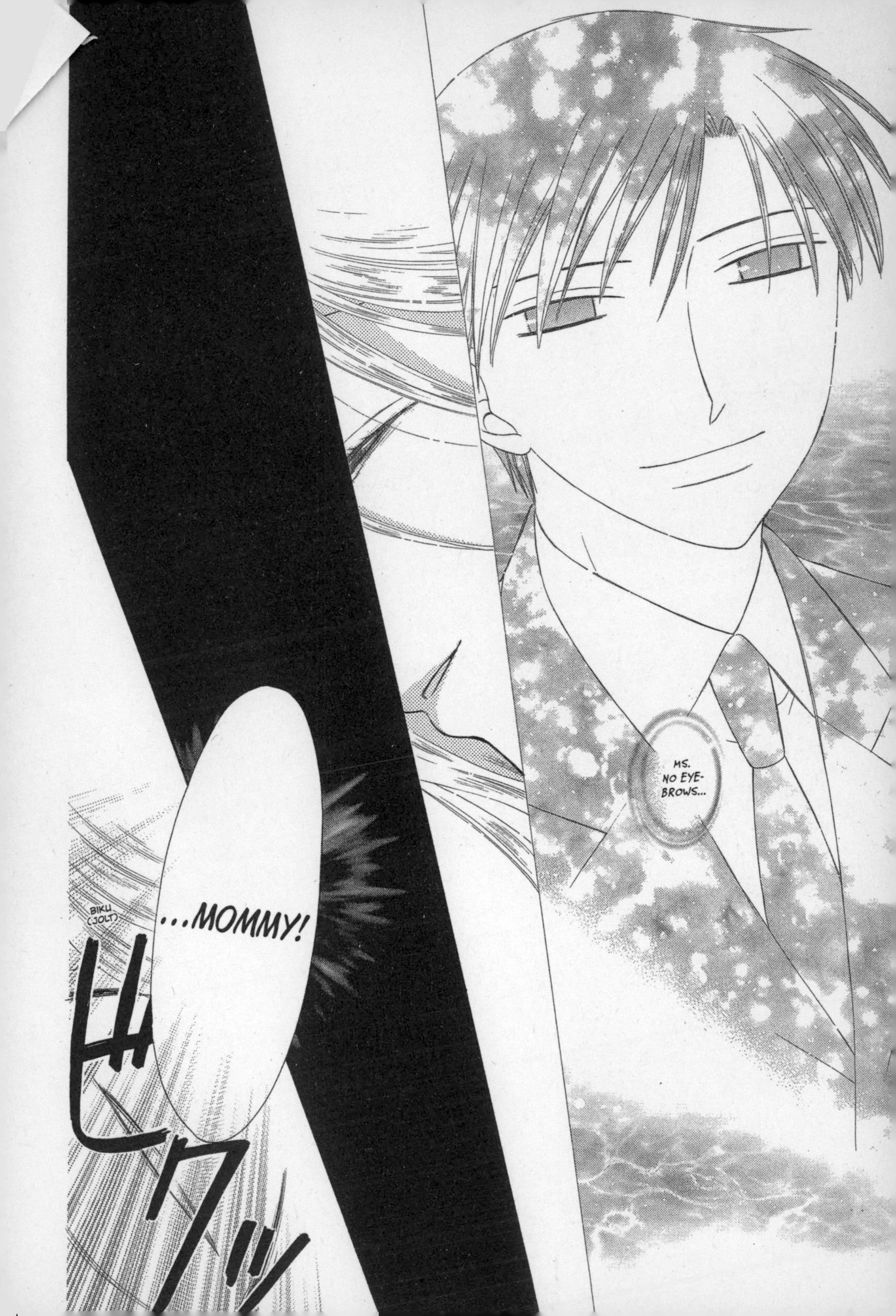
MS. NO EYE-BROWS...
...MOMMY!
BIKU (JOLT)

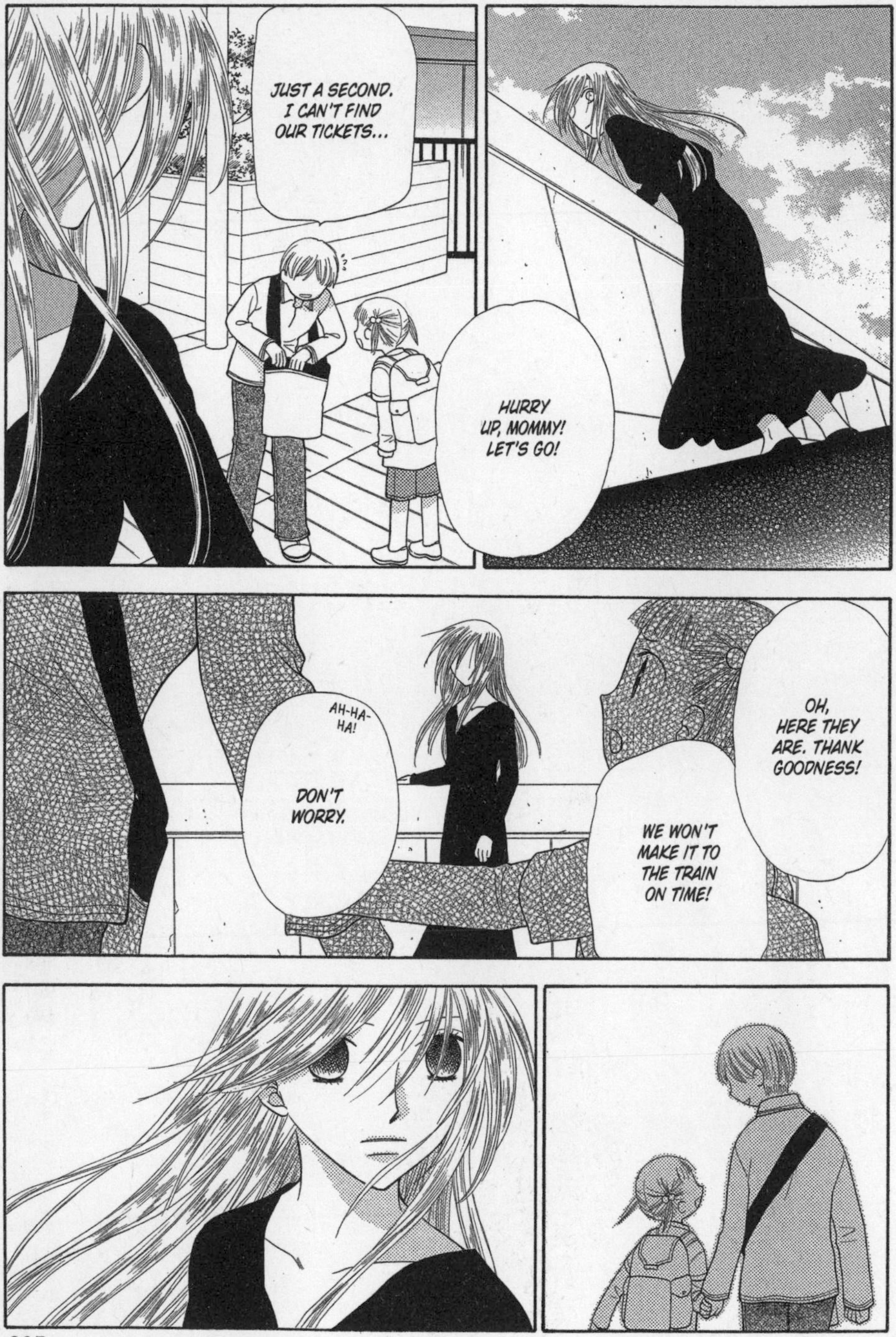
JUST A SECOND. I CAN'T FIND OUR TICKETS...
HURRY UP, MOMMY! LET'S GO!
OH, HERE THEY ARE. THANK GOODNESS!
WE WON'T MAKE IT TO THE TRAIN ON TIME!
AH-HA-HA!
DON'T WORRY.

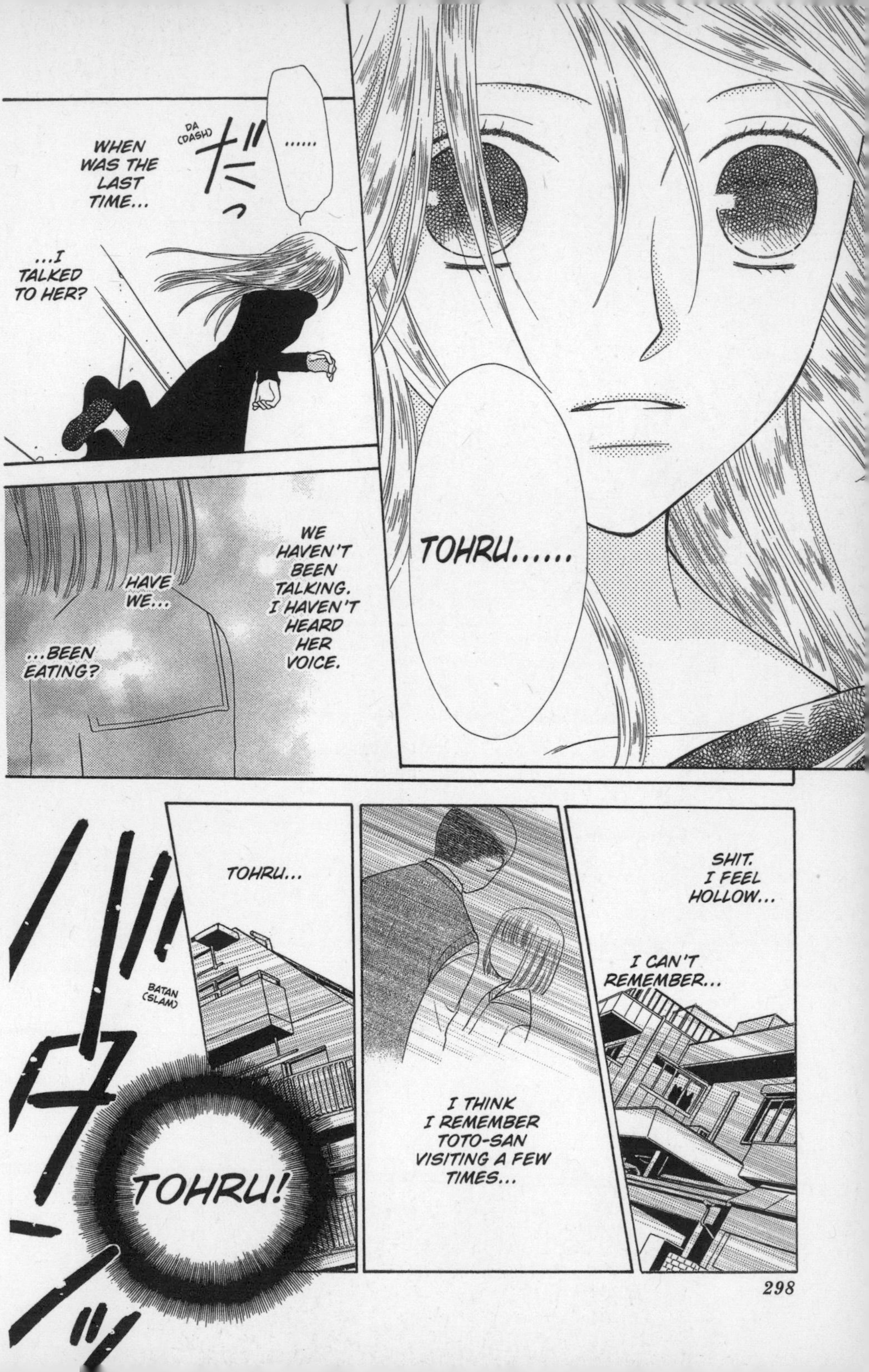
TOHRU......
......
DA (DASH)
WHEN WAS THE LAST TIME...
...I TALKED TO HER?
WE HAVEN'T BEEN TALKING. I HAVEN'T HEARD HER VOICE.
HAVE WE...
...BEEN EATING?
SHIT. I FEEL HOLLOW...
I CAN'T REMEMBER...
I THINK I REMEMBER TOTO-SAN VISITING A FEW TIMES...
TOHRU...
BATAN (SLAM)
TOHRU!

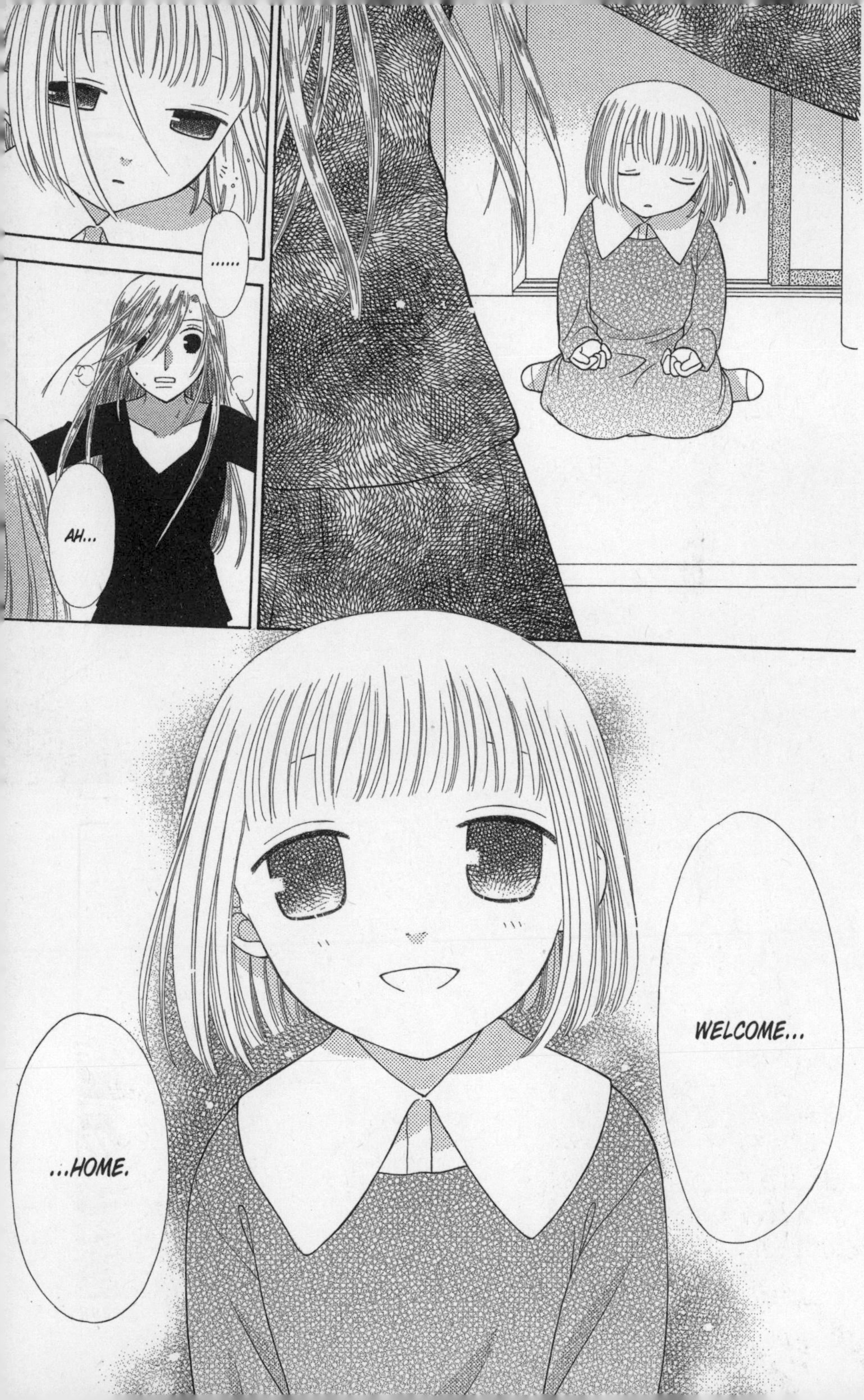
......
AH...
WELCOME...
...HOME.

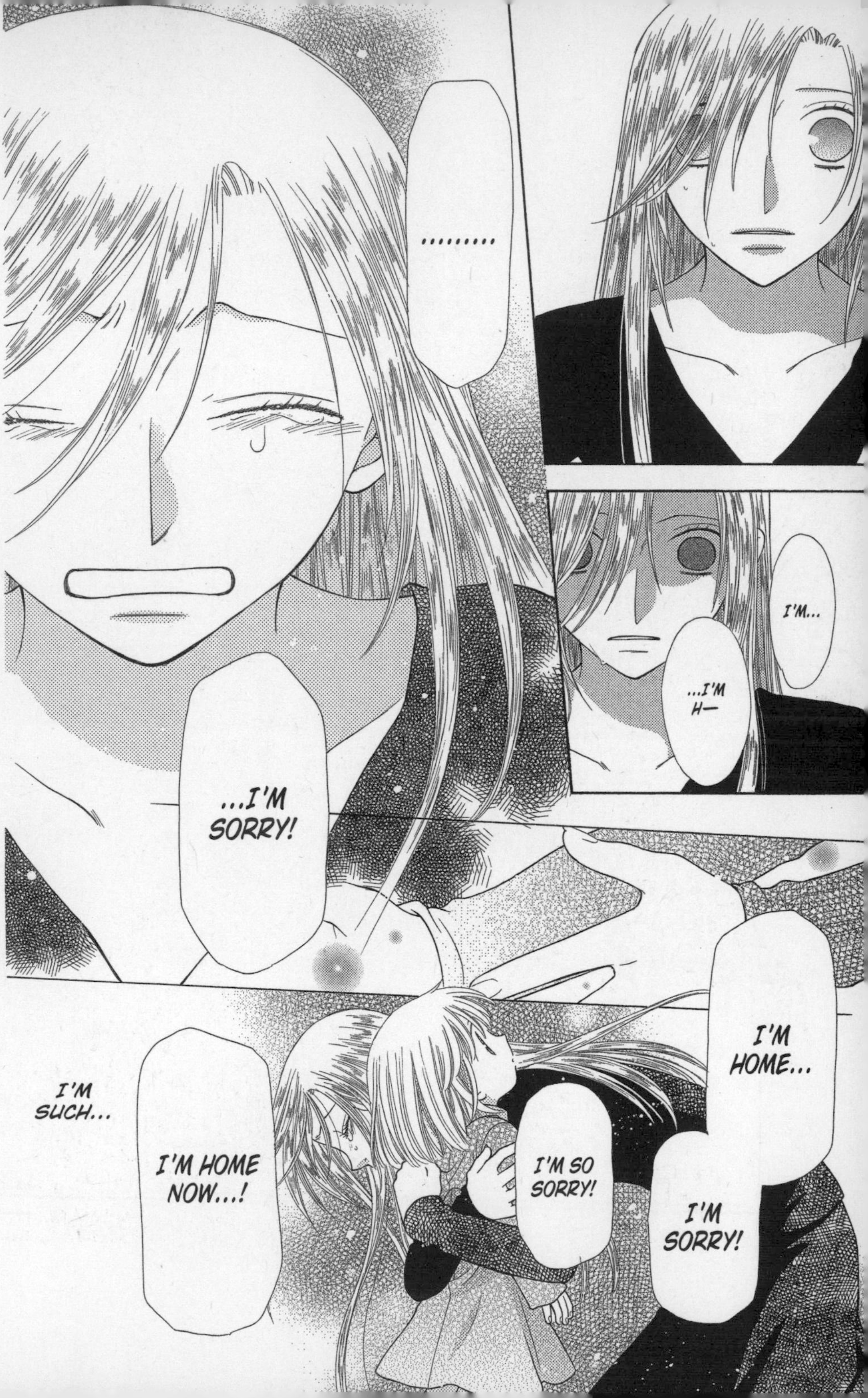

I'M...
...I'M H—
....
...I'M SORRY!
I'M HOME...
I'M SORRY!
I'M SO SORRY!
I'M HOME NOW...!
I'M SUCH...

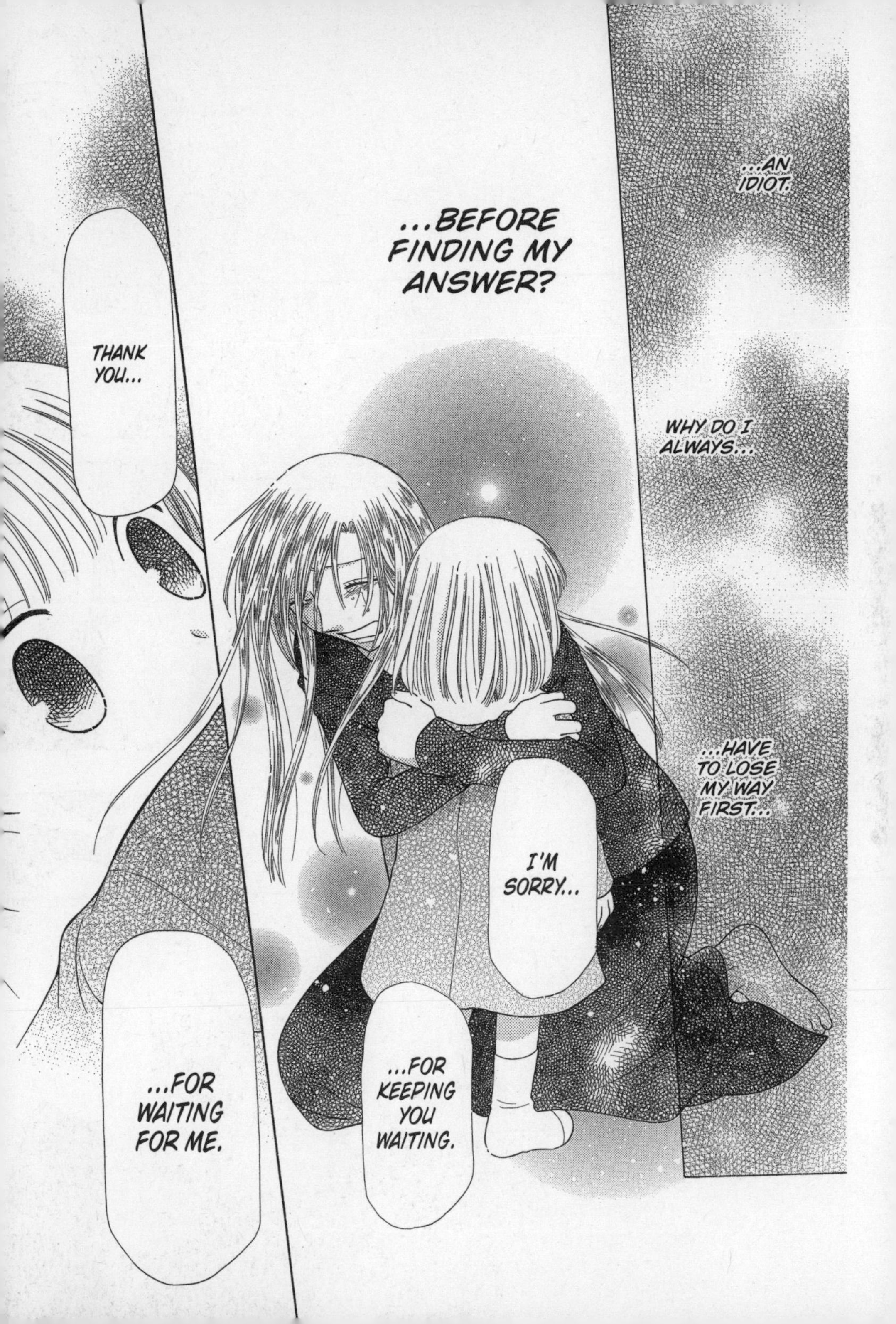
...AN IDIOT.
WHY DO I ALWAYS...
...HAVE TO LOSE MY WAY FIRST...
...BEFORE FINDING MY ANSWER?
I'M SORRY...
...FOR KEEPING YOU WAITING.
THANK YOU...
...FOR WAITING FOR ME.

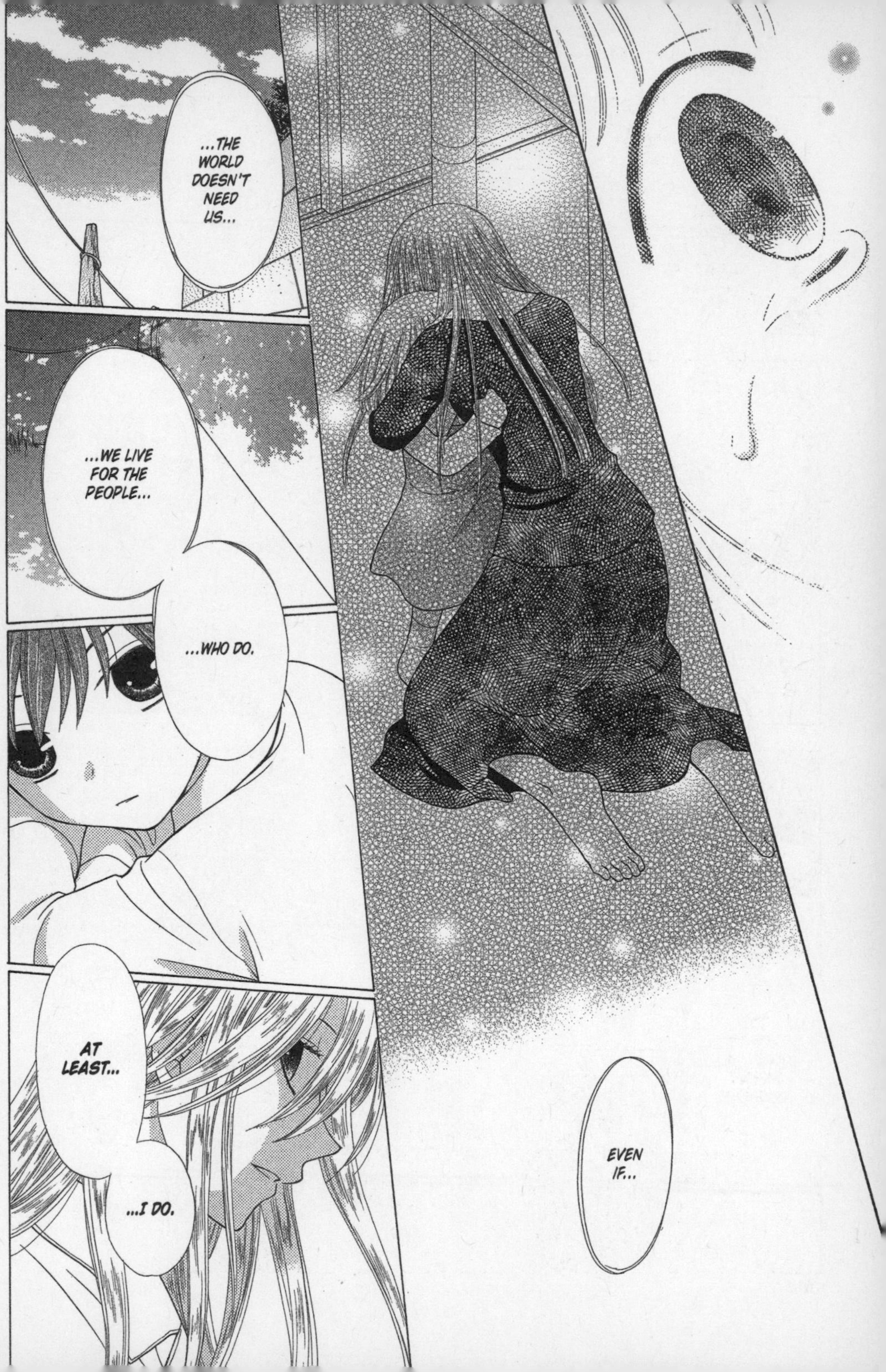
EVEN IF...
...THE WORLD DOESN'T NEED US...
...WE LIVE FOR THE PEOPLE...
...WHO DO.
AT LEAST...
...I DO.

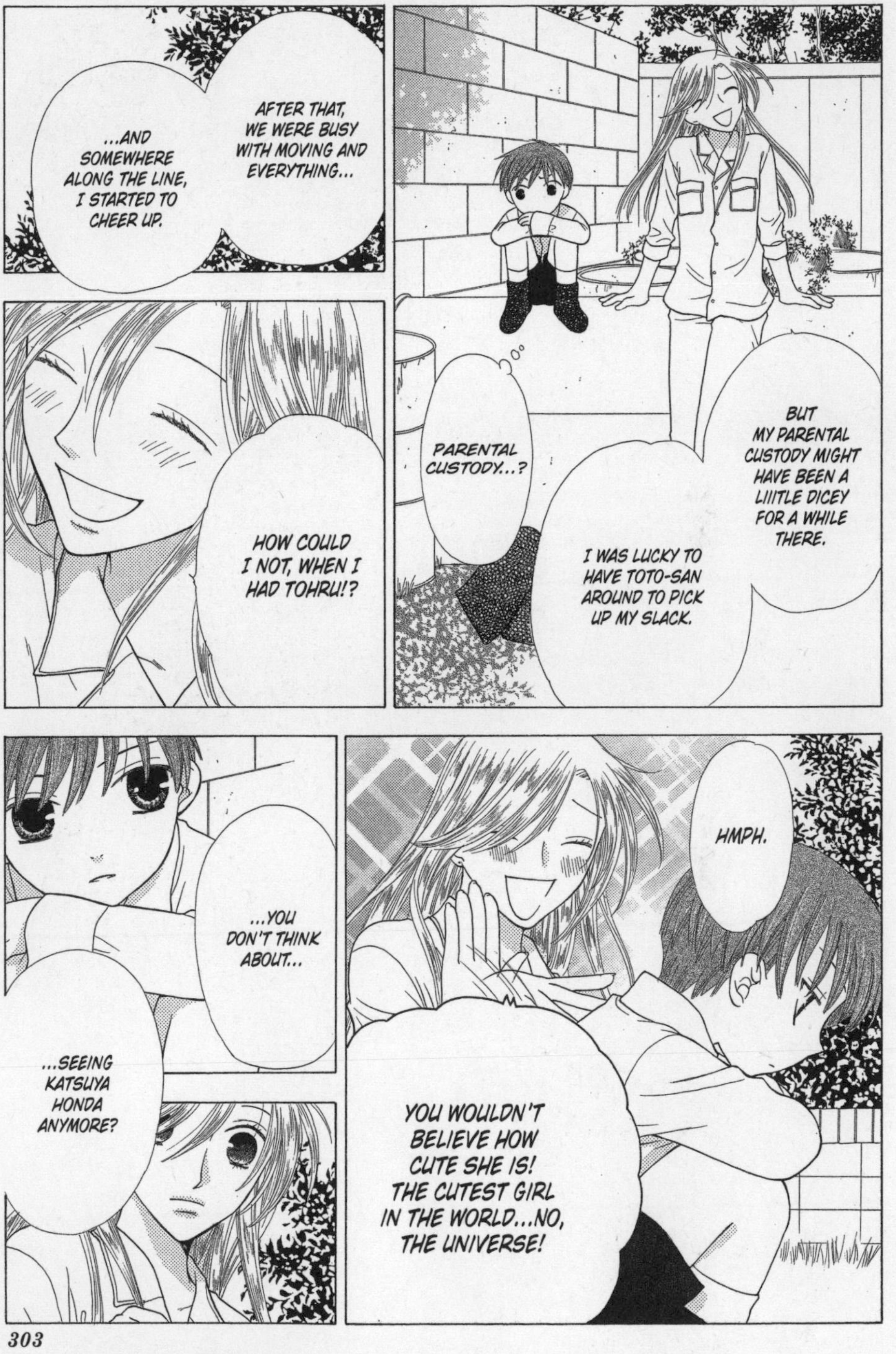

BUT MY PARENTAL CUSTODY MIGHT HAVE BEEN A LIIITLE DICEY FOR A WHILE THERE.
I WAS LUCKY TO HAVE TOTO-SAN AROUND TO PICK UP MY SLACK.
PARENTAL CUSTODY...?
AFTER THAT, WE WERE BUSY WITH MOVING AND EVERYTHING...
...AND SOMEWHERE ALONG THE LINE, I STARTED TO CHEER UP.
HOW COULD I NOT, WHEN I HAD TOHRU!?
HMPH.
YOU WOULDN'T BELIEVE HOW CUTE SHE IS! THE CUTEST GIRL IN THE WORLD...NO, THE UNIVERSE!
...YOU DON'T THINK ABOUT...
...SEEING KATSUYA HONDA ANYMORE?

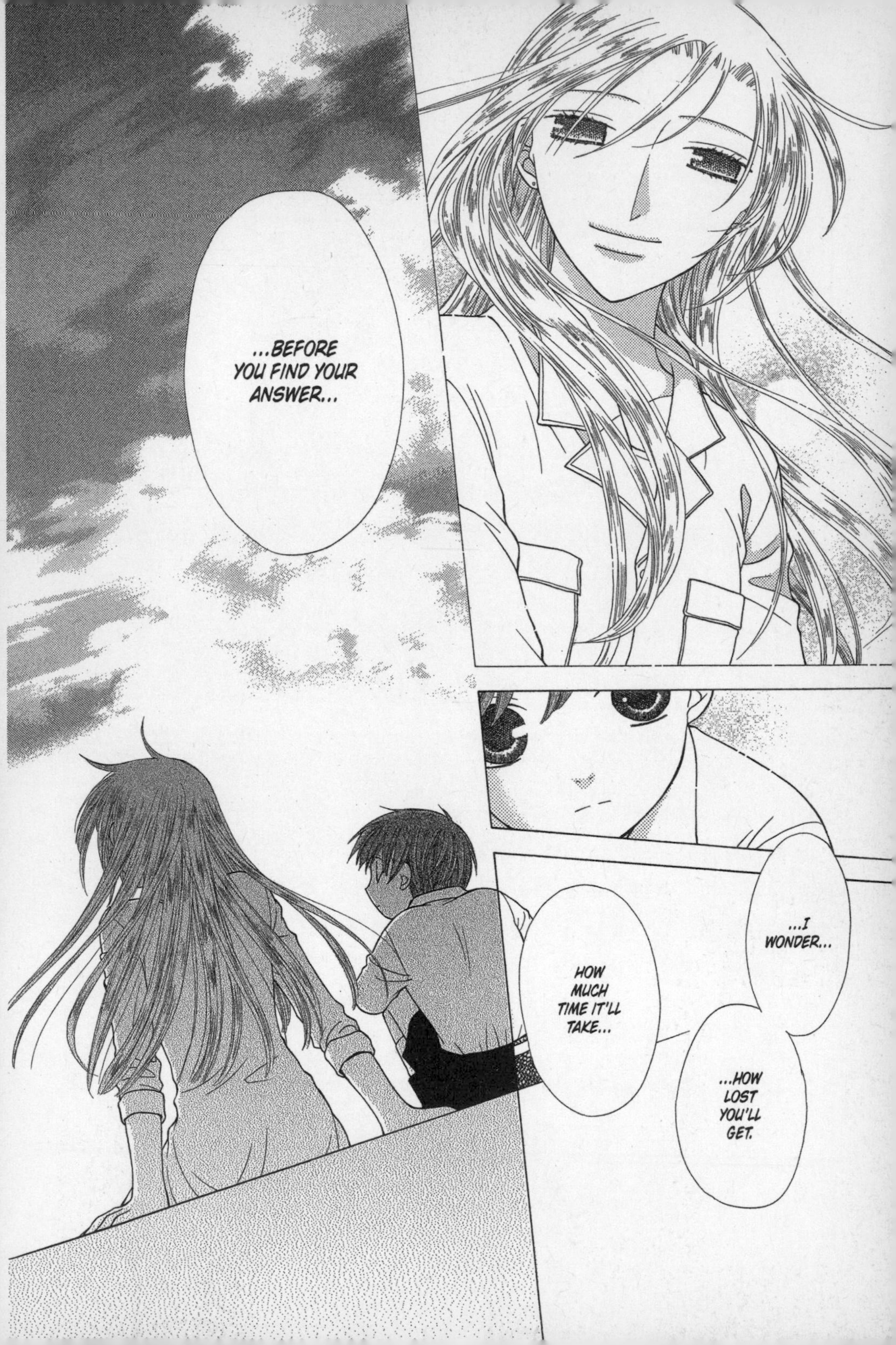
...I WONDER...
HOW MUCH TIME IT'LL TAKE...
...HOW LOST YOU'LL GET.
...BEFORE YOU FIND YOUR ANSWER...

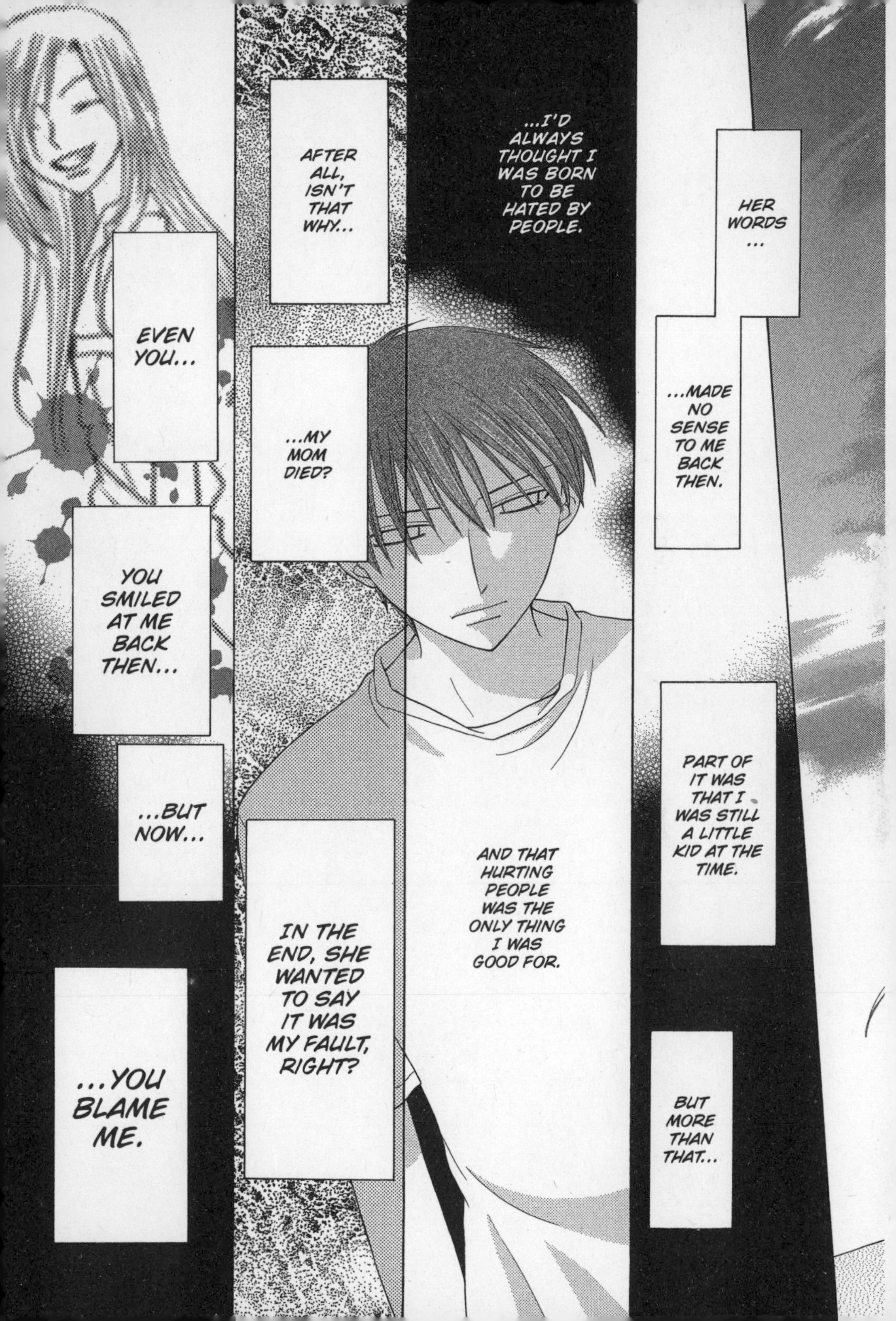
HER WORDS...
...MADE NO SENSE TO ME BACK THEN.
PART OF IT WAS THAT I WAS STILL A LITTLE KID AT THE TIME.
BUT MORE THAN THAT...
...I'D ALWAYS THOUGHT I WAS BORN TO BE HATED BY PEOPLE.
AND THAT HURTING PEOPLE WAS THE ONLY THING I WAS GOOD FOR.
AFTER ALL, ISN'T THAT WHY...
...MY MOM DIED?
IN THE END, SHE WANTED TO SAY IT WAS MY FAULT, RIGHT?
EVEN YOU...
YOU SMILED AT ME BACK THEN...
...BUT NOW...
...YOU BLAME ME.

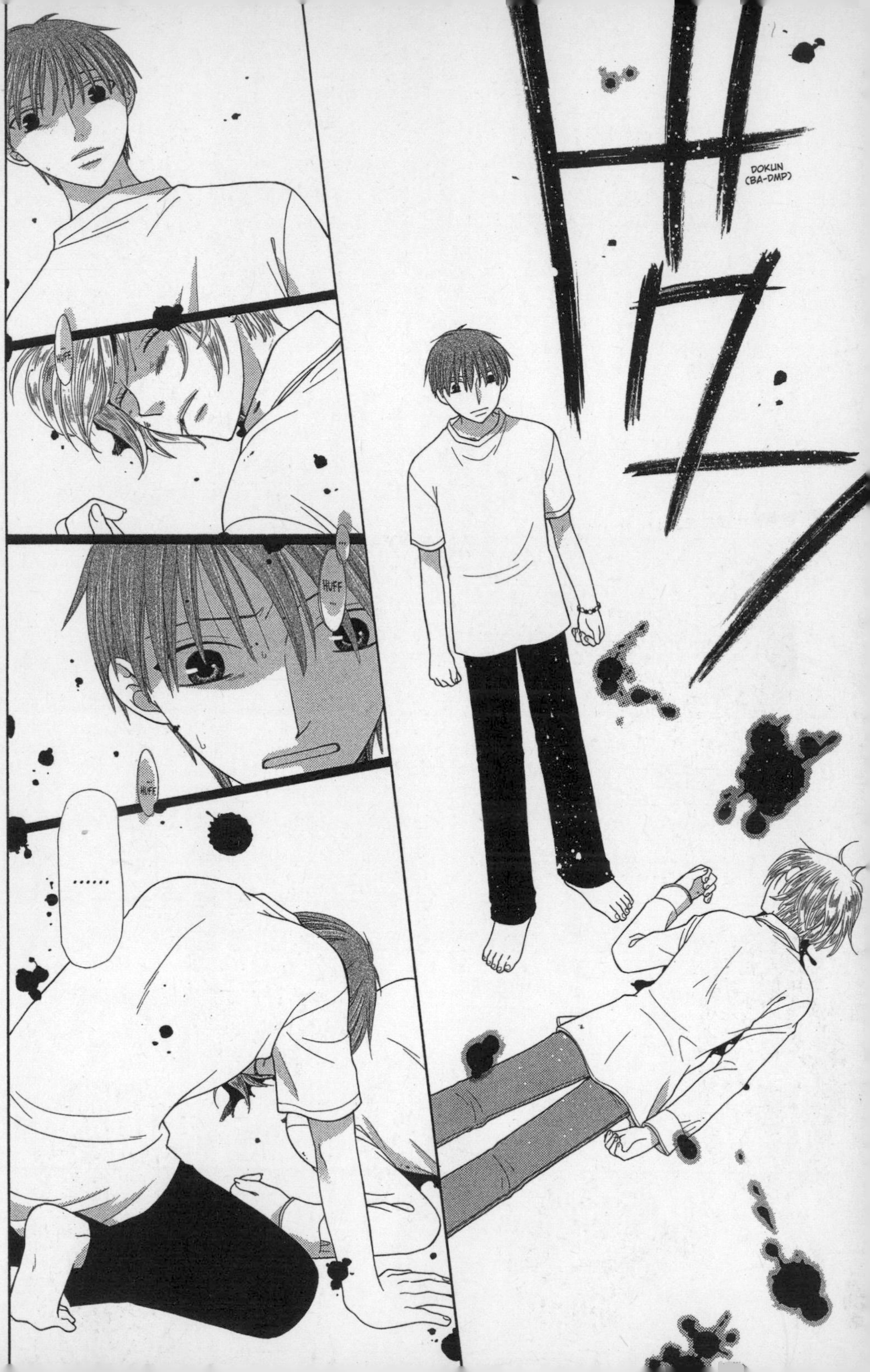
DOKUN (BA-DMP)
HUFF
...
HUFF
HUFF
......

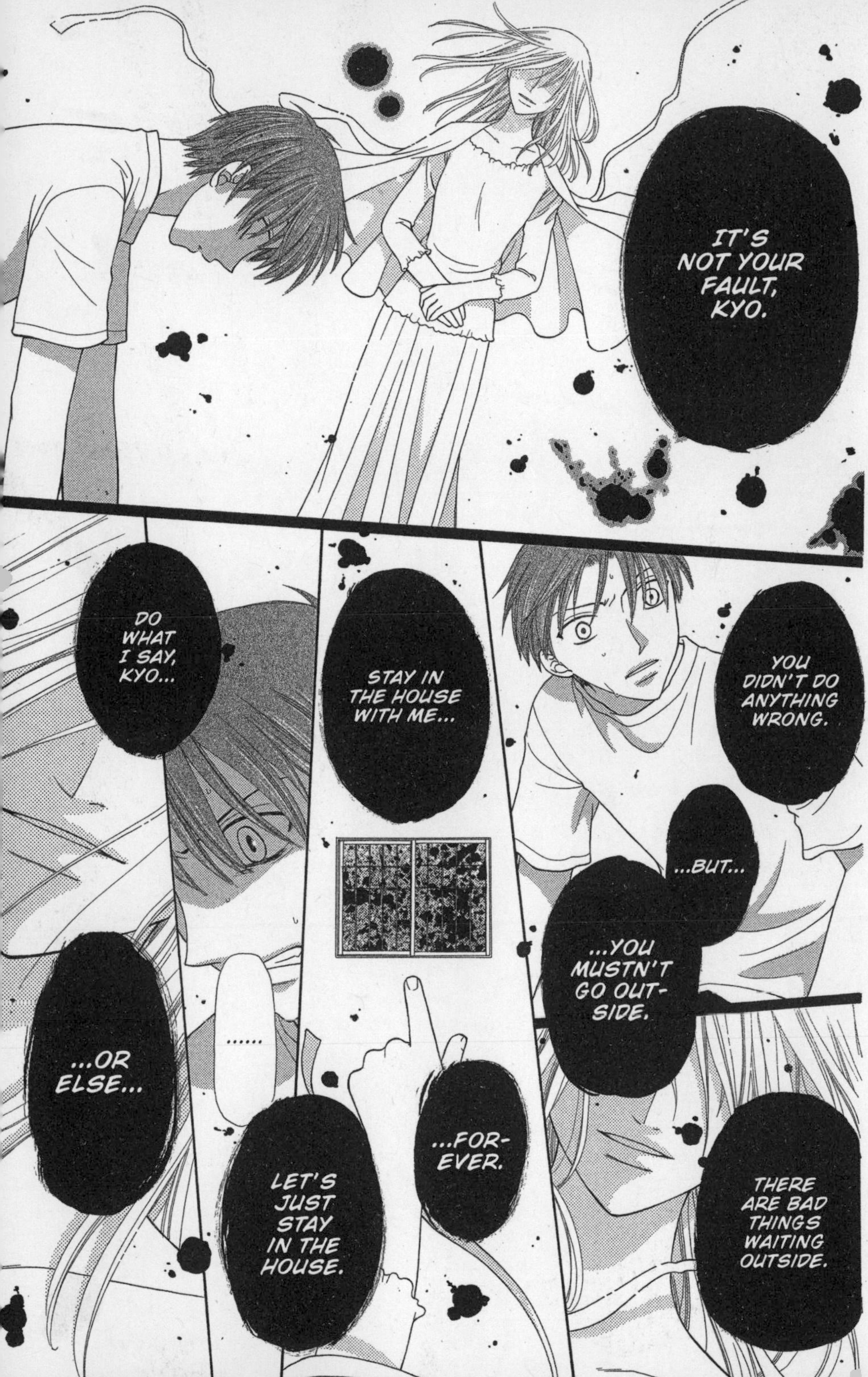
IT'S NOT YOUR FAULT, KYO.
YOU DIDN'T DO ANYTHING WRONG.
...BUT...
...YOU MUSTN'T GO OUT-SIDE.
THERE ARE BAD THINGS WAITING OUTSIDE.
STAY IN THE HOUSE WITH ME...
...FOR-EVER.
LET'S JUST STAY IN THE HOUSE.
DO WHAT I SAY, KYO...
......
...OR ELSE...

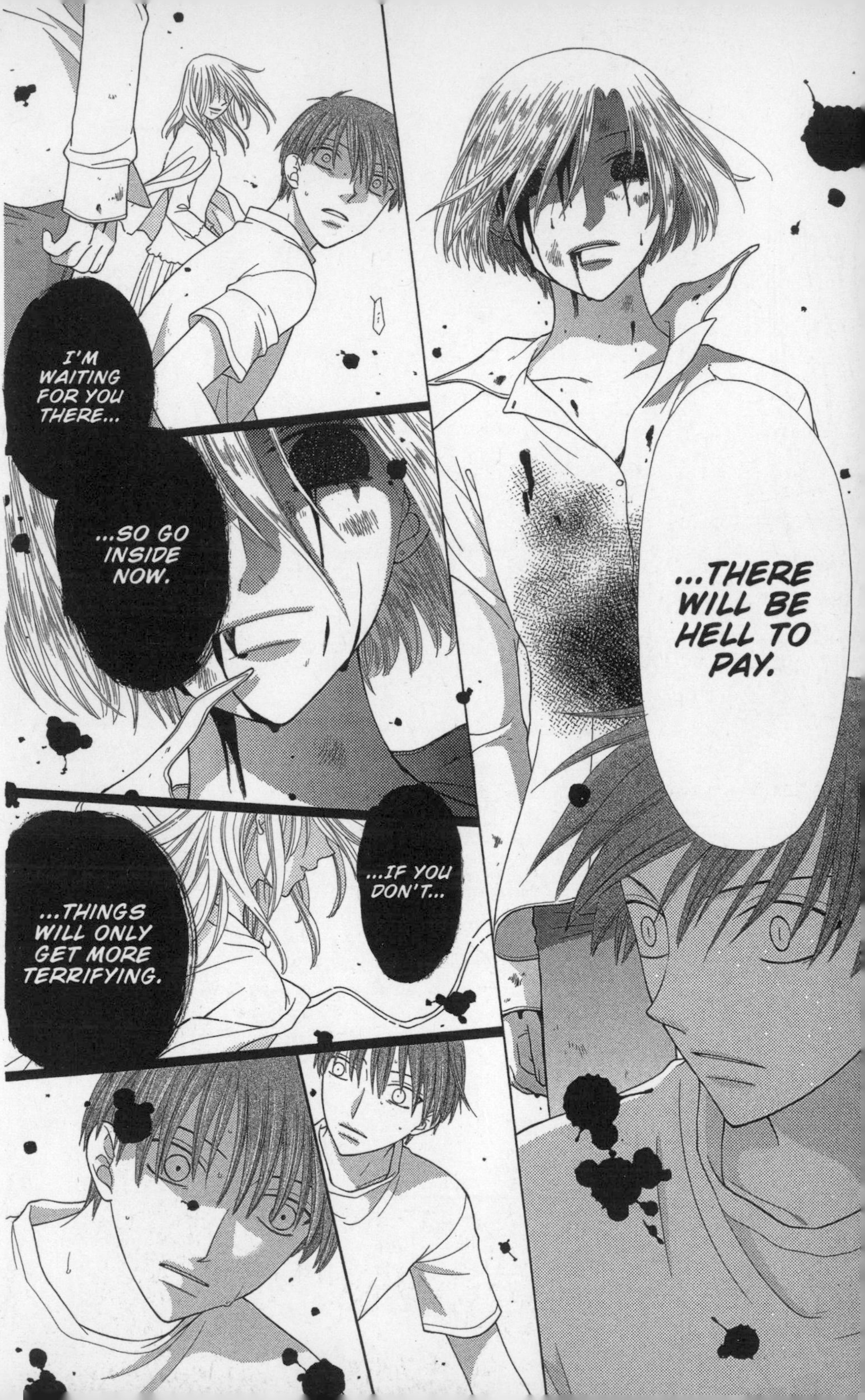
...THERE WILL BE HELL TO PAY.
I'M WAITING FOR YOU THERE...
...SO GO INSIDE NOW.
...IF YOU DON'T...
...THINGS WILL ONLY GET MORE TERRIFYING.

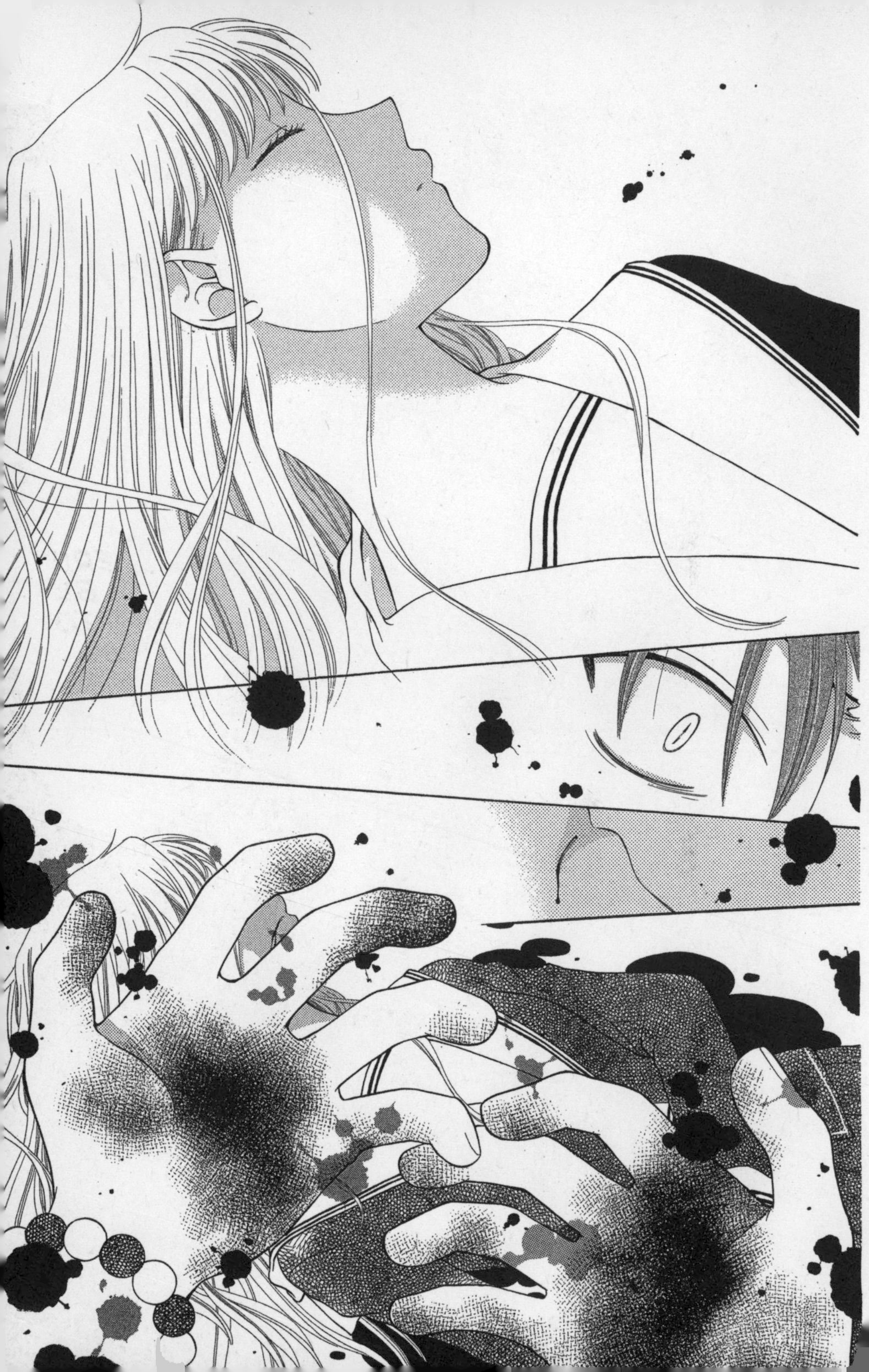

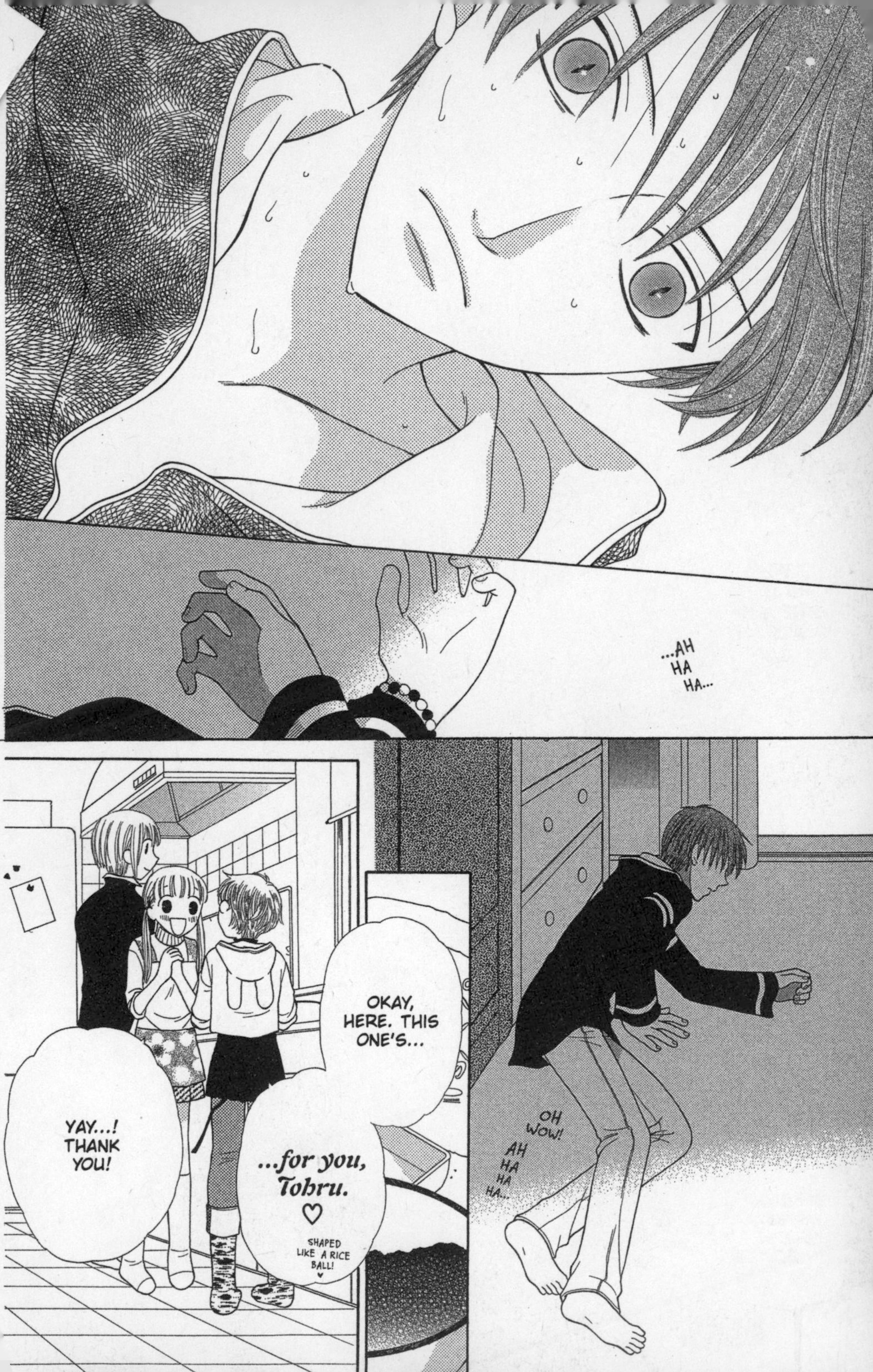
...AH HA HA...
OH WOW!
AH HA HA HA...
OKAY, HERE. THIS ONE'S...
...for you, Tohru. ♡
SHAPED LIKE A RICE BALL! ♥
YAY...! THANK YOU!

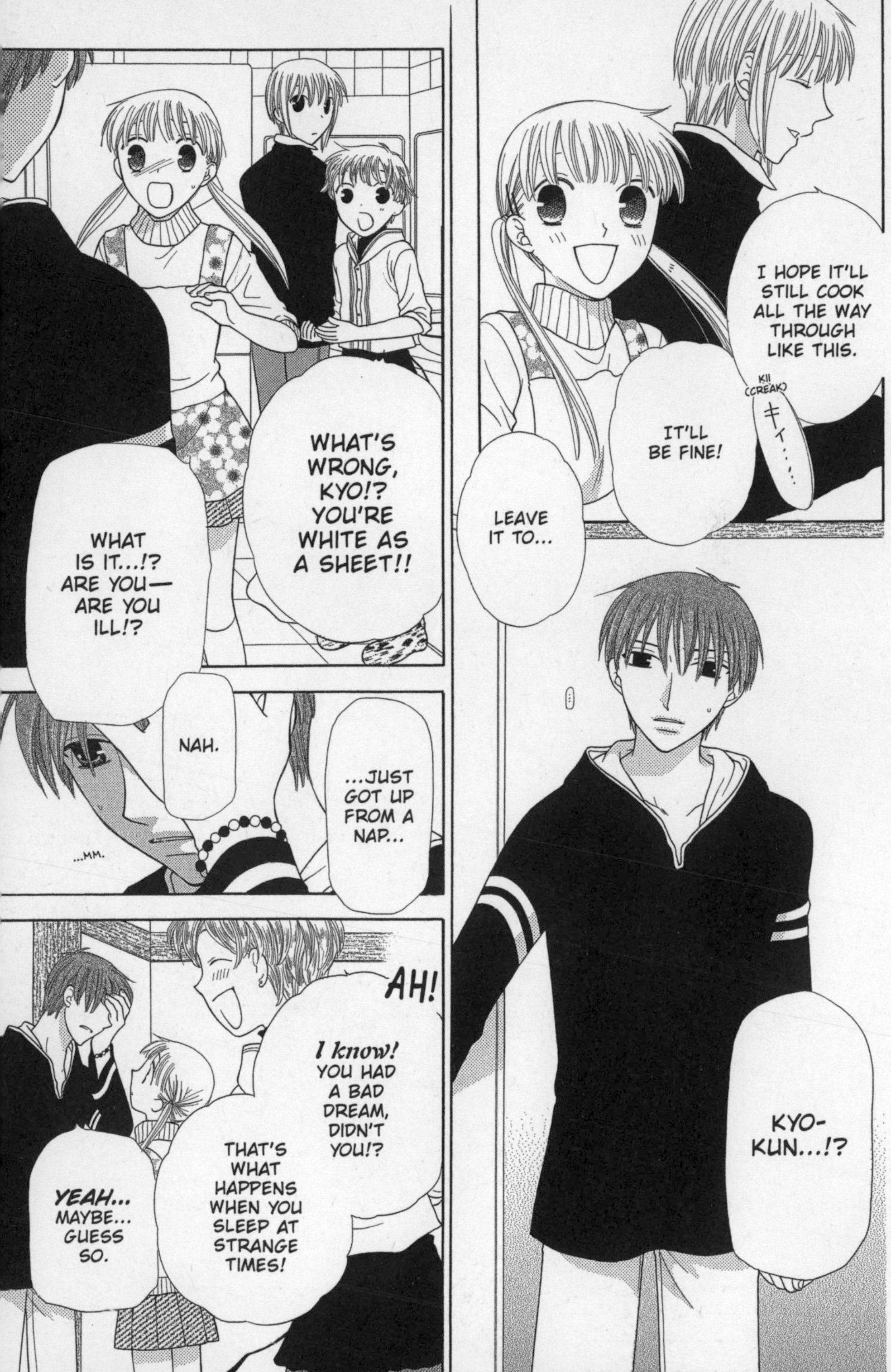
I HOPE IT'LL STILL COOK ALL THE WAY THROUGH LIKE THIS.
KII (CREAK)
キィ・・・
IT'LL BE FINE!
LEAVE IT TO...
...
KYO-KUN...!?
WHAT'S WRONG, KYO!? YOU'RE WHITE AS A SHEET!!
WHAT IS IT...!? ARE YOU— ARE YOU ILL!?
NAH.
...JUST GOT UP FROM A NAP...
...MM.
AH!
I know! YOU HAD A BAD DREAM, DIDN'T YOU!?
THAT'S WHAT HAPPENS WHEN YOU SLEEP AT STRANGE TIMES!
YEAH... MAYBE... GUESS SO.

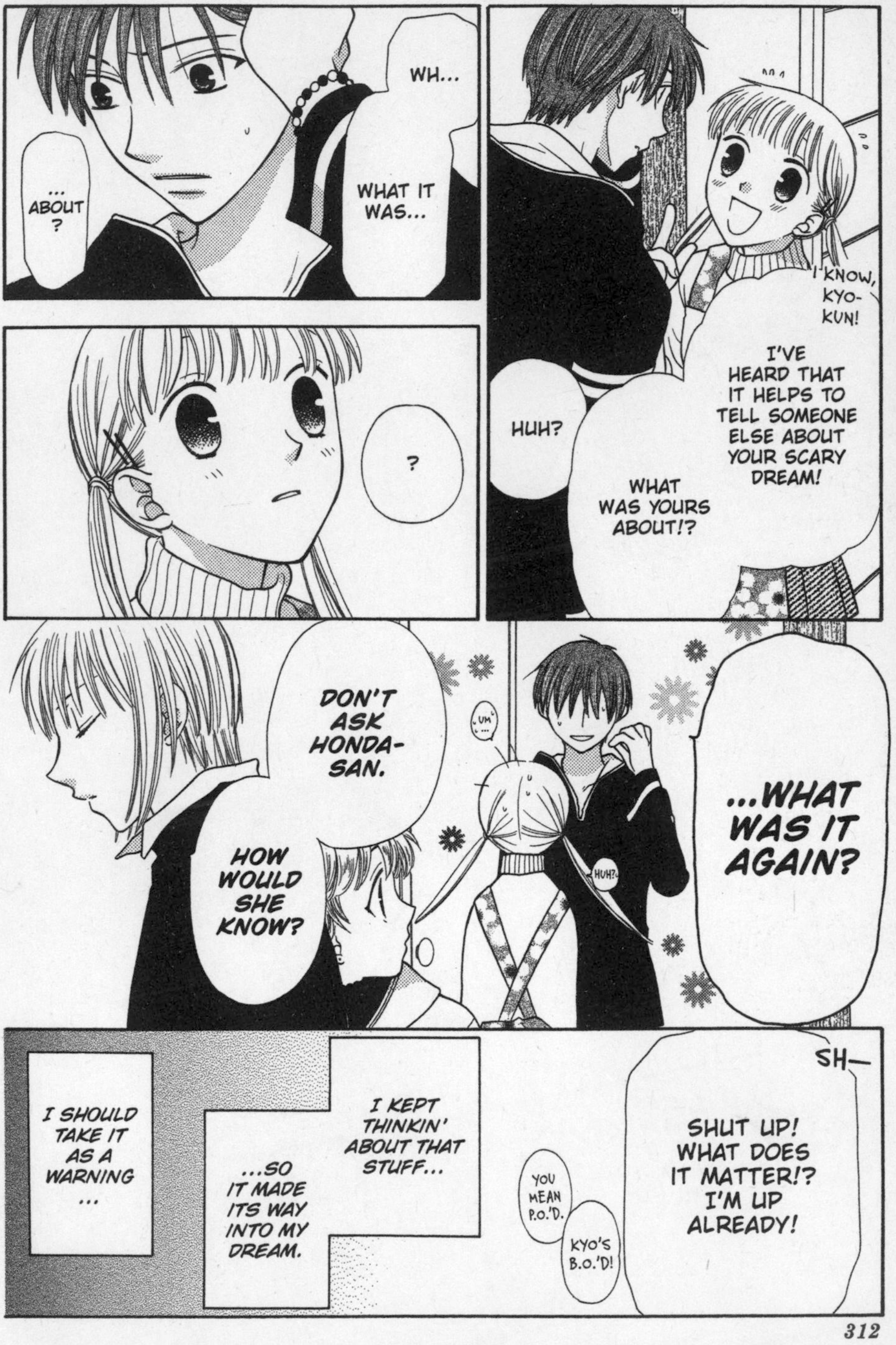
I KNOW, KYO-KUN!
I'VE HEARD THAT IT HELPS TO TELL SOMEONE ELSE ABOUT YOUR SCARY DREAM!
WHAT WAS YOURS ABOUT!?
HUH?
WH...
WHAT IT WAS...
...ABOUT?
?
...WHAT WAS IT AGAIN?
UM...
HUH?
DON'T ASK HONDA-SAN.
HOW WOULD SHE KNOW?
SH—
SHUT UP! WHAT DOES IT MATTER!? I'M UP ALREADY!
KYO'S B.O.'D!
YOU MEAN P.O.'D.
I KEPT THINKIN' ABOUT THAT STUFF...
...SO IT MADE ITS WAY INTO MY DREAM.
I SHOULD TAKE IT AS A WARNING...

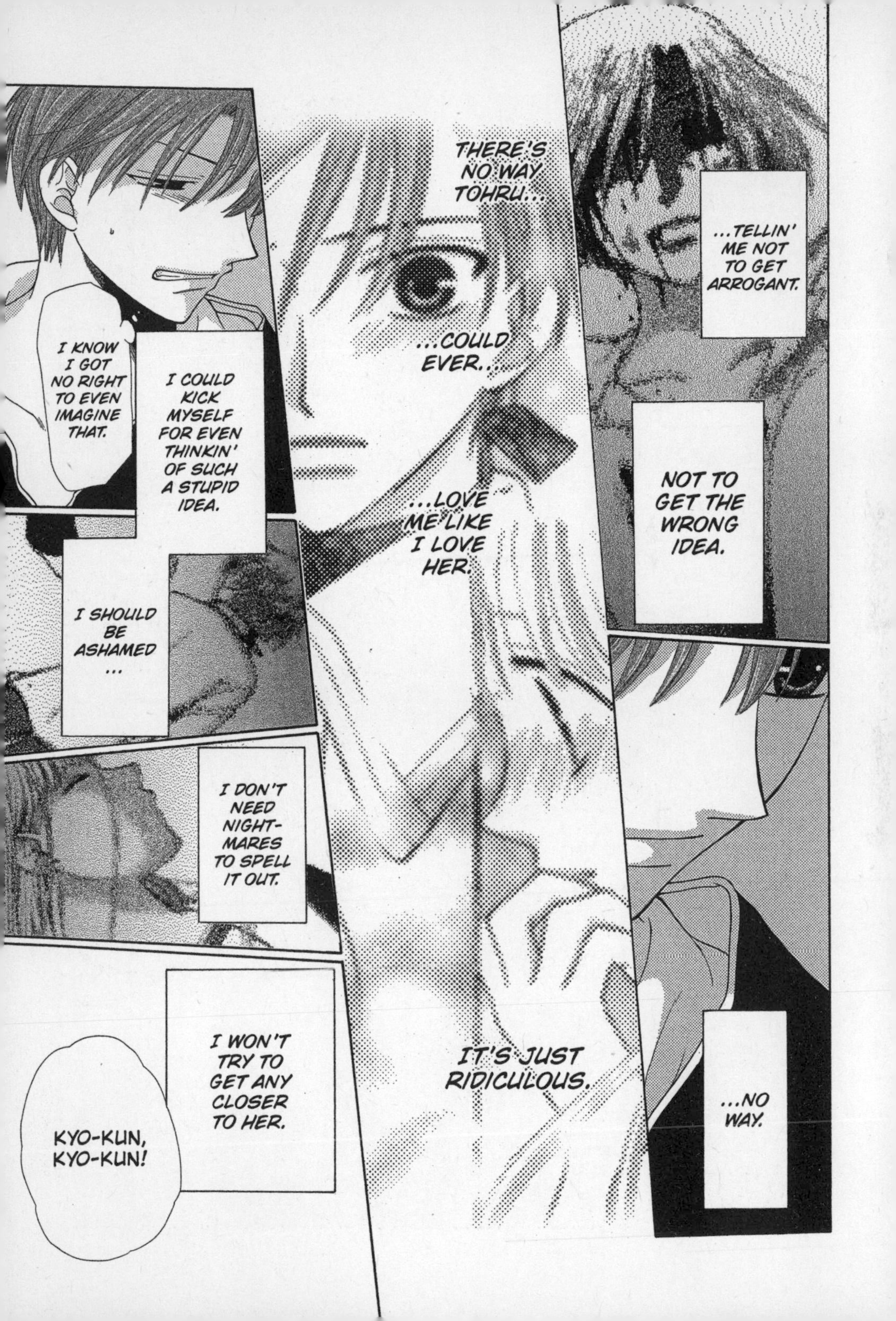
...TELLIN' ME NOT TO GET ARROGANT.
NOT TO GET THE WRONG IDEA.
...NO WAY.
THERE'S NO WAY TOHRU...
...COULD EVER...
...LOVE ME LIKE I LOVE HER.
IT'S JUST RIDICULOUS.
I KNOW I GOT NO RIGHT TO EVEN IMAGINE THAT.
I COULD KICK MYSELF FOR EVEN THINKIN' OF SUCH A STUPID IDEA.
I SHOULD BE ASHAMED...
I DON'T NEED NIGHT-MARES TO SPELL IT OUT.
I WON'T TRY TO GET ANY CLOSER TO HER.
KYO-KUN, KYO-KUN!

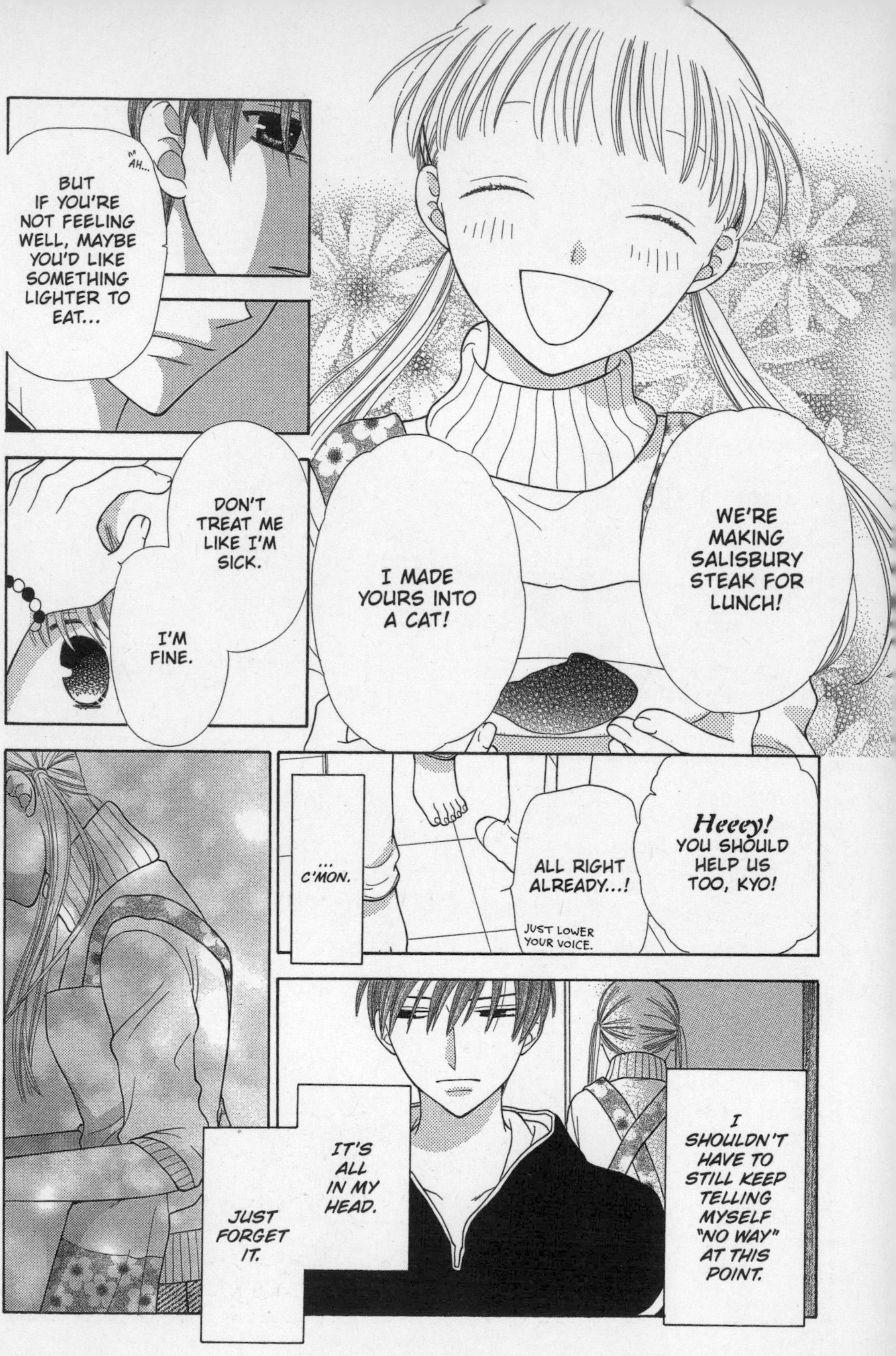
WE'RE MAKING SALISBURY STEAK FOR LUNCH!
I MADE YOURS INTO A CAT!
AH...
BUT IF YOU'RE NOT FEELING WELL, MAYBE YOU'D LIKE SOMETHING LIGHTER TO EAT...
DON'T TREAT ME LIKE I'M SICK.
I'M FINE.
Heeey! YOU SHOULD HELP US TOO, KYO!
ALL RIGHT ALREADY...!
JUST LOWER YOUR VOICE.
...C'MON.
I SHOULDN'T HAVE TO STILL KEEP TELLING MYSELF "NO WAY" AT THIS POINT.
IT'S ALL IN MY HEAD.
JUST FORGET IT.

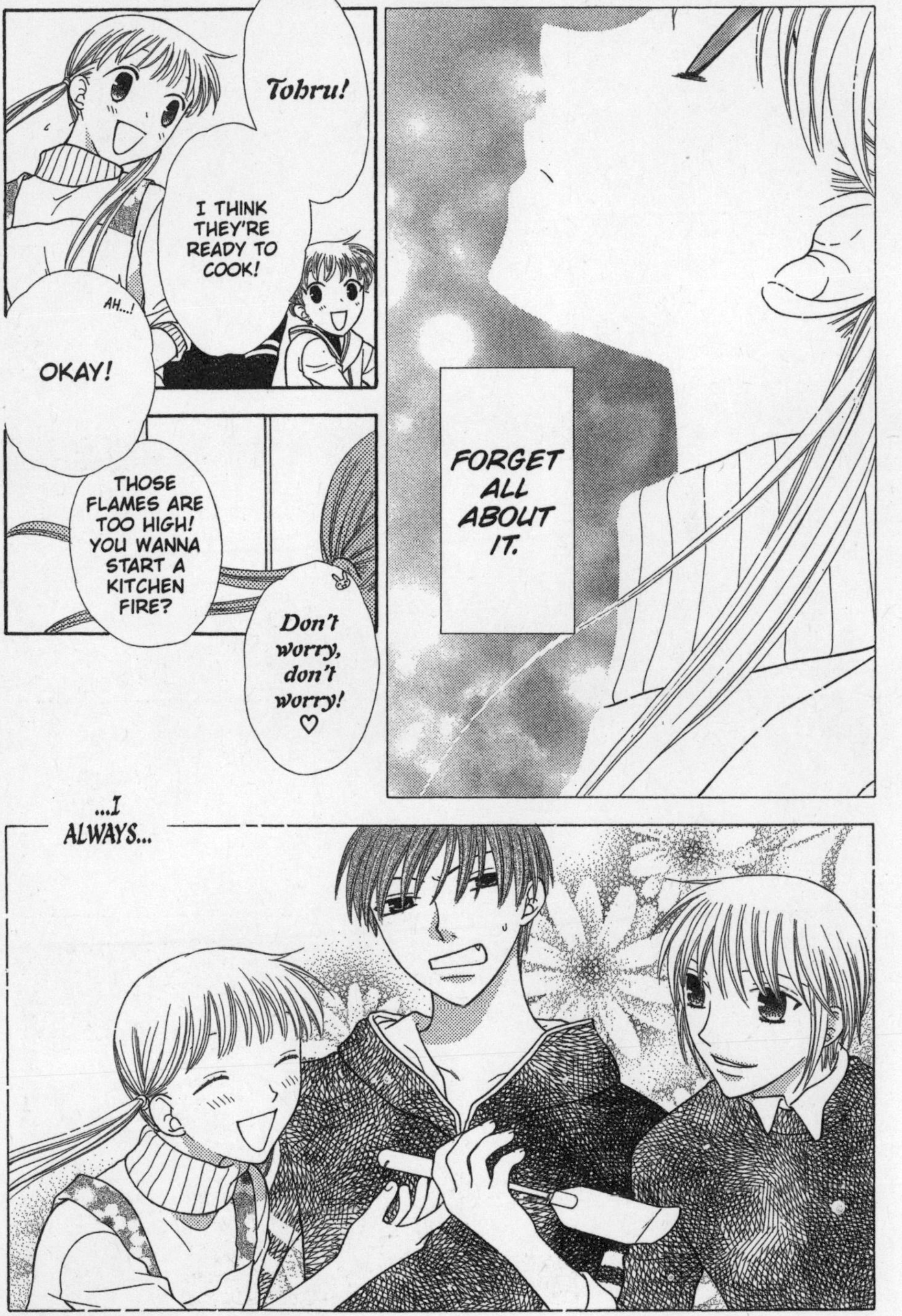
FORGET ALL ABOUT IT.
Tohru!
I THINK THEY'RE READY TO COOK!
AH...!
OKAY!
THOSE FLAMES ARE TOO HIGH! YOU WANNA START A KITCHEN FIRE?
Don't worry, don't worry! ♡
...I ALWAYS...

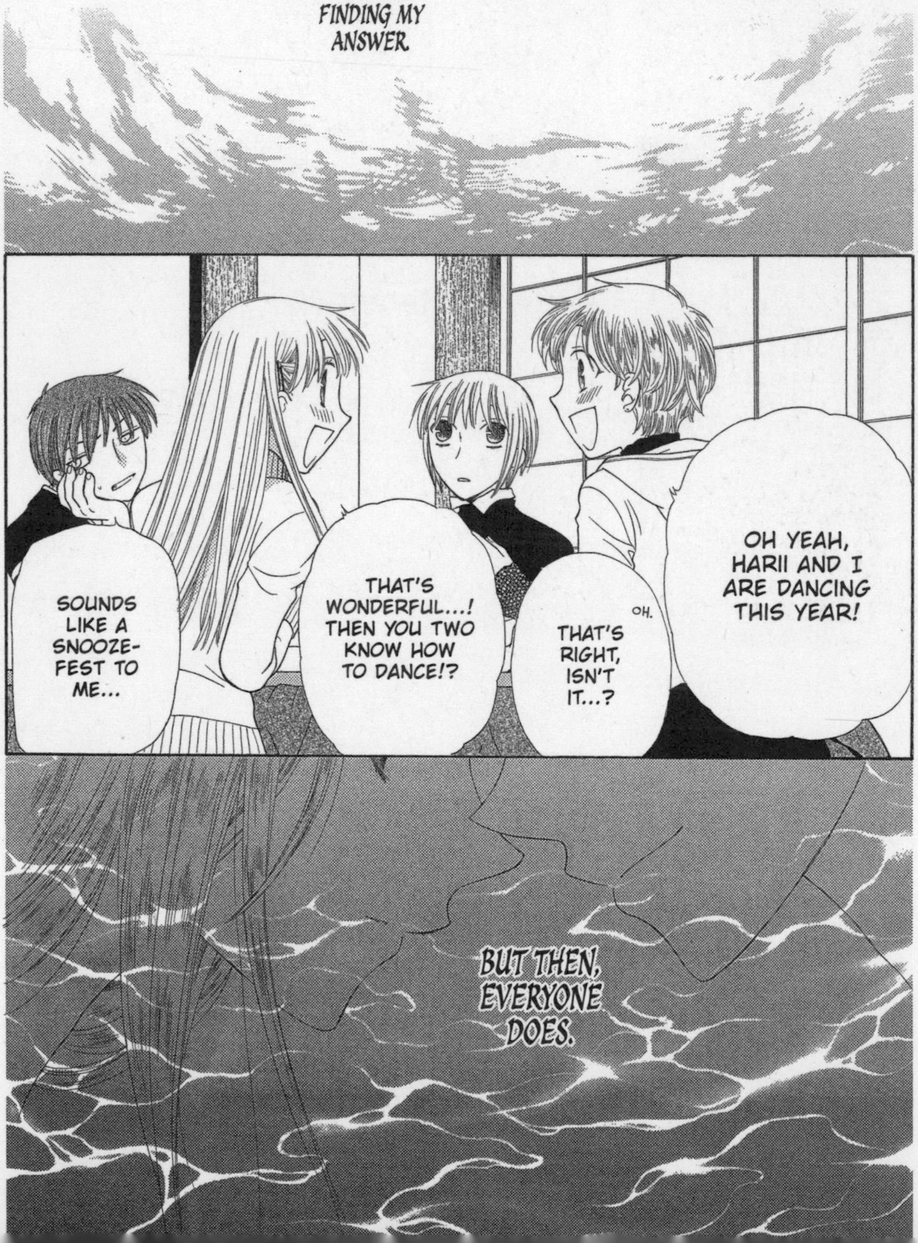
...HAVE TO LOSE MY WAY FIRST...
...BEFORE FINDING MY ANSWER.
OH YEAH, HARII AND I ARE DANCING THIS YEAR!
OH.
THAT'S RIGHT, ISN'T IT...?
THAT'S WONDERFUL...! THEN YOU TWO KNOW HOW TO DANCE!?
SOUNDS LIKE A SNOOZE-FEST TO ME...
BUT THEN, EVERYONE DOES.

Chapter 94

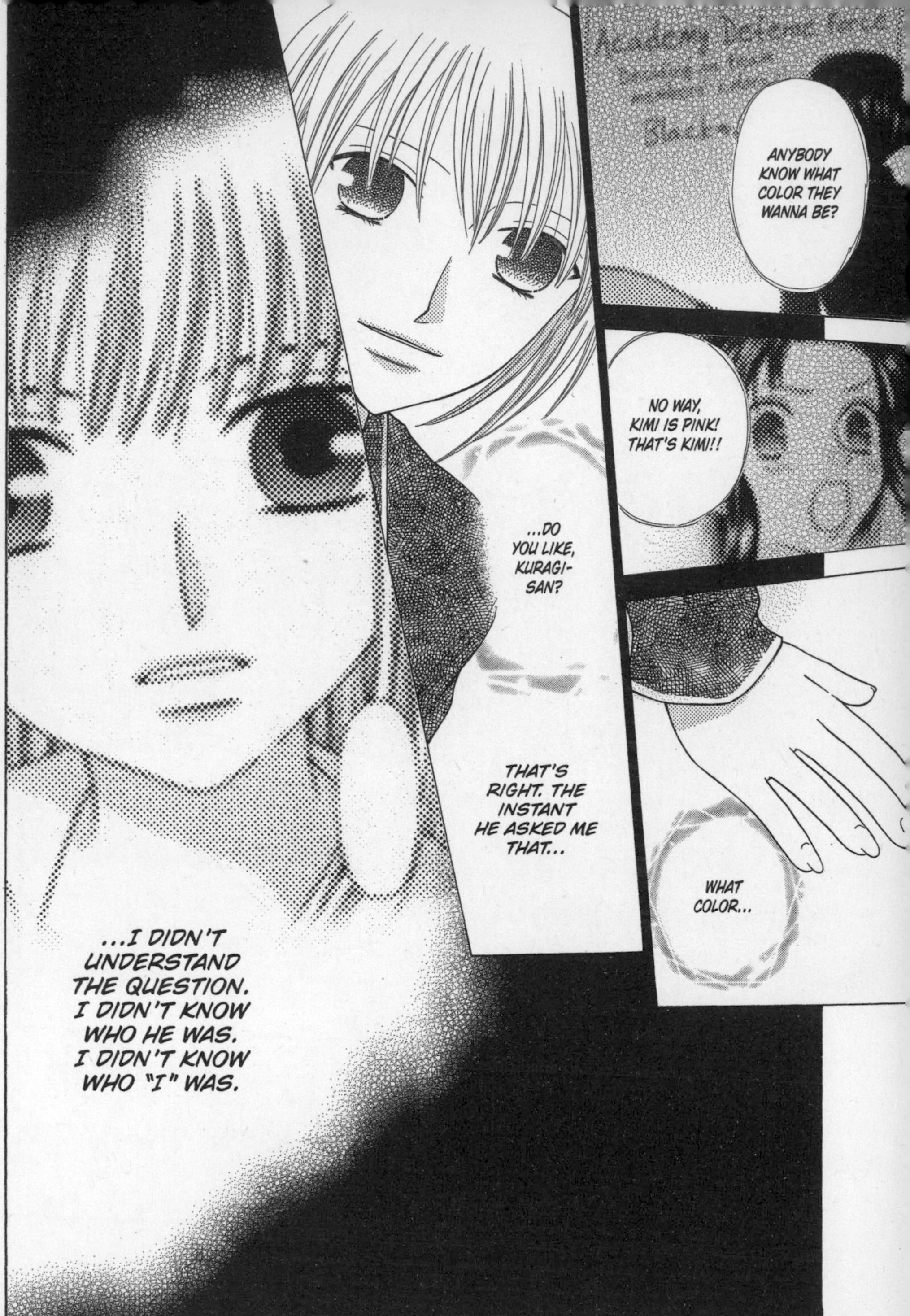
ANYBODY KNOW WHAT COLOR THEY WANNA BE?
NO WAY, KIMI IS PINK! THAT'S KIMI!!
WHAT COLOR...
...DO YOU LIKE, KURAGI-SAN?
THAT'S RIGHT. THE INSTANT HE ASKED ME THAT...
...I DIDN'T UNDERSTAND THE QUESTION. I DIDN'T KNOW WHO HE WAS. I DIDN'T KNOW WHO "I" WAS.

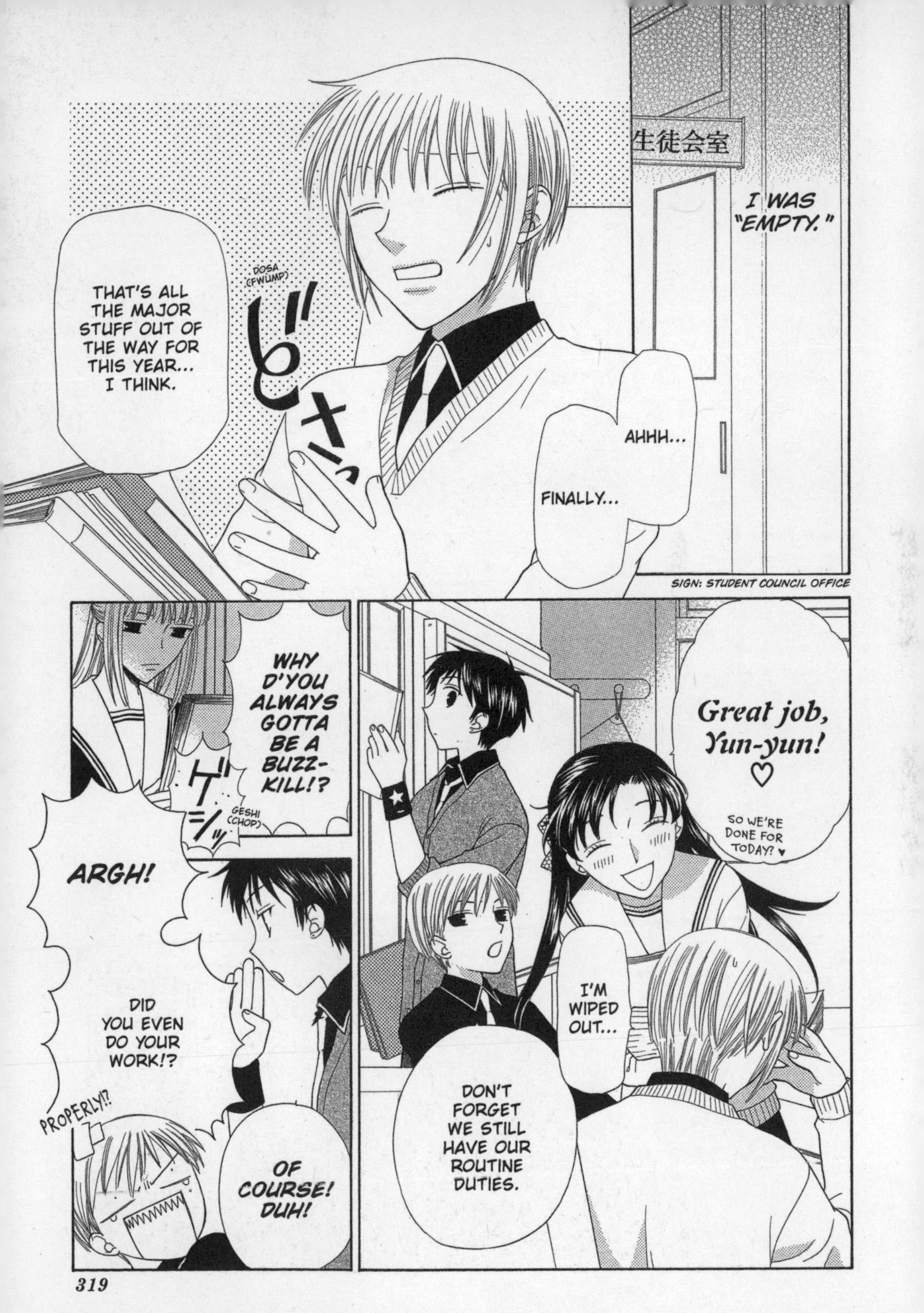
I WAS "EMPTY."
生徒会室
THAT'S ALL THE MAJOR STUFF OUT OF THE WAY FOR THIS YEAR... I THINK.
DOSA (FWUMP)
AHHH...
FINALLY...
SIGN: STUDENT COUNCIL OFFICE
Great job, Yun-yun! ♡
SO WE'RE DONE FOR TODAY? ♥
I'M WIPED OUT...
DON'T FORGET WE STILL HAVE OUR ROUTINE DUTIES.
WHY D'YOU ALWAYS GOTTA BE A BUZZ-KILL!?
GESHI (CHOP)
ARGH!
DID YOU EVEN DO YOUR WORK!?
PROPERLY!?
OF COURSE! DUH!

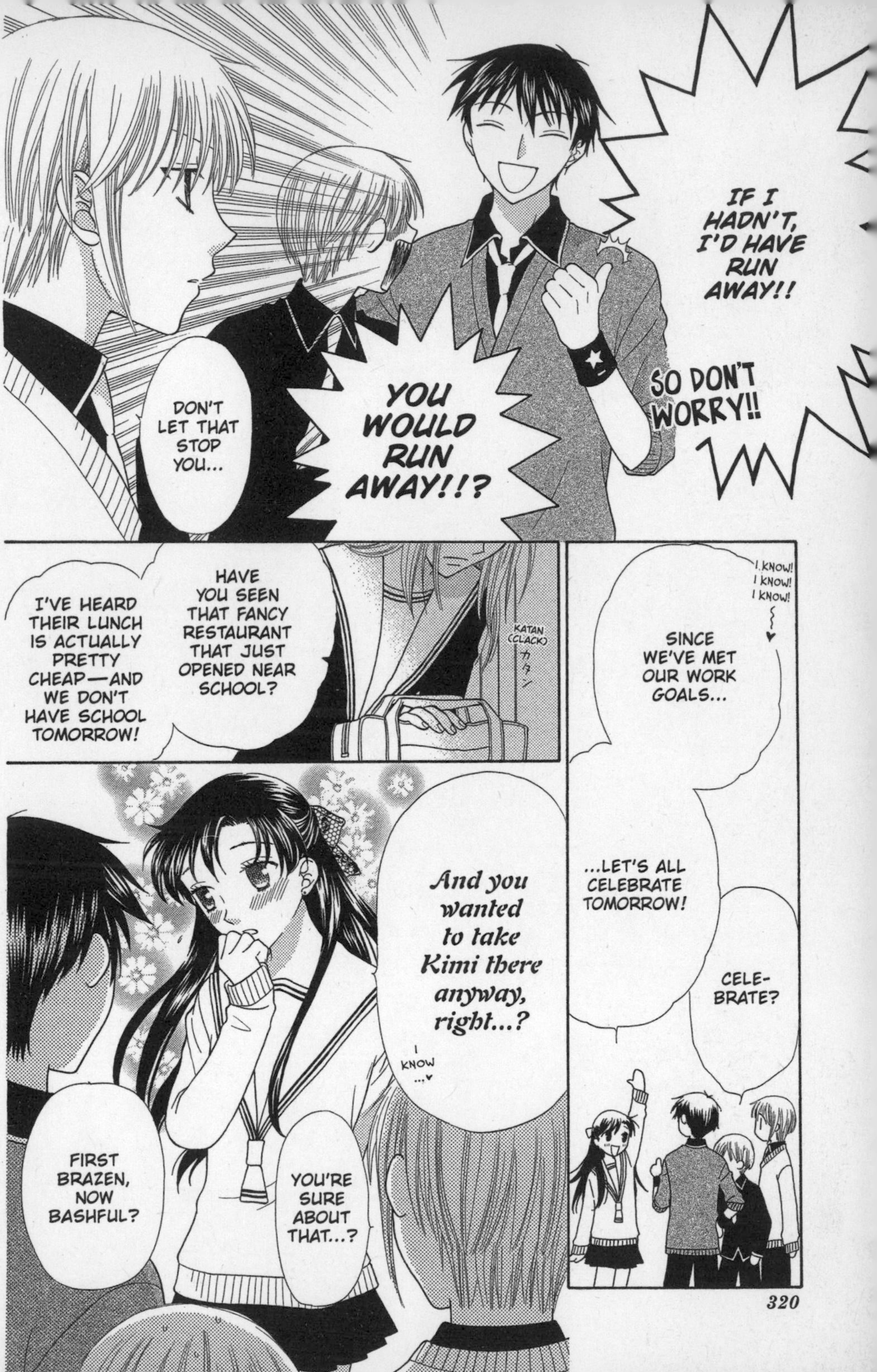

IF I HADN'T, I'D HAVE RUN AWAY!!
SO DON'T WORRY!!
YOU WOULD RUN AWAY!!?
DON'T LET THAT STOP YOU...
I KNOW! I KNOW! I KNOW!
SINCE WE'VE MET OUR WORK GOALS...
...LET'S ALL CELEBRATE TOMORROW!
CELE-BRATE?
KATAN (CLACK)
カタン
HAVE YOU SEEN THAT FANCY RESTAURANT THAT JUST OPENED NEAR SCHOOL?
I'VE HEARD THEIR LUNCH IS ACTUALLY PRETTY CHEAP—AND WE DON'T HAVE SCHOOL TOMORROW!
And you wanted to take Kimi there anyway, right...?
I KNOW...
YOU'RE SURE ABOUT THAT...?
FIRST BRAZEN, NOW BASHFUL?

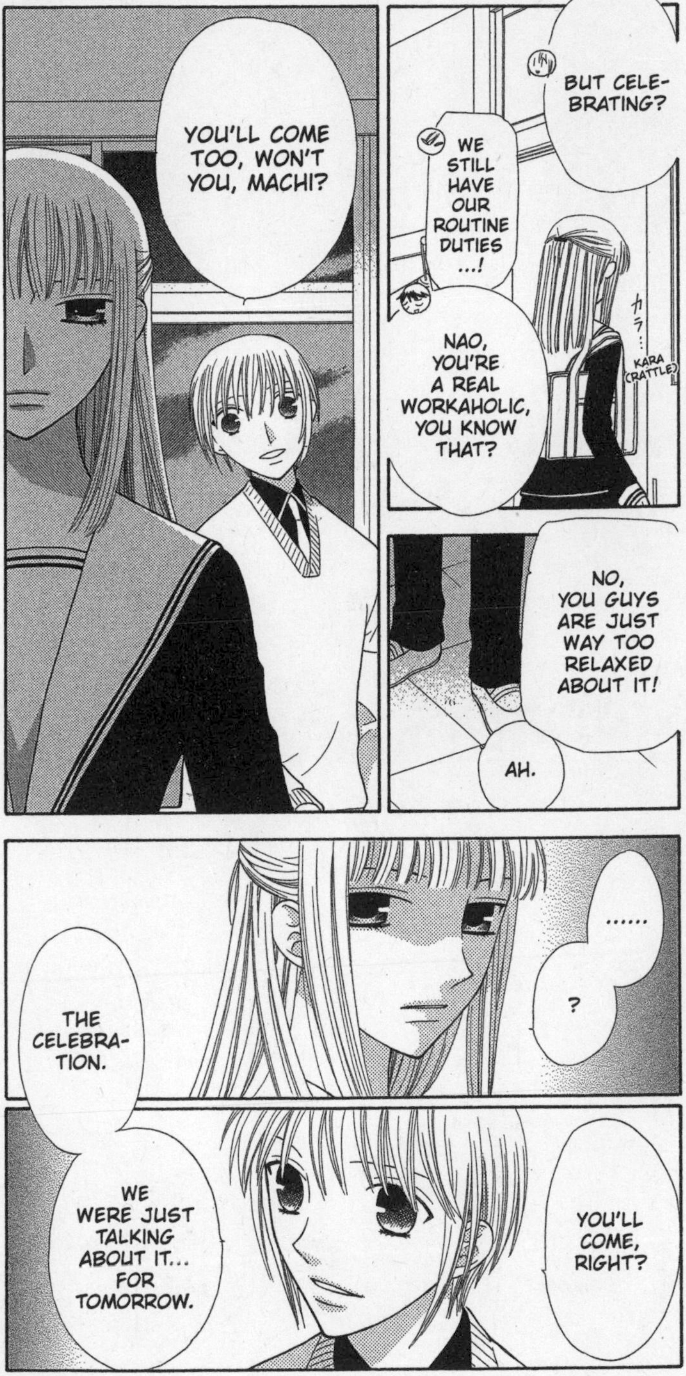
BUT CELE-BRATING?
WE STILL HAVE OUR ROUTINE DUTIES ...!
NAO, YOU'RE A REAL WORKAHOLIC, YOU KNOW THAT?
カラ…
KARA (RATTLE)
NO, YOU GUYS ARE JUST WAY TOO RELAXED ABOUT IT!
AH.
YOU'LL COME TOO, WON'T YOU, MACHI?
......
?
THE CELEBRA-TION.
WE WERE JUST TALKING ABOUT IT... FOR TOMORROW.
YOU'LL COME, RIGHT?
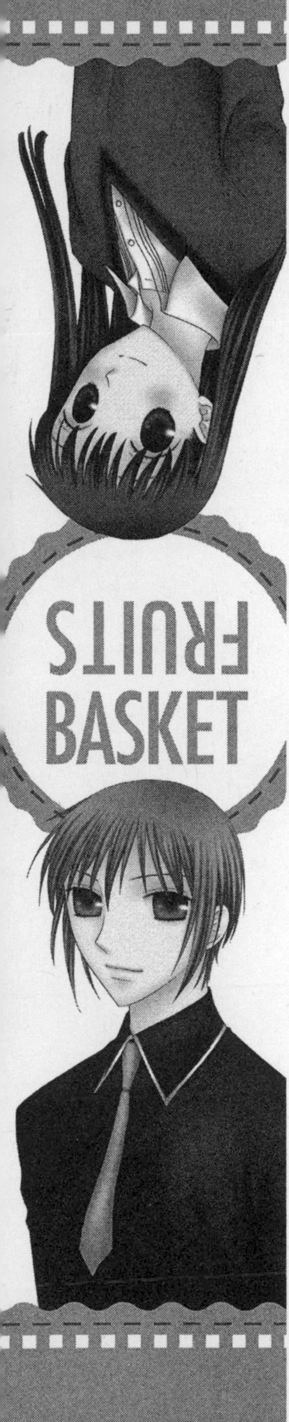
FRUITS
BASKET

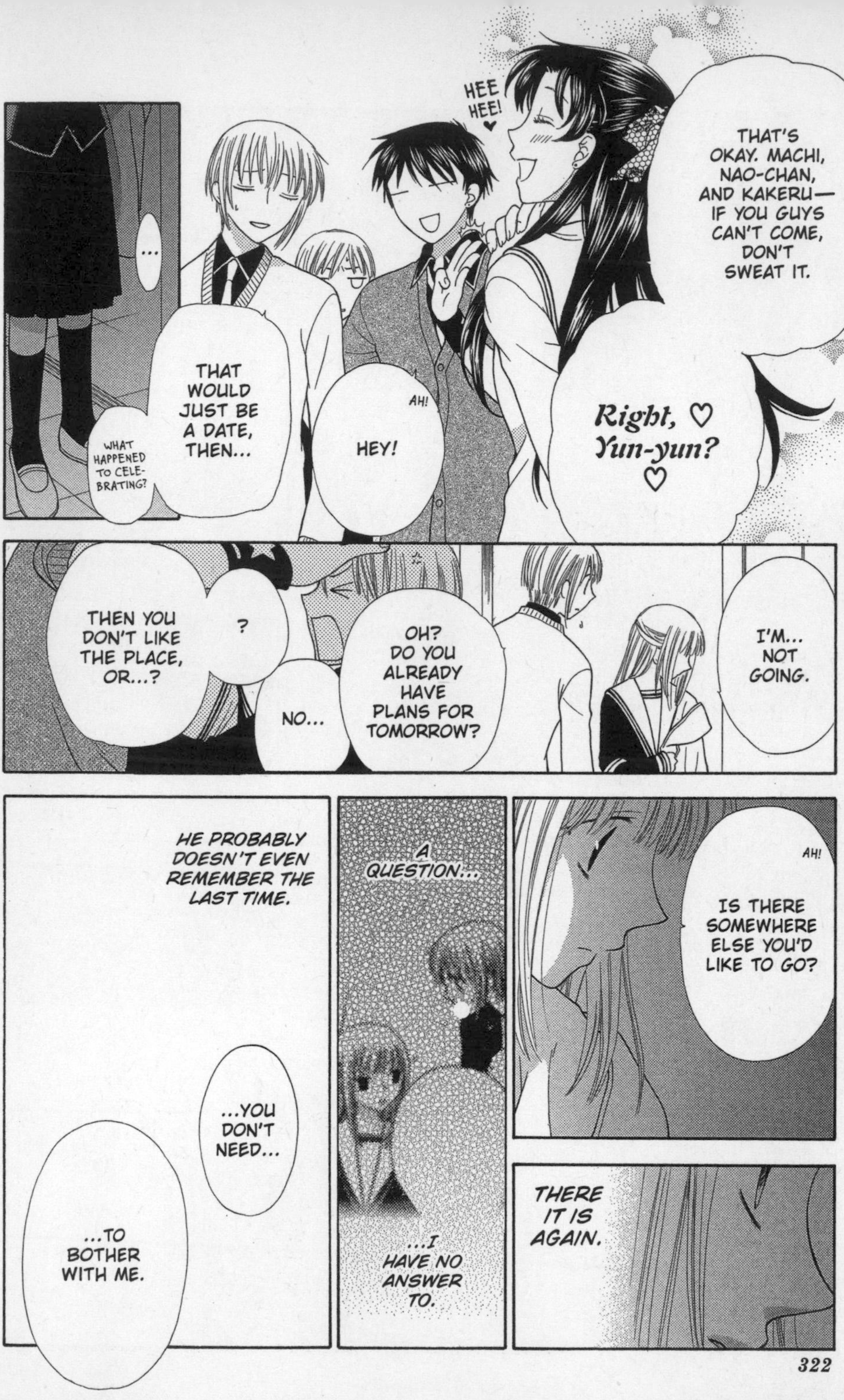
HEE HEE!
THAT'S OKAY. MACHI, NAO-CHAN, AND KAKERU— IF YOU GUYS CAN'T COME, DON'T SWEAT IT.
Right, ♡ Yun-yun? ♡
AH!
HEY!
THAT WOULD JUST BE A DATE, THEN...
...
WHAT HAPPENED TO CELE-BRATING?
I'M... NOT GOING.
OH? DO YOU ALREADY HAVE PLANS FOR TOMORROW?
NO...
?
THEN YOU DON'T LIKE THE PLACE, OR...?
AH!
IS THERE SOMEWHERE ELSE YOU'D LIKE TO GO?
THERE IT IS AGAIN.
A QUESTION...
...I HAVE NO ANSWER TO.
HE PROBABLY DOESN'T EVEN REMEMBER THE LAST TIME.
...YOU DON'T NEED...
...TO BOTHER WITH ME.

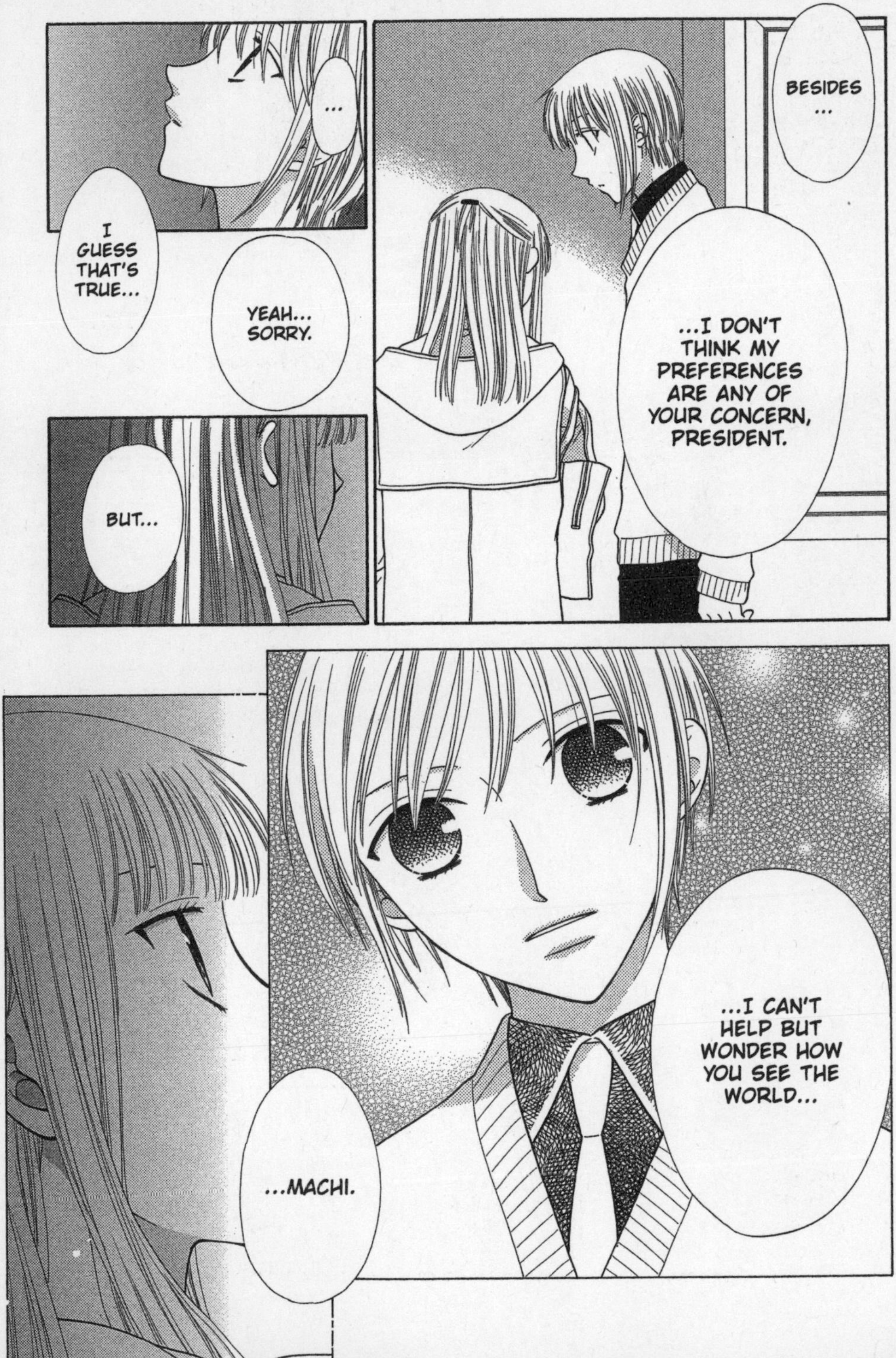
BESIDES ...
...I DON'T THINK MY PREFERENCES ARE ANY OF YOUR CONCERN, PRESIDENT.
...
I GUESS THAT'S TRUE...
YEAH... SORRY.
BUT...
...I CAN'T HELP BUT WONDER HOW YOU SEE THE WORLD...
...MACHI.

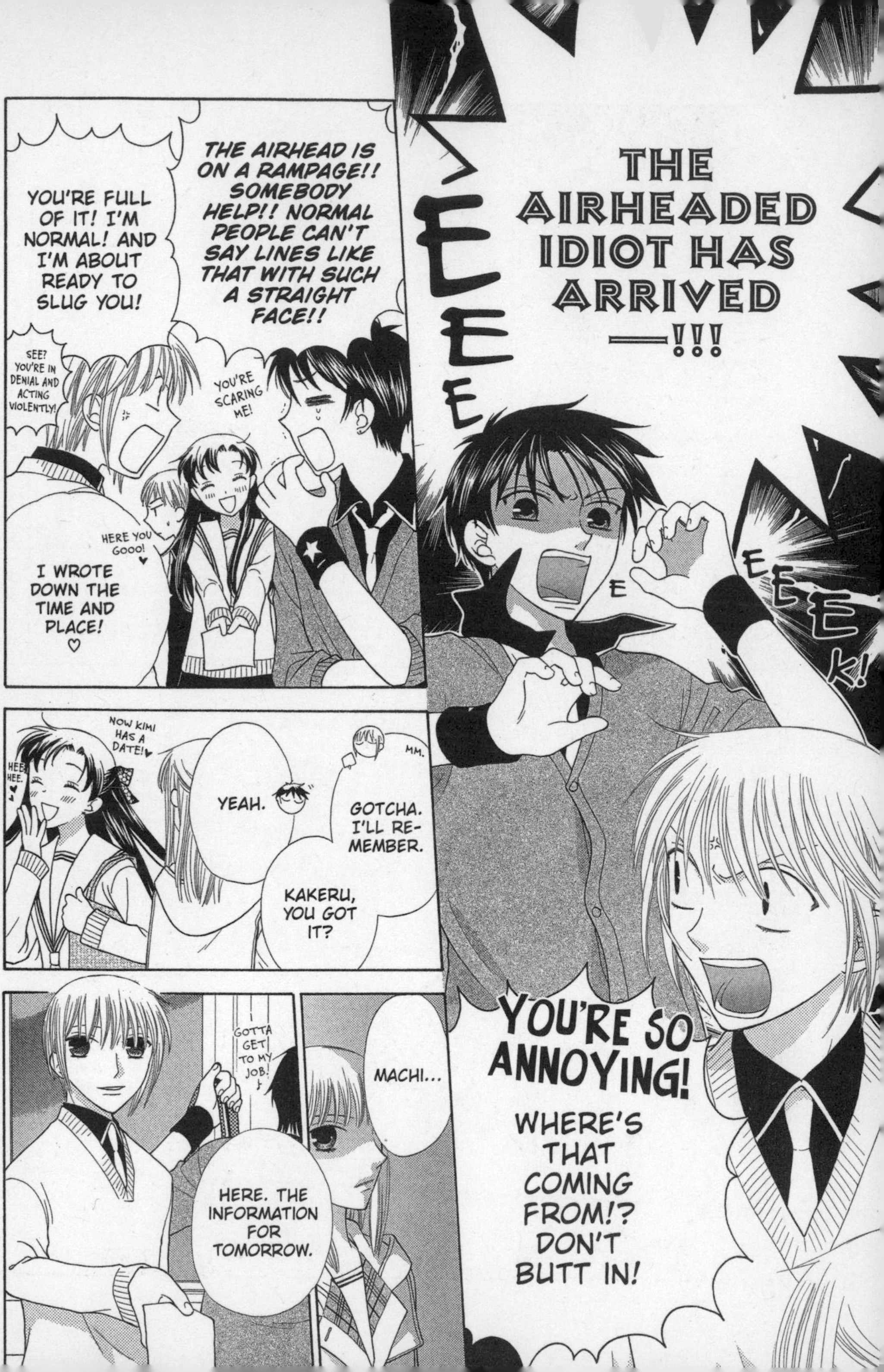
EEEE
THE AIRHEADED IDIOT HAS ARRIVED —!!!
E
EEEEK!
YOU'RE SO ANNOYING!
WHERE'S THAT COMING FROM!? DON'T BUTT IN!
THE AIRHEAD IS ON A RAMPAGE!! SOMEBODY HELP!! NORMAL PEOPLE CAN'T SAY LINES LIKE THAT WITH SUCH A STRAIGHT FACE!!
YOU'RE FULL OF IT! I'M NORMAL! AND I'M ABOUT READY TO SLUG YOU!
YOU'RE SCARING ME!
SEE? YOU'RE IN DENIAL AND ACTING VIOLENTLY!
HERE YOU GOOO! ♥
I WROTE DOWN THE TIME AND PLACE! ♡
MM.
GOTCHA. I'LL RE-MEMBER.
YEAH.
KAKERU, YOU GOT IT?
NOW KIMI HAS A DATE! ♥
HEE HEE.
MACHI...
HERE. THE INFORMATION FOR TOMORROW.
GOTTA GET TO MY JOB! ♪

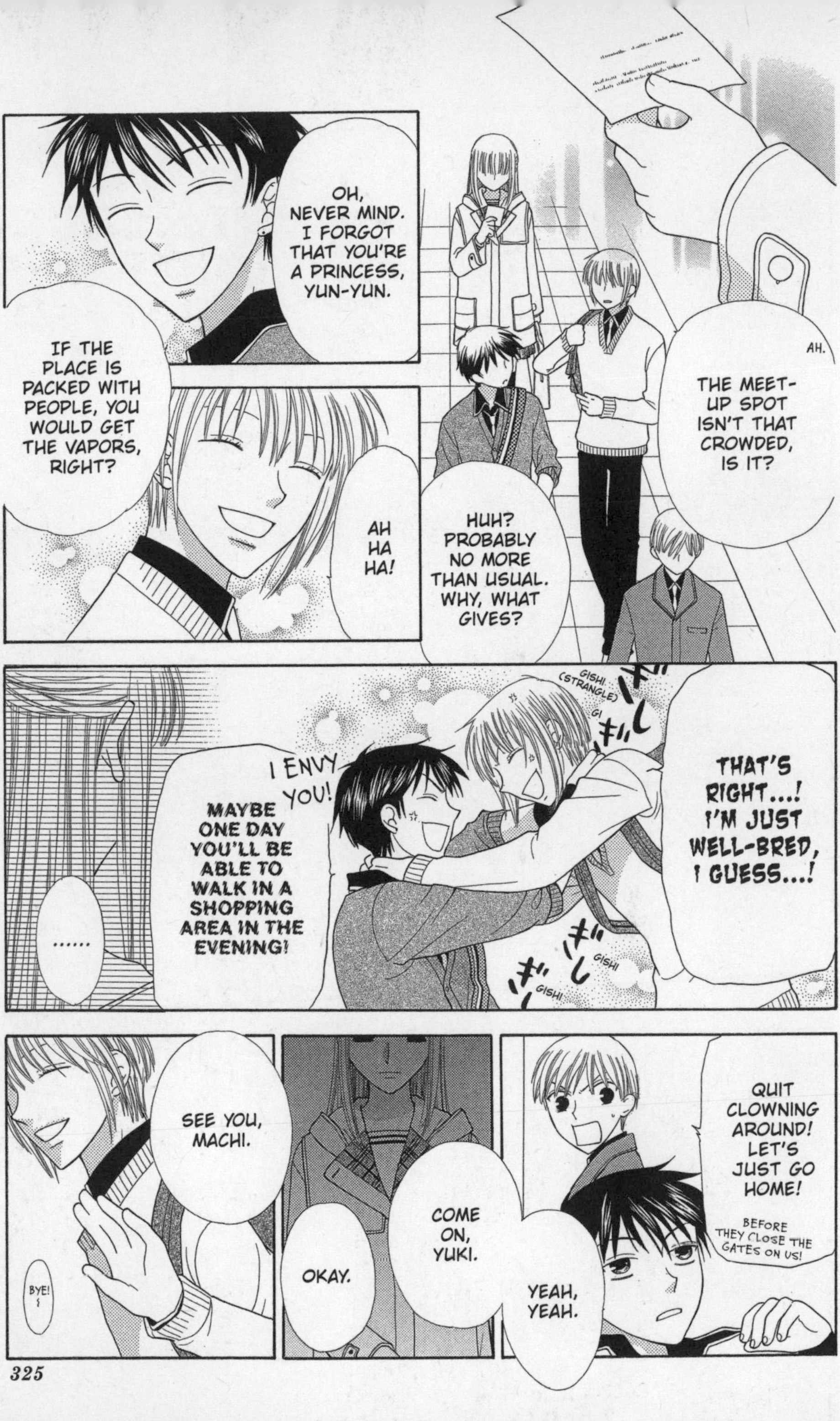
AH.
THE MEET-UP SPOT ISN'T THAT CROWDED, IS IT?
HUH? PROBABLY NO MORE THAN USUAL. WHY, WHAT GIVES?
OH, NEVER MIND. I FORGOT THAT YOU'RE A PRINCESS, YUN-YUN.
IF THE PLACE IS PACKED WITH PEOPLE, YOU WOULD GET THE VAPORS, RIGHT?
AH HA HA!
THAT'S RIGHT...! I'M JUST WELL-BRED, I GUESS...!
GISHI (STRANGLE)
GI!
GISHI
GISHI
I ENVY YOU!
MAYBE ONE DAY YOU'LL BE ABLE TO WALK IN A SHOPPING AREA IN THE EVENING!
......
QUIT CLOWNING AROUND! LET'S JUST GO HOME!
BEFORE THEY CLOSE THE GATES ON US!
YEAH, YEAH.
COME ON, YUKI.
OKAY.
SEE YOU, MACHI.
BYE!

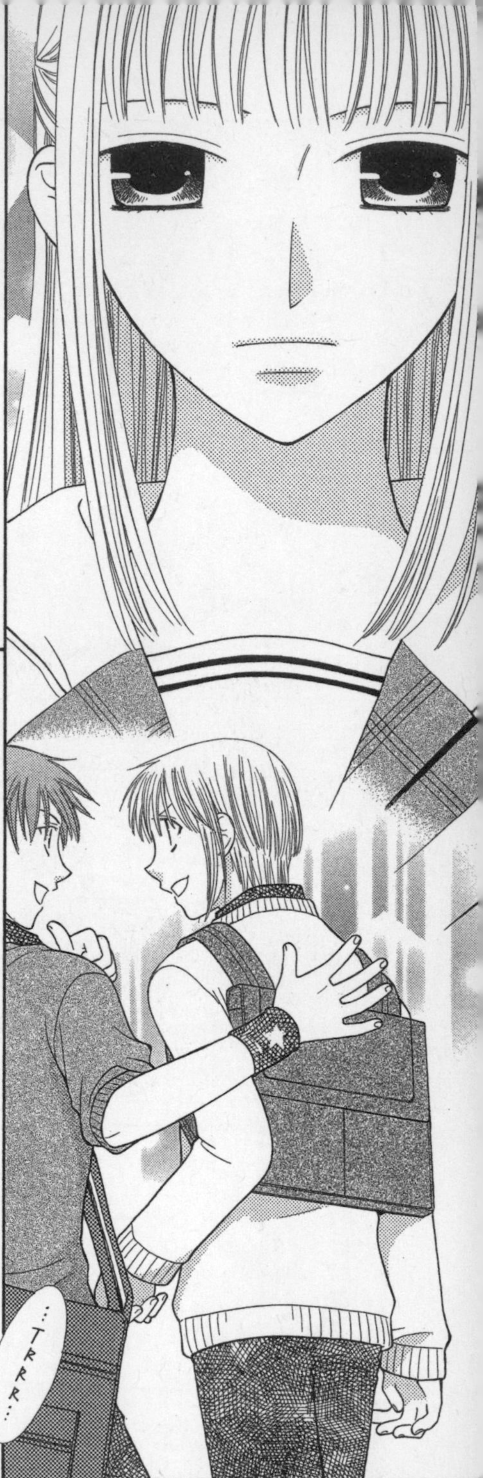
...TRRR...

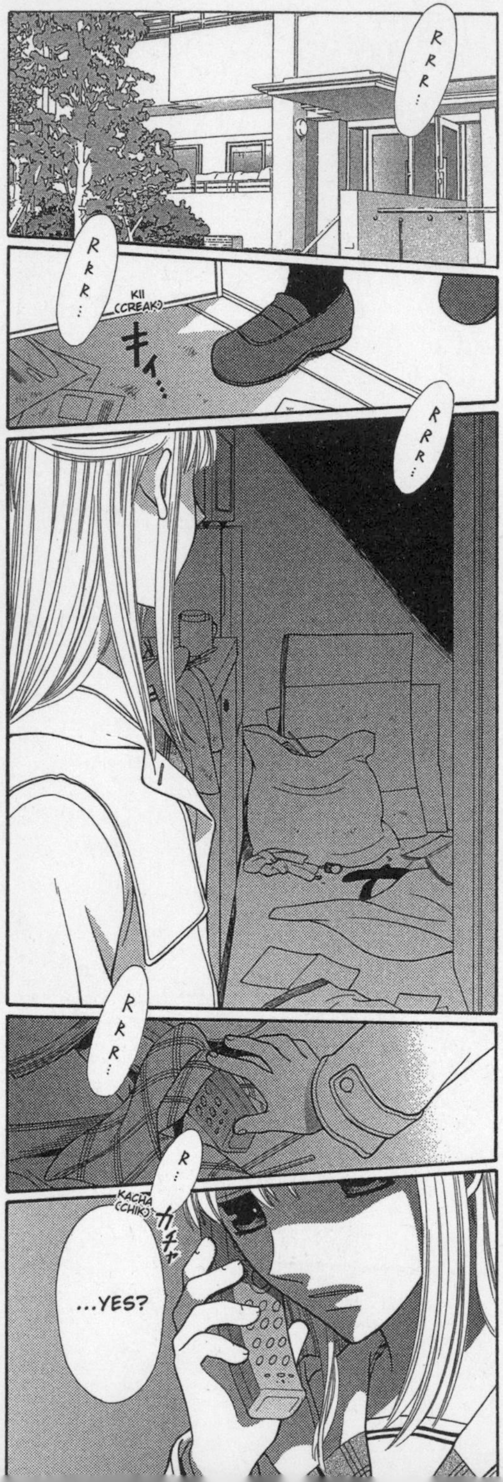
RRR...
RRR...
KII (CREAK)
キィ...
RRR...
RRR...
R...
KACHA (CHIK)
カチャ
...YES?

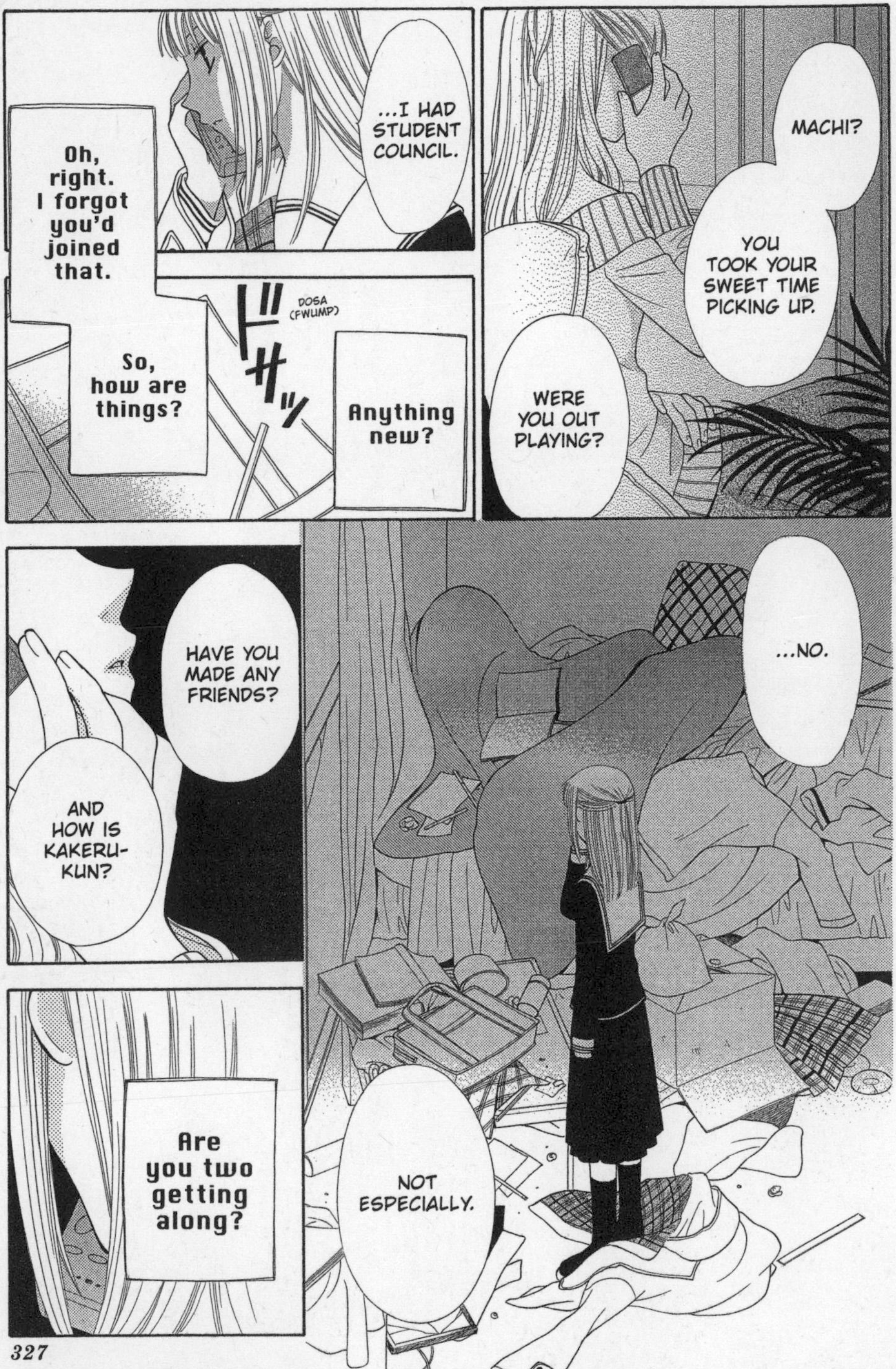
MACHI?
YOU TOOK YOUR SWEET TIME PICKING UP.
WERE YOU OUT PLAYING?
...I HAD STUDENT COUNCIL.
Oh, right. I forgot you'd joined that.
So, how are things?
ドサッ
DOSA (FWUMP)
Anything new?
...NO.
NOT ESPECIALLY.
HAVE YOU MADE ANY FRIENDS?
AND HOW IS KAKERU-KUN?
Are you two getting along?

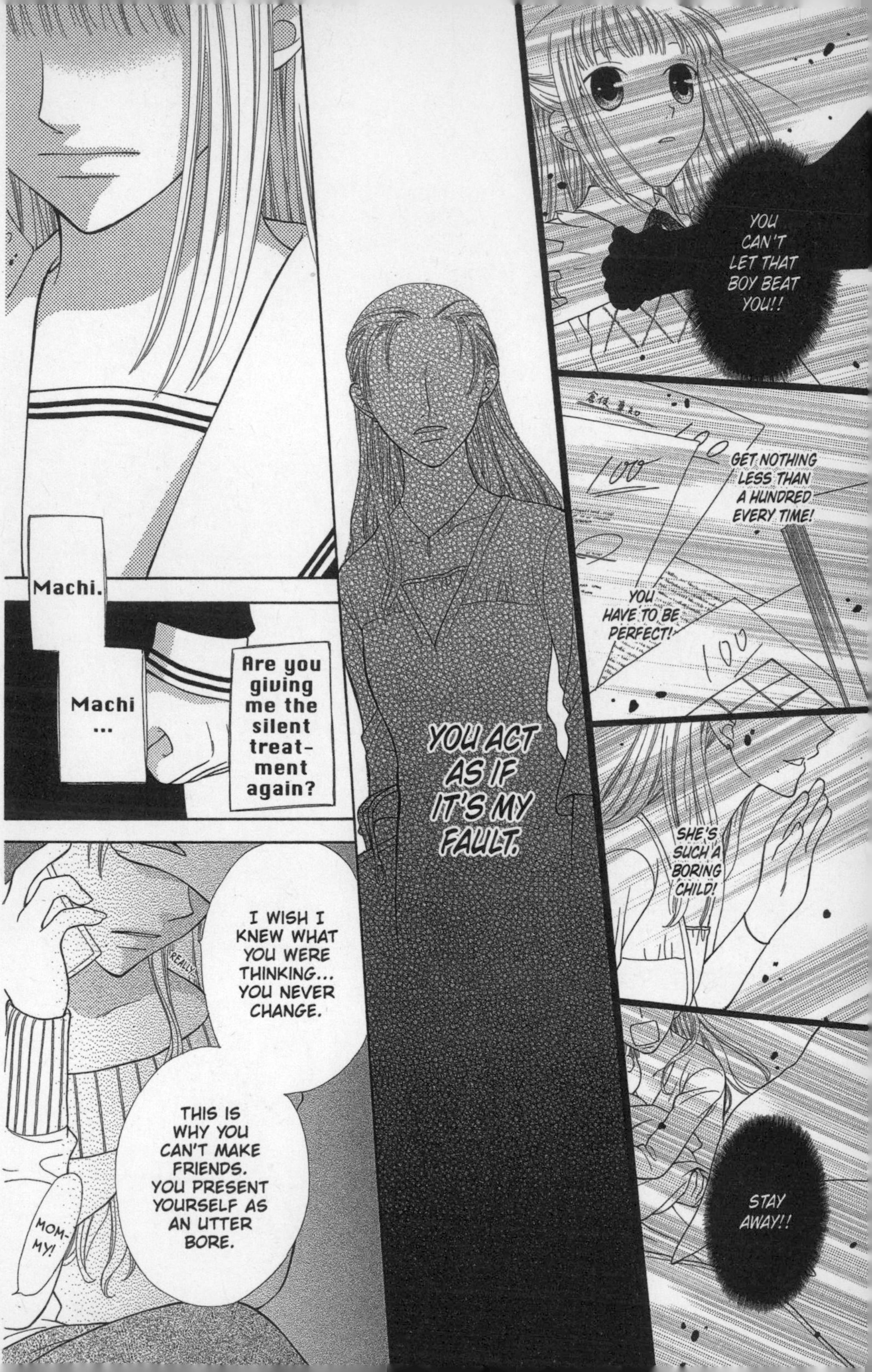
YOU CAN'T LET THAT BOY BEAT YOU!!
GET NOTHING LESS THAN A HUNDRED EVERY TIME!
YOU HAVE TO BE PERFECT!
SHE'S SUCH A BORING CHILD!
STAY AWAY!!
YOU ACT AS IF IT'S MY FAULT.
Machi.
Machi...
Are you giving me the silent treatment again?
I WISH I KNEW WHAT YOU WERE THINKING... YOU NEVER CHANGE.
REALLY
THIS IS WHY YOU CAN'T MAKE FRIENDS. YOU PRESENT YOURSELF AS AN UTTER BORE.
MOMMY!

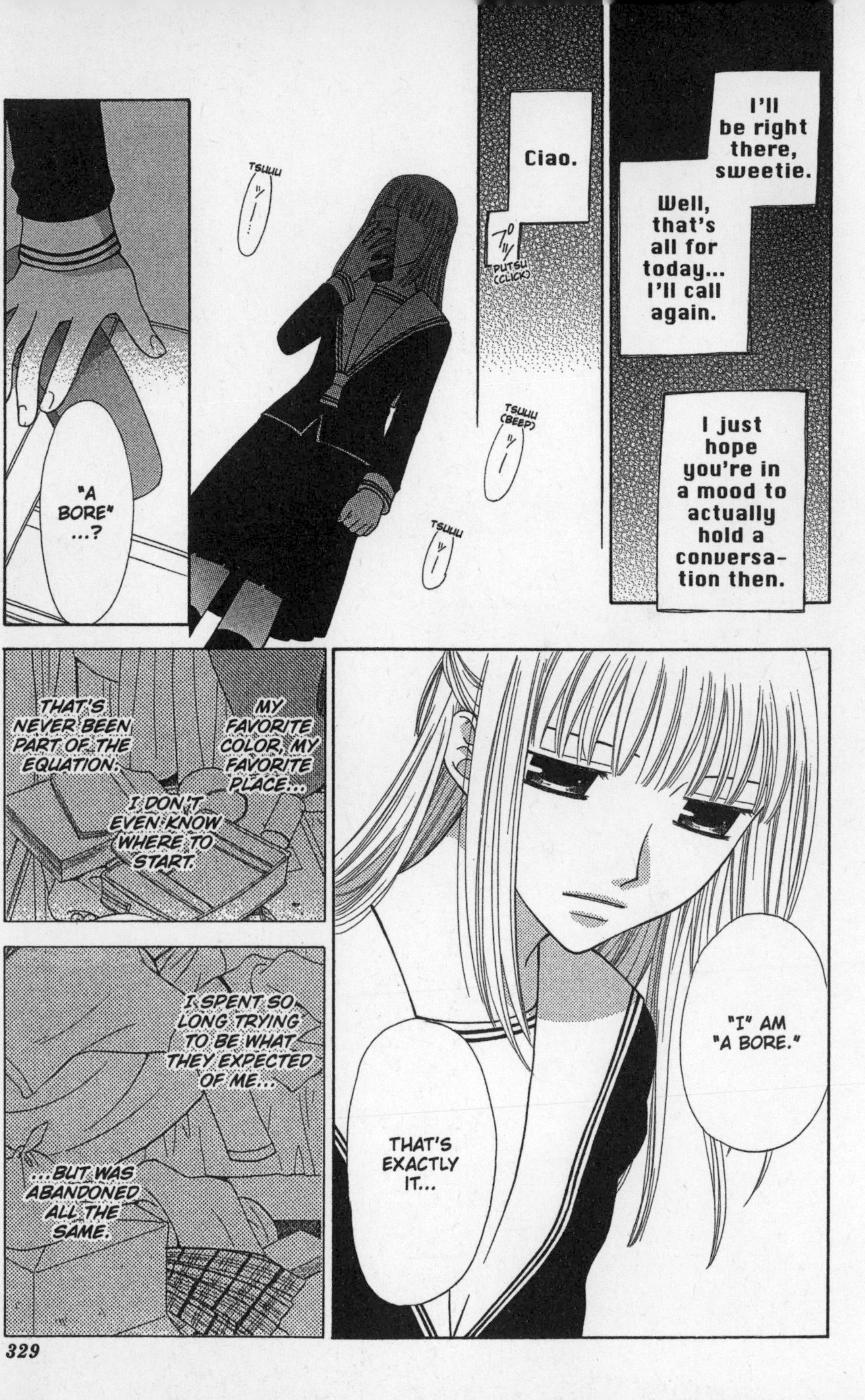
I'll be right there, sweetie.
Well, that's all for today... I'll call again.
I just hope you're in a mood to actually hold a conversation then.
Ciao.
PUTSU (CLICK)
TSUUU (BEEP)
TSUUU
TSUUU
"A BORE" ...?
"I" AM "A BORE."
THAT'S EXACTLY IT...
MY FAVORITE COLOR, MY FAVORITE PLACE...
THAT'S NEVER BEEN PART OF THE EQUATION.
I DON'T EVEN KNOW WHERE TO START.
I SPENT SO LONG TRYING TO BE WHAT THEY EXPECTED OF ME...
...BUT WAS ABANDONED ALL THE SAME.

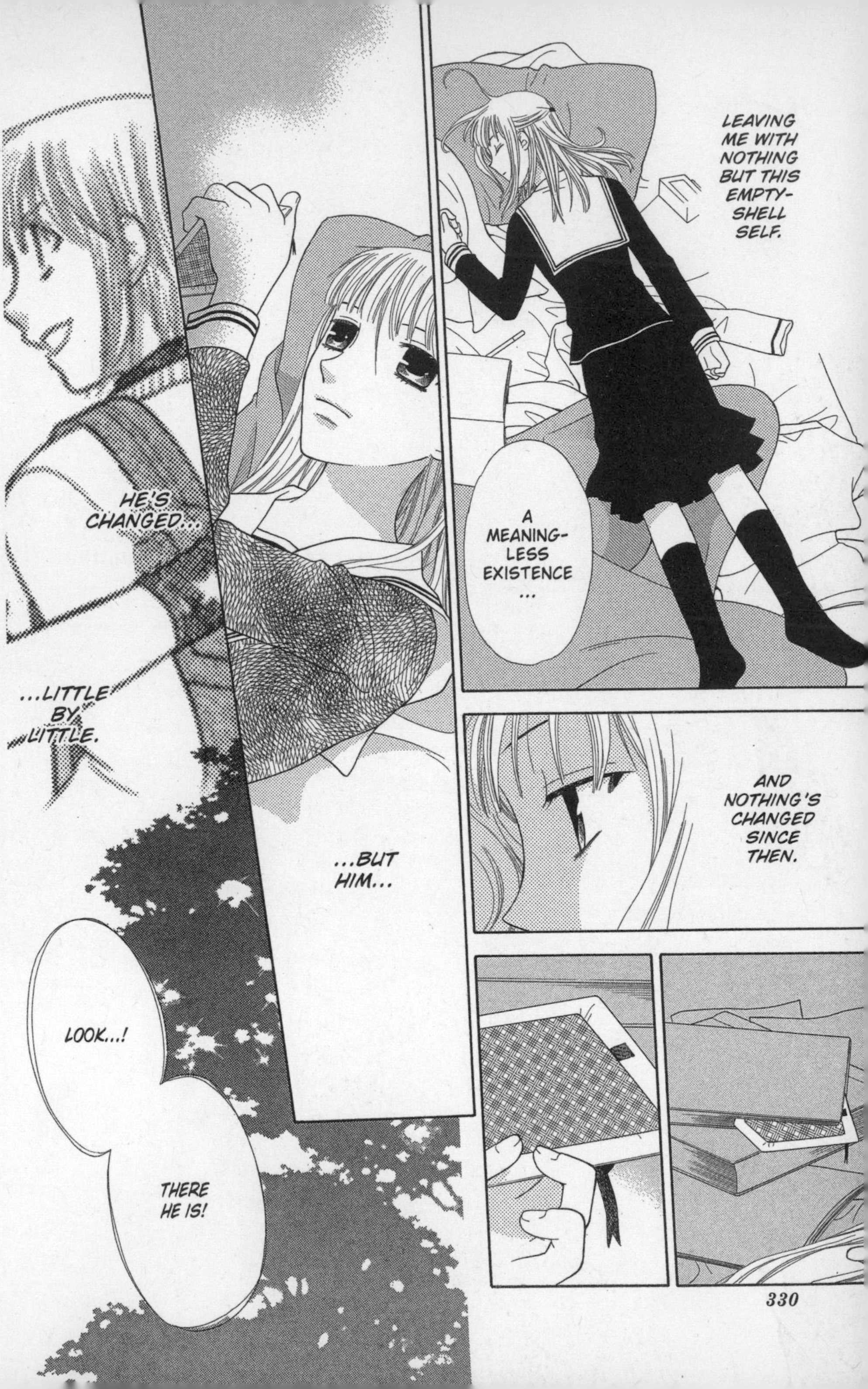
LEAVING ME WITH NOTHING BUT THIS EMPTY-SHELL SELF.
A MEANING-LESS EXISTENCE ...
AND NOTHING'S CHANGED SINCE THEN.
...BUT HIM...
HE'S CHANGED...
...LITTLE BY LITTLE.
LOOK...!
THERE HE IS!

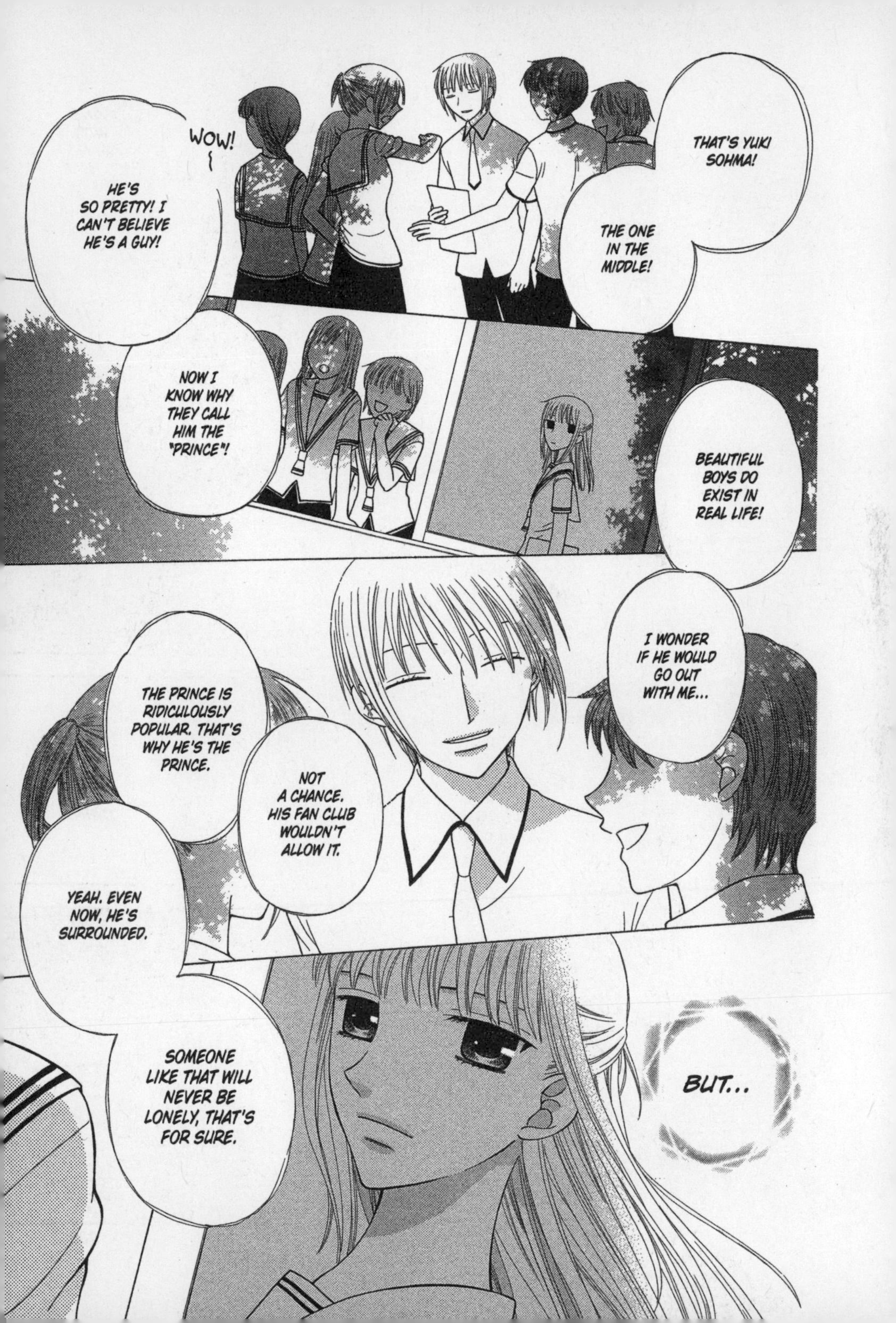
THAT'S YUKI SOHMA!
THE ONE IN THE MIDDLE!
WOW!
HE'S SO PRETTY! I CAN'T BELIEVE HE'S A GUY!
BEAUTIFUL BOYS DO EXIST IN REAL LIFE!
NOW I KNOW WHY THEY CALL HIM THE "PRINCE"!
I WONDER IF HE WOULD GO OUT WITH ME...
NOT A CHANCE. HIS FAN CLUB WOULDN'T ALLOW IT.
THE PRINCE IS RIDICULOUSLY POPULAR. THAT'S WHY HE'S THE PRINCE.
YEAH. EVEN NOW, HE'S SURROUNDED.
SOMEONE LIKE THAT WILL NEVER BE LONELY, THAT'S FOR SURE.
BUT...

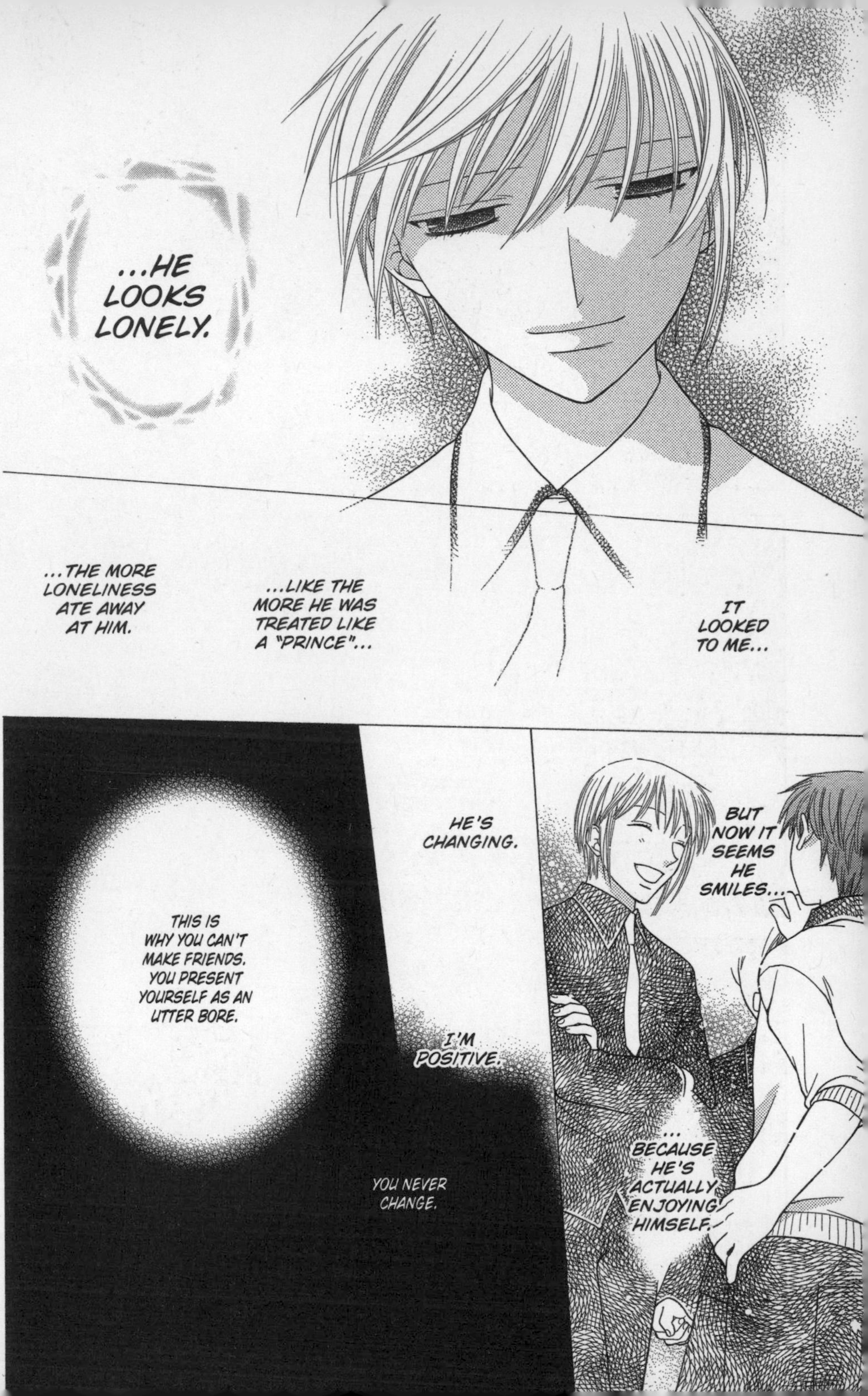
...HE LOOKS LONELY.
IT LOOKED TO ME...
...LIKE THE MORE HE WAS TREATED LIKE A "PRINCE"...
...THE MORE LONELINESS ATE AWAY AT HIM.
BUT NOW IT SEEMS HE SMILES...
...BECAUSE HE'S ACTUALLY ENJOYING HIMSELF.
HE'S CHANGING.
I'M POSITIVE.
THIS IS WHY YOU CAN'T MAKE FRIENDS. YOU PRESENT YOURSELF AS AN UTTER BORE.
YOU NEVER CHANGE.

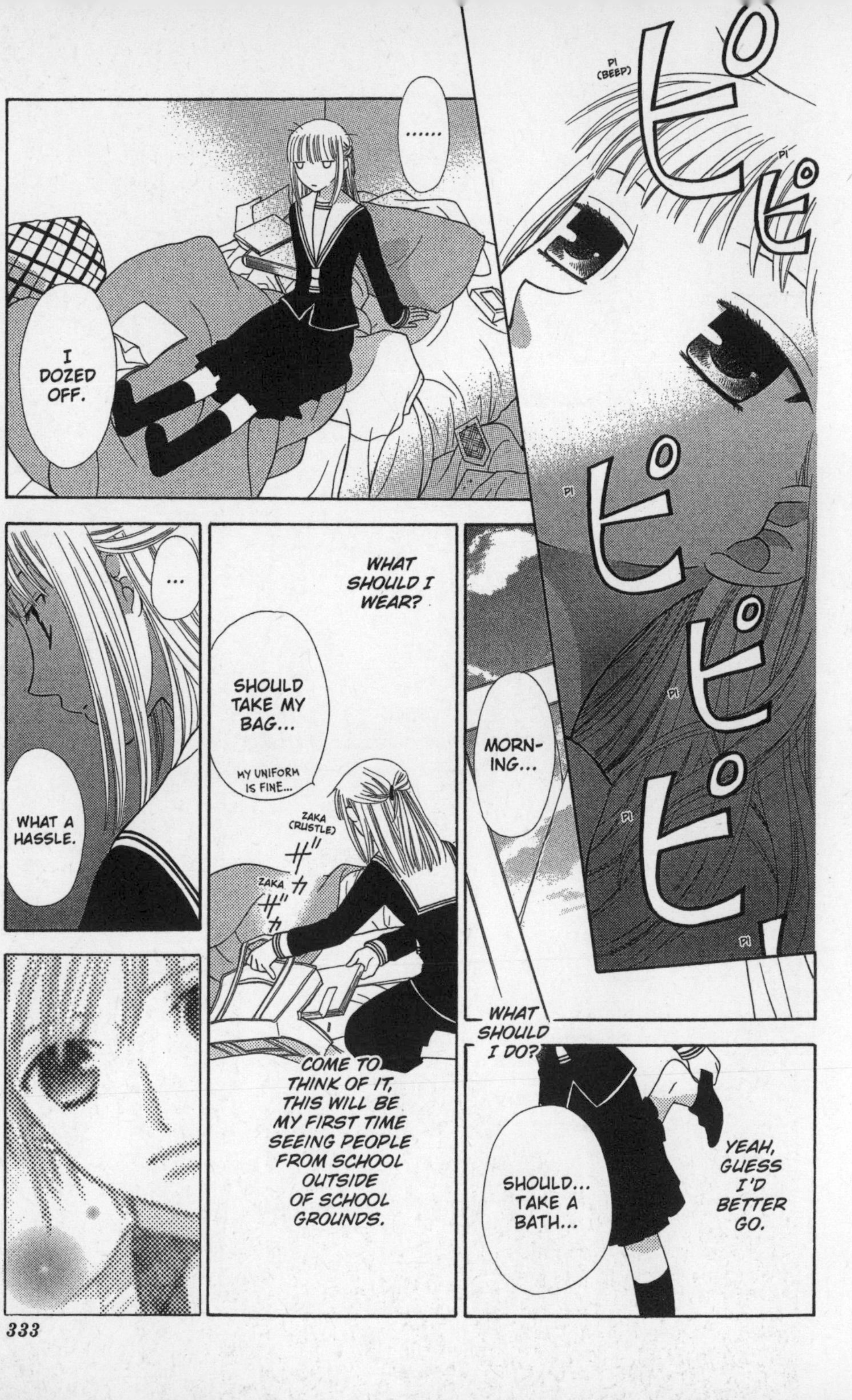
PI (BEEP)
PI
PI
PI
PI
PI
......
I DOZED OFF.
MORNING...
WHAT SHOULD I WEAR?
SHOULD TAKE MY BAG...
MY UNIFORM IS FINE...
ZAKA (RUSTLE)
ZAKA
COME TO THINK OF IT, THIS WILL BE MY FIRST TIME SEEING PEOPLE FROM SCHOOL OUTSIDE OF SCHOOL GROUNDS.
...
WHAT A HASSLE.
WHAT SHOULD I DO?
SHOULD... TAKE A BATH...
YEAH, GUESS I'D BETTER GO.

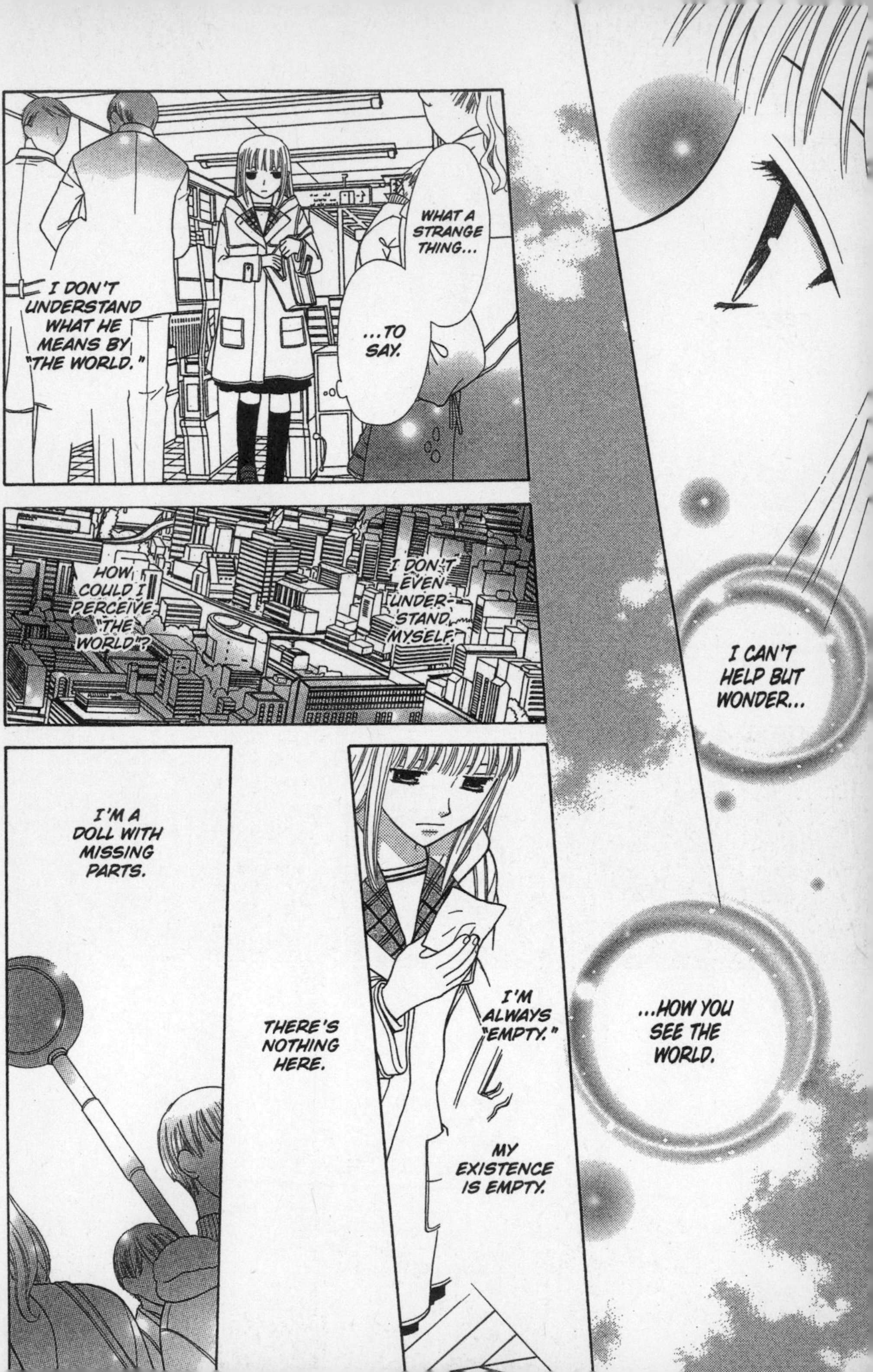
I CAN'T HELP BUT WONDER...
...HOW YOU SEE THE WORLD.
WHAT A STRANGE THING...
...TO SAY.
I DON'T UNDERSTAND WHAT HE MEANS BY "THE WORLD."
I DON'T EVEN UNDERSTAND MYSELF.
HOW COULD I PERCEIVE "THE WORLD"?
I'M ALWAYS "EMPTY."
MY EXISTENCE IS EMPTY.
THERE'S NOTHING HERE.
I'M A DOLL WITH MISSING PARTS.

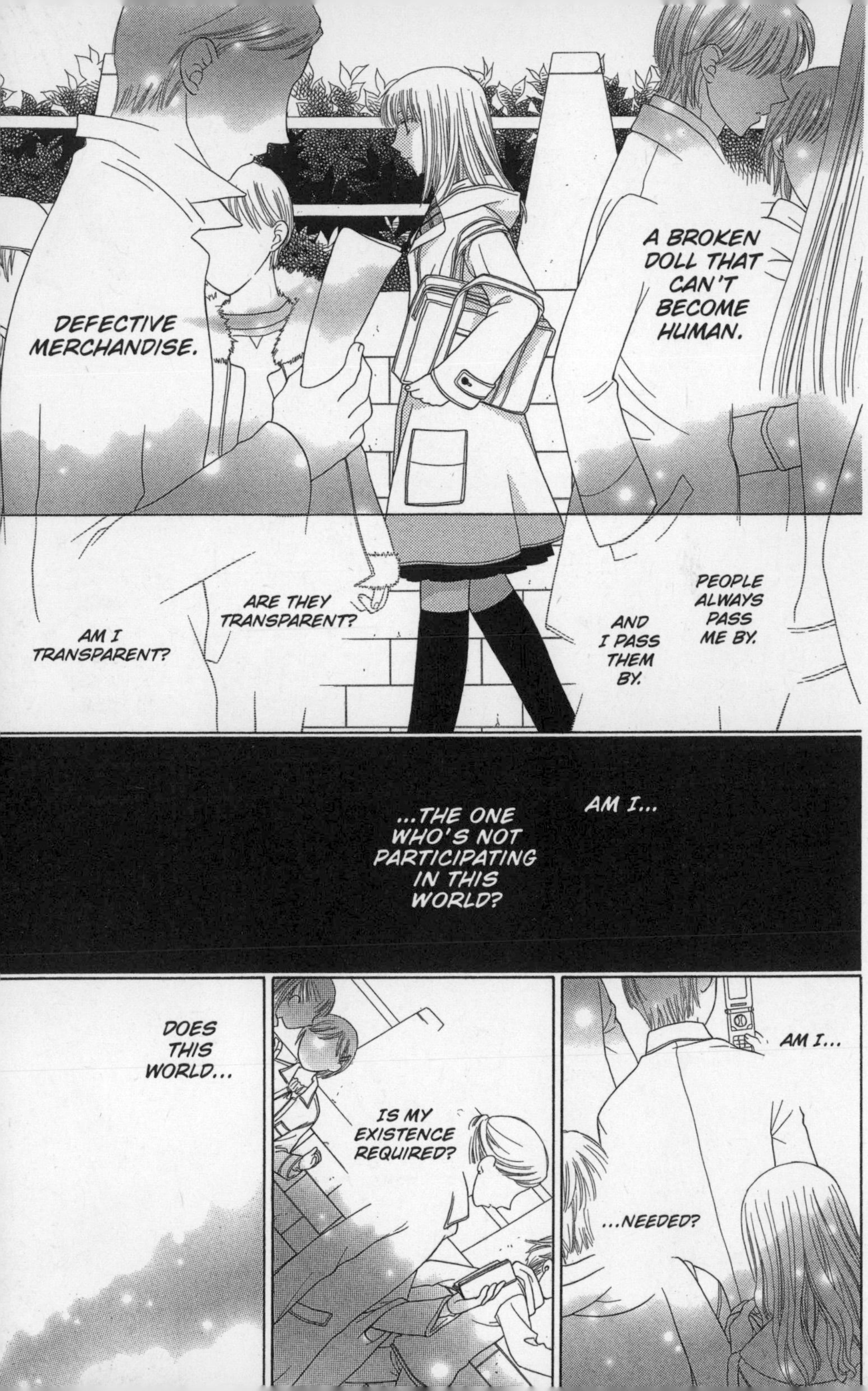
A BROKEN DOLL THAT CAN'T BECOME HUMAN.
DEFECTIVE MERCHANDISE.
PEOPLE ALWAYS PASS ME BY.
AND I PASS THEM BY.
ARE THEY TRANSPARENT?
AM I TRANSPARENT?
AM I...
...THE ONE WHO'S NOT PARTICIPATING IN THIS WORLD?
AM I...
...NEEDED?
IS MY EXISTENCE REQUIRED?
DOES THIS WORLD...

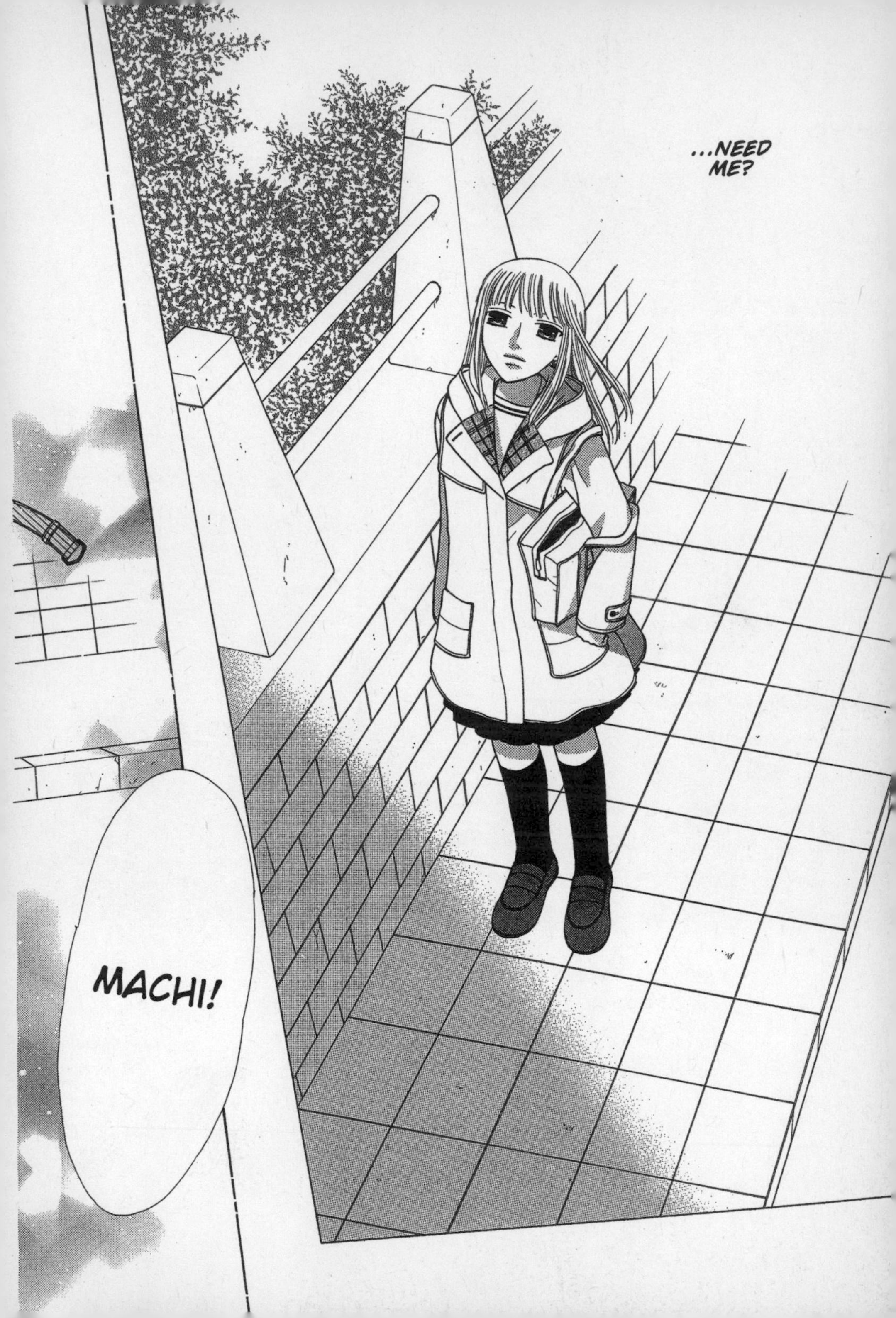
...NEED ME?
MACHI!

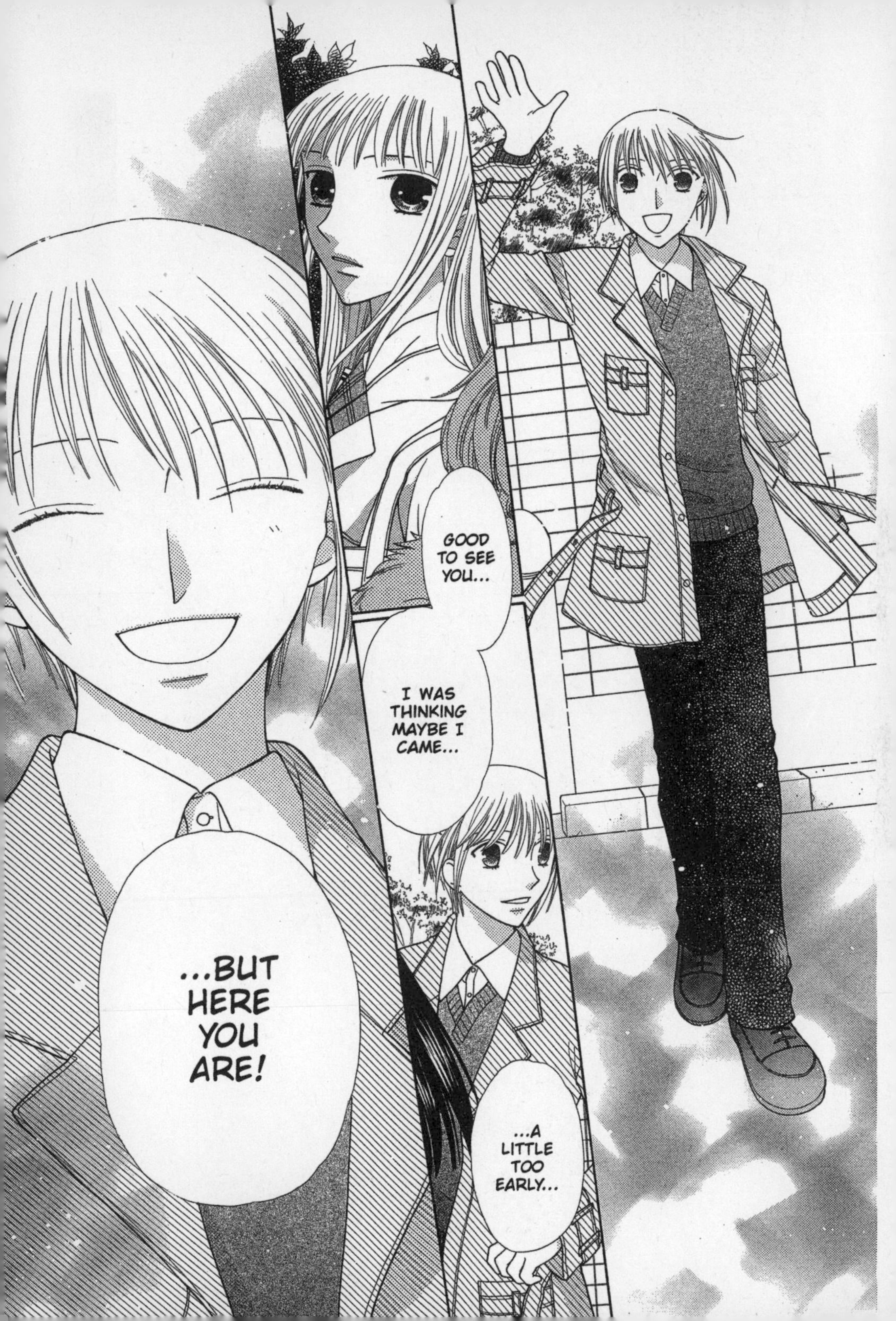
GOOD TO SEE YOU...
I WAS THINKING MAYBE I CAME...
...A LITTLE TOO EARLY...
...BUT HERE YOU ARE!

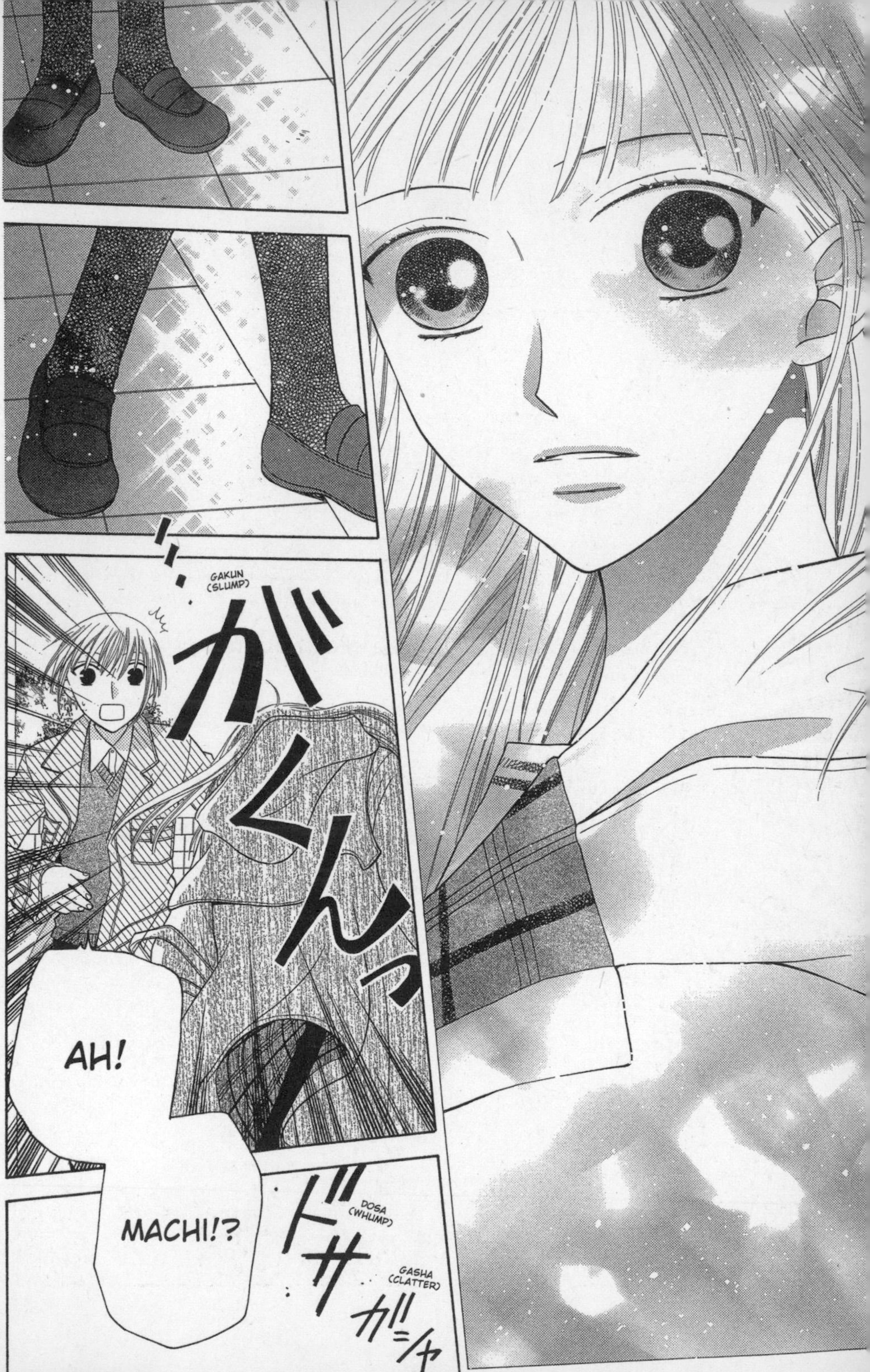
GAKUN (SLUMP)
がくんっ
AH!
MACHI!?
DOSA (WHUMP)
ドサ
GASHA (CLATTER)
ガシャ

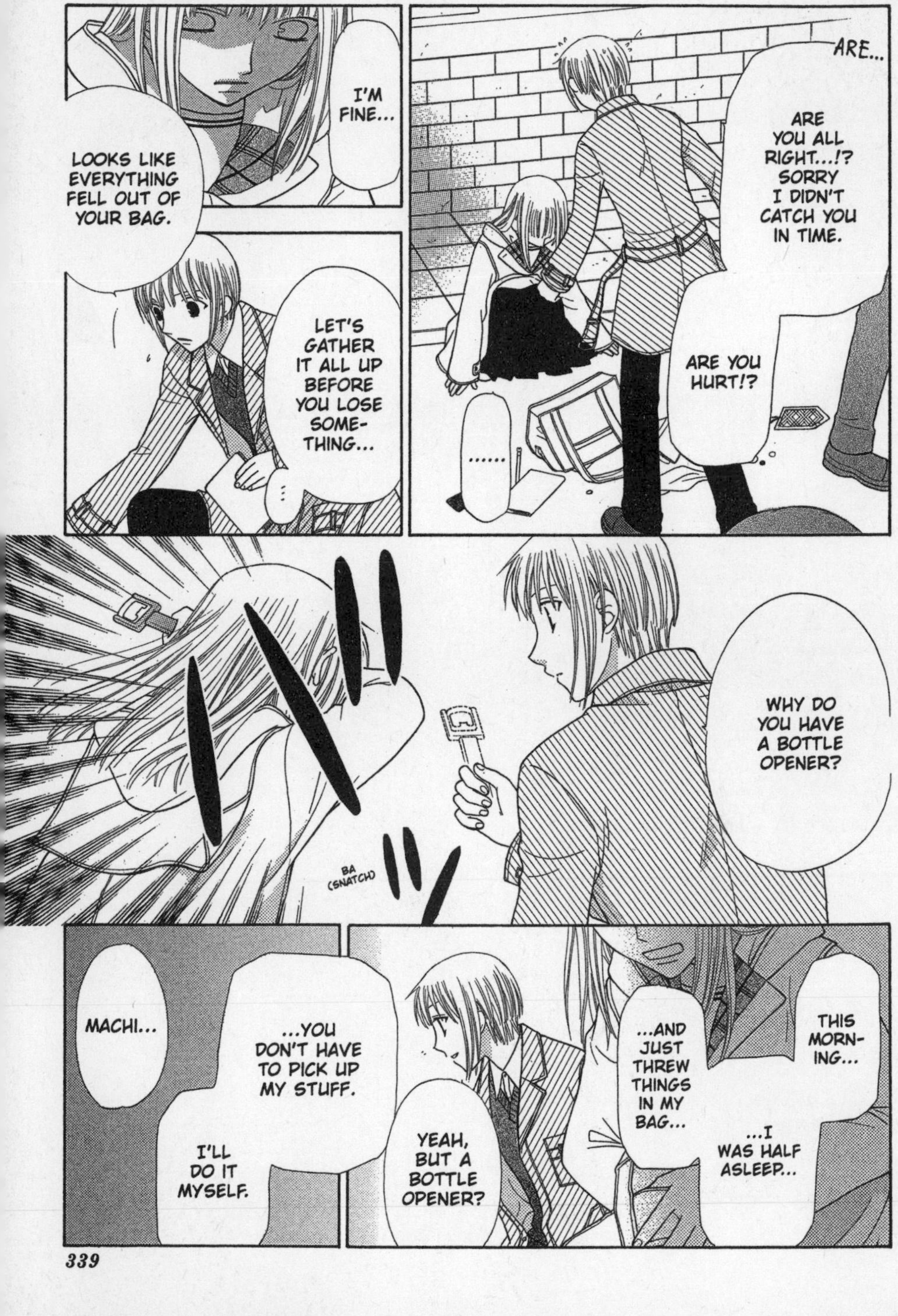
ARE...
ARE YOU ALL RIGHT...!? SORRY I DIDN'T CATCH YOU IN TIME.
ARE YOU HURT!?
......
I'M FINE...
LOOKS LIKE EVERYTHING FELL OUT OF YOUR BAG.
LET'S GATHER IT ALL UP BEFORE YOU LOSE SOME-THING...
WHY DO YOU HAVE A BOTTLE OPENER?
BA (SNATCH)
THIS MORNING...
...I WAS HALF ASLEEP...
...AND JUST THREW THINGS IN MY BAG...
YEAH, BUT A BOTTLE OPENER?
...YOU DON'T HAVE TO PICK UP MY STUFF.
MACHI...
I'LL DO IT MYSELF.

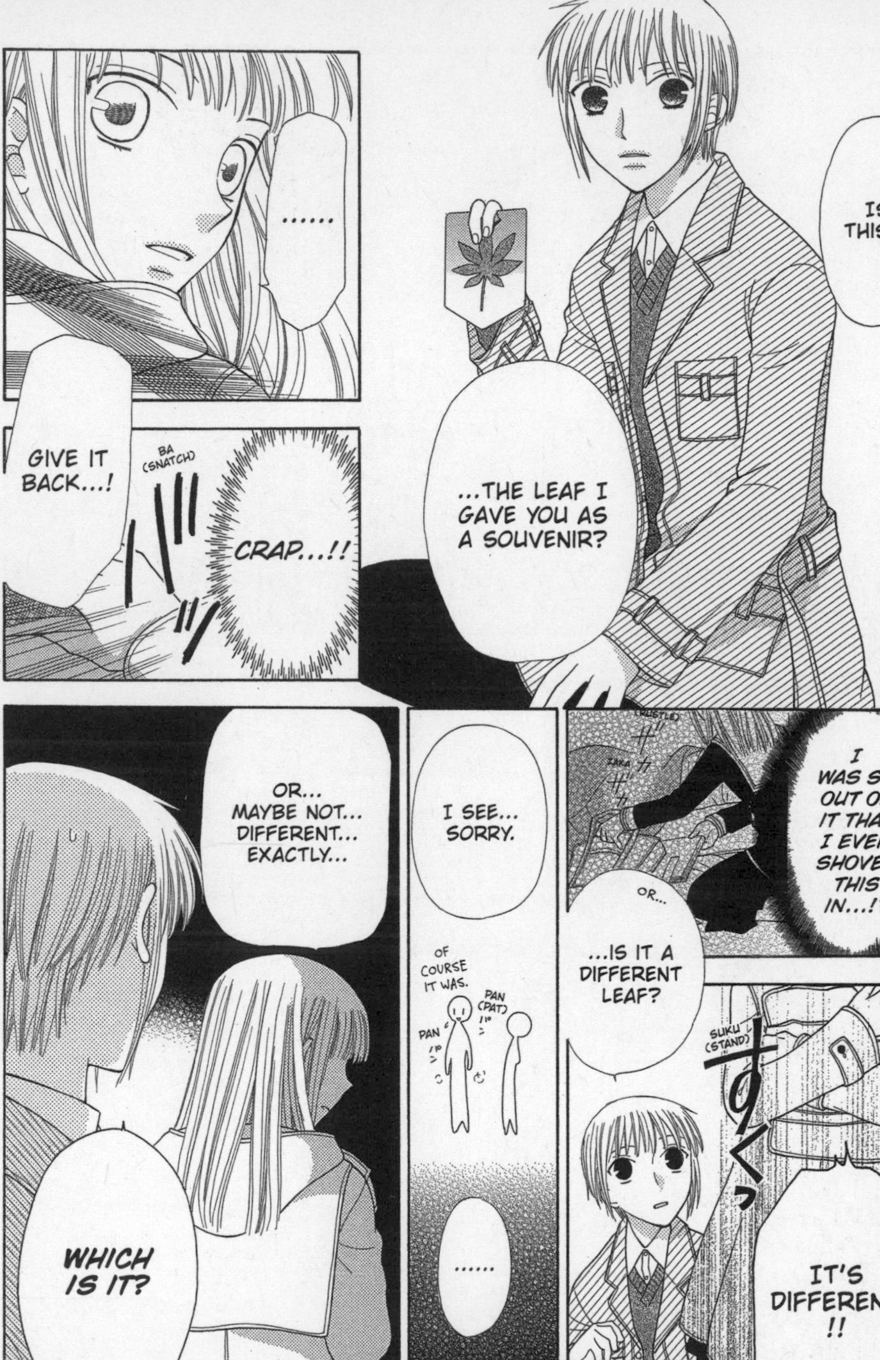

IS THIS...
...THE LEAF I GAVE YOU AS A SOUVENIR?
......
CRAP...!!
BA (SNATCH)
GIVE IT BACK...!
(RUSTLE)
ZAKA
I WAS SO OUT OF IT THAT I EVEN SHOVED THIS IN...!?
OR...
...IS IT A DIFFERENT LEAF?
SUKU (STAND)
IT'S DIFFERENT !!
I SEE... SORRY.
OF COURSE IT WAS.
PAN (PAT)
PAN
......
OR... MAYBE NOT... DIFFERENT... EXACTLY...
WHICH IS IT?

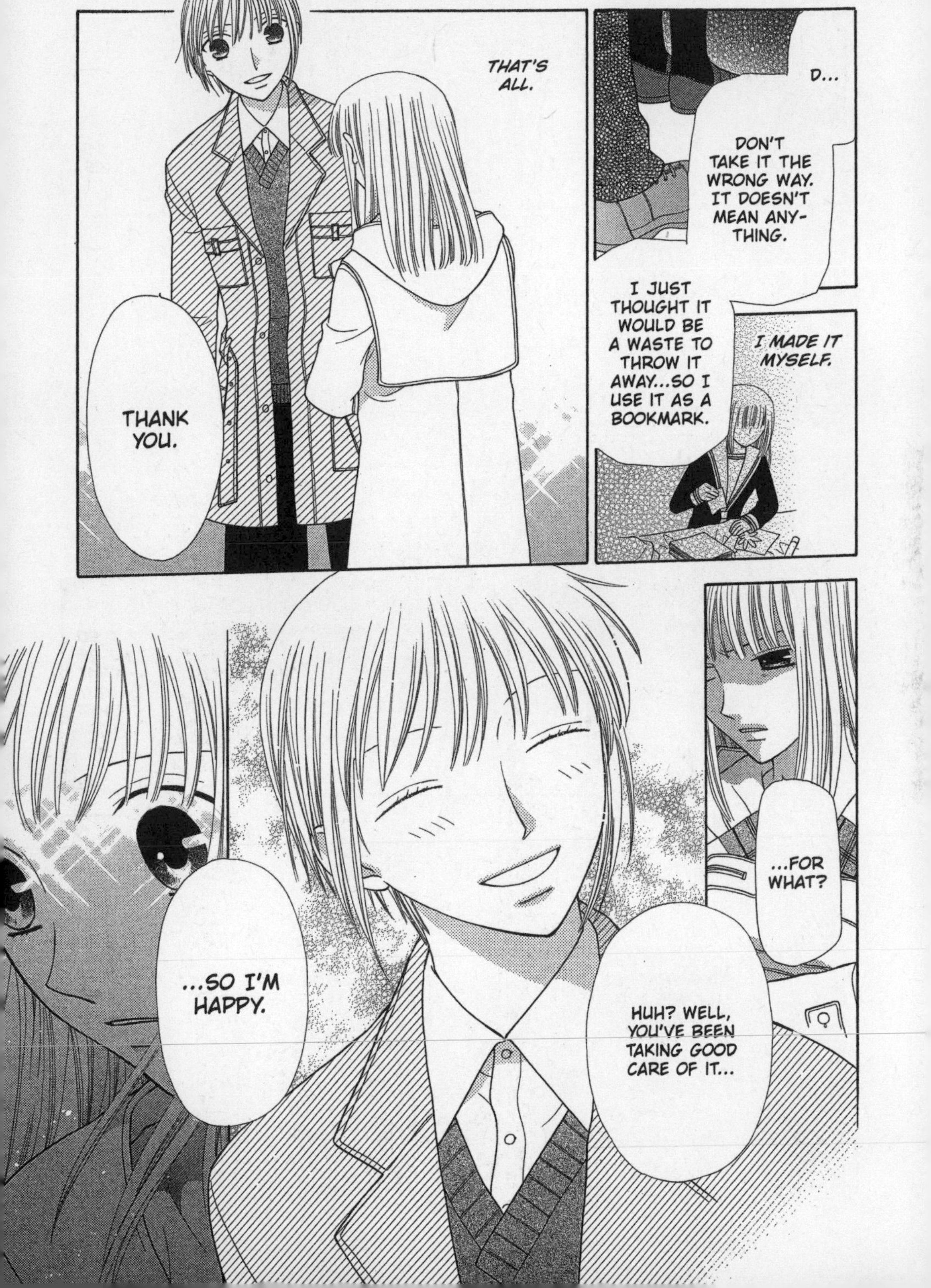
D...
DON'T TAKE IT THE WRONG WAY. IT DOESN'T MEAN ANY-THING.
I JUST THOUGHT IT WOULD BE A WASTE TO THROW IT AWAY...SO I USE IT AS A BOOKMARK.
I MADE IT MYSELF.
THAT'S ALL.
THANK YOU.
...FOR WHAT?
HUH? WELL, YOU'VE BEEN TAKING GOOD CARE OF IT...
...SO I'M HAPPY.

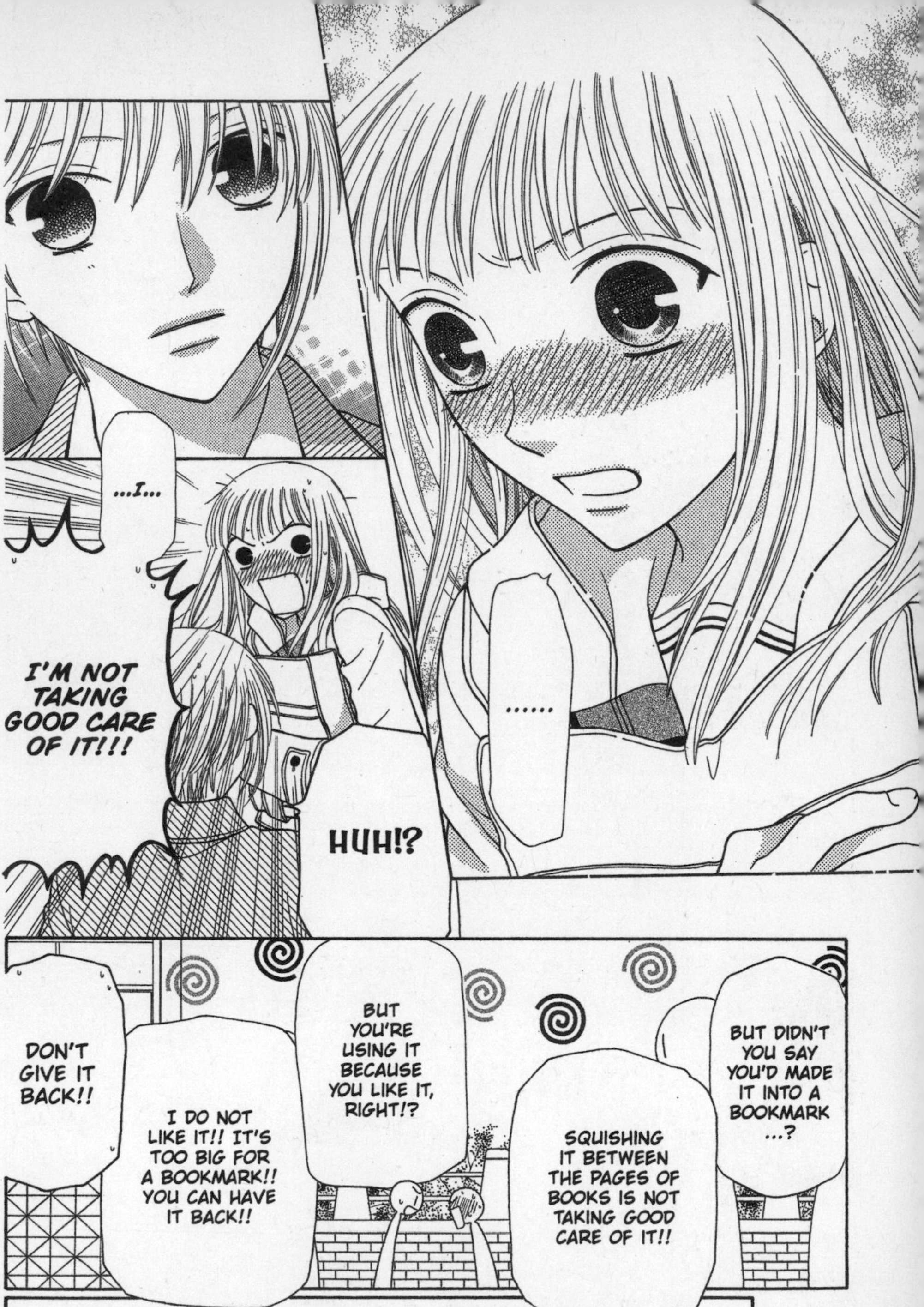
......
...I...
I'M NOT TAKING GOOD CARE OF IT!!!
HUH!?
BUT DIDN'T YOU SAY YOU'D MADE IT INTO A BOOKMARK ...?
SQUISHING IT BETWEEN THE PAGES OF BOOKS IS NOT TAKING GOOD CARE OF IT!!
BUT YOU'RE USING IT BECAUSE YOU LIKE IT, RIGHT!?
I DO NOT LIKE IT!! IT'S TOO BIG FOR A BOOKMARK!! YOU CAN HAVE IT BACK!!
DON'T GIVE IT BACK!!

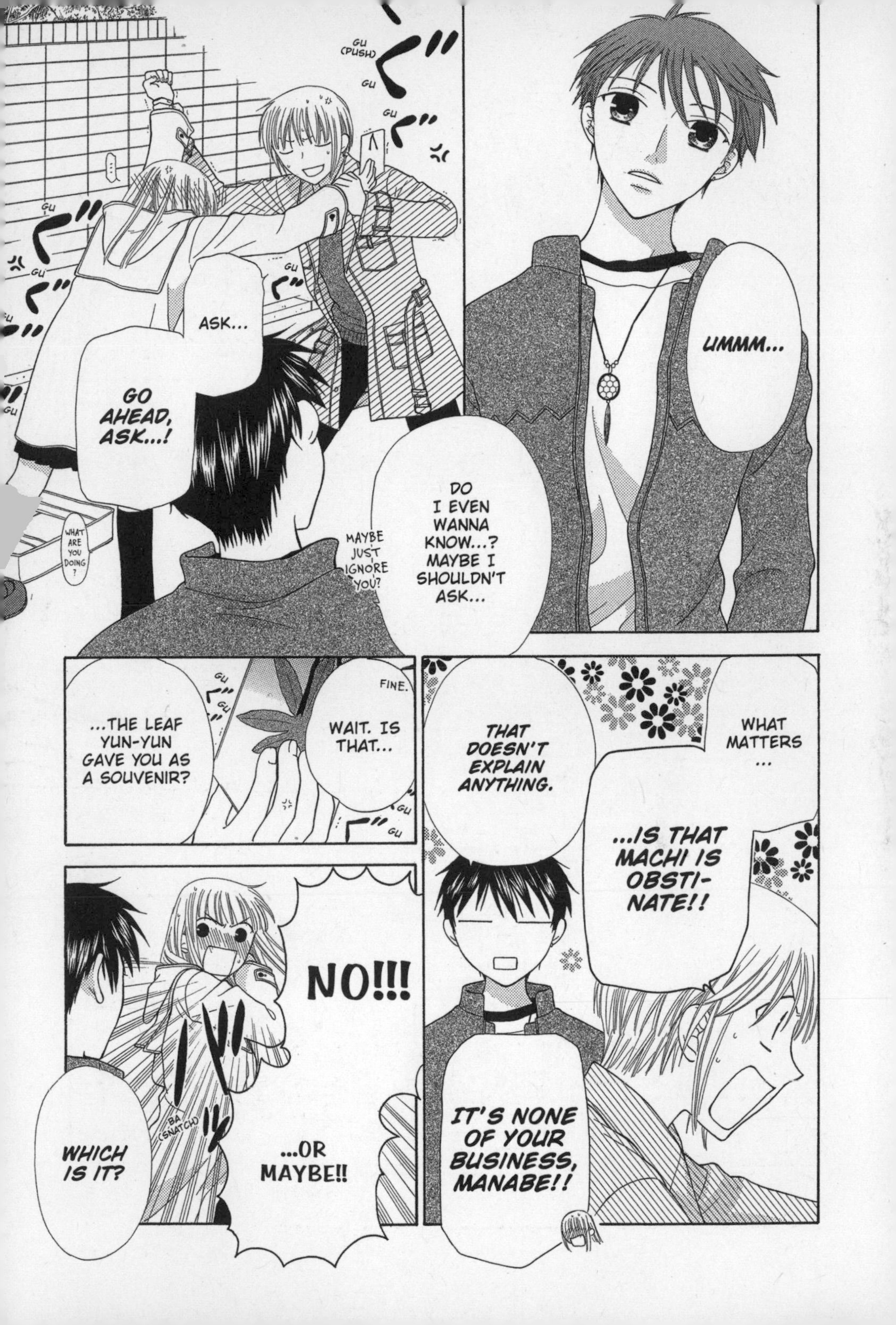
UMMM...
GU (PUSH)
GU
GU
GU
GU
GU
GU
ASK...
DO I EVEN WANNA KNOW...? MAYBE I SHOULDN'T ASK...
MAYBE JUST IGNORE YOU?
GO AHEAD, ASK...!
WHAT ARE YOU DOING?
WHAT MATTERS ...
THAT DOESN'T EXPLAIN ANYTHING.
...IS THAT MACHI IS OBSTI-NATE!!
IT'S NONE OF YOUR BUSINESS, MANABE!!
FINE.
WAIT. IS THAT...
GU
GU
...THE LEAF YUN-YUN GAVE YOU AS A SOUVENIR?
GU
GU
NO!!!
BA (SNATCH)
...OR MAYBE!!
WHICH IS IT?

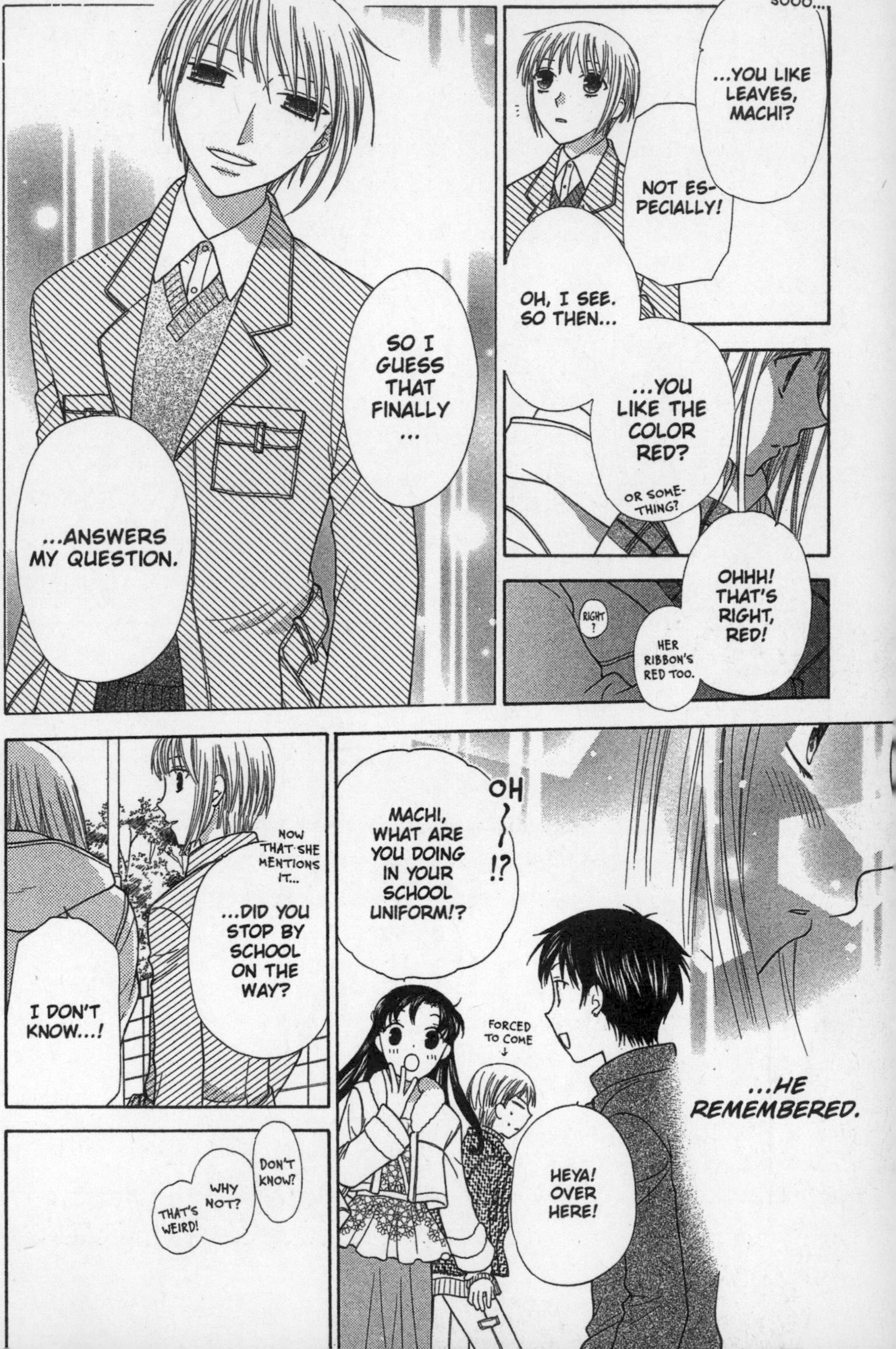
SOOO...
...YOU LIKE LEAVES, MACHI?
NOT ES-PECIALLY!
OH, I SEE. SO THEN...
...YOU LIKE THE COLOR RED?
OR SOME-THING?
OHHH! THAT'S RIGHT, RED!
HER RIBBON'S RED TOO.
RIGHT?
SO I GUESS THAT FINALLY...
...ANSWERS MY QUESTION.
...HE REMEMBERED.
OH~!?
MACHI, WHAT ARE YOU DOING IN YOUR SCHOOL UNIFORM!?
FORCED TO COME ↓
HEYA! OVER HERE!
NOW THAT SHE MENTIONS IT...
...DID YOU STOP BY SCHOOL ON THE WAY?
I DON'T KNOW...!
DON'T KNOW?
WHY NOT?
THAT'S WEIRD!

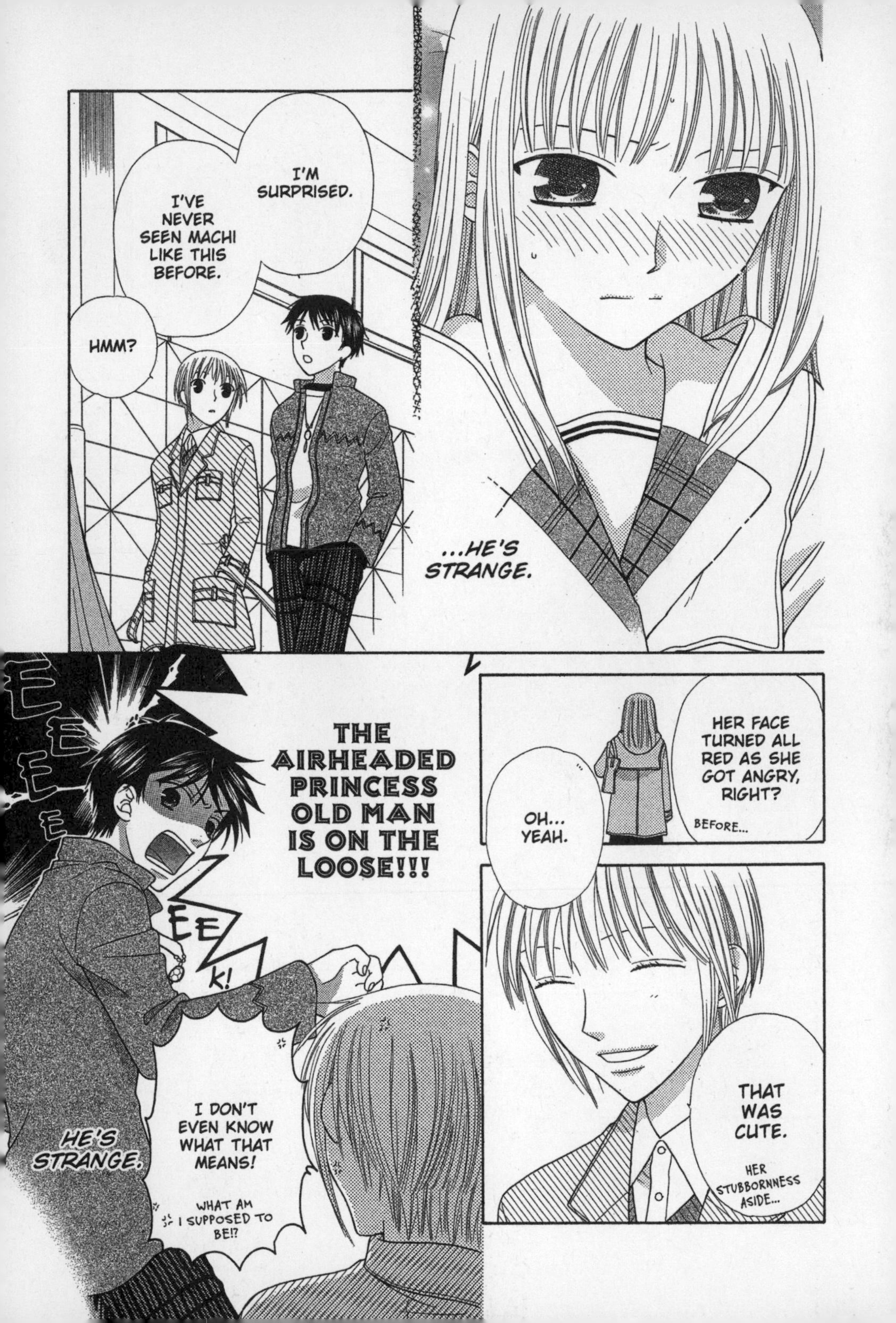
...HE'S STRANGE.
I'M SURPRISED.
I'VE NEVER SEEN MACHI LIKE THIS BEFORE.
HMM?
HER FACE TURNED ALL RED AS SHE GOT ANGRY, RIGHT?
BEFORE...
OH... YEAH.
THAT WAS CUTE.
HER STUBBORNNESS ASIDE...
THE AIRHEADED PRINCESS OLD MAN IS ON THE LOOSE!!!
EEEEE
EEk!
I DON'T EVEN KNOW WHAT THAT MEANS!
WHAT AM I SUPPOSED TO BE!?
HE'S STRANGE.

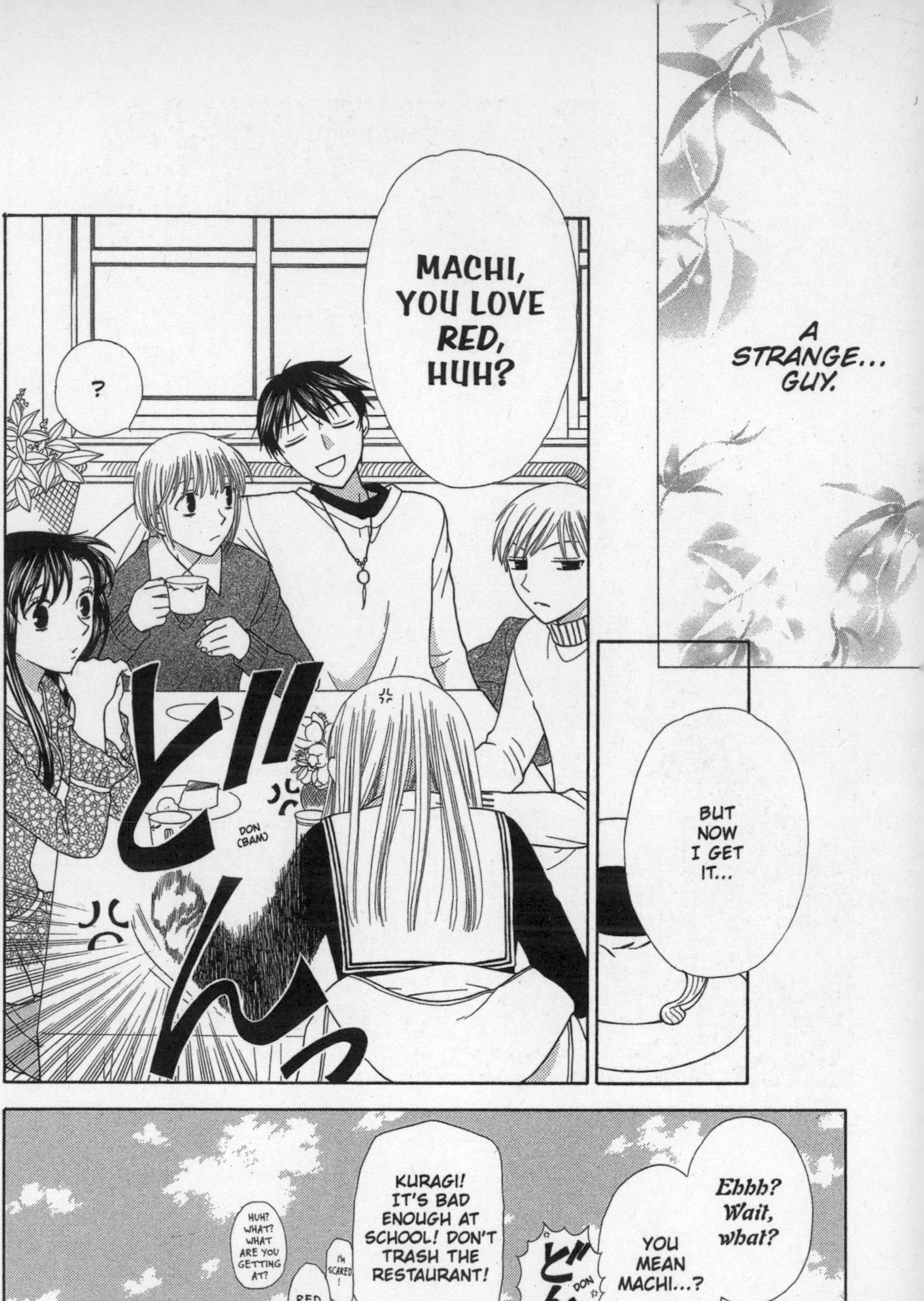
A STRANGE... GUY.
BUT NOW I GET IT...
MACHI, YOU LOVE RED, HUH?
?
DON (BAM)
どんっ
Ehhh? Wait, what?
YOU MEAN MACHI...?
どんっ DON
KURAGI! IT'S BAD ENOUGH AT SCHOOL! DON'T TRASH THE RESTAURANT!
I'M SCARED!
HUH? WHAT? WHAT ARE YOU GETTING AT?
RED, HUH?

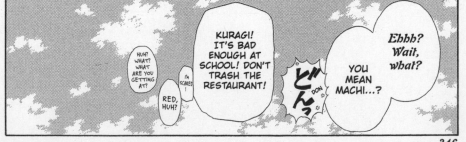

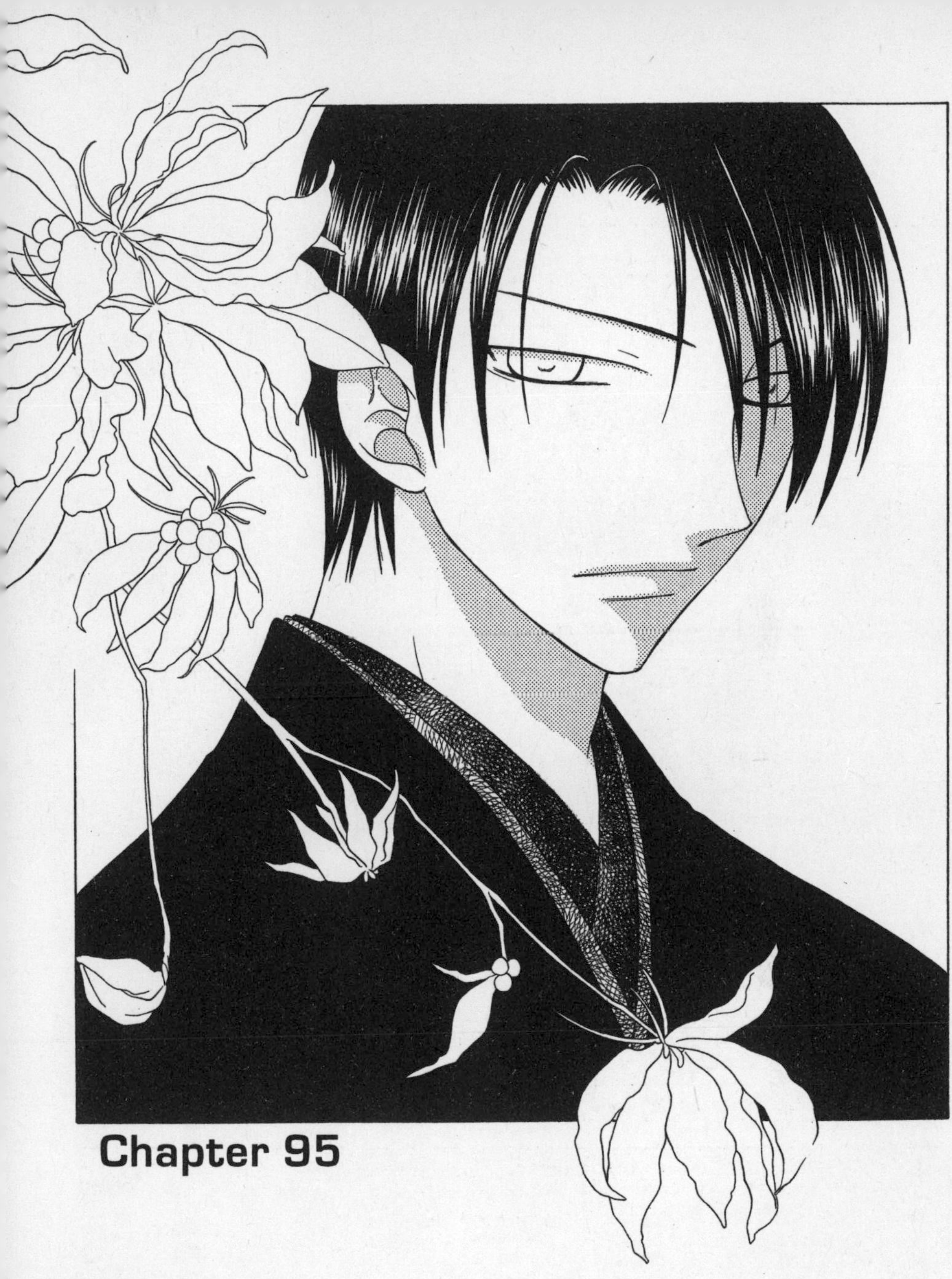

Chapter 95

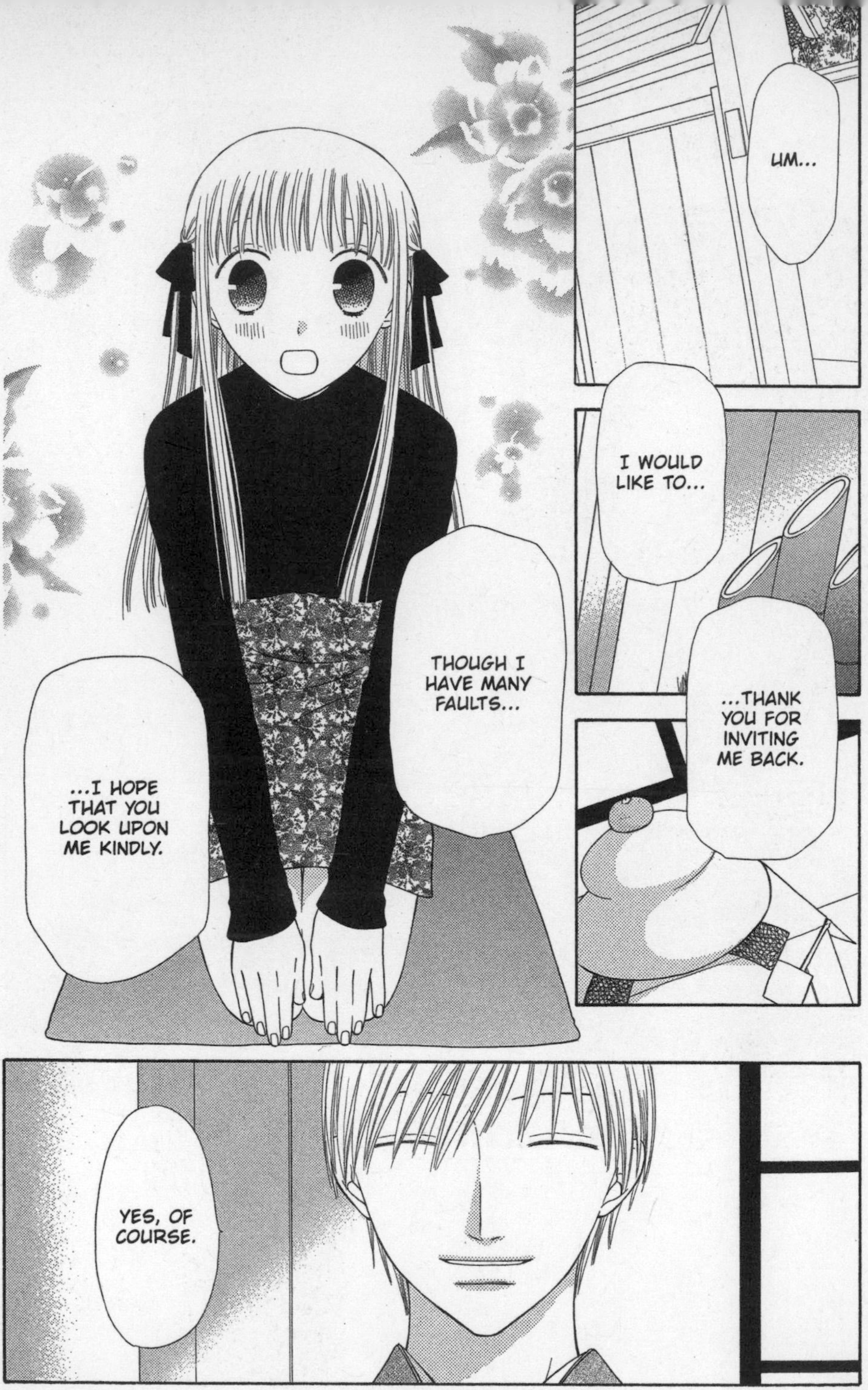
UM...
I WOULD LIKE TO...
...THANK YOU FOR INVITING ME BACK.
THOUGH I HAVE MANY FAULTS...
...I HOPE THAT YOU LOOK UPON ME KINDLY.
YES, OF COURSE.

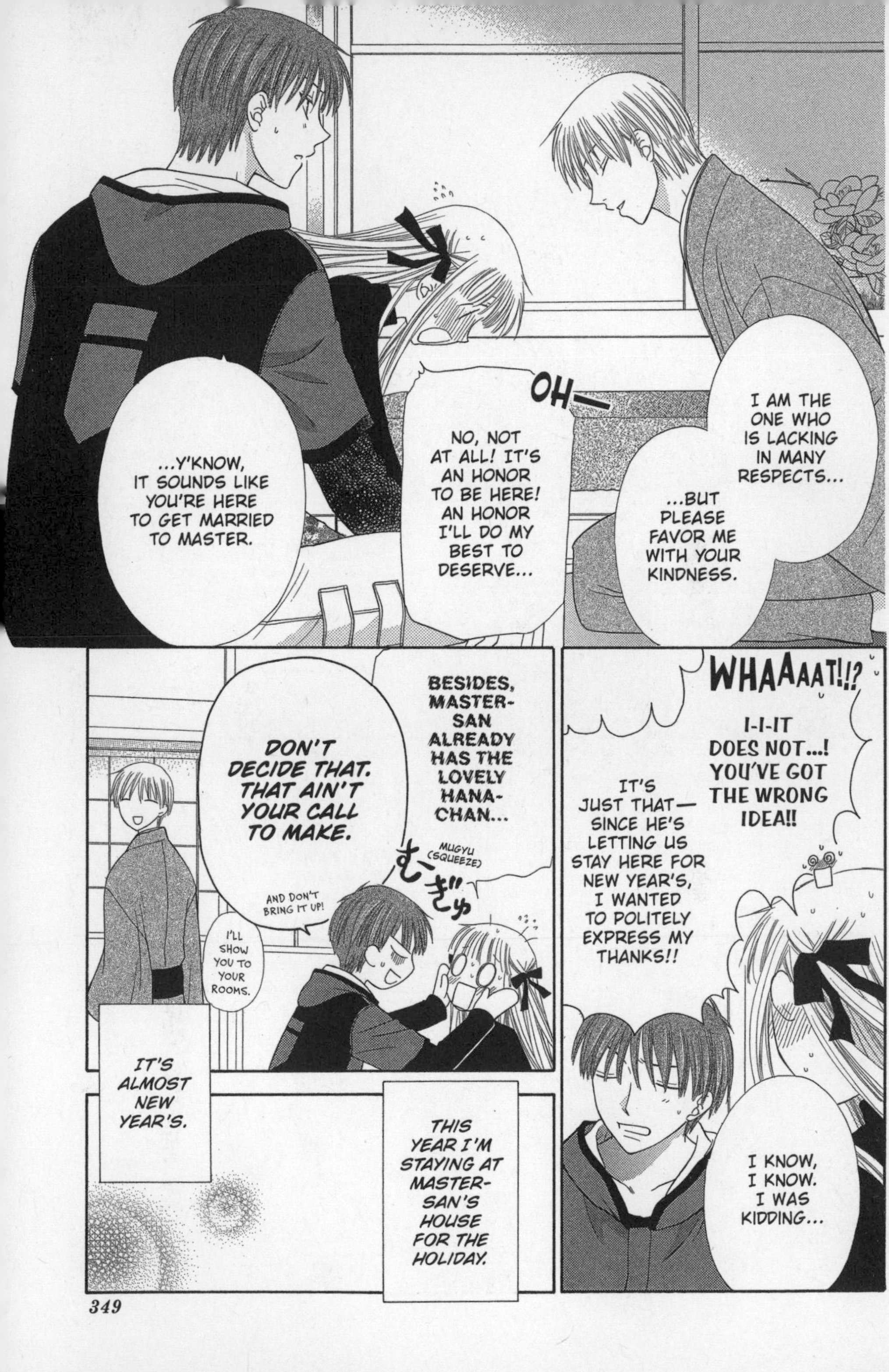
I AM THE ONE WHO IS LACKING IN MANY RESPECTS...
...BUT PLEASE FAVOR ME WITH YOUR KINDNESS.
OH—
NO, NOT AT ALL! IT'S AN HONOR TO BE HERE! AN HONOR I'LL DO MY BEST TO DESERVE...
...Y'KNOW, IT SOUNDS LIKE YOU'RE HERE TO GET MARRIED TO MASTER.
WHAAAAT!!?
I-I-IT DOES NOT...! YOU'VE GOT THE WRONG IDEA!!
IT'S JUST THAT— SINCE HE'S LETTING US STAY HERE FOR NEW YEAR'S, I WANTED TO POLITELY EXPRESS MY THANKS!!
I KNOW, I KNOW. I WAS KIDDING...
BESIDES, MASTER-SAN ALREADY HAS THE LOVELY HANA-CHAN...
DON'T DECIDE THAT. THAT AIN'T YOUR CALL TO MAKE.
むぎゅ
MUGYU (SQUEEZE)
AND DON'T BRING IT UP!
I'LL SHOW YOU TO YOUR ROOMS.
IT'S ALMOST NEW YEAR'S.
THIS YEAR I'M STAYING AT MASTER-SAN'S HOUSE FOR THE HOLIDAY.

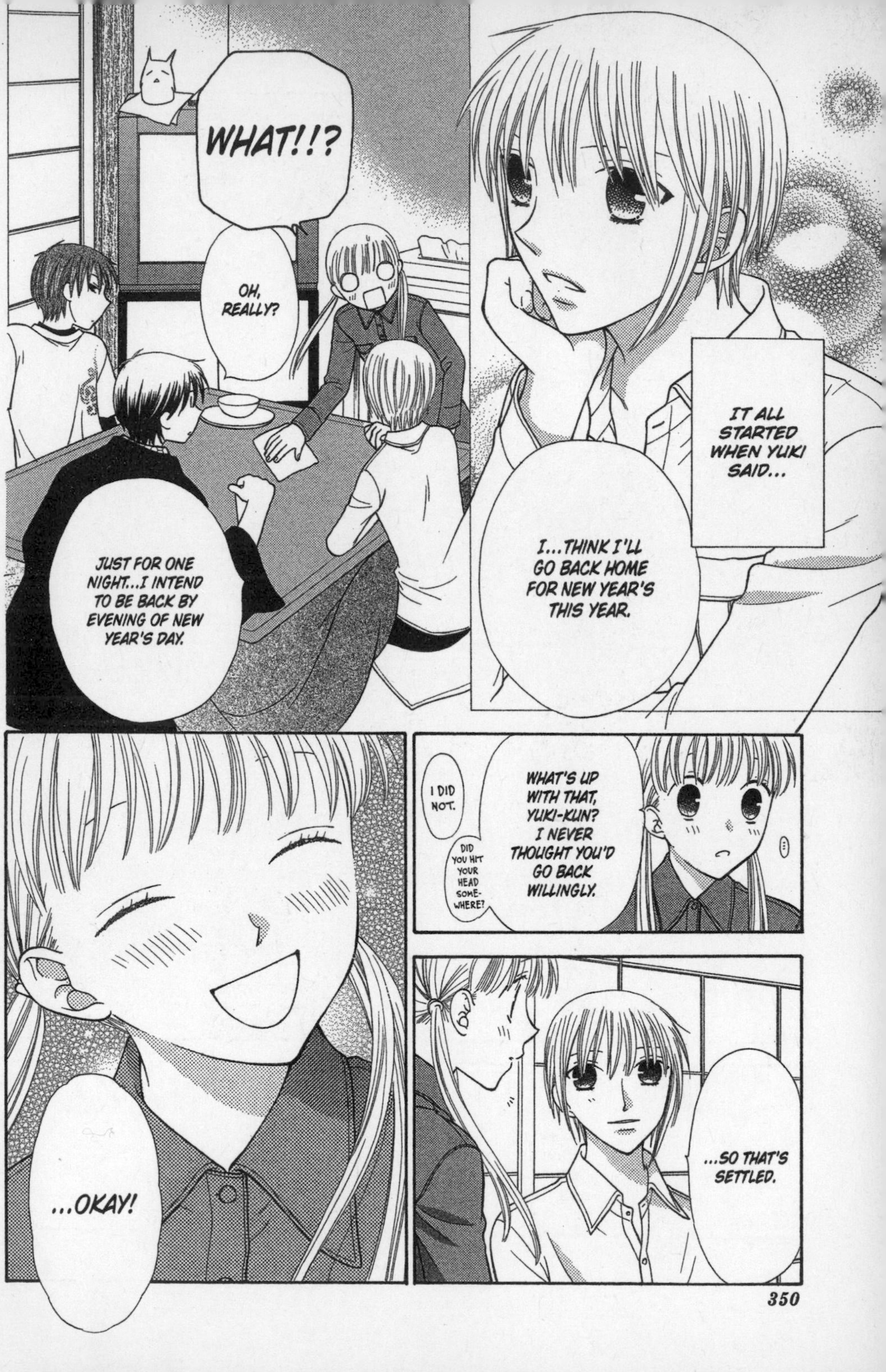
IT ALL STARTED WHEN YUKI SAID...
I...THINK I'LL GO BACK HOME FOR NEW YEAR'S THIS YEAR.
WHAT!!?
OH, REALLY?
JUST FOR ONE NIGHT...I INTEND TO BE BACK BY EVENING OF NEW YEAR'S DAY.
...
WHAT'S UP WITH THAT, YUKI-KUN? I NEVER THOUGHT YOU'D GO BACK WILLINGLY.
I DID NOT.
DID YOU HIT YOUR HEAD SOME-WHERE?
...SO THAT'S SETTLED.
...OKAY!

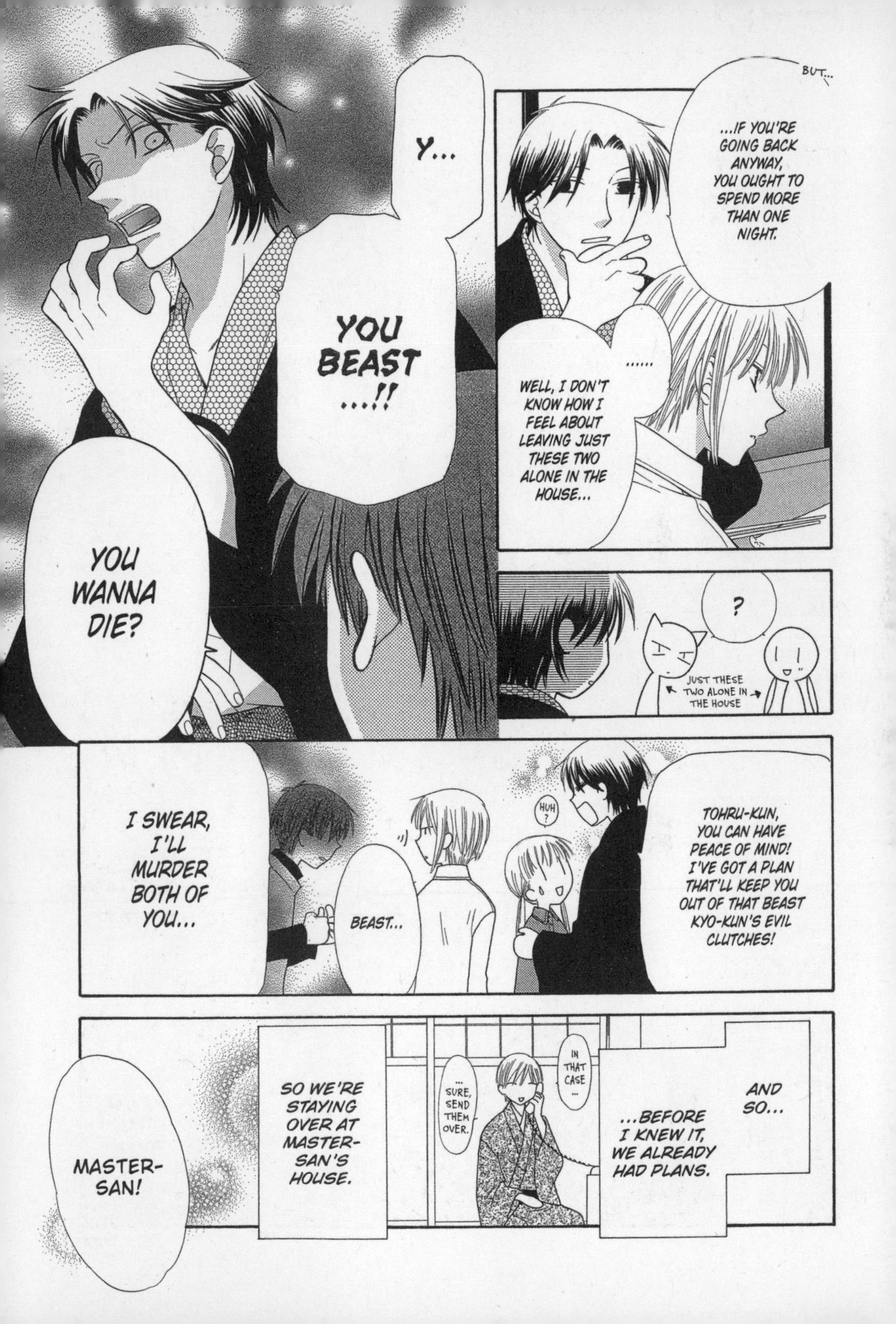
BUT...
...IF YOU'RE GOING BACK ANYWAY, YOU OUGHT TO SPEND MORE THAN ONE NIGHT.
......
WELL, I DON'T KNOW HOW I FEEL ABOUT LEAVING JUST THESE TWO ALONE IN THE HOUSE...
?
JUST THESE TWO ALONE IN THE HOUSE
Y...
YOU BEAST ...!!
YOU WANNA DIE?
TOHRU-KUN, YOU CAN HAVE PEACE OF MIND! I'VE GOT A PLAN THAT'LL KEEP YOU OUT OF THAT BEAST KYO-KUN'S EVIL CLUTCHES!
HUH?
BEAST...
I SWEAR, I'LL MURDER BOTH OF YOU...
AND SO...
...BEFORE I KNEW IT, WE ALREADY HAD PLANS.
IN THAT CASE...
...SURE, SEND THEM OVER.
SO WE'RE STAYING OVER AT MASTER-SAN'S HOUSE.
MASTER-SAN!

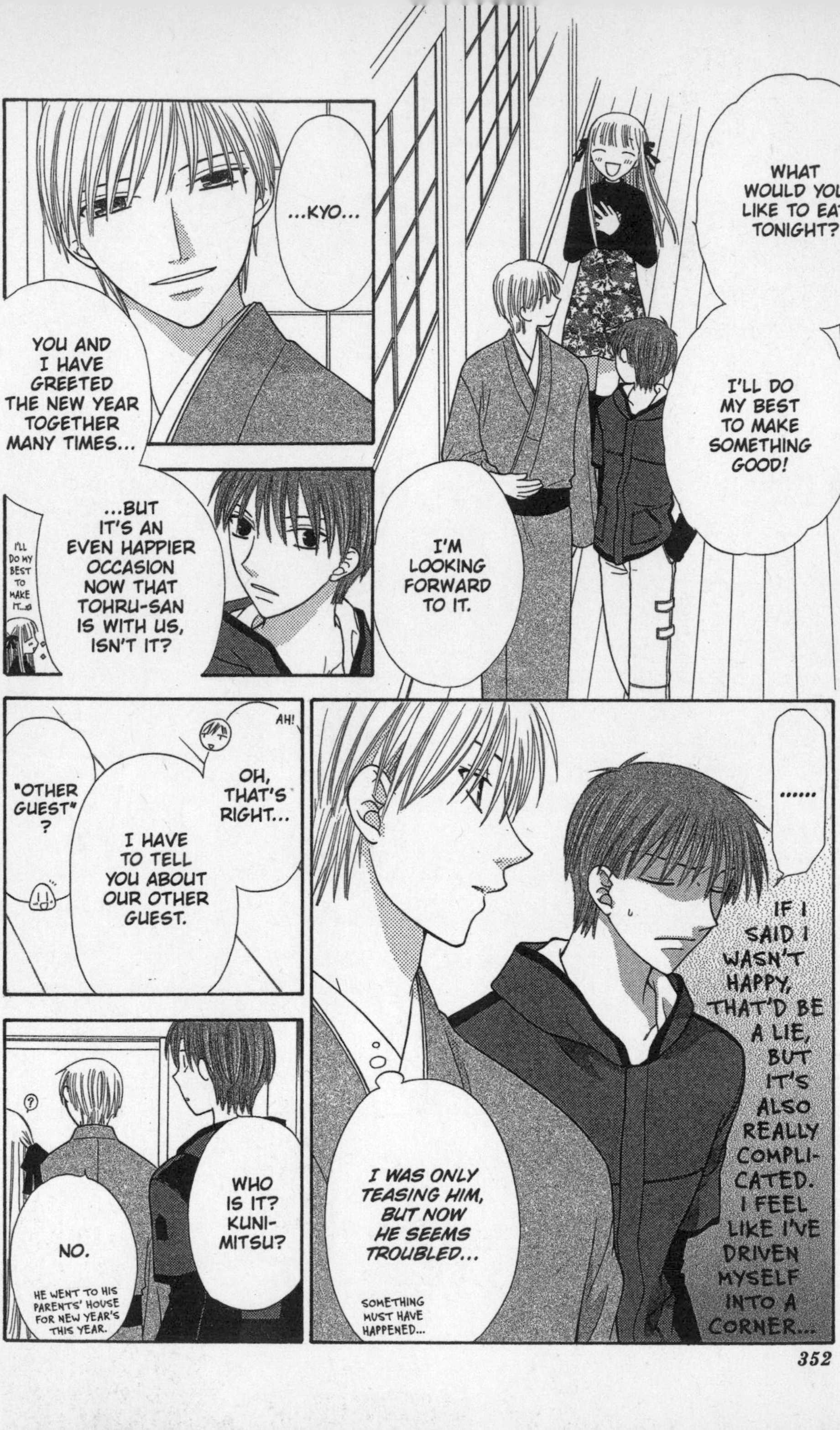
WHAT WOULD YOU LIKE TO EAT TONIGHT?
I'LL DO MY BEST TO MAKE SOMETHING GOOD!
I'M LOOKING FORWARD TO IT.
...KYO...
YOU AND I HAVE GREETED THE NEW YEAR TOGETHER MANY TIMES...
...BUT IT'S AN EVEN HAPPIER OCCASION NOW THAT TOHRU-SAN IS WITH US, ISN'T IT?
I'LL DO MY BEST TO MAKE IT...
......
IF I SAID I WASN'T HAPPY, THAT'D BE A LIE, BUT IT'S ALSO REALLY COMPLI-CATED. I FEEL LIKE I'VE DRIVEN MYSELF INTO A CORNER...
I WAS ONLY TEASING HIM, BUT NOW HE SEEMS TROUBLED...
SOMETHING MUST HAVE HAPPENED...
AH!
OH, THAT'S RIGHT...
I HAVE TO TELL YOU ABOUT OUR OTHER GUEST.
"OTHER GUEST"?
WHO IS IT? KUNI-MITSU?
NO.
HE WENT TO HIS PARENTS' HOUSE FOR NEW YEAR'S THIS YEAR.

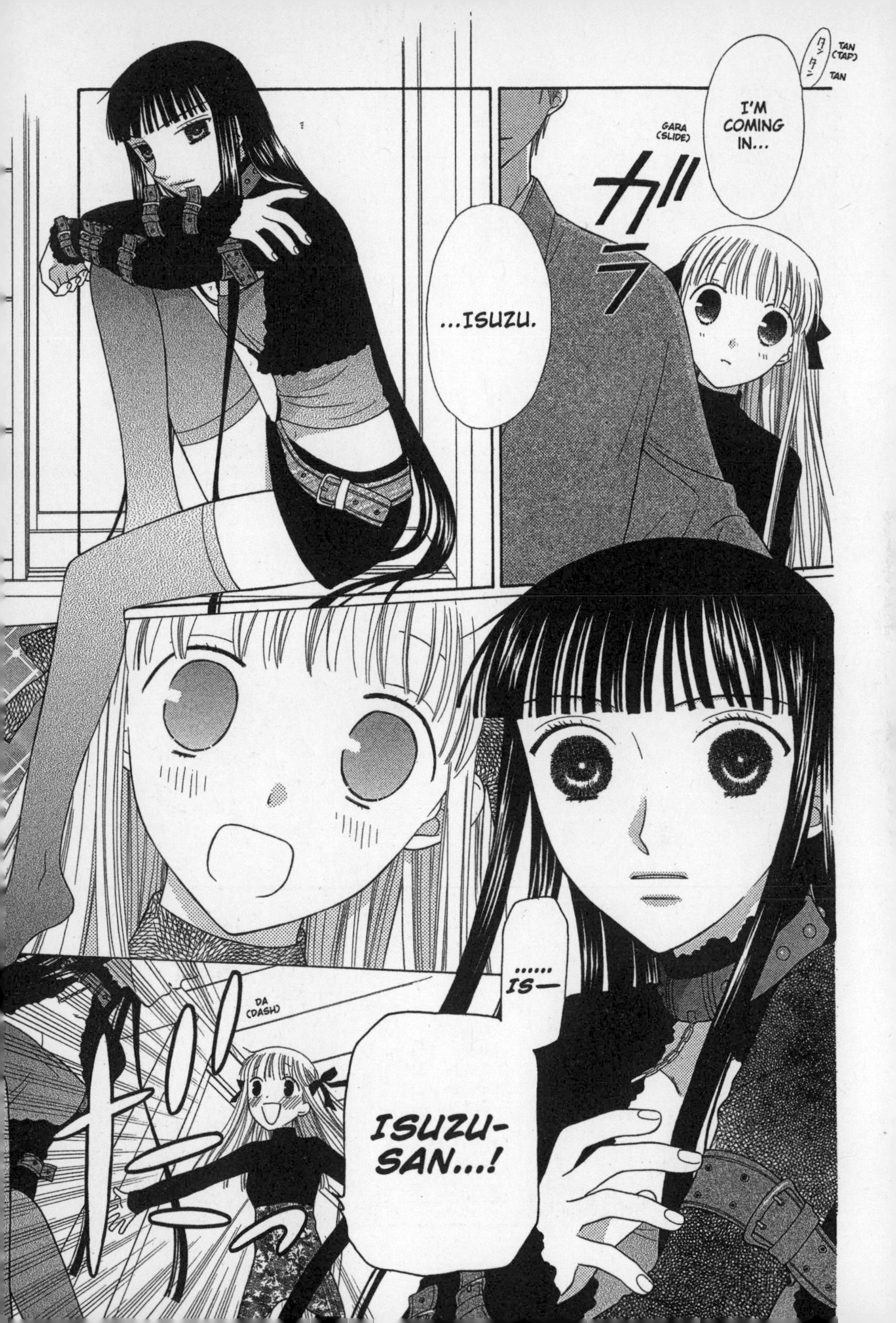
タン タン
TAN (TAP) TAN
I'M COMING IN...
ガラ
GARA (SLIDE)
...ISUZU.
......IS—
ダッ
DA (DASH)
ISUZU-SAN...!

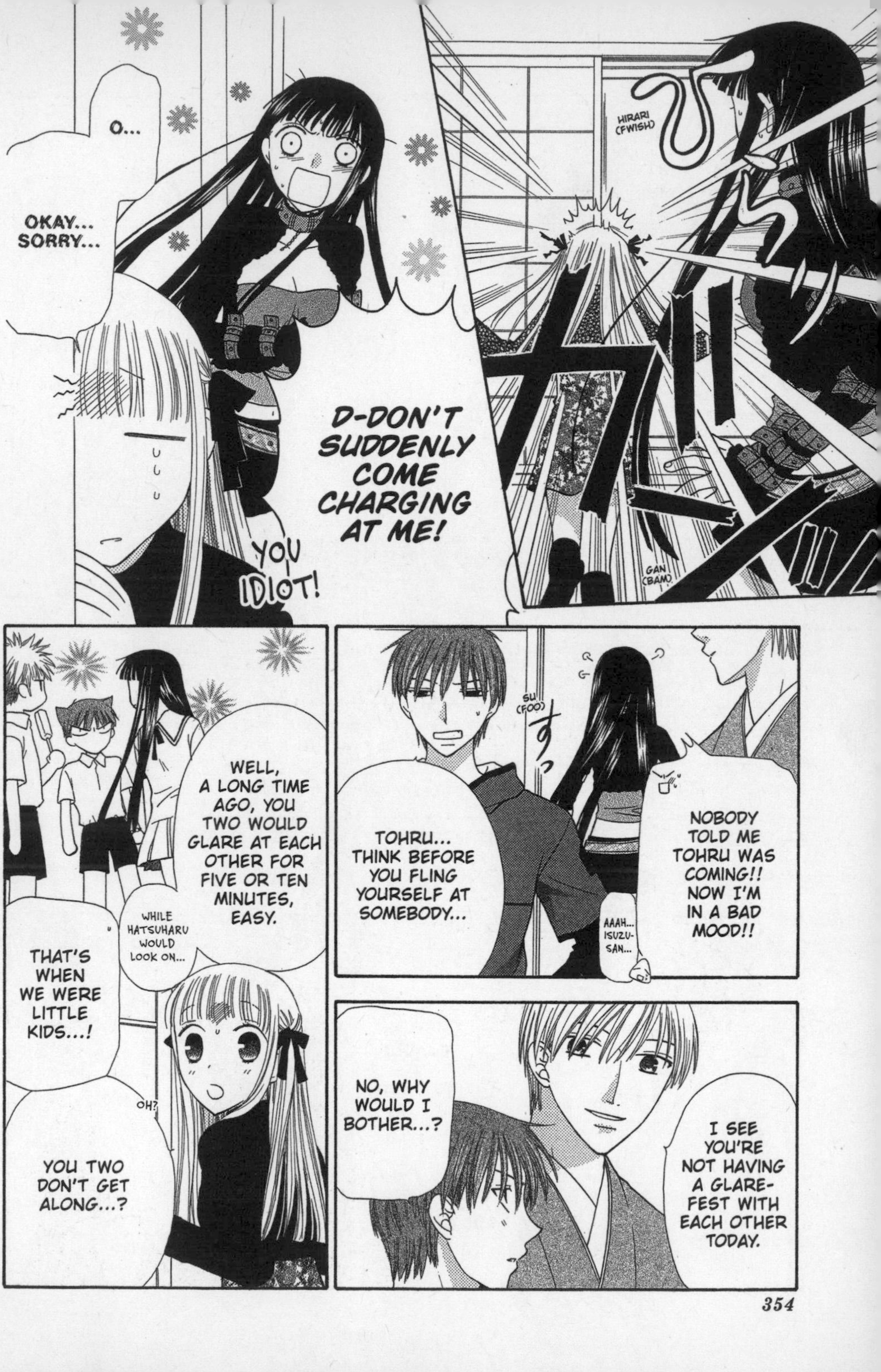
HIRARI (FWISH)
GAN (BAM)
D-DON'T SUDDENLY COME CHARGING AT ME!
YOU IDIOT!
O...
OKAY... SORRY...
NOBODY TOLD ME TOHRU WAS COMING!! NOW I'M IN A BAD MOOD!!
SU (FOO)
AAAH... ISUZU-SAN...
TOHRU... THINK BEFORE YOU FLING YOURSELF AT SOMEBODY...
I SEE YOU'RE NOT HAVING A GLARE-FEST WITH EACH OTHER TODAY.
NO, WHY WOULD I BOTHER...?
WELL, A LONG TIME AGO, YOU TWO WOULD GLARE AT EACH OTHER FOR FIVE OR TEN MINUTES, EASY.
WHILE HATSUHARU WOULD LOOK ON...
THAT'S WHEN WE WERE LITTLE KIDS...!
OH?
YOU TWO DON'T GET ALONG...?

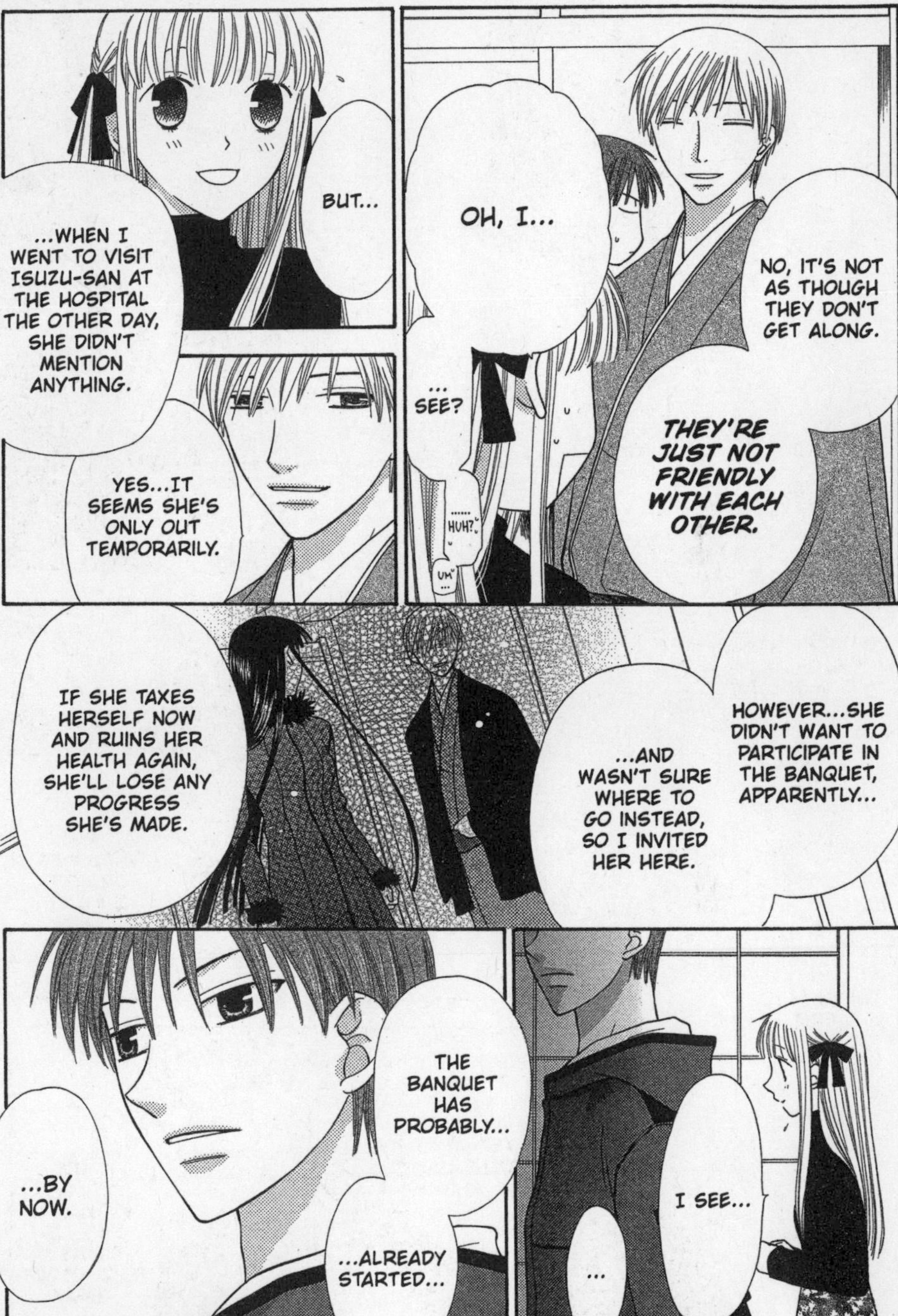
OH, I...
NO, IT'S NOT AS THOUGH THEY DON'T GET ALONG.
THEY'RE JUST NOT FRIENDLY WITH EACH OTHER.
...SEE?
......HUH?
UM...
BUT...
...WHEN I WENT TO VISIT ISUZU-SAN AT THE HOSPITAL THE OTHER DAY, SHE DIDN'T MENTION ANYTHING.
YES...IT SEEMS SHE'S ONLY OUT TEMPORARILY.
HOWEVER...SHE DIDN'T WANT TO PARTICIPATE IN THE BANQUET, APPARENTLY...
...AND WASN'T SURE WHERE TO GO INSTEAD, SO I INVITED HER HERE.
IF SHE TAXES HERSELF NOW AND RUINS HER HEALTH AGAIN, SHE'LL LOSE ANY PROGRESS SHE'S MADE.
I SEE...
...
THE BANQUET HAS PROBABLY...
...ALREADY STARTED...
...BY NOW.

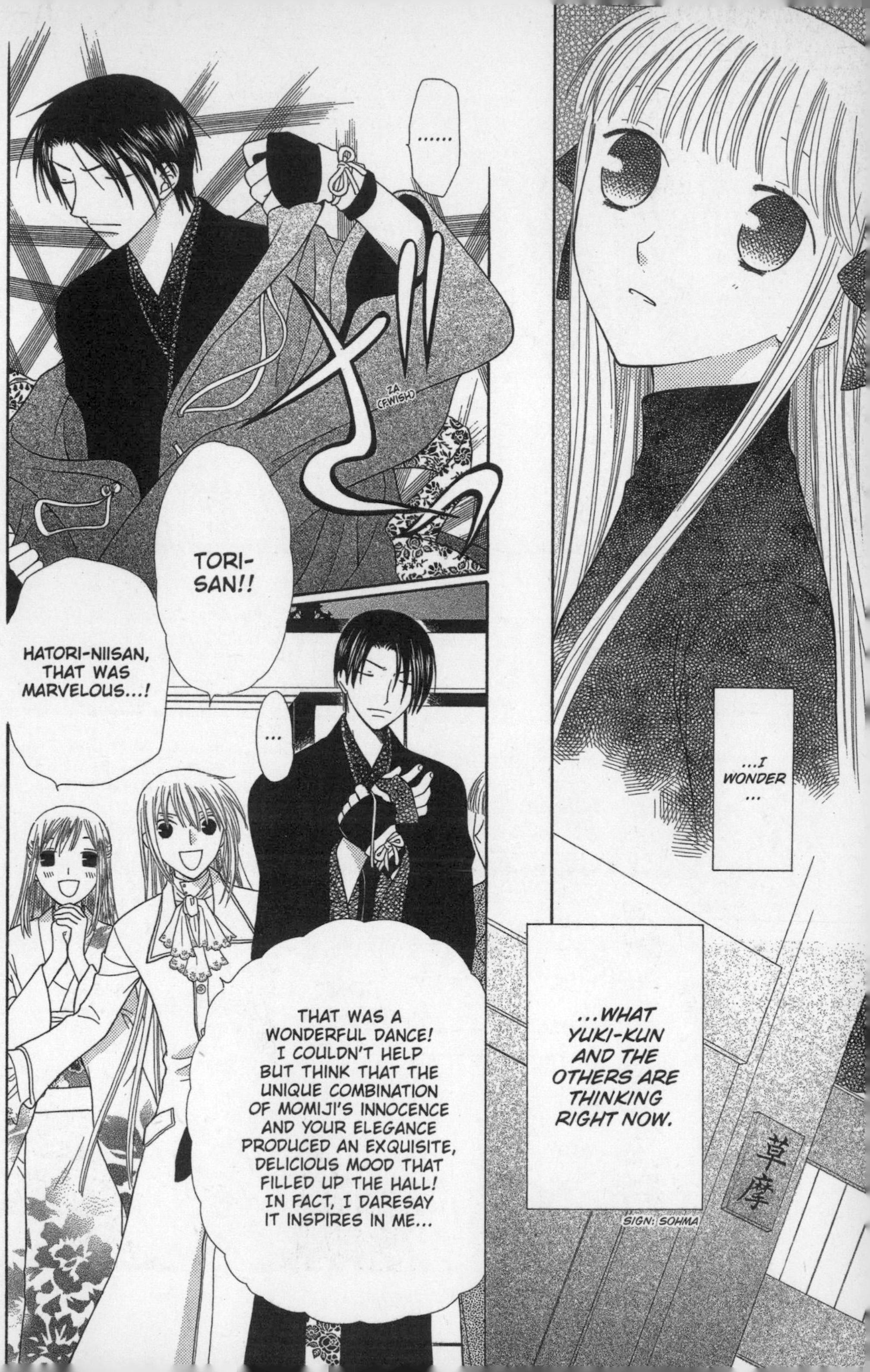
...I WONDER ...
...WHAT YUKI-KUN AND THE OTHERS ARE THINKING RIGHT NOW.
草摩
SIGN: SOHMA
......
ZA (FWISH)
TORI-SAN!!
...
HATORI-NIISAN, THAT WAS MARVELOUS...!
THAT WAS A WONDERFUL DANCE! I COULDN'T HELP BUT THINK THAT THE UNIQUE COMBINATION OF MOMIJI'S INNOCENCE AND YOUR ELEGANCE PRODUCED AN EXQUISITE, DELICIOUS MOOD THAT FILLED UP THE HALL! IN FACT, I DARESAY IT INSPIRES IN ME...

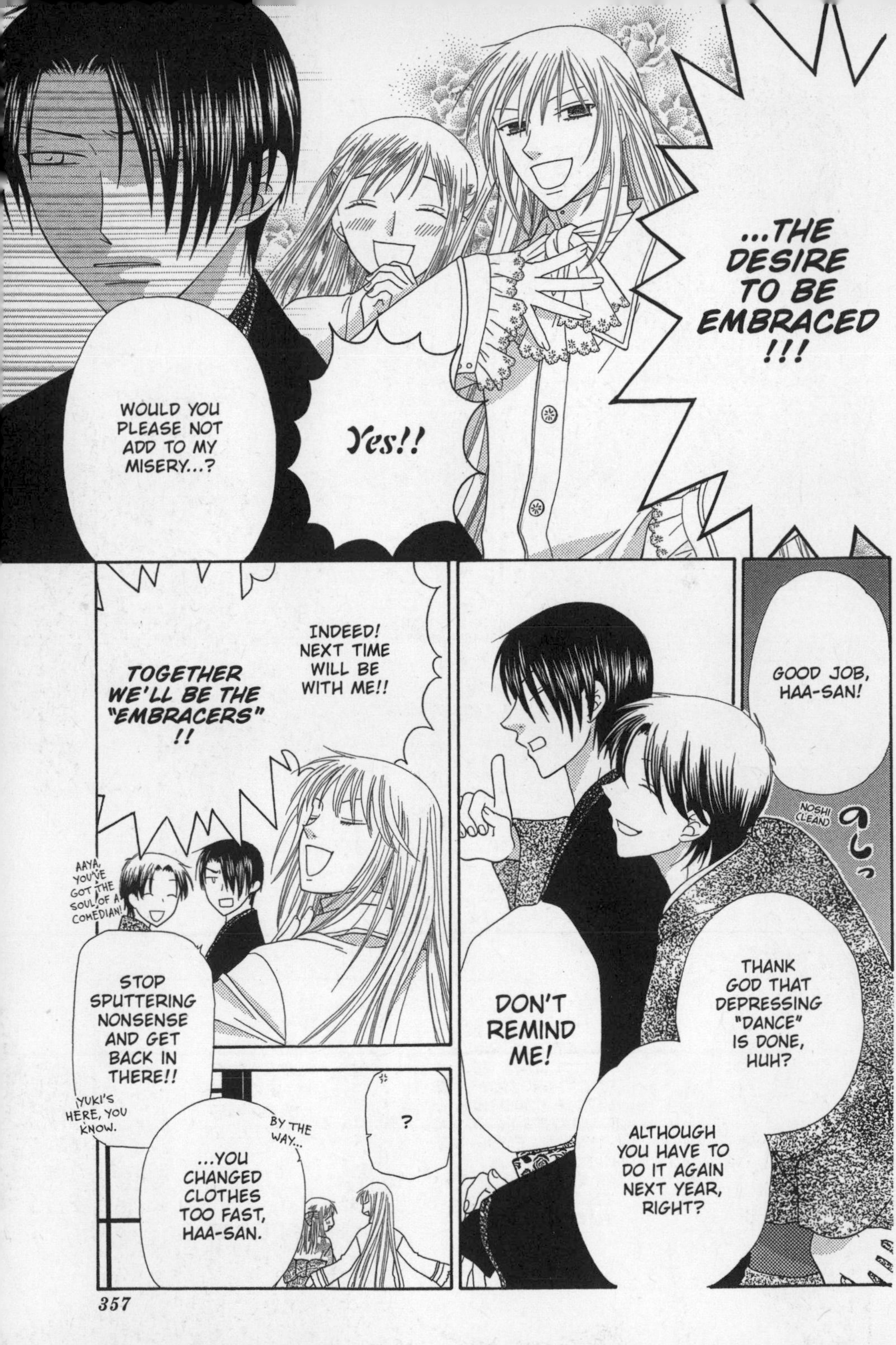
...THE DESIRE TO BE EMBRACED !!!
Yes!!
WOULD YOU PLEASE NOT ADD TO MY MISERY...?
GOOD JOB, HAA-SAN!
NOSHI (LEAN)
THANK GOD THAT DEPRESSING "DANCE" IS DONE, HUH?
DON'T REMIND ME!
ALTHOUGH YOU HAVE TO DO IT AGAIN NEXT YEAR, RIGHT?
INDEED! NEXT TIME WILL BE WITH ME!!
TOGETHER WE'LL BE THE "EMBRACERS" !!
AAYA, YOU'VE GOT THE SOUL OF A COMEDIAN!
STOP SPUTTERING NONSENSE AND GET BACK IN THERE!!
?
BY THE WAY...
...YOU CHANGED CLOTHES TOO FAST, HAA-SAN.
YUKI'S HERE, YOU KNOW.

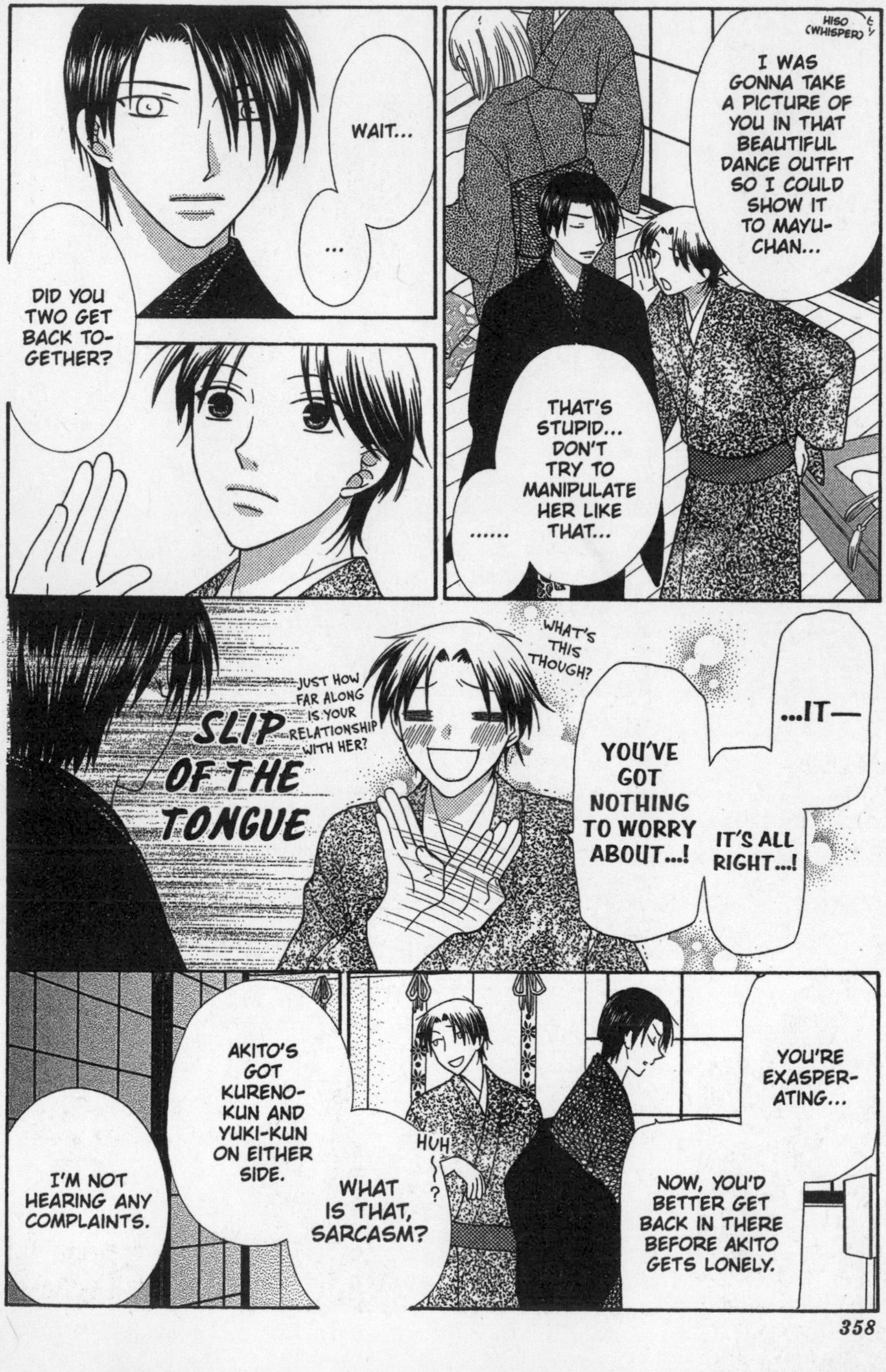
HISO (WHISPER)
I WAS GONNA TAKE A PICTURE OF YOU IN THAT BEAUTIFUL DANCE OUTFIT SO I COULD SHOW IT TO MAYU-CHAN...
THAT'S STUPID... DON'T TRY TO MANIPULATE HER LIKE THAT...
......
WAIT...
...
DID YOU TWO GET BACK TO-GETHER?
...IT—
IT'S ALL RIGHT...!
YOU'VE GOT NOTHING TO WORRY ABOUT...!
WHAT'S THIS THOUGH?
JUST HOW FAR ALONG IS YOUR RELATIONSHIP WITH HER?
SLIP OF THE TONGUE
YOU'RE EXASPER-ATING...
NOW, YOU'D BETTER GET BACK IN THERE BEFORE AKITO GETS LONELY.
HUH ~?
WHAT IS THAT, SARCASM?
AKITO'S GOT KURENO-KUN AND YUKI-KUN ON EITHER SIDE.
I'M NOT HEARING ANY COMPLAINTS.

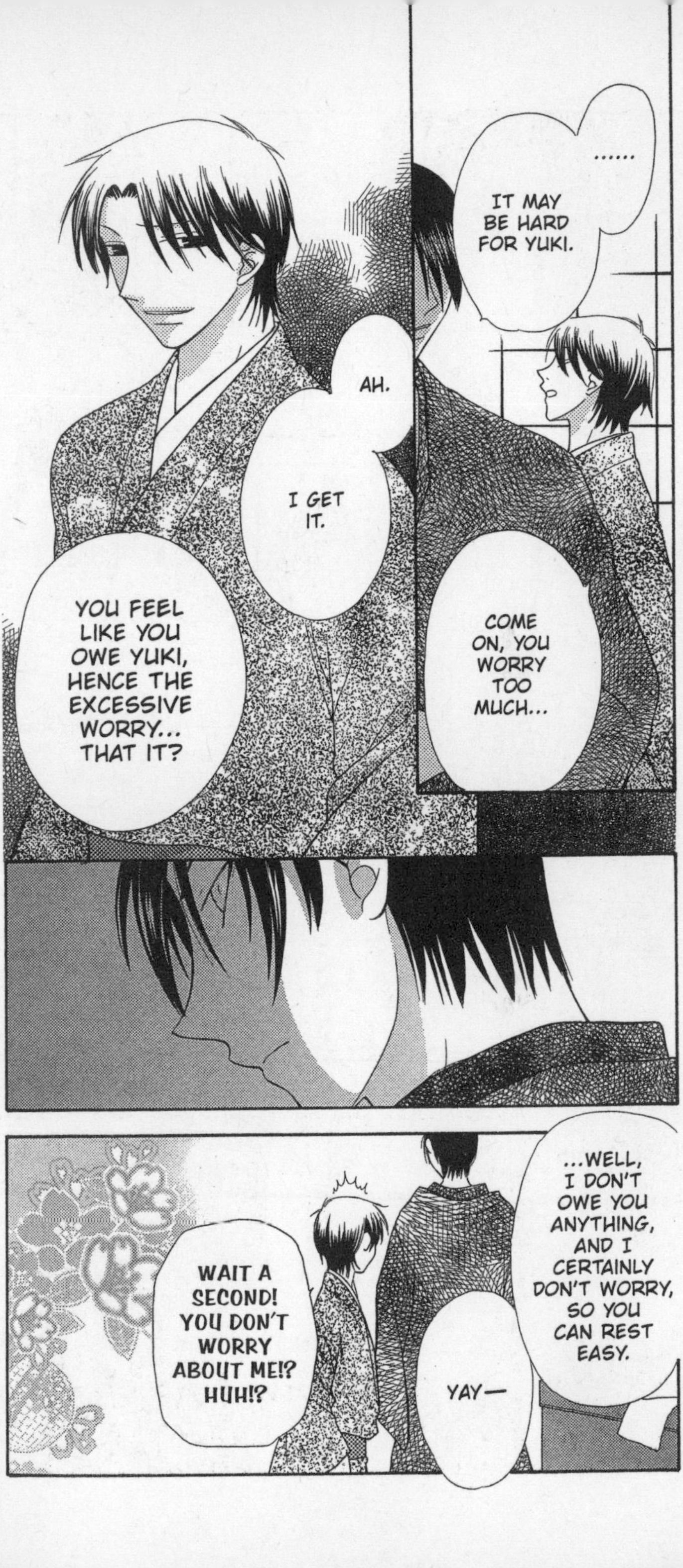
......
IT MAY BE HARD FOR YUKI.
COME ON, YOU WORRY TOO MUCH...
AH.
I GET IT.
YOU FEEL LIKE YOU OWE YUKI, HENCE THE EXCESSIVE WORRY... THAT IT?
...WELL, I DON'T OWE YOU ANYTHING, AND I CERTAINLY DON'T WORRY, SO YOU CAN REST EASY.
YAY—
WAIT A SECOND! YOU DON'T WORRY ABOUT ME!? HUH!?

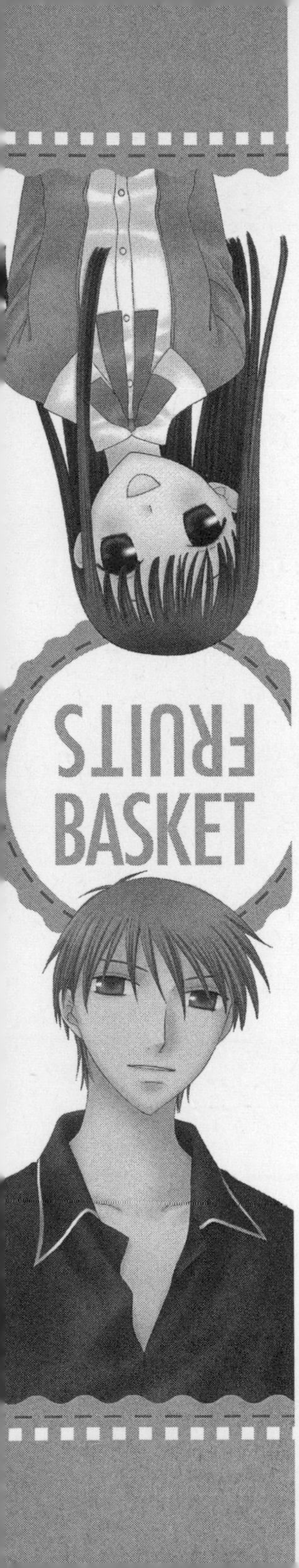
FRUITS
BASKET

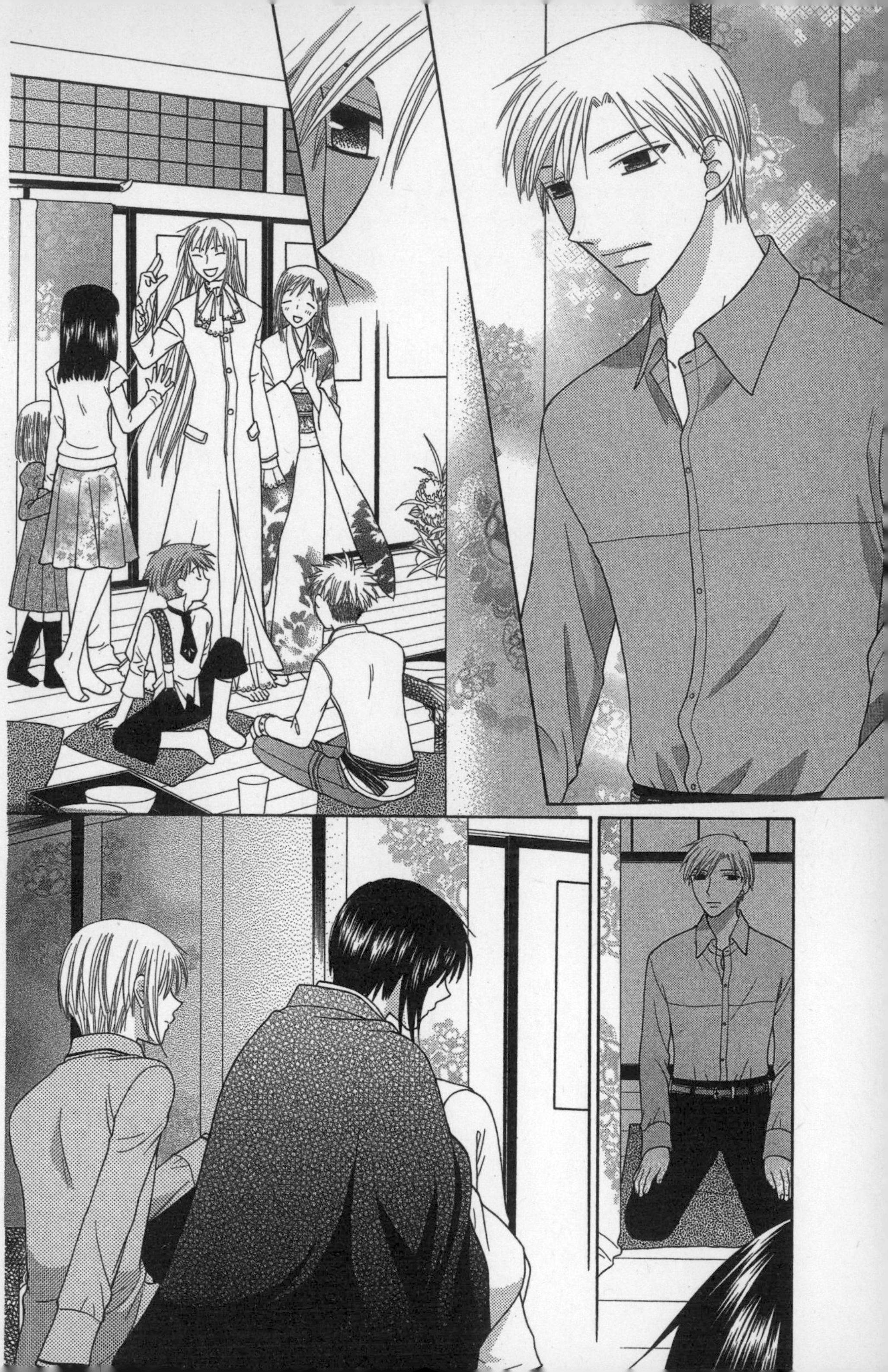

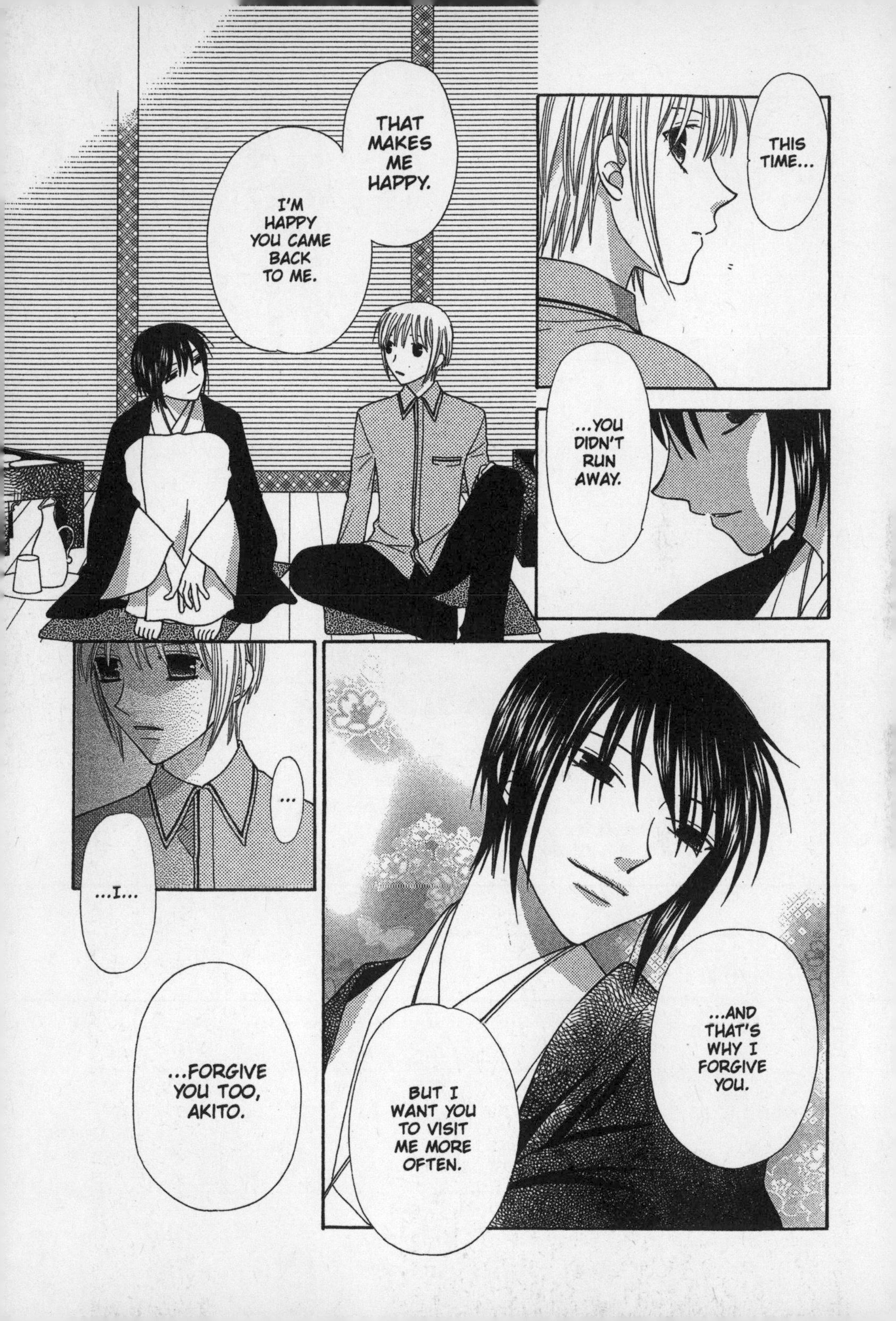
THIS TIME...
...YOU DIDN'T RUN AWAY.
THAT MAKES ME HAPPY.
I'M HAPPY YOU CAME BACK TO ME.
...AND THAT'S WHY I FORGIVE YOU.
BUT I WANT YOU TO VISIT ME MORE OFTEN.
...
...I...
...FORGIVE YOU TOO, AKITO.

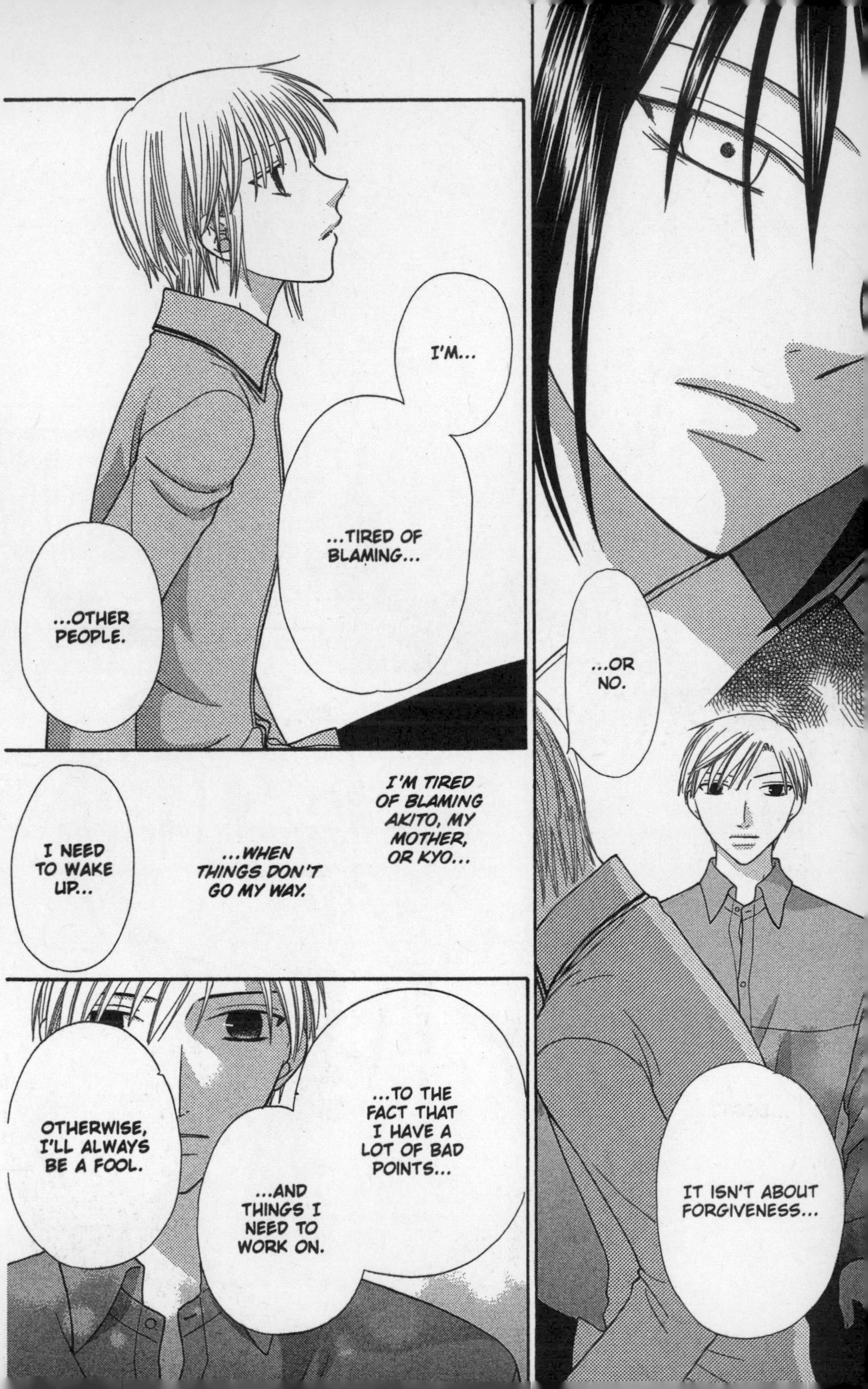
...OR NO.
IT ISN'T ABOUT FORGIVENESS...
I'M...
...TIRED OF BLAMING...
...OTHER PEOPLE.
I'M TIRED OF BLAMING AKITO, MY MOTHER, OR KYO...
...WHEN THINGS DON'T GO MY WAY.
I NEED TO WAKE UP...
...TO THE FACT THAT I HAVE A LOT OF BAD POINTS...
...AND THINGS I NEED TO WORK ON.
OTHERWISE, I'LL ALWAYS BE A FOOL.

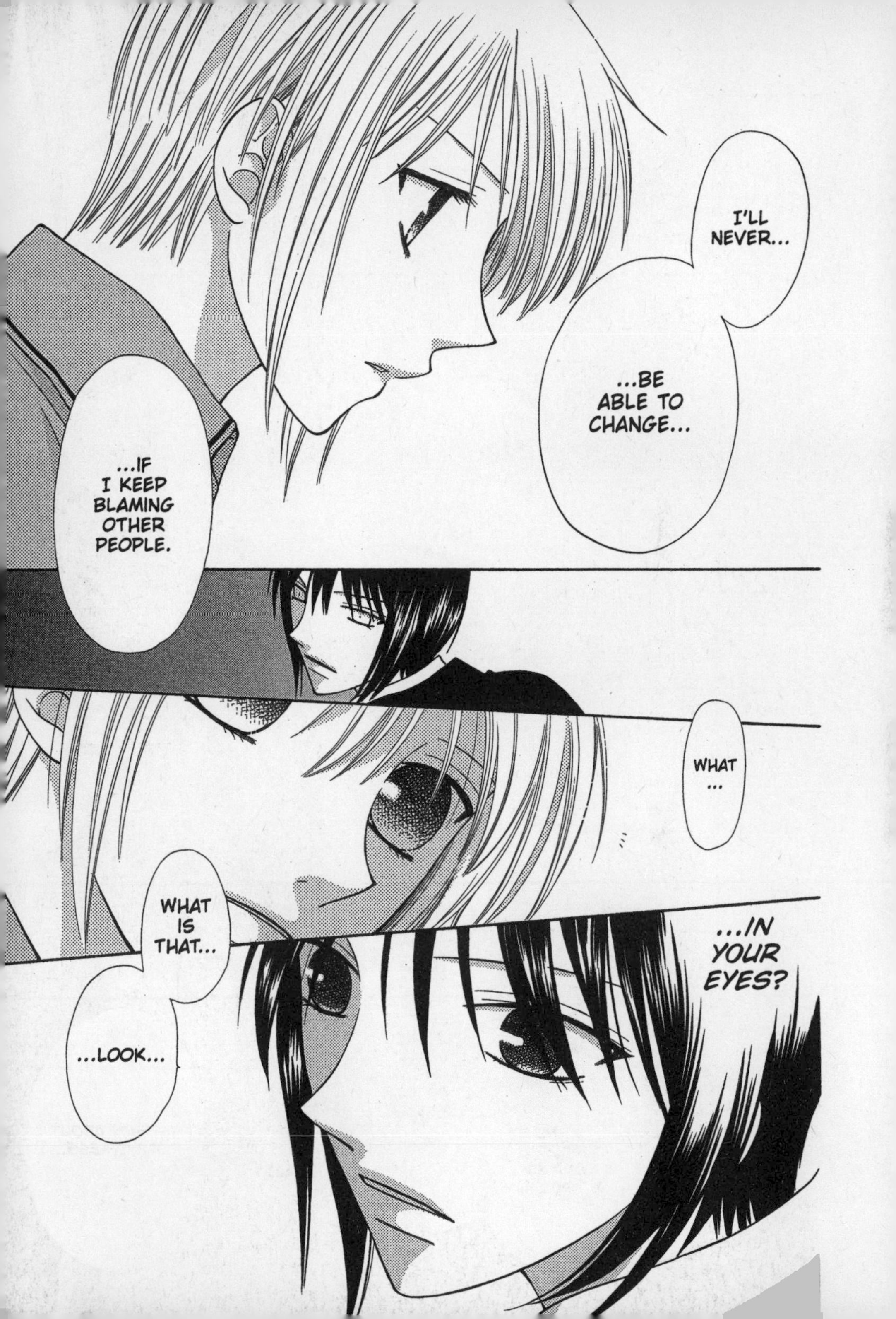
I'LL NEVER...
...BE ABLE TO CHANGE...
...IF I KEEP BLAMING OTHER PEOPLE.
WHAT ...
WHAT IS THAT...
...IN YOUR EYES?
...LOOK...

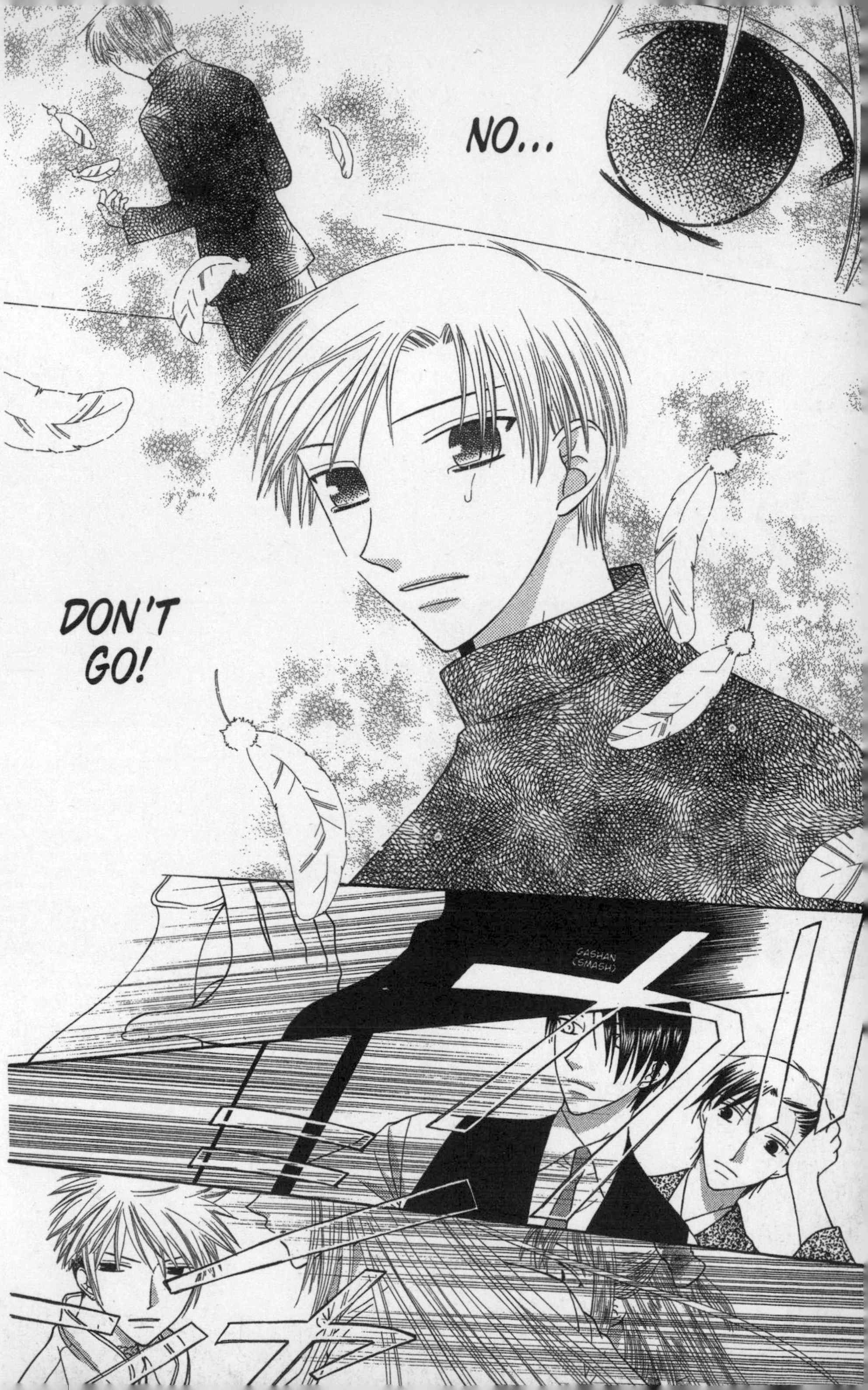
NO...
DON'T GO!
GASHAN (SMASH)

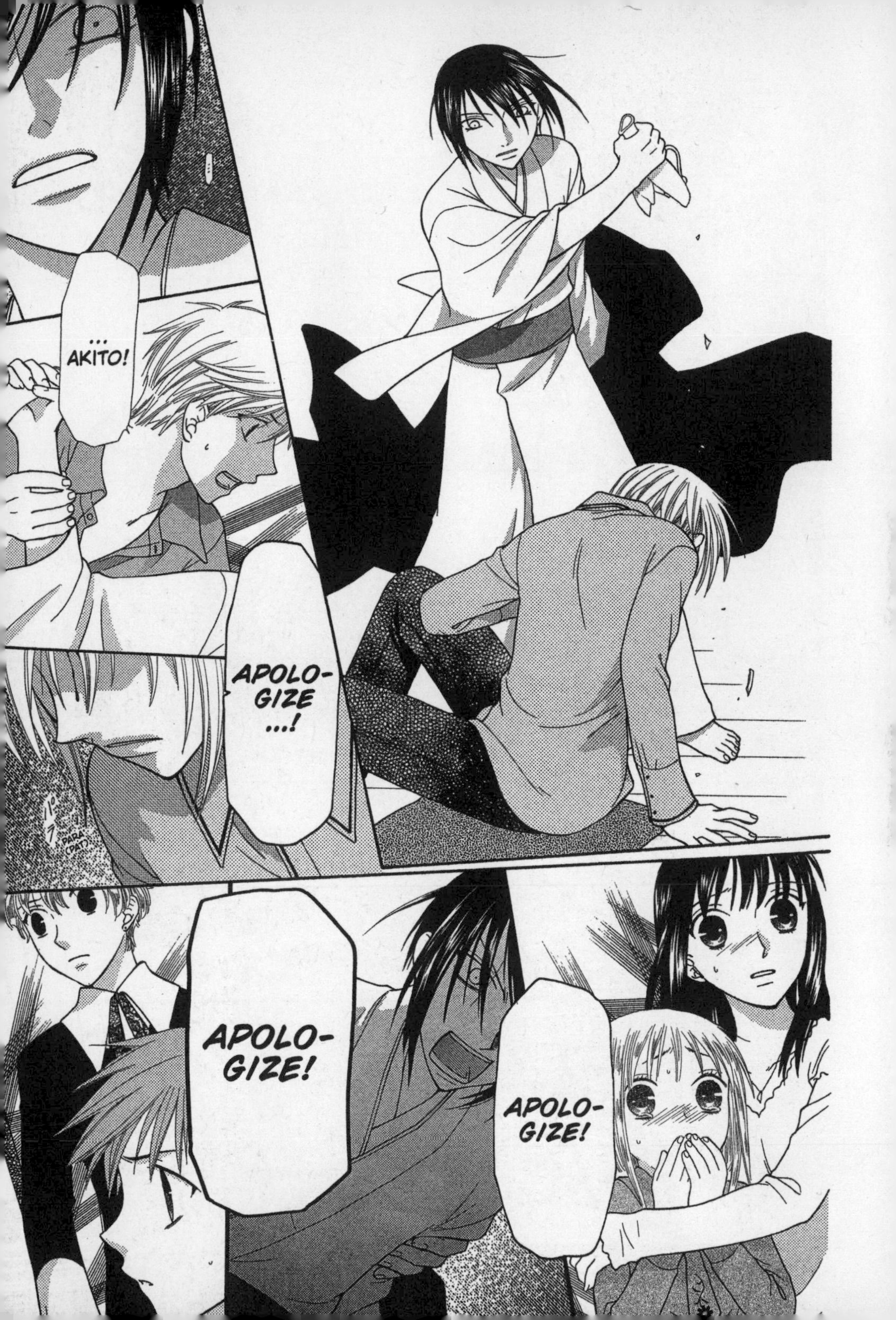
...
...AKITO!
APOLO-GIZE ...!
PARA (PAT)
APOLO-GIZE!
APOLO-GIZE!

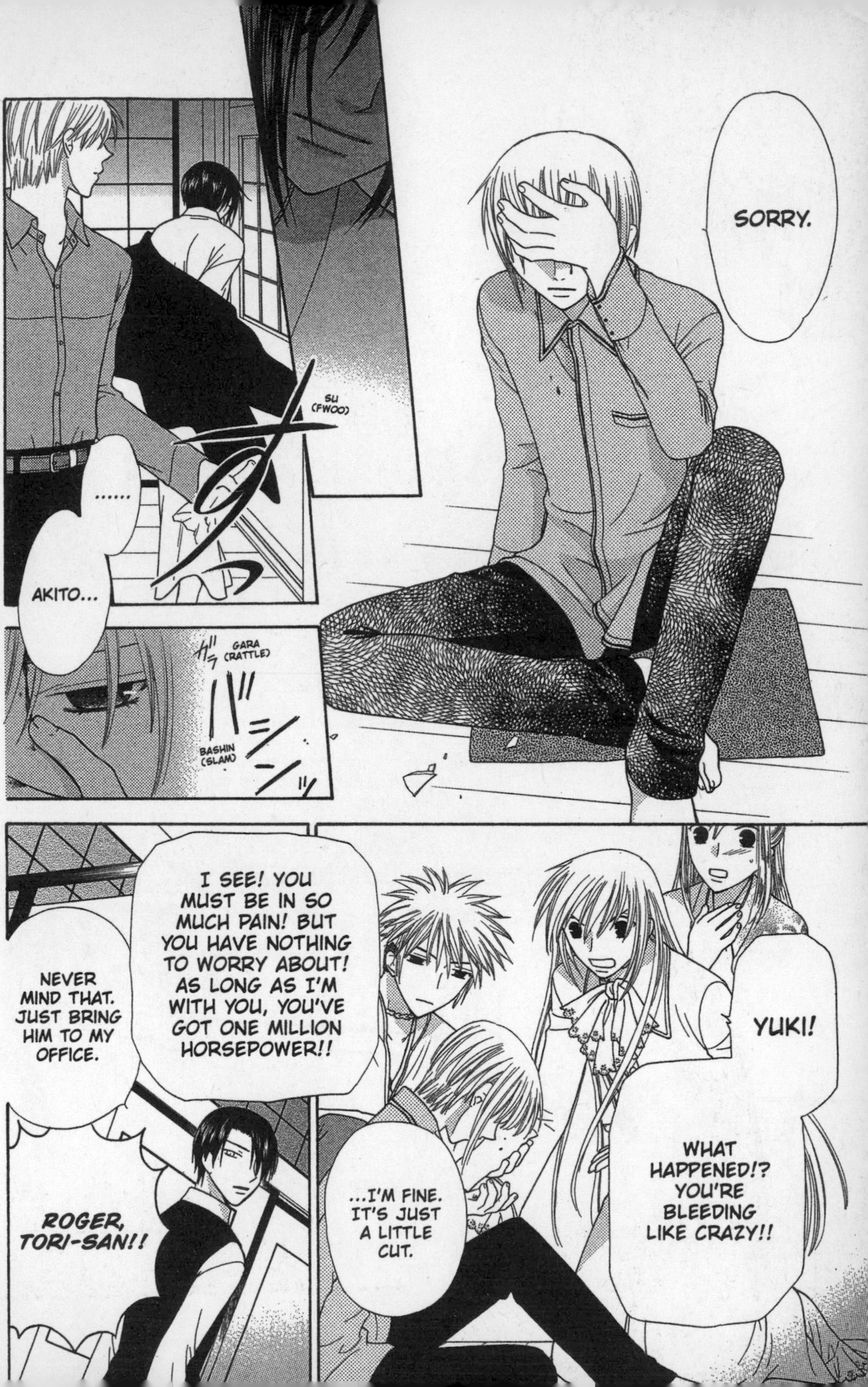
SORRY.
SU (FWOO)
......
AKITO...
GARA (RATTLE)
BASHIN (SLAM)
YUKI!
WHAT HAPPENED!? YOU'RE BLEEDING LIKE CRAZY!!
...I'M FINE. IT'S JUST A LITTLE CUT.
I SEE! YOU MUST BE IN SO MUCH PAIN! BUT YOU HAVE NOTHING TO WORRY ABOUT! AS LONG AS I'M WITH YOU, YOU'VE GOT ONE MILLION HORSEPOWER!!
NEVER MIND THAT. JUST BRING HIM TO MY OFFICE.
ROGER, TORI-SAN!!

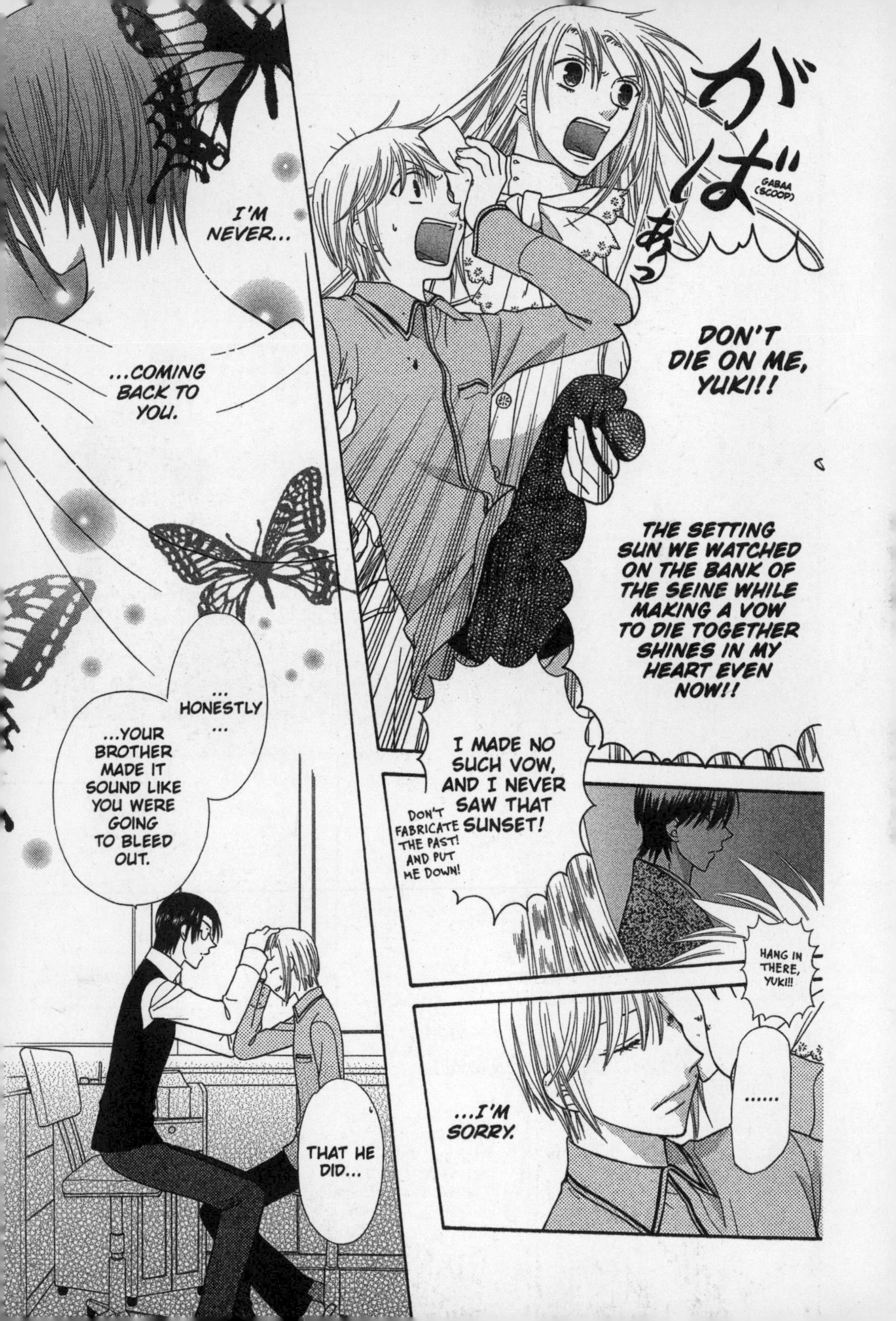
がばあっ
GABAA (SCOOP)
DON'T DIE ON ME, YUKI!!
THE SETTING SUN WE WATCHED ON THE BANK OF THE SEINE WHILE MAKING A VOW TO DIE TOGETHER SHINES IN MY HEART EVEN NOW!!
I MADE NO SUCH VOW, AND I NEVER SAW THAT SUNSET!
DON'T FABRICATE THE PAST! AND PUT ME DOWN!
HANG IN THERE, YUKI!!
...I'M SORRY.
......
I'M NEVER...
...COMING BACK TO YOU.
...HONESTLY...
...YOUR BROTHER MADE IT SOUND LIKE YOU WERE GOING TO BLEED OUT.
THAT HE DID...

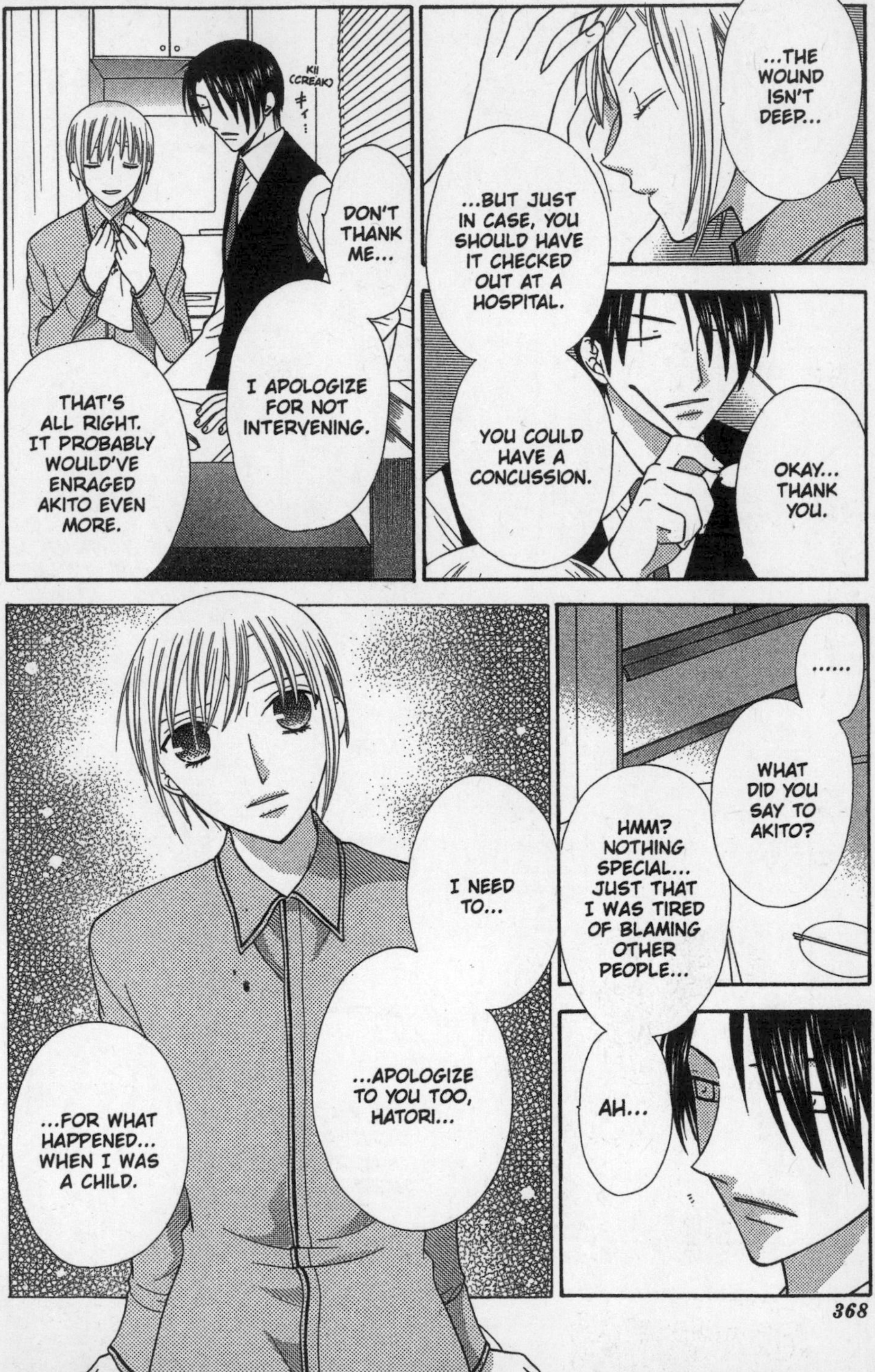
...THE WOUND ISN'T DEEP...
...BUT JUST IN CASE, YOU SHOULD HAVE IT CHECKED OUT AT A HOSPITAL.
YOU COULD HAVE A CONCUSSION.
OKAY... THANK YOU.
KII (CREAK)
キィ…
DON'T THANK ME...
I APOLOGIZE FOR NOT INTERVENING.
THAT'S ALL RIGHT. IT PROBABLY WOULD'VE ENRAGED AKITO EVEN MORE.
......
WHAT DID YOU SAY TO AKITO?
HMM? NOTHING SPECIAL... JUST THAT I WAS TIRED OF BLAMING OTHER PEOPLE...
AH...
I NEED TO...
...APOLOGIZE TO YOU TOO, HATORI...
...FOR WHAT HAPPENED... WHEN I WAS A CHILD.

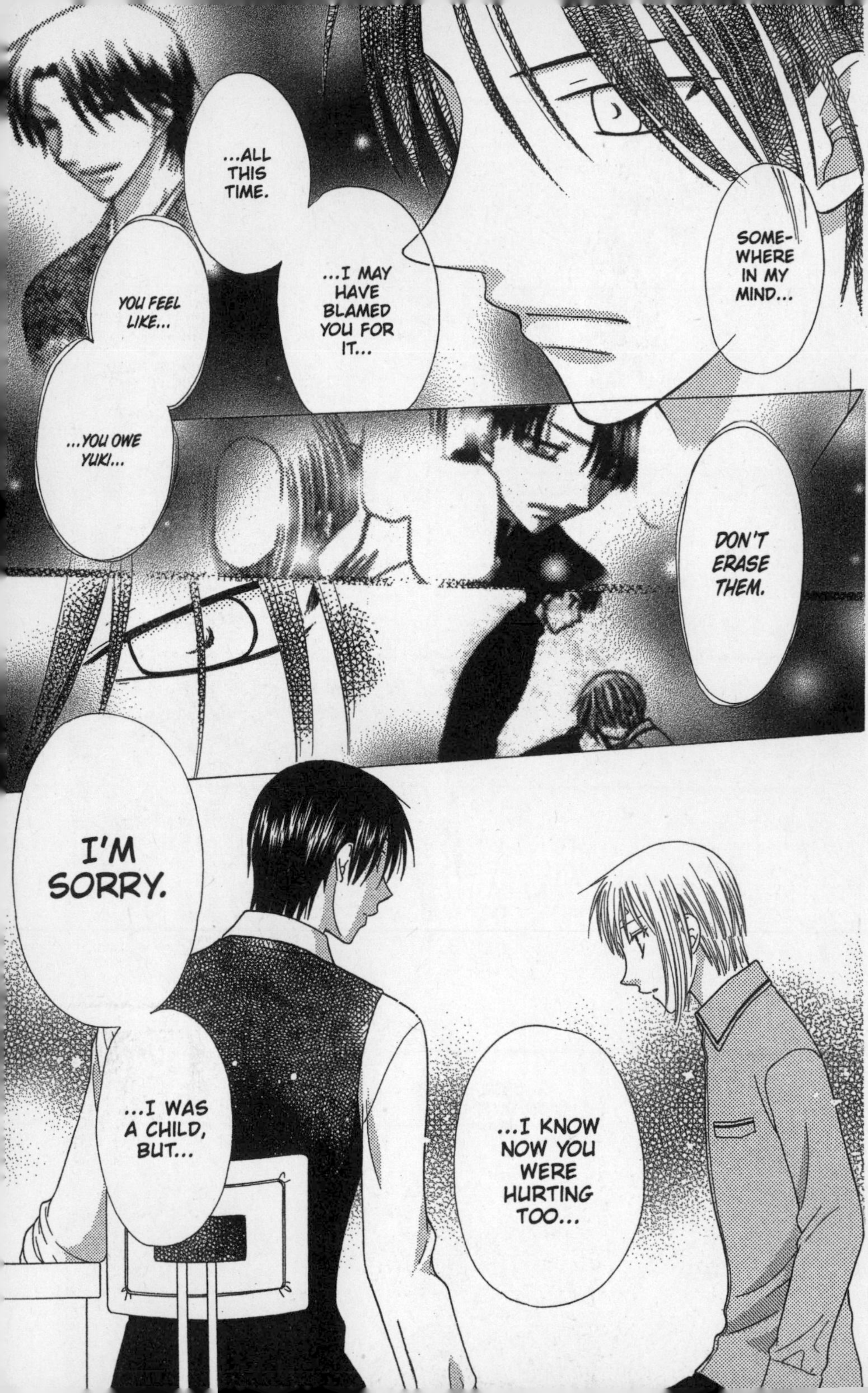
SOME-WHERE IN MY MIND...
...I MAY HAVE BLAMED YOU FOR IT...
...ALL THIS TIME.
YOU FEEL LIKE...
...YOU OWE YUKI...
DON'T ERASE THEM.
I'M SORRY.
...I WAS A CHILD, BUT...
...I KNOW NOW YOU WERE HURTING TOO...

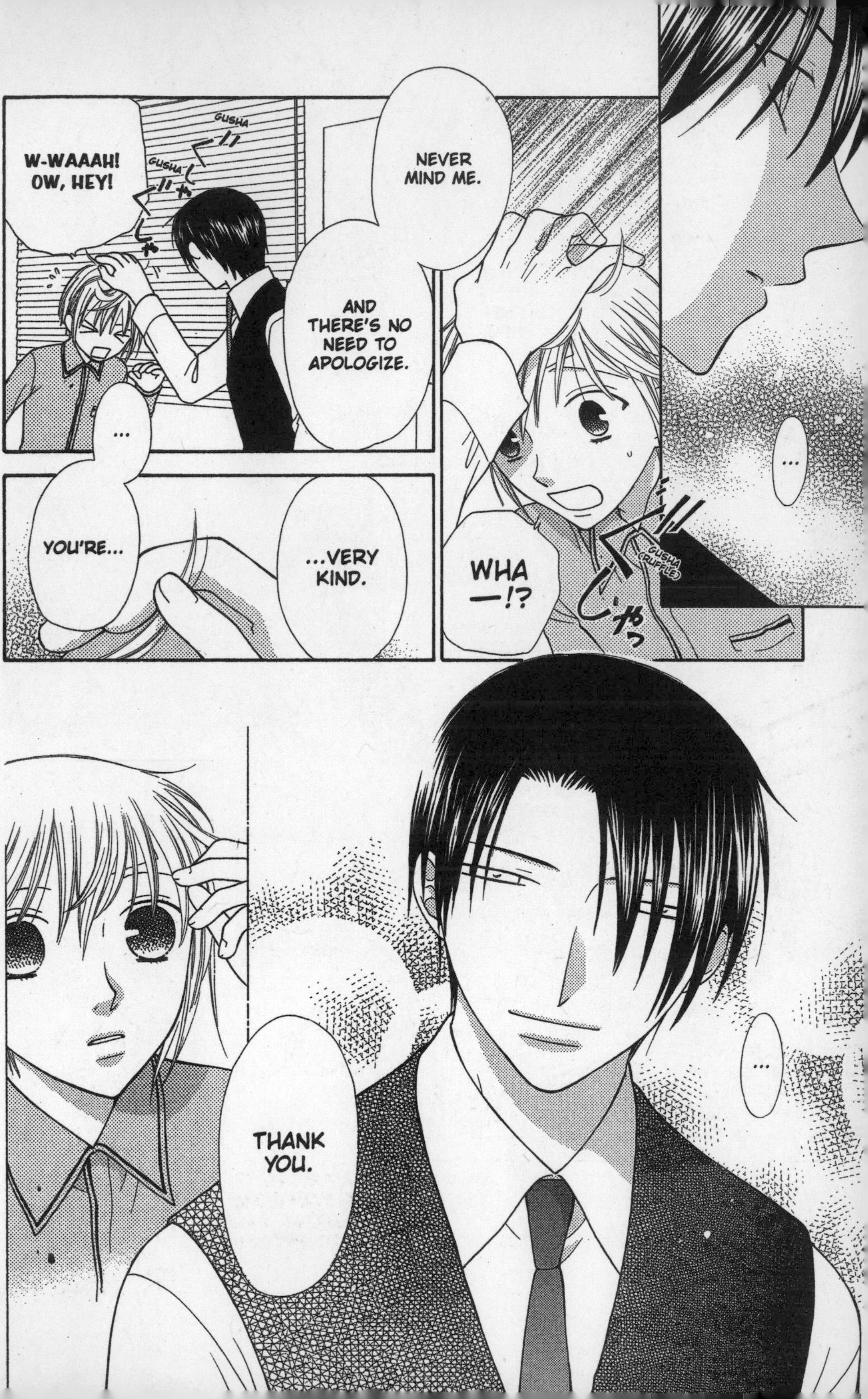
...
NEVER MIND ME.
AND THERE'S NO NEED TO APOLOGIZE.
WHA—!?
GUSHA (RUFFLE)
W-WAAAH! OW, HEY!
GUSHA
GUSHA
...
YOU'RE...
...VERY KIND.
...
THANK YOU.

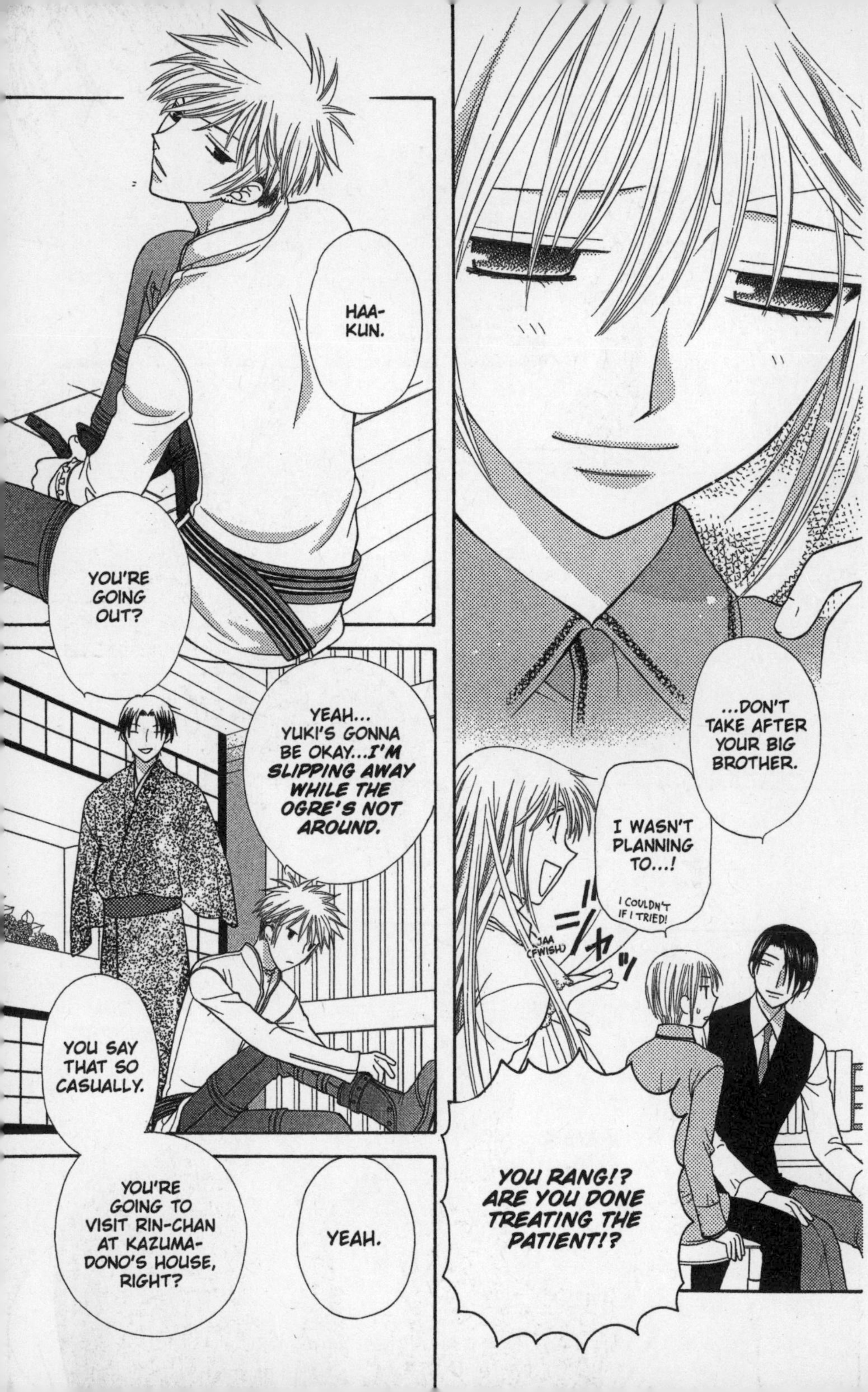
...DON'T TAKE AFTER YOUR BIG BROTHER.
I WASN'T PLANNING TO...!
I COULDN'T IF I TRIED!
JAA (FWISH)
YOU RANG!? ARE YOU DONE TREATING THE PATIENT!?
HAA-KUN.
YOU'RE GOING OUT?
YEAH... YUKI'S GONNA BE OKAY...I'M SLIPPING AWAY WHILE THE OGRE'S NOT AROUND.
YOU SAY THAT SO CASUALLY.
YOU'RE GOING TO VISIT RIN-CHAN AT KAZUMA-DONO'S HOUSE, RIGHT?
YEAH.

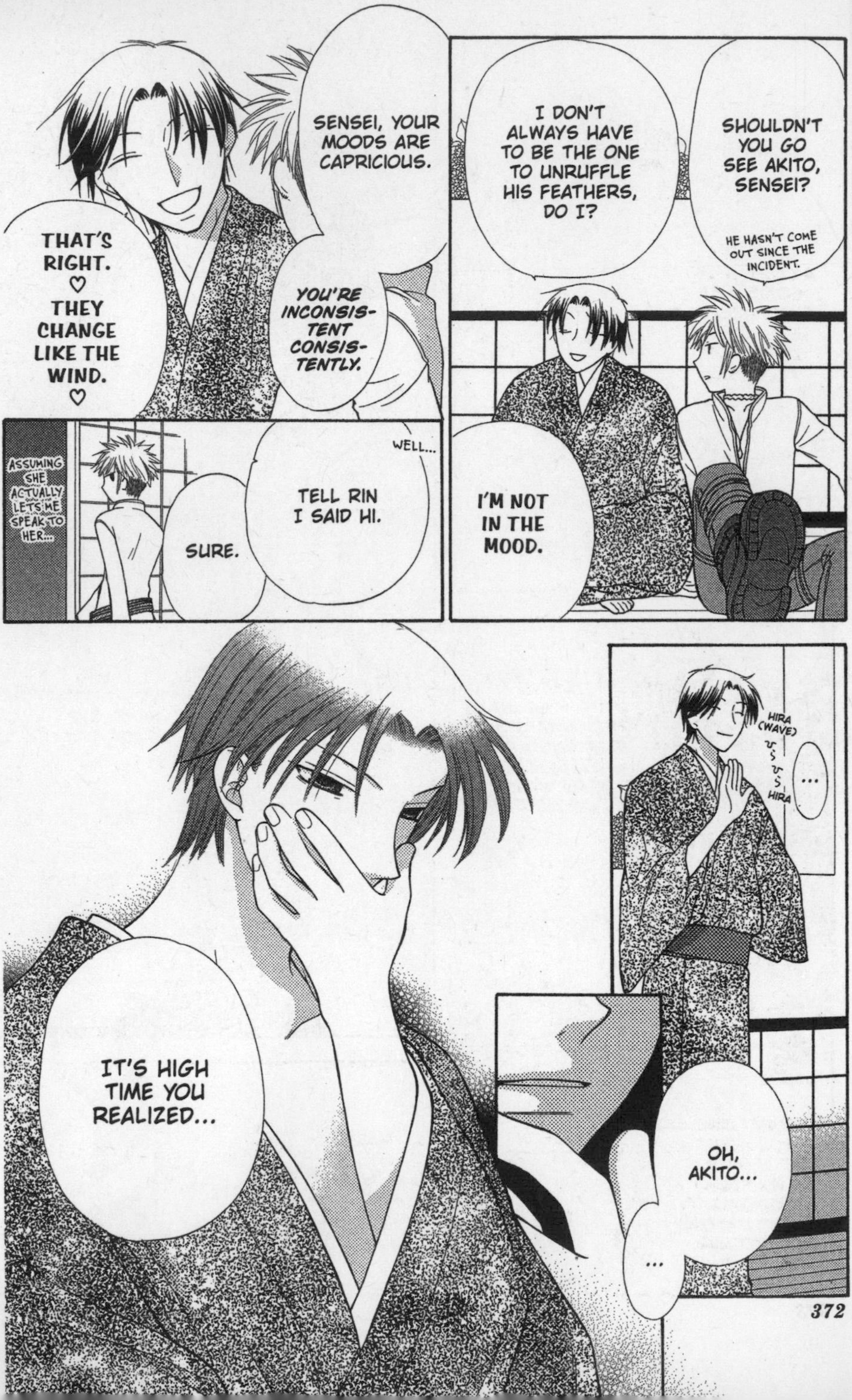
SHOULDN'T YOU GO SEE AKITO, SENSEI?
HE HASN'T COME OUT SINCE THE INCIDENT.
I DON'T ALWAYS HAVE TO BE THE ONE TO UNRUFFLE HIS FEATHERS, DO I?
I'M NOT IN THE MOOD.
SENSEI, YOUR MOODS ARE CAPRICIOUS.
YOU'RE INCONSISTENT CONSISTENTLY.
THAT'S RIGHT. ♡ THEY CHANGE LIKE THE WIND. ♡
WELL...
TELL RIN I SAID HI.
SURE.
ASSUMING SHE ACTUALLY LETS ME SPEAK TO HER...
HIRA (WAVE) HIRA
...
OH, AKITO...
...
IT'S HIGH TIME YOU REALIZED...

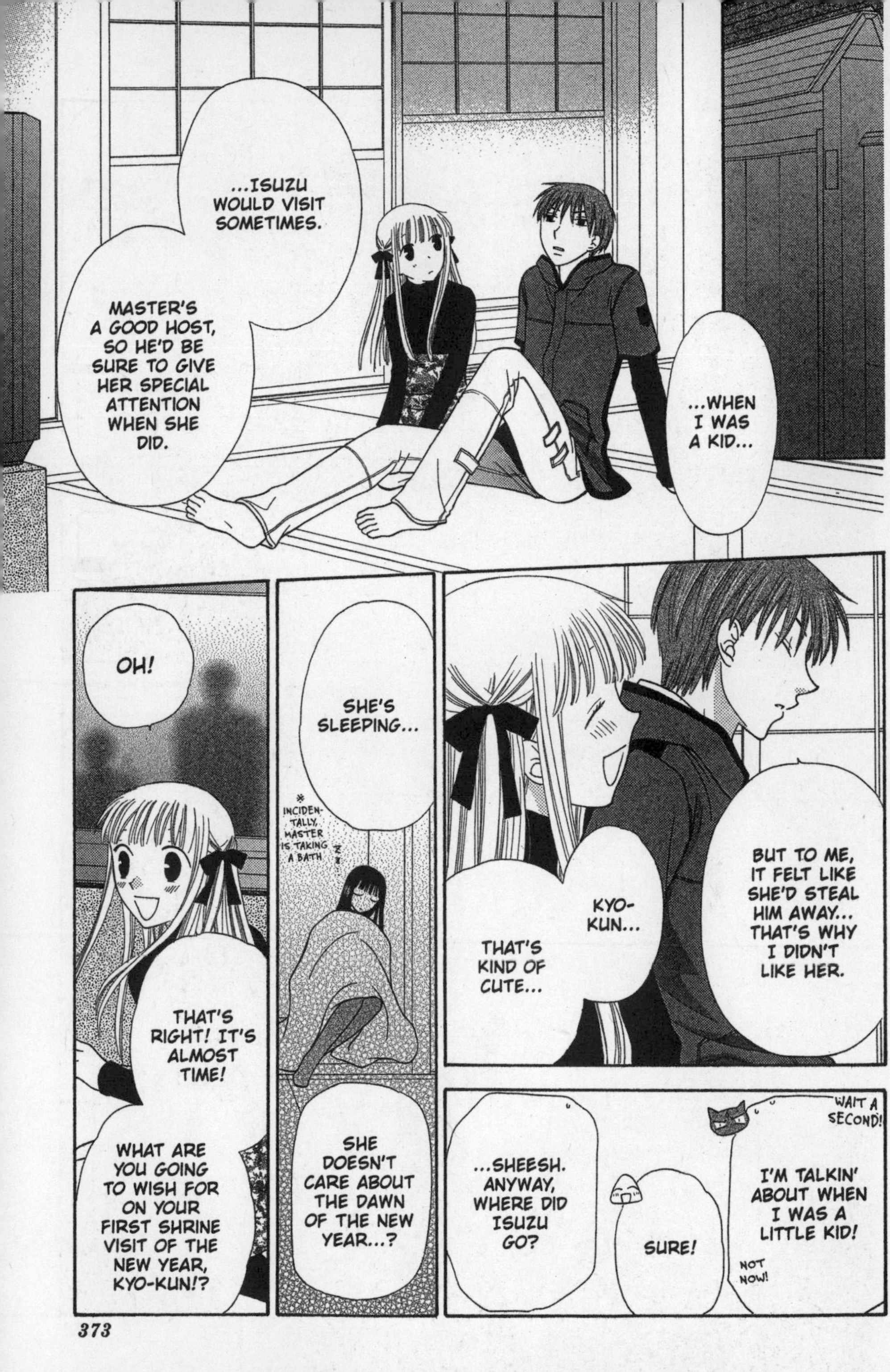
...WHEN I WAS A KID...
...ISUZU WOULD VISIT SOMETIMES.
MASTER'S A GOOD HOST, SO HE'D BE SURE TO GIVE HER SPECIAL ATTENTION WHEN SHE DID.
BUT TO ME, IT FELT LIKE SHE'D STEAL HIM AWAY... THAT'S WHY I DIDN'T LIKE HER.
KYO-KUN...
THAT'S KIND OF CUTE...
WAIT A SECOND!
I'M TALKIN' ABOUT WHEN I WAS A LITTLE KID!
NOT NOW!
SURE!
...SHEESH. ANYWAY, WHERE DID ISUZU GO?
SHE'S SLEEPING...
*INCIDENTALLY, MASTER IS TAKING A BATH
SHE DOESN'T CARE ABOUT THE DAWN OF THE NEW YEAR...?
OH!
THAT'S RIGHT! IT'S ALMOST TIME!
WHAT ARE YOU GOING TO WISH FOR ON YOUR FIRST SHRINE VISIT OF THE NEW YEAR, KYO-KUN!?

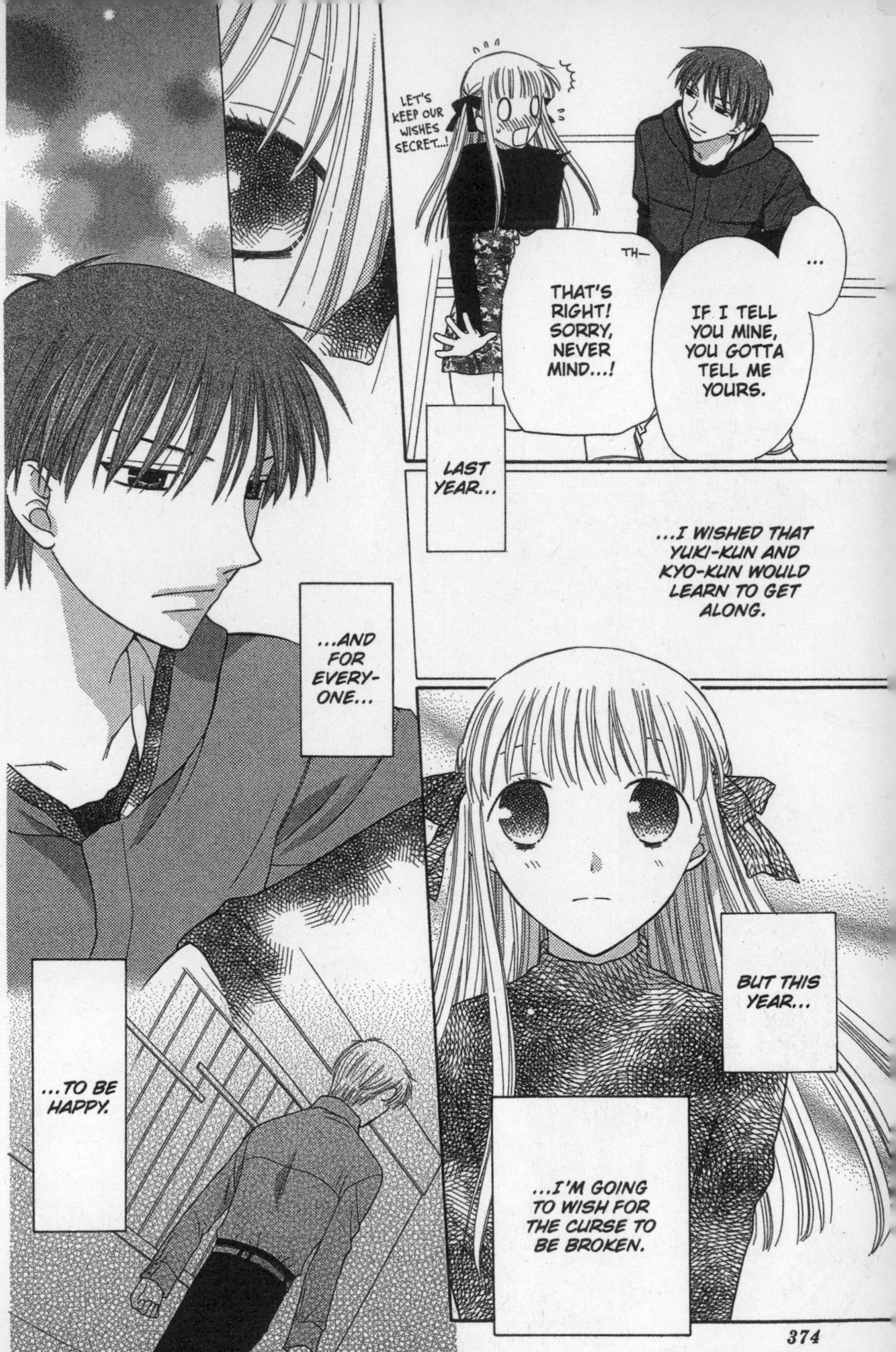

LET'S KEEP OUR WISHES SECRET...!
...
IF I TELL YOU MINE, YOU GOTTA TELL ME YOURS.
TH—
THAT'S RIGHT! SORRY, NEVER MIND...!
LAST YEAR...
...I WISHED THAT YUKI-KUN AND KYO-KUN WOULD LEARN TO GET ALONG.
...AND FOR EVERY-ONE...
...TO BE HAPPY.
BUT THIS YEAR...
...I'M GOING TO WISH FOR THE CURSE TO BE BROKEN.

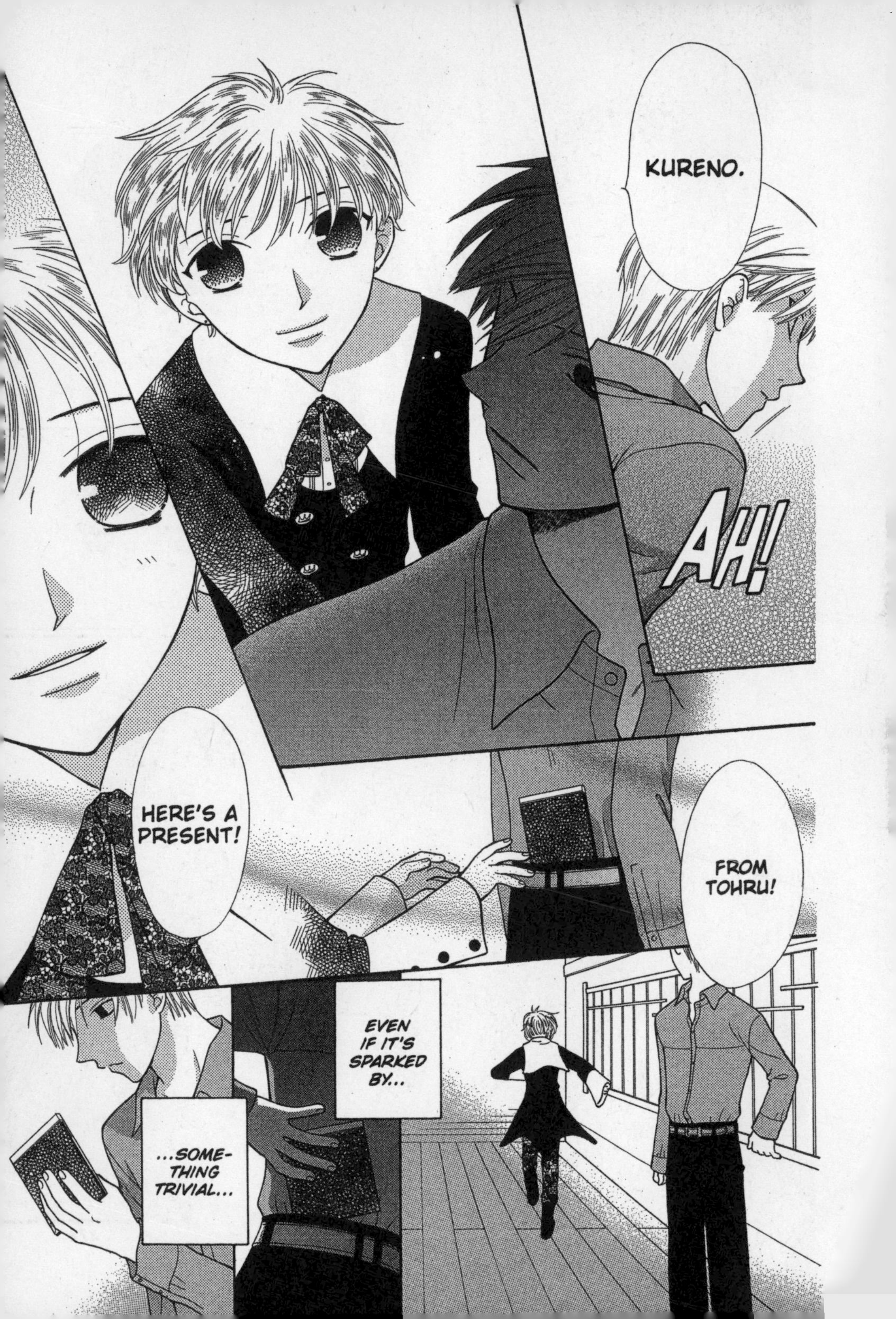
KURENO.
AH!
FROM TOHRU!
HERE'S A PRESENT!
EVEN IF IT'S SPARKED BY...
...SOME-THING TRIVIAL...

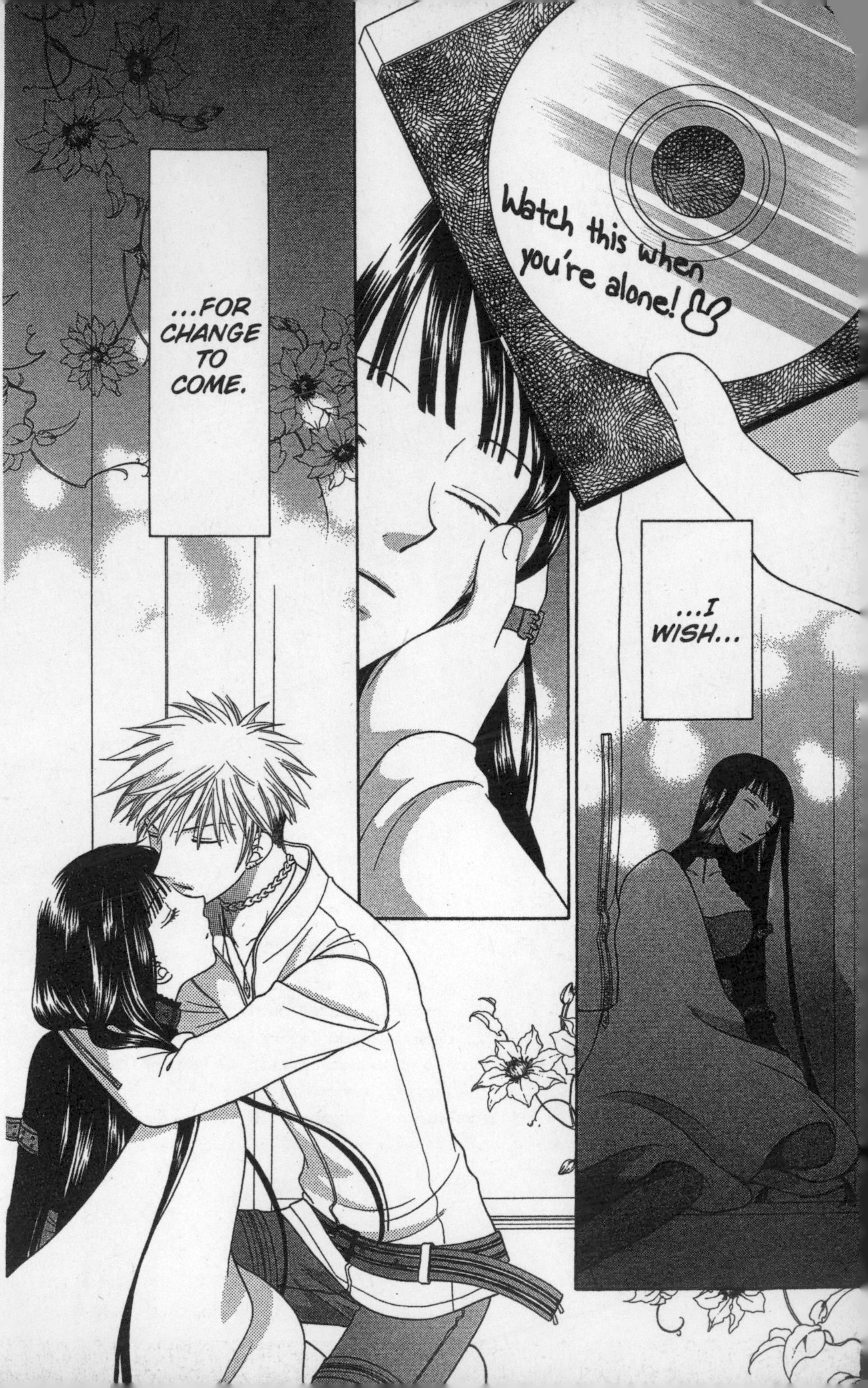
Watch this when you're alone!
...I WISH...
...FOR CHANGE TO COME.

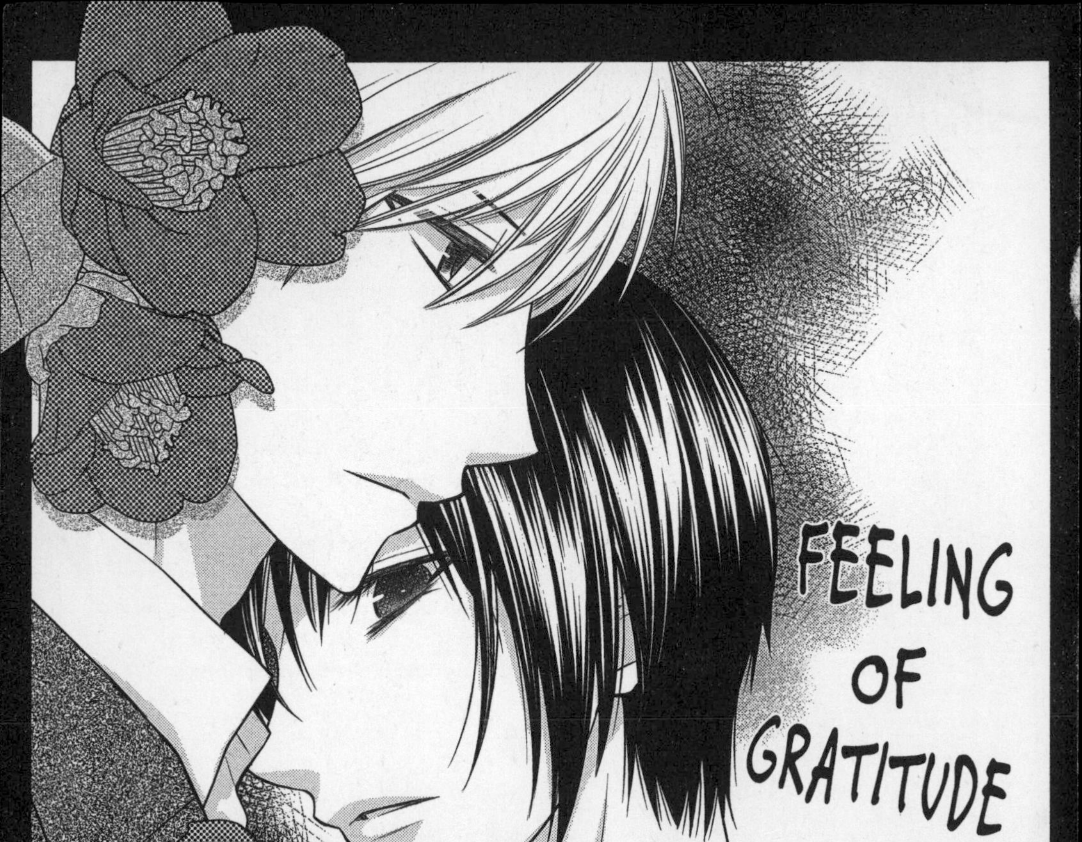
FEELING OF GRATITUDE

This isn't limited to *Furuba*, but when I'm creating a story, there are "episodes" that I cannot leave out, that I feel like I must tell, and sometimes a title will be created just for that specific episode. Yuki's storyline that begins around Volume 7 of the collector's edition is such an episode. Of course, I knew there'd be mixed reactions, but even so, I wanted to have him standing up on his own two feet in a proper fashion and begin walking toward a new place for himself. I mentioned this in the fan book too, but Yuki is another main character who carries *Furuba*'s theme.

Thank you for picking up this collector's edition!

高屋 奈月。

NATSUKI TAKAYA

TRANSLATION NOTES

COMMON HONORIFICS

no honorific: Indicates familiarity or closeness; if used without permission or reason, addressing someone in this manner would constitute an insult.

-san: The Japanese equivalent of Mr./Mrs./Miss. If a situation calls for politeness, this is the fail-safe honorific.

-sama: Conveys great respect; may also indicate that the social status of the speaker is lower than that of the addressee.

-kun: Used most often when referring to boys, this indicates affection or familiarity. Occasionally used by older men among their peers, but it may also be used by anyone referring to a person of lower standing.

-chan: An affectionate honorific indicating familiarity used mostly in reference to girls; also used in reference to cute persons or animals of either gender.

-senpai: A suffix used to address upperclassmen or more experienced coworkers.

-kouhai: A suffix used to address underclassmen or less experienced coworkers.

-sensei: A respectful term for teachers, artists, or high-level professionals.

Page 98

"It's not a wedding!": Japanese weddings generally begin with a Shinto-style ceremony in which the bride and groom are dressed in traditional garb, a white kimono for the bride and a black kimono for the groom. Afterward, a Western-style reception is held, during which the groom wears a tuxedo and the bride a Western-style wedding dress. Then there is one more chance to change clothes, an intermission during the reception. The groom may change into a suit or simply change the waistcoast. However, the bride will often wear a brightly colored showstopper of a gown.

Page 113

Mito Koumon: Long-running (1969–2011) historical drama series about an elderly nobleman who travels all over Japan incognito with his retainers.

Page 113

Suke-san, Kaku-san, Ogin-san: All faithful attendents of the titular character in *Mito Koumon*. The expert swordsmen Suke-san and Kaku-san are Koumon's bodyguards. Ogin-san is a female ninja, a character often seen bathing.

Page 143

Yakiniku: Sometimes called "Korean barbecue," this dish consists of meat cooked at the table on a small grill.

Page 175
"There is always only one grandpa!!": An amalgamation of the catchphrases of two famous manga/anime teen detectives. From the *Case Closed* series, the pint-sized Conan's correct tagline is: "There is always only one truth!" From *The Kindaichi Case Files*, lecherous teen detective Hajime Kindaichi's trademark line is: "In the name of my grandpa!" (His grandfather is said to be Kosuke Kindaichi, another famous fictional Japanese detective created by mystery novelist Seishi Yokomizo.)

Page 182
Yakisoba: Noodles stir-fried with vegetables like carrots and onions — and sometimes meat or seafood — all covered in sweet sauce. Usually served with seaweed flakes, pickled red ginger, dried bonito flakes, and mayonnaise. A favorite dish at festivals but also found in convenience stores and in the home as well.

Page 225
Ms. No Eyebrows: High school gang fashion sense in the 1980s and 1990s entailed shaving off one's eyebrows, having permed hair, and wearing customized school uniforms such as a long skirt (supposedly to hide weapons within). Historically speaking, shaved eyebrows on women were in fashion (a practice adopted from the Chinese custom) from the Heian period (794–1185) until 1870 when it was banned as being inappropriate for a modern society that had begun adapting to Western ways.

Page 241
"Go to hell, ocean!!": It's a staple of Japanese coming-of-age dramas for teenagers to face the sea and yell, "You bastard!" Teens often have a myriad of stressors in their lives, and this yelling out to sea is thought to be a harmless way to blow off steam...although you'd be hard-pressed to find a real teenager who's done this.

Page 271
Otou-san: Though *otou-san* is most commonly used to mean one's own father, it is often used to refer to one's father-in-law. Likewise, *okaa-san* can refer to one's own mother as well as mother-in-law.

Page 346
"Machi, you love Red, huh?": Up until now, the characters had been using the Japanese word for red, *aka*, to talk about Machi's favorite color. This is noteworthy because, when they've discussed their "ranger" colors in the past, they've always used the English loanword for red, *reddo*, instead. This means that Kakeru is the first one to draw the connection between Machi liking red (*aka*) and Machi liking *red* (*Reddo* Ranger, Yuki). But this reference goes right over Yuki's head.

Page 357

"...the desire to be embraced!!!": There is actually a pun on this page. Ayame says the line about the "desire to be embraced," or *dakaretai* (which also has the slang nuance of, put bluntly, "the desire to be screwed"). In the third panel in Japanese, he calls their duo *dakaretai*, the same word as above, but using a kanji for *tai* meaning "group/corps/company/squad." If it was translated literally (and clunkily), it would be something like "the Wanna-Be-Screwed Squad."

Page 373

New Year's wish: It's tradition to make a wish on the first shrine visit of the New Year. People often try to visit one on New Year's Eve or New Year's Day, but some choose to go later in the week to avoid the crowds.

Fruits Basket

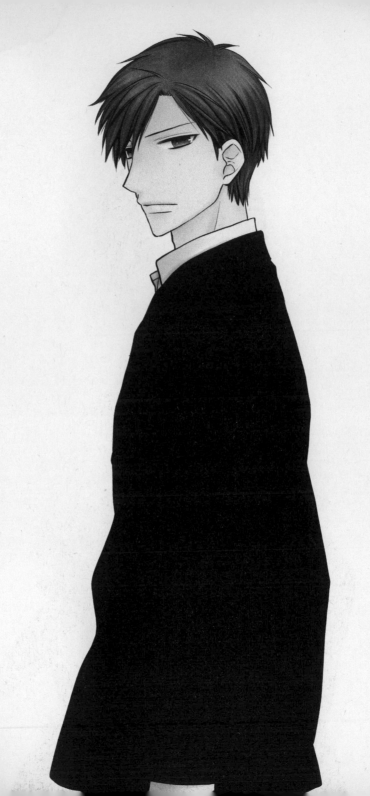

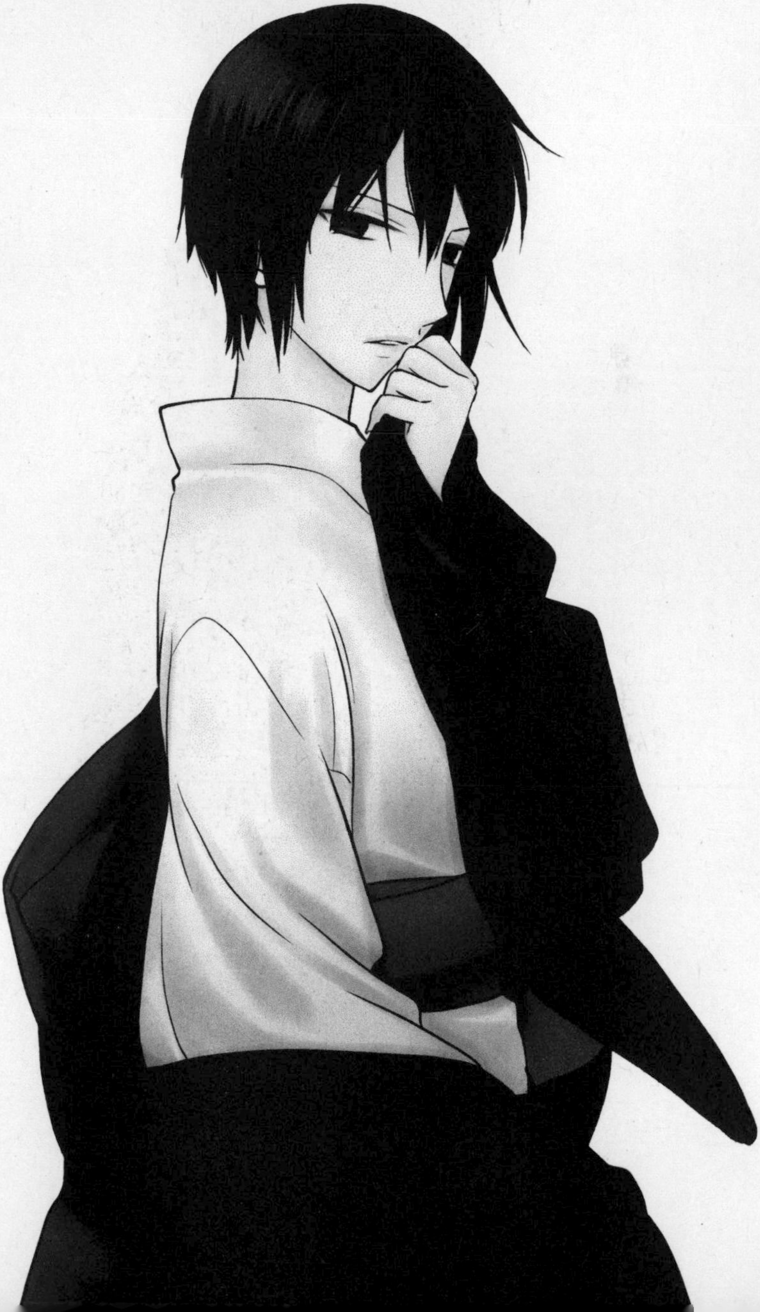

COLLECTOR'S EDITION

Fruits Basket

Read on for an early look at Volume 9,
coming January 2017.

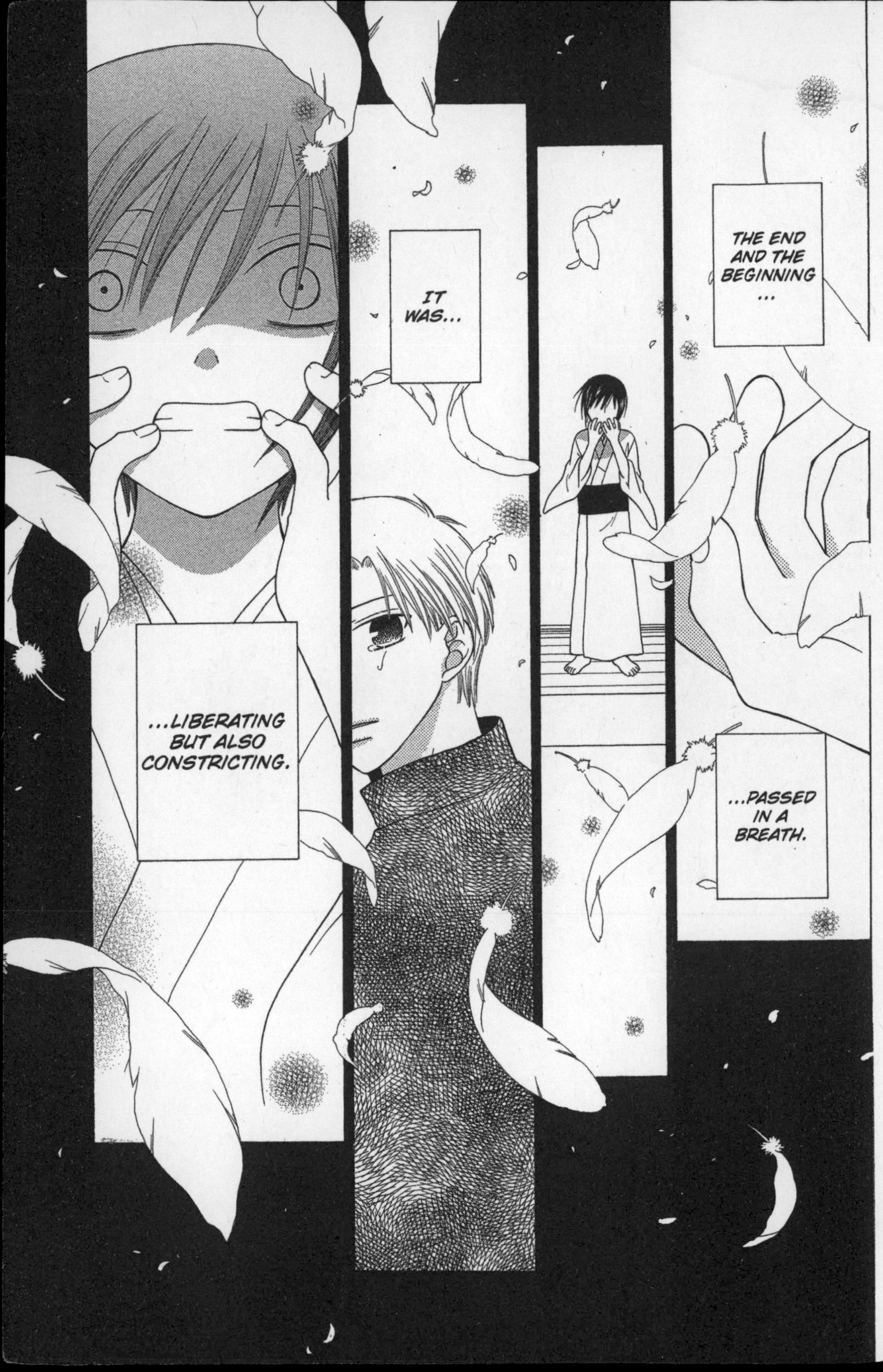
THE END AND THE BEGINNING ...
...PASSED IN A BREATH.
IT WAS...
...LIBERATING BUT ALSO CONSTRICTING.

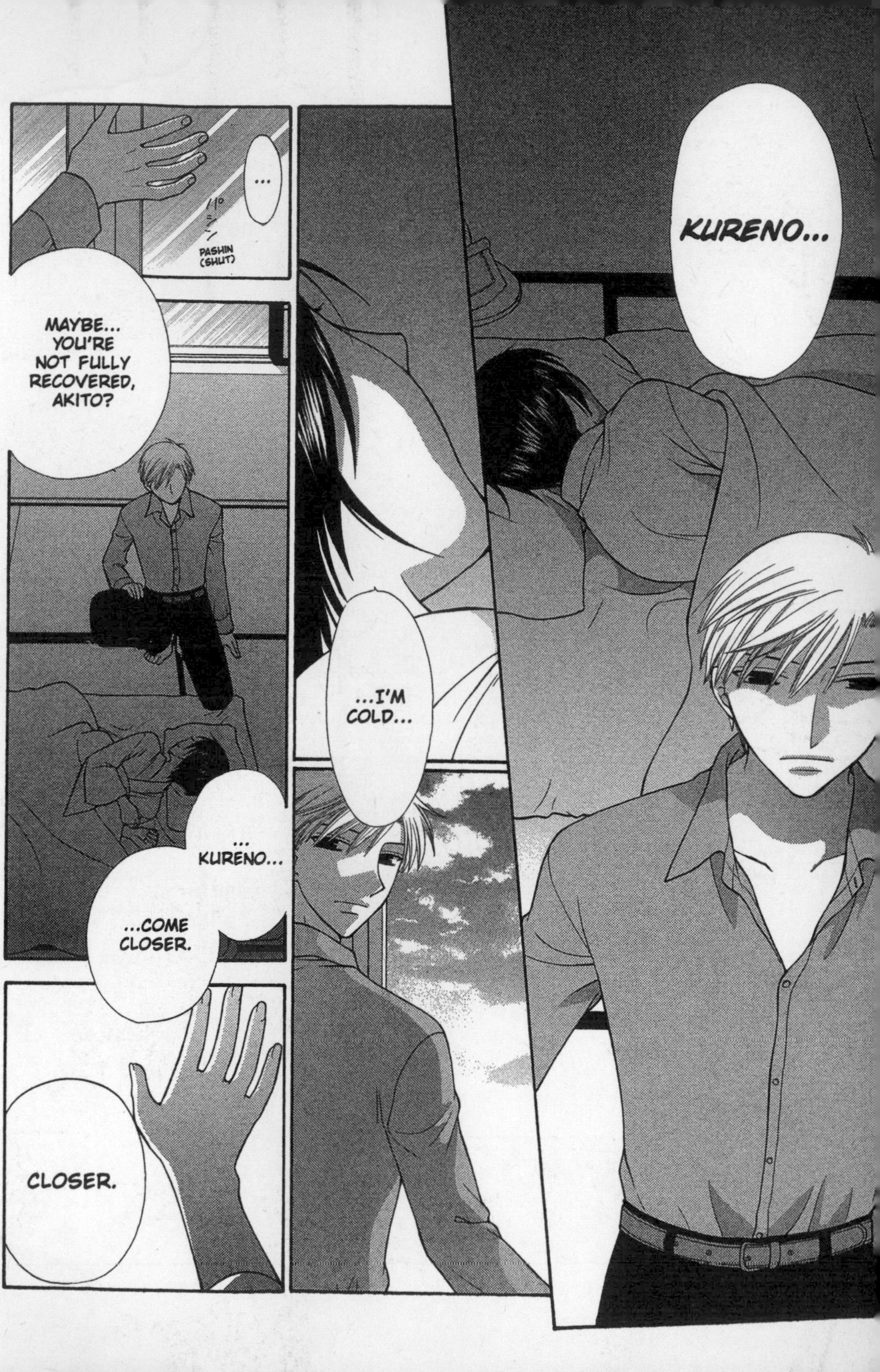
KURENO...
...I'M COLD...
...
PASHIN (SHUT)
MAYBE... YOU'RE NOT FULLY RECOVERED, AKITO?
... KURENO...
...COME CLOSER.
CLOSER.

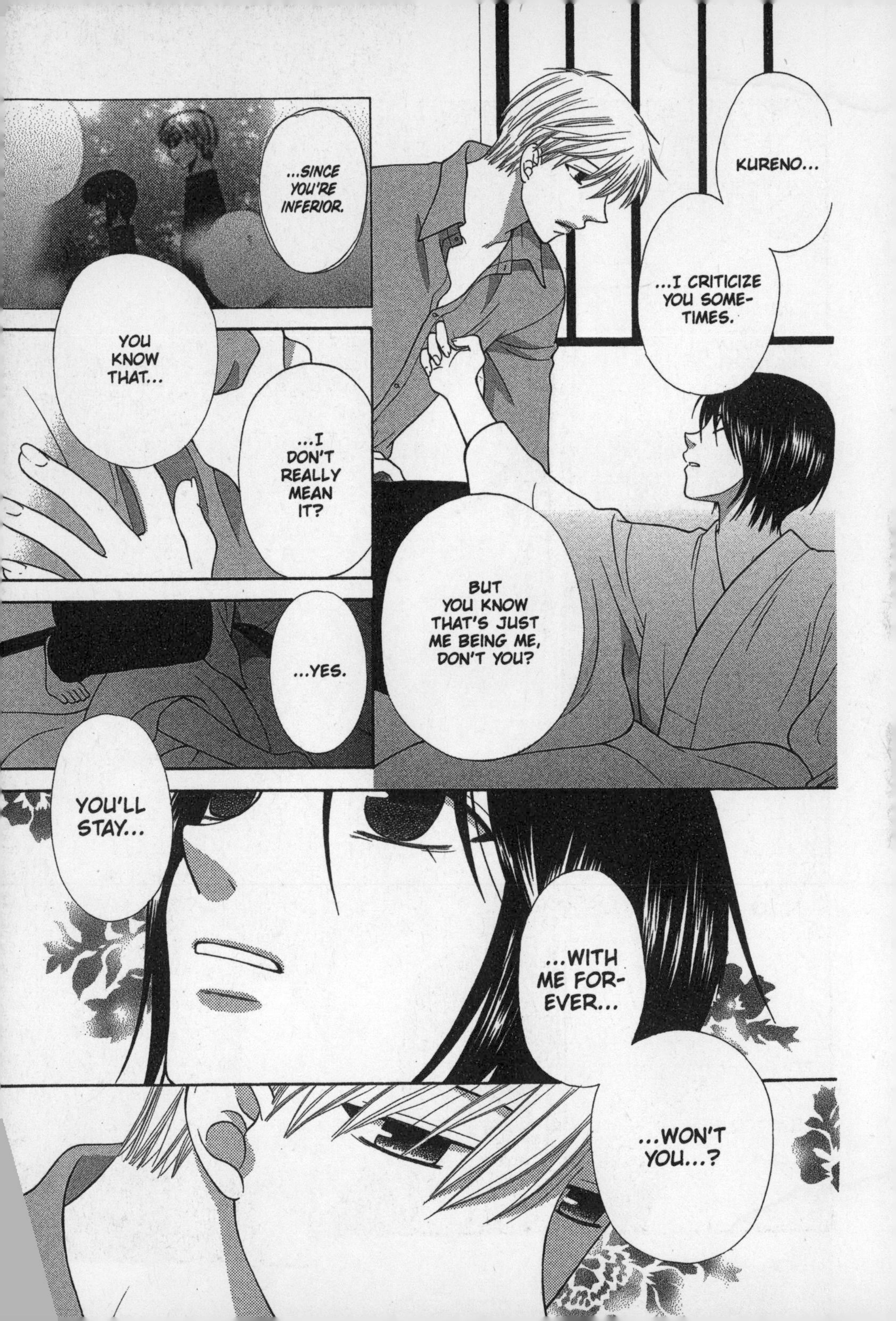
KURENO...
...I CRITICIZE YOU SOME-TIMES.
BUT YOU KNOW THAT'S JUST ME BEING ME, DON'T YOU?
...SINCE YOU'RE INFERIOR.
YOU KNOW THAT...
...I DON'T REALLY MEAN IT?
...YES.
YOU'LL STAY...
...WITH ME FOR-EVER...
...WON'T YOU...?

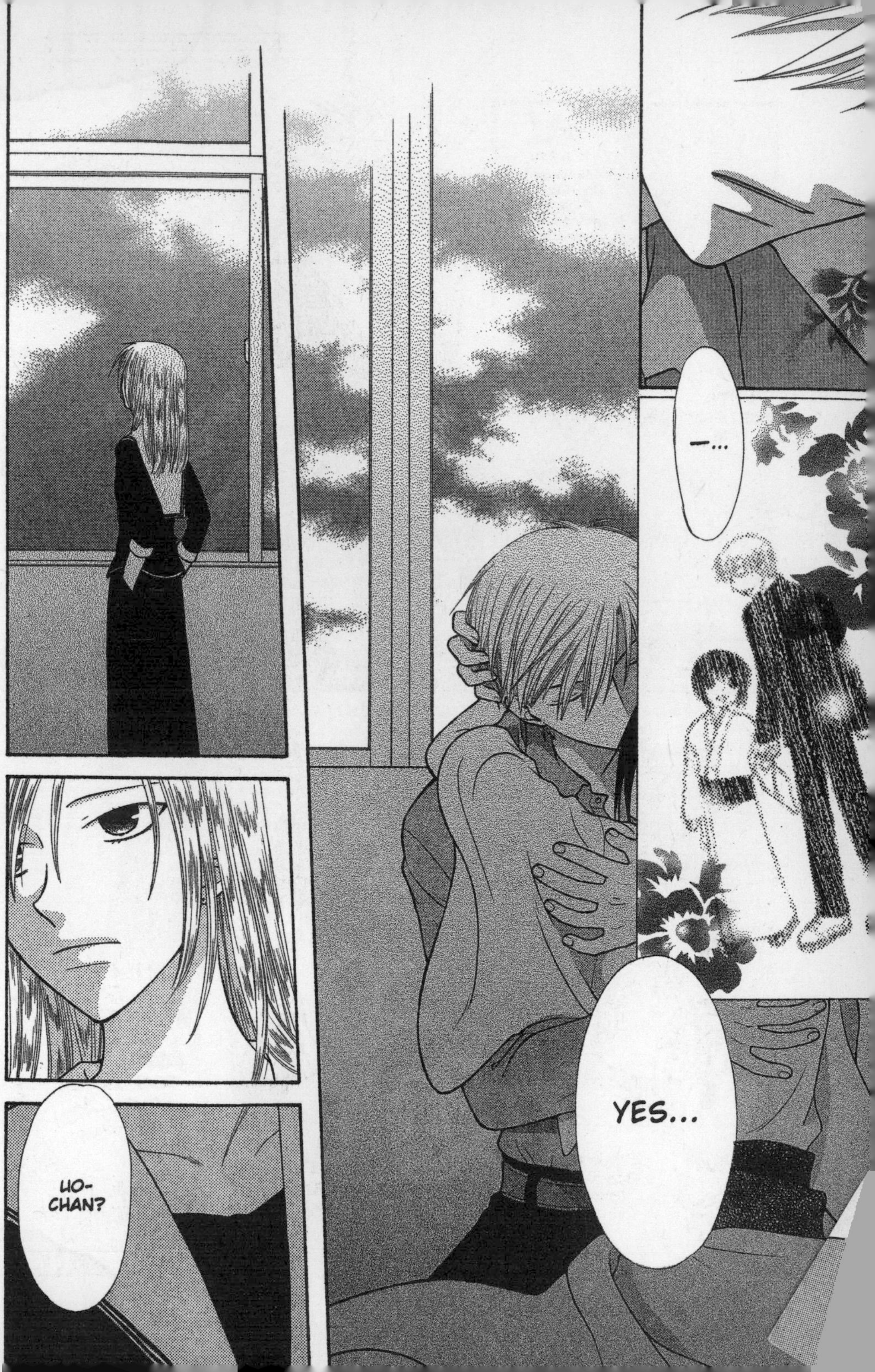
—...
YES...
UO-CHAN?

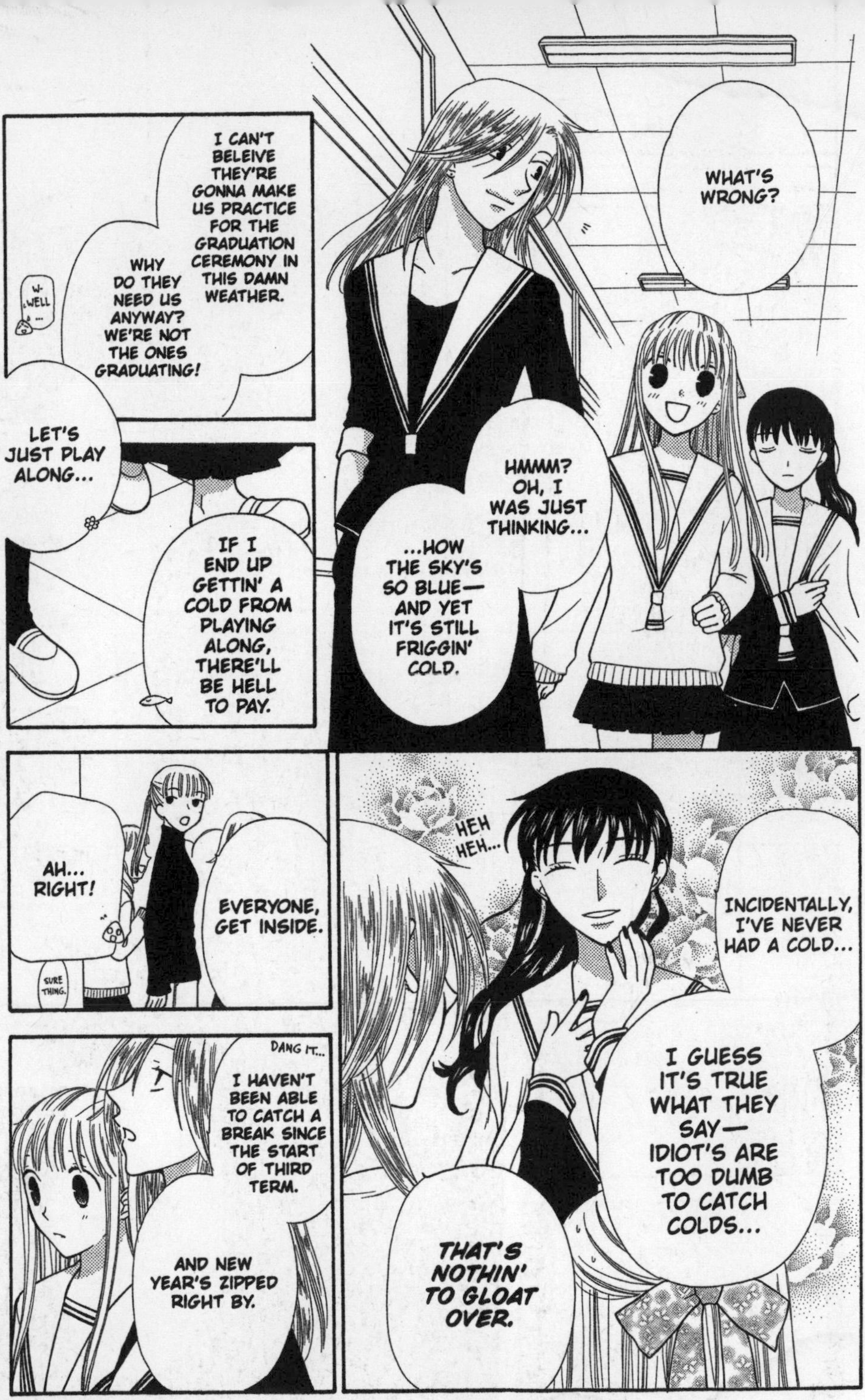
WHAT'S WRONG?
HMMM? OH, I WAS JUST THINKING...
...HOW THE SKY'S SO BLUE—AND YET IT'S STILL FRIGGIN' COLD.
I CAN'T BELEIVE THEY'RE GONNA MAKE US PRACTICE FOR THE GRADUATION CEREMONY IN THIS DAMN WEATHER.
WHY DO THEY NEED US ANYWAY? WE'RE NOT THE ONES GRADUATING!
W-WELL...
LET'S JUST PLAY ALONG...
IF I END UP GETTIN' A COLD FROM PLAYING ALONG, THERE'LL BE HELL TO PAY.
HEH HEH...
INCIDENTALLY, I'VE NEVER HAD A COLD...
I GUESS IT'S TRUE WHAT THEY SAY—IDIOT'S ARE TOO DUMB TO CATCH COLDS...
THAT'S NOTHIN' TO GLOAT OVER.
EVERYONE, GET INSIDE.
AH... RIGHT!
SURE THING.
DANG IT...
I HAVEN'T BEEN ABLE TO CATCH A BREAK SINCE THE START OF THIRD TERM.
AND NEW YEAR'S ZIPPED RIGHT BY.

TO BE CONTINUED IN VOLUME ⑨

Love Natsuki Takaya?
Don't forget to check out her other works
also available from Yen Press!

**Volumes 1 and 2,
available now.**

**Volume 1,
available now.**

COLLECTOR'S EDITION

Fruits Basket

COLLECTOR'S EDITION

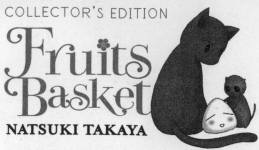

Fruits Basket

NATSUKI TAKAYA

Translation: Sheldon Drzka • Lettering: Lys Blakeslee

This book is a work of fiction. Names, characters, places, and incidents are the product of the author's imagination or are used fictitiously. Any resemblance to actual events, locales, or persons, living or dead, is coincidental.

First published in Japan in 2016 by HAKUSENSHA, INC., Tokyo.
English language translation rights in U.S.A., Canada and U.K. arranged with HAKUSENSHA, INC., Tokyo through Tuttle-Mori Agency, Inc., Tokyo.

Yen Press
1290 Avenue of the Americas
New York, NY 10104

Visit us at yenpress.com
facebook.com/yenpress
twitter.com/yenpress
yenpress.tumblr.com
instagram.com/yenpress

First Yen Press Edition: December 2016

Yen Press is an imprint of Yen Press, LLC.
The Yen Press name and logo are trademarks of Yen Press, LLC.

The publisher is not responsible for websites (or their content) that are not owned by the publisher.

Library of Congress Control Number: 2016932692

ISBN: 978-0-316-36073-9

10 9 8 7 6 5 4 3 2 1

BVG

Printed in the United States of America